MULTINATIONAL ENTERPRISES, MARKETS AND INSTITUTIONAL DIVERSITY

PROGRESS IN INTERNATIONAL BUSINESS RESEARCH

Series Editors: The European International Business Academy (EIBA)

Recent Volumes:

PROGRESS IN INTERNATIONAL BUSINESS RESEARCH
VOLUME 9

MULTINATIONAL ENTERPRISES, MARKETS AND INSTITUTIONAL DIVERSITY

EDITED BY

ALAIN VERBEKE

Haskayne School of Business, University of Calgary, Calgary, Canada; Solvay Business School, University of Brussels (VUB), Brussels, Belgium; Henley Business School, University of Reading, Henley-on-Thames, United Kingdom

ROB VAN TULDER

RSM Erasmus University Rotterdam, Rotterdam, The Netherlands

SARIANNA LUNDAN

Faculty of Business Studies and Economics, University of Bremen, Bremen, Germany

European International Business Academy

United Kingdom – North America – Japan
India – Malaysia – China

Emerald Group Publishing Limited
Howard House, Wagon Lane, Bingley BD16 1WA, UK

First edition 2014

British Library Cataloguing in Publication Data
A catalogue record for this book is available from the British Library

ISBN: 978-1-78441-422-1
ISSN: 1745-8862 (Series)

ISOQAR certified
Management System,
awarded to Emerald
for adherence to
Environmental
standard
ISO 14001:2004.

Certificate Number 1985
ISO 14001

INVESTOR IN PEOPLE

CONTENTS

LIST OF CONTRIBUTORS

Victor Amaral	Organizações Globo, Rio de Janeiro, Brazil
Björn Ambos	Institute of Management (IFB), University of St. Gallen, St. Gallen, Switzerland
Christos Antoniou	Centre for International Business, University of Leeds, Leeds, UK
Nicola Berg	Department of Strategic Management, University of Hamburg, Hamburg, Germany
Jorge Carneiro	Pontifical Catholic University of Rio de Janeiro, IAG Business School, Gávea, Rio de Janeiro, Brazil
Enrique Claver-Cortés	Department of Management, University of Alicante, Alicante, Spain
Filip De Beule	KU Leuven University, Antwerpen, Belgium
Douglas Dow	Melbourne Business School, Faculty of Business & Economics, The University of Melbourne, Carlton, Victoria, Australia
William G. Egelhoff	Graduate School of Business, Fordham University, New York, NY, USA
Robert L. Engle	School of Business and Engineering, Quinnipiac University SB-DNF, Hamden, CT, USA
Gilberto Figueira da Silva	Pontifical Catholic University of Rio de Janeiro, IAG Business School, Gávea, Rio de Janeiro, Brazil

Simona Gentile-Lüdecke	Bremen University, Faculty of International Management and Governance, Bremen, Germany
Marjaana Gunkel	Leuphana University of Lueneburg, Lueneburg, Germany
Lars Håkanson	Copenhagen Business School, Frederiksberg, Denmark
Katrin Held	Department of Strategic Management, University of Hamburg, Hamburg, Germany
Jenny Hillemann	Department of Management and Strategy, Solvay Business School, University of Brussels (VUB), Brussels, Belgium
Andreja Jaklič	University of Ljubljana, Faculty of Social Sciences, Ljubljana, Slovenia
Aljaž Kunčič	Economic and Social Commission for Western Asia (UN ESCWA), Beirut, Lebanon
Michał K. Lemański	Nottingham University Business School China, Ningbo, P.R. China
Sarianna Lundan	Faculty of Business Studies and Economics, University of Bremen, Bremen, Germany
Robbert Maseland	University of Groningen, Groningen, The Netherlands
Gilmar Masiero	School of Economics, Administration and Accountancy (FEA-USP), University of São Paulo, São Paulo, Brazil
Sylvia Moraes	Pontifical Catholic University of Rio de Janeiro, IAG Business School, Gávea, Rio de Janeiro, Brazil
Henrique Pacheco	Pontifical Catholic University of Rio de Janeiro, IAG Business School, Gávea, Rio de Janeiro, Brazil

Bent Petersen	Copenhagen Business School, Frederiksburg, Denmark and University of Gothenburg, Göteborg, Sweden
Rebecca Piekkari	Department of Management Studies, Aalto University, School of Business, Helsinki, Finland
Jonas Puck	Institute for International Business, WU Vienna, Vienna, Austria
Diego Quer-Ramón	Department of Management, University of Alicante, Alicante, Spain
Laura Rienda-García	Department of Management, University of Alicante, Alicante, Spain
Christian Rohrlack	Danfoss Power Solutions GmbH & Co. OHG, Neumünster, Germany
Huub J. M. Ruël	Windesheim University of Applied Sciences, School of Business, Media & Law, Zwolle, The Netherlands
Christopher Schlaegel	Faculty of Economics and Management, Otto von Guericke University Magdeburg, Magdeburg, Germany
Rene E. Seifert, Jr.	Universidade Tecnológica Federal do Paraná (UTFPR), Curitiba, Brazil and Instituto Brasileiro de Estudos e Pesquisas Sociais (IBEPES), Brazil
Natalya Smith	Heelstone Consulting Ltd., Manchester, UK
Ekaterina Thomas	Staffordshire University Business School, Stoke-on-Trent, UK
Susanne Tietze	Keele University, Keele Management School, Keele, United Kingdom
Francisco Urdinez	Institute of International Relations (IRI-USP), University of São Paulo, São Paulo, Brazil

Danny Van Den Bulcke	University of Antwerp, Antwerpen, Belgium
André van Hoorn	University of Groningen, Groningen, The Netherlands
Rob Van Tulder	RSM Erasmus University Rotterdam, Rotterdam, The Netherlands
Alain Verbeke	Haskayne School of Business, University of Calgary, Calgary, Canada; Solvay Business School, University of Brussels (VUB), Brussels, Belgium; Henley Business School, University of Reading, Henley-on-Thames, United Kingdom
Robin Visser	Deakin University, Faculty of Business and Law, Deakin Graduate School of Business, Burwood, Victoria, Australia
Alexander H. Wisgickl	WU Vienna, University of Economics and Business, Vienna, Austria
Joachim Wolf	Institute of Business Administration, University of Kiel, Kiel, Germany
Haiyan Zhang	Neoma Business School, Mont-Saint-Aignan, France

DEDICATION

This research volume is dedicated to Daniël Van Den Bulcke, professor emeritus of international business (IB), who passed away on January 8th, 2014. He was 74 years old.

Daniël or Danny Van Den Bulcke was a beloved member of the University of Antwerp. He served this institution as a faculty member from 1985 to 2004, and remained actively engaged with the university and the IB research and teaching community after his retirement until his sudden passing.

Danny will be remembered for his thoughtful and principled leadership, as well as his warm persona. He was a renowned academic expert in IB and highly respected among his peers for his many contributions to the intellectual development of the field.

Danny was a pioneer of IB research and teaching in the Benelux and beyond. He taught at no less than ten Belgian institutes and universities, including the Universities of Leuven, Ghent, Limburg, Brussels and of course Antwerp. At the University of Antwerp, he lectured at the Institute of Development Policy and Management (IOB), the Faculty of Applied

Economics, the Institute of Transport and Maritime Management (ITMMA) and the Antwerp Management School (AMS). He was also a visiting professor at five Dutch universities, and instrumental in establishing IB research and teaching in Cambodia, China, India, Indonesia, Laos, Macau, the Philippines, Poland, Thailand, and Vietnam. Many of his students from across the world kept in touch with him long after their graduation.

During his career, Danny authored many books and articles, all of these addressing the subject matter of this research volume, namely multinational enterprises, markets and institutional diversity. He was often one of the very first researchers to address emerging issues in international business - mostly at the request of public policy institutions, including the United Nations, the European Centre for the Study and Information on Multinationals, the International Labour Organisation and the Belgian Ministry of Economic Affairs. He also ran a large number of education-based, international development projects in countries such as Burundi, Cambodia, Cameroon, China, Madagascar, Laos, the Philippines, Rwanda, South Africa, Thailand, and Vietnam. He was awarded the Sanqin Prize by the Shaanxi Province in China and the Friendship Prize by the Chinese Ministry of Foreign Experts for his many contributions to the educational development of Chinese universities.

He will be remembered by most as a founding father and the Chairman of the European International Business Academy (EIBA), which he ran for many years. He was also Vice-President of the Academy of International Business (AIB) and a Fellow of both EIBA and AIB. During each EIBA yearly conference, he was the friendly host of every new face attending the event, and he deeply influenced many future IB scholars through the doctoral tutorials he organized from 1987 until 2004.

During his long and distinguished career, Danny traveled the world many times over and developed deep friendships with numerous people around the globe. He truly embodied the belief that increased international exchange can make the world a better place, and he did make it a better one.

Danny is survived by his wife, two daughters, and five grandchildren.

CHAPTER 1

NEW ANALYSIS OF MULTINATIONAL ENTERPRISES AND THEIR LINKAGES WITH MARKETS AND INSTITUTIONAL DIVERSITY

Alain Verbeke, Rob Van Tulder and
Sarianna Lundan

ABSTRACT

Purpose — *This chapter provides an overview of various new streams in international business (IB) research that will have an important impact on IB studies in the years to come, both from a conceptual and a methodological perspective.*

Methodology/approach — *The authors discuss a set of 18 chapters, all included in this research volume, and highlight both the key intellectual contributions and the challenges identified that will need to be taken into account in future research.*

Findings — *The findings of the studies discussed are manifold and profound. Some of the main findings include the following: (1) multinational*

Multinational Enterprises, Markets and Institutional Diversity
Progress in International Business Research, Volume 9, 1–23
Copyright © 2014 by Emerald Group Publishing Limited
All rights of reproduction in any form reserved
ISSN: 1745-8862/doi:10.1108/S1745-886220140000009006

enterprise (MNE)-centric empirical research studies should be avoided. Resource recombination typically requires taking into account the resource base and the strategies of at least two economic actors. (2) IB studies, almost by definition, need to take into account "distance," but most prior empirical research has not done a particularly good job in including relevant distance parameters in a methodologically sound way to assess their impact on MNE strategy, operational functioning or performance. (3) Nonbusiness institutions can be very helpful in promoting MNE expansion but include "dark side" institutions that sometimes appear very effective in particular situational contexts. (4) Institutional diversity matters: it can make international knowledge transfers difficult, it can lead to discrimination against firms from specific nationalities, it certainly suggests that there is no generalizable multinationality—performance relationship, and it raises the question whether new theory is needed to accommodate previously neglected institutional contexts.

Practical implications − *This overview of several recent IB studies confirms that managing the international innovation chain in its entirety is fraught with difficulties. MNE senior management must economize on bounded rationality (meaning: improving information quality and information processing) and bounded reliability (meaning: making sure that economic actors make good on open-ended promises, whether implicit or explicit). Any IB transaction by definition entails new resource recombination. Doing so effectively requires correct information, reliable partners and a recombination outcome that supports value creation for the MNE. Multiple, practice-driven puzzles in the IB context are proposed to the reader, and the outcomes are often unexpected.*

Originality/value − *A variety of new concepts and methodological approaches are proposed to improve the quality of future IB research.*

Keywords: Multinational enterprise (MNE); emerging market multinational enterprise (EMNE); institutions; global factory; firm performance; cultural distance

INTRODUCTION

This research volume includes new analyses of the complex interactions among multinational enterprises (MNEs), external markets, and diverse institutions. It has four parts.

Part I is microlevel oriented and addresses new governance determinants of MNE functioning in four chapters, much in line with modern internalization theory thinking (Verbeke, 2013; Grøgaard & Verbeke, 2012). Chapter 2 explores the usefulness of the global factory paradigm and provides a balanced overview of its strengths and weaknesses through the use of an internalization theory lens. Chapter 3 shows that optimal MNE governance is contingent upon transaction costs facing both the MNE and its potential partners in host countries. Chapter 4 explores the importance of the firm-specific advantages (FSAs) of both the acquired and acquiring firms in cases of international acquisitions. Finally, Chapter 5 explores the effectiveness of alternative coordination instruments to optimize MNE governance.

Overall, the chapters in Part I of this volume highlight the critical linkages between the nature of the resources (including requisite complementary resources) to be deployed in IB transactions and the related need for the proper governance thereof. In all cases, proper governance means economizing on bounded rationality and reliability, and guaranteeing that innovation and value creation can occur at the international level.

Part II, with five chapters, is more focused on the interactions between business and host country markets. It includes novel approaches to measuring "distance" and the effects thereof on international business (IB) transactions. Chapter 6 contains new methodological insight on how to marry the psychic distance perspective and the exogenous distance approaches in IB studies. Chapter 7 studies the impacts of institutions (institutional distance, formal institutions, and informal institutions) on macrolevel trade flows and bilateral foreign direct investment (FDI) in the OECD context. Unsurprisingly, it confirms that institutions do matter (Dunning & Lundan, 2008a). Chapter 8 includes definitive evidence that cultural distance is an asymmetrical phenomenon. It demonstrates why this had led to contradictory conclusions in terms of, for example, the influence of cultural distance on entry mode choice. Chapter 9 assesses the linkages between dimensions of culture and the usage of emotions to achieve goals. Here again, it appears that a contingency approach is required, with different cultures having a differential impact on the extent to which emotions can affect performance in business. Finally, Chapter 10 focuses on the micropolitical aspects of language usage inside the MNE. The choice of a particular "corporate language" appears to have important implications on the power distribution and internal social dynamics within the MNE.

As a set, the five chapters in Part II of this volume demonstrate that there is much more than meets the eye when assessing how good firms are in economizing on bounded rationality and bounded reliability. Both types of challenges are affected by cultural distance, but the impacts thereof appear much more complex than recognized in most extant empirical work. In addition, institutions and institutional quality appear important, in line with earlier research (Slangen & van Tulder, 2009) and so do elements such as emotional intelligence and the micropolitical aspects of language. This multitude of parameters apparently relevant to MNE strategy, operational functioning and performance raises the question whether parsimony is still achievable in IB research. The editors of this volume do think that parsimony remains important but the proven relevance of many, often neglected parameters does impose renewed reflection on which "envelope concepts" can best capture the wide range of variables relevant to IB practice.

Part III, with five chapters, proposes new approaches to identifying and measuring country-specific advantages (CSAs). Such advantages are at least partly determined by institutional parameters and can have a strong influence on microlevel competitive advantages (see Van Den Bulcke and Verbeke, 2001). Chapter 11, coauthored by Danny Van Den Bulcke, an early institution builder in the IB field to whom this research volume is dedicated, assesses the importance of investment promotion for emerging economies and credibly demonstrates the role of public institutions in private business success. Chapter 12 complements the analysis in Chapter 11 and focuses on commercial diplomacy. Here, the complementarity between business and public interests is highlighted and important recommendations are made to guide future research on commercial diplomacy. Chapter 13 attempts to answer the question which host-CSAs attract Chinese FDI. The observation that, for example, countries with weak institutions tend to attract Chinese FDI is undoubtedly important for future research in this area. Chapter 14 addresses the interactions between corruption and MNE innovation in Russia. Here, the important, though perhaps disturbing, conclusion is that corruption does grease the wheels of innovation.

All chapters in Part III of this volume explore well-known territory in terms of assessing the interactions between the nonbusiness environment and IB activities (Van Den Bulcke, 1995; van Tulder & Van der Zwart, 2005). However, whereas Chapters 11 and 12 conclude that investment promotion and commercial diplomacy can be effective in supporting IB transactions and represent conventional, "good governance" at the macrolevel, Chapters 13 and 14 explore the dark side of the nonbusiness environment and conclude that both weak institutions and corruption can actually be helpful to MNE activity, thereby leading to a completely new perspective as to what constitutes a CSA since the dark side appears to confer benefits to the businesses willing to embrace it. Here, future IB research should undoubtedly focus on what types of MNE resources (and complementary resource needs) may be most conducive to choices in favor of the dark side. In addition, the important question must be raised as to negative spill-overs: weak institutional quality and corruption typically increase bounded rationality and bounded reliability challenges at the macrolevel, a situation not normally conducive to sustainable economic wealth creation.

Finally, Part IV analyzes institutional diversity, with a focus on the impacts of emerging economy institutions on IB transactions, including the effects on emerging economy MNEs (EMNEs) expanding abroad. Chapter 15 usefully applies the liability of foreignness (LOF) and liability of outsidership (LOO) concepts to the context of MNEs from emerging economies acquiring strategic assets in developed countries. One of the main insights is that these strategic assets, when deployed in the (emerging) home economy of the acquiring MNE, are largely sheltered from foreign competition because of the LOF facing developed country entrants. Chapter 16 discusses MNE reverse knowledge transfers in the human resources management sphere from emerging economy subsidiaries and identifies the conditions for successful transfers to occur. Chapter 17 suggests that EMNEs are sometimes discriminated against and provides careful analysis of this negative, emerging-country-of-origin effect. Chapter 18 provides a case-based analysis of the multinationality—performance (M—P) linkage in five Brazilian MNEs and comes to the appropriate conclusion that no general M—P relationship should be assumed because of a large number of case-specific idiosyncrasies, including the nature of the MNEs' FSAs, the strategic motivations for international expansion and a variety of case-specific environmental circumstances. Finally, chapter 19 provides an interesting literature review on Chinese outward FDI. It raises the question whether this phenomenon can be fully explained by extant theory or whether it requires new conceptual frameworks.

The volume, when studied in its entirety, demonstrates the vibrancy of the IB research field. There is no need for a single "big question," but the research presented here does suggest that there are opportunities to use shared concepts and common language, such as those developed by scholars espousing internalization theory as the general theory of the MNE (Rugman, Verbeke, & Nguyen, 2011) and the eclectic paradigm as the framework most conducive to in-depth analysis of the interactions between business and broader institutions in an international context (Dunning & Lundan, 2008b).

Importantly, it appears that the analysis of MNE activity, though at the heart of IB functioning, cannot build on a purely MNE-centric approach.

It is only through analyzing the often-complex interactions between FSAs and CSAs, and the related, requisite resource recombinations, that true insight can be gained on the efficient boundaries and boundary-spanning activities of firms, markets, and broader institutions. Here, the present research volume suggests that much work remains to be done in terms of theory development and the crafting of appropriate empirical constructs and methods.

PART I: NEW GOVERNANCE DETERMINANTS OF MNE BEHAVIOR

In Chapter 2, Hillemann and Verbeke revisit the "global factory" paradigm, which argues that many MNEs have moved away from conventional horizontal and vertical integration across borders. Instead, these firms have become more flexible, with the head office acting as a "controlling intelligence" and fine-slicing activities. According to the paradigm, each fine-sliced activity could in principle be outsourced – reflecting the usage of external markets – and offshored – meaning production in potentially distant locations with institutions very different from the home country ones – if such moves were to reduce the sum of production costs and transaction costs facing the MNE. However, Hillemann and Verbeke point out that the global factory may not be the panacea for international competitive success. More specifically, they demonstrate that the global factory paradigm lacks the predictive capacity of mainstream IB theory, namely internalization theory. They also show that each of the global factory's "strengths" can – from a comparative institutional perspective – be interpreted as a "weakness" in particular circumstances. Importantly, internalization theory suggests that the global factory's head office may, in particular situations, be faced with substantial bounded rationality and bounded reliability challenges. In circumstances where the head office lacks proper intelligence as compared to other units in the company, especially foreign subsidiaries with strong subsidiary-specific advantages (SSAs) (Rugman & Verbeke, 2001), it should not decide in a controlling fashion on the outsourcing and offshoring of fine-sliced activities, as this could be detrimental to the MNE's survival, profitability and growth prospects. The authors also propose a simple dual test to assess what governance approach may be optimal for a given operation in a host country, namely, the tradability of the resources critical to success in the market place held by the MNE on the one hand and by external contracting partners on the other.

Chapter 3 also provides a two-sided perspective on transaction costs, in the context of market entry. When expanding abroad, MNEs need to make decisions regarding their entry mode, for example, between an international joint venture (IJV) or a wholly owned subsidiary (WOS), based on considerations of transaction costs resulting from differential bounded rationality and bounded reliability challenges associated with each entry mode. Wisgickl and Puck point out that the empirical findings to date have been contradictory, perhaps because of the conventionally adopted MNE-centric, transaction cost economics (TCE) perspective. They argue that the transaction costs faced by potential local partners with complementary resources in the host country also do matter. Here, the authors develop a conceptual framework that adopts a "two-sided" perspective, whereby both MNE and local partner characteristics matter in entry mode choices.

More specifically, they identify three scenarios whereby a traditional MNE-centric perspective can lead to underestimating the transaction costs for MNEs when trying to find an appropriate and willing local joint venture partner. The first scenario describes the MNE as having easily tradable assets, whereas the potential local partner commands nontradable assets. Under this scenario, and adopting an MNE-centric perspective, the MNE could opt for an IJV strategy to access the coveted nontradable assets. However, a local partner with nontradable assets and being offered tradable ones in the context of an IJV is unlikely to accept this offer since it could simply purchase equivalents of the MNE's assets on the external market and then set up a wholly owned operation itself. As a result, the MNE may not be able to find a local partner to establish an IJV, and if it does, this may involve much higher transaction costs than traditional, MNE-centric TCE would predict. The second scenario focuses on the internal uncertainty expected by the partners when establishing an IJV. If the MNE perceives low internal uncertainty associated with an IJV, while the potential local partner perceives high internal uncertainty, the traditional, MNE-centric TCE perspective would again suggest an IJV mode. But the potential local partner might again prefer not to partner with the MNE since it would anticipate substantial internal transaction costs. As a result, convincing the potential partner to engage in an IJV will be an exercise "rich" in transaction costs. The third scenario considers the case whereby both the MNE and the local partner perceive high external uncertainty arising from forces in the local environment. In this case, the MNE might opt for the IJV mode and thus partner with a local company to share risks and reduce uncertainties. But if the local company perceives higher external uncertainty *as a result* of partnering with the MNE, for example, due to unfavorable government regulations, the local company may again have a preference not to partner with the MNE. Under these three scenarios, the traditional MNE-centric TCE perspective may still predict correctly the MNE's operating mode choice, but in each case it will also underestimate the transaction costs of the IJV strategy for the MNE.

Chapter 4 assesses acquisitions, but not − in contrast to most conceptual and empirical work − from the perspective of the acquirer but rather from the perspective of the seller. Here, the focus is on German firms in the automotive industry that wish to be acquired by Chinese companies. More specifically, Gentile-Lüdecke examines the motivations behind two established and financially healthy German MNEs in the automotive industry to proactively search for a buyer in China. The research is based on interviews with managers from the two German companies who were actively involved in the process of identifying and selling out to a Chinese buyer. The author ultimately uncovers the main motivations inducing developed country MNEs, which are financially healthy and command strong FSAs, to deliberately search for a buyer in China, the world's largest emerging economy.

The author proposes, much along the lines of the analyses provided in Chapters 2 and 3, that resource asymmetries and complementarities between the seller and the acquiring firm are likely to generate synergies arising from resource recombinations by both economic actors. The possibility to create complementarities based on the seller's financial and technical resources and the local knowledge of the Chinese acquirer represents a key motivation for these two German firms to proactively opt for a Chinese strategic investor. On the one hand, the two German companies in the case studies (Latch and Sensor) are both major OEM suppliers (Tier 1 suppliers) in the automotive industry. Financial investors owned these firms before their acquisition by a Chinese company, and there was some likelihood that they would be sold at some stage in the future. To remain at the forefront in terms of technology (a pressure imposed by these companies' clients) and expand their customer base to enjoy economies of scale, these German suppliers needed complementary resources such as access to local networks in China. On the other hand, both Chinese acquiring companies (Lock and Filter) were relatively new firms without international experience but with the ambition to become international suppliers. They commanded the complementary resources needed by the two German companies.

The author also suggests that owning and controlling valuable intangible assets of interest to the acquiring firm gives the seller substantial bargaining power. In this case, both German companies had strong FSAs, including advanced production process technology, consisting partly of tacit knowledge. These higher-order FSAs were embedded in the German firms' organizational structure and culture and could therefore not easily be transferred.

Based on the case studies, the author demonstrates that the strong likelihood of being able to maintain a high level of operational autonomy, in line with Rugman and Verbeke's (2001) SSA concept, and the need to access complementary resources such as local knowledge of the Chinese market (location-bound FSAs) can be major drivers for companies from developed countries to proactively seek Chinese acquirers.

Chapter 5 is the most "internally oriented" chapter in Part I of this research volume and addresses several internal organizational complexities, demonstrating the lack of often-assumed, centralized coordination and control inside the MNE. Wolf, Egelhoff, and Rohrlack focus on cross-border technology transfers in MNE functioning. Achieving success in this activity reflects the MNE's capacity to adapt to new environments and to recombine resources effectively in host environments. The authors conduct an empirical study to investigate the relative influence on technology transfer success of "traditional," design-oriented coordination instruments and "modern" management concepts. Their survey-based analysis was based on responses from 255 managers and engineers in Germany's largest firms. The authors assume that technology transfers help the recipient unit to improve existing solutions and to innovate and learn. From a conceptual perspective, the chapter builds on information-processing theory, with the MNE functioning mainly as an information-processing system.

The traditional design-oriented coordination instruments consist of three types. "Person-oriented" coordination instruments include informal meetings among managers, expatriation and visits to other MNE subunits, video-conferences, and manager training sessions. "Technocratic" coordination instruments replace interpersonal interactions by "managerial technologies" such as guidelines, rules, and standards. Finally, "structural" instruments rely on planned occurrences such as regularly held meetings or the deployment of permanent teams.

In contrast to the above, "modern" management concepts include the subunit's absorptive capacity and its epistemic communities. Absorptive capacity's conventional definition refers to the ability of a firm to recognize the value of new information, assimilate it, and apply it to commercial ends. The defining characteristic of an epistemic community is cognitive coupling, whereby codes, theories, tools, etc. are shared among the individuals (in this case managers) active in a community.

This study concludes that all three types of traditional coordination instruments are positively and significantly related to the success of technology transfers. Especially structural and person-oriented coordination instruments significantly help in achieving transfer goals ("improvement of existing solutions" and "innovation and learning"). Technocratic instruments appear to contribute more to improving existing solutions than to innovating and learning. In turn, modern management concepts, though facilitating the "improvement of existing solutions" and "innovation and learning," exert a much weaker and actually insignificant impact on transfer success. Based on these findings, the authors conclude that recent management research may have gone too far in shifting its focus from assessing the impact of very concrete integration instruments to studying the effects of more abstract concepts that may be appealing to some scientists but have little validity in managerial practice. They propose that future MNE research studies should pay sufficient attention to traditional coordination instruments. These instruments are the key foundation of the MNE's resource recombination capability since they strongly influence organizational behavior and outcomes.

PART II: NEW APPROACHES TO DEFINING AND MEASURING DISTANCE

Irrespective of the level of analysis chosen, whether the country, the MNE or the subsidiary, one key challenge in IB is to understand how cross-national distances along several dimensions, such as culture, institutions, geography and economic characteristics, influence trade flows, investment patterns, entry modes and other MNE strategic decisions (Dunning & Lundan, 2008a; Verbeke, 2013). Yet, it is still not entirely clear how exactly distance should be defined, measured and applied in IB research, and what it entails specifically for MNE strategic decision-making and operational functioning.

Part II of this volume, covering Chapters 6–10, addresses the above-mentioned challenge from different perspectives. A number of distance dimensions are discussed in this part, namely, psychic distance (Chapter 6), institutional distance (Chapter 7), cultural distance (Chapters 6, 8, 9), and language (Chapter 10). The empirical work included in this part showcases the increasing sophistication of this type of research (Chapters 6–9).

Chapter 6 develops a mediating model of psychic distance, with a focus on perceptions versus national-level differences. In this chapter, Dow, Håkanson, and Ambos argue that psychic distance is a critical construct in IB research. It captures differences in language, education, business practices, culture, industrial development, etc. There are two schools of thought as to how psychic distance should be measured in empirical research. The first school focuses on exogenous, national-level differences and uses indicators such as the Kogut and Singh index, which combine the four original cultural dimensions identified by Geert Hofstede into one score. In contrast, the second school favors measuring perceptions. The authors attempt to bridge the gap between these two approaches and develop a mediating model to test empirically the relationships among exogenous, national-level differences, perceptions of distance, bilateral trade volumes and FDI stocks.

The authors define psychic distance as "the perception that two parties from different countries, regions or backgrounds may have difficulty communicating with, interpreting, and understanding each other. This may arise from factors such as differences in language, religion, education, political systems, business practices, culture, and industrial development." Here, psychic distance may arise due to *intracountry* variations as well as *intercountry* differences in collecting, transferring and interpreting information. Starting from this definition, the authors build sophisticated models to test whether exogenous, national-level differences in the realm of industrial development, education, political processes, geographic distance, language, religion and culture are antecedents of perceived psychic distance that will affect bilateral trade flows (exports) and FDI.

The authors demonstrate empirically that perceptions of psychic distance, even if measured by expert panels rather than by actual decision-makers, fully capture the impact of national-level differences (except that of geographic distance) on bilateral trade and FDI flows. The results also show that a set of national-level difference indicators as modeled in this chapter capture close to 80% of the explained variance in psychic distance, which means that a small number of national-level difference indicators can function as the equivalent of real-world perceptions, when measuring the latter is not an option.

The great contribution of this chapter is that it demonstrates empirically the relationship between exogenous, national-level differences and perceptions of psychic distance, thereby bridging the gap between the two opposing approaches. It also provides critical new insights into which measurement approach is more appropriate in specific situations.

Chapter 7 addresses the linkages between FDI and institutions, both formal and informal ones. Kunčič and Jaklič argue that institutions can be a source of CSAs for MNEs. They examine, at the country level, whether formal and informal institutions affect bilateral inward FDI stocks in OECD countries. The authors conduct a longitudinal study of 34 OECD countries during the 1990−2010 period. They use a new dataset that includes institutional distance (in legal, political and economic terms), formal institutions' quality and informal institutions (mainly public opinion). As regards informal institutions, the authors argue that public opinion can make FDI more risky and costly and even affect the functioning of formal institutions. The inward FDI stocks from the OECD database are used in the model since the sample of host countries is more homogeneous, and the usage of inward FDI stocks allows focusing on specific pull factors for FDI.

The authors demonstrate that legal and political institutional qualities are important FDI determinants and that legal and political institutional distance dimensions are significant obstacles to FDI. Perhaps surprisingly, the quality of economic institutions does not appear to affect FDI stocks. However, the findings do suggest that a "non-liberal" public opinion can significantly reduce inward FDI. The authors also report that market-seeking FDI motives and agglomeration effects (i.e., new FDI building upon existing investments) largely drive inward FDI stocks in the OECD countries.

The findings in this OECD context also show that GDP as well as GDP per capita of both home and host countries positively affect bilateral inward FDI stocks. Variables conducive to creating "closeness" between countries, such as sharing a border, language, currency, legal origins or colonial ties and membership of the same regional agreement, all positively affect bilateral, inward FDI stocks.

Chapter 8 addresses a methodological question on the impact of distance that has mystified researchers for many years, namely, whether distance is experienced identically or differently across cultures? Here, the authors, van Hoorn and Maseland, adopt a "measurement-equivalence perspective."

The extant IB literature has attempted to link national cultural distance and entry mode selection but has produced contradictory empirical evidence. Van Hoorn and Maseland argue that it is not feasible to generalize the relationship between cultural distance and IB-related decisions such as entry mode selection. To test the relevance of their perspective, they engage in empirical analysis based on Geert Hofstede's original four dimensions of national culture (individualism, power distance, uncertainty avoidance, and masculinity/femininity) for 69 countries. Based on these four dimensions of national culture, the authors construct a one-dimensional factor to measure any nation's "profile." As to the cultural distance measurement, the authors use the Mahalanobis distance index,[1] with weights given to Hofstede's four separate dimensions of national culture. The main element of relevance to managers is that cultural distance is not equivalent across different base countries. The effect of cultural distance for strategic decision-making, for example, in the realm of foreign entry mode choice or location selection cannot be generalized since the cultural profile of the base country must be understood as well.

The above findings contribute greatly to understanding the "cultural distance paradox." Some prior studies had found that higher cultural distance is associated with wholly owned entry modes, but the main reason for this outcome may have been that in those studies, Japan was chosen as the base country. In contrast, other studies concluded that higher cultural distance is associated with shared-control entry modes, but in these cases, the United States was the base country. The importance of such asymmetries had been highlighted at the conceptual level in earlier studies, such as Tung and Verbeke (2010).

Chapter 9 provides an exploratory analysis of culture and the role of a "cascading model of emotional intelligence." Human resources represent an important source of FSAs instrumental to MNE international success, especially when having to work with partners in the international market place. In this chapter, Gunkel, Schlaegel, and Engle explore the influence of national culture on the emotional intelligence of the individuals engaged in IB activities. Their proposed model tests the following: cultural dimensions influence how individuals sense their own emotions (self-emotional appraisal) and understand others' emotions (others' emotional appraisal). The self-emotional appraisal in turn will influence how individuals control their own emotions (regulation of emotion). Both the regulation of emotion and others' emotional appraisal will affect how emotions contribute to achieving performance goals.

The authors administered surveys to 2,067 individuals from nine countries (China, Columbia, Germany, India, Italy, Russia, Spain, Turkey, and the United States). Their results show that several of Hofstede's cultural dimensions but not power distance, influence self-emotional appraisal and others' emotional appraisal, and thus the use of emotions to achieve goals. Specific cultures characterized by relatively high degrees of uncertainty avoidance and long-term orientation exhibit a higher degree of others' emotional appraisal and self-emotional appraisal, which in turn influences regulation of emotion. Here, a positive effect results from the use of emotions to achieve goals. These findings not only confirm the relationship between cultural dimensions and the use of emotions but also illustrate the paths through which culture influences the different facets of emotional intelligence. In terms of managerial relevance, these findings should support MNE managers in their efforts to identify appropriate employees for international activities and to train them as a function of their national cultural profile.

Chapter 10, as the last chapter of Part II of this research volume, investigates the role of language in micropolitical behavior inside the MNE. Piekkari and Tietze view MNEs as multilingual organizations. They usefully combine two streams of literature on MNEs. One stream is the micropolitical perspective, concerned mainly with the use of intraorganizational power within the MNE, that is, how power relations are constructed and played out in the MNE social context. The second stream addresses language use in the MNE, for example, the choice of a common corporate language mandated by the head office, the accommodation of local languages, etc.

The authors combine the two above streams of literature and demonstrate that language-use decisions serve an important role in the power distribution and language hierarchy inside the MNE. They argue that the head office, foreign subsidiaries, teams, managers, and employees all act as language agents in the sense that they negotiate and make decisions on the usage of languages in the firm, thereby being involved in constructing the distribution of power/autonomy and control in the MNE.

Language agents can achieve four types of changes through micropolitical behavior:

(1) The employees' command in different languages (especially the common language mandated by the head office) in the MNE's internal network influences their ability to communicate with different units inside the MNE, thereby generating an organizational dynamic that may be very different from what is foreseen by the formal MNE structure.

(2) The decision on the language to be used as the corporate language may redefine the winners (the privileged) and losers (the disadvantaged) among the various language groups, which could be especially critical after a merger of acquisition. Those individuals competent in the new, dominant corporate language will become the privileged in the organizational hierarchy and may have increased negotiation power.

(3) Teams with members from multiple language backgrounds can exercise their "language agency" (i.e., which language to use in which situation)

to affect which knowledge is shared in the MNE and with whom, thereby reinforcing subgroup formation.

(4) When English is chosen as the common corporate language; the "purity" of English language instead of fluency can affect the hierarchy, thereby reproducing colonial-style power relationships between different units inside the MNE.

PART III: NEW PERSPECTIVES ON COUNTRY-SPECIFIC ADVANTAGES IN INTERNATIONAL BUSINESS

IB strategy research appropriately focuses not only on FSAs, both location-bound and non-location-bound ones, but also on CSAs and on the recombination thereof to create value. Part III of this volume includes four chapters exploring CSAs from new perspectives, with a special focus on emerging economies (Chapters 11–14). Chapter 11 looks at CSAs in newly industrialized, emerging, and developing Asian economies. Chapter 12 investigates the CSAs of emerging economies as a whole. China and its CSAs are the subject of Chapter 13, whereas Russia is addressed in Chapter 14.

Chapter 11 addresses the impact of outward foreign direct investment (OFDI) promotion policies, an emerging topic in IB studies (De Beule & Van Den Bulcke, 2010) using evidence from newly industrialized, emerging, and developing Asian economies (NIEDAEs). These include Hong Kong, Singapore, South Korea, Taiwan, Thailand, The Philippines, Malaysia, Indonesia, China, and India. However, there is also some description of the ASEAN countries. For the above countries, De Beule, Van Den Bulcke, and Zhang provide historical information regarding investment and trade patterns, the development of the institutional environment, and policies promoting OFDI in these countries. The authors point out that many MNEs from south-eastern Asian countries ascribe their own success to their strong home CSAs, but each of these nations appears to build on very different CSA bundles. Singaporean MNEs tend to build on CSAs in high-quality human resources and on the country's well-functioning financial system. In contrast, the CSAs of Malaysian MNEs stem mainly from government support policies. The authors devote much of their analysis to China, given its dominant position in the Asian economy. They attribute the success of China's economic and technological leapfrogging to its open-door policy in the realm of inward FDI, as well as regulatory improvements and relaxed exchange controls for OFDI. The authors also point out that with OFDI from emerging economies, there is typically little fear of loss of employment. Such OFDI appears focused mainly on trade creation, resource-seeking, and strategic asset-seeking. The authors formulate a number of useful, generic recommendations to optimize OFDI policies.

Chapter 12 by Ruël and Visser explores commercial diplomacy as a tool to support IB to and from emergent markets. Commercial diplomacy, typically considers the interests of both governments and businesses, with the benefits of new markets and investment opportunities highlighted for the two sets of actors. Based on an extensive literature review of English commercial diplomacy studies in established journals written during the past 60 years, Ruël and Visser confirm the importance of commercial diplomacy, in spite of its impacts not being well understood at present.

The authors call for integrating contemporary IB research topics and methods in future commercial diplomacy research. As regards the former, suggested subject matter could include business—government relationships in the area of commercial diplomacy, the actual organization/governance of commercial diplomacy, and the analysis of economic value created. As regards methodology, the authors propose multilevel analysis with sources of data at the macrolevels, mesolevels, and microlevels and the usage of multiple data-collection methods.

Chapter 13 discusses the "vagueness" of the "country specific advantage" or CSA concept and assesses which host-CSAs matter most when analyzing Chinese OFDI.

Masiero and Urdinez acknowledge the importance of CSAs in IB transactions, and focus in this context on the double diamond model (Rugman & Verbeke, 1993; Moon, Rugman, & Verbeke, 1998). Their analysis of 176 peer-reviewed studies containing the expression "country specific advantage" in the title or body shows the "vagueness" in the usage of the CSA concept.

The authors then review the literature as to which host-CSAs are most likely to attract Chinese OFDI and demonstrate that the answer to this question largely depends on the choice of particular data sources and indicators. The authors propose a list of variables and related indicators, based on the double diamond model (factor conditions, domestic demand, related and supporting industries, and government characteristics) as the foundation of their own approach (see also Van den Bulcke, Verbeke, and Yuan, 2009). They base their findings on secondary data for the 2005—2012 period, and they include 96 host countries to identify the locational drivers of Chinese OFDI.

The regression results suggest only a few significant indicators, somewhat in line with past research. *First*, natural factor endowments appear to be the key, especially for Chinese OFDI in the energy sector. *Second*, and this remains perhaps more controversial, Chinese investments tend to favor unstable countries with weak institutions. *Third*, as regards domestic demand, none of the indicators appeared to be significant in the empirical analysis. One can therefore conclude from this chapter that much work remains to be done on determining *ex ante* what could constitute relevant CSAs driving IB transactions. Such exercise becomes more difficult when not only host-CSAs are taken into account but also home country ones. In any case, this chapter highlights that IB researchers should always define clear indicators to measure home CSAs and host CSAs, as a basis for analyzing MNE location choices, and should use replicable data based on publicly available information.

Chapter 14, as the last chapter in Part III of this volume, addresses the interactions among multinational firms, corruption, and innovation in Russia. Smith, Thomas, and Antoniou model the impact of corruption on innovation activities in Russia between 1997 and 2011, of both developed economy MNEs (DMNEs) from Germany, the United Kingdom, the United States, and Finland on the one hand and EMNEs from Belorussia, Kazakhstan, Ukraine, and China on the other. They use a fixed-effect panel data methodology. Here, the number of patents at the national level is used to measure innovation. As to corruption, the authors measure actual rather than perceived corruption, as reflected in the number of economic crimes per capita. They also use indices measuring institutional quality and innovation input. Their data on FDI from both emerging and developed countries allow testing whether the impact on innovation varies between EMNEs and DMNEs. Just as was the case with Chapter 13, the authors reach a perhaps unexpected conclusion: corruption appears not just to grease the wheels of commerce but also to grease the wheels of innovation activity, with corruption acting as a hedge in a high-risk institutional environment. In contrast to their expectation, the authors find that (assumed) prior experience of EMNEs operating in environments with weak institutions and high corruption does not offer them any advantage over DMNEs when operating in Russia. Importantly, in a geographically large country such as Russia, it is critical to consider the factors affecting innovation output at the subnational level, thereby requiring a contingency approach to address such intracountry idiosyncrasies.

PART IV: INSTITUTIONAL DIVERSITY IN THE EMERGING ECONOMY CONTEXT

Emerging nations perform an increasingly important role in the world economy. Perhaps, the single most important criterion in distinguishing between developed and emerging economies is that the latter are characterized by institutional voids and various forms of market failure that typically do not occur in developed economies, at least not over prolonged periods of time (which suggests institutional correction in developed economies). The institutional differences between developed economies and emerging ones affect MNE strategic decisions in many ways. Chapter 15 focuses on the specific motivations for internationalization and diversification. Chapter 16 addresses the transfer of managerial practices. Chapter 17 studies the differential treatment of DMNEs and EMNEs by host country nationals. Finally, Chapters 18 and 19 address institution-related issues facing MNEs from Brazil and China, respectively.

Chapter 15 attempts to answer the question whether the concepts of LOF and LOO can contribute to explaining the prevalence of strategic asset-seeking by EMNEs. Petersen and Seifert argue that strategic asset-seeking is the major driver behind EMNE acquisitions. The question then arises why EMNEs appear more able (and certainly more eager) than DMNEs to acquire strategic assets in developed economy markets. The authors review the springboard perspective and related literature to explain EMNEs' acquisition of strategic assets in developed countries. EMNEs invest abroad to obtain complementary resources, such as brands, access to superior institutional quality, home government support, etc. and also to avoid home country institutional and market deficiencies and to overcome latecomer disadvantages internationally. These EMNEs utilize their resource recombination capabilities, both at home and abroad, as a platform to compete in their large home country or home region market with DMNEs.

Petersen and Seifert identify two antecedents of the springboard perspective in the literature: state-owned enterprises with international ambitions (and with government support in the form of inexpensive capital) and firms with a global consolidator perspective that wish to play a dominant role through achieving scale and scope economies on an international level. However, the authors think that the springboard perspective can be extended, by using the mainstream IB concepts of LOF and LOO. The LOF concept describes the inherent disadvantages that foreign firms experience in host countries because of their non-native status. It addresses the impact of various forms of distance (cultural, economic, institutional, geographic, etc.). The LOO concept describes the inherent disadvantages that firms experience because of not having a privileged or central position in a relevant network (i.e., having outsider status).

The authors propose that LOF asymmetries can exist between DMNEs and EMNEs. More specifically, they argue that the LOF is typically higher for DMNEs entering emerging markets than for EMNEs entering developed countries. As a result of the LOF asymmetries between both sets of firms, EMNEs can capture more value in their own large home countries or large home regions by utilizing the strategic assets they acquire relatively easily in developed markets. State-owned EMNEs and firms affiliated with a business group are the ultimate insiders in their own countries, which can be very useful in deploying assets acquired abroad, but global consolidators can also derive value from foreign strategic assets even if they are relative outsiders (meaning firms with a weak networking position) in their home market. Consequently, the LOF concept considerably expands the springboard perspective based on LOF asymmetries between EMNEs and DMNEs. The LOO concept further points out that the springboard perspective is relevant mainly to EMNEs that enjoy insidership in their home country or region.

Chapter 16 discusses reverse transfers in MNEs of human resources management practices prevailing in emerging market subsidiaries. Lemanski views as critical the transferability of good practices in subsidiaries across the entire MNE network, thereby creating value for various stakeholders. Emerging markets offer substantial learning potential for MNEs, yet most recent studies focus on transfers of technology and product innovations from subsidiaries to the head office, thereby leaving the transfer of human resources management practices largely unexplored. In contrast, Lemanski reflects on reverse transfers of human resource management practices from subsidiaries to MNE head offices, based on a review of the extant literature. He identifies various parameters hindering such transfers, including, for example, the particular (emerging) country of origin of the best practice and the presence of a corporate immune system at the MNE level. In addition, an MNE head office located in a more liberal economy is typically more open to receive a reverse knowledge transfer.

The author also argues that head offices of MNEs located in countries facing rapid economic changes will be more open to adopting practices from their subsidiaries. However, local best practices or routines considered highly effective and efficient in the emerging economy environment may not be considered as such by the head office in the developed country. Hence, the type of human resources management practices most conducive to reverse transfer should embody values and characteristics aligned with mainstream thinking in the MNE.

Chapter 17 explores discrimination applied by host country nationals in developed markets against EMNEs. Based on a literature review, Held and Berg argue that in developed markets, EMNEs are more discriminated against by host country nationals than DMNEs and ascribe this to country-of-origin disadvantages. The chapter advances prior research by identifying those factors that may lead to a higher level of discrimination against EMNEs than against foreign DMNEs. The authors present a conceptual framework to analyze the impact of different institutional and resource-related variables on discrimination by host country nationals. Institutional parameters include the company's degree of state-ownership and the institutional distance with the host country, as reflected in, for example, the similarity of business practices and legal requirements between the foreign company's home country and the host country. The resource-related parameters include the company's transferable FSAs, in the realm of marketing, managerial and technological resources and the company's prior internationalization experience.

Building on institutional theory, the authors propose that a higher degree of state ownership, a larger institutional distance with the host country, weaker FSAs, and less international experience may lead to more discrimination against the firm by host country nationals. However, even if an EMNE has the same ownership structure, the quality of firm-level resources, and internationalization experience as a foreign DMNE, host country nationals may still be biased against the EMNE, simply because of its emerging-country-of-origin status.

Chapter 18 analyzes the performance effects of international diversification. Carneiro, Amaral, Pacheco, Moraes, and Figueira da Silva conducted in-depth case studies of five leading Brazilian MNEs to explore the complex relationship between international diversification and firm performance. Past empirical studies on the relationship between the degree of internationalization (DOI) and performance have yielded contradictory findings, at least in part because they use large samples of MNEs with completely different profiles and typically ignore elements such as market entry motivations, FSAs, locational diversity, etc.

In contrast, the authors adopt a qualitative approach to uncover the peculiarities of specific internationalization decisions by individual companies and the performance consequences resulting from changes in international diversification levels. Building upon in-depth information gathered from top-level executives from the five companies, the authors link the motivations for internationalization to the expected benefits. They find that higher profitability is typically expected when expansion motivations include scale and scope economies, market-seeking, and natural resource-seeking. However, when managers face strong uncertainty about the future, international expansion may be adopted, not to gain short-term profitability but rather to secure future opportunities through buying "real options." Unfortunately, in such cases, capital costs or switching costs associated with exercising a real option in the future are seldom considered, thereby suggesting substantial bounded rationality.

All five firms built up strong FSAs in their home country prior to internationalizing and most enjoyed a scale advantage in their domestic market. These FSAs were instrumental in offsetting the LOF associated with internationalizing, but the internationalization patterns differed strongly among the firms in terms of host country selection, entry mode choices, resource recombinations, etc.

The main conclusion is that no universal relationship should be expected between international diversification and firm performance in line with Verbeke and Brugman (2009) and Verbeke and Forootan (2012). Rather, the performance implications of internationalization-related decisions depend on the particular combinations at hand of the MNE's FSAs in various activities, including its routines, the location advantages of the countries selected, and environmental contingencies. The authors conclude that no generally valid linkage should be assumed between international diversification and performance, since it would be difficult to capture all different contingencies associated with an internationalization strategy.

Chapter 19, as the last chapter in this volume, provides an overview of the current state of research on Chinese MNEs and their institutional context. The Chinese government's official position on OFDI is a "go out" policy. As a result, China's OFDI has been growing steadily and that Chinese MNEs are playing an increasingly important role in the global economy. In parallel, the number of papers focusing on China's OFDI and Chinese MNEs has also been increasing. The authors of this chapter, Quer-Ramón, Claver, and Rienda, reviewed 43 empirical papers addressing the functioning of Chinese MNEs that were published between 2002 and 2012, in nine high-impact international management journals. Interestingly, 19 of the 43 papers were built on institutional theory and 10 on the resource-based view or the organizational capabilities perspective. The authors grouped the 43 papers into seven broad categories depending upon their main focus: internationalization drivers, cross-border M&As, entry mode choice, location determinants, applicability of FDI and MNE models, comparison with other countries, and other topics. They raise the question whether future research on Chinese OFDI, especially if it involves the globalization of Chinese firms, represents a challenge to mainstream IB theories and policy guidance (see also Zhang and Van Den Bulcke, 2014).

NOTE

1. Mahalanobis distance measures the dissimilarity between two random vectors of the same distribution and provides a relative measure of a data point's distance from a common point. It is scale-invariant and incorporates the variability and inter-correlations between different dimensions.

REFERENCES

De Beule, F., & Van Den Bulcke, D. (2010). *Changing policy regimes in outward foreign direct investment: From control to promotion* (pp. 277–304). New York, NY: Palgrave Macmillan.

Dunning, J. H., & Lundan, S. M. (2008a). *Multinational enterprises and the global economy*. Cheltenham: Edward Elgar Publishing.

Dunning, J. H., & Lundan, S. M. (2008b). Institutions and the OLI paradigm of the multinational enterprise. *Asia Pacific Journal of Management, 25*(4), 573–593.

Grøgaard, B., & Verbeke, A. (2012). Twenty key hypotheses that make internalization theory the general theory of international strategic management. In *Handbook of research in international strategic management*. Cheltenham: Edward Elgar Publishing.

Moon, H., Rugman, A. M., & Verbeke, A. (1998). A generalized double diamond approach to the global competitiveness of Korea and Singapore. *International Business Review, 7*(2), 135–150.

Rugman, A., Verbeke, A., & Nguyen, Q. (2011). Fifty years of international business theory and beyond. *Management International Review, 51*, 755–786.

Rugman, A. M., & Verbeke, A. (1993). Foreign subsidiaries and multinational strategic management: An extension and correction of Porter's single diamond framework. *MIR: Management International Review, 2*, 71–84.

Rugman, A. M., & Verbeke, A. (2001). Subsidiary-specific advantages in multinational enterprises. *Strategic Management Journal, 22*, 237–250.

Slangen, A. H., & van Tulder, R. J. (2009). Cultural distance, political risk, or governance quality? Towards a more accurate conceptualization and measurement of external uncertainty in foreign entry mode research. *International Business Review, 18*(3), 276–291.

Tung, R. L., & Verbeke, A. (2010). Beyond Hofstede and GLOBE: Improving the quality of cross-cultural research. *Journal of International Business Studies, 41*(8), 1259–1274.

Van Den Bulcke, D. (1995). The strategic management of multinationals in a triad-based world economy. In A. M. Rugman, J. Van den Broeck, & A. Verbeke (Eds.), *Global strategic management: Beyond the diamond* (Vol. 5, pp. 25–63). Greenwich, CN: JAI Press.

Van Den Bulcke, D., & Verbeke, A. (2001). *Globalization and the small open economy.* Cheltenham: Edward Elgar Publishing.

Van den Bulcke, D., Verbeke, A., & Yuan, W. (Eds.). (2009). *Handbook on small nations in the global economy: The contributions of multinational enterprises to national economic success.* Cheltenham: Edward Elgar Publishing.

van Tulder, R., & Van der Zwart, A. (2005). *International business-society management: Linking corporate responsibility and globalization.* New York, NY: Routledge.

Verbeke, A. (2013). *International business strategy.* Cambridge: Cambridge University Press.

Verbeke, A., & Brugman, P. (2009). Triple-testing the quality of multinationality − performance research: An internalization theory perspective. *International Business Review, 18*(3), 265−275.

Verbeke, A., & Forootan, M. Z. (2012). How good are multinationality − performance (M−P) empirical studies? *Global Strategy Journal, 2*(4), 332−344.

Zhang, H., & Van Den Bulcke, D. (2014). China's direct investment in the European Union: A new regulatory challenge? *Asia Europe Journal, 12*(1−2), 159−177.

PART I
NEW GOVERNANCE
DETERMINANTS OF MNE
BEHAVIOR

CHAPTER 2

INTERNALIZATION THEORY AND THE GOVERNANCE OF THE GLOBAL FACTORY

Jenny Hillemann and Alain Verbeke

ABSTRACT

Purpose — *This chapter discusses the global factory paradigm. We show how mainstream international business (IB) thinking, namely, internalization theory, can guide multinational enterprise (MNE) strategic decision-making in the context of a global factory network.*

Methodology/approach — *We identify the key assumptions made in the global factory paradigm about the fine slicing of economic activities and the related implications for the ownership status and location of each activity. In order to overcome the global factory paradigm's relative lack of predictive capacity, as compared to internalization theory, we propose an asset-bundling approach. This approach uses a clear and unambiguous criterion, namely, the tradability of resources (and resource combinations) to determine which sets of activities can best be left to external market contracting or should on the contrary be internalized on the basis of efficiency considerations.*

Multinational Enterprises, Markets and Institutional Diversity
Progress in International Business Research, Volume 9, 27–48
Copyright © 2014 by Emerald Group Publishing Limited
All rights of reproduction in any form reserved
ISSN: 1745-8862/doi:10.1108/S1745-886220140000009001

Findings − *We describe the enhanced role of developing/transition countries in the functioning of the global economy and show that these countries represent an increasing share of worldwide economic activities. Given this macrolevel development, the global factory, as a complex organizational form governing both internal activities and contracts with external parties, is rapidly gaining in importance. We describe, at the conceptual level, the strengths and weaknesses of the global factory and propose a "decision dynamics" matrix to support global factory, senior managers' strategies in the realm of ownership status and location.*

Research implications − *Future research on the MNE should focus on in-depth analysis of firms that embody "global factory"-type characteristics in order to understand better the evolution of this type of company and to capture the close requisite links among the focal firm, external contracting parties, and the broader environment. Such research should also lead to a better understanding of innovative resource combination processes and the transferability of non-location-bound firm-specific advantages (FSAs) across the global factory network.*

Practical implications − *In the global factory, the MNE head office assumes the role of resource orchestrator and is responsible for key strategic decisions on ownership status and location. Here, the head office must assess critically the operations that are part of the MNE's value chain and reflect on the firm's international dispersion of economic activities on an ongoing basis, given a myriad of broad environmental changes and changes in external competitive pressures. Our "decision dynamics" matrix provides a simple but effective managerial tool supporting MNE ownership status and location decisions, but the head office's capability to make these decisions should not be overestimated.*

Originality/value − *We explicitly link internalization theory with the global factory paradigm and explore unresolved issues in the relevant literature. Internalization theory prescribes the optimal ownership status and location for each economic activity considered. The theory focuses on the bundling of firm-level resources and complementary ones held by external parties, for each fine-sliced economic activity. It also considers explicitly the nature of the linkages among these activities.*

Keywords: Global factory; internalization theory; asset-bundling

INTRODUCTION

What does the "global factory" concept mean? It is important to realize that this concept is actually unrelated to being global or to being a factory. Instead, the global factory concept refers to an organizational form that focuses on the joint usage of internalization and external contracts in a variety of geographically dispersed markets so as to minimize the sum of production and transaction costs. In order to achieve this efficiency goal, control of the value chain is viewed as more important than the ownership thereof. The global factory is therefore just a reflection of one particular form of international activity deployment, one that can easily be explained by internalization theory.

The recent past has been characterized by increasingly complex, multinational enterprise (MNE) organizational structures, whereby senior level managers in MNEs try to determine the optimal location and optimal ownership status for each individual element of the value chain. Here, Peter Buckley and his co-authors, have contributed immensely to the debate on where to locate economic activities and on how to control these (Buckley, 2009, 2010, 2011; Buckley & Ghauri, 2004).

This chapter revisits the global factory using an internalization theory lens. We will argue that explicit usage of internalization theory can enhance the predictive capacity of the global factory paradigm in three ways. *First*, internalization theory properly accounts for the global factory's strengths. *Second*, internalization theory explains in a parsimonious fashion the occurrence of the global factory as a modern organizational form. *Third*, internalization theory suggests that both choices of ownership status and location are primarily asset-bundling decisions, reflecting the optimal combination of firm-specific advantages (FSAs) and accessible complementary resources in host countries.

Buckley views the global factory as "the key to understanding the changes in, and configuration of, the global economy" (2011, p. 270). Here, particular attention is devoted to the MNE head office, which assumes the role of "center" in coordinating geographically dispersed activities. As the orchestrator of the global factory, the MNE head office guides the complex flows of information and knowledge assets throughout the organization's internal and external networks. However, especially in the context of global factories, flexible structures and systems can lead to organizational challenges. Flexibility, even though typically perceived as an "advantage," might negatively affect performance. It is undoubtedly beneficial for the

MNE as a whole that the head office would systematically reflect on − and reassess − its past choices regarding the ownership status and location of each fine-sliced economic activity. However, the head office must also take into account the linkages among activities and the implications of any changes in ownership status and location for all parties directly and indirectly involved in the global factory's value chain.

Below, we first describe the macrolevel shift of economic activities toward developing and transition economies, which has been paralleled at the microlevel by the transformation of MNEs into internationally dispersed networks that control activities far beyond their own firm boundaries. These global factories differ from MNEs focused mainly on conventional vertical and horizontal integration (Buckley, 2012). We provide an internalization theory perspective on the global factory by exploring the implications of Hennart's (2009) asset-bundling approach for global factory functioning. Internalization theory provides superior insight into the actual strengths and weaknesses of the global factory, taking into account earlier concerns about its organizational vulnerabilities (Yamin, 2011).

THE WORLDWIDE DISTRIBUTION OF ECONOMIC ACTIVITIES

Developing and transition countries claim a rapidly increasing share of worldwide economic activities. The UNCTAD classification scheme categorizes the world's national economies into three broad sets: developing, transition, and developed economies (UNCTAD, 2013). In line with Buckley and Strange (2013), we describe below the overall development of these three country groupings in terms of population, share in GDP, merchandise exports, inward and outward FDI. A few key economic trends can be derived from the comparison of these parameters over the 1982−2012 period, that is, a time frame spanning three decades (see Table 1).

The world population increased from 4.61 bn in 1982 to 5.50 bn in 1992, 6.28 bn in 2002, and 7.08 bn in 2012. Given this strong growth, the share of population in developing economies rose from 74.8 percent in 1982 to 81.0 percent in 2012, while the transition and developed economies showed declines from 6.4 percent to 4.3 percent and from 18.8 percent to 14.7 percent, respectively, during this same period.

The world GDP almost tripled from 12.22 bn to 33.99 bn in the 1982−2002 period and then doubled again during the last decade to reach

Table 1. The Catching-Up Race of Developing Economies.

Indicators	Country Groupings	1982	1992	2002	2012
Population	Developing economies	74.8%	77.5%	79.5%	81.0%
	Transition economies	6.4%	5.6%	4.8%	4.3%
	Developed economies	18.8%	16.9%	15.6%	14.7%
Merchandise exports	Developing economies	28.1%	25.7%	31.9%	44.7%
	Transition economies	5.1%	1.9%	2.5%	4.5%
	Developed economies	66.8%	72.4%	65.6%	50.8%
GDP	Developing economies	22.2%	18.0%	21.2%	35.8%
	Transition economies	8.4%	2.7%	1.5%	3.9%
	Developed economies	69.4%	79.3%	77.3%	60.4%
Inward FDI	Developing economies	45.4%	32.1%	27.0%	52.0%
	Transition economies	0.0%	1.0%	1.8%	6.5%
	Developed economies	54.6%	66.9%	71.2%	41.5%
Outward FDI	Developing economies	9.7%	11.6%	8.8%	30.6%
	Transition economies			0.9%	4.0%
	Developed economies	90.3%	88.4%	90.3%	65.4%

Source: Own calculations based on UNCTADSTAD.
Note: The figures are calculated as the percentage of the global total.

72.68 bn in 2012. The share held by developing economies grew from 22.2 percent to 35.8 percent, at the expense of the transition and developed economies, whose shares decreased from 8.4 percent to 3.9 percent and from 69.4 percent to 60.4 percent, respectively.

Global merchandise exports increased tenfold between 1982 and 2012. The share of the developing economies rose from 28.1 percent to 44.7 percent during this period, at the expense of the developed and transition economies. The share of developed economies dropped from 66.8 percent in 1982 to 50.8 percent in 2012, whereas the share of transition economies only fell slightly from 5.1 percent in 1982 to 4.5 percent in 2012.

The UNCTAD statistics do not show transition economies' share in inward and outward FDI in 1982, and the numbers are only reported for later years. In 1982, the proportion of reported inward FDI was shared almost equally between developing and developed countries with 45.4 percent and 54.6 percent, respectively. The developed economies then further increased their share, which culminated in 71.2 percent of inward FDI in 2002. However, over the last decade, the developed economies experienced a sharp decline and lost almost 30 percentage points with a global share down to 41.5 percent in 2012. In that same year, developing economies represented a 52 percent share. The share attracted by transition economies increased from 1 percent in 1992 to 6.5 percent in 2012.

As regards outward FDI, developed economies accounted for a
dominant share of 90.3 percent in 1982, 88.3 percent in 1992, and again
90.3 percent in 2002. However, by 2012, the proportion of outward FDI
flows from these countries had fallen to 65.4 percent. In contrast, developing economies increased their share from 9.7 percent in 1982 to 30.6 percent
in 2012, whereas the share of transition economies rose from 0.9 percent in
2002 to 4 percent in 2012.

The evolution of the above-mentioned indicators illustrates the shift of
economic activities from developed economies to developing and transition
economies. During the 1982–2002 period, developing and transition
countries dramatically increased their share in merchandise exports, GDP,
and inward and outward FDI flows. In parallel with this more dispersed
distribution of economic activities at the macrolevel, many MNEs evolved
from being "vehicles for the international transfer of proprietary knowledge, commonly referred to as non-location-bound FSAs" (Rugman &
Verbeke, 2005; Verbeke, Bachor, & Nguyen, 2013, p. 536), with a particular,
homogeneous administrative heritage (centralized exporter, international
projector, international coordinator, or multicentered firm), into more
complex networks characterized by multiple patterns of competence building (Verbeke, 2013). Here, FSAs can originate in multiple locations where
the MNE is active, and knowledge transfers can also occur in multiple directions, and include third parties.

THE GLOBAL FACTORY

Rapid changes in the competitive landscape across industries and continuous managerial innovations require firms to provide goods that are more
aligned to customer needs through flexible network structures that stretch
far beyond the boundaries of the firm (Buckley & Ghauri, 2004). The
global factory represents (at least from a normative perspective) such a
well-integrated, flexible organizational framework covering internalized
activities, as well as activities conducted at least partly by subcontractors,
alliance partners, etc.

From a strategy perspective, two sets of decisions are critical: ownership
status and location decisions. The *first* set refers to the degree of control a
firm wants to maintain when conducting an economic activity. Here, firms
have to weigh the (transaction) costs associated with using the external
market against internal managerial costs associated with internalization

(Grøgaard & Verbeke, 2012; Verbeke & Hillemann, 2013). The *second* set relates to selecting host countries to conduct particular economic activities, taking into account the relative efficiency of multiple relevant markets, including markets for assets, asset services, and firms (Grøgaard & Verbeke, 2012). Grøgaard and Verbeke focus on the interconnectedness of these two decisions and suggest performing comparisons of the efficiency properties of clusters of "multiple transactions in multiple markets simultaneously" (2012, p. 8).

In the global factory, transaction costs occur "in assembling the business processes of the firm (collections of activities that are technologically or managerially linked) so that they jointly contribute to value added" (Buckley, 2012, p. 77). Internalization theory suggests that transaction costs can be identified at the level of individual transactions and classes of transactions. On the one hand, such costs result from imperfections in information available to specific economic actors, as well as from their limited information processing capabilities. On the other hand, these costs are related to imperfections in "making good on open-ended promises" (Verbeke & Greidanus, 2009). The above-mentioned imperfections should always be assessed in a comparative fashion, through evaluating alternative, real-world governance approaches. The first type of imperfection refers to bounded rationality, whereas the second type reflects to bounded reliability (Verbeke, 2013).

In line with internalization theory, the ownership strategy of the global factory is really an optimization challenge involving the effective bundling of firm resources and complementary resources of potential partners in host countries, who might contribute strengths in, for example, cost-efficient production or in marketing and distribution (Hennart, 2009; Verbeke & Hillemann, 2013). In order to address appropriately this optimization challenge, global factory senior managers must assess the tradability in external markets of their own company's FSAs as well as the tradability of complementary resources held by third parties in the host country and then select the most suitable operating mode (see Table 2).

In efficient external markets, the MNE's FSAs as well as third-party resources are easy to transact, whereas in inefficient markets they are not. Hence, the "efficiency of external markets" criterion, operationalized in terms of the tradability of the resources considered, represents an actionable tool for global factory senior management to determine which operating mode should be selected, for example, international joint ventures/ strategic partnerships, external contractual agreements, or wholly owned operations. Importantly, the most efficient alternative does not only depend

Table 2.   Global Factory Ownership Strategy.

		Global factory-specific advantages	
		Efficient market	Inefficient market
Complementary assets/ capabilities held by third party	Efficient market	1. Contractual agreements	3. Global factory subsidiaries
	Inefficient market	2. Wholly owned third-party subsidiaries	4. Strategic partnerships

Source: Based on Grøgaard and Verbeke (2012) and Hennart (2009).

on the MNE's FSAs but also on access to complementary resources held by their parties.

We have suggested above that ownership and location strategies result from a comparison of real-world alternatives in terms of production and transaction costs but assuming equivalent value creation. However, assessing transaction costs in real-world settings is often very complex. Despite the fact that information and communications technology (ICT) advances have facilitated significant structural changes in MNEs, "away from the traditional federative system towards more tightly integrated and controlled entities," procedural justice remains a key determinant to make intraorganizational knowledge transfers work and hence to make a global factories successful (Verbeke et al., 2013; Yamin & Sinkovics, 2007, p. 324).

Procedural justice refers to the level of fairness in decision-making processes (Kim & Mauborgne, 1991). If managers perceive the decision-making process as fair, they will "go beyond what is expected of them, and engage in creative, innovative, and cooperative behavior when implementing corporate head office decisions, even if disagreeing with the direction selected" (Kim & Mauborgne, 1993, 1996; Verbeke et al., 2013, p. 539). In other words, complex organizational forms such as the global factory require two-way or even multidirectional information flows with a substantial relational contracting component; otherwise such networks will not succeed. Korsgaard, Schweiger, and Sapienza (1995) have shown that procedural justice increases subordinate's willingness to accept strategic decisions mandated by the MNE's head office and thus improves the transferability of knowledge between units within the firm (Verbeke et al., 2013). Similarly, strategic decisions related to external contracting can also lead to failure if firms do not engage in high-quality communication and relational contracting with potential external partners (Verbeke & Kano, 2013).

FINE SLICING OF ECONOMIC ACTIVITIES AND THE RISE OF THE GLOBAL FACTORY

As a result of more advanced activity-based accounting and ICT systems, as well as other managerial innovations in coordination and control (e.g., global account management, formalized sharing of functional best practices), it is increasingly possible to assess the performance of narrow activity sets and to coordinate these with other sets, thereby facilitating decisions on whether to conduct activities internally or via external contracting, and on the location thereof. Fine slicing has led to a general shift from conventional trade in finished goods to trade in goods and services resulting from narrow activities in the value chain (Rugman, Verbeke, & Yuan, 2011)

In normative terms, senior managers at the MNE head office should be able to choose the most suitable governance mode and location for each single activity set within the global factory network. The outcome should be a flexible firm, well positioned to reduce the sum of production and transaction costs for each activity set. An MNE governing large sets of diverse, fine-sliced activities should have core FSAs in controlling and processing information. Here, senior managers should give priority to monitoring complex information flows on internal capabilities and (changes in) external market conditions, as compared to monitoring physical assets, which should increasingly be the subject of outsourcing. In other words, large MNEs should progressively reduce their ownership of physical assets, yet make sure to keep control over them, while focusing on the ownership of intangible assets in the form of know-how and trademarks.

Global factories operating according to the above-mentioned principles (combining the fine slicing of activities and the outsourcing of activities centered around physical assets) will experience high complexity in coordinating, monitoring, and integrating internal and outsourced activities. Especially for the latter, the global factory requires "interface competences" that allow aligning the activities of external contracting parties with the strategic roadmap of the global factory. In order to achieve network coherence beyond the firm's boundaries, senior managers should focus on a cooperative management approach that fosters relationship building and coordination with external contracting parties such as subcontractors and alliance partners (Buckley, 2012).

DECISION DYNAMICS IN THE GLOBAL FACTORY

In global factories, both an ownership decision and a location decision must be made for each fine-sliced economic activity. Here, senior managers should balance the current ownership status and location of each activity against alternative ownership status and location combinations, in line with the decision dynamics matrix represented in Fig. 1.

Requisite Change in Ownership Status

The horizontal axis of Fig. 1 describes the decision to be made on the ownership status of each fine-sliced activity, with a focus on requisite changes (low or high) as compared to the status quo.

Requisite Change in Location Decision

The vertical axis of Fig. 1 describes the decision to be made on the location of each fine-sliced activity, again with a focus on requisite changes (low or high) as compared to the status quo.

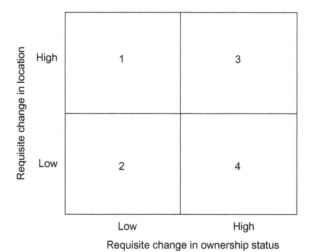

Fig. 1. Decision Dynamics in the Global Factory: Requisite Changes in Ownership Status and Location for Each Fine-Sliced Activity.

The Quadrants

Quadrant 1 of Fig. 1 includes fine-sliced economic activities that require only a low level of change (or no change at all) in their ownership status but do need a change in location. One conventional case includes economic activities involving labor-intensive production that in the past could not have been performed by low-cost employees in developing countries because of poor labor skills. However, due to macrolevel skills upgrading in some of these countries and microlevel learning through continuously increasing demands in complexity from foreign and local companies alike, local suppliers in low-cost markets such as China have become much more capable to complete more sophisticated manufacturing activities.

As a result, global factories have tended to relocate activities previously carried out in developed economies. One example is Logitech, one of the world's leading providers of personal computer and tablets accessories. In 1994, Logitech decided to relocate its own manufacturing from Ireland and the United States to Suzhou, in China. This decision showed "the confidence of the firm in the competencies of the Suzhou plant and the strategic importance of China as an input market" (Verbeke, 2013, p. 172). Today, this plant covers about half of Logitech's total production. With the remaining half being outsourced to contract manufacturers in Asia, Logitech proactively and systematically assesses which activities should remain inside the company and which can be left to external parties through a variety of contracting arrangements (Verbeke, 2013).

Quadrant 2 of Fig. 1 includes activities that may not require a substantial change (or even any change) in either ownership status or location. As one example, Apple Inc., the popular producer of consumer electronics and personal computers, was incorporated in 1977, in Cupertino (California, the United States), which today claims to be the heart of Silicon Valley (Apple, 2014). Apple's head office has remained in the same location, and Silicon Valley has arguably developed into the world's leading cluster for high-tech research and innovation in information technology and software. The development of Silicon Valley into a research hub has resulted in location advantages that have attracted technology-intensive firms from all over the world. Apple has benefited from this cluster's formation, which has contributed to strengthening further its FSAs in software and hardware design, as well as in branding. Apple has established several international R&D centers, namely, in Israel, Taiwan, and China, but irrespective of these recent overseas technology units, its main R&D activities continue to be performed in-house and are located in Cupertino. Apple is listed among the 100 most innovative companies in the world and is well positioned to maintain this favorable position in the foreseeable future (Forbes, 2013).

Quadrant 3 of Fig. 1 exemplifies a key feature of the global factory concept. A firm that structurally and systematically reflects on requisite changes in ownership status and location of fine-sliced activities arguably represents a flexible firm, able to respond rapidly to new information coming from the broader environment and to competitive pressures (Buckley, 2012). This quadrant illustrates the importance of actively managing the firm's portfolio of internalized and outsourced activities and the need to act rapidly when changes in ownership status and location are required.

In 2003, the German family enterprise Steiff, the well-known producer of traditional, hand-made teddy bears, started to outsource about a fifth of its production to China. However, Steiff did not benefit from the initially anticipated reduction in costs but instead experienced quality problems and supply bottlenecks. As a result, within five years Steiff announced its withdrawal from China as a country of production and its intent to re-establish full production in Europe by 2009 (New York Times, 2008). The Steiff case demonstrates that firms must thoroughly reflect both on the extent to which they internalize and on the location of fine-sliced activities. For most manufacturing firms, outsourcing and relocating (offshoring) at least parts of their production activities appears almost self-evident in order to earn cost efficiencies, bring less expensive products to the market place, and improve performance in terms of profitability and growth. However, the Steiff case suggests that companies should be careful not to lose their FSAs in the processes of outsourcing and offshoring. In this case, outsourcing to China was optimal neither as an ownership decision nor as a location decision.

Finally, Quadrant 4 of Fig. 1 discusses the case of fine-sliced activities requiring little or no change in location but a change in ownership status. Here, the global factory should consider switching from the current ownership status to a lower or higher control level, while preserving the existing location. One example is automotive supplier Bosch's joint venture with the Japanese firms GS Yuasa and Mitsubishi in November 2013. These three companies combined forces and launched an R&D center focusing on next-generation lithium ion batteries. It was a supplier initiative, supporting the introduction of electric vehicles as a successful mass product starting in 2020. The joint venture is presently headquartered in Stuttgart, Germany, where Bosch was founded in 1886. The German supplier is the largest shareholder with a 50 percent equity stake, with the two Japanese firms sharing the remainder, holding 25 percent each. Bosch entered into this partnership agreement to gain in-depth knowledge on the manufacturing of lithium ion battery cells from GS Yuasa and to benefit from Mitsubishi's sales network and experience in establishing global value-added chains. In return, Bosch contributes its complete portfolio of components for electro-mobility and specific competences in battery management systems. It further shares its expertise in large-scale manufacturing of complex products. This example illustrates (at least from Bosch's perspective) that a change in location may not be required rather Bosch preferred to establish a joint venture close to most of its own German R&D centers and its worldwide headquarters. However, given the lower likelihood of success associated with wholly owned operations, Bosch decided to seek external partners with complementary resources. As a result, Bosch will be able to augment its own internal competencies by developing new non-location-bound FSAs. More specifically, it will create an upgraded electric vehicle battery with twice the prevailing maximum capacity and become more competitive in the market place (Mitsubishi, 2014).

STRENGTHS OF THE GLOBAL FACTORY

According to Buckley (2012), the global factory has five features that can be interpreted as its core strengths or as global factory-specific advantages (GFSAs). These GFSAs are what distinguishes global factories from MNEs involved in conventional vertical and horizontal integration.

Ownership of Intangible Assets

Senior managers in the global factory focus on establishing appropriate control rather than the ownership of assets, though ownership of intangible assets often does remain important. A global factory thus consists of both assets under the firm's sole ownership and a variety of contractual arrangements with external parties (which may include partial ownership, as in the case of equity joint ventures), allowing access to assets available in the market place. In order to economize on bounded rationality and bounded reliability, outsourced activities may require close supervision, especially when they are strongly linked to internalized activities. In general terms, increasing levels of outsourcing can be observed across manufacturing industries, at least as far as physical assets are concerned (Buckley, 2012).

However, in the realm of critical intangible assets, global factories appear to have a preference for ownership, partly for risk mitigation reasons. Internalizing intangible assets guarantees that the global factory can retain full control of knowledge stocks and flows considered vital to its sustained performance in the market place.

Ownership of Core Activities

In line with the perceived need to retain ownership of intangible assets, a number of activities typically need to remain under the firm's ownership, namely, if these are considered "core" activities, critical to compete successfully in international markets. Such activities typically include those focused on new knowledge generation critical to sustained competitiveness.

Contestability of Ownership Status and Location of Single Activity Sets

No single activity set established in any location is considered "above the law" in the sense of guaranteed, continued internal organization in this dedicated location over long periods of time. Every internal activity set is "contestable." The MNE head office is supposed to reassess systematically, and in an ongoing fashion the optimal location and mode of governance of each single activity set, and may decide to relocate and switch from internal organization to external contracting (or vice versa) any of these activity sets. Given a general preference to retain ownership of intangible assets and a number of core activities, the location thereof still does remain contestable.

Flexibility

Given the above three GFSAs, perhaps the most critical strength of the global factory is its flexibility as the outcome of senior management engaging in a systematic and ongoing reflection on what should be done inside versus outside the firm and in what locations. Such flexibility allows substantial resilience, that is, the ability to absorb environmental shocks quickly and effectively and to adapt to rapid changes in the competitive landscape, even though shifts in ownership status and location can also be associated with substantial costs (Buckley & Casson, 1998). Flexibility on the input side means contemplating a variety of avenues to access valuable intermediate goods and on the output side a similar variety of options for distributing and selling final products. Such flexibility requires investments in modern management tools, including an integrative, intelligent forecasting system, and a sophisticated, internal knowledge management system.

MNE Head Office as Controlling Intelligence

The MNE head office becomes the global factory's "controlling intelligence" and "activity orchestrator," with full authority to make decisions on the ownership status and location of any activity considered part of the firm's value chain, therefore conferring an advantage to this type of firm as compared with the more traditional, vertically and horizontally integrated firms that are subject to more internal inertia. This decision-making feature is critical to the success of the global factory, with the head office initially determining the appropriate fine slicing of the value chain and subsequently tightly controlling these fine-sliced activities. Such tight control includes selecting, and if needed changing, the ownership status and location of each fine-sliced activity set, while exercising full control over information flows and engaging in strategy implementation that should benefit the global factory as a whole. Given the above head office responsibilities, new managerial skills, and especially managerial practices, need to be developed on "how to manage spatially dispersed and organizationally diffuse units within the global factory" (Buckley, 2012, p. 83).

CONCEPTUAL WEAKNESSES

The main weakness of the global factory paradigm is the relative lack of predictive capacity as compared to mainstream internalization theory. The following five limitations highlight some critical issues to be considered in future research on the global factory.

Ownership of Intangible Assets

In some cases, ownership of tangible rather than only intangible assets remains important (e.g., in the energy and natural resources sectors and in sectors characterized by complex production engineering that must be closely aligned with more upstream and more downstream activities). The global factory paradigm argues that the control of "complex flow(s) of information on external conditions and internal competences (...) is far more important than control of physical assets" and recommends externalizing physical assets rather than intangible assets (Buckley, 2012, pp. 82–83). However, the global factory paradigm does not itself provide a clear and unambiguous criterion to determine which assets and related activities should remain inside the firm. Here, core competence thinking provides some key tests on which assets, and more broadly resource bundles, should remain inside the firm (Verbeke, 2013):

— Difficult for competitors to imitate (because of uncertainties/ambiguities regarding expected efficiency and requisite internal coordination and learning);
— Provides potential access to wide variety of markets;
— Makes a significant contribution to perceived customer benefits from the end product;
— Its loss would have an important negative effect on the firm's present and future performance, in terms of value creation.

Ownership of Core Activities

Related to the above, core activities are supposed to remain under the firm's control, but the global factory paradigm does not really explain, beyond naming activities such as branding and engineering, which activities must be undertaken inside the firm and why. The head office of the global factory should decide for each fine-sliced activity whether to outsource it or to keep it in-house. The head office is supposed to exercise proper judgment and build upon prior experience to make these types of governance decisions. However, from a managerial perspective, it would be of great value to outline conceptually how the head office should determine what constitutes a core activity that should remain inside the firm. Here again, the four above tests related to core assets can be useful, and these can ultimately be synthesized under the heading of easy versus difficult tradability of assets and capabilities, whereby both the global factory's resource base and that of potential contracting partners should be considered.

Contestability of Ownership Status and Location of Single Activity Sets

No single activity set is "off limits" in terms of being a potential candidate for outsourcing and/or offshoring, but some activities reflecting the firm's

administrative heritage (or its "DNA") are embedded in managerial practices that surely must be exempted from this rule (save a crisis that could
bankrupt the company). Firms command FSAs derived from physical and
intangible assets. By engaging in resource recombination, firms combine
"in novel ways existing resources, often in conjunction with newly accessed
resources" (Verbeke, 2013, p. 38). However, without reflecting on specific
core activities and even locations within which the firm's administrative
heritage is embedded, the global factory risks losing those very routines
and recombination capabilities that constitute the firm's key strengths and
directly affect its long-run competitiveness in industry. Especially in times
of crisis, global factories are assumed to benefit from their flexible organizational approach that provides resilience, but this is conditional upon key
FSAs, embedded in some of the firm's activities and in localized, key organizational units (i.e., its competence carriers), remaining under ownership
and control of the global factory.

Flexibility

This is the key feature of the global factory, but it can be associated with
unintended negative spillovers, for example, if short run production and
transaction cost economizing considerations result in outsourcing and offshoring at the expense of longer-term innovation performance by internal
units that can simply not be replicated by the MNE's external network
partners. The global factory paradigm argues that the MNE's head office
will decide on the ownership status and location of specific activities following transaction cost and production cost minimizing strategies. But in such
process, the head office may well overlook unintended, negative spillover
effects on other economic activities that are not directly involved in the
joint transaction cost and production cost minimization exercise at hand.
The head office should obviously consider possible spillover effects
that might overrule any projected cost savings associated with outsourcing
and/or offshoring as compared to internalization in low-distance
locations. Unfortunately, a head office giving priority to achieving short
run efficiencies might prefer outsourcing and offshoring rather than building up internal capabilities, though the latter could provide opportunities
to generate higher performance in the long run. The global factory should
deploy flexible strategies, yet choices on whether or not to internalize,
and where to locate, should be the result of careful reflection, considering

short-term and long-term consequences as well as possible, unintended spillover effects.

MNE Head Office as Controlling Intelligence

The head office is critical in the global factory, but this role of controlling intelligence and orchestrator neglects the unique bounded rationality and bounded reliability challenges facing the head office itself as compared to, for example, subsidiaries equipped with a unique resource base and subsidiary-specific advantages (Rugman & Verbeke, 2001). Bounded rationality means that the head office has incomplete information and only limited information processing capacity. It also means that the head office and foreign units will each "focus on particular facets [of information], as a function of their position in the MNE and their geographic location in the MNE network" (Hillemann & Verbeke, 2014, p. 77; Verbeke & Yuan, 2005). The selectivity in deciding what constitutes "relevant" information results in biased decision-making, which in turn can lead to internal conflicts between the head office and subsidiaries. In addition, even if economic actors identify identical information facets as being relevant to strategic decision-making, the interpretation thereof can differ as a function of these economic actors' background and experience, whereby it is unclear whether the MNE head office will necessarily always be the best judge to make desirable choices on governance and location.

In addition to bounded rationality, a second behavioral assumption, namely, bounded reliability, has implications for the role of the head office in ownership status and location decisions. Here, the head office of the global factory might itself be prone to opportunism in terms of making ex-ante false promises (to shareholders or other stakeholders) and/or engaging in ex-post breach of trust. In addition, bounded reliability often involves "benevolent preference reversal associated with reprioritization [and] benevolent preference reversal associated with scaling back on overcommitment," whereby the head office is as likely as any other MNE unit or external contracting party to be unreliable (Verbeke & Greidanus, 2009, p. 1482). When combining bounded reliability and bounded rationality challenges, it is not clear whether the head office of the global factory can reasonably be predicted to operate in all circumstances as the most effective controlling intelligence and orchestrator inside the firm, while at the same time being the actor best positioned to engage in information exchange and relationship building with external partners in the global factory network (Forsgren, 2013).

CONCLUSION

In the more integrated, contemporary world economy, the global factory as an organizational form has undoubtedly gained in importance. A variety of economic indicators suggests a significant shift of economic activities from highly developed economies to developing and transition economies. This macrolevel shift has been associated with the rise of MNEs characterized by more internationally dispersed value chains and more complex organizational approaches.

From a normative perspective, the global factory should function as a well-integrated, flexible network, with a head office that orchestrates a large set of in-house activities, contractual agreements, strategic partnerships, and other joint operations with external partners across borders. With this organizational form, the head office faces two main strategic challenges, namely, developing an ownership strategy and a location strategy. The ownership strategy addresses what constitutes the optimal governance mode for narrowly defined economic activities, whereas the location strategy is "used to differentiate the wholly owned 'hub' (centrally located) from the jointly owned 'spokes'" (Buckley, 2012, p. 78). The main intellectual contribution of the global factory paradigm in the context of the two above sets of strategic decisions is that both have to be made for each fine-sliced economic activity separately, but taking into account efficiency effects on the entire network. Here, we have proposed a "decision dynamics" matrix, guiding managerial strategies on ownership status and location.

In line with internalization theory, the ownership strategy represents the global factory's response to an optimization challenge that involves the bundling of non-location-bound FSAs and complementary resources held by external economic actors, as a prerequisite for successful foreign market expansion (Verbeke, 2013). In other words, the global factory must bundle effectively its own firm-level resources with accessible host country resources controlled by third parties in the markets for asset services, assets, and firms (Hennart, 2009). We have described the global factory's five key features (Buckley, 2012). These represent the strengths of that particular organizational form. We have named these strengths "GFSAs," to distinguish the global factory from MNEs involved in conventional vertical and horizontal integration.

However, when analyzing the global factory paradigm through an internalization theory lens, it appears that each strength can also be considered a weakness, thereby highlighting the paradigm's relative lack of predictive capacity, as compared to what internalization theory would suggest. In essence, ownership status and location strategies in the global factory, just as in any other MNE, will be largely determined by the need to engage in effective asset-bundling of firm-level resources with requisite complementary resources in host countries. Access to the latter will be largely determined by the efficiency (or the lack thereof) of the various markets for these resources prevailing in these host countries.

Ultimately, global factories, as well as conventional horizontally and vertically integrated MNEs and even international new ventures, will all follow the same economizing principles, namely, deciding on the ownership status and location of specific activities as a function of the tradability and bundling characteristics of requisite (and accessible) resources. These characteristics will determine the severity of the bounded rationality and bounded reliability challenges associated with each alternative operating mode and alternative location.

Just as is the case with many other strategic management phenomena, ranging from the survival of family firms (Verbeke & Kano, 2012a), the timing of international new ventures (Verbeke, Zargarzadeh, & Osiyevskyy, 2014), the conduct of regional strategies (Verbeke & Kano, 2012b) or the managing of global MNEs (Verbeke & Greidanus, 2009; Verbeke & Kenworthy, 2008), internalization theory rules because it is the only theory that can explain and predict empirical regularities without the benefits of 20/20 hindsight and the related "conceptual reengineering."

REFERENCES

Apple. (2014). *Apple investor relations*. Retrieved from http://investor.apple.com/faq.cfm? FaqSetID=6. Accessed on July 8, 2014.

Buckley, P. (2012). The multinational enterprise as a global factory. In A. Verbeke & H. Merchant (Eds.), *Handbook of research on international strategic management* (pp. 77—92). Cheltenham: Edward Elgar Publishing.

Buckley, P. J. (2009). The impact of the global factory on economic development. *Journal of World Business*, *44*(2), 131—143.

Buckley, P. J. (2010). The role of headquarters in the global factory. In U. Andersson & U. Holm (Eds.), *Managing the contemporary multinational — The role of headquarters* (pp. 60—84). Cheltenham: Edward Elgar Publishing.

Buckley, P. J. (2011). International integration and coordination in the global factory. *Management International Review, 51*, 269–283.

Buckley, P. J., & Casson, M. C. (1998). Analyzing foreign market entry strategies: Extending the internalization theory approach. *Journal of International Business Studies, 29*(3), 539–561.

Buckley, P. J., & Ghauri, P. N. (2004). Globalisation, economic geography and the strategy of multinational enterprises. *Journal of International Business Studies, 35*(2), 81–98.

Buckley, P. J., & Strange, R. (2013). The governance of the global factory. *Proceedings of the 39th European International Business Academy Annual Conference*, Bremen, Germany, December 12–14, 2013.

Forbes. (2013). *The world's most innovative companies*. Retrieved from http://www.forbes.com/innovative-companies/list/#page:1_sort:0_direction:asc_search:apple_filter:All%20regions_filter:All%20industries. Accessed on July 1, 2014.

Forsgren, M. (2013). *Theories of the multinational firm: A multidimensional creature in the global economy*. Cheltenham: Edward Elgar Publishing.

Grøgaard, B., & Verbeke, A. (2012). Twenty key hypotheses that make internalization theory the general theory of international strategic management. In A. Verbeke & H. Merchant (Eds.), *Handbook of research on international strategic management* (pp. 7–30). Cheltenham: Edward Elgar Publishing.

Hennart, J.-F. (2009). Down with MNE-centric theories! Market entry and expansion as the bundling of MNE and local assets. *Journal of International Business Studies, 40*(9), 1432–1454.

Hillemann, J., & Verbeke, A. (2014). An internalization theory perspective on the bottom of the pyramid. In R. Van Tulder, A. Verbeke, & R. Strange (Eds.), *Progress in international business research* (pp. 69–90). Bingley: Emerald Group Publishing Limited.

Kim, W. C., & Mauborgne, R. A. (1991). Implementing global strategies: The role of procedural justice. *Strategic Management Journal, 12*(4), 125–144.

Kim, W. C., & Mauborgne, R. A. (1993). Procedural justice, attitudes, and subsidiary top management compliance with multinationals' corporate strategic decisions. *Academy of Management Journal, 36*(3), 502–527.

Kim, W. C., & Mauborgne, R. A. (1996). Procedural justice and managers' in-role and extra-role behavior: The case of the multinational. *Management Science, 42*(4), 499–516.

Korsgaard, M. A., Schweiger, D. M., & Sapienza, H. J. (1995). The role of procedural justice in building commitment, attachment, and trust in strategic decision making teams. *Academy of Management Journal, 38*(1), 60–84.

Mitsubishi. (2014). *Bosch, GS Yuasa, and Mitsubishi Corporation to double capacity for Electric Vehicle battery*. Published on February 12, 2014 by Mitsubishi Corporation. Retrieved from http://www.mitsubishicorp.com/jp/en/pr/archive/2014/html/0000023638.html. Accessed on July 2, 2014.

New York Times. (2008). *"For some, 'Made in China' doesn't fit"* by Sylvia Westall published on July 14, 2008. Retrieved from http://www.nytimes.com/2008/07/14/business/worldbusiness/14iht-steiff.2.14481596.html?_r=0. Accessed on July 1, 2014.

Rugman, A., & Verbeke, A. (2001). Subsidiary-specific advantages in multinational enterprises. *Strategic Management Journal, 22*(3), 237–250.

Rugman, A., & Verbeke, A. (2005). *Analysis of multinational strategic management: The selected scientific papers of Alan M. Rugman and Alain Verbeke*. Cheltenham: Edward Elgar Publishing.

Rugman, A., Verbeke, A., & Yuan, W. (2011). Re-conceptualizing Bartlett and Ghoshal's classification of national subsidiary roles in the multinational enterprise. *Journal of Management Studies*, *48*(2), 253−277.

UNCTAD. (2013). *Methodology and classification − geographical regions/DEvelopment status.* Retrieved from http://unctadstat.unctad.org/UnctadStatMetadata/Classifications/ UnctadStat.Countries.GeographicalRegionslist.Classification_En.pdf. Accessed on June 30, 2014.

Verbeke, A. (2013). *International business strategy*. Cambridge: Cambridge University Press.

Verbeke, A., Bachor, V., & Nguyen, B. (2013). Procedural justice, not absorptive capacity, matters in multinational enterprise ICT transfers. *Management International Review*, *53*(4), 535−554.

Verbeke, A., & Greidanus, N. S. (2009). The end of the opportunism vs trust debate: Bounded reliability as a new envelope concept in research on MNE governance. *Journal of International Business Studies*, *40*(9), 1471−1495.

Verbeke, A., & Hillemann, J. (2013). Internalization theory as the general theory of international strategic management: Jean-François Hennart's contributions. In T. Devinney, T. Pedersen, & L. Tihanyi (Eds.), *Advances in international management* (pp. 35−52). Bingley: Emerald Group Publishing Limited.

Verbeke, A., & Kano, L. (2012a). The transaction cost economics (TCE) theory of the family firm: Family-based human asset specificity and the bifurcation bias. *Entrepreneurship Theory and Practice*, *36*(6), 1183−1205.

Verbeke, A., & Kano, L. (2012b). An internalization theory rationale for MNE regional strategy. *Multinational Business Review*, *20*(2), 135−152.

Verbeke, A., & Kano, L. (2013). The transaction cost economics (TCE) theory of trading favors. *Asia Pacific Journal of Management*, *30*(2), 409−431.

Verbeke, A., & Kenworthy, T. P. (2008). Multidivisional vs metanational governance of the multinational enterprise. *Journal of International Business Studies*, *39*(6), 940−956.

Verbeke, A., & Yuan, W. (2005). Subsidiary autonomous activities in multinational enterprises: A transaction cost perspective. *Management International Review*, *45*(2), 31−52.

Verbeke, A., Zargarzadeh, A., & Osiyevskyy, O. (2014). Internalization theory, entrepreneurship and international new ventures. *Multinational Business Review*, *22*(3), (forthcoming).

Yamin, M. (2011). A commentary on Peter Buckley's writings on the global factory. *Management International Review*, *51*, 285−293.

Yamin, M., & Sinkovics, R. R. (2007). ICT and MNE reorganization: The paradox of control. *Critical Perspectives on International Business*, *3*(4), 322−336.

CHAPTER 3

CONSIDERING THE LOCAL PARTNER. A TWO-SIDED PERSPECTIVE ON TRANSACTION COSTS DURING MARKET ENTRY

Alexander H. Wisgickl and Jonas Puck

ABSTRACT

Purpose — *Building on transaction cost economics (TCE) and recent critique on international business (IB) research, we intend to sharpen our knowledge on the application of TCE in entry mode studies.*

Methodology/approach — *We develop a two-sided model of transaction costs by considering the multinational corporation (MNC) and the local partner.*

Findings — *Overall, we illustrate that the decisions firms undertake are not always in line with traditional MNC-centric TCE reasoning. Specifically, we identify three situations when "traditional" TCE predicts transaction costs lower than they actually are. Based on our findings we derive implications for future TCE studies.*

Multinational Enterprises, Markets and Institutional Diversity
Progress in International Business Research, Volume 9, 49–69
Copyright © 2014 by Emerald Group Publishing Limited
All rights of reproduction in any form reserved
ISSN: 1745-8862/doi:10.1108/S1745-886220140000009002

Originality/value – Our study is among the first to highlight the rele-vance of potential partners' transaction costs during market entry. Our model of dually impinged transaction costs is supposed to guide future research and can be of direct use to firms assessing costs of entry.

Keywords: Entry mode choice; transaction cost economics; asset specificity; uncertainty; local partner; conceptual paper

INTRODUCTION

When venturing abroad, firms have to decide on the entry mode for their foreign operations. Prior research has argued that this "boundary decision" involves a long-term decision given the difficulty of changing already estab-lished modes and thus entails a significant performance implication (Brouthers & Hennart, 2007; Morschett, Schramm-Klein, & Swoboda, 2010). Not surprisingly, entry mode choices have been extensively investi-gated in the last 15 years and are among the most researched topics in the international business (IB) literature (Brouthers & Hennart, 2007; Canabal & White, 2008).

To explain why firms choose specific governance modes when entering foreign markets, transaction cost economics (TCE) is the most frequently used theory. According to Canabal and White (2008), TCE appears twice as many times as the second most used theory (OLI paradigm). TCE focuses on "transactions and the costs which attend completing transac-tions by one institutional mode rather than another" (Williamson, 1975, p. 2). Relying on the interplay of bounded rationality and opportunism, TCE predicts that firms choose a governance form that minimizes the costs associated with managing and monitoring transactions. Three main factors determine the differences between transactions: asset specificity (AS), uncertainty, and frequency (Williamson, 1985). Anderson and Gatignon (1986) or Hennart (1989, 1991) were among the first to introduce TCE in the context of international entry mode. Since then many scholars (e.g., Brouthers & Brouthers, 2001; Brouthers, Brouthers, & Werner, 2003; Contractor & Kundu, 1998; Erramilli & Rao, 1993; Hennart, 1991; Kim, Kim, & Lee, 2002) have applied traditional or enhanced TCE models.

The above-mentioned theories, including TCE, have been recently (e.g., Hennart, 2009) criticized to be too comprehensive and to therefore fail to explain many entry mode choices. It has been argued that seminal contributions such as Anderson and Gatignon (1986) and Johanson and Vahlne (1977) have adopted what Hennart (2009) calls an "MNC-centric" (MNC = multinational corporation) approach when analyzing these decisions. While previous studies have undoubtedly contributed to the explanation of firms' boundary decisions, they view the entry mode choice and subsequent changes as entirely determined by the MNC. Moreover, while other seminal works such as Dunning (1988) do acknowledge that foreign market expansion requires the combination of firm-specific and local assets, they assume, however, that these local assets are freely available to MNCs (Hennart, 2009).

Altogether, extant frameworks and specifically most existing TCE publications neglect that the evolution of the MNC is determined by both owners of firm-specific assets (e.g., the MNC) and owners of local assets (e.g., local partner abroad). Specifically, existing research deserts the important role of market efficiency for assets that are (1) held by firms in the foreign markets and (2) sought by firms investing in a specific market. Taking into account the nature of markets for such assets would, according to Hennart (2009), provide a more comprehensive explanation of entry mode decisions than previously suggested perspectives. Hennart (2009) thus moves beyond existing research and recommends scholars to look at both sides of the coin (e.g., owners of firm-specific and owners of local assets) when modeling entry modes decisions. Undoubtedly, his approach provides a valuable extension of existing theories in the field of IB, which we want to build our study on.

However, we want to take his work further. Hennart (2009) solely focuses on the tradability of assets. We translate this terminology into a language being used in common entry mode literature and therefore make it better applicable in this context. Specifically, we intend to develop a model based on the traditional TC determinants asset specificity (Hennart, 1991) and uncertainty (Anderson & Gatignon, 1986; Williamson, 1985). In addition, we see uncertainty as a dynamic variable in this model. Some prior entry mode studies from a TCE perspective have already implicitly adopted a similar argumentation toward this determinant, and it accounts for both internal and external uncertainty.

As Brouthers and Hennart (2007, p. 403) examined in their review on international entry mode research, most studies on uncertainty and entry mode contend that "... uncertainty encourages firms to maintain flexibility and, hence, to choose market rather than hierarchical forms of governance." Therefore, IB scholars argue that market forms of governance or shared-entry modes, for example, as in an international joint venture (IJV), comparably tie up fewer resources and offer MNCs greater flexibility, thereby reducing the firm's exposure to external uncertainty (e.g., Erramilli & Rao, 1993; Gatignon & Anderson, 1988; Kim & Hwang, 1992). Consequently, this stream in the IB literature deviates from the original Williamson TCE model, which suggests that companies choose hierarchical forms of governance in insecure environments in order to avoid opportunism and economize on transaction costs (Morschett et al., 2010). Thus, this approach also implies that by integrating a foreign partner who is familiar with the local environment, the MNC is able to decrease external uncertainty (e.g., Zhao, Luo, & Suh, 2004). Similarly, this dynamic perspective has been applied to internal uncertainty. Scholars (e.g., Brouthers, 2002; Brouthers & Nakos, 2004) argue that high behavioral uncertainties are strongly related to the choice of a hierarchical governance structure. Brouthers and Hennart (2007) state that by integrating a foreign partner (e.g., shared ownership), his incentives to act opportunistically can be reduced and, consequently, internal uncertainties can be reduced. We contend that the same is true from the perspective of the local partner. In line with these scholars' perspectives, we thus see the determinants' internal uncertainty and external as dynamic dimensions as it seems reasonable to argue that for each partner, internal and external uncertainty are subject to change as a consequence of joint operations.

By integrating the dual-sided perspective as well as the dynamic nature of uncertainties, we contribute to the field of entry mode literature from a TCE perspective in the following ways: First, we develop a two-sided model of transaction costs and identify three specific situations when TCE not necessarily fails to explain the entry mode choice but predicts the transaction costs lower than they actually are. Here, traditional applications of TCE may thus partially lead to wrong recommendations. Second, we discuss uncertainty as a determinant that is rather dynamic than static; specifically, we provide evidence that involving a local partner into the entry mode decision might increase or decrease uncertainty in a foreign environment. The same accounts for the local partner. The partner's uncertainty perception might also increase by including a foreign firm into local operations. Hence, including a foreign partner might not be as attractive.

Overall, we hope to unravel some of the many contradictory findings in current entry mode research (Brouthers & Hennart, 2007; Crook, Combs, Ketchen, & Aguinis, 2013; Zhao et al., 2004) with our approach. From a managerial perspective, the findings may reveal to what extent the internationalization strategy of the MNC depends on the characteristics of potential local partners in the overseas market. Thus, the findings may indicate to foreign managers when and to what extent they need to accommodate to the characteristics of local partners.

The remainder of this chapter is organized as follows. First, we describe traditional TCE predictions for entry mode decisions. Second, we provide reasoning for the two most important assumptions in our model: On the one hand that the local partner bases his assessment on transaction costs when considering the integration of a foreign MNC in the local operations similar to the MNC. On the other hand that uncertainty is dynamic and that many ownership decisions are actually made because firms want to benefit from this dynamism. Third, we develop a combined TCE approach, including the MNC and the local partner, and illustrate when the costs for finding and negotiating with a suitable partner as well as monitoring and controlling this partner are predicted too low from a single-sided TCE perspective. Finally, we summarize the implications of our study.

THEORETICAL BACKGROUND

Entry modes are governance structures that coordinate international transactions (Zhao et al., 2004). In our study we investigate the determinants of equity-based entry modes, for example, the choice between an IJV and a wholly owned subsidiary (WOS). In favor of the theoretical argumentation down below, we see IJVs as forms of governance that include a local partner and where equity is shared. In accordance with Hennart (2009), it covers both greenfields and acquisitions. WOSs are hierarchical forms of governance that do not involve a local partner and are consequently entry modes with full control and equity. We do not include other entry mode forms in our discussion such as exporting or licensing, to assure comparability with previous TCE entry mode studies (e.g., Hennart, 1991; Makino & Neupert, 2000; Padmanabhan & Cho, 1996).

As described in the introduction and from a TCE perspective, firms choose the governance mode that minimizes the costs associated with managing and monitoring transactions. Hence, transaction costs are mainly costs that arise for, on the one hand, finding and negotiating with a suitable partner and on the other hand monitoring and controlling this partner (Agarwal & Ramaswami, 1992; Gatignon & Anderson, 1988; Hennart, 1991; Makino & Neupert, 2000). For the basic TCE hypothesis, we assume that firms, which perceive high levels of transaction costs (as compared to organizational costs), tend to choose hierarchical forms of governance, as examined by Brouthers (2002) in his *Journal of International Business Studies* decade award study.

According to TCE reasoning, the decision between a WOS and an IJV is determined by three main factors: asset specificity, uncertainty, and frequency (Williamson, 1985). In the context of international market entry, Anderson and Gatignon (1986) or Hennart (1989, 1991) were the first to introduce TCE in an entry mode context. Since then many scholars (e.g., Brouthers & Brouthers, 2001; Brouthers et al., 2003; Contractor & Kundu, 1998; Erramilli & Rao, 1993; Hennart, 1991; Kim et al., 2002) have tested these relationships. In this chapter and as in many TCE studies so far (e.g., Brouthers, 2002; Brouthers & Nakos, 2004), we do not take frequency into consideration. This is due to the fact that in most studies, transactions are considered to be continuous, which excludes the need for a frequency measure. Further, it is still not clear if the determinant frequency actually affects the choice of entry mode (e.g., Brouthers & Brouthers, 2003; Erramilli & Rao, 1993). In the following sections, we concentrate on the determinants asset specificity and uncertainty. The latter we distinguish into internal and external uncertainty (e.g., Anderson & Gatignon, 1986; Brouthers & Nakos, 2004; Zhao et al., 2004).

Asset Specificity

Asset specificity represents the central dimension in the TCE framework and has been argued to be an important antecedent of entry mode choices (Brouthers, 2002; Gatignon & Anderson, 1988). In this chapter, we are in line with the definition by Anderson and Gatignon (1986, p. 7): Transaction-specific investments are "investments (physical and human) that are valuable only in a narrow range of transactions, that is, specialized to one or a few users or uses and see assets as investments." Therefore, these investments would lose their value if used outside the intended purpose and would lead to high levels of sunk costs (Rindfleisch & Heide, 1997).

From a TCE perspective, firms with high asset specificity incur considerable transaction costs as other firms may opportunistically exploit this dependency to pursue their self-interest and change the terms of the formerly stipulated contract – a situation that is named hold-up or shirking in the TCE literature (Klein, 1980). In addition to the hold-up or shirking potential, firms may also use the dependency to gradually absorb firm-specific assets (Lu & Hébert, 2005) or free-ride on these assets (Zhao et al., 2004). Altogether, the dependency stemming from asset specificity leads to the proposition that classical markets fail for these assets. As a result of the market imperfections, asset specificity is thus assumed to generate high levels of transaction costs for firms. Hence, a company with high asset specificity would opt for a going alone strategy instead of integrating a foreign partner into the operations abroad, such as in an IJV.

Uncertainty

Besides asset specificity, uncertainty represents a core dimension in TCE and has been argued to influence the choice of entry mode. TCE suggests that firms are confronted with two different types of uncertainty (Anderson & Gatignon, 1986): Internal uncertainty (IU) and external uncertainty (EU).

On the one hand, firms face *internal uncertainties* which "arise from the inability of a company to predict the behavior of individuals in foreign countries" (Brouthers & Nakos, 2004, p. 232). IU thus refers to the unpredictability within the operations of the foreign subsidiary (Lu & Hébert, 2005) and predominantly stems from the risk of opportunistic behavior, which may involve actions like distorting or hiding important pieces of information. Moreover, IU raises transaction costs as firms cannot accurately predict behavior within their firm boundaries and must thus integrate more elaborate (and thus costly) monitoring and controlling systems (Anderson & Gatignon, 1986). Consequently, firms with high IU would opt for a going alone strategy instead of integrating a foreign partner into the operations abroad, such as in an IJV.

On the other hand, firms are – according to TCE – also confronted with *external uncertainties*. Although IU mainly concerns the unpredictability of future actions within the subsidiary, EU is predominantly associated with the difficulty of specifying environmental contingencies in contracts in advance (Brouthers & Hennart, 2007) and also refers to the unpredictability stemming from the environment (Delios & Henisz, 2003). For instance, with rising political instability, legal insecurity, or socioeconomic fluctuations, the level of EU in the host market is expected to increase (Gatignon & Anderson, 1988). Altogether, high EU enhances the level of transaction costs as firms face difficulties in foreseeing changes in the institutional environment a priori. Scholars (e.g., Erramilli & Rao, 1993; Gatignon & Anderson, 1988) found empirical support that firms will pursue an entry mode that involves low equity involvement. A low resource commitment enables companies to stay flexible and if necessary withdraw from the market or change the partner if severe external influences would affect the operations abroad (Brouthers & Nakos, 2004). Hence, a company will favor an entry mode with low equity involvement such as in an IJV over a WOS, when external uncertainties are high.

TCE AND THE LOCAL FIRM

As outlined above and in line with recent criticism of the IB literature, we include both the perspective of the MNC and the local partner in the entry mode decision. Before we identify three specific situations when "traditional" TCE predicts transaction costs lower than they actually are, we provide reasoning for the two most important assumptions in our model. First, we argue that the local partner bases his assessment on transaction costs when considering integrating a foreign MNC in the local operations similar to the MNC, as described earlier. This argumentation is based on the following line of reasoning: according to TCE, managers in general, not only MNC managers, suffer from bounded rationality and a potential partner in general, not only a local partner, may act opportunistically (e.g., Williamson, 1985). Therefore, we believe that a local partner, similarly to the MNC, tries to reduce market transaction costs, monitoring cost, and control cost created by asset specificity, internal uncertainties, and EU (e.g., Hennart, 1989; Williamson, 1985). Consequently, if high levels of transaction cost are perceived, a hierarchical form of governance is chosen.

Second, we argue that uncertainty is dynamic and that many ownership decisions are actually made because firms want to benefit from this dynamism. Specifically, IU and EU are seen as dynamic dimensions as it seems reasonable to assume that for each partner internal and EU are subject to change as a consequence of the establishment of a joint operation. Looking especially at EU, this determinant is already, but largely implicitly, adopted as a dynamic dimension in many TCE studies (e.g., Erramilli & Rao, 1993; Gatignon & Anderson, 1988; Kim & Hwang, 1992). Besides staying flexible when uncertainty is high, the involvement of a foreign partner who is familiar with the local environment enables the MNC to decrease its environmental uncertainties. We want to adopt this and include it into our context. On the contrary, we view asset specificity as a static dimension of TCE. Thus, we expect that the degree of asset specificity held by each potential partner does not change due to a joint operation. In the following sections, we describe these assumptions, by applying the TCE determinants, as described above, to the local partner.

Asset Specificity (Local Partner)

Similar to the MNC, a local partner might own transaction-specific investments, meaning physical and human investments that are only valuable in a certain range of transactions. As described above, these are specialized to one or a few users or usages and if used outside the intended purpose could lead to a high level of sunk cost (Rindfleisch & Heide, 1997), also for the local partner. Including a foreign partner in the daily operations and sharing those investments also bares the risk of opportunistic behavior of the foreign partner. Therefore, the costs for negotiating and controlling an involvement with a possible partner are significantly higher.

> Consequently, a local partner with high asset specificity would opt for a going alone strategy instead of integrating a foreign partner into the local operations, such as in an IJV. (c.p.)

Uncertainty (Local Partner)

Internal uncertainty (Anderson & Gatignon, 1986), also referred to as behavioral uncertainties (Brouthers & Nakos, 2004), is a result of the inability to predict the behavior of individuals. These uncertainties exist when firms are not able to assess an agent's performance through available and objective output measures (Anderson & Gatignon, 1986). If a company is not able to establish these control mechanisms (Gatignon & Anderson, 1988; Williamson, 1985), the risk that a partner may distort or hide important pieces of information increases, as does the threat of opportunistic behavior. Thus and as described above, traditional TCE predictions propose that a company that perceives internal uncertainties to be high should opt for hierarchical governance forms. We argue that this TCE prediction for IU is applicable to a local firm as well. Especially when a local partner has no international experience and is not able to establish instruments to control a foreign partner, which would increase the costs for controlling and monitoring the partner and thus increases transaction costs.

> Consequently, a local partner would opt for a going alone strategy if integrating a foreign partner increases internal uncertainty and therefore the transaction cost significantly. (c.p.)

External uncertainty arises when the firm cannot predict its environment (Anderson & Gatignon, 1986). This enhances the level of transaction costs as firms face difficulties in foreseeing changes in the environment. As described above, firms will pursue an entry mode that involves low equity involvement or low resource commitment. By doing so, the company is not stuck with its operations when sudden changes in the environment occur. Recent research (e.g., Brouthers & Hennart, 2007; Zhao et al., 2004) on the determinant EU examined that companies should stay flexible when environmental uncertainties are high and it is proposed to opt for a market form of governance. By doing so and as stated in the introduction, the MNC integrates a foreign partner who is familiar with the local environment and able to decrease EU and therefore the transaction cost. TCE scholars thus regularly but implicitly assume that potential local partners' perceived EU is lower than the perceived uncertainty of the MNC, if not even low per se. Consequently, they often have no strong need to (further) reduce their already low perception of EU. For them, it may rather lead to increased transaction costs if partnering with an MNC increases their EU, as may be the case through higher legal restrictions and/or market entry barriers established by the host government. Potential local partners would therefore only opt for an IJV if the integration of an MNC does not increase the local partner's volatility or unpredictability of the environment and subsequently the transactions costs.

> Consequently, a local partner would opt for a going alone strategy if integrating a foreign partner increases external uncertainty and therefore the transaction cost significantly. (c.p.)

Table 1 summarizes the predictions made by TCE and its determinants as discussed above. On the left-hand side, the TCE predictions for the choice of entry mode for the MNC, as covered in the theoretical background, are listed. We choose to stick to predictions made and examined in

Table 1. TCE Predictions for the MNC and the Local Partner.

	MNC		Local Partner	
	Low	High	Low	High
AS	IJV	WOS	IJV	WOS
IU	IJV	WOS	IJV	WOS
EU	WOS	IJV	IJV	WOS

Note: MNC = multinational corporation; AS = asset specificity; IU = internal uncertainty; EU = external uncertainty.

primary studies, as well as meta-analyses, and reviews on international entry mode (e.g., Brouthers & Hennart, 2007; Brouthers & Nakos, 2004; Zhao et al., 2004). The right-hand side summarizes our argumentation for the local partner, from above. For asset specificity and IU, the predictions are the same. For EU, the predictions for MNC and the local firm are different (Table 1).

THEORETICAL PROPOSITIONS

TCE argues that some combinations of asset specificity, IU, and EU favor the establishment of joint operations while others are detrimental to this ownership mode and favor a going alone strategy for the MNC. Empirical studies (e.g., Anderson & Gatignon, 1988; Brouthers & Nakos, 2004; Zhao et al., 2004) and reviews (Brouthers & Hennart, 2007) generally support this assumption. However, if both sides of the coin are considered, there might be combinations of the three determinants that, while not necessarily failing to explain the entry mode decisions, predict the transaction cost significantly lower than they actually are. We, thus, matched the predictions, as summarized in Table 1 and identified three situations in which a joint operation, such as an IJV, might be confronted with much higher transaction costs than predicted by "traditional" single-sided TCE.

Table 2 gives an overview of the different combinations of entry mode choices, including the MNC side and the local partner's side. The three highlighted fields in the table show the TCE prediction for asset specificity, IU, and EU for the MNC in combination with the TCE prediction for asset

Table 2. Combinations.

		Local Partner AS		Local Partner IU		Local Partner EU	
		Low	High	Lower	Higher	Lower	Higher
MNC AS	Low	IJV/IJV	**IJV/WOS**	IJV/IJV	IJV/WOS	IJV/IJV	IJV/WOS
	High	WOS/IJV	WOS/WOS	WOS/IJV	WOS/WOS	WOS/IJV	WOS/WOS
MNC IU	Lower	IJV/IJV	IJV/WOS	IJV/IJV	**IJV/WOS**	IJV/IJV	IJV/WOS
	Higher	WOS/IJV	WOS/WOS	WOS/IJV	WOS/WOS	WOS/IJV	WOS/WOS
MNC EU	Lower	WOS/IJV	WOS/WOS	WOS/IJV	WOS/WOS	WOS/IJV	WOS/WOS
	Higher	IJV/IJV	IJV/WOS	IJV/IJV	IJV/WOS	IJV/IJV	**IJV/WOS**

Note: MNC = multinational corporation; AS = asset specificity; IU = internal uncertainty; EU = external uncertainty.

specificity, IU, and EU for the local partner as argued above. Three of these combinations, marked with bold letters, are combinations, or as we call them situations, in which transaction cost are predicted too low when using a single-sided MNC lens, only. We argue that in these three situations, the transaction cost and therefore the costs for finding, negotiating with a suitable partner and also monitoring and controlling this partner are significantly higher than "traditional" TCE predicts. In the following sections, we discuss these situations.

Situation 1: AS Low MNC/AS High Local Partner

For asset specificity, we identified two combinations (IJV/IJV: AS low on both sides and WOS/WOS: AS high on both sides) that perfectly match. If asset specificity is low on both sides, TCE clearly predicts a market form of governance for both the MNC and the local partner. Consequently, both are willing to partner. If asset specificity is high on both sides, TCE clearly predicts a hierarchical form of governance for both the MNC and the local partner. Here, TCE proposes a going alone strategy and a partnering is not an option for both. The third combination (WOS/IJV: AS high MNC and AS low local partner) suggests a partnering for the local company and a going alone strategy for the MNC. Due to the fact that we examine the MNCs entry mode choice, this combination is in line with "traditional" TCE reasoning, as potential local partners' transaction costs do not matter for the MNC if hierarchy is recommended. However, the fourth combination (IJV/WOS: AS low MNC and AS high local partner) suggests the establishment of an IJV for the MNC and a going alone strategy for the local partner, which leads to Situation 1 and consequently to a situation where transaction costs are predicted too low by single-sided TCE reasoning. This combination implies that the MNC might not find a local partner to establish an IJV at all (because potential local partners are not sufficiently motivated), or at least the costs for finding, negotiating with a suitable partner and also monitoring and controlling this partner are significantly higher for the MNC than traditional TCE predicts. In the following sections, we are taking a closer look at this situation.

In the highlighted case, the MNC exhibits low asset specificity, while the local partner has high asset specificity. "Traditional" TCE would recommend an IJV for the foreign partner but a WOS for the local partner. We argue that transaction costs for the MNE will be much higher than predicted by "traditional" TCE. In order to provide a simple illustration, consider a Western plastic component producer that internationalizes to Asia and aims to venture with a local company. The local company is said to deploy assets of high specificity in their production processes. In our opinion, the establishment of an IJV is very unlikely, simply because there is no imminent need for the local firm to venture with this Western company. Therefore, a local partner may not be readily available for the MNC. From a TCE perspective, the local partner would incur considerable transaction costs as the MNC might opportunistically exploit this dependency to pursue its self-interest (Klein, 1980) or gradually absorb these assets (Lu & Hébert, 2005). These transaction costs are not taken into account by traditional TCE reasoning in the field of IB, which largely focuses on the MNC side. However, the level of transaction costs may deter the MNC from engaging in IJV operations or at least make the development and controlling of contracts much more complex and costly.

Overall, we thus argue that an MNC-centric approach with respect to asset specificity would fail to fully explain MNCs' strategic decisions in foreign markets. Previous studies exclusively assessed the level of asset specificity on part of the MNC. This shortcoming in the existing literature may at least partially explain the conflicting results with respect to the effect of asset specificity on firm boundary decisions (for a review, see Brouthers & Hennart, 2007). While scholars such as Brouthers and Brouthers (2003), Brouthers et al. (2003), Erramilli and Rao (1993), and Gatignon and Anderson (1988), among others, found a positive relationship between the level of asset specificity and the propensity of choosing a WOS; Palenzuela and Bobillo (1999) found, for instance, the opposite. Moreover, Brouthers (2002) discovered for a sample of European firms and Hennart (1991) for a sample of Japanese firms that research and development intensity (R&D intensity) – which has often been used as a proxy for asset specificity in TCE studies – did not enhance the likelihood of establishing a WOS. Further, Puck, Holtbrügge, and Mohr (2009), when analyzing mode changes, also found no significant influence of high asset specificity. A dual perspective on this TCE dimension may have the potential to explain these unexpected findings and to further enhance our understanding of ownership choices.

Situation 2: IU Low MNC/IU High Local Partner

For IU, we identified two combinations (IJV/IJV: IU low on both sides; WOS/WOS: IU high on both sides) that perfectly match. If IU is low on both sides, TCE clearly predicts a market form of governance for both the

MNC and the local partner. Consequently, both are willing to partner. Transaction costs are therefore as high as predicted. If IU is high on both sides, TCE predicts a hierarchical form of governance for both the MNC and the local partner. Here, TCE proposes a going alone strategy and a partnering is not an option for both. The third combination (WOS/IJV: IU high MNC and IU low local partner), again, suggests a partnering for the local company and a going alone strategy for the MNC. Here, finding a partner is only an issue for the local partner, but does not affect the TCE prediction for the MNC. The fourth combination (IJV/WOS: IU low MNC and IU high local partner) suggests the establishment of an IJV for the MNC and a going alone strategy for the local partner. This means, similar to Situation 1, that a local partner might not be willing to partner or at least the costs for finding, negotiating with a suitable partner and also monitoring and controlling a partner are significantly higher for the MNC than traditional TCE predicts. In the following we are taking a closer look at the situation for IU.

Overall, as described in the theoretical background and from a unilateral point of view, TCE suggests the establishment of an IJV for the MNC when IU is low. As highlighted above, we extend the perspective of traditional TCE as we argue that IU is a dynamic concept. If the establishment of the IJV decreases the IU of the MNC (or leaves it stable) but increases the IU of the local partner we contend that this specific situation will lead to the situation that the MNC will not find a local partner or at least needs to accept high search-, monitoring-, and controlling cost to find a local partner. An illustration would be an MNC with high international experience. According to theory (e.g., Brouthers & Nakos, 2004; Johanson & Vahlne, 1977) firms can establish more efficient and less costly control mechanisms through international experience. This expertise helps in dealing with foreign partners and hence to reduce IU. However, it is less likely that a company with low IU finds a suitable partner, if it is increasing the local partner's IU through a joint operation. This might be the case, if the local partner is "internationally green" and lacks these control mechanisms, for example, to deal with cultural differences between MNC and local partner. Consequently, the costs to find, monitor, and to control the partner are significantly higher than predicted by traditional "single-sided" TCE.

Previous studies analyzed the level of IU only on part of the MNC, neglecting that the choice of internationalization decision may also hinge on the characteristics of perceived uncertainty of the local partner overseas. Empirical results have been equivocal with respect to the relationship between IU and the choice of entry mode (for a review, see Brouthers & Hennart, 2007). Only few scholars (Brouthers & Brouthers, 2003; Brouthers et al., 2003) have made attempts to measure the level of IU directly by looking, for instance, at the difficulty of enforcing and monitoring contracts in the subsidiary. Most studies have used the level of international experience on part of the MNC as a proxy for IU, arguing that more experienced firms are confronted with lower levels of IU than inexperienced firms (Zhao et al., 2004). The rationale behind this reasoning is that firms are assumed to develop skills to handle internal issues over time, which mitigates the level of IU (Johanson & Vahlne, 1977).

On the one hand, scholars (Contractor & Kundu, 1998; Gatignon & Anderson, 1988; Hennart, 1991) detected that ventures with higher international experience exhibit a greater propensity of choosing a WOS. These findings are also supported by the results of Zhao et al.'s (2004) meta-analysis. On the other hand, previous studies (e.g., Gomes-Casseres, 1989) revealed that firms with higher international experience exhibit a greater likelihood of setting up IJVs. Other studies (Padmanabhan & Cho, 1996; Palenzuela & Bobillo, 1999) could not find a significant relationship between these variables. With respect to perceptual measures of IU, Brouthers and Brouthers (2003) found that high IU increases the likelihood of choosing IJVs (for their sample of service firms), while Brouthers et al. (2003) found no significant relationship. Besides measurement inequivalence and the heavy use of proxies, we suggest that accounting for the level of IU perceived by the local partner may increase our understanding of internationalization decisions. Moreover, a dual perspective on IU may partially explain the highly contradictory findings with respect to this TCE dimension and the choice of ownership mode.

Situation 3: EU High MNC/EU High Local Partner

As previously discussed, for EU we identified two combinations (IJV/IJV: EU high MNC and EU low local partner and WOS/WOS: EU low MNC and EU high local partner) that perfectly match. In the first combination, both companies are willing to partner. In the second, according to TCE both are going alone to avoid high transaction cost. The third combination (WOS/IJV: EU low MNC and EU low local partner) predicts a going alone strategy for the MNC. Again, no partner is involved in the entry mode decision. The fourth combination (IJV/WOS: EU low MNC and EU high local partner), however, suggests the establishment of an IJV for the MNC and a going alone strategy for the local partner. This means that a local partner might not be willing to partner or at least the costs for finding, negotiating with a suitable partner and also monitoring and controlling a partner are significantly higher for the MNC than traditional TCE predicts. In the following sections, we take a closer look at the situation for EU.

As discussed above, theory proposes that an MNC will favor an entry mode with low equity involvement such as in an IJV, when external uncertainties are high. This is due to the fact that an MNC can stay more flexible and withdraw from the market more easily. In addition, it enables the MNC to include a partner that is more familiar with the local conditions and, therefore, can help to reduce external uncertainties for the MNC (e.g., Erramilli & Rao, 1993; Gatignon & Anderson, 1988; Kim & Hwang, 1992). On the one hand, an IJV leads to a decreased EU on the MNC side but on the other hand it might lead to an increased EU on the local partner's side. This increase of EU on the partner's side increases the transaction cost for the local partner and also the search-, control-, and monitoring cost for the MNC. Hence, transaction costs are predicted significantly too low.

Consider, for instance, a software company such as Google that aims for a joint venture with a local firm in China. Undoubtedly, the company faces high EU in China, which favors the establishment of an IJV based on TCE reasoning (Brouthers & Brouthers, 2003; Puck et al., 2009). Given the dispute Google has had with the Chinese government, any cooperation with the U.S. company would, however, certainly increase the level of EU on part of the local Chinese firm, as well. Specifically, a cooperation with Google could make the Chinese partner vulnerable to hardly predictable government regulations and prone to discriminatory policies due to the low standing the U.S. company has enjoyed in China. The New York Times states "For companies inside its borders, the government uses a broad array of penalties and threats to keep content clean. For websites that originate anywhere else in the world, the government has another impressively effective mechanism of control: what techies call the Great Firewall of China" (Thompson, 2006, p. 4). Therefore, it seems reasonable to assume that Google would face presumably higher transaction cost when establishing an IJV in China and despite the high EU the company is confronted with. Therefore, we believe that it is crucial to assess the overall level of EU stemming from the establishment of an IJV − all the more as high EU on part of the local partner, for instance, may deter the firm to engage in such a hybrid governance structure.

Apart from the theoretical divergence, empirical findings are conflicting as well. To operationalize EU (for a review, see Brouthers & Hennart, 2007), most TCE studies used cultural distance (Erramilli & Rao, 1993; Padmanabhan & Cho, 1996) measures of country risk (Contractor & Kundu, 1998; Delios & Beamish, 1999) or perceptual measures referring to the economic and political volatility in the host market (Brouthers, 2002; Brouthers & Nakos, 2004; Erramilli & Rao, 1993). Tihanyi, Griffith, and Russell (2005), for instance, failed to detect a significant relationship between cultural distance and entry mode choice in their meta-analytical review. Zhao et al. (2004), by contrast, found that cultural distance significantly affected the ownership mode. With respect to country risk, most scholars found that higher levels of risk induce firms to choose lower ownership control. For instance, Contractor and Kundu (1998) revealed that higher risk enhanced the likelihood of choosing nonequity-based modes in the hotel sector. Moreover, Brouthers (2002) found that a greater risk increased the propensity of choosing IJVs using a perceptual measure of EU. In a similar vein, Brouthers and Nakos (2004) revealed that SMEs are more likely to opt for nonequity-based modes in case of high EU.

Again, besides measurement inequivalence and the use of different proxies, previous research analyzed the level of EU on part of the MNC, failing to acknowledge that the choice governance also depends on the characteristics of the local partner in the host market. It is thus necessary to consider both perspectives by evaluating the level of EU. Overall, a dual perspective on the dimension of EU may untangle the theoretical and empirical divergence and improve our understanding why companies might choose a local partner (Brouthers & Hennart, 2007).

IMPLICATIONS

Building on TCEs and recent critique on IB research, we applied a double-sided TCE lens to illustrate three situations where an MNC might not find an available IJV partner or at least the costs for finding, negotiating with a suitable partner, and also monitoring and controlling this partner are significantly higher for the MNC than traditional TCE predicts. We theoretically argued and illustrated that the decisions firms undertake are not always in line with traditional TCE reasoning but can be explained when accounting for both the perspective of the MNC and the local partner and the dynamic nature of uncertainty.

Not only the entry mode literature per se but also, for example, in the IJV literature the local partner's transaction costs should be included in the decisions process. Geringer (1991, p. 41) already stated that the "issue of IJV partners and particularly their selection has received limited attention in the joint venture literature." According to this contribution, only a few scholars (Awadzi, 1987; Daniels, 1971; Renforth, 1974; Tomlinson & Thompson, 1977) have dealt with the issue of partner selection so far. Meanwhile, a substantial amount of research on the criteria that influence the nature of IJV partner selection has evolved since the choice of a suitable partner is seen as a crucial variable to achieve corporate objectives. Selection criteria include, for instance, compatibility and chemistry of partners, strategic fit, requisite assets and skills, or cultural and strategic fit (Glaister, Husan, & Buckley, 2005). However, these studies from the IJV literature also assume that foreign partners in the host country are willing to venture with the MNC if a certain complementarity or diversity of recourses is achieved. We believe that this is not necessarily the case and that certain matches of potential IJV partners do not lead to an establishment of jointly managed operations, and a closer look needs to be taken on this specific topic in all areas of IB research. In our opinion, it is necessary to not only look at economic efficiency criteria on the MNC side but also the local partner's side, as we have done in our argumentation above.

From a theoretical perspective, our chapter provides a theory-based explanation for the partner selection processes, including a dynamic perspective on the TCE determinant uncertainty. Furthermore, it highlights the importance of taking both the owners of firm-specific assets (e.g., the MNC) and the owners of local assets (e.g., local partner abroad) into account when examining the entry mode choice from a TCE perspective. As our model shows and by examining each determinant separately, in one out of four possible combinations the transaction costs are predicted too low. Looking at it overall, in 50 percent of the modeled cases that actually predict the establishment of an IJV for the MNC the transaction cost and therefore also the costs to find a partner, to integrate more elaborate (and thus costly) monitoring- and controlling systems are predicted too low. We do not conclude that this eliminates the establishment of joint operations but that future studies should be aware and consider that the level of transaction cost differs if the local partner is included in the entry mode decision from a TCE perspective.

From a managerial perspective, our propositions may reveal to what extent the internationalization strategy of the MNC hinges on the characteristics of the local partner abroad. Overall, when evaluating the potential for IJVs in host markets, foreign mangers need to recognize the boundaries that are set by local partners.

REFERENCES

Agarwal, S., & Ramaswami, S. (1992). Choice of foreign market entry mode: Impact of ownership, location and internalization factors. *Journal of International Business Studies*, *23*(1), 517–551.
Anderson, E., & Gatignon, H. (1986). Modes of foreign entry: A transaction cost analysis and propositions. *Journal of International Business Studies*, *17*, 1–26.
Awadzi, W. K. (1987). *Determinants of joint venture performance: A study of international joint ventures in the United States*. Baton Rouge, LA: Louisiana State University.
Brouthers, K. D. (2002). Institutional, cultural and transaction cost influences on entry mode choice and performance. *Journal of International Business Studies*, *33*, 203–221.
Brouthers, K., & Brouthers, L. (2001). Explaining the national cultural distance paradox. *Journal of International Business Studies*, *32*(1), 177–189.
Brouthers, K. D., & Brouthers, L. E. (2003). Why service and manufacturing entry mode choices differ: The influence of transaction cost factors, risk and trust. *Journal of Management Studies*, *40*, 1179–1204.
Brouthers, K. D., Brouthers, L. E., & Werner, S. (2003). Transaction cost-enhanced entry mode choices and firm performance. *Strategic Management Journal*, *24*, 1239–1248.
Brouthers, K. D., & Hennart, J.-F. (2007). Boundaries of the firm: Insights from international entry mode research. *Journal of Management*, *33*, 395–425.
Brouthers, K. D., & Nakos, G. (2004). SME entry mode choice and performance: A transaction cost perspective. *Entrepreneurship: Theory & Practice*, *28*, 229–247.
Canabal, A., & White, G. O. (2008). Entry mode research: Past and future. *International Business Review*, *17*, 267–284.
Contractor, F. J., & Kundu, S. K. (1998). Modal choice in a world of alliances: Analyzing organizational forms in the international hotel sector. *Journal of International Business Studies*, *29*, 325–357.
Crook, T. R., Combs, J. G., Ketchen, D. J., & Aguinis, H. (2013). Organizing around transaction costs: What have we learned and where do we go from here? *Academy of Management Perspectives*, *27*(1), 63–79.
Daniels, J. D. (1971). *Recent foreign direct manufacturing investment in the United States: An interview study of the decision process*. New York, NY: Praeger Publishers.
Delios, A., & Beamish, P. W. (1999). Ownership strategy of Japanese firms: Transactional, institutional, and experience influences. *Strategic Management Journal*, *20*, 915–933.
Delios, A., & Henisz, W. J. (2003). Political hazards, experience, and sequential entry strategies: The international expansion of Japanese firms, 1980–1998. *Strategic Management Journal*, *24*, 1153–1164.
Dunning, J. H. (1988). The eclectic paradigm of international production: A restatement of some possible extensions. *Journal of International Business Studies*, *19*(1), 1–31.
Erramilli, M. K., & Rao, C. P. (1993). Service firms' international entry-mode choice: A modified transaction-cost analysis approach. *Journal of Marketing*, *57*, 19.

Gatignon, H., & Anderson, E. (1988). The multinational corporation's degree of control over foreign subsidiaries: An empirical test of a transaction cost explanation. *Journal of Law, Economics & Organization, 4,* 305.

Geringer, J. M. (1991). Strategic determinants of partner selection criteria in international joint ventures. *Journal of International Business Studies, 22,* 41–62.

Glaister, K. W., Husan, R., & Buckley, P. J. (2005). International joint ventures: An examination of the core dimensions. *Journal of General Management, 30,* 43–72.

Gomes-Casseres, B. (1989). Ownership structures of foreign subsidiaries: Theory and evidence. *Journal of Economic Behavior & Organization, 11,* 1–25.

Hennart, J.-F. (1989). Transaction costs theory of equity joint ventures. *Strategic Management Journal, 9*(4), 361–374.

Hennart, J.-F. (1991). The transaction costs theory of joint ventures: An empirical study of Japanese subsidiaries in the United States. *Management Science, 37,* 483–497.

Hennart, J.-F. (2009). Down with MNE-centric theories! Market entry and expansion as the bundling of MNE and local assets. *Journal of International Business Studies, 40,* 1432–1454.

Johanson, J., & Vahlne, J.-E. (1977). The internationalization process of the firm – A model of knowledge development and increasing foreign market commitments. *Journal of International Business Studies, 8,* 25–34.

Kim, B., Kim, H., & Lee, Y. (2002). Modes of foreign market entry by Korean SI firms. *Asia Pacific Journal of Marketing and Logistics, 14*(4), 13–35.

Kim, C. W., & Hwang, P. (1992). Global strategy and multinationals' entry mode choice. *Journal of International Business Studies, 23,* 29–53.

Klein, B. (1980). Transaction cost determinants of "Unfair" contractual arrangements. *The American Economic Review, 70,* 356–362.

Lu, J. W., & Hébert, L. (2005). Equity control and the survival of international joint ventures: A contingency approach. *Journal of Business Research, 58,* 736–745.

Makino, S., & Neupert, K. (2000). National culture, transaction costs, and the choice between joint venture and wholly owned subsidiary. *Journal of International Business Studies, 31*(4), 705–713.

Morschett, D., Schramm-Klein, H., & Swoboda, B. (2010). Decades of research on market entry modes: What do we really know about antecedents of entry mode choice? *Journal of International Management, 16*(1), 60–77.

Padmanabhan, P., & Cho, K. R. (1996). Ownership strategy for a foreign affiliate: An empirical investigation of Japanese firms. *Management International Review, 36,* 45–65.

Palenzuela, V. A., & Bobillo, A. M. (1999). Transaction costs and bargaining power: Entry mode choice in foreign markets. *Multinational Business Review, 7,* 62.

Puck, J. F., Holtbrügge, D., & Mohr, A. T. (2009). Beyond entry mode choice: Explaining the conversion of joint ventures into wholly owned subsidiaries in the people's republic of China. *Journal of International Business Studies, 40,* 388–404.

Renforth, W. (1974). *A comparative study of joint international business ventures with family firm or non-family firm partners: The Caribbean community experience.*

Rindfleisch, A., & Heide, J. B. (1997). Transaction cost analysis: Past, present, and future applications. *Journal of Marketing, 61,* 30.

Thompson, C. (2006). Google's China problem (and China's Google problem). *The New York Times,* 1–15.

Tihanyi, L., Griffith, D. A., & Russell, C. J. (2005). The effect of cultural distance on entry mode choice, international diversification, and MNE performance: A meta-analysis. *Journal of International Business Studies, 36,* 270–283.

Tomlinson, J. W. C., & Thompson, M. (1977). *A study of Canadian joint ventures in Mexico.* Vancouver: University of British Columbia.

Williamson, O. E. (1975). *Markets and hierarchies, analysis and antitrust implications: A study in the economics of internal organization.* New York, NY: The Free Press.

Williamson, O. E. (1985). *The economic institutions of capitalism: Firms, markets, relational contracting.* New York, NY: Free Press.

Zhao, H., Luo, Y., & Suh, T. (2004). Transaction cost determinants and ownership-based entry mode choice: A meta-analytical review. *Journal of International Business Studies, 35,* 524–544.

CHAPTER 4

SELLING TO CHINESE FIRMS: A SELLER'S PERSPECTIVE. EMPIRICAL EVIDENCE FROM THE GERMAN AUTOMOTIVE INDUSTRY

Simona Gentile-Lüdecke

ABSTRACT

Purpose — *The chapter looks at two recent acquisitions by Chinese companies of German firms operating in the automotive sector. In both cases it was the target firm that initiated the process, intentionally selling to a Chinese strategic investor. The main purpose of the chapter is to examine the main motivations that induce developed country MNEs to deliberately search for a buyer in China.*

Methodology — *The chapter uses a case-study approach. Interviews were conducted with the managers that followed the entire process of sale and who were responsible for the search and the selection of a strategic investor in China.*

Multinational Enterprises, Markets and Institutional Diversity
Progress in International Business Research, Volume 9, 71–96
Copyright © 2014 by Emerald Group Publishing Limited
All rights of reproduction in any form reserved
ISSN: 1745-8862/doi:10.1108/S1745-886220140000009003

Findings — *Empirical findings show that major drivers in opting for Chinese investors are the potential synergies generating from resource redeployment, the ability of the acquired firm to maintain its autonomy and the opportunity to expand into the Chinese market.*

Research implications — *The cases analysed show that developed country firms may take a proactive role in China in order to address their institutional-based disadvantages and to reduce and eliminate the liability of foreignness they may confront there. What is important is strong core competitiveness on their side, which can ensure their operational autonomy, such as technological leadership and superior quality and solid development. The policy implications are relevant, because in the current particular situation where many companies in Europe turn for sources of capital to emerging market firms, Chinese investors can facilitate target companies' growth, with a positive impact for the local economy.*

Keywords: Sino-German M&A; automotive industry; resource redeployment; resource asymmetry

INTRODUCTION

Motivations to acquire have received attention in international business research and they have predominantly focused on the rational to buy, from the buyer perspective, while the seller is usually depicted as reactive and price-driven. However, as previous studies have shown (Graebner, 2004) the seller may play an active and influential role in the selling process, particularly when the firms are privately held, determining when and to which buyers they will be sold. Thus, the decision to sell must be understood from a rationale-choice perspective (Trautwein, 1990). Sellers may interpret an acquisition as a partnership and an opportunity to grow (Kale, Singh, & Raman, 2009). The seller perspective in the setting of South-North acquisitions provides an interesting context of analysis, considering the significant growth in outward FDI by emerging market firms (Buckley et al., 2007; Deng, 2007) and their interest in acquisitions (UNCTAD, 2006), especially when investing in developed economies (Makino, Lau, & Yeh, 2002; Mathews, 2002).

In particular the soaring trend of acquisitions by Chinese enterprises is generating much intrigue and excitement across international economic and political spheres, particularly in Europe. The concern arises if the competitive capabilities received by the target firm may be less useful to a target firm than the capabilities received if it would be acquired from an advanced economy firm (Chen & Cuervo-Cazurra, 2012). Additionally, problems may occur if subsidiaries of emerging market multinationals acquire sensitive technology in the host country (Ramamurti, 2012). Finally, although the influence of Chinese capital has been encouraged by European governments burdened by the sovereign debt crisis in the Eurozone, there is apprehension that too many national assets could end up in the control of foreign firms (Filippov, 2012). While motivations to acquire from the Chinese buyer perspective have been subject of study (Deng, 2004, 2007, 2009; Rui & Yip, 2008; Wang, Hong, Kafouros, & Boateng, 2012), with the only exception of Knoerich (2010), there have been no studies looking at the seller perspective on the setting of developed country firms acquired by emerging market companies.

Thus, the main research question of this study is to examine what are the main motivations that induce German MNEs to intentionally search for a buyer in China, considering that Chinese firms are imprinted with very different institutional configurations, business models, belief systems and stakeholder relationships (Cheung & Qian, 2009).

The chapter contributes to the acquisitions literature by advancing the recent theory development towards forming the seller's perspective of acquisitions.

By integrating the resource-based view and the bundling model of assets, the study shows the importance of both firm-specific assets, owned by the target developed firm, and complementary local resources, owned by the acquiring firms, in influencing the decision to sell.

The remainder of the chapter is organized as follows. First, it reviews the literature on the seller's perspective and on motivations for cross-border mergers and acquisitions (M&A). Then, it introduces the theory and states propositions. Afterwards, it illustrates the methodology and presents the empirical analysis. Finally, it discusses the results and concludes, examining major implications of the study.

LITERATURE REVIEW

The Decision to Sell from the Acquired Perspective

Previous studies on firm-level motivations for acquisition generally take a buyer's perspective and focus on which firms might be attractive targets given certain buyer motivations. The seller's perspective is usually depicted as reactive and price-driven. Typically, the target's shareholders are assumed to sell shares when an attractive premium is offered, and management may resist if changes in their wealth are not satisfactory (Cotter & Zenne, 1994).

There have been two views concerning the motivations for voluntary selling of an entire firm. The first is that selling is triggered by poor firm performance (Tremblay & Tremblay, 1988). However, empirical support for this argument has been limited – studies have generally demonstrated that targets in friendly acquisitions and privately owned targets often had average or above average performance (Agrawal & Jaffe, 2003; Graebner & Eisenhardt, 2004; Rahman & Limmack, 2004).

The second is that strategic hurdles and the resulting uncertainty trigger selling. Graebner and Eisenhardt (2004) investigated determinants of selling an entire firm from the seller's perspective using a sample of privately owned US entrepreneurial firms. They found that firm leaders (i.e., key executives and/or board members) may actively pursue buyers when their firms encounter multiple strategic hurdles such as ramping up sales or hiring a new CEO, while ignoring attractive acquisition proposals when their firms do not face strategic hurdles. Furthermore, when choosing the buyer, they seek buyers that provide long-run synergy potential and organizational rapport rather than the highest price. These findings contrast sharply with the passive and price-driven image of sellers depicted in the traditional acquisition literature, indicating that selling might be a strategic decision based on the evaluation of a firm's long-term prospects. Dalziel (2008) confirmed this long-term and non-price-centred orientation of sellers in her study on the communication equipment industry.

Looking at the viewpoint of the acquired firms in the context of the small advanced economy of New Zealand, Scott-Kennel (2013) argues that selling to foreign MNEs addresses gaps in activities and resources exacerbated by the size and distance of the small advanced economy. The most obvious gaps that the author identifies are financial and operational.

With focus on acquisitions in China and looking at the brewery industry, Zeng, Douglas, and Wu (2013) argue that the likelihood of selling is high for firms which have a high level of embeddedness within the planned system, fail to undertake necessary organizational changes in a timely manner, or deviate too much from competitors in investing in competitive resources and adopting a market-based strategy. These firms are less likely to fit well with the transitioning environment and thus have less promising long-term prospects.

Finally, in the only study on South-North setting, Knoerich (2010) focuses on acquisition of German firms in the machinery sector by Chinese firms and finds that the German sellers are able to promote their own interests in the relationships between both partners, advancing their own competitive position. This is due to complementarities in the motivations for engaging in the deals as well as the underlying strategic needs of both firms.

Motivations for Cross-Border Acquisitions

Cross-border acquisitions have been a long-standing research issue in the international business literature. Scholars consider the transfer of tacit resources as an incentive for cross-border acquisitions, focusing on market failures that stem from potential opportunism and knowledge limits (Hymer, 1976; Kogut & Zander, 1993).

When efficient market exchange of resources is possible, 'firms are more likely to continue alone' and rely on the market (Eisenhardt & Schoonhoven, 1996, p. 137). However, efficient exchanges are often not possible on the spot market. Certain resources are not perfectly tradable, as they are either mingled with other resources or embedded in organizations (Chi, 1994). Cross-border acquisitions thus provide the acquirer and the acquired firm with access to a potentially valuable repository of capabilities embedded in the local environment (Ghoshal, 1987; Jameson & Sitkin, 1986).

To maintain their competitive advantages (Capron, Dussage, & Mitchell, 1998), businesses frequently need to reconfigure their unique and valuable resources (Barney, 1991), whether by obtaining new resources or by employing existing excess resources in new applications.

Businesses tend to search for new resources outside the firm when their current performance declines or when they become concerned about future performance. When companies are struggling in their home and overseas markets they may recognize that their future would be more promising as part of another firm (Graebner & Eisenhardt, 2004; Knoerich, 2010).

Emerging market firms are most interested in seeking superior resources and skills that are not available at home (Makino et al., 2002) in advanced host countries. As newly international players, Chinese firms are generally conducting cross-border M&A with the primary motive of obtaining and controlling strategic assets (Deng, 2007; UNCTAD, 2006). They lag behind foreign firms in the development of firm-specific advantages, especially with respect to technology (Nolan, 2004), experience in innovative activities and top management talent (Rugman & Li, 2007).

According to Madhok and Keyhani (2012) acquisitions are particularly fitted to the asymmetries that characterize the emerging country MNEs and represent for these an opportunity to overcome the liability of emergingness. Most relevantly, acquiring strategic assets via M&A may significantly help Chinese firms earn legitimacy, social support and prestige in the marketplace (Deng, 2009). If these are the expectations of the emerging market firm in deciding to buy an advanced market firm, what are the motivations from the seller's side, when deciding to sell out to Chinese investors?

THEORETICAL FRAMEWORK AND PROPOSITIONS

Barney (1988) suggested that an acquisition creates value for the acquirer when it adds unique and valuable resources than can be leveraged into the target organization and Harrison, Hitt, Hoskisson, and Ireland (1991) argued that synergistic benefits are more likely to produce return when based on complementarities. Strategy research indicates that redeployment of complementary resources between the acquiring and acquired units contribute to superior financial performance (Capron, 1999; Capron & Pistre, 2002). Capron et al. (1998) found that the relative strength of the merging firms along several resource dimensions (technical innovative capabilities, manufacturing know-how and managerial capabilities) affected the redeployment of resources in the other firm. Resource redeployment is the extent to which a target or acquiring firm uses the other firm resources (R&D capabilities, manufacturing, know-how, marketing resources, supplier relationships and distribution expertise), which may involve physical transfer of resources to new locations or sharing resources without physical transfer (Capron, 1999).

The greater the asymmetry in the strength of a resource between target and acquirer, the greater the extent of resource redeployment from the business with the stronger positions to the business with the weaker position.

Although the existing literature mostly focuses on the benefits of resource redeployment for the acquiring firms, one can argue that they apply equally well to the acquired firms in the sense that the expected synergies may constitute a reason to sell as the synergies may help target companies to address some resource gaps.

Proposition 1. The resource asymmetry between target and acquiring firm is likely to generate synergies deriving from resource redeployment (from target to acquirer and vice-versa). The possibility to use acquiring firm resources in order to create new complementarities is a major driver in intentionally selling to a Chinese strategic investor.

As Hennart (2009, 2012) explains, the organizational form by which two firms transact with each other depends on the contributions and costs faced by both partners. The difference lies in the types of contribution made by foreign and local partner. Acquisitions allow firms to exchange firm-specific intangible assets and information that are subject to market failure because in the cases of tacit resources, the market for firms is often more efficient than the market for resources (Vermeulen & Barkema, 2001). The possession and control of critical resources are the ones that determine the bargaining power of each company (Pfeffer & Salancik, 1978).

In the case of South-North acquisitions the firm-specific advantages owned by the acquired firms are based on the possession and use of certain intangible assets, such as patents, trademarks, management skills (Caves, 1996), brand names as well as skilled labour, knowledge of technology and efficient production processes (Wernerfelt, 1984).

When the target company is providing advanced technology, it has considerable bargaining power and its contribution is subject to high transaction costs (Meyer, 2014). The knowledge that is owned by the acquired firms is embedded in the organization, and thus dependent on the organizational structure and culture. Such knowledge that could help the acquiring firm to develop new advantages (Shan & Song, 1997) cannot easily be disembodied and transferred, nor does it easily fit in the acquiring firm. Tacit knowledge that resides in a group of workers or in firms' routines is hard to separate from the firm in which it has been developed. Accessing knowledge by taking over firms requires sophisticated management skills, because employees are free to defect at any time (Verbeke, 2009). The technological-related knowledge is not the only valuable resource owned by the acquired firm; the other asset that is often tacit is the knowledge of how to successfully operate internationally and in particular host countries. Such knowledge is to a large extent experiential, meaning that is primarily developed through experience. The resources already possessed by the firm can be deployed in many markets (Barkema & Vermeulen, 1998; Johanson & Vahlne, 1977) helping the company balance the costs and risks incurred overseas due to greater managerial complexity and liability of foreignness (Tseng, Tansuhaj, Hallagan, & McCullough, 2007). As a result of the knowledge accumulation, it becomes easier for firms to deal with operations that have occurred before and the level of the liability of foreignness can be largely reduced.

The implementation of an acquisition requires a lot of managerial resources, both in the acquisition process and in the subsequent management and integration of the acquired unit. The low level of familiarity that management in the acquiring firm has of the acquired companies' operations is a reason to expect a higher level of autonomy in the target firm (Datta & Grant, 1990).

Puranam and Srikanth (2007) agree that if the acquiring firm intends to leverage the target's capacity to innovate, then a structural integration – which is associated with a loss of autonomy – would negatively impact the outcome, due to the likelihood that highly talented employees would become demotivated and eventually leave the firm, and thus cause harm to the target's potential to innovate. Graebner (2004) claims that if managers from the acquired firm exercise their influence promptly, the disruptive impact of a loss of autonomy on the acquired firm's routines can be mitigated. Autonomy implies that the management of the acquired firm has the freedom of influencing events and making the day-to-day operating decisions without close control by the parent company management (Hayes, 1979). Additionally, autonomy has an important influence in the management of acquired firms, ensuring top management retention and facilitating post-acquisition success (Datta & Grant, 1990). In such cases the acquiring firm may even end up supporting and investing further in the acquired firm.

Proposition 2. The possession and control of valuable intangibles, that are of interests of the acquiring firm, allow the target firm substantial bargaining power, ensuring a high level of autonomy. Preserving autonomy is a major driver in intentionally selling to a Chinese strategic investor.

In order to enter the emerging markets, target companies need to bundle (Hennart, 2012) their firm-specific advantages with complementary local resources such as land, utilities, employees, managers, access to suppliers and access to final customers (Hennart, 2009). However, country-specific advantages of the acquiring firms are not freely available but incur high transaction costs. Emerging market firms have the advantage of better information about their country, its economy, language, laws and regulations. Additionally, local firms enjoy favourable access to the resources of their home country relative to foreign firms, due to favourable treatment by the governments, consumers and suppliers.

According to the institutional perspective organizations gain legitimacy for their operations through isomorphism with the environment, that is, by conforming to commonly accepted structures and procedures (DiMaggio & Powell, 1983; Kostova & Zaheer, 1999).

In the specific case of China, China's distinctive cultural and institutional legacy, including the tendency to rely on close personal relationships in business transacting − 'guanxi' − (Chen & Chen, 2004), may be expected to increase the liability of foreignness faced by firm that seek to internationalize in that country. It is then important for the foreign companies operating in China to conform to local procedures and try to develop a guanxi business network. The economic benefits of a guanxi network (Luo, 2000) include the lowering of transactions costs, information costs and competitive threats as well as reducing uncertainty in the operation.

Such location-related assets provide local firms with some strong competitive advantage that foreign firms do not have (Nachum, 2003) and for the target firms, operating as an autonomous subsidiary of a Chinese firm may facilitate the presence in an important market as China, as well as facilitating further global expansion. Thus, the acquisition could operate as a genuine collaborative partnership rather than an imposition of hunter upon hunted (Kale et al., 2009).

Proposition 3. Once autonomy is ensured, accessing local market knowledge from the acquiring firm is a major driver for the target company in intentionally selling to a Chinese strategic investor.

METHODOLOGY

The chapter uses a case-study approach following the methodology adopted in the few studies examining Chinese acquisitions in Germany (Klossek, Linke, & Nippa, 2012; Knoerich, 2010; Liu & Wywode, 2012) and acquisitions from the seller perspective in general (Dalziel, 2008; Graebner, 2004; Knoerich, 2010; Scott-Kennel, 2013).

The value of the case study lies in its ability to provide insights through rich, real-world details for further investigation (Eisenhardt & Graebner, 2007).

Interviews were conducted with the managers that followed the entire process of sale to the Chinese firm and who were responsible for the search (and the selection) of a strategic investor in China. Before conducting the interviews, a set of open-ended questions was developed focusing on the investment motivations of the companies.

The interviews lasted one and a half hour and have been conducted in German; the author has carried out the translation into English. In addition, the interviews were supplemented with other sources of data, including research journals, company documentation, Internet data and archival data. Due to diverse sources of information, information and data from different sources have been crosschecked for triangulation purpose so as to increase the reliability and accuracy of the explanations.

Research Setting

The chapter investigates the acquisitions of German firms operating in the automotive sector. The target country and the specific industry represent an appropriate context for the study, in consideration of increasing acquisitions of Chinese companies in Germany in that specific sector.

Chinese outward FDI in Germany has been constantly increasing since 2004 (see Fig. 1), with acceleration in the years 2010−2011. In Germany there have been two waves of Chinese investment. The first one started in 2004 and was characterized by small acquisitions, mainly in the machinery industry. Many of the companies acquired were in financial trouble and some of these acquisitions were unsuccessful. The second wave of

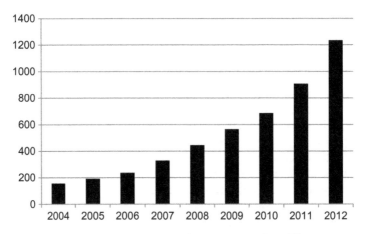

Fig. 1.   Chinese Outward FDI Stock in Germany, in Million of Euro.
Source: Deutsche Bundesbank (2013, April).

investment started in 2010 and is characterized by bigger deals and by acquisitions of companies that are financially healthy and mostly operating in the automotive, energy sector, machine building, in line with the objectives stated in the 12th Five-Year Plan (2011–2015).

Political and corporate preferences seem to go hand in hand. Chinese state agencies push companies to go to Germany. 'Made in Germany' is taken as a symbol of quality and point to German industrial brands, emphasizing the reputation of the country as a high-tech location. In the guidelines of the country-industry register, the Ministry of Commerce recommends that Chinese companies focus on German flagship industries, especially machine tools and automotive, ICT and renewable energy (Jungbluth, 2013).

In the automotive industry the Chinese government is encouraging the overall growth of an indigenous automotive industry, also through M&A (Chu, 2011), and German companies are a preferred target for Chinese auto-parts manufacturers. The overview of the recent M&A deals in the automotive supplier industry in Germany (see Table 1) shows how Chinese investors have been involved in the majority of recent acquisitions in the automotive sector.

Around 85% of auto industry suppliers in Germany are medium-sized companies. All of these suppliers provide up to 70% of value added within the domestic auto sector – ensuring that the German auto industry remains at the forefront of the competition (GTAI, 2012). Auto manufacturers and suppliers located in Germany are among the world leading

Table 1. Home Country of Acquiring Firms in Recent Acquisitions in the Automotive Supplier Industry in Germany.

Acquirer Home Country	Sector of Activity of the German Target Firm	Year
China	Decorative interior trim	2013
India	Machined metal parts	2013
Mexico	Hinges, structural parts	2012
China	Latches and actuators	2012
China	Customized metal parts	2012
China	Light metal castings	2011
Turkey	Automotive signal lights	2011
China	Decorative interior trim	2011
India	Plastic parts and modules for interior/exterior	2011
China	Electronics/switches	2011
China	Rubber sealing	2011

Source: Thomson; press research.

patent applicants. However, many of these suppliers are facing challenges. Those suppliers with focus on Europe in terms of client structure are facing declining revenues in line with European production cuts and some of them are in distress or are filing for insolvency. Many suppliers overestimated their capability to manage fast growing global complexity in their organization and footprint — and as a result came into turbulent situations. Finally, several suppliers are faced with changing 'rules of the game', since one of their competitors has been acquired by Chinese companies providing new investment capabilities and a new level of access to the Chinese market (Roland Berger Strategy Consultants & Lazard, 2013).

For the German OEMs China is a strategic market. Volkswagen is strongly investing in China and intends to increase the current capacity of 2.8 million cars (2012) to 4 million cars by 2018. For both Audi and BMW China is the most important market[1] and the key role played by the country for the German OEMs is emphasized by the fact that some OEMs (Daimler and VW) have recently appointed a Member of the Board exclusively for China.[2]

Following the investment of major German OEMs, many German autoparts manufacturers have established and/or increased their presence in the country. In fact, being present in China is hardly encouraged by OEMs and for those suppliers not active in the country, the risk of a short-term and significant drop in margins has increased over the past few years.

Case Profiles

The two German companies acquired are both Tier 1 suppliers, having among their customers all market relevant OEMs and counting with highly innovative and most advanced production processes. These are firms defined by Simon (1996) as 'hidden champions', companies that occupy global leadership positions despite their small size, excelling at incremental and constant innovation.

A short description of the target firms is presented as follows.

Latch was founded in 1857. For more than 100 years the company was a supplier of the most comprehensive range of latch system products to the automotive industry. The firm has invented the central locking system and is a technology leader for automotive side door latches, holding a global market share of 20%.[3] It is also the first latch manufacturer that has developed a charger locking actuator for electric cars. Its customer base include over 50 OEMs and individual brands.

Sensor was founded in 1919 and started manufacturing electrical parts and accessories. It was one of the first German manufacturers to market a radio-receiver. In 1988, the company entered the field of automotive electronics focusing on climate control, driver control and sensor systems. Unlike its competitors, Sensor maintains up to 95% vertical integration, with hardware, software and mechanical development all made at the company's place, along with plastic injection moulding, electronics manufacturing, surface technology and assembly. In addition, tooling and assembly lines are also built in-house. With the production of control units for battery management, the company is contributing to the development of e-mobility, providing a uniform charge and discharge of battery cells in electric and hybrid vehicles.

Both companies were owned by financial investors before the acquisition and their pre-acquisition situation was similar: the companies knew that they will be sold at some stage in the future, they were financially healthy and they realised that in order to keep growing they needed to expand into Asia, first of all in China, responding to the increasing demand of their customers.

Latch had been in the hand of different financial investors prior to the acquisition by the Chinese firm. In 2000, it was acquired by a financial private equity firm, which loaded the company with debt. In 2006, the company was turned over to its creditors in a debt-equity swap. The consortium installed a new management team whose priority was to restructure the company. Once the re-organization was complete the question arose of when and in what form the private equity firm would take their leave of the automotive supplier. Accordingly, the management team decided to proactively search for an acquirer. For the team it was clear that the acquirer should not be a global automotive supplier because in that case, the focus would have been on cost-based synergies, with consequences like plants closure and employees redundancies. Looking at the need to access the Chinese market, where, in 2008, the company had opened an own subsidiary to serve its own foreign customers, the management matured the decision to look for an investor in China, without the intermediation and assistance of an investment bank. The management of the company organised a road show in China by pre-selected Chinese companies, with help of the association of the automotive industry. Latch looked for a company with complementary objectives, not operating in the same field of latches but with a good knowledge in metal and plastic treatment and with good contacts and network in China. They visited many companies and tried to generate interest. At the beginning Chinese firms were rather sceptical and there were communication problems due to the different language. Moreover, as the German company was being sold by a hedge fund, local firms were suspicious on the information provided to them. Finally, they found the company Lock and were reassured by the commitment of the firm and the engagement of its management.

Lock is a publicly traded automotive supplier that develops, produces and sells plastic and metal components (e.g., body trim, specialized tubes, door elements, drive shafts). It is part of a state-owned company. Focusing on the Chinese domestic market, Lock has around 10,000 employees and more than 40 locations in the country. Lock is a R&D supplier to the Chinese OEMs and to most of the joint venture companies of the international OEMs.

Sensor was founded in 1919 but entered the automotive sector only in the late 1980s. In 1993, it was sold to a group specialised in automotive components and defence equipment. In 2003, the group decided to sell its electronics division to financial investors, the German private equity. Following the crisis of 2008, which heavily impacted on the automotive industry, particularly in Europe, the company knew that it would need a partner to grow. In 2010, the management decided to look for a partner in China. The company had already lost some important contracts for not being actively present in that country and decided to become active. In 2010, the management visited the owner of Filter, a company that six years before had been in Germany and had visited Sensor, being interested in a joint venture. The German management denied the offer at that time, because the Chinese company was still very young. After a visit in China, the CEO of Sensor was surprised to see the investment carried out by Filter in the short period. Seeing potential for growth, Sensor decided to start cooperating with that company. A joint venture agreement was signed in 2010, one year later the Chinese company acquired 74.9% of Sensor and in 2012 it acquired the 100% of the German firm.

Filter was founded in 2004 and it was listed in the Shanghai Stock Exchange in December 2011. Right from the beginning, the firm adopted the concept of synchronous design with the automotive OEMs and started to offer products ranging from the engine air intake manifold, to air vent scrubbers. In 2008, Filter qualified as a Tier 1 supplier to VW and a global supplier to GM and Ford, turning itself in one of the biggest auto-parts manufacturers in China.

While both target firms have a long history, both Chinese companies are young and have no international experience, being focused on the Chinese market. For both of them the major sector of activity is the automotive and the aim is to become a global supplier, in conformity with the Chinese development policy in the automotive industry that strives to create a small number of global suppliers. This goal motivates the current wave of Chinese overseas M&A, carried out by a new generation of firms, successful in the Chinese market, and rapidly working to establish themselves globally (Luo & Tung, 2007).

EMPIRICAL FINDINGS

For both target companies there were different factors that acted as a push in deciding to sell. While both companies were well established and successful, both at home and internationally, they faced resource constraints. On one side both of them were owned by private equity firms, knowing that at some stage in the future they will be sold, on the other side they were facing a pressure from the OEMs, that would welcome the sale to a strategic investor. The role of OEMs is particularly relevant in the automotive industry because OEMs expect suppliers to lead the innovation, design, development and scale-up of advanced technologies for global platforms. Important investments are necessary in achieving an effective cooperation between OEMs and suppliers along the value chain and in the current economic crisis many suppliers need to address a gap of financial resources. The decision to sell was not easy, because acquisitions are not neutral for companies operating in the automotive industry; OEMs could exercise a veto on the acquisition of one of their Tier 1 suppliers by an emerging country firm (von Kienlin & Wagner, 2012). While the above-mentioned issues pushed the companies to sell, the decision to whom to sell was motivated by some relevant drivers that will be illustrated below.

Preservation of Autonomy

Asked to identify the main motivations in opting for a Chinese strategic investor, both companies answered in a very similar way.

As Latch management indicated:

> *Our firm remains independent, maintains its structure, gains the possibility of a better entry into the Chinese market and becomes a clearly improved equity. Moreover, in China the government sponsors companies, there is a strong interest for the automotive sector*

and Chinese companies need to gain international acceptance and win new customers: on that issue we are in the position to offer something.

Those same motivations were emphasized by Sensor:

Through the acquisition, Sensor remains Sensor and indeed, nearly everything remains as before: the name, the independence, the centre for innovation in Germany, the management and largely the supervision board. Clearly better, however, is the equity base and the market access to China. By contrast, with an acquisition by a real large competitor it would have resulted in a consolidation and we, perhaps, could probably have only brought our plants to the group.

At the centre of the acquisition there is the innovation capability of the German firm. The technological knowledge is the core competence of the target firm and this knowledge is what Chinese companies need to absorb if they want catch-up. For both target firms it was clear that the innovation capability would have to remain in Germany and that this advantage would ensure them to continue their activity in an autonomous way.

Asked if there was concern about losing the proprietary technology to the Chinese company, both companies did not consider this as a source of problem. Sensor affirmed that buying a company, and stealing its know-how and go away would not work, would be like destruction of value.

As the manager said: *If you do not have innovation, you are out ... We are on another technical level and we have a more robust and internationally more experienced automotive management team. The owner of the acquiring firm knows that he cannot transfer this know-how to China. To maintain and protect those capabilities is for the Chinese company a highest priority.*

The question of autonomy and independence is also a critical factor for the OEMs, as they prefer establishing long-term relationships with their suppliers, to whom they are giving increasing responsibility, particularly in terms of technological development. The two German companies behaved differently in reporting the acquisition to the OEMs.

Latch informed the OEMs about their intention of selling the company to Lock and completed the acquisition only after their approval, while Sensor decided to involve the OEMs only when the process of acquisition was complete. Latch organized a road show at the customers' place to introduce the potential Chinese buyer. Those customers that were initially against the acquisition were able to change their mind after meeting the President of the Chinese company, a long time professional in the automotive sector, with a strong charisma. The process to win the approval and to gain the trust of the OEMs meant that for a period of time that the new business of Latch was put on 'hold'.

In the case of Sensor, customers were not actively involved into the sale process although OEMs had already repeatedly called the company to find a strategic investor. After the acquisition, Sensor started proactively approaching its customers addressing the obvious questions about future performance and innovation and reinsured the OEMs that Sensor will safeguard its own intellectual property.

> *The OEMs want to know that the business will continue operationally. From the customer point of view, that looks good for the foreseeable future, because a maximum of continuity is guaranteed with contact partners and processes.*

The motivation to preserve autonomy and ensure continuity of operations, indicated by both companies, leads to support Proposition 2.

Access to Local Market Knowledge and Resource Redeployment

Both companies are similar in their internationalization experience, having been active worldwide before the acquisition. Latch had production plants in the Czech Republic, the United States, Mexico and China. R&D was carried out in Germany but also in the United States and China. Sensor had production plants in Portugal, Rumania, Mexico and the United States. R&D was carried out in Germany but R&D facilities were also available in Rumania and the United States.

Latch had opened a plant in China before the acquisition. While the establishment of a company in China was firstly motivated to serve the current customers of the firms operating in China, the company knew that to grow faster in China, it needed to be able to serve also Chinese OEMs. Sensor was not present in China before starting cooperating with Filter.

The possibility to offer their international experience and their international market channels to the acquirer firms and at the same time to use the facilities and contacts of the Chinese company for the expansion in China was indicated by both target firms as an important determinant motivating the search for a Chinese buyer.

According to Latch: '*The Chinese acquirer has no foreign distribution channels; in our company and its products it has an ideal platform that is well established and functioning on a global level and able to offer access to our customers*'.

Before the acquisition Latch has visited all its plants with the Chinese acquirer and it regularly travels to the customers with the management of Lock so that the Chinese firm can be introduced in the network and has the possibility to be known. The same is happening in the case of Sensor.

For the management of Sensor the acquiring firm complements the target firm perfectly and represents the next development step for Sensor in Asia. In addition, the Chinese company will finance further growth in Europe and in the NAFTA region.

As management at Sensor said: '*I see in the new line-up great opportunities, in particular, those that concern the fast growth of our business in China. In addition, we have better access to the Chinese procurement market with our acquirer firm*'.

Latch expects to expand its locking systems business in the Asia region and is simultaneously planning to globalize its acquirer firm's core products by bringing them to Europe and the NAFTA region.

> When a supplier moves into a new region, it calls for a deep-seated understanding of the country well beyond the confines of the automotive industry .... The Chinese acquirer is a financially sound partner that will also support our company in its non-organic growth. Our Company has now the possibility, in addition to its own facility in China, to use one of the production lines of the acquirer firm to build a line for its products. Using classic routes, we would have had to work extremely hard over a period of years in order to establish such contacts.

Being able to use the respective market experience to help the other is the ideal situation to learn and to build trust, step after step, because the differences are still very big. The manager of Latch said: '*The way Chinese establish relationships to their clients is lot more intensive. Here we do not dare to go that far*'.

Thus, possibility to use each other's knowledge to access markets and create new complementarities supports Propositions 1 and 3.

Looking at the early development of the target companies post-acquisition, one can say that the expectations of resource redeployment have been satisfied.[4]

The strong commitment of the Chinese acquirer to Sensor and its German manufacturing site has been showed in the increase of Sensor's equity ratio to more than 40% and in major investments following the takeover of the company: the enlargement and modernization of the Sensor training centre in Germany in 2011; the opening of a new production hall for the product division Sensor Innovative Automation (PIA) in 2012, the acquisition of a leading software development company headquartered in Germany (August 2013). The acquired firm focuses on test systems, software components and engineering services in the field of motor vehicle electronic network systems and associated sectors and will help the firm to further develop its capacity in the field of auto-electronic.

As far as integration is concerned, there have been no major changes at the management level of the target firm after the acquisition and few, if any, Chinese employees have been transferred to the target firm. A manager of the Chinese company is now responsible for the procurement activity, and he is located in Germany, while two managers from Lock are on the Supervisory Board (President and Personnel/IT).

Also in the case of Latch, the commitment of the Chinese firm has made possible important investments that were on hold, aimed to reinforce the global production capability of Latch. In 2013, Latch started building a production plant in Russia, securing solid contractual volume for the Russian automotive market, from Russian and international vehicle manufacturers. In 2014, the company opened a new production building at its plant in the Czech Republic, investing around 14 million euro. Also, in the case of Latch, there have been no major changes in the management of the target company after the acquisition, apart from the inclusion of two members of the acquiring firm in the Supervisory Board (President and Finance).

DISCUSSION AND CONCLUSIONS

This study has focused on two recent acquisitions of German companies operating in the automotive sector by Chinese firms. The chapter focuses on the seller side, looking at the motivations influencing leading German automotive suppliers to intentionally sell their company to a strategic investor from China. In consideration of the complexity in gaining information, this is still an understudied topic in the field of M&A by emerging market multinationals. However, this is an important subject because, due to the current economic downturn in the Eurozone, many European companies find that a lack of capital is the biggest bottleneck to expansion, and they have turned for sources of capital to emerging market firms.

For Chinese companies eager to become global players, German technologically advanced small and medium firms are the ideal partners to access new technologies and to make the first step into the international market.

Results indicate that the main drivers influencing target companies to sell to Chinese investors are the possibility to use resources of the acquiring firms as well to offer own resources to the acquirer, together with the possibility to preserve autonomy after acquisition and the opportunity to have access to the local market knowledge of the acquiring firms.

The concept of resource asymmetry discussed in this study emphasizes the issue that, when looking for a Chinese investor, target companies need to be well aware of the value of both the intangibles resources they own and the resources owned by the Chinese firms. German companies' strategic resources can facilitate the acquiring firms to overcome the liability of newness and foreignness in global markets, hence, target firms have something important to offer in the deal, which gives them a strong bargaining power. At the same time, target companies know that, to respond to the demand of the market and to remain competitive, they need to have access to the unique local competencies of the Chinese firms as well as their substantial financial resources. Chinese companies are benefiting in these credit-constrained times from abundant government funding and they are able to provide the financial support for the growth of their target firms.

During the first wave of Chinese acquisitions in Germany, starting in 2004, there have been many cases of unsuccessful deals, particularly when the target firms were ailing or insolvent. The takeover of those companies required intervention and restructuring that were beyond the capabilities of acquirers. Because of the very different management gap between Chinese and Western firms, and the liability of foreignness of Chinese firms in global markets, a strong post-acquisition integration has proved to be wrong. Chinese companies seem to have realised that, no matter how much money they are able to provide to the deal, they first need to learn how to exploit the complementary assets owned by the target firms. Indeed, even when firms undertake knowledge seeking FDI, they still need to have their own resources and capabilities to be able to understand the value of the external knowledge. Thus, it makes more sense to concentrate on absorbing the knowledge of the newly acquired firm than to rush the integration process.

Target firms are aware that the access to advanced technology, superior products and powerful brands is of strategic importance for the acquiring company and that this expertise and knowledge can be preserved only by keeping the identity of the target firm and retaining its senior employees. Retaining autonomy can contribute to maintain the 'made in Germany' reputational advantages that Chinese firms need to compete at home and abroad.

China is a challenging market to global companies as it is important. The relevance of the Chinese market and the possibility to use the channels of the acquirer and its capital to further expand in the Asian country is an important motivation to sell to a Chinese investor. In order to increase their presence in the Chinese market, German companies need to develop a strong network of relationships with local firms and institutions. However, overcoming the liability of foreignness is complex, particularly in a sector where the government is oriented in reducing the dependence from foreign firms and to promote the development of Chinese global players.

Becoming a subsidiary of a Chinese company, by maintaining a high degree of autonomy, should lower the transaction costs of operating in China, increase the commitment to the market and facilitate the contact with Chinese OEMs, easing the access to financial incentives provided by the government to locally owned firms. The access to the local market and the preservation of a degree of independence are emphasized by Sensor: '*On the one hand, we support each other to access new market potentials. On the other, we at Sensor have retained the required independence to service our established customers optimally*'.

Implications of the Findings and Limitation of the Research

The recent increase of acquisitions from emerging country in developed countries is shifting the balance of power between developed and developing nations and requires a change of mind set in the developed world (Kothari, Kotabe, & Murphy, 2013). In the case of Chinese acquisitions in Germany the possibility to access Asian markets combined with strong cash flows from booming domestic markets become particularly attractive from the seller perspective, inducing some companies to proactively search for Chinese investors.

The study has shown that this is particularly true for industries like the automotive where OEMs exert high pressure on suppliers, requiring increasing investment in innovation to be part of a complex supply chain, whose coordination is more and more difficult. Hence, pooling resources together, Chinese and German companies can optimize their value chain and benefit both in the developed and emerging markets.

The cases analysed show that developed country firms may take a proactive role in China in order to address their institutional-based disadvantages and to reduce and eliminate the liability of foreignness they may confront there. What is important is strong core competitiveness on their side, which can ensure their operational autonomy, such as technological leadership and superior quality and solid development.

When the target company has financial problems, the priority is to restructure the firm and emerging country firms may not have the capability to carry out the process. Managers of developed country firms should carefully evaluate experience and motivations of the acquiring firm before accepting an acquisition to regain financial stability and gain new applications for brands in the acquirer home country.

In terms of implications for policy makers, while it is too soon to see if the Chinese parent company will have a real input in the strategic decision-making and long-term development of their German business partner, some preliminary considerations are possible.

Looking at the early post-acquisition development of the cases analysed in this study, one can say that the companies, with their respective advantages, not only open up new markets for each other, but they also safeguard jobs and production capabilities at home.

Hence, host-country governments in Europe must keep the door open and must not risk losing its hard-earned reputation for openness by imposing additional barriers to capital inflows based on economic security considerations. Host-country governments should, however, set up policies that attract experienced emerging country firms that rely on a new, more educated class of executives driven to expand the scope of their business activities. At the same time, they should set up policies or assist inexperienced emerging country firms to gain local knowledge before completing the takeover in the host country. Finally, this emerging new investment relationship needs to be institutionalized by a comprehensive investment agreement that will establish a legal framework to encourage mutually beneficial two-way flows of investment.

The small number of cases is a limitation of the study. However, as the chapter looks at two hidden champions of the German economy and at acquisitions in an industry, which is extremely important for Chinese investors, the results may constitute a useful base for future studies on the seller side of acquisitions, using larger samples. For this study only the German managers where interviewed, yet, comparing the vision of the German managers with that of the Chinese entrepreneurs could have provided further insights.

These are still the early days in the study of Chinese acquisition in Germany, but, at this stage, it is possible to argue that Chinese companies may facilitate the future growth of German companies. However, longitudinal studies are recommended to analyse the development of these acquisitions. Differences in organizations' backgrounds, strategy, practices and culture can make it more difficult for the receiving party to absorb or make use of knowledge (Ranft & Lord, 2002; Simonin, 1999). Indeed, future studies should look at the issue of cultural integration, particularly at the corporate governance level, as the corporate governance standards are different and may bring therein, in addition to cultural differences, a potential conflict. As a manager at Sensor said: '*I see a certain challenge in the different cultures. Here both side must learn from each-other*'.

Finally, future research might focus on the challenges that German companies face as they try to embed into Chinese business networks and the components that would foster this embeddedness.

NOTES

1. 'China erstmals wichtigster Markt für BMW', Manager Magazine Online. Retrieved from http://www.manager-magazin.de/unternehmen/autoindustrie/auto-absatz-china-erstmals-wichtigster-markt-fuer-bmw-a-942574.html. Accessed on January 24, 2014.
2. 'China Germany special relationship tested by trade frictions', *Financial Times*, May 26, 2013.
3. Latch is the Number 1 in Europe with a market share of 35%; it is the number one in the NAFTA region with a market share of 25% and is on target to achieve a double figure market share in Asia.
4. Information obtained from the companies' website.

REFERENCES

Agrawal, A., & Jaffe, J. F. (2003). Do takeover target underperform? Evidence from operating and stock returns. *Journal of Financial and Quantitative Analysis, 38*, 721–746.

Barkema, H., & Vermeulen, F. (1998). International expansion through start-up or acquisition: A learning perspective. *Academy of Management Journal, 41*(1), 7–26.

Barney, J. (1988). Returns to bidding firms in mergers and acquisitions: Reconsidering the relatedness hypothesis. *Strategic Management Journal, 9*(5), 71–78.

Barney, J. B. (1991). Firm resources and sustained competitive advantage. *Journal of Management, 17*(1), 99–120.

Buckley, P., Clegg, L. J., Cross, A., Liu, X., Voss, H., & Zheng, P. (2007). The determinants of Chinese outward foreign direct investment. *Journal of International Business Studies, 38*(3), 499–518.

Capron, L. (1999). The long-term performance of horizontal acquisitions. *Strategic Management Journal, 20*(11), 987–1018.

Capron, L., Dussage, P., & Mitchell, W. (1998). Resource redeployment following horizontal acquisitions in Europe and North America, 1988–1992. *Strategic Management Journal, 19*(7), 636–661.

Capron, L., & Pistre, N. (2002). When do acquirers earn abnormal returns? *Strategic Management Journal, 23*(9), 781–794.

Caves, R. E. (1996). *Multinational enterprise and economic analysis*. Cambridge: Cambridge University Press.

Chen, W., & Cuervo-Cazurra, A. (2012). Technological escape and cross-border M&As by developing country multinational companies. Paper presented at the Copenhagen conference on 'Emerging Multinationals': Outward Investment from Emerging and Developing Economies, October 25–26, 2012, Copenhagen.

Chen, X. P., & Chen, C. C. (2004). On the intricacies of the Chinese guanxi: A process model of guanxi development. *Asia Pacific Journal of Management, 21*, 305–324.

Cheung, Y. W., & Qian, X. (2009). The empirics of China's outward direct investment. *Pacific Economic Review*, (*14*), 312–341.

Chi, T. (1994). Trading in strategic resources: Necessary conditions, transaction cost problems, and choice of exchange structure. *Strategic Management Journal, 15*, 271–290.

Chu, W.-W. (2011). How the Chinese government promoted a global automotive industry. *Industrial and Corporate Change, 20*(5), 1235–1276.

Cotter, J. F. & Zenne, M. (1994). How managerial wealth affects the tender offer process. *Journal of Financial Economics, 35*, 63–97.

Dalziel, M. (2008). The seller's perspective on acquisition success: Empirical evidence from the communications equipment industry. *Journal of Engineering and Technology Management, 25*(3), 168–183.

Datta, K., & Grant, J. H. (1990). Relationships between type of acquisition, the autonomy given to the acquired firm, and acquisition success: An empirical analysis. *Journal of Management, 16*(1), 29–44.

Deng, P. (2004). Outward investment by Chinese MNCs: Motivations and implications. *Business Horizons, 47*(3), 8–16.

Deng, P. (2007). Investing for strategic resources and its rationale: The case of outward FDI from Chinese companies. *Business Horizons, 47*(3), 8–16.

Deng, P. (2009). Why do Chinese firms tend to acquire strategic assets in international expansion? *Journal of World Business, 44*(1), 74–84.

Deutsche Bundesbank. (2013). Bestandserhebung über Direktinvestionen. *Statistische Sonderveröffentlichung*, April 10. Retrieved from http://www.bundesbank.de/Navigation/DE/Veroeffentlichungen/Statistische_Sonderveroeffentlichungen/Statso_10/statistische_sonderveroeffentlichungen_10.html. Accessed in September 2013.

DiMaggio, P. J., & Powell, W. W. (1983). The iron cage revisited: Institutional isomorphism and collective rationality in organizational fields. *American Sociological Review, 48*, 147–160.

Eisenhardt, K. M. & Graebner, M. E. (2007). Theory building from cases: Opportunities and challenges. *Academy of Management Journal, 50*(1), 25–32.

Eisenhardt, K. M., & Schoonhoven, C. B. (1996). Resource-based view of strategic alliance formation: Strategic and social effects of entrepreneurial firms. *Organization Science, 7*, 136–150.

Filippov, S. (2012). European investment promotion agencies vis-à-vis multinational companies from emerging economies: Comparative analysis of BRIC investor targeting. Working Paper Series Nr. 076. Maastricht United Nation University UNU-MERIT.

Ghoshal, S. (1987). Global strategy: An organizing framework. *Strategic Management Journal, 8*(5), 425–440.

Graebner, M. E. (2004). Momentum and serendipity: How acquired leaders create value in the integration of technology firms. *Strategic Management Journal, 25*(8–9), 751–777.

Graebner, M. E., & Eisenhardt, K. M. (2004). The seller's side of the story: Acquisition as courtship and governance as syndicate in entrepreneurial firms. *Administrative Science Quarterly, 49*, 366–403.

GTAI. (2012). *The automotive industry in Germany*. Berlin: GTAI – Germany Trade & Invest.

Harrison, J. S., Hitt, M. A., Hoskisson, R. E., & Ireland, R. D. (1991). Synergies and post acquisition performance: Difference versus similarities in resource allocations. *Journal of Management, 17*(1), 173–190.

Hayes, R. H. (1979). The human side of acquisitions. *Management Review*, *68*(11), 44−46.

Hennart, J.-F. (2009). Down with MNE-centric theories! Market entry and expansion as the bundling of MNE and local assets. *Journal of International Business Studies*, *2*(3), 168−187.

Hennart, J.-F. (2012). Emerging market multinationals and the theory of the multinational enterprise. *Global Strategy Journal*, *2*(3), 168−187.

Hymer, S. H. (Ed.). (1976). *The international operations of national firms: A study of direct foreign investment*. Cambridge, MA: MIT Press.

Jameson, D. B., & Sitkin, S. B. (1986). Corporate acquisitions: A process perspective. *Academy of Management Review*, *11*(1), 145−163.

Johanson, J., & Vahlne, J. (1977). The internationalization process of the firm: A model of knowledge development and increasing foreign market commitments. *Journal of International Business Studies*, *81*, 23−32.

Jungbluth, C. (2013). Going global. Chinese investors target Germany's flagships industries. *German Chamber Ticker − Business Journal of the German Chamber of Commerce in China*, 40−41.

Kale, P., Singh, H., & Raman, A. (2009). Don't integrate your acquisitions, partner with them. *Harvard Business Review*, *87*(12), 109−115.

Klossek, A., Linke, B. M., & Nippa, M. (2012). Chinese enterprises in Germany: Establishment modes and strategies to mitigate the liability of foreignness. *Journal of World Business*, *47*, 35−44.

Knoerich, J. (2010). Gaining from the global ambitions of emerging economy enterprises: An analysis of the decision to sell a German firm to a Chinese acquirer. *Journal of International Management*, *16*, 177−191.

Kogut, B., & Zander, U. (1993). Knowledge of the firm and the evolutionary theory of the multinational corporation. *Journal of International Business Studies*, *24*(4), 625−645.

Kostova, T., & Zaheer, S. (1999). Organizational legitimacy under conditions of complexity: The case of the multinational enterprise. *Academy of Management Review*, *24*, 64−81.

Kothari, T., Kotabe, M., & Murphy, P. (2013). Rules of the game for emerging market multinational companies from China and India. *Journal of International Management*, *19*, 276−299.

Liu, Y. P., & Wywode, M. (2012). Light-touch integration of Chinese cross-border MNEs. *Thunderbird International Business Review*, *55*(4), 469−483.

Luo, Y. (2000). Determinants of local responsiveness: Perspectives from foreign subsidiaries in an emerging market. *Journal of Management*, *27*, 451−477.

Luo, Y., & Tung, R. L. (2007). International expansion of emerging market enterprises: A springboard perspective. *Journal of International Business Studies*, *38*, 481−498.

Madhok, A., & Keyhani, M. (2012). Acquisitions as entrepreneurship: Asymmetries, opportunities and the internationalization of multinational firms from emerging economies. *Global Strategy Journal*, *2*, 26−40.

Makino, S., Lau, C. M., & Yeh, R. S. (2002). Asset exploitation versus asset seeking: Implications for locational choice of foreign direct investment for newly industrialized economies. *Journal of International Business Studies*, *33*(3), 403−421.

Mathews, J. A. (2002). Competitive advantages of the latecomer firm: A resource-based account of industrial catch-up strategies. *Asia Pacific Journal of Management*, *19*(4), 467−488.

Meyer, K. (2014). Process perspectives on the growth of emerging economy multinationals. In R. Ramamurti & A. Cuervo-Cazurra (Eds.), *Understanding multinationals from emerging markets*. New York, NY: Cambridge University Press.

Nachum, L. (2003). Liability of foreignness in global competition? Financial service affiliates in the city of London. *Strategic Management Journal*, *24*(12), 1187−1208.

Nolan, P. (2004). *China at the crossroads*. Cambridge: Polity Press.

Pfeffer, J., & Salancik, G. R. (1978). *The external control of organizations. A resource dependence perspective*. New York, NY: Harper & Row Publishers.

Puranam, P. & Srikanth, K. (2007). What they know vs. what they do: How acquirers leverage technology acquisitions. *Strategic Management Journal, 28*, 805–825.

Rahman, R. A. & Limmack, R. J. (2004). Corporate acquisitions and the operating performance of Malaysian companies. *Journal of Business, Finance and Accounting, 31*, 359–400.

Ramamurti, R. (2012). What is really different about emerging market multinationals? *Global Strategy Journal, 2*(1), 41–47.

Ranft, A. L., & Lord, M. D. (2002). Acquiring new technologies and capabilities: A grounded model of acquisition implementation. *Organization Science, 13*(4), 420–441.

Roland Berger Strategy Consultants & Lazard. (2013). Global automotive supplier study 2013. Driving on thin ice. Retrieved from http://www.rolandberger.com/media/pdf/ Roland_Berger_Global_Automotive_Supplier_Study_20130917.pdf. Accessed in December 2013.

Rugman, A. M., & Li, J. (2007). Will China's multinationals succeed globally or regionally? *European Management Journal, 25*(5), 333–343.

Rui, H., & Yip, G. S. (2008). Foreign acquisitions by Chinese firms: A strategic intent perspective. *Journal of World Business, 43*(2), 213–226.

Scott-Kennel, J. (2013). Selling to foreign MNEs. End of the road or the beginning of a journey for firms in small and advanced economies? *International Studies of Management and Organization, 43*(1), 52–80.

Shan, W., & Song, J. (1997). Foreign direct investment and the sourcing of technological advantage: Evidence from the biotechnology industry. *Journal of International Business Studies, 28*(2), 267–284.

Simon, H. (1996). *Hidden champions, lessons from 500 of the world's best unknown companies*. Boston, MA: Harvard Business School Press.

Simonin, B. L. (1999). Ambiguity and the process of knowledge transfer in strategic alliances. *Strategic Management Journal, 20*(7), 595–623.

Trautwein, F. (1990). Merger motives and merger prescriptions. *Strategic Management Journal, 11*(4), 283–295.

Tremblay, V. J., & Tremblay, C. H. (1988). The determinants of horizontal acquisitions: Evidence from the US brewing industry. *Journal of Industrial Economics, 37*, 21–33.

Tseng, C., Tansuhaj, P., Hallagan, W., & McCullough, J. (2007). Effects of firm resources on growth in multitionality. *Journal of International Business Studies, 38*(6), 961–974.

UNCTAD. (2006). World investment report. FDI from developing and transition economies. New York, NY: UNCTAD.

Verbeke, A. (2009). *International business strategy*. Cambridge: Cambridge University Press.

Vermeulen, F., & Barkema, H. G. (2001). Learning through acquisitions. *Academy of Management Journal, 44*, 457–476.

von Kienlin, K., & Wagner, W. (2012). China on the acquisition trail: Increasing competition for European company buyers. In *Executive insights*. Munich: L.E.K. Consulting.

Wang, C., Hong, J., Kafouros, M., & Boateng, A. (2012). What drives outward FDI of Chinese firms? Testing the explanatory power of three theoretical frameworks. *International Business Review, 21*(3), 425–438.

Wernerfelt, B. (1984). A resource-based view of the firm. *Strategic Management Journal, 5*(2), 171–180.

Zeng, Y., Douglas, T. J., & Wu, C. (2013). The seller's perspective on determinants of acquisition likelihood: Insights from China's beer industry. *Journal of Management Studies, 50*, 673–698.

CHAPTER 5

WHAT BEST EXPLAINS THE SUCCESS OF CROSS-BORDER TECHNOLOGY TRANSFERS IN MNCs: TRADITIONAL COORDINATION INSTRUMENTS OR MODERN MANAGEMENT CONCEPTS?

Joachim Wolf, William G. Egelhoff and Christian Rohrlack

ABSTRACT

Purpose − *This chapter investigates whether traditional design-oriented coordination instruments or more modern management concepts have a stronger influence on the success of forward technology transfers within MNCs.*

Design/methodology/approach − *We conducted an empirical study analyzing the relative influence of (a) traditional coordination instruments*

Multinational Enterprises, Markets and Institutional Diversity
Progress in International Business Research, Volume 9, 97−130
Copyright © 2014 by Emerald Group Publishing Limited
All rights of reproduction in any form reserved
ISSN: 1745-8862/doi:10.1108/S1745-886220140000009004

(structural, technocratic, and person-oriented) and (b) modern manage-
ment concepts (epistemic community and absorptive capacity) on the suc-
cess of forward technology transfers within MNCs.

Findings − *The study finds evidence that the traditional coordination*
instruments relate to specific aspects of the success of such transfers.
Comparing the different types of coordination instruments, this chapter
shows that not only the person-oriented, but also the structural and tech-
nocratic coordination instruments relate positively with the achievement
of technology transfer goals. The study finds stronger relationships
between the traditional coordination instruments and the technology
transfer goals than between the modern management concepts and the
technology transfer goals.

Originality/value − *We believe that these results have important*
implications for the management of international technology transfers in
particular and for the focus of future (international) management
research in general. Future MNC research studies need to include
traditional coordination instruments, since they continue to strongly
influence organizational behavior and outcomes. This would help to make
organizational research on MNCs more cumulative and complete.

Keywords: Technology transfer; management; international;
multinational corporations; success

THE CHANGING FOCUS OF INTERNATIONAL MANAGEMENT RESEARCH AND THE NEED TO TEST ITS USEFULNESS

Over the decades, international management scholars have conducted numerous (empirical) studies to identify factors ensuring and improving the cooperation among MNCs' subunits. Often, the publication of Dunning's (1958) seminal book "American Investment in British Manufacturing Industry" is perceived as the starting point of this stream of research. Since then, the focus of research has changed in several dimensions. One important transition is reported in Martinez and Jarillo's (1989) review article, which found that "up to 1975, researchers concentrated their attention on structural and formal administrative tools … and starting in 1976, researchers seem to have begun to enlarge their focus including mechanisms of coordination, more informal and subtle" (p. 493). A further change is that early research was focused on the relationship between MNCs' headquarters and foreign subsidiaries (e.g., Garnier, 1982; Gates & Egelhoff, 1986; Goehle, 1980; Negandhi & Welge, 1984; Picard, 1977; Van den Bulcke & Halsberghe, 1984), while later studies (e.g., Bartlett & Ghoshal, 1989; Ghoshal, Korine, & Szulanski, 1994; Hedlund, 1986; Malnight, 1996) picked the relationships among foreign subsidiaries as their central theme.

In this chapter we want to embrace a further mutation that has occurred in this field of research. While most studies published prior to the mid-1990s concentrated on coordination instruments which can be deliberately designed and implemented by managers (e.g., the structural integration of the subsidiaries into MNCs' formal organizational structure, the centralization and standardization of decisions, formal reporting and planning systems, cross-border transfers, and visits of managers), since the mid-1990s, more research studies have begun to focus on abstract management concepts. These later studies view less direct phenomena like the corporate culture, (sub)units' absorptive capacities (Cohen & Levinthal, 1990), or epistemic communities among MNCs managers (Håkanson, 2005) to be crucial to the integration of subunits within MNCs. One might better understand this reorientation of research by considering the strong influence the writings of authors like Hedlund (1986) and Bartlett and Ghoshal (1989) had on international management research. These writings emphasized the importance of direct knowledge (and technology) transfers among MNC subunits. Whatever reasons might have driven the change in emphasis, the consequence is that today's literature on MNC coordination is dominated by such abstract management concepts. These concepts are different from the explicit design efforts of managers. For managers, it is difficult to directly influence these abstract conceptual phenomena, since their development typically depends on complex, long-lasting evolutionary processes going on within the firm.

This chapter focuses on this shift from traditional design-oriented coordination instruments to the more abstract management concepts. This chapter's overarching goal is to find out which of these two groups of variables have a stronger influence on the success of subunit interactions within MNCs. To address this question, we utilized an empirical study that includes both types of variables and also data measuring the success of subunit interactions.

Such a comparative study is called for, since the rise of the abstract management concepts in today's literature has largely occurred without any convincing empirical evidence that the newer concepts are superior to the older concepts they are replacing. Only a few years before the rise of the abstract management concepts, Martinez and Jarillo (1989) carefully reviewed the existing literature and concluded that the existing formal and informal coordination mechanisms appeared well fitted to coordinating transnational or complex global strategies (p. 506). This, along with the lack of any subsequent comparative research, means that interest in the design-oriented coordination instruments has waned without any real evidence that they have lost their effectiveness with regard to coordination. This study directly addresses this issue.

For the empirical analysis, we created a rather unique database, which contains data on both types of variables (the design-oriented coordination instruments *and* the abstract management concepts). To test the relative performance effects of these two groups of variables, we use a setting of vertical technology transfers between an MNC's home country units and its foreign subsidiaries. This setting is appropriate since, as mentioned above, knowledge and technology transfers between the MNC subunits are commonly seen as being crucial for MNCs' success. Moreover, this setting is interesting since some scholars' ad hoc intuition might assume that, if the goal is to improve an MNC's organization, the abstract management concepts are more useful than the traditional, design-oriented coordination instruments.

We want to conceptualize the usefulness of the traditional, design-oriented coordination instruments and the abstract management concepts on the basis of information-processing theory. Under an information-processing perspective, the MNC is viewed as an information-processing system (Galbraith, 1973; Thompson, 1967; Tushman & Nadler, 1978). Information processing in organizations is generally defined as including the gathering of data, the transforming of data into information, and the communication and storage of information in the organization. When this perspective is applied to the subject of this chapter, each of the various design-oriented coordination instruments and each abstract management concept is seen as facilitating certain types of information processing between the subunits – in this case the home country units and the foreign subsidiaries – while at the same time restricting other types of information processing (Egelhoff, 1982, 1988).

The organization of this chapter is as follows. In the next section, we discuss the two main goals of international technology transfers considered in the study and outline the information-processing capacities of the design-oriented coordination instruments and the abstract management concepts used in the study. We do this in order to develop insight into the performance outcomes associated with using these two categories of variables or views of coordination. After the conceptual part, we describe the study's sample and the measurement of variables. Then we report the results of the data analysis, followed by a discussion of the findings. In the final section, we discuss what the study's results mean for international management research and practice.

CONCEPTUAL MODEL AND HYPOTHESIS DEVELOPMENT

Main Goals of Technology Transfers within MNCs

A specification of the goals of technology transfers (within MNC) should be rooted in a definition of the term "technology." For this we will refer to Burgelman, Maidique, and Wheelwright's (1996) view, where "technology" embraces "theoretical and practical knowledge, skills and artefacts that can be used to develop products and services as well as their production and delivery systems" (p. 2). Since this chapter's empirical analysis refers to manufacturing firms, we will narrow this view somewhat and define technology as theoretical and practical knowledge necessary for the development and manufacturing *of products.*

Means to manage the transfer of technology have to be designed and evaluated in front of the goals, which are to be reached by such transfers. In the literature, there is little consensus about criteria to describe the goals of technology transfers. Scholars agree that research should consider multiple dimensions of transfer goals to obtain a more comprehensive understanding (Van Wijk, Jansen, & Lyles, 2008). Our conceptualization assumes that technology transfers strive to achieve two broad categories of goals − (1) to improve the recipient unit's current solutions and (2) to initiate further innovation and learning processes within this unit. While the first goal category refers to the development of existing problem-solving approaches, the second describes changes within the recipient unit, which tend to be "a trip to the unknown." In the context of the management of MNCs, this distinction is especially appropriate. It is consistent with international management theory's distinction between the ongoing improvement of efficiency and the inspiration of cross-border learning processes as the primary goals of MNCs (Bartlett & Ghoshal, 1989).

Information-Processing Capacities of Traditional Coordination Instruments and More Recent Abstract Management Concepts

Many coordination instruments have been studied in international management research (for an overview see Martinez & Jarillo, 1989; Wolf, 1994). This abundance has led to a need to group them together in a conceptually meaningful way. The sociologist Leavitt (1964) has suggested a typology, which, because of its intellectual clarity, is quite prominent in organization theory. It distinguishes between structural, technocratic, and person-oriented coordination instruments. It is important to realize that none of these coordination instruments (not even the structural category) describe the basic organizational structure of an organization. Instead, they are instruments that can improve the information-processing capacity of any type of organizational structure. We will now attempt to conceptualize and hypothesize a number of fit relationships for the three types of coordination instruments. We will begin with the person-oriented coordination instruments, since they are frequently viewed as appropriate for handling the transfer of technology between organizational subunits.

The defining characteristic of *person-oriented coordination instruments* (such as informal meetings of managers, their expatriation, or visits to other MNC subunits, video conferences, or manager training sessions) is that they use the interaction and communication among human beings as the primary means to align organizational subunits (Håkanson & Zander, 1986). They provide open forums for problem solving. More than other coordination instruments, the person-oriented instruments allow an exchange of social information (Daft & Lengel, 1986). They involve an interactive nature, are able to transfer unstructured kinds of information, and offer the chance for direct feedback. They thus allow an ad hoc form of coordination that is best suited for dealing with non-routine situations where a solution is not yet available and where creative attempts are required (Ring & Van de Ven, 1994). A potential problem is that social interaction might develop in an unpredictable way, since the transfer of information is loosely constrained and not clearly specified. With person-oriented coordination instruments, it is difficult to control or steer social interaction from the outside. These problems are especially critical in an international business environment, where managers of different cultural backgrounds interact. Research has shown that individuals' information-processing behavior depends on their cultural roots (Cattey, 1980). And finally, person-oriented coordination instruments tend to be expensive, since they typically require managers to break away from their standard work processes and in the case of international business, become involved in extensive travel.

Relating this discussion to the two categories of international technology transfer goals considered above, it is clear that person-oriented instruments best fit the goal of innovation and learning. The interactive nature of this type of coordination instrument, as well as its potential to exchange unstructured and social kinds of information, facilitates rich discussion and open-ended problem-solving processes. As a result, we formulate the following hypothesis:

Hypothesis 1. In MNCs' vertical technology transfers, the positive relationship between the intensity of the use of person-oriented coordination instruments and the achievement of the goal "innovation and learning" is stronger than the positive relationship between the intensity of the use of person-oriented coordination instruments and the achievement of the goal "improvement of existing solutions."

In the case of *technocratic coordination instruments* (such as guidelines, standards, or rules), interpersonal interactions are replaced by a "managerial technology." By doing so, technocratic instruments help to reduce the need for direct information exchange among individuals, since here decision situations are disposed a priori (Mascarenhas, 1984). If, for instance, in a technology transfer, standards and rules are applied, the decision-makers can use them as anchor points to classify and evaluate upcoming situations. Thus, technocratic coordination instruments – which are relatively inexpensive (Tushman & Nadler, 1978) – help to reduce the information-processing requirements. Yet, in comparison to person-oriented instruments, technocratic instruments' richness of information processing is significantly lower (Daft & Lengel, 1986) and they restrict flexibility in decision-making. In the literature, there is consensus that technocratic coordination instruments work best if problems reoccur and decision situations are similar and predictable (Khandwalla, 1973).

On one hand, if the primary goal of international technology transfers is to improve a foreign subsidiary's innovation and learning ability, there is a requirement for more variety and uncertainty than if international technology transfers are directed toward improving existing products or processes. In the latter case, the transfer process can largely stay within the status quo existing within the foreign subsidiary. Here, it is possible to work within the existing rules and standards of the organization. On the other hand, when innovation and learning are the goals, new horizons have to be explored and existing frames of reference are less valid. Thus, we expect:

Hypothesis 2. In MNCs' vertical technology transfers, the positive relationship between the intensity of the use of technocratic coordination instruments and the achievement of the goal "improvement of existing solutions" is stronger than the positive relationship between the intensity of the use of technocratic coordination instruments and the achievement of the goal "innovation and learning."

Typical characteristics of *structural coordination instruments* (e.g., regularly held meetings or permanent teams) are a planned occurrence. A further characteristic of such instruments is that "arenas" are created which are responsible for making the respective decisions. In such decision arenas, it is quite clear which managers are allowed to participate in the respective decision process and which are not allowed to participate. Under such a coordination regime, the responsibilities and communication patterns among the participating managers are deliberately designed. Within structural coordination instruments, interactions typically focus on fixed topics (Hulbert & Brandt, 1980), which make them less spontaneous than person-oriented coordination instruments. When applied to technology transfers, structural coordination instruments have names like "Technical Executives Board" (Håkanson & Zander, 1986). Structural coordination instruments are typically used to discuss adaptations to changed contextual conditions or approaches to meet time schedules.

With respect to information processing, structural coordination instruments improve the information flow between organizational subunits. Yet, since the interactions typically follow a formal agenda, this occurs within a framed setting. This creates the rigid character of such instruments and limits the richness of information processing. In earlier times, it was quite difficult to use structural coordination instruments in an international setting, since they required frequent travel by the members of these institutionalized groups. Today, with technology facilitating communication among distant individuals, this problem is less critical. Yet, structural coordination instruments' formal character might still restrict their usefulness if innovative solutions are sought, since institutionalization restricts and reduces flexibility and richness. We hypothesize:

Hypothesis 3. In MNCs' vertical technology transfers, the positive relationship between the intensity of the use of structural coordination instruments and the achievement of the goal "improvement of existing solutions" is stronger than the positive relationship between the intensity of the use of structural coordination instruments and the achievement of the goal "innovation and learning."

As already discussed, more recent organization theory has dealt less with the designable coordination instruments, and, instead, has emphasized more abstract management concepts as the most important factors influencing subunit interaction. This shift is also apparent in the more focused research that deals with (international) technology transfer within and between firms (e.g., Gupta & Govindarajan, 2000; Szulanski, 1996).

The concept of *absorptive capacity* (Cohen & Levinthal, 1990) is one of the newer potential predictors of technology transfers' success. This concept has been used in many research studies relating to both intra- and interorganizational technology and knowledge transfers (Gupta & Govindarajan, 2000; Lane & Lubatkin, 1998; Lyles & Salk, 1996; Minbaeva, Pedersen, Björkman, Fey, & Park, 2003; Tsai, 2001). Absorptive capacity describes "the ability of a firm to recognize the value of new information, assimilate it, and apply it to commercial ends" (Cohen & Levinthal, 1990, p. 128). Based on findings of human brain research, it is argued that a firm's ability to internalize and use knowledge is dependent upon the knowledge stock already existing within the firm. If the content of incoming knowledge corresponds with knowledge already existing in the recipient unit, then there is a good chance the transfer will succeed. For a firm, knowledge absorption is most effective, if it can be related to knowledge already existing within the firm (Cohen & Levinthal, 1990). Moreover, it is helpful if employees know where the firm-specific knowledge resides within the firm. "This sort of knowledge can be knowledge of who knows what, who can help with what problem, or who can exploit new knowledge" (Cohen & Levinthal, 1990, p. 133).

Given these characteristics, it is not surprising that the absorptive capacity concept is frequently related to inter- and intraorganizational technology transfers. Indeed, there are few cases where transferred technology can be used in an independent or free-standing manner within the recipient unit (Connell, Klein, & Powell, 2003). Following the absorptive capacity concept, technology transfers will succeed if the recipient of a transferred technology understands the technical and organizational-social interdependencies associated with the technology (Martin & Salomon, 2003).

Seen through the lens of information-processing theory, it becomes clear that the absorptive capacity concept does not clearly specify the channels through which the technology-oriented information flows into the recipient unit. This is an important difference vis-à-vis the traditional coordination instruments discussed above. For example, if the structural coordination instrument "regularly held meetings" is used, it is usually clear which MNC managers will participate in the meetings where the technology transfer is to be discussed. If the technocratic instrument "formal reporting system" is applied, there is an a priori definition of the variables considered in the report. Or if an MNC works with the person-oriented instrument "manager transfers" for technology transfer reasons, it is clear who in the organization will serve as the intellectual bridge between the sending and recipient units. Unlike these situations, in the case of absorptive capacity the information channels are less clearly specified. If a firm has a high level of absorptive capacity, this is more a general capability the firm can use if a specific transfer process has to occur. It serves more as a fertile soil in which a specific successful technology transfer process can grow. This difference between traditional coordination instruments and the absorptive capacity concept is more relevant for technology transfers than it is for more general transfers of knowledge within firms. The reason for this is that technology transfers typically consist of more specified forms of adaptations. It should be expected that the link between foreign subsidiaries' absorptive capacity and the achievement of the goals of technology transfers will be less strong than the link between the traditional coordination instruments and technology transfers. Yet, since the transfer goal "improvement of existing solutions" relates to absorptive capacity's view that the knowledge stock already existing within the firm is important for knowledge transfers, we expect:

Hypothesis 4. In MNCs' vertical technology transfers, the relationship between foreign subsidiaries' absorptive capacity and the achievement of the goal "improvement of existing solutions" is stronger than the relationship between foreign subsidiaries' absorptive capacity and the achievement of the goal "innovation and learning."

A second factor frequently used in more recent research to explain the success of technology transfers is the existence of an *epistemic community* between the sender and the recipient of the technology. The term "epistemic communities" designates "those knowledge-oriented work communities in which cultural standards and social arrangements interpenetrate around a primary commitment to epistemic criteria in knowledge production and application" (Holzner & Marx, 1979, p. 108). It is important to notice that an epistemic community – which consists at least of two persons – is more than a mere membership of a person in a group, team, or network

(Haas, 1992). Instead, the defining characteristic of an epistemic community is the existence of a cognitive coupling among the persons belonging to it.

It has been argued that codes, theories, and tools are important for the development of such a strong cognitive coupling between individuals (Håkanson, 2010). These dimensions are crucial for the strength of an epistemic community. If people use a joint *coding* scheme, they have a common vocabulary and this increases the likelihood that information is correctly transmitted between the community members. Then, the receiver interprets the information in a way consistent with the sender's intention. The component "*theories*" means that the community members are sufficiently homogeneous with respect to their values. If this is true, the community reflects a common culture, which the members can use as a joint cognitive map and interpretation scheme. This facilitates and simplifies information processing since symbols and other "informational shortcuts" can be applied in the communication processes. *Tools and practices* are artifacts serving as boundary objects to demarcate the epistemic community against other communities. This helps the community to focus its information processing and shields it from disturbing influences (Håkanson, 2010). Because of the community members' use of codes, theories, and tools, a shared understanding can develop, which in turn influences the community's practices as well as the members' views about themselves (Brown & Duguid, 1991).

It is obvious that the epistemic community concept offers a systemic view on technology transfer processes within MNCs (Tiessen, 1999). If the sender and the recipient of a transferred technology belong to the same epistemic community, this will ease the transfer processes (Håkanson, 2005). In such a case, it is easier for sender and receiver to evaluate the relevance and importance of the transferred technology correctly. This leads to higher levels of effectiveness. But the joint use of codes, theories, and tools also improves the efficiency of the transfers, since complicated explanations can be saved (Tushman & Scanlan, 1981). And finally, there might also be a reverse relationship from technology transfers to epistemic communities: if a unit offers a valuable and useful technological component, this increases the likelihood that the unit will become a member of an existing epistemic community so that in the future it can get access to the other community members' technologies (Schrader, 1991).

The previous line of reasoning leads to the assumption that joint membership of the sender and the recipient of a technology in an epistemic community facilitates the transfer of this technology. But, on the other hand, it has to be considered that in a multinational context the development of an epistemic community is more difficult than in a domestic setting. Especially the cultural, geographic, and institutional distances between the home and the host countries, as well as the institutional fragmentation of the MNC into legally autonomous subunits, make it more difficult to develop cross-border epistemic communities (Wolf & Egelhoff, 2010). Indeed, it has been shown that a relatively high *cultural distance* between home and host countries leads to differences in what employees of different locations expect from their work and firm (Kabanoff, 1997), and this can hinder the development of social cohesion within an epistemic community. Since MNCs employ people from different countries, different levels of commitment coexist within their work forces, reducing chances for the development of strong epistemic communities within the firm. With respect to *geographic distance*, it has to be argued that strong epistemic communities necessitate extensive travel and transfer of managers between MNCs' subunits. Since MNCs' subunits are on average geographically more dispersed than those of non-international firms, such epistemic-community-building activities tend to be more expensive and complicated in MNCs (Taylor, Levy, Boyacigiller, & Beechler, 2008). The *institutional fragmentation* of the MNC into legally autonomous subunits leads to the fact that their subsidiaries located in different institutional settings face dual pressures: they not only face an imperative for consistency within the firm, but are also pulled to achieve isomorphism with the host-country environment (Kostova & Roth, 2002). Research by European sociologists (e.g., Geppert, Matten, & Walgenbach, 2006; Morgan, Kristensen, & Whitley, 2001) studying the decisions and actions of MNCs shows that subsidiary managers tend to adapt their business decisions and actions to the dominant social expectations of the business system in which the subsidiary is embedded. Given the simultaneous existence of these three kinds of heterogeneity (cultural, geographic, and institutional) within MNCs, it has to be expected that they face greater difficulty than non-international firms in creating and maintaining strong epistemic communities. To build such epistemic communities overarching MNC subunits located in different countries seems to be more difficult than developing a sufficiently strong level of absorptive capacity in the unit receiving technology from abroad, since for the latter, arguments involving distance are less important. Thus, we expect:

Hypothesis 5. The relationship between the strength of an epistemic community and the achievement of the two technology transfer goals is weaker than the relationship between the recipient unit's absorptive capacity and the two technology transfer goals.

METHOD

Sample

The current empirical research focuses on technology transfers from MNCs' headquarters to their foreign subsidiaries (forward technology transfers). Although reverse technology transfers from MNCs' foreign subsidiaries to the headquarters (e.g., Frost & Zhou, 2005) as well as among foreign subsidiaries (e.g., Persson, 2006) have gained importance during the last decades, in most MNCs the home country R&D units are probably still the most important internal sources of new technology. When Rohrlack (2009) asked foreign subsidiary managers about the directions of technology flows within their MNC, he found that forward technology transfers were four times stronger than reverse technology transfers.

The population addressed by our research is Germany's top 500 firms, as they were documented in the newspaper "Die Welt" in the year 2005. The internet platform "XING" was used to identify employees working in these firms. We then contacted these persons via email and attempted to use them as contact persons within each firm. We used these persons to gain access to the names and contact data of managers and engineers involved in the respective firm's technology transfer projects from the headquarters to the subsidiaries. These latter persons were the target group to which the study's questionnaire was emailed to.

In the questionnaire, the respondents were asked to provide information about: the transferred technology, the goals of the technology transfer, the coordination instruments used in the technology transfer, and contextual factors characterizing the MNC and the respective foreign subsidiary. The questionnaire was designed after a careful literature review and 10 interviews with MNC managers responsible for intra-company technology transfers.

The questionnaire was sent to 872 managers. These managers belonged to R&D, manufacturing, and marketing units. The number of questionnaires returned equaled 255, but 59 questionnaires had to be removed from the sample, because they contained too many missing variables. This left a sample of 196, an effective response rate of 22.5%. Of these, 121 questionnaires exclusively described forward technology transfers, 31 exclusively described reverse technology transfers, and 44 described technology transfers that combined forward and reverse technology transfer. For the study we omitted the 31 questionnaires that exclusively dealt with reverse

technology transfer, leaving a sample of 165. Four additional questionnaires were excluded because of the small size of the firm (less than 600
employees) and another one was excluded because of the small size of the
subsidiary (five persons). We excluded these cases because the focus of the
study is on forward technology transfer in large and relatively complex
MNCs. As a result of these deletions, the database for the study consists of
data on 160 forward technology transfers.

It is important to realize that the unit of analysis for the study is an individual technology transfer project. In each firm the respondent reported on
a specific project that involved the forward transfer of technology. Of the
160 questionnaires used in the database, 65 were completed by respondents
working in the headquarters, and 95 by respondents working in the foreign
subsidiary. The location of the respondent is represented by a dummy variable in the database. As will be seen, this difference has no meaningful
influence on the results of the empirical analysis.

Measurement and Data

As discussed above, the current study considers (1) the strength of the epistemic community between headquarters managers and foreign subsidiary
managers, (2) the respective foreign subsidiary's absorptive capacity, and
the intensity of the use of (3) structural, (4) technocratic, and (5) person-
oriented coordination instruments as potential predictors of the success of
a technology transfer. Detailed information on the measurement of these
five predictors of the success of a technology transfer is presented in the
appendix. Below we discuss the development of each measure.

Epistemic Community
When the empirical part of the study was conducted, a valid and reliable
operationalization of this construct did not exist in the literature. Based on
related research (Cummings & Teng, 2003; Håkanson, 2007), we developed
a new scale containing three measured variables. The Cronbach's alpha for
this scale is 0.675.

Absorptive Capacity
The operationalization of this construct included both the potential absorptive capacity and the realized absorptive capacity (Zahra & George, 2002)
of the foreign subsidiary receiving the technology. While the former

describes a unit's capability to identify and acquire externally generated knowledge, the latter reflects its "capacity to leverage the knowledge that has been absorbed" (Zahra & George, 2002, p. 190). The development of items to measure these two aspects was guided by Jansen, Van den Bosch, and Volberda's (2005) work. Altogether, 13 items were used to measure the two kinds of absorptive capacity. Cronbach's alpha for the scale "potential absorptive capacity" is 0.665, and for the scale "realized absorptive capacity" it is 0.683.

Structural, Technocratic, and Person-Oriented Coordination Instruments

Based on a review of the literature, we considered *"regularly held meetings"* and *"permanent teams"* to be representative of structural coordination instruments. *"Rules and procedures"* and *"formal reporting systems"* were considered representative of technocratic coordination instruments. And *"informal meetings of headquarters and subsidiary members," "expatriation of headquarters or subsidiary members to the other unit," "visits of headquarters or subsidiary members to the other unit," "video conferences of headquarters and subsidiary members,"* and *"trainings of headquarters or subsidiary members"* were considered representative of person-oriented coordination instruments. Using a five-point answering format, respondents were asked to specify in which intensity they were using each of these nine coordination instruments during the technology transfer project they reported on.

Success of Technology Transfers

As mentioned above, two aspects were considered: to which degree the transfer goal "improvement of existing solutions" was achieved, and to which degree the transfer goal "innovation and learning" was achieved. Each of these two aspects was operationalized with two measured variables (see appendix).

Control Variables

Altogether eight control variables (size of the MNC, size of the recipient foreign subsidiary, the origin of this foreign subsidiary (acquisition or greenfield), its strategic role, the difficulty of the transferred technology, and the geographic and cultural distances between the home country and the subsidiary's country) were used to check the robustness of the empirical relationships between the conceptualized variables and the success variables. We selected these control variables because previous literature (e.g., Frost, 1998; Minbaeva, 2007) considered them to be factors that might influence (international) technology transfers. As such, they could potentially influence the relationships between the coordination instrument variables and the success of forward technology transfers. Here, we want to further discuss the variable "difficulty of transferred technology," since this is an integrative variable which includes the articulability, codifiability, observability, and complexity of the transferred technology. These four dimensions are taken from the work of Kogut and Zander (1993), Simonin (1999), and Håkanson and Nobel (2000), and each dimension was measured with several items. The Cronbach's alphas of these scales (see the appendix for their content) are quite high. The resulting variable "difficulty of transferred technology" is the sum of the average values of these four dimensions (the first three dimensions were reverse calculated; i.e., a difficult technology is *not* articulable, *not* codifiable, *not* observable, and complex). A relatively high overall value (e.g., -0.10) indicates a difficult technology and a relatively low value (e.g., -3.05) indicates a simple technology.

Table 1 shows the minimum and maximum values, means, standard deviations, and correlations among the 16 variables used in the analysis.

While some correlations are significant, the levels are sufficiently low that each predictor variable can be viewed as representing a different aspect of a technology transfer project. The correlation between the two dependent variables "transfer goal: 'improvement of existing solutions'" and "transfer goal: 'innovation and learning'" is sufficiently low ($r = 0.415$) that the two clearly represent different aspects of the success of technology transfers.

ANALYSES

When all of the measured variables used in the study are entered in a factor analysis, no dominant factor emerges. Thus, there is no evidence of any common methods variance. Ordinary least squares regressions were used to test the hypotheses. First, each dependent variable was regressed on the control variables (Model 1). Then, in a serial process, the conceptualized variables were added (Models 2–5 and 8). Models 6 and 7 present regression analyses that only include the hypothesized variables, without the control variables. Model 9 includes all of the variables including the dummy variable indicating the source of the data.

Table 1. Intercorrelations of Variables.

Variable Name	Min	Max	Mean	S.D.	1	2	3	4	5	6	7	8	9	10	11	12	13	14	15	16
Control variables																				
1 Size MNC	1700.00	475000.00	66216.2754	110515.56457	1															
2 Size foreign subsidiary	10.00	50000.00	2093.0930	5875.89916	.317**	1														
3 Foreign subsidiary: acquisition (0) or greenfield (1)	0.00	1.00	.6467	.47961	.048	-.091	1													
4 Foreign subsidiary role: global innovator	7.00	35.00	17.3897	5.93317	-.218*	.006	-.102	1												
5 Foreign subsidiary role: implementer	12.00	35.00	23.3939	5.03993	-.122	.071	.099	.240**	1											
6 Difficulty of transferred technology	-3.05	-.10	-1.5864	.51365	.061	-.037	-.067	-.226**	-.077	1										
7 Geographic distance	160.00	16060.00	5355.7305	3221.67622	-.011	.049	.179*	-.102	.169	.033	1									
8 Cultural distance	.03	4.71	1.7360	1.20400	-.042	-.099	.346**	-.231**	.050	-.009	.226**	1								
Conceptualized variables																				
9 Epistemic community	3.00	15.00	8.9154	2.33764	.059	-.014	.040	.245**	.047	-.304**	-.074	-.161*	1							
10 Absorptive capacity	14.00	30.00	23.3032	3.05943	-.173*	-.059	.008	.306**	.105	-.090	.010	-.022	.365**	1						
11 Structural coordination instruments	-2.92	2.14	.0706	.99190	.114	.127	-.079	.165	.159	.093	-.065	-.090	.084	.070	1					
12 Technocratic coordination instruments	-2.71	2.03	.0543	.96867	.055	.016	.137	.121	.069	-.077	-.055	.136	.077	.240**	-.014	1				

Table 1. (Continued)

Variable Name	Min	Max	Mean	S.D.	1	2	3	4	5	6	7	8	9	10	11	12	13	14	15	16
13 Person-oriented coordination instruments	-3.15	2.27	.0539	.98081	.024	-.048	.136	-.184*	.047	.118	.083	.136	-.181*	.044	.022	.028	1			
Dependent variables																				
14 Transfer goal "improvement of existing solutions"	1.00	5.00	4.1023	.83399	.012	.086	.112	-.126	.159	.006	.040	.206**	.101	.213**	.128	.322**	.274**	1		
15 Transfer goal "innovation and learning"	1.50	5.00	4.0686	.72791	.065	.102	.076	-.016	-.005	-.082	.025	.070	.066	.165*	.173*	.122	.245**	.416**	1	
16 Data source: headquarters or foreign subsidiary	1.00	2.00	1.5938	.48267	.175*	.053	.176*	-.072	-.175*	.020	.130	.170*	-.152	-.162*	-.224**	.035	-.101	-.059	-.045	1

**The correlation is significant at 0.01 (two-tailed).
*The correlation is significant at 0.05 (two-tailed).
$n = 160$.

RESULTS

The *first hypothesis* expected that the positive relationship between the intensity of the use of person-oriented coordination instruments and the achievement of the goal "innovation and learning" is stronger than the positive relationship between the intensity of the use of these coordination instruments and the achievement of the goal "improvement of existing solutions." Table 2 presents the results referring to this statement. A comparison of the upper and middle parts of this table shows that Hypothesis 1 is not confirmed. Yet, as implicitly expected in this hypothesis, the person-oriented coordination instruments have a strong positive and significant relationship with the transfer goal "innovation and learning" (beta = 0.241; significant at the 4 per mill level), but these coordination instruments are also strongly linked with the other transfer goal (beta = 0.237; significant at the 2 per mill level). This means that, according to these results, the person-oriented instruments are helpful with respect to both kinds of transfer goals.

Hypothesis 2 stated that the technocratic coordination instruments have a stronger influence on the transfer goal "improvement of existing solutions" than on the transfer goal "innovation and learning." As can be seen from Table 2, this difference exists. While there is a strong and significant relationship between the technocratic coordination instruments and the transfer goal "improvement of existing solutions" (beta = 0.276; significant at the 0 per mill level), there is no significant relationship with the transfer goal "innovation and learning."

According to *Hypothesis 3*, the use of the structural coordination instruments operates similar to the use of technocratic instruments: comparable to the previous hypothesis, we expected that there is a positive and significant relationship with the transfer goal "improvement of existing solutions." While this is true at the 9% level (beta = 0.129), astonishingly an intensive use of the structural coordination instruments is also helpful with respect to the transfer goal "innovation and learning." This relationship is even stronger (beta = 0.184; significant at the 3% level). We will discuss this surprising finding in the "Discussion" section.

With *Hypothesis 4* we expected that a high level of foreign subsidiaries' absorptive capacity mainly helps to reach the transfer goal "improvement of existing solutions." Unfortunately, this hypothesis is not confirmed although there is the expected positive sign between this absorptive capacity and the transfer goal "improvement of existing solutions." But this

Table 2. Regression Models for the Dependent Variables.

Regression Model for the Dependent Variable: Transfer Goal "Improvement of Existing Solutions"

Variable	Model A1	Model A2	Model A3	Model A4	Model A5	Model A6	Model A7	Model A8	Model A9
Control variables									
Size MNC	−0.017	−0.038	0.006	−0.008	−0.063			−0.063	−0.067
Size foreign subsidiary	0.090	0.101	0.098	0.103	0.084			0.099	0.098
Foreign subsidiary: acquisition or greenfield	0.043	0.029	0.037	0.030	−0.003			−0.015	−0.018
Foreign subsidiary role: global innovator	−0.119	−0.151 9%	−0.195 3%	−0.203 3%	−0.157 6%			−0.211 2%	−0.213 2%
Foreign subsidiary role: implementor	0.160 6%	0.159 6%	0.156 6%	0.156 6%	0.113			0.114	0.116
Difficulty of transferred technology	0.002	0.049	0.009	0.033	−0.028			0.013	0.013
Geographic distance	−0.048	−0.043	−0.055	−0.052	−0.014			−0.018	−0.021
Cultural distance	0.176 5%	0.202 3%	0.171 4%	0.185 4%	0.115			0.137 9%	0.135 10%
Data source: headquarters or foreign subsidiary									0.019
Conceptualized variables									
Epistemic community		0.176 4%		0.093			0.086	0.141 10%	0.143 9%
Absorptive capacity			0.267 1PM	0.236 6PM			0.093	0.128	0.130
Structural coordination instruments					0.143 6%	0.127 9%	0.112	0.125 10%	0.129 9%
Technocratic coordination instruments					0.312 0PM	0.317 0PM	0.287 0PM	0.277 0PM	0.276 0PM
Person-oriented coordination Instruments					0.227 3PM	0.263 0PM	0.275 0PM	0.234 2PM	0.237 2PM
F-value	1.697 ns	2.031 4%	2.857 4PM	2.686 5PM	4.330 0PM	12.218 0PM	8.228 0PM	4.456 0PM	4.115 0PM
Adjusted R^2	0.034	0.055	0.095	0.096	0.187	0.175	0.185	0.220	0.215

Level of significance: %=percent; PM = per mill.
$n = 160$.

Table 2. (Continued)

Regression Model for the Dependent Variable: Transfer Goal "Innovation and Learning"

Variable	Model B1	Model B2	Model B3	Model B4	Model B5	Model B6	Model B7	Model B8	Model B9
Control variables									
Size MNC	0.036	0.029	0.053	0.054	0.002			0.014	0.011
Size foreign subsidiary	0.088	0.091	0.093	0.093	0.082			0.088	0.088
Foreign subsidiary: acquisition or greenfield	0.057	0.052	0.053	0.053	0.033			0.031	0.029
Foreign subsidiary role: global innovator	0.000	−0.011	−0.054	−0.054	−0.014			−0.052	−0.054
Foreign subsidiary role: implementor	−0.022	−0.022	−0.025	−0.025	−0.070			−0.069	−0.067
Difficulty of transferred technology	−0.078	−0.062	−0.073	−0.076	−0.124			−0.112	−0.113
Geographic distance	0.004	0.005	−0.001	−0.002	0.020			0.014	0.012
Cultural distance	0.060	0.069	0.056	0.055	0.031			0.037	0.035
Data source: headquarters or foreign subsidiary									0.015
Conceptualized variables									
Epistemic community		0.060		−0.009			0.053	0.028	0.030
Absorptive capacity			0.191 3%	0.194 4%			0.103	0.133	0.135
Structural coordination instruments					0.190 2%	0.170 3%	0.157 4%	0.181 3%	0.184 3%
Technocratic coordination instruments					0.106	0.117	0.088	0.075	0.074
Person-oriented coordination instruments					0.246 2PM	0.238 2PM	0.244 2PM	0.239 3PM	0.241 4PM
F-value	0.486 ns	0.482 ns	1.023 ns	0.915 ns	1.997 4%	5.894 1PM	4.124 2PM	1.936 3%	1.788 5%
Adjusted R^2	−0.027	−0.03	0.001	−0.005	0.065	0.085	0.089	0.071	0.065

Level of significance: % = percent; PM = per mill.
$n = 160$.

Table 2. (Continued)

Regression model for the dependent variable: both transfer goals together

Variable	Model C1	Model C2	Model C3	Model C4	Model C5	Model C6	Model C7	Model C8	Model C9
Control variables									
Size MNC	0.009	−0.008	0.033	0.025	−0.039			−0.033	−0.036
Size foreign subsidiary	0.105	0.114	0.114	0.117	0.099			0.111	0.111
Foreign subsidiary: acquisition or greenfield	0.059	0.047	0.053	0.049	0.017			0.008	0.005
Foreign subsidiary role: global innovator	−0.075	−0.102	−0.154 9%	−0.158 8%	−0.107			−0.162 6%	−0.165 6%
Foreign subsidiary role: implementor	0.089	0.089	0.085	0.085	0.033			0.034	0.037
Difficulty of transferred technology	−0.042	−0.003	−0.035	−0.021	−0.086			−0.054	−0.054
Geographic distance	−0.028	−0.024	−0.036	−0.034	0.002			−0.004	−0.006
Cultural distance	0.145	0.166 7%	0.139	0.148 9%	0.090			0.108	0.105
Data source: headquarters or foreign subsidiary									
Conceptualized variables									
Epistemic community		0.145 10%		0.054			0.084	0.104	0.107
Absorptive capacity					0.196 1%	0.174 2%	0.116	0.155 7%	0.157 7%
Structural coordination instruments			0.275 1PM				0.158 3%	0.180 2%	0.184 2%
Technocratic coordination instruments				0.257 3PM	0.256 1PM	0.266 0PM	0.231 2PM	0.217 5PM	0.216 5PM
Person-oriented coordination instruments					0.280 0PM	0.298 0P M	0.309 0PM	0.281 0PM	0.284 0PM
F-value	1.122 ns	1.327 ns	2.357 2%	2.149 3%	4.039 0PM	12 612 0PM	8.742 0PM	4.145 0PM	3.829 0PM
Adjusted R^2	0.006	0.018	0.071	0.067	0.174	0.180	0.196	0.205	0.199

Level of significance: %=percent; PM = per mill.

$n = 160$.

relationship is weak and insignificant (beta = 0.130). Furthermore, absorptive capacity's influence on the other transfer goal is at the same strength (beta = 0.135; but also insignificant).

Hypothesis 5 is partly supported. As expected, absorptive capacity has a stronger relationship with the goal dimension "innovation and learning" (beta = 0.135) than the strength of the epistemic community concept has (beta = 0.030). Yet, both relationships are insignificant. But, contrary to the hypothesis, with respect to the goal dimension "improvement of existing solutions," the influence of the absorptive capacity is weaker (beta = 0.130) than the influence of epistemic community (beta = 0.143). The latter is significant at the 9% level.

It is important to notice that these empirical results are extremely robust. They remain intact when the eight control variables are included and when they are excluded. And they are also not influenced by the type of data source (data from respondents at headquarters vs. data from respondents in foreign subsidiaries).

Finally, if we compare the results related to the modern abstract management concepts with those related to the traditional coordination instruments, it is obvious that the latter have a stronger relationship with the two transfer goals. This difference exists with respect to both of the transfer goals (i.e., the transfer goal "improvement of existing solutions" and the transfer goal "innovation and learning"). And it also exists if we integrate these two goal dimensions into one (see the third part of Table 2).

DISCUSSION

In the following, we want to discuss some findings, which we have not expected in advance. We want to focus on the following two:

1. We did not expect that an intensive use of the structural coordination instruments supports the achievement of the transfer goal "innovation and learning."
2. And we did not expect that the traditional coordination instruments have more power than the newer management concepts to explain the success of vertical technology transfers in MNCs.

Ad 1: While the person-oriented coordination instruments have the strongest influence on innovation and learning-oriented technology transfers, our study found evidence that the structural coordination instruments (regularly held meetings and permanent teams) are also important for this type of technology transfer. Thus, *both* types of coordination instruments (the structural and the person-oriented) are important with respect to *both* types of technology transfer goals. To understand this counter-intuitive finding, it is important to notice that structural coordination instruments establish relatively stable and reliable forums for managerial co-operation within the firm. They support the development of time-stable patterns of interpersonal interactions. If structural coordination instruments are used, technology-specific information can flow along these well-established lines of communication. This is less guaranteed by the use of person-oriented coordination instruments. In the latter case, a change in the composition of the interaction partners can easily happen. One might argue that manager transfers can also help to create such reliable patterns, since the expatriate's position at his/her foreign workplace and thus the spectrum of his/her interaction partners are clearly specified. But in the case of other person-oriented instruments (e.g., visits or video conferences) it is less clear who will interact with whom. Thus, structural coordination instruments are needed as an additive means of coordination, which complements the coordinative effects of the person-oriented coordination instruments.

This view, that there is a need for structural coordination is consistent with organization theory's insight that formally established teams are helpful when extensive and complex tasks have to be mastered (Galbraith, 1973). Typically, innovation projects are of such an extensive and complex nature. In regularly held meetings and formally established teams, the team members are carefully selected to ensure that complementing personal qualifications and capabilities come together. Thus, it is not astonishing that research has shown that permanent teams play a crucial role in new product development processes (Hoegl & Parboteeah, 2003). One might argue that in MNCs a deliberate and more permanent design of the composition of teams and meetings' attendants is even more important, because this might help the representatives of geographically, culturally, and institutionally distant subsidiaries to become more fully integrated into the network of MNC managers.

Ad 2: We were also surprised that the traditional coordination instruments share a closer empirical relationship with the success of vertical technology transfers than the more recent abstract management concepts. If we want to understand this finding we have to consider that it is possible for managers to deploy the traditional coordination instruments in a deliberate manner against the specific needs of a technology transfer project. If, for instance, problems arise in a technology transfer project, managers can establish a task force to solve these problems, they can visit the respective unit, they can expatriate personnel, etc. On the other hand, the development of an epistemic community within the firm or the improvement of a subsidiary's absorptive capacity is more time consuming, generally not project-specific, and of a more general nature. Consequently, these concepts cannot be spontaneously or specifically applied if a transfer project has stalled. As mentioned above, these management concepts provide a broader, more conceptual background that can help to support technology transfers in a more indirect manner. By saying this, we do not want to deemphasize the importance of the abstract management concepts; we only want to express that it is difficult to deploy them against specific transfer projects.

SUMMARY AND CONCLUSIONS

The study found that all three types of traditional coordination instruments are positively and significantly related to the success of such transfers. Structural and person-oriented instruments are significantly related to both transfer goals (improvement of existing solutions, innovation, and learning). Technocratic instruments share a strong positive relationship with improvement of existing solutions, but only a weak, insignificant positive relationship with innovation and learning. The two modern management concepts (epistemic community and absorptive capacity), on the other hand, share much weaker and largely insignificant positive relationships with both of the transfer goals. Given these findings, we believe that research over the last few decades has gone too far in shifting its focus from the traditional coordination instruments to the modern management concepts. Our recommendation is that future MNC research studies should include more of the traditional coordination instruments, since they are clearly relevant to today's coordination problems in MNCs.

Such a reorientation, not to exclude the more modern management concepts, but also to include more of the traditional coordination instruments, would have several advantages. First, it would ensure that variables that are important drivers of successful coordination in large, complex firms are being included in the organizational design model. These variables have frequently been omitted from recent research for the wrong reasons (i.e., a lack of novelty and not a lack of relevance). Second, since the traditional variables can be more directly selected and manipulated by managers, they will tend to keep organization theory more application-oriented and of greater interest to managers. Good organization theory needs to provide conceptual insight, but it also needs to be applicable to real-world situations (Hilmer & Donaldson, 1996). And third, the inclusion of the traditional variables in new models or organization design will make organizational research on the MNC more cumulative and complete. New theory needs to embrace and reflect existing theory that is still creditable, not ignore it and attempt to replace it with something that is entirely new. Such an approach will lead to theory churn, as opposed to cumulating and constantly improving theory. The former may satisfy the publication needs of academics, but the latter will provide better theory for those who must manage and work in large, complex MNCs.

While our study raises some interesting issues, it is not without its own limitations. Future research also needs to take these into account. First, the study's two unexpected results clearly need to be retested and further explored in future empirical research, since they were not conceptualized and hypothesized in advance. These two findings are that: (1) structured coordination instruments support the transfer goal of innovation and learning, and (2) the traditional coordination instruments are better predictors than the modern management concepts of the success of vertical technology transfers in MNCs. Second, the present study has only dealt with forward technology transfers. It is possible that the relative importance of the modern management concepts might increase for reverse technology transfers from subsidiaries to the headquarters or for horizontal transfers among subsidiaries. The logic for this possibility is that in these situations the sender of the technology cannot use hierarchical authority to facilitate implementing the transfer. Future research needs to address these situations.

In conclusion, this study demonstrates the importance of considering traditional coordination instruments when seeking to understand the factors that drive successful technology transfers in MNCs. More broadly, it argues that modern management concepts need to be embraced with care and objectivity. The influence they have on organizational behavior and outcomes, as well as the insight they provide, needs to be compared against that provided by existing management concepts. As much as possible, this effort needs to be supported by comparative empirical research, as illustrated by the present study. Our view is that this type of research design would lead to a much greater integration of traditional and new management concepts and a richer theory for understanding organizational behavior in MNCs.

REFERENCES

Bartlett, C. A., & Ghoshal, S. (1989). *Managing across borders: The transnational solution.* Boston, MA: Harvard Business School Press.

Brown, J. S., & Duguid, P. (1991). Organizational learning and communities-of-practice: Toward a unified view of working, learning, and innovation. *Organization Science, 2*(1), 40–57.

Burgelman, R. A., Maidique, M. A., & Wheelwright, S. C. (1996). *Strategic management of technology and innovation* (2nd ed.). Chicago, IL: Irwin.

Cattey, M. (1980). Cultural differences in processing information. *Journal of American Indian Education, 20*(1), 23–29.

Cohen, W. M., & Levinthal, D. A. (1990). Absorptive capacity: A new perspective on learning and innovation. *Administrative Science Quarterly, 35*(1), 128–152.

Connell, N. A. D., Klein, J. H., & Powell, P. L. (2003). It's tacit knowledge but not as we know it: Redirecting the search for knowledge. *Journal of the Operational Research Society, 54*(2), 140–152.

Cummings, J. J., & Teng, B.-S. (2003). Transferring R&D knowledge: The key factors affecting knowledge transfer success. *Journal of Engineering and Technology Management, 20*(1–2), 39–68.

Daft, R. L., & Lengel, R. H. (1986). Organizational information requirements, media richness and structural design. *Management Science, 32*(5), 554–571.

Dunning, J. H. (1958). *American investment in British manufacturing industry.* London: Allen and Unwin.

Egelhoff, W. G. (1982). Strategy and structure in multinational corporations: An information-processing approach. *Administrative Science Quarterly, 27*(3), 435–458.

Egelhoff, W. G. (1988). *Organizing the multinational enterprise: An information-processing perspective.* Cambridge, MA: Ballinger.

Frost, T. (1998). *The geographic sources of innovation in the multinational enterprise: U.S. subsidiaries and host country spillovers, 1980–1990.* Unpublished Doctoral Dissertation. MIT, Cambridge.

Frost, T., & Zhou, C. (2005). R&D co-practice and 'reverse' knowledge integration in multinational firms. *Journal of International Business Studies, 36*(6), 676–687.

Galbraith, J. R. (1973). *Designing complex organizations.* Reading, MA: Addison-Wesley.

Garnier, G. H. (1982). Context and decision making autonomy in the foreign affiliates of U.S. multinational corporations. *Academy of Management Journal, 25*(4), 893–908.

Gates, S. R., & Egelhoff, W. G. (1986). Centralization in headquarters-subsidiary relationships. *Journal of International Business Studies, 17*(2), 71–92.

Geppert, M., Matten, D., & Walgenbach, P. (2006). Transnational institution building and the multinational corporation: An emerging field of research. *Human Relations, 59*(11), 1451–1465.

Ghoshal, S., Korine, H., & Szulanski, G. (1994). Interunit communication in multinational corporations. *Management Science, 40*(1), 96–110.

Goehle, D. G. (1980). *Decision making in multinational corporations.* Ann Arbor, MI: UMI Research Press.

Gupta, A. K., & Govindarajan, V. (1991). Knowledge flows and the structure of control within multinational corporations. *Academy of Management Review, 16*(4), 768–792.

Gupta, A. K., & Govindarajan, V. (2000). Knowledge flows within multinational corporations. *Strategic Management Journal, 21*(4), 473–496.

Haas, P. M. (1992). Introduction: Epistemic communities and international policy coordination. *International Organization, 46*(1), 1–35.

Håkanson, L. (2005). Epistemic communities and cluster dynamics: On the role of knowledge in industrial districts. *Industry and Innovation, 12*(4), 433–463.

Håkanson, L. (2007). Creating knowledge: The power and logic of articulation. *Industrial and Corporate Change, 16*(1), 51–88.

Håkanson, L. (2010). The firm as an epistemic community: The knowledge-based view revisited. *Industrial and Corporate Change, 19*(6), 1801–1826.

Håkanson, L., & Nobel, R. (2000). Technology characteristics and reverse technology transfer. *Management International Review, 40*(Special issue 1), 29–48.

Håkanson, L., & Zander, U. (1986). *Managing international research & development.* Stockholm: Mekanförbundet.

Hedlund, G. (1986). The hypermodern MNC: A heterarchy? *Human Resource Management, 23*(1), 9–35.

Hilmer, F. G., & Donaldson, L. (1996). *Management redeemed: Debunking the fads that undermine our corporate performance.* East Roseville: Free Press.

Hoegl, M., & Parboteeah, K. P. (2003). Goal setting and team performance in innovative projects: On the moderating role of teamwork quality. *Small Group Research, 34*(1), 3–19.

Hofstede, G. (1980). *Culture's consequences: International differences in work-related values.* Beverly Hills: Sage.

Hofstede, G. (1991). *Cultures and organizations: Software of the mind.* London: McGraw-Hill.

Holzner, B., & Marx, J. H. (1979). *Knowledge application: The knowledge system in society.* Boston, MA: Allyn and Bacon.

Hulbert, J. M., & Brandt, W. K. (1980). *Managing the multinational subsidiary.* New York, NY: Holt Rinehart and Winston.

Jansen, J. J. P., Van den Bosch, F. A. J., & Volberda, H. W. (2005). Managing potential and realized absorptive capacity: How do organizational antecedents matter? *Academy of Management Journal, 48*(6), 999–1015.

Kabanoff, B. (1997). Organizational cultures across cultures: Integrating organizational-level and culture-level perspectives. In P. C. Earley & M. Erez (Eds.), *New perspectives on international industrial/organizational psychology* (pp. 671–676). San Francisco, CA: Jossey-Bass.

Khandwalla, P. N. (1973). *The design of organizations.* New York, NY: New Lexington Press.

Kogut, B., & Singh, H. (1988). The effect of national culture on the choice of entry mode. *Journal of International Business Studies, 19*(3), 411–432.

Kogut, B., & Zander, U. (1993). Knowledge of the firm and the evolutionary theory of the multinational corporation. *Journal of International Business Studies, 24*(4), 625–645.

Kostova, T., & Roth, K. (2002). Adoption of an organizational practice by subsidiaries of multinational corporations. *Academy of Management Journal, 45*(1), 215–233.

Lane, P. J., & Lubatkin, M. (1998). Relative absorptive capacity and interorganizational learning. *Strategic Management Journal, 19*(5), 461–477.

Leavitt, H. J. (1964). Applied organization change in industry: Structural, technical, and human approaches. In W. W. Cooper, H. J. Leavitt, & M. W. Shelly, I.I. (Eds.), *New perspectives in organization research* (pp. 55–71). New York, NY: Wiley.

Lyles, M. A., & Salk, J. E. (1996). Knowledge acquisition from foreign parents in international joint ventures: An empirical examination in the Hungarian context. *Journal of International Business Studies, 27*(5), 877−903.

Malnight, T. W. (1996). The transition from decentralized to network-based MNC structures: An evolutionary perspective. *Journal of International Business Studies, 27*(1), 43−65.

Martin, X., & Salomon, R. (2003). Knowledge transfer capacity and its implications for the theory of the multinational corporation. *Journal of International Business Studies, 34*(4), 356−373.

Martinez, J. I., & Jarillo, J. C. (1989). The evolution of research on coordination mechanisms in multinational corporations. *Journal of International Business Studies, 20*(3), 489−514.

Mascarenhas, B. (1984). The coordination of manufacturing interdependence in multinational corporations. *Journal of International Business Studies, 15*(3), 91−106.

Minbaeva, D. B. (2007). Knowledge management in multinational corporations. *Management International Review, 47*(4), 567−593.

Minbaeva, D. B., Pedersen, T., Björkman, I., Fey, C. F., & Park, H. J. (2003). MNC knowledge transfer, subsidiary absorptive capacity, and HRM. *Journal of International Business Studies, 34*(6), 586−599.

Morgan, G., Kristensen, P. H., & Whitley, R. (2001). *The multinational firm: Organizing across institutional and national divides*. Oxford: Oxford University Press.

Negandhi, A. R., & Welge, M. (1984). *Beyond theory Z: Global rationalization strategies of American, German and Japanese multinational companies*. Greenwich, London: JAI Press.

Persson, M. (2006). *Unpacking the flow. Knowledge transfer in MNCs*. Unpublished Doctoral Dissertation. Uppsala Universitet, Uppsala.

Picard, J. (1977). How European companies control marketing decisions abroad. *Columbia Journal of World Business, 12*(2), 113−121.

Ring, P. S., & Van de Ven, A. H. (1994). Developmental processes of cooperative interorganizational relationships. *Academy of Management Review, 19*(1), 90−118.

Rohrlack, C. (2009). *Reverse Technology Transfer in multinationalen Unternehmen: Bedingungen und Gestaltungsmöglichkeiten*. Wiesbaden: Gabler.

Schrader, S. (1991). Informal technology transfer between firms: Cooperation through information trading. *Research Policy, 20*(2), 153−170.

Simonin, B. L. (1999). Ambiguity and the process of knowledge transfer in strategic alliances. *Strategic Management Journal, 20*(7), 595−623.

Szulanski, G. (1996). Exploring internal stickiness: Impediments to the transfer of best practice within the firm. *Strategic Management Journal, 17*(Winter special issue), 27−43.

Taylor, S., Levy, O., Boyacigiller, N. A., & Beechler, S. (2008). Employee commitment in MNCs: Impacts of organizational culture, HRM and top management orientation. *International Journal of Human Resource Management, 19*(4), 501−527.

Thompson, J. D. (1967). *Organizations in action: Social science bases of administrative theory*. New York, NY: McGraw-Hill.

Tiessen, J. H. (1999). Developing intellectual capital globally: An epistemic community perspective. *International Journal of Technology Management, 18*(5−8), 720−730.

Tsai, W. (2001). Knowledge transfer in intraorganizational networks: Effects of network position and absorptive capacity on business unit innovation and performance. *Academy of Management Journal, 44*(5), 996−1004.

Tushman, M. L., & Nadler, D. A. (1978). Information processing as an integrating concept in organizational design. *Academy of Management Review, 3*(3), 613–624.

Tushman, M. L., & Scanlan, T. J. (1981). Boundary spanning individuals: Their role in information transfer and their antecedents. *Academy of Management Journal, 24*(2), 289–305.

Van Den Bulcke, D., & Halsberghe, E. (1984). *Employment decision-making in multinational enterprises: Survey results from Belgium.* ILO Working Paper No. 32. ILO, Geneva.

Van Wijk, R., Jansen, J. J. P., & Lyles, M. A. (2008). Inter- and intra-organizational knowledge transfer: A meta-analytic review and assessment of its antecedents and consequences. *Journal of Management Studies, 45*(4), 830–853.

Wolf, J. (1994). *Internationales Personalmanagement: Kontext, Koordination, Erfolg.* Wiesbaden: Gabler.

Wolf, J., & Egelhoff, W. G. (2010). Limitations of the network organization in MNCs. In J. Pla-Barber & J. Alegre (Eds.), *Progress in international business research* (Vol. 5, pp. 143–172). Amsterdam: Emerald.

Zahra, S. A., & George, G. (2002). Absorptive capacity: A review, reconceptualization, and extension. *Academy of Management Review, 27*(2), 185–203.

APPENDIX: MEASUREMENT OF VARIABLES

1. The scale to measure the concept "epistemic community" contained the following three items ((R)=reverse coded): "Employees of our headquarters understand how employees of our subsidiary want to use the transferred knowledge."; "Differences in the knowledge bases between employees of our subsidiary and employees of our headquarters make discussions difficult. (R)"; "Understanding problems between employees of our subsidiary and employees of our headquarters exist because of language deficits. (R)." Cronbach's alpha of this scale is 0.675.

2. Altogether 13 items were used to operationalize the variable "absorptive capacity." To measure the recipient subsidiary's potential absorptive capacity, we used the items: "Employees of our subsidiary collect industry information through informal ways (e.g., business lunch with colleagues and talking to business partners)."; "Employees of our subsidiary regularly organize appointments with customers or other parties to acquire new knowledge."; "Employees of our subsidiary regularly consult experts to acquire new information."; "Employees of our subsidiary only slowly recognize changes in the host market." (R); "Employees of our subsidiary recognize very fast new opportunities to support customers."; "Employees of our subsidiary analyze and interpret changes of market demands very fast."; To measure the recipient subsidiary's realized absorptive capacity, we used the items: "Employees of our subsidiary recognize the benefit of new knowledge related to existing knowledge very fast."; "New acquired external knowledge is documented by employees of our subsidiary and saved for future use."; "Employees of our subsidiary only slowly seize opportunities resulting from newly acquired external knowledge." (R); "Employees of our subsidiary often meet to discuss consequences of changing of market needs and new product development."; "Complaints of customers fall on deaf ears by employees of our subsidiary." (R); "Employees of our subsidiary do permanently think about exploiting knowledge in a better way."; "Employees of our subsidiary have a common language regarding the products and services of our subsidiary." Cronbach's alpha is 0.665 for the potential absorptive capacity and 0.683 for the realized absorptive capacity.

3. Based on a literature review, "regularly held meetings" and "permanent teams" were considered as "structural coordination instruments." Using a five-point answering format, respondents were asked in which

intensity they were using the respective coordination instruments during the considered technology transfer.

4. Based on a literature review, "rules and procedures" and "formal reporting systems" were considered as "technocratic coordination instruments." Using a five-point answering format, respondents were asked in which intensity they were using the respective coordination instruments during the considered technology transfer.

5. Based on a literature review, "informal meetings of headquarters and subsidiary members," "expatriation of headquarters or subsidiary members to the other unit," "visits of headquarters or subsidiary members to the other unit," "video conferences of headquarters and subsidiary members," and "trainings of headquarters or subsidiary members" were considered as "Person-oriented Coordination Instruments." Using a five-point answering format, respondents were asked in which intensity they were using the respective coordination instruments during the considered technology transfer.

The respondents' answers along these altogether nine coordination instruments (two structural, two technocratic, and five person-oriented) were factor analysed (principal component analysis and varimax rotation). Applying the Kaiser criterion (Eigenwert > 1), three factors appeared. Since factor 1 strongly corresponds with the technocratic coordination instruments, factor 2 strongly corresponds with the person-oriented coordination instruments, and factor 3 strongly corresponds with the structural coordination instruments, in the subsequent data analysis, these factors were used as indicator variables for the three classes of coordination instruments.

6. To measure the variable "transfer goal 'improvement of existing solutions'," respondents were asked to which degree they agree with following statements: "The transferred technology has caused a clear improvement of products and/or processes in the recipient subsidiary." and "The transferred technology has caused an increase of the subsidiary's performance." The respondents could answer along a five-point Likert scale ranging from 1 (= I do not agree) to 5 (= I do fully agree). Based on the two values, the arithmetic average was calculated.

7. To measure the variable "transfer goal 'innovation and learning'," respondents were asked to which degree they agree with the following statements: "The transferred technology has caused/will cause further innovation processes in the recipient subsidiary." and "During the technology transfer learning effects occurred which could be used for future transfers." The respondents could answer along a five-point

Likert scale ranging from 1 (= I do not agree) to 5 (= I do fully agree). Based on the two values, the arithmetic average was calculated.

8. The variable "both transfer goals together" is the arithmetic means of the variables "transfer goal 'improvement of existing solutions'" and "transfer goal 'innovation and learning'."

9. The variable "size of MNC" was measured by its number of employees.

10. The variable "size of foreign subsidiary" was measured by its number of employees.

11. In order to measure the origin of the recipient foreign subsidiary (the variable "foreign subsidiary: acquisition or greenfield"), respondents were asked if this subsidiary has been founded by the multinational corporation or acquired by the multinational corporation (0 = acquisition; 1 = greenfield).

12. The measurement of the two considered foreign subsidiary roles (global innovator and implementer) was based on Gupta and Govindarajan's (1991) work. According to them, the intensity of knowledge flows to and from the respective subsidiary defines this unit's role. Thus, with respect to seven functional areas (procurement, production, marketing and sales, R&D, logistics, finance, and information technology), respondents were asked to answer to which degree the following statements are true: "Our subsidiary sends a significant amount of knowledge and skills of the following functional areas to the headquarters and other peer subsidiaries of our MNC" and "Our subsidiary receives a significant amount of knowledge and skills of the following functional areas from the headquarters and other peer subsidiaries of our MNC." For each of the two dimensions (knowledge outflow and knowledge inflow), a median split was calculated. A subsidiary was labeled "global innovator," if it had high knowledge outflows and low knowledge inflows. A subsidiary was labeled "implementer," if it had low knowledge outflows and high knowledge inflows. These two types of subsidiary roles were considered, since they are the opposite types in Gupta and Govindarajan's typology.

13. The variable "difficulty of transferred technology" is a variable integrating the articulability, codifiability, observability, and complexity of the transferred technology. To measure the dimension "articulability," respondents had to evaluate to which degree the following statements are true: "Employees, who know the transferred technology very well, can easily explain/speak about this technology."; "Employees, who know the transferred technology very well can easily conceptualize a training session about the transferred technology." Cronbach's alpha of

this scale is 0.717. To measure the dimension "codifiability," respondents had to answer the following statements: "It is possible to document the transferred technology in a written form."; "It is possible to write a handbook that describes the handling of the transferred technology." Cronbach's alpha of this scale is 0.815. To measure the dimension "observability," respondents had to answer the following statements: "New employees/competitors can learn the transferred technology, by observing personnel who know the transferred technology very well."; "New employees/competitors can learn the transferred technology, if they participate in a guided tour through the functional department in which the transferred technology is used."; "New employees/competitors can learn the transferred technology, if they analyse the working materials (e.g. machines and computers)."; "New employees/competitors can learn the transferred technology, if they carefully analyse a process or a product that depends on the transferred technology."; "New employees/competitors can learn the transferred technology, if they test the use of the technology." Cronbach's alpha of this scale is 0.671. To measure the dimension "complexity," respondents had to answer the following statements: "The transferred technology is based on a larger number of different partial processes."; "Between the different partial processes exist several interdependencies."; "These interdependencies between the partial processes differ in contents." Cronbach's alpha of this scale is 0.875. The resulting variable "difficulty of transferred technology" is the sum of average values of these four dimensions (the first three dimensions were reverse calculated, i.e., a difficult technology is not articulable, not codifiable, not observable, and complex). A relatively high value (e.g. -0.10) indicates a difficult technology, a relatively low value (e.g. -3.05) indicates a simple technology.

14. The variable "Geographic Distance" was measured as the kilometric distance between (1) the capital of the country, where the MNC is headquartered, and the capital of the country, where the foreign subsidiary is located.

15. The variable "Cultural Distance" was measured with the Kogut-Singh index (Kogut & Singh, 1988) based on Hofstede's (1980, 1991) data.

16. The variable "data source: headquarters or foreign subsidiary" is "1" if the questionnaire was filled out by a respondent working in the headquarters and "2" if the respondent is working in the foreign subsidiaries.

PART II
NEW APPROACHES TO DEFINING
AND MEASURING DISTANCE

CHAPTER 6

PERCEPTIONS VERSUS NATIONAL-LEVEL DIFFERENCES: A MEDIATING MODEL OF PSYCHIC DISTANCE

Douglas Dow, Lars Håkanson and Björn Ambos

ABSTRACT

Purpose — *This chapter bridges the gap between two distinct approaches to the concept of psychic distance — measuring it in terms of people's perceptions of distance or in terms of exogenous national-level differences. The two approaches are reconciled in a "refined and integrative" definition of the concept, which is tested empirically using a mediating model.*

Methodology — *Structural equation modeling is used on a bilateral sample of 25 countries to test whether perceptions of psychic distance mediate the relationships between national-level differences and bilateral trade and investment.*

Findings — *By testing for alternative direct paths, the chapter confirms that for the main forms of national-level differences, culture, socioeconomic development, language, and religion, psychic distance fully*

Multinational Enterprises, Markets and Institutional Diversity
Progress in International Business Research, Volume 9, 133–170
Copyright © 2014 by Emerald Group Publishing Limited
All rights of reproduction in any form reserved
ISSN: 1745-8862/doi:10.1108/S1745-886220140000009005

mediates their relationships with both trade flows and investment patterns. However, for geographic distance, while the relationship is fully mediated for investment, it is only partially mediated for exports. Two asymmetric "distance-bridging" factors are also found to be significant antecedents of psychic distance.

Originality and implications — *This chapter is the first to empirically demonstrate the mediating relationship between exogenous national-level differences and perceptions of psychic distance, and thus, provides new insights into the debate over which measurement approach is more appropriate. Perceptions of psychic distance, even if measured by expert panels rather than the actual decision-makers, fully capture the impact of national-level differences on trade and FDI flows; however, if such measures of perceptions are not available, a simple selection of four national-level differences will still capture 80% of the same effect.*

Keywords: Psychic distance; Hofstede; market selection; structural equation modeling; trade flows; FDI

INTRODUCTION

Within the realm of international business, the related constructs of psychic distance (Johanson & Wiedersheim-Paul, 1975) and national cultural distance (Kogut & Singh, 1988), along with other forms of national differences such as institutional distance (Xu & Shenkar, 2002) and sociocultural distance (Agarwal, 1994), have been cited as potential predictor variables for a broad range of management decisions such as the decision to begin exporting (e.g., Gripsrud, 1990), export market selection (e.g., Ellis, 2008), foreign direct investment (FDI) market selection (e.g., Davidson, 1980), entry mode and establishment mode choices (e.g., Kogut & Singh, 1988; Slangen & Hennart, 2008), foreign subsidiary performance (e.g., Evans & Mavondo, 2002), human resource management issues (e.g., Boyacigiller, 1990), and even communication in R&D joint ventures (e.g., Tushman, 1978).

Yet, despite this wide range of applications, substantial differences of opinion remain concerning how best to conceptualize and operationalize the relevant distance constructs (Brewer, 2007; Dow & Karunaratna, 2006; Evans & Mavondo, 2002; Håkanson & Ambos, 2010; Sousa & Bradley, 2006). At the core of this debate is the issue of whether distance should be defined and measured in terms of exogenous differences among countries, as it was initially operationalized by Vahlne and Wiedersheim-Paul (1973), or in terms of the perceptions of distance by individuals (e.g., Sousa & Bradley, 2006). Several commentators (e.g., Shenkar, 2001; Tung & Verbeke, 2010) have recently argued that a focus on perceptions is a superior approach. However, as will be expanded upon in our literature review, the vast majority of actual research has relied on exogenous indicators of national-level differences. The unfortunate reality is that these two streams of research have largely tended to continue on in isolation to one another. This leaves subsequent researchers with two problems. At the empirical level, there in a quandary as to which approach is actually the superior measurement instrument, and what tradeoffs are being made when one approach is chosen over the other? At the theoretical level, there is also a concern about the content validity of how some of the national-level differences are employed. For example, when one employs differences in GDP per capita to predict trade flows, is it an indicator of psychic distance as claimed by Dow and Karunaratna (2006), or is it an indicator of differences in consumer tastes as argued by Hirsch and Lev (1973)?

This chapter addresses these two issues by proposing a model where perceptions of psychic distance mediate the relationships between exogenous national-level differences and two key aspects of international business activity – bilateral trade flows and the flow of foreign direct investment. We argue that this mediating model is not only consistent with the existing theoretical perspectives but also by testing for full and partial mediating relationships; the model provides empirical evidence as to which approach to measuring psychic distance is more appropriate. The nature of the mediating relationships also provides insights into the content validity of several of the national-level differences commonly used as indicators of psychic distance. A further contribution of this study is a finer grained investigation of the role of geographic distance as an unexpected antecedent of perceptions of psychic distance – an insight highlighted by Håkanson and Ambos (2010).

The next section of this chapter briefly reviews past efforts to define, measure, and incorporate psychic distance into empirical international business research, before proposing a slightly revised definition of the concept. A series of hypotheses concerning the mediating nature of psychic distance is then developed. The sections "Research Methodology" and "Results" of this chapter describe the research methodology and report the results of the statistical analyses, respectively. The section "Discussion and Conclusion" discusses and summarizes the findings, contributions, and limitations of the research.

LITERATURE REVIEW AND HYPOTHESES
DEVELOPMENT

A History of the Definition and Measurement of Psychic Distance

The earliest reference to psychic distance is believed to be by Beckerman (1956, p. 38). In a study of intra-European trade flows, Beckerman suggested that some of the unexplained variance in trade patterns might be due to "a special problem ... posed by the existence of psychic distance." Transportation costs between Italy and Turkey may be no greater than between Italy and Switzerland; yet, he argued, "Switzerland will be 'nearer' to [an Italian entrepreneur] in a psychic evaluation (fewer language difficulties, and so on)." However, the construct attracted relatively little attention until researchers at the University of Uppsala adopted it as a key construct in their internationalization process model (Johanson & Wiedersheim-Paul, 1975). Johanson and Vahlne (1977, p. 24) defined psychic distance as: *"... the sum of factors preventing the flow of information from and to the market. Examples include differences in language, education, business practices, culture, and industrial development."*

Following the lead of the early Uppsala studies, a substantial proportion of subsequent empirical research concerning psychic distance focused on exogenous national-level differences, and in particular on Kogut and Singh's (1988) national cultural distance index. Over time, the Kogut and Singh index virtually became the default measurement of national distance in international business research (Harzing, 2003). More recently, this practice that has been heavily criticized (Kirkman, Lowe, & Gibson, 2006; Shenkar, 2001; Tihanyi, Griffith, & Russell, 2005), and several teams of researchers have begun expanding the set of indicators (Berry, Guillen, & Zhou, 2010; Brewer, 2007; Dow & Karunaratna, 2006); however, even these efforts have only broadened the range of exogenous national-level differences.

In contrast, a growing stream of research has argued that since decisions are made by individual managers, psychic distance should be defined and measured in terms of managers' perceptions (e.g., Tung & Verbeke, 2010). While smaller in quantity, the stream of empirical articles measuring psychic distance in terms of perceptions appears to be growing rapidly (Child, Rodrigues, & Frynas, 2009; Dow, 2000; Ellis, 2008; Evans & Mavondo, 2002; Håkanson & Ambos, 2010; Holzmuller & Kasper, 1990; Klein & Roth, 1990; Sousa & Bradley, 2006; Sousa & Lages, 2011). However, as alluded to in the introduction, a significant gap in the literature is the paucity of papers that have empirically explored the relative merits of these two approaches and the nature of their relationship with one another.

To date, we are only aware of five empirical papers that have compared and contrasted the two approaches to measuring psychic distance. Three of these papers (Dow, 2000; Drogendijk & Slangen, 2006; Ellis, 2008) have compared the explanatory power of the Kogut and Singh index (1988) with the explanatory power of an instrument measuring perceived psychic distance. In each case, this was done when predicting managerial choices such as market selection or establishment mode. Unfortunately, in addition to employing only a very narrow and heavily criticism form of national difference (i.e., the Kogut and Singh index), in all three instances, the authors incorporated only these measures in alternative models. As a result, it is not possible to construct from their data a statistical test of the relative merits of the two approaches, and no mediating relationship was allowed for in their analyses.

The other two noteworthy articles in this area (Håkanson & Ambos, 2010; Sousa & Bradley, 2006) modeled national-level differences as antecedents of perceived psychic distance but did not include any criterion variables such as market selection, entry mode, or establishment mode. In the case of Sousa and Bradley (2006), once again the Kogut and Singh index was their sole form of national-level difference, whereas Håkanson and Ambos expanded their set of national-level factors to include geographic distance, common languages, and differences in GDP per capita.

Methodologically, the analyses in this chapter can be viewed as an extension of the work of Håkanson and Ambos (2010) but with three major variations. First, the scales developed by Dow and Karunaratna (2006) are introduced to broaden the set of national-level difference indicators. Second, trade and FDI flows are introduced to provide a form of criterion-related validity. Third, and most critically, these elements are modeled as a mediating model with both direct and indirect paths in order to test alternative explanations. Next, we will develop a series of hypotheses that provide the theoretical underpinnings of this mediating model, but before we progress to that stage, we need to anchor this discussion with our working definition psychic distance.

Our Definition of Psychic Distance

As was the case with respect to the measurement of the construct, the literature is similarly bifurcated in terms of a formal definition of psychic distance. The original Uppsala definition, quoted at the beginning of this review, is still frequently cited; however, a number of revised definitions emphasizing the perceptual aspect of the construct (e.g., Evans & Mavondo, 2002; Sousa & Bradley, 2006) have also been put forward. It is our opinion that there are strengths and weakness to both approaches. The original Uppsala definition is particularly useful because it clearly identifies the unifying theme, or criterion, for determining whether a factor should be considered to be part of the psychic distance construct − that is, whether it influences the flow of information between markets. It also provides specific examples of factors which may fall into that category (e.g., differences in language). In contrast Evans and Mavondo (2002, p. 517) define psychic distance as: *"...the distance between the home market and a foreign market, resulting from the perception of both cultural and business differences."* Similarly, Sousa and Bradley (2006, p. 51) argue that ... *"it is the individual's perception of the differences between the home country and the foreign country that shapes the psychic distance."* This emphasis of the perceptual aspect of psychic distance is an important contribution to the literature; however, these latter two definitions also have their limitations. In particular, both of the aforementioned perceptual definitions are relatively nonspecific about the mechanisms by which the perceptions of psychic distance influence managerial decisions. Are all differences across nations equally important and relevant to psychic distance? As an example, Sousa and Bradley (2006) include differences in climate and consumer preferences between countries as indicators of psychic distance. We would argue that this is a contentious departure from the original Uppsala definition, which focused on the "flow of information," and dramatically blurs the clarity of the construct (Suddaby, 2010). As a result, we propose a "refined and integrative" definition of psychic distance which synthesizes the valuable aspects of both schools of thought.

> Psychic distance is the perception that two parties from different countries, regions or backgrounds may have difficulty communicating with, interpreting, and understanding each other. This may arise from factors such as differences in language, religion, education, political systems, business practices, culture, and industrial development.

We note that this definition also embraces Tung and Verbeke's (2010) point that psychic distance may arise due to intracountry variations as well as intercountry differences and echos the view of a doyen of the Uppsala school (Carlson, 1974) in that it is not just about the collection and transmission of information but also the interpretation of that information.

A Mediating Model

Our preceding definition of psychic distance raises two critical issues. The first issue is that if a person does perceive that they are likely to have difficulties communicating with, and being understood by people in a foreign country, what factors are creating those perceptions? In this respect, the original Uppsala definition was quite explicit, though not exhaustive, in identifying such factors as differences in language. The specific arguments for each potential factor are outlined in the lead up to our hypotheses but this line of argument broadly reflects Håkanson and Ambos' (2010) discussion of the "antecedent's of psychic distance" — that is, the view that among other factors, national-level differences between countries are likely to influence people's perceptions of psychic distance.

The second critical issue is — what are the implications of psychic distance? If managers believe that they will have difficulty communicating with and being understood in a foreign market, how will that influence their actions and thus affect firm behavior? Beckerman (1956) initially coined the term to explain trade flows in the belief that it influenced manager's choices of which markets to export to. Subsequent to that, Johanson and Vahlne (1977) adopted the term to explain foreign market selection and commitment decisions. They argued that psychic distance increases the perceived risk of operating in a market, which in turn, discourages firms from making hard to reverse commitments to such markets. Since that time, the application of psychic distance has been extended to explain a broad range of firm behaviors including entry mode (e.g., Dow & Larimo, 2009; Kogut & Singh, 1988), establishment mode choice (e.g., Larimo, 2003; Slangen & Hennart, 2008), and performance (e.g., Evans & Mavondo, 2002; O'Grady & Lane, 1996).

Combined, these two "issues" form the core of our mediating model as shown in Fig. 1. Psychic distance, or more explicitly "perceived psychic distance," is the mediating construct in the center of this model (PD_{Perc}). On the left side are the exogenous national-level differences — "distance creating factors" — frequently cited as potential antecedents of perceived psychic distance. On the right-hand side are the firm level behaviors and outcomes which may be influenced by psychic distance. In this instance, bilateral trade and FDI flows are selected as the criterion variables as their relationships with various national-level differences have been extensively tested and confirmed. Moreover, trade and investment flows are two of the major business outcomes for which multihome and multitarget country data are available. Such a cross-national dataset is necessary to determine whether

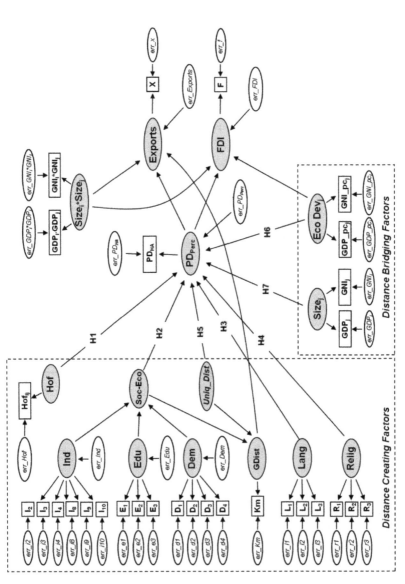

Fig. 1. Structural Paths of the Baseline Model. *Note:* Four control variables (FTA, Colony, Adjacent, and Pol Stab$_j$), and correlations among the exogenous constructs, have been omitted for clarity.

the observed outcomes reflect national-level differences or target country effects.[1]

Direct links between national-level differences and the selected criterion variables have been empirically tested and confirmed in a wide range of studies for both exports (e.g., Brewer, 2007; Dow & Karunaratna, 2006; Ellis, 2008; Rose, 2004; Silva & Tenreyro, 2006) and FDI (e.g., Davidson, 1980; Nordström & Vahlne, 1994; Sethi, Guisinger, Phelan, & Berg, 2003). However, all of these studies make assumptions about the underlying mechanisms of the observed relationships, without actually testing those assumptions. Returning to the example from the introduction, Dow and Karunaratna (2006) use differences in GDP per capita as an indicator of psychic distance in order to predict trade flows. However, Hirsch and Lev (1973), in an attempt to confirm the Burenstam-Linder hypothesis (Linder, 1961), use exactly the same metric in the same context as an indicator of differences in demand preferences. The net result is that GDP per capita does appear to influence trade and FDI flows, but it is unclear whether it is due to psychic distance or differences in consumer preferences. A mediating model helps to resolve such issues (Shaver, 2005) and confirms the construct validity of the antecedent variables (Kerlinger, 1986). In effect, it is the inclusion of all three types of variables (predictor, mediating, and criterion) in our model which sets this study apart and allows us to test alternative explanations – that is, to determine whether the national-level characteristics in question are truly acting as proxies for psychic distance or whether their correlations with specific managerial decisions reflect other phenomena. In light of these arguments, we now develop specific mediating hypotheses for each of four types on national-level differences, plus geographic distance and the distance-bridging factors.

Mediating Hypotheses for the Distance Creating Factors

National Cultural Distance
As already discussed, the most commonly employed measure of national differences in international business (IB) research is Kogut and Singh's (1988) index of national cultural distance. While excessive reliance on this index has been subject to criticism, the underlying rationale is quite compelling. Stretching back to Johanson and Vahlne (1977), national culture is long recognized as an important influence on how people interpret information and the actions of others. For example, it is not difficult to imagine how differences in attitudes toward "power distance" may derail

a delicate joint venture negotiation or how differences in attitudes toward "uncertainty avoidance" may put off a potential customer when a manager is attempting to close an important sale. As such, large differences in national cultures have the potential to generate misunderstandings and disadvantage a firm when it is operating in a foreign country. They are therefore likely to increase perceptions of psychic distance, thereby deterring exports and foreign direct investment.

In the absence of any strong alternative explanations, our first hypothesis is for a full mediating relationship with respect to national cultural distance:

Hypothesis 1. A negative relationship between *national cultural distance* and the volume of both exports and FDI will be *fully mediated* by perceptions of psychic distance.

Socioeconomic Differences
In their early discussions of psychic distance, Johanson and Wiedersheim-Paul (1975) also proposed differences in levels of education, industrial development, and political systems as potential drivers of psychic distance.

The level of education of an individual will influence both the amount and the complexity of the information they can process, as well as the manner in which they process it. However, differences in education may also include more subtle aspects. Educational levels impact expectations and aspirations in life, interests, as well as general attitudes. As in the case of differences in culture, differences in educational levels between groups of people may create barriers to communication and mutual understanding.

In a similar fashion, the level of industrial development shapes the nature of the employment opportunities in a country, which in turn influences people's expectations, attitudes, and behaviors. For example, individuals in a largely agrarian society tend to have a dramatically different set of experiences, values, and attitudes compared to people in regions where the majority of employment is in white collar jobs. Indeed, education levels and the nature of a person's employment have such a strong potential impact on attitudes that they are frequently used as control variables in studies of national cultures (Hofstede, 1980; House, Hanges, Dorfman, & Gupta, 2004; Schwartz, 1992).

Differences in the nature of political processes, specifically the degree of democracy and political freedom, arguably have a distinct impact, which may operate more at the institutional level. Dramatic differences in the nature of the political processes may increase the difficulty of a foreign firm understanding, and thus, interacting with the various local institutions, be they legal, political, or administrative. This closely parallels the arguments put forward by the institutional distance literature (Kostova & Zaheer, 1999; Xu & Shenkar, 2002), though there are subtle differences in that institutional theory focuses on organizational legitimacy, whereas psychic distance focuses on communication and the potential for misunderstandings. Foreign firms may have more difficulty in understanding the expectations of local institutions, and how these institutions may react in certain circumstances. As a result, a foreign firm may have greater difficulty operating in a political and institutional environment that strongly differs from that of the home country.

For each of the dimensions discussed above there are valid but logically distinct arguments for a linkage with psychic distance, but in practice, differences in education, industrial development, and degree of democracy are empirically so strongly correlated that they cannot be assessed independently (Dow & Karunaratna, 2006; Drogendijk & Martin, 2008).[2] We therefore follow Drogendijk and Martin's (2008) approach and merge them into a single factor labeled "socio-economic" distance. We argue that large socioeconomic distances (i.e., large differences in education levels, industrial development, and degree of democracy between countries) may disadvantage a firm in a foreign market due to difficulties in understanding and communicating with local stakeholders. As a consequence, firms may perceive that they will be disadvantaged operating in that market and may avoid exporting to it or investing there.

In contrast to the first hypothesis, there is a strong competing explanation for the linkage between these forms of national differences and market selection.[3] Trade and investment patterns are also influenced by similarities in demand (Linder, 1961; Vernon, 1966). Firms typically first develop their products and services for their domestic market. As a result, foreign markets with similar demand patterns often represent attractive growth opportunities since they require little or no adaptation. Small socioeconomic distances are therefore likely to be correlated not only with low psychic distance but also with high similarity in demand, another important predictor of trade and FDI flows. In light of this competing explanation, the second hypothesis proposes that psychic distance only partially mediates the role of socioeconomic distance:

Hypothesis 2. A negative relationship between *socioeconomic distance* (i.e., the combination of differences in industrial development, education levels, and degree of democracy between countries) and the volume of both exports and FDI will be *partially mediated* by perceptions of psychic distance (i.e., there will be both a direct and a mediated relationship).

Differences in Dominant Language
"Differences in language" among countries is possibly the least controversial aspect of psychic distance (e.g., Boyacigiller, 1990; Johanson & Vahlne, 1977). Simply having a "working knowledge" of another language is not enough in many business situations, such as when negotiating a contract or dealing with a complex employee issue. Attaining proficiency in a foreign language takes many years of study and practice. Hiring an interpreter or employing local managers may resolve some language problems but introduces additional compromises and difficulties (Welch, Welch, & Marschan-Piekkari, 2001). An interpreter or local employee may not have the same degree of technical knowledge or familiarity with the parent company's business. As a result, firms are frequently forced to strike compromises in this area, especially when the differences in languages are substantial. This potential handicap of having to operate in a foreign language may deter managers from investing in and/or exporting to particular country.

Hypothesis 3. A negative relationship between *differences in the dominant languages* and the volume of both exports and FDI will be *fully mediated* by perceptions of psychic distance.

Differences in Dominant Religion
Religious differences have occasionally been linked to psychic distance (Dow & Karunaratna, 2006; Ronen & Shenkar, 1985; Shenkar, 2001). Religion is closely associated with culture, attitudes, and norms (Boyacigiller, 1990), and arguably influences the underlying belief sets of a very large portion of the world's population. This affects the manner in which people filter and interpret information and actions and thus, differences in religion may be a potential source of misunderstandings and miscommunication. While religion may at times be equated with culture, the actual correlation between Dow and Karunaratna's (2006) measure of differences in religions and national cultural distance is actually quite low ($r = 0.17$); thus, it should be considered a distinct aspect of culture compared to Hofstede's (1980) dimensions. Since differences in religion present the risk of misunderstandings between a foreign firm and local stakeholders and employees, it may make a firm more reluctant to invest in or trade with a country with a dominant religion different from that of the home country.

Once again, we are not aware of any alternative explanations for a linkage between differences in dominant religions and market selection and thus, the fourth hypothesis is framed as a full mediating relationship.

Hypothesis 4. A negative relationship between *differences in the dominant religions* and the volume of both exports and FDI will be *fully mediated* by perceptions of psychic distance.

Geographic Distance

The concept of psychic distance was first proposed by Beckerman (1956) in an effort to account for the observed tendency of countries to concentrate their trade on particular countries more strongly than could be explained by geographical distance and tariffs. Thus, it is unsurprising that the early discussions and research on the antecedents of psychic distance tended to exclude geographic distance. However, recent empirical studies (Håkanson & Ambos, 2010) indicate that geographic distance may play a significant role in shaping perceptions of psychic distance.

Even in the age of the Internet, many business transactions require trust and mutual understandings that can only be created in face-to-face interaction (Johanson & Vahlne, 2009; Johanson & Wiedersheim-Paul, 1975; Leamer & Storper, 2001). Despite the recent advances in air travel, geographic proximity still dramatically lowers the time required to travel to a foreign market, and therefore facilitates personal interaction with customers. This effect may even be magnified further with the rising importance of "just-in-time" manufacturing (Sakakibara, Flynn, Schroeder, & Morris, 1997).

Geographic distance may also influence the flow of general information from potential target markets through the effect of transportation costs on prior international business activities, past business travel, peoples' past vacation patterns, and even the frequency with which a country is discussed in the general press. For historical reasons alone, the stock of knowledge about a foreign country is likely to be larger for neighboring countries than for more distant ones. As a result, geographic distance may influence a manager's perception of psychic distance simply through higher awareness.

This geographic distance effect needs to be balanced against the generally accepted hypothesis that the relationship between distance and trade patterns is a reflection of transportation costs — a cornerstone of the "gravity models" used to analyze foreign trade patterns (Anderson, 1979, p. 112). As a result, the fifth and final "distance creating" hypothesis is framed as a partial mediating relationship.

Hypothesis 5. A negative relationship between *geographic distance* and the volume of both exports and FDI will be *partially mediated* by perceptions of psychic distance (i.e., there will be both a direct and a mediated relationship).

Asymmetric Distance-Bridging Factors

The preceding five hypotheses all concern national-level differences that may be characterized as "distance creating" factors. These make it more likely that firms and their foreign stakeholders misunderstand each other, thereby creating potential operational difficulties for the firm. However, other target market factors may counteract this by facilitating the flow of information from one country to another (Brewer, 2007; Child, Ng, & Wong, 2002; Nordström & Vahlne, 1994). The key distinction is that these factors may not increase the similarity between two markets, but they may increase the familiarity (Brewer, 2007) and the awareness of the differences. This increased familiarity, in turn, may reduce the potential for misunderstandings, and thus, reduce perceptions of psychic distance. We refer to these as "asymmetric distance-bridging factors."

Economic Development of the Target Country

One main factor that may improve the flow of information is the scope and quality of a country's institutional infrastructure (Vahlne & Wiedersheim-Paul, 1973). As a country's level of economic development increases, the scope of its information infrastructure and the quality of its output tend to improve. Thus, the higher the economic development of a country, the easier it will be to obtain relevant information about that country. The net effect will be that the level of development of a country will decrease a foreigners' perception the psychic distance to it (Håkanson & Ambos, 2010), in turn, increasing the likelihood that foreign firms may invest in or export to this country.

An important aspect of this proposition is its asymmetric nature. For example, the quality and scope of the information infrastructure in the United States may help a manager from a Polish company to assess business opportunities; however, an American manager considering entry into the Polish market has no such advantage.

In light of these arguments, the first "asymmetric distance bridging" hypothesis predicts a positive relationship between the level of target country economic development and inward trade and investment.[4] However, we must also acknowledge that numerous researchers have proposed and confirmed a direct relationship between target market economic development and both exports (e.g., Silva & Tenreyro, 2006; Subramanian & Wei, 2003) and FDI (e.g., Habib & Zurawicki, 2002; Sethi et al., 2003). We therefore frame this as a partial mediating hypothesis.

Hypothesis 6. A positive relationship between the *economic development of a target country* and the volume of both exports and FDI will be *partially mediated* by perceptions of psychic distance.

Size of the Target Country
A second potential "asymmetric distance bridging" factor is the size and economic power of the target country (Håkanson & Ambos, 2010). Through military strength, political influence, and economic power, large countries tend to have a stronger impact on surrounding countries than do smaller ones. Information from and about large countries therefore receives more media attention outside their borders. People in small countries tend therefore to be better informed about large countries than vice versa. The most striking example is the pervasive cultural influence of the United States through movies, television, and global brands, but similar effects can be noted elsewhere. For example, in the results reported by Håkanson and Ambos (2010), in all but one instance, average perceptions of the psychic distance to Germany held by people in its neighboring countries were smaller than the perceptions by Germans of the distance to these smaller neighbors.

On this basis, we assume that the size of a target market may positively influence the amount of information about it in other countries. This reduces uncertainty and lowers perceptions of psychic distance, making firms from other countries more likely to consider investing in, or exporting to, that country. As a result, we predict an overall positive relationship between target market size and market selection – moderated by perceptions of psychic distance. However, this subtle effect should not be confused with that of the market size – market selection relationship which forms the cornerstone of the gravity model (Anderson, 1979). The size of a market is also indicator of the number of potential opportunities in that market, and bigger markets inherently attract more trade and investment than do smaller ones. Thus, we express this hypothesis as a partial mediating relationship with both direct and mediated paths.

Hypothesis 7. A positive relationship between the *size of a target country* and the volume of both exports and FDI will be *partially mediated* by perceptions of psychic distance.

RESEARCH METHODOLOGY

Data and Unit of Analysis

The data for this investigation is based on a sample of 25 countries (Table 1); however, the actual unit of analysis for the models is the country pairs within that sample. The order of the countries within each pair is important. For example, the perception of China by people from France is distinct from the perception of France by people from China. Similarly, the quantity of exports and FDI from France into China is different from China into France. As a result, the sample yields a total of 600 distinct

Table 1. Countries and Respondent Characteristics for the Survey of Psychic Distance.

	n	Mean Age (Years)	% Male	Business Experience (Years)	Time Abroad (Years)	Formal Education (Years)	Inter-Rater Reliability
Argentina	79	36	83	10.0	1.6	19.7	0.991
Australia	48	40	77	13.9	3.7	18.2	0.941
Austria	68	35	68	9.4	3.0	17.7	0.994
Belgium	34	38	85	13.2	1.4	17.9	0.988
Brazil	40	39	67	13.2	0.7	20.7	0.967
Canada	29	35	59	8.3	4.2	18.7	0.959
China	35	35	49	9.0	3.9	16.8	0.941
Denmark	64	39	73	11.3	2.9	17.2	0.995
France	98	34	68	11.0	4.0	18.1	0.995
Germany	72	34	68	6.3	2.8	19.3	0.994
India	47	30	98	4.3	2.0	19.0	0.838
Italy	57	34	63	8.9	1.8	18.4	0.984
Japan	34	37	78	12.7	1.9	15.7	0.924
Korea, Rep. of	35	38	85	8.7	3.4	17.1	0.954
Mexico	103	37	58	11.3	2.2	19.4	0.973
The Netherlands	46	35	87	10.4	4.0	19.3	0.992
Norway	43	39	72	12.6	3.6	17.3	0.992
Poland	129	37	70	12.5	1.6	18.6	0.995
Russia	57	37	53	10.7	1.9	17.5	0.974
Spain	35	34	71	8.1	2.9	19.7	0.975
Sweden	69	41	74	13.3	3.2	17.4	0.992
Switzerland	48	42	94	14.9	1.7	18.7	0.991
Turkey	45	38	80	10.8	2.0	17.8	0.959
The United Kingdom	64	40	78	13.5	2.2	18.4	0.988
The United States	35	40	57	11.6	0.7	17.7	0.955

country pairs (25×24). Unfortunately, limitations in the availability of one or more of the criterion variables have reduced the usable sample to 563 country pairs. Where appropriate, the subscripts i and j, respectively, indicate the home market (i.e., the exporting or investing country) and the target market (i.e., the importing or target country).

Analytical Techniques

The hypotheses are tested using structural equation modeling (SEM). This method is useful for models using constructs based on multiple indicators and is ideally suited for modeling mediating relationships (Venkatraman, 1989). The base model, including the hypotheses, is presented in Fig. 1. The various national differences (on the left-hand side of Fig. 1), plus the two distance-bridging factors (Ind Dev_j and $Size_j$), form the antecedents of perceptions of psychic distance. Correlations among these exogenous constructs have been allowed in the model but are omitted from Fig. 1 for clarity. These antecedents predict the mediating construct − perceived psychic distance (PD_{Perc}) which in turn, with control variables, predicts the criterion variables − the amount of trade (Exports), and direct foreign investment (FDI). In Fig. 1, all of the control variables except for the size of the target home markets have also been excluded for clarity. Correlations with the mediating construct and the criterion variables have not been allowed as they are reflected in the structural paths. In a limited number of instances, when indicators are highly correlated, it was necessary to fix some path loadings in order to avoid negative error variances. These modifications do not materially influence the structural path loadings of the model.

One unusual feature of the structural model is that in addition to a construct representing geographic distance (GDist), we have isolated the component of geographic distance that is orthogonal to socioeconomic distance (Soc-Eco). This orthogonal component (Uniq_Dist) is isolated by modeling both socioeconomic distance (Soc-Eco) and the orthogonal component (Uniq_Dist) as antecedents of geographic distance (GDist). This orthogonal component of geographic distance allows a conservative but unbiased test of whether geographic distance has any relationship with perceptions of psychic distance, over and above its correlation with socioeconomic distance. In essence, it allows a test of Hypothesis 5, independent of Hypothesis 2, despite the two antecedents being moderately correlated. A direct path from geographic distance (GDist) to exports (Exports) has also been allowed in order to model the effects of transportation costs, and a direct path from the target country economic development (Eco Dev$_j$) to direct foreign investment (FDI) has been allowed in order to model the potential effects of low-wage rate target countries.

Following confirmation of the baseline model, each of the mediating hypotheses is tested (Models 2–7) by sequentially adding a direct path from each of the distance creating variables (e.g., Relig) to the criterion variables (Exports and FDI) as illustrated in Fig. 2. As Venkatraman (1989) argues, if the coefficients for the mediating paths (i.e., paths a, b_1, and b_2 in Fig. 2) all remain statistically significant but the newly introduced direct paths (i.e., paths c_1 and c_2) are nonsignificant, then a full mediating model is supported. If both the direct paths and the mediating paths remain statistically significant, then a partial mediating model is supported. Conversely, if the introduction of the direct links causes any of the mediating paths to become nonsignificant, then a mediating model is rejected. A separate mediating "test" is not necessary for Hypothesis 7 since the equivalent "direct" path is already included as an essential part of the basic "gravity model."

Measuring the Variables

The Antecedents of Psychic Distance
The antecedents of psychic distance included in the model are measured as follows (c.f. Table 2):

National cultural distance (Hof) is measured using the four original Hofstede dimensions (1980) combined into a single index as per Kogut and Singh (1988). Multiple indicators and/or estimates of construct reliability

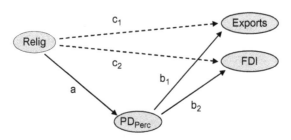

Fig. 2.   An Illustration of the Testing of the Mediating Relationships.

Table 2. Descriptive Statistics for Structural Equation Model Indicators
($n = 563$).

Variables and Indicators	Label	Min	Max	Mean	Std Dev
National cultural distance	Hof_{ij}	0.02	9.11	2.33	1.66
Indicators of differences in industrial development					
Δ Energy consumption (kg of coal equiv) p.c.	I_2	−10.93	10.93	0.08	4.05
Δ Passenger cars per 1,000 people	I_3	−51.7	51.7	0.8	24.4
Δ Nonagricultural labor (%)	I_4	−72.2	72.2	0.5	27.0
Δ Radios per 1,000 people	I_8	−2,041	2,041	20	646
Δ Phones per 1,000 people	I_9	−66.8	66.8	1.1	29.4
Δ TV per 1,000 people	I_{10}	−777	777	6	261
Indicators of differences in education levels					
Δ Literacy (%)	E_1	−47.6	47.6	0.2	14.0
Δ Proportion in 2nd level education (%)	E_2	−65.3	65.3	0.3	21.2
Δ Proportion in 3rd level education (%)	E_3	−32.2	32.2	0.2	11.2
Indicators of differences in degree of democracy					
Δ POLCON	D_1	−0.89	0.89	0.01	0.27
Δ Modif polity IV	D_2	−17.00	17.00	0.12	4.96
Δ Political rights	D_3	−6.00	6.00	0.05	2.03
Δ Civil liberties	D_4	−5.83	5.83	0.07	2.11
Indicators of differences in languages					
Distance between major languages	L_1	1	5	3.60	1.29
Incidence of home country's major lang. in target	L_2	1	5	4.75	0.75
Incidence of target country's major lang. in home	L_3	1	5	4.75	0.75
Indicators of differences in religions					
Distance between major religions	R_1	1	5	2.64	1.54
Incidence of home country's major religion in target	R_2	1	5	2.50	1.40
Incidence of target country's major religion in home	R_3	1	5	2.50	1.39
Geographic distance (km)	km^a	170	19,386	6,352	4,735
Economic development of the target country					
GDP per capita (US$ per person, average: 2003−2005)	GDP_pc_j	638	56,010	25,350	15,964
GNI per capita (US$ per person, average: 2003−2005)	GNI_pc_j	616	56,210	25,444	16,169

Table 2.   (*Continued*)

Variables and Indicators	Label	Min	Max	Mean	Std Dev
Size of target country economy					
Total GDP (US$ billions, average: 2003–2005)	$GDP_j{}^a$	155.3	11,671	1,427	2,293
Total GNI (US$ billions, average: 2003–2005)	$GNI_j{}^a$	147.7	11,637	1,468	2,373
Adjacent countries (i.e., share a common border)	Adjacent	0	1	0.07	0.26
Colonial ties	Colony	0	1	0.05	0.21
Free trade agreement	FTA	0	1	0.28	0.43
Political stability of the target country (j)					
POLCON	$Pol\ Stab_{1j}$	0	8.70	6.71	2.42
Modif polity IV	$Pol\ Stab_{2j}$	−7.0	10.0	8.35	3.44
Perceived psychic distance of the target country	PD_{HA}	6.4	92.9	47.8	21.2
Exports from country i to country j (*US$ billions*)	X^a	0.01	267.79	8.60	21.2
Flow of FDI by country i in country j (*US$ millions*)	F^a	−16.33	1,019.37	6.53	57.45

[a]These five indicators are subjected to a natural logarithm transformation for the main analyses but are reported here in their untransformed state for ease of interpretation.

(at the national level) are not available for national cultural distance; thus, a reliability of 0.95 has been assumed (Bentler & Chou, 1987).

The scales to measure the other five dimensions of national differences: differences in language (Lang), religion (Relig), industrial development (Ind), education (Edu), and degree of democracy (Dem) are all taken directly from Dow and Karunaratna (2006); however, for differences in industrial development (Ind), the number of indicators has been limited to the six highest loading indicators. It is important to note that for three of these five distance constructs (Ind, Edu, and Dem), it is recommended that the absolute value of the differences be used (Dow & Karunaratna, 2006). Unfortunately, SEM cannot directly handle absolute values. Thus, it is necessary to estimate these distance constructs in a separate measurement model, and then manually insert their absolute values, along with appropriate estimates of their reliabilities, into the main structural model. As mentioned earlier, another limitation of these distance measures is the high degree of multicollinearity among three of the constructs (Ind, Edu, and Dem). As a result these three indicators are merged into a formative factor — socioeconomic distance (Soc-Eco) — as per Cadogan and Lee (2012).

Geographic distance (GDist) is measured as the natural logarithm of the great circle distance between the largest economic centers of each country. Once again a reliability of 0.95 has been assumed for this construct (Bentler & Chou, 1987).

The two asymmetric "distance-bridging" factors — economic development of the target market (Eco Dev$_j$) and the size of the target market (Size$_j$) — are each measured by two indicators: GDP per capita (GDP_pc$_j$) and GNI per capita (GNI_pc$_j$) for economic development, and the natural logarithm of the country's GDP (GDP$_j$) and GNI (GNI$_j$) for market size. All four of these indicators are averages across the period of 2003–2005 (World Bank, 2008) and are denominated in current USD.

The Mediating Construct — Perceived Psychic Distance
Ideally, one would prefer to directly measure the a priori perceptions of psychic distance of the actual decision makers. However, the occurrence of major international business decisions is infrequent and difficult to predict (Dow & Karunaratna, 2006). As a result, it is not feasible for a large multilateral sample of export or investment decisions. However, if the variance in perceptions by individual managers is relatively small within a given country, then the psychic distance as perceived on average in that country may help to explain the average behavior of firms from that country. This is the assumption traditionally made in studies of the relationship between psychic distance and international business decisions (Johanson & Vahlne, 1977; Johanson & Wiedersheim-Paul, 1975) and is the approach taken here.

By adopting the Håkanson and Ambos (2010) data on psychic distance perceptions, we essentially employ the same methodology as Nordström (1991), Dow (2000), and Ellis (2008) and use the perceptions of an independent panel of experts. Håkanson and Ambos (2010) collected their bilateral estimates across the 25 countries via a web-based survey conducted between autumn 2003 and spring 2007. The target respondents were academically trained managers with four or more years of business experience. Prospective respondents were invited to participate via a customized email, containing a link to the survey. A total of 1,052 usable responses were received. On average the respondents had 18 years of formal education and 12 years of work experience (see Table 1 for details by country). While clearly not representative of the populations of the countries in question, the sample respondents appear to be reasonably typical of managers involved in international business decisions.

Following Nordström (1991), respondents were asked to indicate on a scale from 0 to 100 their perceptions of the "psychic distance" from their home country to the remaining 24 countries. "Psychic distance" was defined in the questionnaire as the "*sum of factors (cultural or language differences, geographic distance, etc.) that affect the flow and interpretation of information to and from a foreign country.*" The scale was anchored by setting the distance to the home country to "0" and asking respondents to assign the distance "100" to the country on the list that they perceived be the psychically most distant. Respondents were then asked to assign values for the remaining countries to reflect their psychic distances relative to both their home country and the one they considered to be most distant. For countries perceived to be psychically equidistant, the same score could be assigned. On completion, a sorted list was displayed, allowing respondents to make corrections where necessary. National-level averages were then calculated from each of the 25 samples. The inter-rater reliabilities are exceptionally high, exceeding 0.920, for all but one country − India (see the right-hand column of Table 1). However, even for that one exception, the inter-rater reliability for the Indian sample (0.834) is well within the acceptable range. Further methodological details and a full matrix of these psychic distance estimates for each country pair are available in the study by Håkanson and Ambos (2010).

For the analyses presented in this chapter, the mean country scores from Håkanson and Ambos (2010) are employed as our measure of perceived psychic distance (PD_{HA}). While this approach only yields a single indicator of perceived psychic distance, the mean inter-rater reliability (0.983) has been used as an externally imposed reliability (Bentler & Chou, 1987).

Aggregation of individual perceptions into a national average may run the risk of an "ecological fallacy" bias (Robinson, 1950; Selvin, 1958). However, Chan (1998) argues that high "within group agreement" and large "between group variance" are a valid justification for aggregating individual-level data to the group level. Both criteria are satisfied here. As already noted, the inter-rater reliability of the measure of perceived psychic distance is very high, and the between-group (or country pair) variance is quite substantial with the standard deviation of the scale being roughly 44% of the mean value. Thus, the potential of an "ecological fallacy" bias appears minimal.

Gravity Model Control Variables

In gravity models of international trade (e.g., Bergstrand, 1989; Rauch & Trindade, 2002) and foreign direct investment (e.g., Bevan & Estrin, 2004; Razin, Efraim, & Tong, 2005), the size of the target and home countries are critical control variables. For this reason, the product of the target and home market sizes ($Size_i * Size_j$) are included in the baseline model. As was the case with the size of the target market ($Size_j$), the size of the home market ($Size_i$) is based on two indicators: the natural logarithm of the country's GDP (GDP_i) and its GNI (GNI_i). Both are calculated as the average across the period of 2003–2005 (World Bank, 2008) and are denominated in current USD. As recommended by Ping (1996), the two elements of the interaction term ($Size_i * Size_j$) were first modeled in separately. From that preliminary model, the loadings and variances for interaction term were calculated and fixed in the final measurement model.

Gravity models also typically (e.g., Bevan, Estrin, & Meyer, 2004; Cuervo-Cazurra, 2008; Rose, 2004; Silva & Tenreyro, 2006; Zwinkels & Beugelsdijk, 2010) include a range of binary control variables, such as whether countries share a common border (Adjacent), colonial ties (Colony) or are members of a common free trade agreement (FTA). These variables are included in our model with the data for colonial ties sourced from Barraclough (1988) and the data for free trade agreements sourced from WTO (2004).

A fifth, less common and more complex control variable is the political stability of the target country (e.g., Zwinkels & Beugelsdijk, 2010). For this construct, we have employed two indicators including Henisz's (2000) POLCON measure of political stability (Pol $Stab_{1j}$) and Gleditsch's (2003) Polity IV scale (Pol $Stab_{2j}$). This control variable is particularly important given that these same two scales form part of our "differences in degree of democracy" scale (Dom). Inclusion of this control variable allows us to assess whether it is the differences in degree of democracy between countries or merely the nature of the target country's political system which influences trade and investment most.

It should also be noted that our sixth hypothesis proposes that the economic development of the target country may lower perceptions of psychic distance. However, the economic development of the target country can also be seen as indicator of wage rates (Bevan et al., 2004; Buckley, Devinney, & Louviere, 2007; Sethi et al., 2003). In recognition of this possibility, our final control takes the form of a direct structural path between one of our antecedents of psychic distance — the economic development of

Table 3. Correlation Matrix for Main Constructs in Structural Equation Models[a] ($n = 563$).

	1	2	3	4	5	6	7	8	9	10	11	12	13	14	15	16
1 Hof	1.00															
2 Ind	0.16**	1.00														
3 Edu	0.01	0.77**	1.00													
4 Dem	0.32**	0.59**	0.49**	1.00												
5 Lang	0.32**	0.08	0.02	0.21**	1.00											
6 Relig	0.19**	0.38**	0.41**	0.41**	0.31**	1.00										
7 GDist	0.01	0.40**	0.36**	0.28**	0.09*	0.27**	1.00									
8 Eco Dev$_j$	0.08	−0.29**	−0.35**	−0.34**	−0.11**	−0.23**	−0.17**	1.00								
9 Size$_j$	−0.06	0.12**	0.01	0.06	−0.06	0.14**	0.10*	0.12**	1.00							
10 Size$_j$*Size$_j$	−0.08*	0.17**	−0.02	0.09*	−0.09*	0.19**	0.15**	0.08	0.69**	1.00						
11 Adjacent	−0.16**	−0.20**	−0.16**	−0.15**	−0.26**	−0.21**	−0.48**	0.13**	0.04	0.06	1.00					
12 Colony	−0.20**	0.09*	0.14**	−0.04	−0.78**	0.00	0.13**	−0.02	0.10*	0.14**	0.01	1.00				
13 FTA	−0.08*	−0.37**	−0.28**	−0.34**	−0.04	−0.25**	−0.85**	0.32**	−0.13**	−0.19**	0.36**	−0.11*	1.00			
14 Pol Stabj	−0.14**	−0.24**	−0.20**	−0.59**	−0.18**	−0.28**	−0.19**	0.69**	0.03	0.01	0.11**	0.04	0.27**	1.00		
15 PDHA	0.21**	0.40**	0.37**	0.41**	0.42**	0.51**	0.76**	−0.42**	−0.08*	−0.05	−0.43**	−0.12*	−0.64**	−0.51**	1.00	
16 Exports	−0.10*	−0.10*	−0.20**	−0.05	−0.19**	−0.01	−0.50**	0.20**	0.48**	0.66**	0.39**	0.09*	0.34**	0.12**	−0.54**	1.00
17 FDI	0.07	−0.03	−0.07	−0.01	0.05	0.15**	0.02	0.02	0.12**	0.24**	−0.01	−0.01	−0.05	−0.02	−0.08	0.20**

[a]These are correlation coefficients for estimates of latent variables; plus three observed variables (adjacent, colony, and FTA) for which we deemed there to be negligible measurement error. Correlation coefficients for the actual indicators of each construct are available on request from the authors.

*$p < .05$, **$p < .01$ (two-tailed significance).

the target country (Eco Dev$_j$) − and foreign investment (FDI). Several other FDI control variables, specifically, the growth rate of the target market, the stability of the target market currency, and the degree of corruption in the target market were also investigated, but collinearity with our existing control variables prevented their inclusion in the final model.

The Criterion Variables
The first criterion variable for our model is the average yearly exports (X) between 2003 and 2005, from country i to country j (United Nations, 2009) − measured as the natural logarithm of their current USD value (in billions). The volatility of trade across those three years is used as an estimate a reliability of 0.997 for the overall construct (Exports).

The second criterion variable (*F*) is the flow of foreign direct investment in country j by firms originating in country i. It is measured as the natural logarithm of the average flow of FDI across the three years (2003−2005), and the volatility across those three years provides an estimate of the overall reliability (0.995) of the construct (FDI). FDI flows are measured in terms of current USD value (billions) as reported by the OECD (2005).

It should also be noted that Beugelsdijk, Hennart, Slangen, and Smeets (2010) have recently raised a concern that FDI estimates may contain unintentional biases; however, a subsidiary analysis of their data shows that these biases may actually be understating any psychic distance − FDI relationship in our sample.[5] Thus, our tests with respect to predicting FDI flow can be considered a conservative one.

Descriptive statistics for all of indicators are available in Table 2, and a correlation matrix including the main constructs is provided in Table 3.

RESULTS

Overall, both the two stages of measurement models and the structural model had modest but acceptable fits (see Tables 4 and 5). In particular, the final structural model, with a chi square (χ^2) of 1,880.4 and 173 degrees of freedom ($p < 0.001$) yielded a χ^2/df of 10.85, which is moderately high (Hair, Anderson, Tatham, & Black, 1992); however, the most comprehensive measure of overall fit (CFI = 0.904) is still above the normally recommended minimum of 0.900 (Bagozzi & Yi, 1988). Given both the complexity of the model (Gerbing & Anderson, 1993) and the fact the

Table 4. Measurement Models: Loadings, Reliabilities, and Fit Statistics
($n = 563$).

Latent Constructs and Indicators	Construct Reliability	Standardized Regression Weight
Measurement model to estimate the underlying dimensions of socioeconomic distance		
Differences in industrial development (Ind)	.953	
Δ Energy consumption (kg of coal equiv) p.c. (I_2)		.830***
Δ Passenger cars per 1,000 people (I_3)		.948***
Δ % Nonagricultural labor (I_4)		.871***
Δ Radios per 1,000 people (I_8)		.799***
Δ Phones per 1,000 people (I_9)		.917***
Δ TV per 1,000 people (I_{10})		.898***
Differences in education levels (Edu)	.851	
Δ Literacy (E_1)		.772***
Δ Proportion in 2nd level education (E_2)		.812***
Δ Proportion in 3rd level education (E_3)		.845***
Differences in degree of democracy (Dem)	.953	
Δ POLCON (D_1)		.814***
Δ Modif polity IV (D_2)		.906***
Δ Political rights (D_3)		.993***
Δ Civil liberties (D_4)		.937***
χ^2 (df)=846.1 (48); χ^2/df = 17.63; $p < .001$;	CFI = 0.931; RMSEA = 0.112	
**********************		
Final measurement model (single indicator constructs are not listed)		
Differences in language (Lang)	.826	
Distance between major languages (L_1)		.771***
Incidence of i's major language in j (L_2)		.791***
Incidence of j's major language in i (L_3)		.786***
Differences in religion (Relig)	.918	
Distance between major religions (R_1)		.877***
Incidence of i's major religion in j (R_2)		.895***
Incidence of j's major religion in i (R_3)		.891***
*Economic development of the target (*Eco Dev$_j$)*	.999	
GDP per capita (GDP_pc$_j$)		.999***
GNI per capita (GNI_pc$_j$)		.999***
Size of the target country economy (Size$_j$)	.999	
Total GDP (GDP$_j$)		.999***
Total GNI (GNI$_j$)		.999***
Political stability of the target (Pol Stab$_j$)	.963	
POLCON (Pol Stab$_{1j}$)		.928***
Modif polity IV (Pol Stab$_{2j}$)		.928***
χ^2 (df)=1,444.3 (131); χ^2/df = 11.03; $p < .001$;	CFI = 0.924; RMSEA = 0.134	

***$p < .001$ (two-tailed significance).

Table 5. Structural Path Loadings and Overall Model Fit for Baseline Model ($n = 563$).

Path		Standardized Regression Weight	Estimated Regression Weight	Standard Error	Critical Ratio	Significance
Hof–PD$_{Perc}$	H1	0.125	1.512	0.302	5.012	***
Soc-Eco–PD$_{Perc}$	H2	0.207	4.274	1.769	2.416	*
Lang–PD$_{Perc}$	H3	0.213	5.045	0.632	7.975	***
Relig–PD$_{Perc}$	H4	0.241	3.826	0.455	8.414	***
Uniq_Dist–PD$_{Perc}$	H5	0.620	12.229	0.449	27.234	***
Eco Dev$_j$–PD$_{Perc}$	H6	−0.282	−0.352	0.027	−12.670	***
Size$_j$–PD$_{Perc}$	H7	−0.121	−2.315	0.426	−5.432	***
PD$_{Perc}$–Exports	a	−0.107	−0.010	0.003	−3.209	**
PD$_{Perc}$–FDI	a	−0.177	−0.0011	0.0004	−2.756	**
GDist–Exports	−	−0.569	−0.961	0.084	−11.383	***
Size$_i$Size$_j$–Exports	−	0.691	1.632	0.044	37.245	***
Adjacent–Exports	−	0.054	0.386	0.153	2.523	*
Colony–Exports	−	0.039	0.336	0.175	1.920	
FTA–Exports	−	−0.104	−0.440	0.159	−2.763	**
Pol Stab$_j$–Exports	−	−0.041	−0.032	0.016	−2.019	*
Size$_i$Size$_j$–FDI	−	0.246	0.038	0.006	5.933	***
Adjacent–FDI	−	−0.058	−0.027	0.022	−1.233	
Colony–FDI	−	−0.070	−0.039	0.024	−1.602	
FTA–FDI	−	−0.094	−0.025	0.016	−1.620	
Pol Stab$_j$–FDI	−	−0.082	−0.004	0.003	−1.328	
Eco Dev$_j$–FDI	−	0.002	0.00001	0.00048	0.024	
Overall model fit						
Chi-Sq		1880.4				
Degrees of freedom		173				
χ^2/df		10.86				
p		< .001				
CFI		0.904				
RMSEA		.133				

[a]The statistical significances of these two path coefficients are critical components of hypotheses H1 through to H7.

*$p < .05$, **$p < .01$, ***$p < .001$ (two-tailed significance).

indicators are drawn from very diverse secondary sources, these results should not be surprising.

With respect to specific constructs, the results appear quite reliable and robust. The regression weights for each of the latent construct indicators (Table 4) are statistically significant, and the standardized loadings are all above 0.750. The resulting construct reliabilities are high, ranging from

0.826 to 0.999, and the constructs have statistically significant discriminant validity (Bagozzi & Yi, 1988).

For the baseline structural model (Table 5), all the structural paths between perceived psychic distance and its antecedents have highly significant regression weights. Overall, a very high proportion of the perceived psychic distance variance is explained with a squared multiple correlation of 0.793. National cultural distance, socioeconomic distance, differences in language, and differences in religion are significant predictors of perceptions of psychic distance. However, a notable result is the degree to which geographic distance is a significant predictor of perceived psychic distance. Even when using the very conservative test of the orthogonal component of geographic distance (Uniq_Dist), that particular path proves to have a highly statistically significant loading on perceptions of psychic distance ($CR = 27.234$, $p < 0.001$).

The regression weights for the two "information asymmetry" variables – the economic development and size of the target market – are also highly significant in the predicted direction ($CR = 12.670$, $p < 0.001$ and $CR = 5.432$, $p < 0.001$, respectively). Both appear to reduce perceptions of psychic distance.

The final structural paths of interest are the trade and FDI flows. Perceptions of psychic distance (PD_{Perc}) is a highly significant predictor of both exports ($CR = 3.209$, $p < 0.001$) and FDI ($CR = 2.756$, $p < 0.01$). In combination with the control variables, psychic distance explains a very large proportion of the variance in Exports (a squared multiple correlation of 0.830) and a significant proportion of the variance in FDI stock (a squared multiple correlation of 0.082). As expected, in addition to its indirect relationship through perceptions of psychic distance, geographic distance (GDist) is a strong direct antecedent of exports ($CR = 11.383$, $p < .001$). These results provide the first stage in testing the mediating Hypotheses 1–6. At this stage, we can already confirm Hypothesis 7 – in addition to a highly significant direct path to each criterion variable, the size of the target market also has a strong mediating relationship with exports and FDI through perceptions of psychic distance.

Table 6 presents a summary of the final steps in the analyses. For each of the first six moderating hypotheses, direct paths to the criterion variables are introduced sequentially. As predicted, Models 2, 4, and 5 all confirm a full mediating relationship for each of their respective predictor variables – cultural distance (H1), differences in language (H3), and differences in religion (H4). However, for some of these models, and for FDI in Models 4 and 5 in particular, unexpected significant direct paths

Table 6. Testing the Mediating Relationships for Each Antecedent[a] $(n = 563)$.

Est. Regression Weight		Standard Error	Critical Ratio	Significance	$\Delta \Psi^2$ (Δ df)	[b]
Model 2−Hof (H1)						
Hof−PD$_{Perc}$	1.517	0.302	5.020	***	5.86	Full mediation for
PD$_{Perc}$−Exports	−0.010	0.003	−2.964	**	(2)	Exports and FDI
PD$_{Perc}$−FDI	−0.0012	0.0004	−3.086	**		
Hof−Exports	−0.009	0.024	−0.375			
Hof−FDI	0.008	0.003	2.440	*		
Model 3−Soc-Eco (H2)						
Soc-Eco−PD$_{Perc}$	3.859	1.705	2.264	*	4.73	Full mediation for
PD$_{Perc}$−Exports	−0.011	0.003	−3.441	***	(2)	Exports and FDI
PD$_{Perc}$−FDI	−0.0010	0.0004	−2.437	*		
Soc-Eco−Exports	0.061	0.044	1.386			
Soc-Eco−FDI	−0.008	0.006	−1.343			
Model 4−Lang (H3)						
Lang − PD$_{Perc}$	5.033	0.635	7.921	***	35.22	Full mediation for
PD$_{Perc}$−Exports	−0.013	0.004	−3.436	***	(2)	Exports and FDI
PD$_{Perc}$−FDI	−0.0037	0.0006	−6.538	***	***	
Lang−Exports	0.226	0.196	1.154			
Lang−FDI	0.194	0.034	5.675	***		
Model 5−Relig (H4)						
Relig−PD$_{Perc}$	3.755	0.457	8.208	***	21.88	Full mediation for
PD$_{Perc}$−Exports	−0.015	0.004	−4.138	***	(2)	Exports and FDI
PD$_{Perc}$−FDI	−0.0019	0.0004	−4.357	***	***	
Relig−Exports	0.087	0.036	2.419	*		
Relig−FDI	0.021	0.005	4.161	***		
Model 6−GDist (H5)						
Uniq_Dist−PD$_{Perc}$	12.228	0.449	27.225	***	0.00	Full mediation for FDI;
PD$_{Perc}$−Exports	−0.010	0.003	−3.210	**	(1)	partial for Exports
PD$_{Perc}$−FDI	−0.0011	0.0005	−2.352	*		
GDist−Exports	−0.961	0.084	−11.380	***		
GDist−FDI	0.002	0.012	0.158			
Model 7−Eco Dev$_j$ (H6)						
Eco Dev$_j$−PD$_{Perc}$	−0.349	0.028	−12.515	***	6.32	Full mediation for
PD$_{Perc}$−Exports	−0.011	0.003	−3.448	***	(1)	Exports and FDI
PD$_{Perc}$−FDI	−0.0011	0.0004	−2.760	**	*	
Eco Dev$_j$−Exports	−0.008	0.003	−2.470	*		
Eco Dev$_j$−FDI	0.00001	0.0005	0.014			

[a]Each model in this table is an extension of the model presented in Table 5 and tests the mediating role of one antecedent of psychic distance. For simplicity, only the structural paths directly relevant to the testing of the mediating relationship are shown here.

[b]For FDI in Models 2, 4, and 5, and for Exports in Models 5 and 7, the additional direct paths have statistically significant coefficients but in the opposite direction to the mediating effect. As a result in these instances, the relationship has been classified as fully mediating.

$*p < .05$, $**p < .01$, $***p < .001$ (two-tailed significance).

in the opposite direction to the proposed mediating relationships are present. These paths do not contradict the mediating hypotheses, but they are "curious" results, which will be discussed further in the concluding section.

The results for Models 3, 6, and 7 only partially support the respective hypotheses (H2, H5, and H6). A partial mediating hypothesis was predicted for socioeconomic distance (H2), yet the results indicate a full mediating relationship for both exports and FDI. In effect, Linder's alternative explanation concerning similarities in demand is not supported. A similar result is found with respect to hypothesis H6 where a partial mediating relationship was predicted with respect to the economic development of the host country, yet a full mediating relationship is reported. In a reverse pattern, Model 6 indicates partial mediating relationship between exports and geographic distance (as predicted in H5), but a full mediating relationship between geographic distance and FDI (when a partial mediation result was predicted). Once again, these slightly surprising results will be discussed in the next section but it is interesting to note that in each case, it was the direction and/or significance of the direct paths which caused deviations from our predictions. In all instances, the mediating paths remained significant as predicted.

In summary, the empirical results fully support four of the seven hypotheses (H1, H3, H4, and H7) and partially support the remaining three hypotheses (H2, H5, and H6).

DISCUSSION AND CONCLUSIONS

In practical terms, the greatest contribution of this chapter is in giving guidance to future scholars struggling with defining and measuring psychic distance in their research. As explained earlier, this field of research is badly split into two camps – those who continue to measure psychic distance in terms of exogenous national-level differences and those who advocate directly measuring managers' perceptions of distance. This chapter is the first to provide a resolution to that debate which is backed up by empirical evidence. Our empirical results clearly demonstrate that, with the exception of geographic distance, perceptions of psychic distance *fully mediate* the relationship between national-level differences and exports, as well as FDI. This means that measuring perceptions of psychic distance, even if measured by expert panels rather than the actual decision-makers, fully captures the impact of national-level differences on trade and FDI flows and thus is more parsimonious and a superior approach for capturing the full impact of the construct.

However, this chapter also offers some hope to scholars who, for whatever reasons, are not able to measure perceptions of psychic distance directly or via an expert panel. If one does use a comprehensive set of national-level difference indicators similarly to the ones employed here, then our results indicate that they will capture roughly 80% of the explained variance of psychic distance. Thus, while such national-level indicators are a second best alternative to measuring psychic distance, they will capture the vast majority of the effect.

At the theoretical level, this chapter also confirms the content validity (Kerlinger, 1986) of several of the national-level distance variables by incorporating a mediating variable and allowing partial mediating paths. While the results of Dow and Karunaratna (2006) and Berry et al. (2010) seem to strongly confirm that these national-level differences are significant predictors of trade flows and market entry, there is still doubt as to the underlying mechanism driving these relationships. Including an otherwise implicit mediating variable, such as perceptions of psychic distance, allows one to test such issues (Shaver, 2005). As discussed earlier, this is particularly relevant to the role of socioeconomic distance. Differences in industrial development (a component of socioeconomic distance) are reputed to be an indicator of psychic distance (Johanson & Vahlne, 1977); however, it could also be an indicator of differences in customer preferences (Linder, 1961). This expectation is incorporated in the second hypothesis but is not supported by the empirical analysis. This indicates that while the Linder hypothesis may be plausible, the impact of socioeconomic differences on trade and investment appear to be fully captured by the psychic distance construct.

Possibly the most intriguing finding regarding the construct validity of the national-level factors is the role of geographic distance. Our partial mediation result concerning geographic distance and exports confirms the standard assumption that geographic distance is a proxy for transportation costs; however, geographic distance also seems to have a substantial influence on the market selection process in other ways as well. Even after controlling for potential collinearity with socioeconomic distance, geographic distance still exhibits a highly significant partial mediating relationship with exports through perceptions of psychic distance and in the case of FDI, the relationship is a fully mediated one. Thus, geographic distance appears to be a legitimate and major antecedent of perceptions of psychic distance.

A more minor contribution of this study, but one which is critical to the overall relevance of the findings, is the breadth of antecedents selected to predict perceptions of psychic distance. It is dramatically more comprehensive than previous efforts. For example, Dow (2000), Ellis (2008), and Drogendijk and Slangen (2006), the only other papers to have contrasted the predictive power of perceptions of psychic distance to national-level indicators, each used Kogut and Singh's (1988) index as their sole indicator of national-level differences. This is critical as our results show that the Kogut and Singh index is only a very minor predictor of perceptions of psychic distance.

A final contribution of this chapter is our "refined and integrative" definition of psychic distance. It is quite intentional that our definition does not represent a radical departure from past definitions but rather is an attempt to build a bridge between the two opposing approaches by incorporating the positive contributions of both sides. The definition acknowledges and incorporates the perceptual aspect of psychic distance but retaining the Uppsala definition's more explicit explanation of the mechanisms by which psychic distance influences managerial decisions.

One "curious" aspect of our results which warrants discussion is the mildly atheoretic direct paths with respect to FDI in Models 4 and 5. To some extent, these paths which yield unexpected positive coefficients (implying, e.g., that greater differences in religion will increase FDI) may be due to the nature of our structural model. When direct paths are introduced to test the mediating relationship, this allows the antecedent (e.g. differences in religion) to have two potential ways to correlate with the criterion variable (e.g. FDI). However, by the nature of our model, one half of the indirect path (i.e. the perceived psychic distance − FDI path) is also constrained by seven other predictor variables which are moderately correlated. In an effort to optimize the fit with the covariance matrix, the model may be over-compensating by reversing the direction of an otherwise nonsignificant path − in effect, it may represent a mild form of multicollinearity. In order to explore this possibility, the models have been rerun with only one antecedent variable at a time.[6] All of the "atheoretic" direct paths become nonsignificant except for the positive Religion − FDI path from Model 5. This particular relationship does seem to be inherent in the basic dataset, as indicated by the significant positive correlation between the two constructs (Table 3). One can only presume that due to the moderately constrained nature of the selection of countries, there is possibly an unexpected correlation between the differences in religion construct and another unspecified factor. A limitation of this research is the unit of analysis and the need to aggregate individual perceptions of psychic distance to the national level. Although necessary in order to test other specific issues, it does raise the need for further research in two specific areas. The first is research on the antecedents of psychic distance at the individual level. To date, there is virtually no such research reported in the literature. The second avenue for future research is the linkage between individual perceptions of psychic distance and individual-level biases. It may be problematic to conduct such research on actual international business decisions; however, experimental approaches may provide an avenue for testing such issues.

A second limitation of this study is its bias toward large developed trading nations. Unfortunately, given the cost and complexity in collecting perceptual data, such a bias is often difficult to avoid; however, researchers do need to be aware of it. This selection bias may, for example, understate the importance of dimensions such as degree of democracy, as the variance of this dimension is artificially constrained by the nature of the sample. Similarly, the "unusual" Religion—FDI relationship may be a result of this bias. Nevertheless, the vast majority of both FDI and exports is both initiated by and targeted at the 25 countries included in this study; it can therefore be considered representative of most international business decisions.

The third and final limitation is the inherent difficulties in measuring FDI. Issues such as tax haven policies, locally raised funds, and other factors (Beugelsdijk et al., 2010) make the measurement of FDI problematic and we strongly suspect that dramatically low explain variance for FDI flows compared to trade flows may at least partly be due to this. This is corroborated by the similarly low explained variance in other FDI studies such as Bevan and Estrin (2004).

In closing, we believe that by comprehensively modeling national-level differences and perceptions of psychic distance within a mediating model, this chapter builds an effective bridge between the two streams of literature and allows future researchers to make a more informed choice as to how to model psychic distance in their research.

NOTES

1. Discriminating between target country effects and national-level differences is problematic when there is minimal variance in the characteristics of the home country — a very common aspect of many studies within this field.

2. In subsidiary analyses, available from the lead author on request, structural models were tested with differences in education, industrial development, and democracy as separate constructs; however, the high degree of collinearity caused instability in the models with numerous versions of the models refusing to converge.

3. There is also a third competing hypothesis that concerns differences in wage rates between countries influencing resource-seeking FDI decisions; however, this alternative explanation is dealt with via control variables, as will be explained later in this chapter.

4. Note that for this mediating hypothesis, the two specific path coefficients (for economic development to psychic distance and for psychic distance to market selection) are both predicted to be negative; thus, the overall result is a positive relationship.

5. Unfortunately, the Beugelsdijk et al. (2010) correction factors are only available for US outward FDI and thus cannot be applied comprehensively to our analyses.

6. These analyses are available on request from the lead author.

REFERENCES

Agarwal, S. (1994). Socio-cultural distance and the choice of joint ventures: A contingency perspective. *Journal of International Marketing, 2*, 63–80.

Anderson, J. E. (1979). A theoretical foundation for the gravity model. *American Economic Review, 69*, 106–116.

Bagozzi, R. P., & Yi, Y. (1988). On the evaluation of structural equation models. *Academy of Marketing Science, 16*, 74–94.

Barraclough, G. (Ed.). (1988). *Concise atlas of world history*. London: Times Books Ltd.

Beckerman, W. (1956). Distance and the pattern of inter-European trade. *The Review of Economics and Statistics, 38*, 31–40.

Bentler, P. M., & Chou, C. P. (1987). Practical issues in structural modeling. *Sociological Methods & Research, 16*, 78–117.

Bergstrand, J. H. (1989). The generalized gravitation equation, monopolistic competition and the factor proportions theory in international trade. *The Review of Economics and Statistics, 71*, 143–153.

Berry, H., Guillen, M., & Zhou, A. (2010). An institutional approach to cross-national distance. *Journal of International Business Studies, 41*, 1460–1480.

Beugelsdijk, S., Hennart, J. F., Slangen, A., & Smeets, R. (2010). Why and how FDI stocks are a biased measure of MNE affiliate activity. *Journal of International Business Studies, 41*, 1444–1459.

Bevan, A. A., & Estrin, S. (2004). The determinants of foreign direct investment into European transition economies. *Journal of Comparative Economics, 32*, 775–787.

Bevan, A. A., Estrin, S., & Meyer, K. E. (2004). Foreign investment location and institutional development in transition economies. *International Business Review, 13*, 43–64.

Boyacigiller, N. (1990). The role of expatriates in the management of interdependence, complexity and risk in multinational corporations. *Journal of International Business Studies, 21*, 357–381.

Brewer, P. (2007). Operationalizing psychic distance: A revised approach. *Journal of International Marketing, 15*, 44–66.

Buckley, P. J., Devinney, T. M., & Louviere, J. J. (2007). Do managers behave the way theory suggests? A choice-theoretic examination of foreign direct investment location decision-making. *Journal of International Business Studies, 38*, 1069–1094.

Cadogan, J., & Lee, N. (2012). Problems with formative and higher-order reflective variables. *Journal of Business Research, 66*, 242–247.

Carlson, S. (1974). International transmission of information and the business firm. *The Annals of the American Academy of Political and Social Science, 412*, 55–63.

Chan, C. M. (1998). Functional relations among constructs in the same content domain at different levels of analysis: A typology of composition models. *Journal of Applied Psychology, 83*, 234–246.

Child, J., Ng, S. H., & Wong, C. (2002). Psychic distance and internationalization. *International Studies of Management & Organizations, 32*, 36–56.

Child, J., Rodrigues, S. B., & Frynas, J. G. (2009). Psychic distance, its impact and coping modes: Interpretations of SME decision makers. *Management International Review, 49*, 199–224.

Cuervo-Cazurra, A. (2008). The effectiveness of laws against bribery abroad. *Journal of International Business Studies, 39*, 634–651.

Davidson, W. (1980). The location of foreign direct investment activity: Country characteristics and experience effects. *Journal of International Business Studies, 11*, 9–22.

Dow, D. (2000). A note on psychological distance and export market selection. *Journal of International Marketing, 8*, 51–64.

Dow, D., & Karunaratna, A. (2006). Developing a multidimensional instrument to measure psychic distance stimuli. *Journal of International Business Studies, 37*, 575–577.

Dow, D., & Larimo, J. (2009). Challenging the conceptualization and measurement of distance and international experience in entry mode choice research. *Journal of International Marketing, 17*, 74–98.

Drogendijk, R., & Martin, O. (2008). *Country distance: A objective measure and its impact on international market selection*. Milan: Academy of International Business.

Drogendijk, R., & Slangen, A. (2006). Hofstede, Schwartz or managerial perceptions? A comparative analysis of the effects of various cultural distance measures on an MNE's establishment mode choice. *International Business Review, 15*, 361–380.

Ellis, P. (2008). Does psychic distance moderate the market size-entry sequence relationship? *Journal of International Business Studies, 39*, 351–369.

Evans, J., & Mavondo, F. T. (2002). Psychic distance and organizational performance: An empirical examination of international retailing operations. *Journal of International Business Studies, 33*, 515–532.

Gerbing, D. W., & Anderson, J. C. (1993). Monte Carlo evaluations of goodness-of-fit indices for structural models. In K. A. Bollen & J. S. Long (Eds.), *Testing structural equation models*. Newbury Park, CA: Sage Publications.

Gleditsch, K. S. (2003). *Modified polity P4 and P4D data [online]*. Retrieved from http://weber.ucsd.edu/~kgledits/Polity.html Accessed on December 17, 2003.

Gripsrud, G. (1990). The determinants of export decisions and attitudes to a distant market: Norwegian fishery exports to Japan. *Journal of International Business Studies, 21*, 469–486.

Habib, M., & Zurawicki, L. (2002). Corruption and foreign direct investment. *Journal of International Business Studies, 33*, 291–307.

Hair, J. F. J., Anderson, R. E., Tatham, R. L., & Black, W. C. (1992). *Multivariate data analysis*. New York, NY: Macmillan Publishing.

Håkanson, L., & Ambos, B. (2010). The antecedents of psychic distance. *Journal of International Management, 16*, 195–210.

168   DOUGLAS DOW ET AL.

Harzing, A. W. (2003). The role of culture in entry mode studies: From neglect to myopia. In J. Cheng & M. Hitt (Eds.), *Advances in international management*. Amsterdam/ New York, NY: Elsevier/JAI.

Henisz, W. J. (2000). The institutional environment for economic growth. *Economics and Politics, 12*, 1–31.

Hirsch, Z., & Lev, B. (1973). Trade and per capita income differentials: A test of the Burenstam-Linder hypothesis. *World Development, 1*, 11–17.

Hofstede, G. (1980). *Cultural consequences: International differences in work related values*. Beverly Hills, CA: Sage Publications.

Holzmuller, H. H., & Kasper, H. (1990). The decision-maker and export activity: A cross-national comparison of the foreign orientation of Austrian managers. *Management International Review, 30*, 217–230.

House, R. J., Hanges, P. J., Dorfman, P. W., & Gupta, V. (2004). *Culture, leadership and organizations: The GLOBE study of 62 nations*. Thousand Oaks, CA: Sage.

Johanson, J., & Vahlne, J.-E. (1977). The internationalization process of the firm-a model of knowledge development and increasing foreign commitments. *Journal of International Business Studies, 8*, 23–32.

Johanson, J., & Vahlne, J.-E. (2009). The Uppsala internationalization process model revisited: From liability of foreignness to liability of outsidership. *Journal of International Business Studies, 40*, 1411–1431.

Johanson, J., & Wiedersheim-Paul, F. (1975). The internationalization of the firm: Four Swedish cases. *Journal of Management Studies, 12*, 305–322.

Kerlinger, F. N. (1986). *Foundations of behavioural research*. New York, NY: Holt, Rinehart & Winston.

Kirkman, B. I., Lowe, K. B., & Gibson C. B. (2006). A quarter century of culture's consequences: A review of empirical research incorporating Hofstede's cultural values framework. *Journal of International Business Studies, 37*, 285–320.

Klein, S., & Roth, V. J. (1990). Determinants of export channel structure: The effects of experience and psychic distance. *International Marketing Review, 7*, 27–38.

Kogut, B., & Singh, H. (1988). The effect of national culture on the choice of entry mode. *Journal of International Business Studies, 19*, 411–432.

Kostova, T., & Zaheer, S. (1999). Organizational legitimacy under conditions of complexity: The case of the multinational enterprise. *Academy of Management Review, 24*, 64–81.

Larimo, J. (2003). Form of investment by Nordic firms in world markets. *Journal of Business Research, 56*, 791–803.

Leamer, E. E., & Storper, M. (2001). The economic geography of the internet age. *Journal of International Business Studies, 32*, 641–665.

Linder, S. B. (1961). *An essay on trade and transformation*. New York, NY: Wiley.

Nordström, K. A. (1991). *The internationalization process of the firm – Searching for new patterns and explanations*. Unpublished Doctoral Dissertation, Stockholm School of Economics.

Nordström, K. A., & Vahlne, J.-E. (1994). Is the Globe shrinking? Psychic distance and the establishment of Swedish subsidiaries during the last 100 years. In M. Landeck (Ed.), *International trade: Regional and global issues*. New York, NY: St Martin's Press.

OECD. (2005). *International direct investment statistics [online]*. New York, NY. Retrieved from http://titania.sourceoecd.org/ Accessed on September 7, 2008.

O'Grady, S., & Lane, H. W. (1996). The psychic distance paradox. *Journal of International Business Studies, 27*, 309–333.

Ping, R. A. (1996). Latent variable interaction and quadratic effect estimation: A two-step technique using structural equation analysis. *Psychological Bulletin, 119*, 166–175.

Rauch, J. E., & Trindade, V. (2002). Ethnic Chinese networks in international trade. *The Review of Economics and Statistics, 84*, 116–130.

Razin, A., Efraim, S., & Tong, H. (2005). *Bilateral FDI flows: Threshold barriers and productivity shocks.* NBER Working Paper Series 11639. National Bureau of Economic Research, Cambridge, MA.

Robinson, W. S. (1950). Ecological correlations and the behaviour of individuals. *American Sociological Review, 15*, 351–357.

Ronen, S., & Shenkar, O. (1985). Clustering countries on attitudinal dimensions: A review and synthesis. *Academy of Management Review, 10*, 435–454.

Rose, A. K. (2004). Do we really know that the WTO increases trade? *American Economic Review, 94*, 98–114.

Sakakibara, S., Flynn, B. B., Schroeder, R. G., & Morris, W. T. (1997). The impact of just-in-time manufacturing and its infrastructure on manufacturing performance. *Management Science, 43*, 1246–1257.

Schwartz, S. H. (1992). Universals in the content and structure of values: Theoretical advances and empirical tests in 20 countries. *Advances in Experimental Social Psychology, 25*, 1–65.

Selvin, H. C. (1958). Durkheim's suicide and problems of empirical research. *American Journal of Sociology, 63*, 607–619.

Sethi, D., Guisinger, S. E., Phelan, S. E., & Berg, D. M. (2003). Trends in foreign direct investment flows: A theoretical and empirical analysis. *Journal of International Business Studies, 34*, 315–326.

Shaver, J. M. (2005). Testing for mediating variables in management research: Concerns, implications, and alternative strategies. *Journal of Management, 31*, 330–353.

Shenkar, O. (2001). Cultural distance revisited: Towards a more rigorous conceptualization and measurement of cultural differences. *Journal of International Business Studies, 32*, 519–536.

Silva, J. M. C. S., & Tenreyro, S. (2006). The log of gravity. *The Review of Economics and Statistics, 88*, 641–658.

Slangen, A., & Hennart, J. F. (2008). Do multinationals really prefer to enter culturally distant countries through greenfields rather than through acquisitions? The role of parent experience and subsidiary autonomy. *Journal of International Business Studies, 39*, 472–490.

Sousa, C., & Lages, L. F. (2011). The PD Scale: A measure of psychic distance and its impact on international marketing strategy. *International Marketing Review, 28*, 201–222.

Sousa, C. M. P., & Bradley, F. (2006). Cultural distance and psychic distance: Two peas in a Pod? *Journal of International Marketing, 14*, 49–70.

Subramanian, A., & Wei, S.-J. (2003). *The WTO promotes trade strongly but unevenly.* NBER Working Paper Series 10024. NBER, Cambridge, MA.

Suddaby, R. (Ed.) (2010). Editor's comments: Construct clarity in theories of management and organization, *Academy of Management Review*, 35, 346–357.

Tihanyi, L., Griffith, D. A., & Russell, C. J. (2005). The effect of cultural distance on entry mode choice, international diversification, and MNE performance: A meta-analysis. *Journal of International Business Studies*, *36*, 270–283.

Tung, R. L., & Verbeke, A. (2010). Beyond Hofstede and GLOBE: Improving the quality of cross-cultural research. *Journal of International Business Studies*, *41*, 1259–1274.

Tushman, M. L. (1978). Technical communication in R&D laboratories: The impact of project work characteristics. *Academy of Management Journal*, *21*, 624–644.

United Nations. (2009). *United Nations Commodity Trade Statistics Database*. Retrieved from http://comtrade.un.org/. Accessed on September 30, 2009.

Vahlne, J.-E., & Wiedersheim-Paul, F. (1973). Economic distance: Model and empirical investigation. In E. Hörnell, J.-E. Vahlne, & F. Wiedersheim-Paul (Eds.), *Exports and foreign establishment*. Uppsala: University of Uppsala.

Venkatraman, N. (1989). The concept of fit in strategy research: Toward verbal and statistical correspondence. *Academy of Management Review*, *14*, 423–444.

Vernon, R. (1966). International investment and international trade in the product cycle. *Quarterly Journal of Economics*, *80*, 190–207.

Welch, D. E., Welch, L. S., & Marschan-Piekkari, R. (2001). The persistent impact of language on global operations. *Prometheus*, *19*, 193–209.

World Bank (2008). *UNSD key global indictors: World development indicators* [*online*]. New York, NY: United Nations Statistical Division. Retrieved from http://data.un.org/ Accessed on August 1, 2008.

WTO. (2004). *Regional trade agreements* [*online*]. Retrieved from http://www.wto.org/english/ tratop_e/region_e/region_e.htm Accessed on May 3, 2004.

Xu, D., & Shenkar, O. (2002). Institutional distance and the multinational enterprise. *Academy of Management Review*, *27*, 608–618.

Zwinkels, R. C. J., & Beugelsdijk, S. (2010). Gravity equations: Workhorse or Trojan horse in explaining trade and FDI patterns across time and space? *International Business Review*, *19*, 102–115.

CHAPTER 7

FDI AND INSTITUTIONS: FORMAL AND INFORMAL INSTITUTIONS

Aljaž Kunčič[☆] and Andreja Jaklič

ABSTRACT

Purpose — *This chapter examines the role of formal and informal institutions in foreign direct investment (FDI) dynamics.*

Design/methodology/approach — *We examine the effects of the quality of legal, political, and economic formal institution as well as the effect of institutional distance (based on new dataset) on bilateral inward FDI stocks in 34 Organization for Economic Cooperation and Development countries for the period 1990–2010 using a gravity specification. Additionally, we also examine FDI for the effects of a specific informal institution — attitude of the public toward economic liberal issues. Reactions of FDI to liberal and nonliberal public opinion (part of informal institutions) are examined with and without controlling for formal institutions.*

[☆] The views expressed are those of the author and do not necessarily reflect those of the United Nations. This chapter was written when the author was affiliated with Faculty of Social Sciences, University of Ljubljana, Slovenia.

Multinational Enterprises, Markets and Institutional Diversity
Progress in International Business Research, Volume 9, 171–205
Copyright © 2014 by Emerald Group Publishing Limited
All rights of reproduction in any form reserved
ISSN: 1745-8862/doi:10.1108/S1745-886220140000009007

Findings — *Findings show that the quality of legal and political institutions are important determinants of FDI, that legal and political institutional distance are both significant obstacles to FDI, and that public opinion also matters. We find that it is important to control for formal institutions when looking at the effect of informal institutions, and that both past liberal and nonliberal public opinion correlate with FDI, but only nonliberal public opinion significantly reduces inward FDI directly.*

Research limitations/implications — *Results are relevant for enterprises' investment strategies, marketing strategies influencing public opinion as well as for policy makers, and governmental agencies involved in investment promotion programs.*

Originality/value — *Exploring the interplay between formal and informal institutions, institutional quality, institutional distance, and their effect on FDI in a bilateral panel.*

Keywords: FDI; gravity equation; institutional quality; institutional distance; public opinion

INTRODUCTION

Determinants of foreign direct investment (FDI) have been widely discussed in the last two decades along with ways on how to attract FDI. The importance of FDI determinants has even increased with more dynamics in the international business environment and made the investment decisions-making process more complex. A set of traditional gravity variables (such as market size, proximity, and trade agreements) is frequently not enough to understand FDI behavior. More recent discussions are starting to recognize that also factors such as institutional quality are important for attracting FDI and can account for cross-country differences in FDI, wealth, and development. The literature and business managers pay increasing attention to this issue. Institutions and their transitions pose significant challenges for policy makers, multinational enterprises (MNEs), and corporate strategies.

The aim of this chapter is to add to the literature on FDI and institutions. For that purpose, we utilize a new dataset on formal institutional quality, which provides measures on the quality of legal, political, and economic institutions. We pay particular attention to the much neglected concept of not only institutional qualities being important as determinants of FDI, but also institutional distances, that is the difference between the quality of origin's and destination's institutions. Moreover, this chapter explores whether FDI flows (reflecting MNEs' investment location decisions) react also to a measure of informal institutions in the form of public opinion toward liberalization issues.

We examine the effects of institutional quality levels, institutional distances, and public opinion on bilateral FDI inward stocks in OECD countries using a gravity specification in the period from 1990 to 2010. We proxy public opinion toward FDI with a summary index based on attitudes toward liberalization issues from the World Values Survey (WVS) and the European Values Survey. We hypothesize that institutional quality of both the origin and destination country will have a positive effect on FDI, that liberal public opinion will also have a positive, while a nonliberal public opinion will have a negative effect on FDI. Public opinion creates pressure for governments, which may – in order to respect electorate – treat FDI differently. Moreover, when we focus on public opinion, we also control for the usual gravity FDI determinants, fixed effects, and finally also for formal legal, political, and economic institutional environment in the destination and origin country, to eliminate the possible indirect effect of public opinion working through government actions.

The available measures of political risk, such as country risks or country ratings, are often insufficient for investors' decision-making process and a more detailed analysis is needed. Improved indicators and databases covering institutional variables are available,[1] but most of them have an incomplete or a very focused concept of institutions and further more, concentrate solely on formal institutions, while less attention is given to informal institutions. However, informal institutions such as public opinion can, similarly as weak public governance, bring inefficient protection of property rights, or corruption, also bring additional risks and costs to FDI, and can even affect other formal institutions (or wider country risk).

Business press often reports negative attitudes toward FDI in the recent years.[2] Fears were frequently expressed in Europe against FDI from emerging economies and in particular against those coming from Asia, as these economies in the last decade provided a majority share in European FDI inflows (UNCTAD, 2008, 2009, 2011, 2012, 2013). Knowing the relations and the impact of informal institutions such as public opinion on FDI is thus relevant for both enterprises and their investment decision-making process as well as for policy makers and governmental agencies involved in investment promotion strategies.

The role of public opinion as a determinant of FDI is modestly explored in the literature (one of the rare empirical studies exploring the role of nationalism is offered by Jakobsen & Jakobsen, 2011), yet anecdotal evidence exists, saying that a hostile public attitude toward FDI or raising economic nationalism prevent FDI inflows and/or cause relocation of foreign investors. Jaklič, Kunčič, and Burger (2011) examine this issue most directly in looking at the effect of formal and informal institutions on FDI in a panel of countries. This study builds on that as it extends their approach to a gravity bilateral setting and includes institutional distance. The main results of this study as pertaining to the effect of informal institutions on FDI confirms the result of Jaklič et al. (2011): public opinion affects FDI with a lag, and it is only the nonliberal public opinion which has a direct negative effect on FDI, while the positive effect of liberal public opinion is mediated by the formal institutional environment.

Institutional analysis is increasingly used as a policy tool for changing and promoting comparative advantages. Research evidence highlights that institutional environment matters for FDI, yet few studies include institutional distance into bilateral FDI analysis. Using institutional distance (in legal, political, and economic institutions) from a newly formed institutional dataset (Kunčič, 2014) in bilateral FDI estimation is the first contribution of this study to the existing literature. Next is including the public opinion into FDI inflows analysis. To our knowledge public opinion has not been tested in any bilateral FDI study so far. Looking into the relationship of the effect of formal institutions and public pressure (informal institutions) on FDI is the third novelty of the study.

This chapter is structured as follows. We first present the theoretical framework and in the next section, the empirical framework, data, and summary statistics. The following section deals with the empirical estimations and discusses the results. The final section summarizes and concludes.

THEORETICAL FRAMEWORK AND EXISTING EVIDENCE

Institutions were recognized as important determinants not only of cross-country differences in wealth and development (Acemoglu & Johnson, 2005; IMF, 2003), but also of cross-country differences in FDI (Dunning & Lundan, 2008; Stein & Daude, 2001; Wei, 2000; Wheeler & Mody, 1992). Institutions (and their quality) were identified as a source of comparative advantage and nations/governments are reforming institutional (legal, political, economic, and cultural) context for firms to improve their working conditions (Pedersen, 2010). Institutional competitiveness has (along with the effort of attracting FDI) become implicitly the aim of industrial policies and a tool for increasing international competitiveness all over the world. Nations and governments not only restructure formal institutions and coordinate different policies and departments, but also intervene in the attitudes, values, aspirations, and interests of citizens and firms in attempts to use behavior change as a means to create comparative advantage (Pedersen, 2010). The concept of international competitiveness has placed institutions in the center of focus the last two decades for business managers, policy makers, and international organizations when they measure competitiveness and construct internationalization strategies.

Foreign investors have become increasingly aware of the importance of the institutional quality as they make their investment decisions (Bevan & Estrin, 2004). Current IB research has identified institutional efficiency as a determinant of enterprise performance and also the impact of national institutions on firms strategic choices (Benito, Grogaard, & Narula, 2003; Delios & Henisz, 2003). The awareness that institutional quality influences the enterprise strategy and performance is rising along with findings that forms of enterprise response differ across national contexts.

Business research and managers initially pay greater attention to economic institutions. Chacar, Newburry, and Vissa (2010) argue that formal institutions in the product, financial, and labor markets affect the size of pools of exchange partners and the types of exchanges allowed and condoned. Exploring the impact of political and legal institutions got greater research effort recently, including the response of enterprises such as increasing engagement in corporate social responsibility and also the challenge of corporate political activity (Dahan, Hadani, & Schuler, 2013; Ozer & Alakent, 2012). Increased interaction among MNEs, host governments, and other institutions/actors has made the implementation of FDIs more complex and potentially more prone to conflict (Skippari & Pajunen, 2010). As pointed out in recent research (Doh & Teegen, 2002; Grosse, 2005; Lambell, Ramia, Nyland, & Michelotti, 2008; Ramamurti, 2001; Teegen, Doh, & Vachani, 2004), activities of MNEs are often influenced by a diverse set of nongovernmental organizations (NGOs), such as environmental activist groups, human rights organizations, community groups, and social movements in general, which advocate the interests of the civil society in local, national, and global contexts. These findings imply that mulinationals should not consider only the economic institutions of the host government but think also about their legitimacy in light of public sentiment and political context.

The economic crisis enhanced these efforts as investment risks increased not only due to a less stable macroeconomic environment but also due to a more volatile social and political environment. Global structural changes and growing influence of emerging economies additionally challenged institutional uncertainty.[3] Rising presence of Asian enterprises in the "old developed economies" in Europe has been accompanied with a number of new bilateral investment treaties (BITs), but also with a number of investment restrictions (UNCTAD, 2010, 2011, 2013).[4] MNEs are responding to the regulatory and other institutional changes, but also leading the change of institutions (and build attitudes, values, aspirations, and interests of consumers). Changes in institutional environment are thus increasingly monitored to evaluate "institutional competitiveness" (Campbell & Pedersen, 2007) and as a consequence, institutional analyses have been growing. Thus, our first hypothesis is:

H1. MNEs and FDI react to formal (legal, political, and economic) institutions.

Empirical research on FDI has recently begun to include institutional factors in both the FDI effects on domestic economy, such as spillovers and growth, and the determinants of FDI flows. Prüfer and Tondl (2008) discuss the positive effects of good institutional environment in the form of a functioning legal framework and find they are important for FDI spillovers. Moreover, the determinants of FDI or the attraction of FDI itself depends, *inter alia*, on the local environment and institutional system, ranging from the level of corruption to property right protection, for instance see Kostevc, Redek, and Susjan (2007). Investment-related costs, especially those influencing uncertainty such as the quality of legal institutions and political institutions, affect FDI costs and through that, FDI flows (Daniele & Marani, 2006; Demekas, Horvath, Ribakova, & Wu, 2007). Recently, Ali, Fiess, and MacDonald (2010) examined institutions as determinants of FDI for a large panel of countries and found that they are a robust determinant of FDI flows, namely legal institutions in the form of property rights, rule of law, and expropriation risk.

The quality of institutions in both the country of origin as well as in the importing country plays a direct role in the frequency and magnitude of the above-mentioned costs, as emphasized within the OLI paradigm by Dunning (1979, 1981, 1988) and Dunning and Lundan (2008). The OLI or eclectic paradigm is a theory describing the type of market entry a firm will choose, licensing, export, or FDI, based on the ownership, location, and internalization advantages available to the firm. To this theoretical framework, we can include an additional factor as an innovation within the location advantages, which is institutional difference (explained later in more detail). Both within the OLI paradigm and also within the Helpman (2006) model, institutional difference, measured as quality of institutions in the origin country minus the quality of institutions in the receiving country, can be incorporated into the country-pair-specific investment costs that are pertinent in the theory.

Levchenko (2007) introduced institutional differences as a source of comparative advantages by using bilateral data between the host and the source country on trade. To the extent that trade and FDI are complements, this could raise FDI too. Aizenman and Spiegel (2006), on the contrary (by using a principal–agent framework where ex-post monitoring of contracts is more costly for foreign investors than for domestic ones), argue that the share of FDI in total investment should be lower in countries with weak institutions (e.g., enforcement of property rights). If investors from weak quality of institution countries face lower costs (when investing in weak quality of institutions countries) than investors from strong quality of institutions countries, this would entail that institutional difference between the origin and the host country should have a negative impact on bilateral FDI. Institutional difference can be thus understood with traditional arguments of the literature on management for "psychic distance" as a major impediment to the foreign entry decision of companies. Proximity would reduce either perceived uncertainty or learning costs about the target countries. Institutions based on economic and social history (including the colonization era) attract more FDI, other things equal, among countries displaying relatively similar institutions (Habib & Zurawicki, 2002).

The link between institutions and FDI is increasingly studied also as a channel through which institutions promote productivity growth (Benassy-Quere, Coupet, & Mayer, 2007). Good institutions (mainly considered as formal institutions) exert their positive influence on development through the promotion of investment in general, which faces less uncertainty and higher expected rates of return. Since FDI now represent a very large share of capital formation in poor countries (UNCTAD, 2010) and forms one of the most stable sources of capital, the FDI-promoting effect of good institutions might be an important channel of their overall effect on growth and development.

All the above-mentioned studies focus mainly on formal institutions, while there is less discussion and research on the topic of informal institutions. Still, state—society relations are seen as one of the facets of institutional competitiveness and a number of above-mentioned actors apply professional means to influence public opinion and government decisions. The impact of public opinion on institutions has been recognized (Jaklič et al., 2011; Jakobsen & Jakobsen, 2011), but rarely studied as a determinant of institutional quality separately or further investigated as a determinant of international trade and capital flows. Multinational firms often report negative attitude in public opinion or chicane due to liability of foreignness.[5] Anecdotal evidence highlights the difficulties (or even withdrawals) of foreign investors due to underestimated costs of unfavorable and hostile climate. In societies where nationalist sentiments dominate, the public prefers indigenous to foreign firms. This induces host authorities to institute more stringent foreign investment rules, which deter FDI (Jakobsen & Jakobsen, 2011). Public opinion, if hostile, may prolong the process of getting licenses, hiring personnel, coordinating with stakeholders, etc. and consequently increases costs and/or return period. Positive attitudes toward FDI (often established due to job creation or wage increases) may on the other hand be a comparative advantage of a location and may indirectly work as an incentive for improved functioning of formal institutions. Public opinion may thus be relevant to MNC's behavior, investment location decisions, and performance, thus, next hypotheses are:

H2. Liberal public opinion stimulates FDI, while nonliberal public opinion hinders FDI.

H3. There are complementarities between the formal and informal institutions and their effect on FDI.

Fig. 1 illustrates the theoretical linkages between institutions and MNEs, which make decisions on FDI. Although MNEs and FDI are primarily effected by formal and informal institutions, there are some feedback effects, as well as interplay effects between formal and informal institutions.

EMPIRICAL FRAMEWORK AND DATA

With the rise of availability of bilateral FDI flows, the empirical literature on FDI quickly adopted the gravity approach from the trade literature.

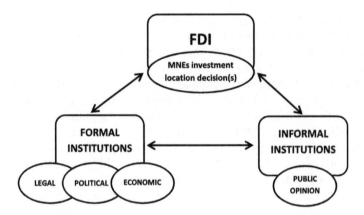

Fig. 1. MNEs, FDI, and Institutions.

Whether we are exploring market seeking – horizontal FDI, or efficiency seeking – vertical FDI (which is often joined by resource seeking and asset-seeking FDI), the two motives for FDI can be combined together in a gravity specification of FDI from country *i* to country *j* (Markusen & Venables, 1998, 2000). Taking into account that around two thirds of new FDI is in fact mergers and acquisitions (Head & Ries, 2008; UNCTAD, 2011) develop a gravity model of FDI, where the bilateral FDI flows depend on origin country *i*'s characteristics, destination country *j*'s characteristics, and bilateral-specific variables such as geographic and cultural distance. The authors also suggest, in line with the trade gravity estimations, that the origin and destination effects can be estimated with *i* and *j* fixed effects.

When we log-linearize the multiplicative gravity equation for bilateral FDI from country *i* to country *j* in time *t*, we arrive at an estimable expression such as the one in Eq. (1), where FDI is explained by a set of country origin and country destination-specific time variant and invariant variables in vectors X_{it} and X_{jt}, and a set of bilateral variables stacked in vector X_{ijt}, all of which are based on the literature and explained below. Additionally, the vector INST contains the variables capturing the institutional environment in the origin country (*it*), the destination country (*jt*), or institutional distance (*ijt*).

$$\ln\text{FDI}_{ijt} = \text{const.} + X_{it}'\alpha + X_{jt}'\beta + X_{ijt}'\gamma + \text{INST}_{it}'\delta + \text{INST}_{jt}'\theta + \text{INST}_{ijt}'\vartheta + \varepsilon_{ijt}$$

$$(1)$$

Empirically, the following questions have to be tackled: (1) Should we operate with FDI flows or FDI stocks? (2) Which are the control variables that should be included? (3) Which are the institutional variables that should be included? (4) How to control for possible endogeneity sources in general and how to control for endogeneity of institutions in particular? (5) Which estimation procedure should be employed to account for the zeroes in the FDI flows? We discuss these questions in the pecking order later.

The choice between FDI flows and FDI stocks is not completely straight forward, however, the literature does favor using FDI stocks, namely for three reasons explained in Benassy-Quere et al. (2007, p. ~769). "First, foreign investors decide on the worldwide allocation of output, hence on capital stocks. Second, stocks account for FDI being financed through local capital markets, hence it is a better measure of capital ownership (Devereux & Griffith, 2003). Finally, stocks are much less volatile than flows which are sometimes dependent on one or two large takeovers, especially in relatively small countries." Also, some other recent examinations of bilateral FDI and institutions rely on using stocks instead of FDI flows, such as Júlio, Pinheiro-Alves, and Tavares (2011), Bellak, Leibrecht, and Stehrer (2010), or Head and Ries (2008), which is not to say that some other authors do not also rely on flows (Aleksynska & Havrylchyk, 2013) or averaged flows (Andrés, Nunnenkamp, & Busse, 2013). There are two sources of wide country and time coverage for bilateral FDI stocks, OECD, and UNCTAD. OECD covers member countries for the period at most from 1985 to 2010, while UNCTAD (UNCTAD's Data Extract Service) covers a wider set of developed, various emerging, and developing countries, and covers the period of at most from 1980 to 2007. Due to the recent literature that emphasizes the differential impact of FDI determinants for emerging/non-traditional sources as opposed to the ones for developed countries (Brennan, 2008; Sauvant, 2008), and due to the fact that the UNCTAD database is available only for a fee, we use the inward FDI stock from the OECD database and concentrate our analysis only on OECD countries. Thus, our sample of host countries is more homogenous, and using the inward instead of outward FDI stock allows us to focus more on some specific pull factors we are interested in, as the data for OECD countries is more readily available and when focusing on the pull factors, we would ideally want all FDI in a country to be accounted for, which is directly achieved by studying inward FDI.

The set of control variables we use include first the standard bilateral gravity controls based on bilateral trade models, as for instance in Head, Mayer, and Ries (2010), where the brackets denote which margin the variables vary on: we include the nominal gross domestic products (GDPs) in millions of current USD and GDP's per capita for both the origin and the host country (*it* and *jt*) from the World Bank's World Development Indicators (WB WDI), geographic distance between each country pair, and dummy for contiguity (*ij*) from Head et al. (2010) and extended to fit our sample. From the same source we also include dummies for common language, common legal origins, colonial history (*ij*), as well as common currency, both countries being members of GATT (WTO), sharing a regional trade agreement (RTA) (de Sousa, 2012) and sharing a common political entity (country) in the past (*ijt*) (Mayer & Zignago, 2011). The other variables which are specific to bilateral FDI estimation and are used by the literature (see for instance Andrés et al., 2013 or Bellak et al., 2010) are again taken from WB WDI and include host country inflation (*jt*), as a proxy for macroeconomic stability, total tax rate (% of commercial profits), and research and development expenditure (% of GDP, to capture the potential attractive spillover effects). The horizontal motive for FDI is captured with real GDP growth of the host country (along with GDP of the host), and the vertical motive is controlled for with the host's openness to trade, Information and Communication Technology (ICT)-infrastructure endowment (*jt*), and with the already included GDP's per capita of origin and host countries, as the difference in GDP's per capita of each country pair proxies the cost benefits of vertical FDI. Resource seeking FDI is captured by resource rents of the host economy and asset augmenting FDI by the number of patents per host country (*jt*). Finally, we also include the average FDI stock in the host country (*jt*), to account for the ever more important agglomeration effects of FDI. All the control variables with sources and remarks are listed in the Appendix.

The question of which institutional variables to include is rarely tackled directly in the literature, as the generic term institutions is used to describe everything from financial market developments to organizational structures. Most often, one of the indices for property rights protection either from the ICRG (The PRS Group, 2013), World Bank World Governance Indicators (Kaufmann, Kraay, & Mastruzzi, 2013), or Freedom House (2012) is used. This however does not take into account the New Institutional Economics theory, where institutions are defined as formal and informal rules of the game, and their enforcement characteristics (North, 1990, 1993, 2005). Our own formal institutional measures come from a paper where a set of three institutional measures are developed on the basis of more than 30 established institutional indicators with a wide cross-country and year coverage (Kunčič, 2014), and where the calculated institutional quality is linked to the theory. The dataset is available online and offers already calculated cross-country and yearly values for the quality of legal, political, and economic institutions, which we use to control for the source country and destination country quality of formal institutional environment. We use these values to also calculate legal, political, and economic institutional distance between each country pair for every year, as the absolute difference between the country pair. Capturing informal institutions is much trickier, as it is extremely difficult to arrive at a few common informal institutional dimensions, as with formal institutions.[6] We concentrate on one dimension of informal institutions, which is the attitude of the public toward liberalization. Liberal and nonliberal attitudes in a society are captured with the data from European values study (EVS) (European Values Study Group, 2012) and World values study (WVS) (World Values Survey Association, 2012), which have been done in nine waves from the start of the 1980s. We integrate both surveys and use three questions which can be used to measure the public attitude toward liberalization, namely the attitude toward private versus government business ownership, responsibility for oneself versus tasking the government with that, and competition being good versus being bad.[7] As per Jakobsen and Jakobsen (2011) or Jaklič et al. (2011), the measure of non(liberal) public attitude comes from using the aggregated values of answers to all three questions. The total number of points from all three question is 30, so we calculate the share of respondents for every country and year available with a total score of 10 and less, and call this the share of nonliberal people, and those with a total score of 20 or more, and call this the share of liberal people. All the institutional variables with sources and remarks are listed in the Appendix.

The gravity specification of FDI flows has a range of possible endogeneities, stemming from possible heterogeneity of country pairs in time as well as country-specific heterogeneity. Matyas (1997) argues that in a gravity specification, time-fixed effects as well as country-specific-fixed effects should be included. This however does not control for possible biases arising from time-varying factors, which also include the salient multilateral resistance (Anderson & van Wincoop, 2003), although these effects can be varying slowly, so bilateral and country-specific effects do in fact still capture a large share of the cross-sectional heterogeneity (Bergstrand & Egger, 2007). Benassy-Quere et al. (2007) use only time-fixed effects to control for the problematic endogeneity. The endogeneity of institutions requires a more sophisticated solution, as institutions are notorious for being correlated to other measures of development. The use of panel data with country fixed effects prevents the usage of time invariant instruments such as settler mortality (Acemoglu, Johnson, & Robinson, 2001) or latitude and longitude of a country as instruments for institutions. We follow Benassy-Quere et al. (2007) in cleansing our institutional variables of their endogenous part. GDP per capita of both origin and destination country is separately regressed on each institutional measure. This makes the collected institutional residuals and calculated institutional distance orthogonal to the capture-all development variable GDP per capita, and so cleansed of the most problematic endogenous parts correlated with development.

The choice of the estimation procedure of the gravity specification is crucially affected by the fact that 60% of our FDI stocks observations are zero or negative, which would turn into missing values if we transform them with natural logs. The literature initially solved this problem with a Tobit estimation (Jonathan & Akiko, 1994), which was shown later to produce biased results in the presence of heteroskedastic errors, so Poisson Pseudo Maximum Likelihood (Poisson PML) was suggested as an alternative procedure, which accounts for the zeros and is not biased (see Santos Silva & Tenreyro, 2006 for an application to trade in goods or Head & Ries, 2008 for an application to bilateral FDI). However, the latter method is primarily intended to be used for count-dependent variables and has the requirement of conditional means and conditional variances of variables to be roughly the same; both of which is hardly the case with FDI data. Another option is to first cap all negative observations to zero, then add a constant to the FDI stocks and only then taking the natural logarithm of it, which is what we do, by first capping the negative observations to zero and then adding a constant of 0.3, following Benassy-Quere et al. (2007), which in our sample of FDI stocks corresponds to the value of the fifth percentile of strictly positive values.

The summary statistics of all variables used (without logs) are presented in Table 1. Some variables are not as available as our main gravity variables, variables such as R&D expenses, tax rate, ICT infrastructure, and especially the institutional variables, so some variables are thus not included in the final regression analysis. Fig. 2 shows a scatter plot of public opinion in the destination countries for FDI stocks from OECD. We can see there is a lot of variation, and that the share of liberal people is much higher on average than the share of nonliberal people. Out of OECD countries, the most liberal crowd can be found in Israel in 2001, when according to our measure, everyone was liberal, followed by United Kingdom in 1998 at 93% and Sweden in 1997 at 72%. Low values of liberal public opinion are can be found in Korea in 2001, 2005, and 1996 at 2%, 2%, and 4%, respectively. A look at nonliberal public opinion shows that the most nonliberal public opinion can be found in Poland in 2005 at 30%, followed by Turkey in 1990 by just under 30% and Chile in 2008 at

Table 1. Summary Statistics.

Variable	N	Mean	Min	Max	SD
FDIstock	55,864	1772.19	0.00	447529.00	12473.47
gdp_d (bill. current USD)	70,518	1058.02	5.68	14419.40	2258.30
gdpcap_d	70,518	30160.55	1693.74	112028.50	18368.96
gdp_o (bill. current USD)	66,458	296.14	0.01	14419.40	1115.88
gdpcap_o	66,447	11265.84	64.36	138774.70	16839.89
distance	141,372	7359.08	20.25	19563.95	4409.22
common_border	141,372	0.02	0.00	1.00	0.13
common_language	141,372	0.10	0.00	1.00	0.30
colony	141,372	0.03	0.00	1.00	0.18
common_legal	141,372	0.24	0.00	1.00	0.43
common_currency	140,658	0.01	0.00	1.00	0.12
rta	141,372	0.13	0.00	1.00	0.34
wto	146,374	0.63	0.00	1.00	0.48
gdp_growth_d	70,512	2.50	−14.07	10.49	3.35
inflation_d	69,596	3.69	−4.48	555.38	7.67
rd_d	55,202	1.81	0.31	4.84	0.93
resource_rents_d	70,518	1.92	0.00	22.05	4.01
tax_rate_d	35,587	44.41	20.80	77.50	12.21
trade_d	70,518	87.94	15.92	333.53	52.00
ict_d	58,638	1529.26	136.87	2303.50	384.73
patents_d	63,094	19880.58	1.00	222693.00	50984.56
FDIstockavg_d	70,518	2438.57	41.32	17006.06	3717.47
legal_inst_o	136,422	1.09	−0.83	1.93	0.60
political_inst_o	128,106	1.25	−0.74	2.04	0.51
economic_inst_o	135,630	0.92	−0.91	1.91	0.56
legal_inst_d	82,552	−0.01	−2.15	1.93	0.95
political_inst_d	86,870	0.00	−2.22	2.04	0.98
economic_inst_d	76,364	0.00	−2.93	1.96	0.95
abs(legal_diff)	79,490	1.32	0.00	3.98	0.86
abs(political_diff)	78,886	1.40	0.00	4.07	0.90
abs(economic_diff)	73,352	1.17	0.00	4.71	0.83
liberal_d	26,035	0.27	0.02	1.00	0.16
not_liberal_d	26,035	0.10	0.00	0.30	0.07
liberal_o	8,874	0.23	0.02	1.00	0.15
not_liberal_o	8,874	0.13	0.00	0.39	0.08

Source: OECD, World Bank WDI; Head et al. (2010), Mayer and Zignago (2011), de Sousa (2012), Kunčič (2014), EVS; WVS; own calculation.

28%. On the other end, the lowest values of nonliberal public opinion as we measure it are in France in 2000 with no nonliberal people, Sweden in 1999 with 0.2%, and the Netherlands in 2006 at 0.3%. The dynamics of public opinion are more worrisome, as they imply that the share of liberals is declining, while the share of nonliberals is increasing in the total sample.

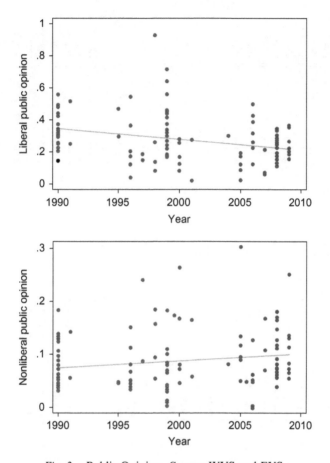

Fig. 2. Public Opinion. *Source*: WVS and EVS.

EMPIRICAL ESTIMATION AND DISCUSSION OF RESULTS

What we start is the replication of gravity FDI results from the literature, essentially estimating Eq. (1) without the institutional part. Even here, we proceed in several steps, essentially to show how the estimates can evolve, when controlling for endogeneity sources in different ways and when using different methods. Table 2 shows the OLS gravity model estimations with

Table 2. Gravity Estimations.

dep. var. ln(FDIstock)	1	2	3	4	5	6
ln(gdp_o)	0.521***	−1.254***	−1.083***	0.498***	−1.291***	−1.164***
	(0.0158)	(0.270)	(0.293)	(0.0169)	(0.274)	(0.296)
ln(gdp_d)	0.536***	−2.015***	−3.995***	0.243***	−2.116***	−3.853***
	(0.0212)	(0.673)	(0.630)	(0.0487)	(0.710)	(0.698)
ln(gdpcap_o)	0.658***	1.408***	1.268***	0.662***	1.434***	1.333***
	(0.0236)	(0.280)	(0.305)	(0.0252)	(0.285)	(0.308)
ln(gdpcap_d)	0.124***	2.704***	4.373***	−0.0883	2.750***	3.994***
	(0.0443)	(0.682)	(0.642)	(0.0546)	(0.711)	(0.707)
ln(distance)	−0.357***	−0.706***	−0.379***	−0.679***		
	(0.0485)	(0.0515)		(0.0537)	(0.0545)	
common_border	1.325***	0.806***		1.460***	0.857***	
	(0.222)	(0.163)		(0.245)	(0.181)	
common_language	1.160***	0.164		0.950***	0.0774	
	(0.119)	(0.106)		(0.128)	(0.109)	
common_legal	0.0257	0.364***		0.00905	0.430***	
	(0.0751)	(0.0591)		(0.0899)	(0.0671)	
colony	1.126***	1.106***		1.346***	1.160***	
	(0.202)	(0.170)		(0.212)	(0.185)	
rta	0.568***	0.233***	0.240***	0.464***	0.217**	0.235***
	(0.101)	(0.0833)	(0.0651)	(0.108)	(0.0890)	(0.0713)
wto	0.0408	−0.234***	−0.349***	0.0565	−0.226***	−0.364***
	(0.0625)	(0.0760)	(0.0711)	(0.0681)	(0.0806)	(0.0766)
common_currency	1.904***	0.656***	0.932***	1.921***	0.635***	0.948***
	(0.191)	(0.140)	(0.109)	(0.212)	(0.155)	(0.131)
gdp_growth_d				0.00402	−0.00732***	−0.00369
				(0.00316)	(0.00229)	(0.00233)
inflation_d				−0.0252***	−0.00227	−0.0163***
				(0.00502)	(0.00509)	(0.00479)

resource_rents_d				-0.0104	-0.0451***	0.0119
				(0.00942)	(0.0123)	(0.00934)
trade_d				5.20e-05	-0.00191*	-0.00288***
				(0.000774)	(0.000990)	(0.00100)
patents_d				0.175**	-0.00457	0.0209
				(0.0787)	(0.0503)	(0.0353)
ln(FDIstockavg_d)				0.381***		
				(0.0467)		
Constant	-8.117***	-2.431	-26.16***	-6.393***	-38.25***	-23.59***
	(0.659)		(3.138)	(0.766)	(7.556)	(3.504)
Observations	51,721	51,721	51,721	44,402	44,402	44,402
R^2	0.608	0.787	0.924	0.614	0.791	0.927
Time FE	Yes	Yes	Yes	Yes	Yes	Yes
Origin FE	No	Yes	Yes	No	Yes	Yes
Destination FE	No	Yes	Yes	No	Yes	Yes
Dyadic FE	No	No	Yes	No	No	Yes

Source: Own calculation.

Country pair robust standard errors within parentheses.

*** $p < 0.01$, ** $p < 0.05$, * $p < 0.1$.

and without the FDI-specific variables, and with different combinations of fixed effects, controlling for several possible biases.

Regressions from 1 to 3 show the results with only including the full gravity variables, while regressions 4 to 6 add also the FDI-specific variables suggested by the literature. Fixed effects (FE) included are time FE in regressions 1 and 4, time and country FE in regressions 2 and 5, and finally the entire set of FE, time, country, and dyadic FE in regressions 3 and 6. Generally, we get the expected results in practically all regressions, namely that the GDPs as well as GDP's per capita of both origin and destination country have a positive marginal effect on bilateral inward FDI,[8] as do variables denoting closeness of countries such as sharing a border, language, currency, legal origins, or colonial ties. Distance has a highly significant and negative marginal effect. Also, being in the same RTA has a positive effect, while both countries being members of WTO has an interesting negative marginal effect. In terms of the FDI-specific variables, the most consistent effect is the negative marginal effect of inflation in the destination OECD country, and there seems to be a negative marginal effect of openness to trade. Also, the already amassed FDI stock has a positive and strong marginal effect, implying big agglomeration effects.

It has to be noted that depending on the fixed effects included, the partial coefficients can be very different from one another. This volatility of estimates points to the fact that including only year FE can be misleading, not only in the magnitudes, but also in significance and signs. Comparing regressions 1 and 4 to the ones with more fixed effects, some variables stand out. Namely, the positive effect of GDP of both the origin and destination country is severely overestimated without country FE. There are also some changes in the FDI-specific variables, highlighting the need for the inclusion of additional FE.

The baseline model results imply that inward FDI stock in the OECD countries is primarily driven by the market seeking motive and agglomeration effects. It is much less motivated by efficiency seeking FDI (which is to be expected as labor is expensive in OECD countries), not motivated by resource seeking FDI (also expected, as OECD countries are not among the most resource rich countries) but also surprisingly not motivated by asset seeking. We also believe that the best specification is the one which includes the most fixed effects, as this allows us to control for time heterogeneity, origin, and destination country heterogeneity, and heterogeneity in country pairs.

We proceed with cleansing of our formal institutional variables of their endogeneity. We regress GDP per capita of origin (destination) country on origin (destination) country's quality of the legal, political, and economic institutions, and collect the residuals, which are not correlated with GDP per capita any more, and as such can be seen as cleansed of their most problematic part. We use these orthogonal institutional values to further create the absolute institutional distance between country pairs. The results when we account for all the possible fixed effects, that is time, country, and dyadic fixed effects, are presented in Table 3 using the same control variables as in Table 2 in regressions 1–3, and excluding the FDI non-gravity variables in regressions 4–6 in order to increase the sample. In both instances we include first just the relative institutional levels in regressions 1 and 4, then both the institutional levels and institutional distances in regressions 2 and 5, and finally only institutional distances in regressions 3 and 6. In comparison to the baseline estimates in Table 2, the partial coefficient on resource rents is now positive and significant. However, since the FDI-specific variables do not effect the institutional variables much, we concentrate on getting a larger sample and on regressions 4 to 6.

There are some empirical regularities with the institutional estimates. We have institutional push and pull factors in the form of the quality of legal institutions in the origin country and political institutions in the destination OECD country, which both have a significant and positive marginal effect on inward FDI stock, and the quality of political institutions in the origin country and legal institutions in the destination country, which both have a negative and significant effect on FDI. The political institutions imply that a better political environment at home is possibly more conducive to home investment, and serves as an attractor of investments at home, instead of abroad, whereas a good quality of political institutional environment in the destination country attracts FDI. Vice versa goes for legal institutions, where legal institutions in the origin country promote FDI, and interestingly, depress it in the destination country. A surprising finding is that the quality of economic institutions plays no role in FDI, either in levels or in differences, implying that when it comes to investment, the quality of economic environment or the difference in economic rules at home and in the destination country does not significantly contribute to the costs of investment. This does not hold for legal and political institutional distance, since they both depress inward FDI stock in the OECD countries, implying that the differences in legal and political rules of the game contribute to the costs of investing somewhere significantly. This can be seen as being in line with the new institutional economics theory, which according to Williamson (2000) differentiates institutions based on their embeddedness or frequency of change. Economic institutions are most

Table 3. Gravity Estimations with Formal Institutions.

dep. var. ln(FDIstock)	1	2	3	4	5	6
ln(gdp_o)	-0.878*	-0.860*	-0.978*	-0.850*	-0.826*	-0.981**
	(0.497)	(0.494)	(0.502)	(0.488)	(0.486)	(0.490)
ln(gdp_d)	-5.157***	-5.127***	-4.134***	-4.347***	-4.388***	-3.942***
	(1.141)	(1.137)	(1.146)	(1.023)	(1.026)	(1.024)
ln(gdpcap_o)	1.105**	1.074**	1.189**	1.133**	1.095**	1.261**
	(0.506)	(0.504)	(0.513)	(0.496)	(0.495)	(0.500)
ln(gdpcap_d)	5.267***	5.239***	4.271***	4.750***	4.755***	4.312***
	(1.127)	(1.124)	(1.126)	(1.031)	(1.033)	(1.026)
rta	0.0588	0.0701	0.0477	0.0301	0.0411	0.0209
	(0.100)	(0.100)	(0.0994)	(0.0886)	(0.0890)	(0.0882)
wto	-0.166	-0.169	-0.305**	-0.170	-0.173	-0.315**
	(0.148)	(0.148)	(0.149)	(0.133)	(0.133)	(0.135)
common_currency	0.555***	0.531***	0.566***	0.551***	0.534***	0.576***
	(0.131)	(0.131)	(0.133)	(0.114)	(0.114)	(0.114)
gdp_growth_d	0.00747	0.00694	0.00598			
	(0.00527)	(0.00526)	(0.00508)			
inflation_d	-0.0128**	-0.0118*	-0.0118*			
	(0.00647)	(0.00647)	(0.00646)			
resource_rents_d	0.0234*	0.0229*	0.0237*			
	(0.0135)	(0.0135)	(0.0134)			
trade_d	-0.000985	-0.000999	0.00147			
	(0.00269)	(0.00268)	(0.00267)			
patents_d	0.0288	0.0433	0.0867			
	(0.0843)	(0.0838)	(0.0843)			
legal_inst_o	0.387***	0.363***		0.331***	0.309***	
	(0.108)	(0.108)		(0.0983)	(0.0983)	
political_inst_o	-0.562***	-0.582***		-0.559***	-0.577***	
	(0.0954)	(0.0957)		(0.0874)	(0.0877)	

	(1)	(2)	(3)	(4)	(5)	(6)
economic_inst_o	−0.0345	−0.0497		−0.000522	−0.0162	
	(0.0871)	(0.0859)		(0.0793)	(0.0783)	
legal_inst_d	−0.263**	−0.284**		−0.203*	−0.255**	
	(0.128)	(0.128)		(0.112)	(0.113)	
political_inst_d	0.508***	0.467***		0.466***	0.416***	
	(0.164)	(0.163)		(0.154)	(0.152)	
economic_inst_d	−0.118	−0.122		−0.0745	−0.0869	
	(0.0977)	(0.0996)		(0.0850)	(0.0869)	
abs(legal_diff)		−0.139*	−0.101		−0.178**	−0.126*
		(0.0791)	(0.0802)		(0.0711)	(0.0725)
abs(political_diff)		−0.145*	−0.165**		−0.136*	−0.171**
		(0.0791)	(0.0809)		(0.0743)	(0.0764)
abs(economic_diff)		−0.00828	0.0238		−0.0266	−0.00293
		(0.0663)	(0.0662)		(0.0606)	(0.0596)
Constant	−24.18***	−23.56***	−20.43***	−24.06***	−23.48***	−22.05***
	(4.955)	(4.927)	(4.946)	(4.621)	(4.626)	(4.593)
Observations	24,486	24,486	24,486	28,734	28,734	28,734
R^2	0.929	0.929	0.928	0.927	0.927	0.926
Time FE	Yes	Yes	Yes	Yes	Yes	Yes
Origin FE	Yes	Yes	Yes	Yes	Yes	Yes
Destination FE	Yes	Yes	Yes	Yes	Yes	Yes
Dyadic FE	Yes	Yes	Yes	Yes	Yes	Yes
Orthog. Inst.	Yes	Yes	Yes	Yes	Yes	Yes

Source: Own calculation.

Country pair robust standard errors in parentheses.

*** $p < 0.01$, ** $p < 0.05$, * $p < 0.1$.

prone to changes, whereas political and legal institutions change more slowly, thus, it may be more difficult for FDI to adjust to their changes, in comparison to economic institutions, which change more frequently, so investors can first expect that and second, for FDI stocks, it is more difficult to react to more frequent changes in institutions than to less frequent ones (as opposed to possibly flows). Lastly, we also find that it does not seem to matter for the effect of either levels or differences, whether we include only levels, only distances or both.

We move in our estimation to the effect of informal institutions and try to capture how either liberal or nonliberal public opinion affects inward bilateral FDI stocks in OECD countries. Firstly, since the EVS and WVS have values predominantly for the developed world, we only include the destination country (OECD) liberal and nonliberal public opinion, as we are left with less than 1,500 observations when both origin and destination country's public opinion is used. Further more, not to further reduce the size of our sample, which is with the inclusion of destination country's public opinion decimated as it is, we exclude the FDI-specific variables and include only the widely available gravity controls.

Table 4 presents only the coefficients on liberal and nonliberal public opinion, controlling, as before, for all possible fixed effects (year, country, and dyadic fixed effects), and gravity explanatory variables. The complete regression coefficients are reported in the Appendix, although the same variables as in Table 2 are included. The first three regressions include besides the standard gravity variables only liberal and nonliberal public opinion in the first regression, their first lags in the second regression, and their second lag in the third.

Without controlling for formal institutions, we see that we get a positive and significant marginal effect of liberal public opinion with one lag, and a significant and negative marginal effect of nonliberal public opinion at two lags. However, not including formal institutions can bias results, as public opinion as an informal institution can also be channeled through the formal institutional environment. However, once we control for formal institutions, we can see that the result from regression 2 disappears, as well as that it becomes evident that only nonliberal public opinion has a statically significant and negative direct marginal effect on FDI, at two lags. The positive marginal effect of liberal public opinion disappears, implying that the liberal public sentiment about economic issues is channeled through the formal institutional environment, which then has a direct effect on FDI. We have to note that also the marginal effect of nonliberal public opinion is much smaller once we control for formal institutions, implying that

Table 4. Gravity Estimations with Public Opinion.

dep. var. ln(FDIstock)	1	2	3	4	5	6
liberal	0.418			0.0123		
	(0.373)			(0.414)		
nonliberal	0.708			0.168		
	(1.070)			(1.238)		
L.liberal		0.692*			0.572	
		(0.372)			(0.417)	
L.nonliberal		0.834			0.535	
		(1.112)			(1.276)	
L2.liberal			−0.527			−0.721
			(0.492)			(0.507)
L2.nonliberal			−4.564***			−2.599*
			(1.243)			(1.401)
Constant	−24.77***	−36.61***	−12.87	8.178	2.922	−5.465
	(7.733)	(7.878)	(10.88)	(10.00)	(10.24)	(11.72)
Observations	9,147	9,385	7,853	5,154	5,481	4,908
R^2	0.942	0.939	0.956	0.950	0.942	0.953
Time FE	Yes	Yes	Yes	Yes	Yes	Yes
Origin FE	Yes	Yes	Yes	Yes	Yes	Yes
Destination FE	Yes	Yes	Yes	Yes	Yes	Yes
Dyadic FE	Yes	Yes	Yes	Yes	Yes	Yes
Formal inst.	No	No	No	Yes	Yes	Yes

Source: Own calculation.
Country pair robust standard errors within parentheses.
***$p < 0.01$, **$p < 0.05$, *$p < 0.1$.

formal institutions overtake some of this negative marginal effect, but apparently not all of it, since nonliberal public opinion is strong enough to keep a direct (but smaller) effect on FDI.

The negative marginal effect of nonliberal public opinion on FDI with a lagged impact implies that negative public sentiment does indeed serve as a direct detrimental force for foreign investors, with which we also confirm the findings of Jaklič et al. (2011), who also find that nonliberal public attitudes reduce FDI with a lag. Liberal public opinion, however, does not have a direct effect on FDI.

CONCLUSION

Institutions, may be formal (economic, political, and legal) or informal, and their quality affects FDI and poses significant challenges for MNEs

and corporate strategies. Changes in political risks after the economic crisis, rising protectionism, and restrictions influence institutional uncertainty
and investment decisions. MNEs are responding to the regulatory and
other institutional changes. Public opinion is one of informal institutions
where changes can be seen quickly. Being increasingly monitored and discussed, public opinion may (due to latent costs) influence MNC's behavior,
investment location decisions, and performance. As a part of business
environment and business climate, public opinion may also cause change in
and work through formal institutions (and potentially affect political risks
or wider country risk).

This chapter explores whether and how FDI (MNEs' investment location decisions) react to first the quality of formal institutional environment
and institutional distances in formal institutional environment between
FDI partners, and second how FDI reacts to public opinion as a belief-
based informal institution. We examine these institutional effects on bilateral inward FDI stocks in OECD countries using a gravity specification.
We utilize a new dataset on formal institutions for the quality of legal, political, and economic institutions, and WVS and EVS for constructing liberal
and nonliberal public opinion.

We confirm our hypotheses and find that most formal institutions influence FDI decisions, with the interesting exception of economic institutions,
which do not have a statistically significant marginal effect. We find there is
a twin set of promoting institutional factors for FDI in the form of origin's
quality of legal institutions and destination's quality of political institutions, and a twin set of detrimental institutional factors for FDI in the
form of origin's quality of political institutions and destination's quality of
legal institutions. It follows that an improvement in the legal framework in
the origin country increases inward FDI to OECD countries, while an
improvement of the relative quality of political institutions of the origin
country has a consistent and negative effect on bilateral FDI stock, which
implies that home investments are seen as relatively more attractive than
international investments when the quality of home political environment
is good. The quality of the legal environment of the receiving OECD country has a surprising depressing marginal effect, while more in line of our
expectations is the positive marginal effect of the political environment in
the destination country.

More interesting than the mere effects of institutional levels are the
effects of institutional distances, that is, the differences between the quality
of institutions in each set of partner countries in each year. We find that
both legal institutional distance and political institutional distance have a

significant and negative effect on inward FDI stocks. Interestingly though, economic institutional difference does not seem to matter. We explain this with the fact that we are studying FDI stocks, which take the different economic rules into account already (that is to say, differences and changes in economic rules are expected), since they are not expected to be the same everywhere and they change frequently, as opposed to political and legal rules, which can have more far-reaching effects. Additionally, the non-responsiveness of FDI stocks to economic institutions can also be seen in the light of stocks reacting much slower (if at all) to quick changes in the economic environment.

We also find that informal institutions matter. Informal institutions such as the beliefs of the public about FDI can have an effect on FDI. We find that a liberal public opinion has a positive marginal effect on FDI, with one lag, while a nonliberal public opinion has a negative marginal effect on FDI, with two lags. However, one effect disappears once we control for the formal institutional environment, which eliminates the effect of liberal public opinion working through government actions. The remaining effect of nonliberal public opinion is reduced due to partial catalyzation through the formal institutional environment, but it is still present as a direct detrimental force for inward FDI stocks, confirming the findings on public opinion and FDI by Jaklič et al. (2011).

Non-favorable attitudes toward economic liberalism seem to be a trend in developed economies, with a significant impact on inward FDI. Data from European Value Study and World Value Survey namely confirm raising protectionism after the crisis; since 1990, OECD countries face continuously rising shares of nonliberal population. Testing the impact of public opinion in gravity specification has proven our hypothesis: liberal public opinion attracts FDI (but it works through formal institutions), while nonliberal attitude reduces inward FDI. Nonliberal public opinion has a statically significant and negative effect at a two year lag. These results imply that a broad range of formal and informal institutions and actors should be considered in FDI decision-making process. Efforts of a variety of actors and institutions, trying to influence public opinion, matter for FDI.

NOTES

1. For example, the worldwide governance indicators (Kaufmann, Kraay, & Mastruzzi, 2013), the Global Competitiveness Report (Sala i Martin, Greenhill, & World Economic Forum, 2011), the Fraser Institute's database (Gwartney,

Lawson, & Hall, 2012), Heritage Foundation's economic freedom, (Miller, Holmes, Roberts, & Kim, 2010), Transparency International Corruption Perception Index Transparency International, 2013), etc.

2. One of the famous examples is hostile public opinion toward FDI (especially Wal-Mart) in retail in India.

3. The emerging markets MNEs phenomenon along with the global crisis has revived new protectionism and nationalism in Europe, where in spite of the efforts to increase FDI inflows, huge challenges for new entries from emerging markets MNEs still exists. Nationalism and hostile public opinion can even more easily develop during and after an economic crisis.

4. Growing outward FDI by Chinese companies in industrialized and especially in developed countries go along the changing patterns of global economic govern-ance; emerging economies intensify efforts to influence institutions or rules of the game in international trade and investment. Since 1990, China intensified the pro-tection of FDI through BITs and the variance of the institutional design of Chinese international investment agreements (IIAs) is huge. Nowadays China is demonstrat-ing a new confidence as an actor of importance in the global governance system for FDI shown by its willingness to engage in BIT negotiations with the United States (Berger, 2011). A number of European countries agreed to BITs in the last decade in spite of (or exactly despite of) the "after Lisbon" intention of EU to centralize the IIAs and that a European Model BIT is underway.

5. Public opinion is often related to FDI impact on labor market, through both job creation and wage effects (Jaklič et al., 2011).

6. The most known attempt at this is Hofstede's cultural dimensions index (Hofstede, 2001), which concentrates on five specific cultural dimensions.

7. As in E036: Private ownership of business should be increased/Government ownership of business should be increased. E037: People should take more responsi-bility to provide for themselves/The government should take more responsibility to ensure that everyone is provided for. E039: Competition is good. It stimulates peo-ple to work hard and develop new ideas/Competition is harmful. It brings the worst in people. All variables are recoded (scale reversed) so that a higher score means a more liberal attitude.

8. The negative coefficient on lngdp_o and lngdp_d cannot be interpreted as a negative marginal effect of GDP on FDI, as the entire influence of GDP is captured by adding the coefficient on GDP and the coefficient on GDP p.c., which then turns positive and remains significant (with dyadic FE it turns slightly negative, but is not significant). It is also worth noting that this also implies a negative effect of origin and destination country population on bilateral FDI, which has been documented by the literature before (see for instance Razin, Sadka, & Tong, September, 2008) and is thus not discussed further.

REFERENCES

Acemoglu, D., & Johnson, S. (2005). Unbundling institutions. *Journal of Political Economy*, *113*(5), 949–995.

Acemoglu, D., Johnson, S., & Robinson, J. A. (2001). The colonial origins of comparative development: An empirical investigation. *American Economic Review*, *91*(5), 1369–1401.

Aizenman, J., & Spiegel, M. M. (2006). Institutional efficiency, monitoring costs and the investment share of FDI. *Review of International Economics*, *14*(4), 683–697.

Aleksynska, M., & Havrylchyk, O. (2013). FDI from the south: The role of institutional distance and natural resources. *European Journal of Political Economy*, *29*(C), 38–53.

Ali, F., Fiess, N., & MacDonald, R. (2010). Do institutions matter for foreign direct investment? *Open Economies Review*, *21*(2), 201–219.

Anderson, J. E., & van Wincoop, E. (2003). Gravity with gravitas: A solution to the border puzzle. *American Economic Review*, *93*(1), 170–192.

Andrés, M. S., Nunnenkamp, P., & Busse, M. (2013). What drives FDI from non-traditional sources? A comparative analysis of the determinants of bilateral FDI flows. *Economics – The Open-Access, Open-Assessment E-Journal*, *7*(1), 1–53.

Bellak, C., Leibrecht, M., & Stehrer, R. (2010). The role of public policy in closing foreign direct investment gaps: An empirical analysis. *Empirica*, *37*(1), 19–46.

Benassy-Quere, A., Coupet, M., & Mayer, T. (2007). Institutional determinants of foreign direct investment. *The World Economy*, *30*(5), 764–782.

Benito, G. R. G., Grogaard, B., & Narula, R. (2003). Environmental influences on MNE subsidiary roles: Economic integration and the Nordic countries. *Journal of International Business Studies*, *34*(5), 443–456.

Berger, A. (2011). The politics of China's investment treaty-making program. In T. Broude, M. L. Busch, & Amelia Porges (Eds.), *The politics of international economic law* (Vol. 1, pp. 162–185). New York, NY: Cambridge University Press.

Bergstrand, J. H., & Egger, P. (2007). A knowledge-and-physical-capital model of international trade flows, foreign direct investment, and multinational enterprises. *Journal of International Economics*, *73*(2), 278–308.

Bevan, A. A., & Estrin, S. (2004). The determinants of foreign direct investment into European transition economies. *Journal of Comparative Economics*, *32*(4), 775–787.

Brennan, L. (2008). *The emergence of southern multinationals. Their impact on Europe*. UK: Palgrave Macmillan.

Campbell, J. L., & Pedersen, O. K. (2007). Institutional competitiveness in the global economy: Denmark, the United States and the varieties of capitalism. *Regulation and Governance*, *1*(3), 230–246.

Chacar, A. S., Newburry, W., & Vissa, B. (2010). Bringing institutions into performance persistence research: Exploring the impact of product, financial, and labor market institutions. *Journal of International Business Studies*, *41*(7), 1119–1140.

Dahan, N. M., Hadani, M., & Schuler, D. A. (2013). The governance challenges of corporate political activity. *Business & Society*, *52*(3), 365–387.

Daniele, V., & Marani, U. (2006). *Do institutions matter for FDI? A comparative analysis for the MENA countries*. MPRA Paper No. 2426. University Library of Munich, Germany.

Delios, A., & Henisz, W. J. (2003). Political hazards, experience, and sequential entry strategies: The international expansion of Japanese firms, 1980–1998. *Strategic Management Journal*, *24*(11), 1153–1164.

Demekas, D. G., Horvath, B., Ribakova, E., & Wu, Y. (2007). Foreign direct investment in European transition economies – The role of policies. *Journal of Comparative Economics*, *35*(2), 369–386.

de Sousa, J. (2012). The currency union effect on trade is decreasing over time. *Economics Letters*, *117*(3), 917–920.

Devereux, M. P., & Griffith, R. (2003). The impact of corporate taxation on the location of capital: A review. *Economic Analysis and Policy (EAP)*, *33*(2), 275–292.

Doh, J. P., & Teegen, H. (2002). Nongovernmental organizations as institutional actors in international business: Theory and implications. *International Business Review*, *11*(6), 665–684.

Dunning, J. H. (1979). Explaining changing patterns of international production: In defence of the eclectic theory. *Oxford Bulletin of Economics and Statistics*, *41*(4), 269–295.

Dunning, J. H. (1981). *International production and the multinational enterprise*. London: Allen & Unwin.

Dunning, J. H. (1988). *Explaining international production*. London: Unwin Hyman.

Dunning, J. H., & Lundan, S. M. (2008). *Multinational enterprises and the global economy* (2nd ed.). Cheltenham, UK: Edgar Elgar Publishing Limited.

European Values Study Group. (2012). European values study.

Freedom House. (2012). Freedom of the press.

Grosse, R. (2005). Cambridge University Press.

Gwartney, J., Lawson, R., & Hall, J. (2012). *2012 Economic freedom dataset*. Published in *Economic Freedom of the World: 2012 Annual Report*.

Habib, M., & Zurawicki, L. (2002). Corruption and foreign direct investment. *Journal of International Business Studies*, *33*(2), 291–307.

Head, K., Mayer, T., & Ries, J. (2010). The erosion of colonial trade linkages after independence. *Journal of International Economics*, *81*(1), 1–14.

Head, K., & Ries, J. (2008). FDI as an outcome of the market for corporate control: Theory and evidence. *Journal of International Economics*, *74*(1), 2–20.

Helpman, E. (2006). Trade, FDI, and the organization of firms. *Journal of Economic Literature*, *44*(3), 589–630.

Hofstede, G. (2001). *Culture's consequences: Comparing values, behaviors, institutions and organizations across nations* (2nd ed.). Thousand Oaks, CA: Sage Publications.

IMF. (2003). *World economic outlook* (Report). International Monetary Fund (IMF).

Jaklič, A., Kunčič, A., & Burger, A. (2011). The public and foreign direct investments. *Javnost — The Public*, *18*(5), 23–44.

Jakobsen, J., & Jakobsen, T. G. (2011). Economic nationalism and FDI: The impact of public opinion on foreign direct investment in emerging markets, 1990–2005. *Society and Business Review*, *6*(1), 61–76.

Jonathan, E., & Akiko, T. (1994). Bilateralism and regionalism in Japanese and U.S. trade and direct foreign investment patterns. *Journal of the Japanese and International Economies*, *8*(4), 478–510.

Júlio, P., Pinheiro-Alves, R., & Tavares, J. (2011, September). *FDI and institutional reform in Portugal*. GEE Papers 0040, Gabinete de Estratégia e Estudos, Ministério da Economia e da Inovaça o.

Kaufmann, D., Kraay, A., & Mastruzzi, M. (2013). Worldwide governance indicators.

Kostevc, C., Redek, T., & Susjan, A. (2007). Foreign direct investment and institutional environment in transition economies. *Transition Studies Review*, *14*(1), 40–54.

Kunčič, A. (2014). Institutional quality dataset. *Journal of Institutional Economics*, *10*, 135–161.

Lambell, R., Ramia, G., Nyland, C., & Michelotti, M. (2008). NGOs and international business research: Progress, prospects and problems. *International Journal of Management Reviews, 10*(1), 75–92.

Levchenko, A. A. (2007). Institutional quality and international trade. *Review of Economic Studies, 74*(3), 791–819.

Markusen, J. R., & Venables, A. J. (1998). Multinational firms and the new trade theory. *Journal of International Economics, 46*(2), 183–203.

Markusen, J. R., & Venables, A. J. (2000). The theory of endowment, intra-industry and multi-national trade. *Journal of International Economics, 52*(2), 209–234.

Matyas, L. (1997). Proper econometric specification of the gravity model. *The World Economy, 20*(3), 363–368.

Mayer, T., & Zignago, S. (2011, December). *Notes on CEPII's distances measures: The GeoDist database*. Working Paper 2011–25. CEPII Research Center.

Miller, T., Holmes, K. R., Roberts, J. M., & Kim, A. B. (2010). Index of economic freedom.

North, D. C. (1990). *Institutions, institutional change, and economic performance*. New York, NY: Cambridge University Press.

North, D. C. (1993, September). *The new institutional economics and development*. Economic History 9309002, EconWPA.

North, D. C. (2005). *Understanding the process of economic change*. Princeton, NJ: Princeton University Press.

Pedersen, O. K. (2010). Institutional competitiveness: How nations came to compete. In G. Morgan, J. L. Campbell, C. Crouch, O. K. Pedersen, & R. Whitley (Eds.), *The oxford handbook of comparative institutional analysis*. New York, NY: Oxford University Press.

Organisation for Economic Cooperation and Development (OECD). (2012). Oecd.stat.

Ozer, M., & Alakent, E. (2012). The influence of ownership structure on how firms make corporate political strategy choices. *Business & Society, 52*(3), 451–472.

Prüfer, P., & Tondl, G. (2008). *The FDI-growth nexus in Latin America: The role of source countries and local conditions*. Technical Report. Tilburg University, The Netherlands.

Ramamurti, R. (March 2001). The obsolescing "bargaining model"? MNC-host developing country relations revisited. *Journal of International Business Studies, 32*(1), 23–39.

Razin, A., Sadka, E., & Tong, H. (2008). Bilateral FDI flows: Threshold barriers and productivity shocks. *CESifo Economic Studies, 54*(3), 451–470.

Sala i Martin, X., Greenhill, R., & World Economic Forum. (2011). *The Global Competitiveness Report 2011–2012*. World Economic Forum, Geneva.

Santos Silva, J. M. C., & Tenreyro, S. (2006). The log of gravity. *The Review of Economics and Statistics, 88*(4), 641–658.

Sauvant, K. (2008). *The rise of transnational corporations from emerging markets*. Cheltenham, UK: Edward Elgar.

Skippari, M., & Pajunen, K. (2010). MNE-NGO-host government relationships in the escalation of an FDI conflict. *Business & Society, 49*(4), 619–651.

Stein, E., & Daude, C. (2001, August). Institutions, integration, and the location of foreign direct investment: Mimeo. Inter-American Development Bank, Research Department.

Teegen, H., Doh, J. P., & Vachani, S. (2004). The importance of nongovernmental organizations (NGOs) in global governance and value creation: An international business research agenda. *Journal of International Business Studies, 35*(6), 463–483.

The PRS Group. (2013). International country risk guide.

The World Bank. (2013). World development indicators 2012.

Transparency International. (2013). Corruption perceptions index.

UNCTAD. (2008). *Transnational corporations and the infrastructure challenge.* World Investment Report. United Nations Conference on Trade and Development (UNCTAD), New York, NY.

UNCTAD. (2009). *Transnational corporations, agricultural production and development.* World Investment Report. United Nations Conference on Trade and Development (UNCTAD), New York, NY.

UNCTAD. (2010). *Investing in a low-carbon economy.* World Investment Report. United Nations Conference on Trade and Development (UNCTAD), New York, NY.

UNCTAD. (2011). *Non-equity modes of international production and development.* World Investment Report. United Nations Conference on Trade and Development (UNCTAD), New York, NY.

UNCTAD. (2012). *Towards a new generations of investment policies.* World Investment Report. United Nations Conference on Trade and Development (UNCTAD), New York, NY.

UNCTAD. (2013). *Global value chains: Investment and trade for development.* World Investment Report. United Nations Conference on Trade and Development (UNCTAD), New York, NY.

Wei, S.-J. (2000). How taxing is corruption on international investors? *The Review of Economics and Statistics, 82*(1), 1−11.

Wheeler, D., & Mody, A. (1992). International investment location decisions: The case of U.S. firms. *Journal of International Economics, 33*(1−2), 57−76.

Williamson, O. E. (2000). The new institutional economics: Taking stock, looking ahead. *Journal of Economic Literature, 38*(3), 595−613.

WIPO. (2012). WIPO statistics database.

World Values Survey Association. (2012). World values survey.

APPENDIX

Data

Table A1. Gravity and FDI-Specific Variables Used.

Variable	Definition	Variation Dimension	Source
Gravity variables			
FDIstock	Inward FDI stock in mill USD	*ijt*	OECD (2012)
gdp	Nominal GDP in mill USD	*it* and *jt*	The World Bank (2013)
gdpcap	Nominal GDP per capita in USD	*it* and *jt*	The World Bank (2013)
distance	Average distance between two countries based on bilateral distances between the largest cities of those two countries, weighted by the share of the city in the overall country's population	*ij*	Head et al. (2010)
common_border	Dummy for sharing a border	*ij*	Head et al. (2010)
common_language	Dummy for sharing a language	*ij*	Head et al. (2010)
common_legal	Dummy for common legal origins	*ij*	Head et al. (2010)
colonial_history	Dummy for country pair ever being in a colonial relationship	*ij*	Head et al. (2010)
rta	Dummy for sharing a regional trade agreement	*ijt*	(de Sousa, 2012)
wto	Dummy for both countries being members of WTO	*ijt*	Head et al. (2010)
common_currency	Dummy for sharing a currency	*ijt*	Head et al. (2010)
FDI-specific variables			
inflation	Host country's inflation rate	*jt*	The World Bank (2013)
tax_rate	Host country's total tax rate (% of commercial profits)	*jt*	The World Bank (2013)
rd	Host country's research and development expenditure (% of GDP)	*jt*	The World Bank (2013)
gdp_growth	Host country's real GDP growth	*jt*	The World Bank (2013)
trade	Host country's openness to trade, sum of imports and exports as a share of GDP	*jt*	The World Bank (2013)
ict	Host country's infrastructure, sum of telephone mainlines, mobile phone subscribers and internet connections per 1,000 inhabitants	*jt*	citetwdi

Table A1. (*Continued*)

Variable	Definition	Variation Dimension	Source
resource_rents	Host country's total resource rents as a share of GDP	*jt*	The World Bank (2013)
patents	Host country's patent applications by residents and nonresidents, divided by total population in thousands	*jt*	WIPO (2012)
FDIstockavg	Host country's average total FDI stock	*j*	OECD (2012)

Table A2. Institutional Variables Used.

Variable	Definition	Variation Dimension	Source
legal_inst	Relative quality of legal institutions	*it* and *jt*	Kunčič (2014)
political_inst	Relative quality of political institutions	*it* and *jt*	Kunčič (2014)
economic_inst	Relative quality of economic institutions	*it* and *jt*	Kunčič (2014)
abs(legal_diff)	Absolute difference between the two institutional measures	*ijt*	Kunčič (2014) and own calculations
abs(political_diff)	Absolute difference between the two institutional measures	*ijt*	Kunčič (2014) and own calculations
abs(economic_diff)	Absolute difference between the two institutional measures	*ijt*	Kunčič (2014) and own calculations
liberal	Share of people with liberal economic attitudes	*it* and *jt*	EVS and WVS
not_liberal	Share of people with nonliberal economic attitudes	*it* and *jt*	EVS and WVS

Full Results

Table A3.   Full Results with Public Opinion.

dep. var. ln(FDIstock)	1	2	3	4	5	6
ln(gdp_o)	-2.161***	-1.884***	-0.810	-0.675	-0.384	-0.212
	(0.688)	(0.673)	(0.730)	(1.135)	(1.041)	(0.856)
ln(gdp_d)	-2.416	-5.639***	-1.700	4.249*	1.122	-0.477
	(1.480)	(1.518)	(2.289)	(2.376)	(2.271)	(2.624)
ln(gdpcap_o)	2.331***	2.007***	1.061	1.150	0.739	0.711
	(0.703)	(0.678)	(0.742)	(1.152)	(1.060)	(0.893)
ln(gdpcap_d)	2.735*	6.117***	1.790	-3.881*	-1.140	0.604
	(1.525)	(1.578)	(2.408)	(2.352)	(2.319)	(2.712)
rta	0.141	0.111	0.124	0.0262	0.0840	-0.0775
	(0.192)	(0.161)	(0.209)	(0.244)	(0.230)	(0.232)
wto	-0.631***	-0.498***	-0.463**	-0.417	0.000867	-0.179
	(0.160)	(0.178)	(0.189)	(0.261)	(0.314)	(0.285)
common_currency	0.909***	0.970***	0.919***	0.919***	0.809***	0.636***
	(0.297)	(0.245)	(0.277)	(0.314)	(0.253)	(0.245)
legal_inst_o				0.441**	0.316	0.583**
				(0.221)	(0.240)	(0.240)
political_inst_o				-0.662***	-0.690***	-0.688***
				(0.203)	(0.227)	(0.210)
economic_inst_o				-0.107	0.108	0.0160
				(0.173)	(0.183)	(0.186)
legal_inst_d				0.189	-0.385	-0.586
				(0.327)	(0.320)	(0.387)
political_inst_d				-0.415	0.552	0.613
				(0.428)	(0.516)	(0.428)
economic_inst_d				-0.388	0.249	0.339
				(0.277)	(0.273)	(0.344)

	(1)	(2)	(3)	(4)	(5)	(6)
abs(legal_diff)				-0.136	-0.239	-0.271
				(0.195)	(0.189)	(0.193)
abs(political_diff)				-0.0644	-0.0398	-0.00891
				(0.195)	(0.204)	(0.190)
abs(economic_diff)				-0.175	-0.194	-0.0306
				(0.161)	(0.152)	(0.149)
liberal	0.418			0.0123		
	(0.373)			(0.414)		
nonliberal	0.708			0.168		
	(1.070)			(1.238)		
L.liberal		0.692*			0.572	
		(0.372)			(0.417)	
L.nonliberal		0.834			0.535	
		(1.112)			(1.276)	
L2.liberal			-0.527			-0.721
			(0.492)			(0.507)
L2.nonliberal			-4.564***			-2.599*
			(1.243)			(1.401)
Constant	-24.77***	-36.61***	-12.87	8.178	2.922	-5.465
	(7.733)	(7.878)	(10.88)	(10.00)	(10.24)	(11.72)
Observations	9,147	9,385	7,853	5,154	5,481	4,908
R^2	0.942	0.939	0.956	0.950	0.942	0.953
Time FE	Yes	Yes	Yes	Yes	Yes	Yes
Origin FE	Yes	Yes	Yes	Yes	Yes	Yes
Destination FE	Yes	Yes	Yes	Yes	Yes	Yes
Dyadic FE	Yes	Yes	Yes	Yes	Yes	Yes
Formal inst.	No	No	No	Yes	Yes	Yes

Country pair robust standard errors within parentheses.
***$p < 0.01$, **$p < 0.05$, *$p < 0.1$.

CHAPTER 8

IS DISTANCE THE SAME ACROSS CULTURES? A MEASUREMENT-EQUIVALENCE PERSPECTIVE ON THE CULTURAL DISTANCE PARADOX

André van Hoorn and Robbert Maseland

ABSTRACT

Purpose − *The purpose of this chapter is to make sense of the cultural distance paradox through a basic assessment of the cross-cultural comparability of cultural distance measures. Cultural distance between a base country and partner countries is a key construct in international business (IB). However, we propose that what exactly is measured by cultural distance is unique for each country that is chosen as the base country to/from which cultural distance to a set of partner countries is calculated.*

Methodology/approach − *We use a mathematical argument to establish that cultural distance may correlate rather differently with the culture of partner countries depending on which base country one considers, for example, the United States or China. We then use empirical analysis to*

Multinational Enterprises, Markets and Institutional Diversity
Progress in International Business Research, Volume 9, 207−227
ISSN: 1745-8862/doi:10.1108/S1745-886220140000009008

show the relevance of this argument, using Hofstede's data on national culture for 69 countries.

Findings — *Results show that cultural distance indeed has very different correlations with partner country culture, depending on which country one selects as the base country in one's distance calculations.*

Practical implications — *Implication of our findings is that measured cultural distance is not equivalent across different base countries. The effect of cultural distance on such issues as foreign market entry mode or market selection, therefore, lacks international generalizability.*

Originality/value — *This chapter presents the first assessment of the cross-cultural comparability of cultural distance. Paradoxical findings that plague extant cultural distance research may be understood from the found lack of measurement equivalence.*

Keywords: Distance; culture; measurement equivalence; institutional profile; Kogut-Singh index; validity

INTRODUCTION

Wildly popular, the limitations of measures of cultural distance have been much discussed in international business (IB) (Shenkar, 2001; Tung & Verbeke, 2010; Zaheer, Schomaker, & Nachum, 2012). Mostly, the debate concerns the quality of inputs to distance indexes, not least Hofstede's dimensions of national culture, or the possibility for improved distance measures, for instance, through incorporating cultural variation that occurs within countries (Beugelsdijk, Maseland, Onrust, van Hoorn, & Slangen, 2014; van Hoorn, 2014b). Important and insightful as these improvements are, they unfortunately remain rather disconnected from the actual problems faced by the cultural distance literature, specifically the many ambiguous and conflicting findings that characterize distance research (see, among others, Harzing, 2003; Kirkman, Lowe, & Gibson, 2006; Tihanyi, Griffith, & Russell, 2005; Zhao, Luo, & Suh, 2004). For instance, using a Mahalanobis distance index (Berry, Guillén, & Zhou, 2010) instead of the common Kogut-Singh index (Kogut & Singh, 1988) does little to address the contradiction that higher cultural distance is associated with both *wholly owned* entry modes (Anand & Delios, 1997; Padmanabhan & Cho,

1996) and *shared-control* entry modes (Erramilli & Rao, 1993; Kogut & Singh, 1988) (see Brouthers & Brouthers, 2001).

We seek to make sense of these muddled findings, known as the cultural distance paradox (Brouthers & Brouthers, 2001), following the most basic approach available to a researcher, which is to ask whether we are actually measuring what we think we are measuring. Validity is a fundamental feature of measurement, referring to the ability of a measure to capture the construct it is supposed to capture. Many criteria for assessing validity exist. The standard approach to validity assessment is to consider relationships between the measured construct and other (empirical) constructs.[1] For the kind of cross-cultural comparative research that characterizes IB, a particular validity concern is cross-cultural measurement equivalence (Hult et al., 2008; Mullen, 1995; Singh, 1995), meaning whether the same construct is being measured across different cultures or countries. Hence, in this chapter we seek to answer the following question: can cultural distance measures be meaningfully compared across countries?

Standard tests of measurement equivalence (also known as measurement invariance) involve confirmatory factor analysis of multiple items or indicators, where factor loadings, residual variances, et cetera should be more or less the same across groups, notably across countries. As cultural distance is not a latent construct but measured by a single indicator, we cannot rely on such tests. However, the idea behind these tests is to assess the comparability of relationships, specifically whether the various items or indicators relate to the latent construct in the same way across the different groups. This focus on relationships, in turn, fits with the established idea of using relationships with other variables to assess the validity of a particular measure (cf. Cronbach & Meehl, 1955). That is, measurement equivalence requires that a measure's relationships with other (country) factors are consistent across countries. If a measure does not pass the criterion of having cross-culturally consistent relationships with other factors, we should doubt the measure's cross-cultural comparability. To be sure, meeting the criterion of cross-culturally consistent relationships with other country factors is the only necessary and not a sufficient condition for measurement equivalence, but a discussion of further criteria is beyond the scope of the present analysis.

Starting point for our actual assessment of the measurement equivalence of cultural distance is the recent work by van Hoorn and Maseland (2013). They show how the institutional distance literature tends to conflate institutional distance between a base country and its potential partner countries with the institutional profile of the partner countries. The basis for their claim is that while a base country's location on the institutional spectrum is fixed, the location of partner countries on this spectrum varies with partner countries' institutional profile. As the location of partner countries on the institutional spectrum also determines their distance to the base country, we end up with a situation in which partner countries' institutional profile correlates strongly with the institutional distance of these countries to the base country. van Hoorn and Maseland (2013) find that this effect can be so strong as to render partner country institutional profile and institutional distance between the base country and the partner country (statistically) indistinguishable.

We adapt van Hoorn and Maseland's (2013) work to consider culture and cultural distance and focus on one particular feature of their analysis, which is that the exact correlation between institutional (i.e., cultural) distance and partner country institutional profile (i.e., partner country culture) may vary for different base countries. In fact, in van Hoorn and Maseland's (2013) analysis, the correlation between institutional distance and partner country institutional profile may vary from exactly −1 to exactly +1, and anything in between. Our extension is to use this finding to challenge the measurement equivalence of cultural distance measures, applying the cross-cultural relationship-consistency criterion discussed above.

In short, we propose that cultural distance measures indeed lack measurement equivalence. Following van Hoorn and Maseland (2013), the claim is that, across different base countries, cultural distance correlates differently with partner country culture and therefore does not meet the criterion of cross-culturally consistent relationships with other factors. Concretely, then, we cannot compare the effect that cultural distance has on a dependent variable (say, foreign market entry mode or market selection) when the United States is the base country, with the effect that cultural distance has on the same dependent variable when China is the base country. Empirical analysis demonstrates the real-life significance of this argument, which is essentially mathematical (cf. van Hoorn & Maseland, 2013). In a sample of 69 countries, we find that cultural distance correlates with partner country culture in a unique way for each base country considered. Moreover, the differences between the base countries can be large, with correlations between cultural distance and partner country culture ranging from −1 to +1, just as in van Hoorn and Maseland (2013).

Overall, this chapter brings an important new perspective to the cultural distance paradox and the general lack of strong and consistent results in the cultural distance literature. Because cultural distance measures are unique for each base country, distance measured for firms going to and from one country (say, China) is incomparable to distance measured for firms going to and from another country (say, the United States). Key implication is that studies of the effect of cultural distance lack international generalizability. "Paradoxes" subsequently are a logical consequence. Specifically, when cultural distance correlates (strongly) positively with partner country culture for one base country but (strongly) negatively for another base country, there is actually good reason to expect that empirical results on the effects of cultural distance will not be consistent and/or even contradictory.

The wider implication of our findings concerns the use of distance as the master metaphor in IB. Our analysis is not meant to criticize the idea of distance as a crucial challenge for MNEs (e.g., Ghemawat, 2001; Zaheer et al., 2012), which we find very appealing indeed. However, such intuitive appeal in and of itself is not enough to make the distance metaphor or the cultural distance construct valuable for IB research. Hence, we call for more theorizing on how exactly the idea of distance can be applied in IB and on what exactly it entails for an MNE to expand globally and having to manage operations in cultural environments that are different from its home-country cultural environment. With a strengthened theoretical foundation to build on, we can then improve our measures of cultural distance and our empirical analysis of how distance shapes cross-border business activities.

The remainder of this chapter is organized as follows. We start with a brief review of cultural distance and its measurement in the next section. In the section "Partner Country Culture and the Measurement Equivalence of Cultural Distance," we review and extend the mathematical part of van Hoorn and Maseland's (2013) analysis for the case of cultural distance and partner country culture and make a proposition as to the measurement equivalence of cultural distance. The section "Empirical Demonstration" presents an empirical demonstration of the incomparability problem that we identify and shows the extent to which cultural distance indeed lacks cross-culturally consistent relationships with other country factors, specifically partner country culture. We discuss the implications of our findings in the section "Discussion."

CULTURAL DISTANCE AND ITS MEASUREMENT

Cultural distance between two countries, a base country and a partner country, can be defined as the degree of dissimilarity of the national cultures of the two countries (Shenkar, 2001). Typically, researchers construct measures of cultural distance by subtracting base and partner countries scores on one or more dimensions of culture. The base country thereby can be either the home or the host country in an analysis, as when multinational firms from the United States face a cultural distance when entering partner country markets (the United States as the home country) or as when multinational firms from partner countries face a cultural distance when entering the U.S. market (the United States as the host country). The best-known cultural distance measure is the index by Kogut and Singh (1988) (Bae & Salomon, 2010; Berry et al., 2010; Drogendijk & Zander, 2010; Em, 2011). The formula for this index is as follows:

$$CD_j = \frac{1}{4} \sum_{k=1}^{4} \frac{(N_{kp} - N_{kc})^2}{V_k} \tag{1}$$

where CD_j is the cultural distance of the pth partner country from a base country denoted by c, N_{kp} indicates the national culture score on the kth dimension of country p, and V_k is the variance in country scores on culture dimension k. Hence, the formula presents the cultural distance between base country c and partner country p as the sum of squared differences between country c's culture dimension scores and the culture dimension scores of the partner country, corrected for differences in the variances of each dimension. The number four in the formula reflects that the Kogut-Singh index is meant to be comprehensive and collapses distance scores on Hofstede's (1980) four original dimensions (individualism, power distance, uncertainty avoidance, and masculinity/femininity) into a single measure. Only very few studies expand on Kogut and Singh's (1988) original measure to include the dimensions of long-term orientation or indulgence versus restraint that Hofstede and collaborators added to Hofstede's framework after follow-up research (e.g., Hofstede, Hofstede, & Minkov, 2010).

Other measures of cultural distance exist (e.g., Berry et al., 2010) but these measures all share the two essential features of the Kogut-Singh index, which is the application of both a horizontal and a vertical transformation of the underlying data (van Hoorn & Kunst, 2014). The horizontal transformation thereby refers to the reduction in the number of indicators (say from four to one), while the vertical transformation refers to the actual calculation of the distance between a base country and potential partner countries. The main difference between the various cultural distance measures used in the literature is whether the vertical transformation takes place before the horizontal transformation as with the Kogut-Singh index or after the horizontal transformation as with the Mahalanobis index of Berry et al. (2010). The core idea of cultural distance as being the differences between country scores on various cultural indicators is the same in the various measures.

PARTNER COUNTRY CULTURE AND THE MEASUREMENT EQUIVALENCE OF CULTURAL DISTANCE

Why Cultural Distance and Partner Country Culture Are Correlated

As just described, cultural distance between a base country and a partner country is essentially measured by calculating the difference between the base country's score on some dimension of national culture and a partner country's score on the same dimension (see Eq. (1)). When calculating cultural distance for, say the United States, obviously the base country is always the same. The partner country may vary, however, being China, Japan, Russia, or Brazil, etc. When calculating cultural distance, we thus repeatedly detract the same constant, which is set by the base country's culture scores. The result is that the only potential source of variation in cultural distance is the variation in the culture scores of the partner countries (see van Hoorn & Maseland, 2013).

Panel A in Fig. 1, adapted from van Hoorn and Maseland (2013), illustrates the process of calculating cultural distance (vertical transformation) for a base country and three partner countries. We call this base country c and denote the three partner countries by $p1$, $p2$, and $p3$. The partner countries are characterized by different cultures, signified by their different culture scores on the Y-axis.[2] Their unique culture puts each partner country at a similarly unique distance to the base country. In fact, cultural distance between the base country and the three partner countries is straightforwardly given by the differences between the base country's culture score (c) and partner country culture scores ($p1$, $p2$, and $p3$): $c-p1$, $c-p2$, and $c-p3$.[3] The main thing to note is that in this scenario the base country's culture score c is fixed and the same for all partner countries. Hence, for all partner countries, cultural distance is calculated by taking their culture scores and subtracting the same constant. As a consequence, the variation in cultural distance within the set of partner countries is completely determined by the variation in culture scores among these partner countries.

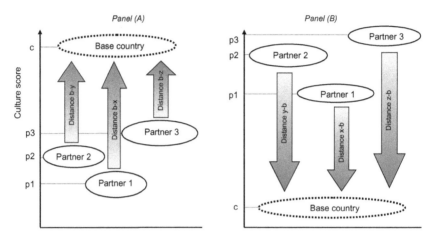

Fig. 1. Two Scenarios for Cultural Distance Calculations (Vertical Transformation).

Mathematically, the distance scores $c - p1$, $c - p2$, and $c - p3$ correlate perfectly with the culture scores $p1$, $p2$, and $p3$ and this will also show when using the cultural distance of the base country to these partner countries in a statistical analysis.

Why Cultural Distance and Partner Country Culture Correlate Differently across Base Countries

The above-mentioned point of cultural distance and partner country culture being correlated is the main insight of van Hoorn and Maseland (2013). However, the example that we used constitutes an extreme case with all partner countries having culture scores below the culture score of the base country. In practice, partner countries can score both higher and lower than the base country, which, as it turns out, affects the exact nature of the correlation between cultural distance and the culture of the partner countries. We can again illustrate this point using a figure (panel B in Fig. 1, also adapted from van Hoorn & Maseland, 2013).

With all partner countries having culture scores higher than the culture score of the base country, panel B in Fig. 1 depicts the opposite case of the situation in panel A in Fig. 1. At the same time, we still have a situation in which base country culture is fixed at a certain level c and therefore the same for all partner countries. Accordingly, the variation in cultural distance between this partner country and the set of partner countries remains entirely driven by the variation in culture scores among the partner countries. Applying the same mathematical notation as before, cultural distance between the base country and the three partner countries is now equal to $p1 - c$, $p2 - c$, and $p3 - c$.[4] The essential difference between panel A and panel B does not lie in the extent to which cultural distance and partner country culture are correlated, however. Rather, the essential difference lies in the direction of the correlation. In both panel A and panel B, the correlation between cultural distance and partner country culture is perfect, but the sign of the coefficient is negative for the case depicted in panel A in Fig. 1, while the sign is positive for the case depicted in panel B in Fig. 1. In fact, the correlation between a single base country and the culture of its potential partner countries may vary from exactly -1 to exactly $+1$, and anything in between (see van Hoorn & Maseland, 2013). When most partner countries have a culture score below the culture score of the base country, the correlation between cultural distance and partner country culture is negative, while this correlation is positive for a base country that has a culture score below the culture score of most of its partner countries.

The Cross-Cultural (In)Comparability of Cultural Distance

What are the implications of the above-mentioned results for the cross-cultural comparability of cultural distance? We find that the differences in the exact nature of the correlation between cultural distance and the culture of the partner countries imply that cultural distance measures lack measurement equivalence. The reason is that cultural distance does not exhibit cross-culturally consistent relationships with other country factors. Rather, cultural distance correlates uniquely with partner country culture for each base country: cultural distance calculated for one base country may correlate strongly positively with partner country culture, but for another base country this correlation can be strongly negative or close to zero. We thus have the following proposition:

Proposition 1. Across base countries, cultural distance correlates differently with partner country culture and, therefore, cultural distance measures lack measurement equivalence.

The importance of Proposition 1 lies in its implications for cultural distance research, especially empirical cultural distance research. Notably, if cultural distance cannot be meaningfully compared across base countries, then how can we compare the results of extant studies involving different base countries? In the final section of this chapter, we discuss such ramifications, particularly by using our findings to make sense of the cultural distance paradox. First, however, we turn to an empirical demonstration of the above-mentioned argument that cultural distance measures do not pass the criterion of having cross-culturally consistent relationships with other country factors (specifically with partner country culture).

EMPIRICAL DEMONSTRATION

As in van Hoorn and Maseland (2013), the essential proof of our proposition that cultural distance measures lack cross-cultural comparability is mathematical. Bringing the proposition to data allows us to see the real-life significance of the proposition, however. Typical measures of cultural distance provide a one-dimensional representation of the cultural dissimilarities between a base country and a partner country. Hence, a first step in empirically assessing the extent to which cultural distance measures lack measurement equivalence is to construct a measure of national culture that is commensurable to the typical cultural distance index, meaning that this measure of national culture also needs to be one dimensional (cf. the stylized scenarios for cultural distance calculation depicted in Fig. 1). We take up the construction of this one-dimensional measure of (partner country) culture in the first part of this section, which also describes the other data and variables in our analysis and our general method of calculating correlations between cultural distance and partner country culture as a way to judge how cultural distance fares on the criterion of having cross-culturally consistent relationships with other country factors. The second part then demonstrates empirically our claim concerning the cross-cultural comparability of cultural distance measures.

Data and Method

Constructing a One-Dimensional Measure of National Culture
How can we obtain a one-dimensional measure of national culture that is commensurable to cultural distance indexes that similarly aggregate a set of culture dimensions into a single measure? We used principal

components analysis that was pre-set to force the selected set of culture dimensions into a single factor. This principal components analysis disregarded traditional criteria concerning the identification of factors but with good reason, namely to get to a single measure of national culture that is commensurable to a one-dimensional measure of cultural distance.

Data concerned Hofstede's (1980) original four dimensions of national culture (individualism, power distance, uncertainty avoidance, and masculinity/femininity) and are available from Hofstede's personal website, http://www.geerthofstede.nl. We used the original four dimensions only, as most extant cultural distance research has also only used these dimensions, and not the dimensions that have been added to Hofstede's (1980) framework later (see, for instance, Hofstede et al., 2010). We dropped data that did not concern countries but concerned, for instance, subnational regions such as French-speaking Canada and English-speaking Canada or supranational units such as "Arab countries." After removing these observations, the sample covered 69 countries for which we had scores on all four dimensions of national culture. The resulting factor is mostly based on countries' scores on individualism and power distance, which is consistent with how Hofstede (1980) constructed these dimensions, namely by breaking up a broader initial factor in two subfactors, which he then labeled individualism and power distance. We reverse coded the resulting culture factor so that we find Guatemala at the low end, scoring −1.96 on the standardized culture factor (mean = 0.00; SD = 1.00), and Denmark at the high end, scoring 2.16. The exact loadings on our one-dimensional culture factor are 0.86 and −0.87 for individualism and power distance, respectively, compared to −0.51 for uncertainty avoidance and −0.07 for masculinity/femininity. To save space, we do not report descriptive statistics, as these would be different for all 69 potential base countries. Complete data are available on request, however, while Column 1 of Table A1 in the appendix presents scores on the culture factor for all countries in our sample.

Measure of Cultural Distance
We measure cultural distance by calculating a Mahalanobis index as in Berry et al. (2010). The key feature of the Mahalanobis distance index is that it assigns weights to the separate dimensions of national culture based on the intercorrelations between these dimensions. Hence, Mahalanobis distance matches the culture factor that we have just calculated perfectly.

Assessing the Cross-Cultural Consistency of Cultural Distance's Relationship with Other Country Factors

Following the mathematical analysis in the preceding section, our approach to empirically demonstrating cultural distance's lack of measurement equivalence involves calculating correlations between cultural distance and partner country culture, separately for all potential base countries from our sample. We find that cultural distance fails on the cross-cultural relationship-consistency criterion if the correlations between cultural distance and partner country culture indeed vary considerably across base countries.

For our empirical demonstration, we initially consider a sample of two countries, each of which resembles one of the extreme cases depicted in panels A and B in Fig. 1. The reason for focusing on two extreme cases is the mathematical insight that when a base country has a higher culture score than most of its partner countries, the correlation between cultural distance and partner country culture is negative and that this correlation is positive when the base country has a lower culture score than most of its partner countries. Hence, focusing on two extreme cases is the most straightforward way to assess the extent to which cultural distance lacks cross-culturally consistent relationships with other factors, specifically with partner country culture. The two countries that we selected are the United States and China. The United States has a score of 1.63 on the culture factor and therefore scores close to the high end of the culture factor. Similarly, China has a score of −0.53 on the culture factor and therefore scores close to the low end of the culture factor. For completeness, we added a third base country to this sample, namely a country that holds a middle ground on the culture factor. This country is Belgium, which scores 0.17 on the culture factor, close to the average score of 0.00.[5] For these three base countries, we expect the following (cross-culturally inconsistent) relationships between cultural distance and partner country culture:

- For the United States, the correlation between cultural distance and partner country culture is negative, possibly approaching the upper bound of $r = -1$.
- For China, the correlation between cultural distance and partner country culture is positive, possibly approaching the upper bound of $r = +1$.
- For Belgium, the correlation between cultural distance and partner country culture is almost zero.

Below we first present detailed empirical results for these three base countries, before considering the complete set of 69 countries for which we had data on national culture.

Results

Table 1 presents the results for our empirical demonstration of the proposition that concluded the mathematical analysis in the previous section. Results show striking differences in the correlation between cultural distance and partner country culture for the three base countries that we selected, just as we expected. More importantly, the problem of cultural distance lacking measurement equivalence does not seem a mere theoretical issue. In fact, real-life correlations between cultural distance and partner country culture can be almost diametrically opposed ($r = -0.99$ for the United States versus $r = +0.82$ for China). Importantly, we find these strikingly large differences in the relationship between cultural distance and partner country culture, even though the base countries that we considered are not the countries scoring most extreme on the culture factor.

Considering all 69 countries in our sample, we obtained similar results (column 2 of Table A1 in the appendix). In fact, in this case, the correlations between cultural distance and partner country culture actually ranged

Table 1. Cross-Cultural Inconsistencies in the Relationship between Cultural Distance and Partner Country Culture for Selected Base Countries.

$N = 68$	Partner Country Scores on the Culture Factor
1 Cultural distance to/from base country with the *United States* as the base country	−0.99
2 Cultural distance to/from base country with *China* as the base country	0.82
3 Cultural distance to/from base country with *Belgium* as the base country	0.05

Notes: Table reports correlation coefficients. For calculating the correlations, we have excluded the scores of the base countries' themselves because, by construction, they have zero distance to the base country, leaving a sample of 68 observations. The culture factor is obtained including the selected base countries ($n = 69$). Sources for the data are Hofstede's personal website (http://www.geerthofstede.nl) and own calculations. Complete country data are available on request.

between exactly −1 and exactly +1, depending on the specific base country considered. Overall, we thus have strong and comprehensive empirical evidence that we cannot simply compare cultural distance measures for different base countries, as these measures are capturing very different things.

DISCUSSION

Both our mathematical analysis and our empirical demonstration are unequivocal about the lack of measurement equivalence of cultural distance measures. In this final section, we discuss implications of these findings, particularly for cultural distance research. We do so mainly by relating our findings to the cultural distance paradox, which is highly empirical. Because we find that the implications of our findings reach beyond empirical research strictly, we add a short discussion of distance as the master metaphor in IB.

Measurement Equivalence and the Cultural Distance Paradox

What does it mean for empirical cultural distance research that cultural distance measures lack measurement equivalence? The most basic ramification is that we can no longer generalize effects of cultural distance found for one base country to another base country. Thus, when cultural distance is found to have a particular effect when considering Country A as base country, this effect may very well be different when considering Country B as base country. Indeed, the effect of cultural distance can be smaller or larger for Country B than for Country A or even be overturned altogether, simply because cultural distance does not have consistent relations with other country factors across Country A and Country B.

The cultural distance paradox refers to a specific case in which the effect of cultural distance on a dependent variable is far from unequivocal. Brouthers and Brouthers (2001) introduce the term cultural distance paradox to refer to the contradictory findings on cultural distance as a determinant of entry mode by Anand and Delios (1997) and Padmanabhan and Cho (1996) on the one hand and Kogut and Singh (1988) and Erramilli and Rao (1993) on the other hand. Specifically, whereas Anand and Delios (1997) and Padmanabhan and Cho (1996) report evidence that higher cultural distance is associated with *wholly owned* entry modes, Kogut and

Singh (1988) and Erramilli and Rao (1993) report evidence that higher cultural distance is associated with *shared-control* entry modes. Other work has also used the term cultural distance paradox (e.g., Drogendijk & Zander, 2010; López-Duarte, 2013). Moreover, literature reviews consistently conclude that, more than anything else, cultural distance research is characterized by a lack of clear, unambiguous results as to the effects of cultural distance on a range of phenomena in IB (Harzing, 2003; Kirkman et al., 2006; Tihanyi et al., 2005; Zhao et al., 2004).

Digging deeper into the four studies that originally inspired the idea of a cultural distance paradox, we find that these studies have considered two different base countries. The two studies that find that higher cultural distance is associated with wholly owned entry modes both have Japan as base country (Anand & Delios, 1997; Padmanabhan & Cho, 1996), while the two studies that find that higher cultural distance is associated with shared-control entry modes both have the United States as base country (Erramilli & Rao, 1993; Kogut & Singh, 1988). Given our findings, it is subsequently quite understandable that the two sets of studies do not report the same results. A cultural distance measure calculated with the United States as base country is simply not the same measure as a cultural distance measure calculated with Japan as the base country. Moreover, in this particular case, the two base countries are characterized by rather different national cultures, which results in strikingly different correlations between cultural distance and partner country culture for the two countries, just as in Panel A and Panel B in Fig. 1. In fact, whereas for the United States cultural distance correlates negatively with partner country culture ($r = -0.99$), for Japan this correlation is positive ($r = +0.59$) (see column 2 of Table A1 in the appendix). The cultural distance paradox, then, may not be a paradox after all.

The reasoning behind this conclusion is as follows. First, because the correlation between cultural distance and partner country culture is negative for the United States, in Kogut and Singh (1988) and Erramilli and Rao (1993) a high cultural distance signifies that a partner country scores *low* on the culture factor. Similarly, for Japan, the correlation between cultural distance and partner country culture is positive, implying that in Anand and Delios (1997) and Padmanabhan and Cho (1996) a high cultural distance signifies that a partner country scores *high* on the culture factor. Accordingly, we can straightforwardly reinterpret the studies of Anand and Delios (1997), Erramilli and Rao (1993), Kogut and Singh (1988), and Padmanabhan and Cho (1996) as reporting the following relationships: wholly owned entry modes are associated with partner countries having a high score on the culture factor and, vice versa, shared-control entry modes are associated with partner countries having a low score on the culture factor. Viewed in this light, however, there are no paradoxical findings that require reconciliation. Rather, both the studies by Kogut and Singh (1988) and Erramilli and Rao (1993) and the studies by Anand and Delios (1997) and Padmanabhan and Cho (1996) point to the same general pattern, which is that partner country culture affects MNEs' entry mode (cf. van Hoorn & Maseland, 2013).

More generally, national culture is known to be an important factor shaping countries' socio-economic environment. Notably individualism, in turn a key driver of a country's score on the culture factor (see the previous section), has been implicated in such areas as economic growth (Gorodnichenko & Roland, 2011a, 2011b), national innovation rates (Gorodnichenko & Roland, 2011b; Shane, 1992, 1993), levels of entrepreneurship (McGrath, MacMillan, & Scheinberg, 1992; Mitchell, Smith, Seawright, & Morse, 2000), and even the specific practices that firms in a country use to manage their daily operations (van Hoorn, 2014a). As such, it is hardly surprising that the culture of a partner country is an important factor for MNEs to consider and deal with (cf. van Hoorn & Maseland, 2013). Moreover, now that we know that the cultural distance literature is plagued by incomparability issues rather than paradoxes per se, we may well find that national culture actually matters more and through different channels than typically recognized in either empirical or theoretical IB research (ibidem).

Cultural Distance in International Business

Following up on the last point, we find that our mathematical findings and empirical demonstration do not matter only for empirical distance research but also have implications for the way in which cultural distance is used in IB research more broadly. The general appeal of cultural distance is that it provides a useful metaphor for thinking about an MNE and the difficulties it experiences in its cross-border activities. In IB theory, cultural distance thus often plays a crucial role, which is to be a catch-all for the many different contingencies a firm has to deal with when it seeks to expand globally and/or when managing operations in a cultural environment that is different from its home-country cultural environment. Perhaps, however, this is too powerful a role for any one construct to fulfill, meaning the time has come for us to rethink how exactly the concept of distance can be of use to IB. We find that, at the least, IB theory should be careful to signal out cultural distance between the MNE's home- and host country as the only factor shaping MNE strategies, location choices and operational decisions. Overall, however, what seems needed is a general overhaul in which we strengthen the field's theorizing on what exactly cultural distance means and what it can and cannot do for our understanding of cross-border business activities. Once we have thus improved our theoretical foundations, we can go back to the empirical drawing board and design novel measures of cultural distance that truly capture what we want them to capture and do so in a cross-culturally meaningful way.

NOTES

1. See, notably, Cronbach and Meehl's (1955) classic work on (construct) validity, which introduces the idea of establishing a so-called nomological network for a construct. This network relates different theoretical constructs to each other and specifies empirically observable relationships between these constructs, which, in turn, allow researchers to ascertain the validity of the construct of interest.

2. Of course, we recognize that national culture is a multidimensional phenomenon. However, in order to keep this illustration as simple as possible, we refrain from introducing complexity by considering multiple dimensions of national culture simultaneously. Moreover, the focus on culture as a one-dimensional construct fits the idea of cultural distance as a one-dimensional construct (Berry et al., 2010; Kogut & Singh, 1988).

3. To be sure, distance measures such as the Kogut-Singh index depicted in Eq. (1) tend to take the absolute values of these differences between the base country and the set of partner countries. However, for this example, taking the absolute value has no effect as $|c - p1| = c - p1$, $|c - p2| = c - p2$, and $|c - p3| = c - p3$.

4. Again, taking absolute values has no effect in this example as $|p1 - c| = p1 - c$, $|p2 - c| = p2 - c$, and $|p3 - c| = p3 - c$.

5. Remember that the culture factor is measured as an actual factor and therefore has a mean of zero by construction. While Belgium does not score zero on the culture factor, in our sample of 69 countries, Belgium has roughly the same number of partner countries scoring higher on the culture factor as it has partner countries scoring lower on the culture factor.

REFERENCES

Anand, J., & Delios, A. (1997). Location specificity and the transferability of downstream assets to foreign subsidiaries. *Journal of International Business Studies, 28*, 579−603.

Bae, J. H., & Salomon, R. (2010). Institutional distance in international business research. In T. Devinney, T. Pedersen, & L. Tihanyi (Eds.), *The past, present and future of international business & management* (Vol. 23, pp. 327–349). Advances in International Management. Bingley, UK: Emerald Group Publishing Limited.

Berry, H., Guillén, M., & Zhou, N. (2010). An institutional approach to cross-national distance. *Journal of International Business Studies, 41*, 1460–1480.

Beugelsdijk, S., Maseland, R., Onrust, M., van Hoorn, A., & Slangen, A. (2014). Cultural distance in international management: From mean-based to variance-based measures. *International Journal of Human Resource Management* 1–27. Advanced online publication, doi:10.1080/09585192.2014.922355

Brouthers, K. D., & Brouthers, L. E. (2001). Explaining the national cultural distance paradox. *Journal of International Business Studies, 32*, 177–189.

Cronbach, L. J., & Meehl, P. E. (1955). Construct validity in psychological tests. *Psychological Bulletin, 52*, 281–302.

Drogendijk, R., & Zander, L. (2010). Walking the cultural distance – In search of direction beyond friction. In T. Devinney, T. Pedersen, & L. Tihanyi (Eds.), *The past, present and future of international business & management* (Vol. 23, pp. 189–212). Advances in International Management. Bingley, UK: Emerald Group Publishing Limited.

Em, L. (2011). Disentangling the different concepts of distance: A lexicographic exploration of the past 20 years of the *Journal of International Business Studies*. Paper presented at the Academy of International Business Annual Meeting, Nagoya, Japan.

Erramilli, M., & Rao, C. (1993). Service firms' international entry-mode choice: A modified transaction-cost analysis approach. *Journal of Marketing, 57*, 19–38.

Ghemawat, P. (2001). Distance still matters: The hard reality of global expansion. *Harvard Business Review, 79*, 137–146.

Gorodnichenko, Y., & Roland, G. (2011a). Which dimensions of culture matter for long run growth? *American Economic Review Papers and Proceedings, 101*, 492–498.

Gorodnichenko, Y., & Roland, G. (2011b). Individualism, innovation, and long-run growth. *Proceedings of the National Academy of Sciences, 108*, 21316–21319.

Harzing, A. W. (2003). The role of culture in entry mode studies: From neglect to myopia? In M. A. Hitt & J. L. C. Cheng (Eds.), *Managing multinationals in a knowledge economy: Economics, culture, and human resources* (Vol. 15, pp. 75–127). Advances in International Management. Oxford: Elsevier JAI.

Hofstede, G. (1980). *Culture's consequences: International differences in work-related values.* Beverly Hills, CA: Sage.

Hofstede, G., Hofstede, G. J., & Minkov, M. (2010). *Cultures and organizations: Software of the mind* (3rd ed.). London: McGraw-Hill.

Hult, G. T. M., Ketchen, D. J., Griffith, D. A., Finnegan, C. A., Gonzalez-Padron, T., Harmancioglu, N., … Cavusgil, S. T. (2008). business research: Assessment and guidelines. *Journal of International Business Studies, 39*, 1027–1044.

Kirkman, B. L., Lowe, K. B., & Gibson, C. B. (2006). A quarter century of culture's consequences: A review of empirical research incorporating Hofstede's cultural values framework. *Journal of International Business Studies, 37*, 285–320.

Kogut, B., & Singh, H. (1988). The effect of national culture on the choice of entry mode. *Journal of International Business Studies, 19*, 411–432.

López-Duarte, C. (2013). Trying to solve the cultural distance paradox: A commentary essay. *Journal of Business Research, 66*, 523–524.

McGrath, R. G., MacMillan, I. C., & Scheinberg, S. (1992). Elitists, risk-takers, and rugged individualists? An exploratory analysis of cultural differences between entrepreneurs and non-entrepreneurs. *Journal of Business Venturing, 7*, 115–135.

Mitchell, R. K., Smith, B., Seawright, K. W., & Morse, E. A. (2000). Cross-cultural cognitions and the venture creation decision. *Academy of Management Journal, 43*, 974–993.

Mullen, M. R. (1995). Diagnosing measurement equivalence in cross-national research. *Journal of International Business Studies, 26*, 573–596.

Padmanabhan, P., & Cho, K. R. (1996). Ownership strategy for a foreign affiliate: An empirical investigation of Japanese firms. *Management International Review, 36*, 45–65.

Shane, S. (1992). Why do some societies invent more than others? *Journal of Business Venturing, 7*, 29–46.

Shane, S. (1993). Cultural influences on national rates of innovation. *Journal of Business Venturing, 8*, 59–73.

Shenkar, O. (2001). Cultural distance revisited towards a more rigorous conceptualization and measurement of cultural differences. *Journal of International Business Studies, 32*, 519–535.

Singh, J. (1995). Measurement issues in cross-national research. *Journal of International Business Studies, 26*, 597–619.

Tihanyi, L., Griffith, D., & Russell, C. (2005). The effect of cultural distance on entry mode choice, international diversification, and MNE performance: A meta-analysis. *Journal of International Business Studies, 36*, 270–283.

Tung, R. L., & Verbeke, A. (2010). Beyond Hofstede and GLOBE: Improving the quality of cross-cultural research. *Journal of International Business Studies, 41*, 1259–1274.

van Hoorn, A. (2014a). Individualism and the cultural roots of management practices. *Journal of Economic Behavior & Organization, 99*, 53–68.

van Hoorn, A. (2014b). Differences in work values: Understanding the role of intra- versus inter-country variation. *International Journal of Human Resource Management*, 1–19. Advanced online publication, doi:10.1080/09585192.2013.872165

van Hoorn, A., & Kunst, V. (2014). From Institutional Theory to Institutional Distance. Paper presented at the Academy of International Business Annual Conference, Vancouver, Canada.

van Hoorn, A., & Maseland, R. (2013). *Why the institutional distance literature in management is about institutional profiles, not distance, and what to do about it.* Mimeo, University of Groningen.

Zaheer, S., Schomaker, M. S., & Nachum, L. (2012). Distance without direction: Restoring credibility to a much-loved construct. *Journal of International Business Studies, 43*, 18–27.

Zhao, H., Luo, Y., & Suh, T. (2004). Transaction cost determinants and ownership-based entry mode choice: A meta-analytical review. *Journal of International Business Studies, 35*, 524–544.

APPENDIX

Table A1. Differences in the Relationship between Cultural Distance and
Partner Country Culture across Base Countries.

Selected Base Country to/ from Which Cultural Distance Is Calculated	1	2
	Selected base country's score on the culture factor	Correlation between cultural distance and partner country scores on the culture factor for the selected base country
Guatemala	−1.963	1.000
Panama	−1.692	0.998
Venezuela	−1.290	0.982
Serbia	−1.274	0.981
Romania	−1.237	0.979
Ecuador	−1.174	0.974
Russia	−1.171	0.973
Malaysia	−0.995	0.952
Mexico	−0.988	0.951
Colombia	−0.983	0.951
El Salvador	−0.961	0.947
Peru	−0.896	0.935
Bangladesh	−0.874	0.931
Portugal	−0.834	0.922
Slovenia	−0.798	0.913
Suriname	−0.792	0.912
Indonesia	−0.788	0.910
Philippines	−0.771	0.906
Slovakia	−0.765	0.905
Greece	−0.752	0.901
South Korea	−0.734	0.896
Bulgaria	−0.719	0.892
Chile	−0.691	0.884
Croatia	−0.665	0.875
Uruguay	−0.571	0.839
Pakistan	−0.542	0.825
China	−0.531	0.820
Taiwan	−0.527	0.818
Thailand	−0.519	0.814
Turkey	−0.495	0.803
Brazil	−0.441	0.773
Vietnam	−0.254	0.626
Japan	−0.223	0.594
Morocco	−0.212	0.582
Poland	−0.207	0.577

Table A1. (*Continued*)

Selected Base Country to/ from Which Cultural Distance Is Calculated	1 Selected base country's score on the culture factor	2 Correlation between cultural distance and partner country scores on the culture factor for the selected base country
Costa Rica	−0.206	0.576
Trinidad and Tobago	−0.153	0.520
Hong Kong	−0.128	0.491
Singapore	−0.093	0.449
Spain	−0.013	0.343
India	0.005	0.318
Argentina	0.040	0.267
Malta	0.042	0.264
Iran	0.087	0.195
France	0.143	0.106
Belgium	0.174	0.054
Czech Republic	0.247	−0.073
Italy	0.734	−0.740
Luxembourg	0.735	−0.740
Hungary	0.786	−0.774
Lithuania	0.811	−0.789
Jamaica	0.852	−0.813
Estonia	0.896	−0.835
Latvia	1.013	−0.884
Germany	1.020	−0.886
Israel	1.097	−0.911
Finland	1.135	−0.921
Switzerland	1.141	−0.923
Austria	1.234	−0.945
Canada	1.428	−0.975
Norway	1.447	−0.977
The Netherlands	1.464	−0.979
Ireland	1.601	−0.989
The United States	1.634	−0.991
Australia	1.646	−0.991
Sweden	1.749	−0.995
New Zealand	1.770	−0.996
United Kingdom	1.833	−0.997
Denmark	2.156	−1.000

Notes: For calculating the correlations, we have excluded the scores of the base countries' themselves because, by construction, they have zero distance to the base country, leaving a sample of 68 observations for each base country. Sources for the data are Hofstede's personal website (http://www.geerthofstede.nl) and own calculations. Complete country data are available on request.

CHAPTER 9

CULTURE AND A CASCADING MODEL OF EMOTIONAL INTELLIGENCE: AN EXPLORATORY ANALYSIS

Marjaana Gunkel, Christopher Schlaegel and Robert L. Engle

ABSTRACT

Purpose — *The study addresses the mechanism of how cultural dimensions influence the different dimensions of emotional intelligence. Building on the cascading model described by Joseph and Newman (2010), we extend our previous findings (Gunkel, Schlaegel, & Engle, 2014) by exploring the influence of cultural dimensions on a cascading model of emotional intelligence.*

Methodology — *We use survey data from 2,067 business students in nine countries (China, Colombia, Germany, India, Italy, Russia, Spain, Turkey, and the United States), representing 8 of the 11 cultural clusters identified by Ronen and Shenkar (2013).*

Findings — *We find that uncertainty avoidance and long-term orientation have a positive influence on self-emotional appraisal, which in turn*

Multinational Enterprises, Markets and Institutional Diversity
Progress in International Business Research, Volume 9, 229–257
Copyright © 2014 by Emerald Group Publishing Limited
All rights of reproduction in any form reserved
ISSN: 1745-8862/doi:10.1108/S1745-886220140000009009

influence regulation of emotion, which then has a positive influence on the use of emotion. At the same time, others' emotional appraisal mediates the relationship between all cultural dimensions except power distance and use of emotion. We also find that uncertainty avoidance, masculinity, and long-term orientation directly influence the use of emotion, suggesting a partial mediation effect.

Research limitations − *Our findings have to be interpreted in the light of the limitations of our approach owing to the cross-sectional study design and the limited generalizability of the sample.*

Originality − *We contribute to the existing literature by examining the mechanism through which culture influences the different facets of emotional intelligence and whether and how the different facets affect each other. The proposed influence of culture on a cascading model of emotional intelligence provides a more detailed and nuanced understanding of the mechanism and the pathways in which culture affects emotional intelligence.*

Keywords: Emotional intelligence; cultural dimensions; cascading model; structural equation modeling

INTRODUCTION

While a large body of research has examined the outcomes of emotional intelligence, relatively little is known about the antecedents of emotional intelligence. Until recently, the literature on emotional intelligence has not been able to identify any antecedents of emotional intelligence apart from the parents' emotional intelligence (Vernon, Petrides, Bratko, & Schermer, 2008). There has been theoretical discussion in the literature on how emotional intelligence may develop; nevertheless, there is a clear need for studies examining the antecedents of emotional intelligence (Barbuto & Bugenhagen, 2009). We extended the literature on the antecedents of emotional intelligence (Gunkel, Schlaegel, & Engle, 2014) by showing that cultural dimensions influence the four facets of emotional intelligence suggested by Wong and Law (2002). That is, culture can be seen as one antecedent of emotional intelligence.

Building upon and extending our previous analysis (Gunkel et al., 2014) on culture's influence on emotional intelligence, we draw on a cascading model of emotional intelligence proposed by Joseph and Newman (2010). Using meta-analytic evidence, they showed that emotional intelligence should rather be considered as a cascading process, in which the facets of emotional intelligence flow into each other. For example, in order to regulate one's emotions, one needs to be first able to perceive one's emotions and understand them. In our explorative analysis, we test whether the Wong and Law (2002) conceptualization of emotional intelligence can also be seen as a cascading model. Furthermore, we will examine culture's role as an antecedent of emotional intelligence in such a cascading model.

Along with globalization, firms employ labor from various cultural settings. The monitoring of own and others' emotions becomes a difficult task, which, however, might be critical for the success of an organization. The human resource management of an internationally active organization has to face the challenge of finding a management team that is emotionally intelligent in various cultural settings. But so far very little is known about the cross-cultural differences in emotional intelligence. That is, how does the national culture influence the emotional intelligence of individuals? Even though the literature on culture's influence on emotional intelligence is sporadic, the topic is of crucial importance as more and more organizations have individuals interfacing with global partners. Our explorative study aims at providing a deeper understanding of how national culture influences the facets of emotional intelligence in a cascading model of emotional intelligence. We suggest that the facets of emotional intelligence build on each other as proposed by Joseph and Newman (2010). To be specific, we suggest that self-emotional appraisal (SEA) and others' emotional appraisal mediate the relationship between the different cultural dimensions and the regulation and use of emotion.

The results of our study contribute to the existing literature in two ways. First, we examine the mechanism through which culture influences emotional intelligence by proposing an influence via a cascading model of emotional intelligence. Second, we extend the work of Joseph and Newman (2010), who utilized the Mayer and Salovey (1997) conceptualization of emotional intelligence, by examining a cascading model of emotional intelligence based on the Wong and Law (2002) conceptualization of emotional intelligence. By examining the mechanism through which culture affects different dimensions of emotional intelligence and whether and how the different dimensions of emotional intelligence affect each other, we provide a more complete and more detailed picture of the process from whence emotional intelligence arises, an area which has been identified as being understudied in this research field (Joseph & Newman, 2010; Ybarra et al., 2013).

The results of our analysis can also be seen as a help for organizations to increase the job satisfaction as well as a wide range of other work-related behaviors and outcomes of their employees as previous literature has shown that emotional intelligence has an important influence on work outcomes in different cultural contexts (e.g., Abraham, 2005; Bell, 2007; Cherniss & Goleman, 2001; Goleman, 1998; Harms & Credé, 2010; Joseph & Newman, 2010; O'Boyle, Humphrey, Pollack, Hawver, & Story, 2011; Schlaerth, Ensari, & Christian, 2013; Sharma, Bottom, & Elfenbein, 2013; Van Rooy & Viswesvaran, 2004; Walter, Cole, & Humphrey, 2011).

CONCEPTUAL BACKGROUND

Emotional intelligence, "the ability to monitor one's own and others' feelings and emotions, to discriminate among them and to use this information to guide one's thinking and actions" (Salovey & Mayer, 1990, p. 189), is composed of four dimensions: (1) appraisal and expression of emotion in the self − SEA, (2) appraisal and recognition of emotion in others − others' emotional appraisal, (3) regulation of emotion in the self − regulation of emotion, and (4) use of emotion to facilitate performance − use of emotion (Mayer & Salovey, 1997; Salovey & Mayer, 1990). Connecting emotional intelligence to organizational outcomes, Wong and Law's (2002) model proposes that emotionally intelligent employees are able to revise their perceptions about their work environment. The perceptions affect the emotions of the individuals, which can be regulated by the people the employees select to interact with, by the work environment itself, by focusing on specific aspects of the work environment or by changing the evaluation of the work environment (antecedent-focused emotion regulation). Employees can also change the influence of an emotional stimulus from the work environment by intensifying, diminishing, prolonging, or curtailing certain emotions (response-focused emotion regulation). Employees with high emotional intelligence can use such regulation of emotion to create positive emotions and promote emotional and intellectual growth. Employees with low emotional intelligence have slower emotional growth due to the fact that they are not able to regulate their emotions effectively. Individuals with high levels of emotional intelligence can make use of this emotion regulation. There has been significant research that supports the importance of emotional intelligence in the workplace with impacts of emotional intelligence seen in the areas of personal selection, leadership, workgroup cohesion, performance feedback, organizational commitment, organizational citizenship, and job control (Abraham, 2005). Cherniss' (2001) research suggests that emotional intelligence has a broad influence on organizational effectiveness across a wide range of organizational activities including teamwork, innovation, productivity, sales, quality service, and customer loyalty. This work along with that of many others supports the view of Wong and Law (2002) that for virtually any organization it is of crucial importance to hire employees with high levels of emotional intelligence in order to realize the many benefits of an emotionally intelligent workforce.

A Cascading Model of Emotional Intelligence

Joseph and Newman (2010) propose a cascading model of emotional intelligence, suggesting that the subdimensions of emotional intelligence are related to job performance in a sequential fashion as presented in Fig. 1. They base their model on the ability-based model of emotional intelligence

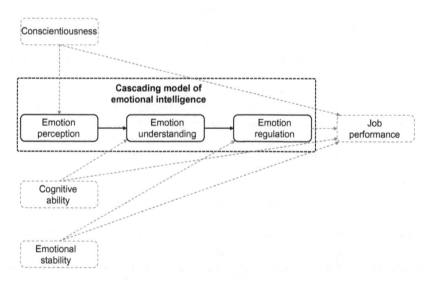

Fig. 1. Cascading Model of Emotional Intelligence (Adapted from Joseph and Newman, 2010, p. 56). *Note*: The cascading model of emotional intelligence described by Joseph and Newman (2010) is based on the ability emotional intelligence concept proposed by Mayer and Salovey (1997).

by Mayer and Salovey (1997). Joseph and Newman (2010) propose that emotion perception influences emotion understanding, which in turn influences emotion regulation, which finally influences job performance. In addition, they consider the effect of two personality traits and cognitive ability on job performance.

We follow the idea of a cascading model of emotional intelligence; however, we utilize the Wong and Law (2002) constructs of emotional intelligence. Given the particular conceptualization, the perception and understanding of one's own and others' emotions is presented independent of each other, which provides the advantage of being able to examine the influence of others' emotional appraisal in the cascading model as well. Analogous to Joseph and Newman (2010), we propose, when using the Wong and Law (2002) conceptualization of emotional intelligence, that SEA influences regulation of emotion. Joseph and Newman (2010) omit the facet of emotional facilitation, which can be seen as use of emotion in the Wong and Law (2002) model. We, however, posit that also this facet is of importance. To be specific, following the argumentation of Wong and Law (2002, p. 247), suggesting that the ability to regulate emotions leads to the ability to "create positive emotions as well as to promote emotional and intellectual growth," we propose that the use of emotion might be the outcome variable of the other three facets of emotional intelligence. With our cascading model of emotional intelligence, we follow Gross's (1998a) definition of emotion regulation which proposes that in order to be able to regulate one's own emotions, one must have a good understanding of these emotions. However, one's emotions are often stimulated by the emotions of others, and therefore, the ability to understand one's own emotions is related to the ability to understand others' emotions. Gross (1998a) further proposes that one is able to regulate the emotions one experiences and also to determine how one expresses and uses these emotions.

Culture and a Cascading Model of Emotional Intelligence

Ang et al. (2007) propose that a person who is emotionally intelligent in one culture might not be that in another one. One's norms and values determine the central importance in life, thereby influencing the manner in which emotions are appraised, recognized, and used. Also, meta-analytic evidence suggests that cultural beliefs and values impact emotions, perceptions, and cognitive schema (Taras, Kirkman, & Steel, 2010). That implies that culture has an influence on emotional intelligence, and therefore, can be seen as an antecedent of emotional intelligence. The way emotions are displayed and dealt with in various countries has been shown to be influenced by the culture of the countries (e.g., Matsumoto, 1989). So far, the influence of culture on emotional intelligence has remained widely unexplored. The literature on emotions and culture has focused only on two facets of the model of emotional intelligence, namely, perceiving and expressing emotions (e.g., Palmer, Gignac, Ekermans, & Stough, 2008). This, however, leads us to suspect that emotional intelligence is a concept which is also influenced by culture. Studies have indicated that intelligence is affected by culture (Crowne, Phatak, & Salunkhe, 2009); nevertheless, only few efforts (e.g., Crowne, Phatak, Salunkhe, & Shivarajan, 2011) have been taken to examine the influence of culture on the formation of emotional intelligence. Our study will examine how Hofstede's (2001) cultural dimensions, operationalized at the individual level, influence emotional intelligence across a broad group of countries. Fig. 2 depicts our conceptual model.

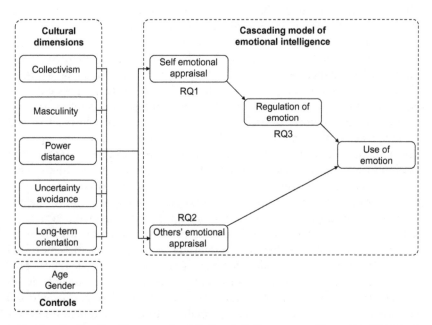

Fig. 2. Explorative Framework of Culture's Influence on a Cascading Model of Emotional Intelligence.

We follow Hofstede's (1980, p. 25) definition of culture stating that culture is the "collective programming of the mind which distinguishes one group from another," setting the basic values and norms for a society. Hofstede (2001) distinguishes between five dimensions of culture: individualism versus collectivism, masculinity versus femininity, power distance, uncertainty avoidance, and short-term versus long-term orientation. The dimensions of Hofstede have been found to reflect the fundamental dimensions of culture (Taras et al., 2010). These dimensions have been the basis for the research on culture's influence on emotions (e.g., Fernández-Berrocal, Salovey, Vera, Extremera, & Ramos, 2005; Matsumoto, 1989, 1990; Matsumoto, Nezlek, & Koopmann, 2007), and therefore, serve as an appropriate basis for the analysis of the connection between these dimensions and culture. While previous studies propose that emotional intelligence is defined by cultural norms and values (e.g., Mayer & Geher, 1996; Mayer, Salovey, & Caruso, 2000; Offermann & Phan, 2002), the literature on emotional intelligence lacks a theoretical understanding of the process how national culture affects emotional intelligence. Given the lack of literature in this area, our explorative study will examine how Hofstede's cultural dimensions might have an influence on the cascading model of emotional intelligence across a broad group of countries.

Even though emotions are biologically programed, controlling the expression of emotions is determined by culture (Matsumoto, 1989). Emotions are shaped and maintained by culture (Kitayama & Markus, 1994). The communication of emotions significantly differs across cultures. Individualistic cultures stress the needs of individuals and therefore emphasize the emotional world of an individual. A balance between positive and negative emotions is searched for. The type of emotion, however, seems to play a great role in the display of emotions. For example, Matsumoto (1990) showed that American individuals (high individualism) found negative emotions in in-groups and happiness to out-groups to be more appropriate emotions to show than their Japanese counterparts. Nevertheless, Japanese rated anger to out-groups more appropriate than the American participants of the study. In collective cultures, the cohesion with peers is of high importance and therefore less attention is paid on the emotional world of individuals (Fernández-Berrocal et al., 2005). Hofstede (2001) proposes that countries with high uncertainty avoidance (high anxiety level) have created social systems that allow the expression of emotions, and the expression of emotion is considered normal. Cultures scoring high on uncertainty avoidance are more expressive cultures where emotions are displayed clearly (Palmer et al., 2008). Countries with high femininity show a greater emotional intensity and expressiveness than masculine countries (Paez & Vergara, 1995). In addition, feminine nations seem to be associated with higher frequency of positive emotions than negative ones (Basabe et al., 2000). Power distance has been shown to influence the fact to whom emotions are shown. Matsumoto (1990) showed that Japanese employees (high power distance) found showing negative emotions toward lower-status others appropriate. They, however, surpass their negative emotions in the presence of higher-status others (Ekman, 1972). Matsumoto et al. (2007) demonstrate that long-term orientation is related to lowered emotional expressivity. That is, emotions in general are not shown as openly in long-term-oriented cultures. It is well known that emotions we display and to whom we display them are influenced by culture. Nevertheless, so far the literature has not provided us with a clear connection between cultural dimensions and SEA. Therefore, we propose the following research question:

Research Question 1 (RQ1): Does self-emotional appraisal mediate the relationship between cultural dimensions and the more proximal emotional intelligence facets in the cascading model, namely regulation of emotion and use of emotion?

The manner in which individuals read the emotions of others has been shown to be influenced by culture (Matsumoto, 1989). In his study on the recognition of emotion in facial expression, Matsumoto (1989) examined how different cultures recognize emotions of others and found that individualism was positively correlated with identifying happiness and negatively correlated with identifying sadness. In addition, power distance was negatively correlated to identifying the facial expression of happiness. Uncertainty avoidance is related to the expression of emotions, such as anxiety as an outlet for fear, but it was not possible to find a correlation between uncertainty avoidance and the recognition of emotions. According to Hofstede (2001), femininity is related to good work relationships with others and cooperation at work. Therefore, it may be assumed that feminine cultures observe their counterparts in greater detail and therefore are able to observe and understand their emotions better than individuals from rather masculine cultures. The appraisal of others' emotions is a complex topic. Again, the type of emotion (positive or negative) seems to matter. The question which seems important to the research in the field of emotional intelligence is whether culture is related to the recognition of others' emotions. Individuals from certain cultures would thus be more sensitive to others' emotions within their cultures and better at reading others' minds.

A large body of literature examines the contagiousness of emotions (see for an overview, Doherty, 1997). People consciously and nonconsciously mimic others' emotional expressions in order to attend to others (Hatfield, Cacioppo, & Rapson, 1994). This process of "emotional contagion" is defined as "a tendency to automatically mimic and synchronize expressions, vocalizations, postures, and movements with those of another person's and consequently, to converge emotionally" (Hatfield et al., 1994, p. 5). Barsade (2002) shows that individual-level attitudes and group processes were influenced by emotional contagion. Wong and Law (2002) suggest that one's emotional responses are stimulated by the emotions of other individuals. That is, being able to appraise and understand the emotions of others might influence the use of emotion.

Research Question 2 (RQ2): Does others' emotional appraisal mediate the relationship between cultural dimensions and the use of emotion?

Regulation of emotion (ROE) is the attempt to influence which emotions one has and how these emotions are experienced or expressed (Gross, 1998b). Nevertheless, the precondition for the regulation of emotion appears to be the awareness of the emotions one has. Emotion regulation requires the ability to appraise and understand the emotions. The ability to regulate emotions then leads to the effective use of the emotion regulation. That is, individuals who are able to regulate the appraised emotions are able to create positive emotions and also to promote emotional and intellectual growth (Wong & Law, 2002). Gross (1998a) proposes that individuals receive emotional cues, which can be called forth when an individual thinks there is an opportunity that can be created by the emotions. These emotions then result in changes in the behavioral, experiential, autonomic, and neuroendocrine systems. Such responses may be modulated, resulting in the final shape of the emotional response. Therefore, we propose a cascading relationship between the facets of emotional intelligence. First, the recognition of one's own emotions (which may be related to the emotions of others') enables one to regulate emotions and secondly, regulation of emotion can lead to the use of emotion.

Research Question 3 (RQ3): Does regulation of emotion mediate the relationship between self-emotional appraisal and use of emotion?

METHOD

Sample and Data Collection

To answer our exploratory research questions, we use a dataset that we also used to explain the direct effect of cultural dimensions on the emotional intelligence dimensions (Gunkel et al., 2014). The dataset includes question-naire responses from a total of 2,067 individuals surveyed in nine countries. To ensure that the number of countries and the countries selected were appropriate for the purpose of our study, we followed the suggestions in the literature and aimed to cover a relatively broad range of countries (Franke & Richey, 2010) and cultural clusters (Ronen & Shenkar, 2013). The nine countries included in the dataset (China $n = 261$; Colombia $n = 202$; Germany $n = 255$; India $n = 276$; Italy $n = 98$; Russia $n = 224$; Spain $n = 185$; Turkey $n = 196$; the United States $n = 270$) represent 8 of 11 cultural clusters (Ronen & Shenkar, 2013): Anglo (the United States), Confucian (China), East Europe (Russia), Far East (India), Germanic (Germany), Latin America (Colombia), Latin Europe (Italy, Spain), and Near East (Turkey).

In an effort to ensure that the effect of cultural dimensions on the emo-tional intelligence dimensions is based on cultural norms and values rather than on other types of factors, we used a sample of university business students. While the use of student samples is debated in cross-country research (e.g., Bello, Leung, Radebaugh, Tung, & Van Witteloostuijn, 2009), in the current study the use of a student sample can be considered appropriate as this sample allows to isolate the effects of cultural dimen-sions on the emotional intelligence dimensions. Student samples are more homogenous than nonstudent samples and allow to establish cross-country homogeneity of samples (Van de Vijver & Leung, 1997). The respondents were from at least one university in each country and only the responses from individuals who were born, raised, educated, and permanently resided in their respective country were used in this study. The average age of respondents was 22 years. More than half of the respondents (51%) were females.

To ensure the equivalence and consistency across samples in terms of survey formats and the data collection procedure, in all nine countries, sur-veys were administered in a classroom setting (Leung, 2008). Participation in the study was voluntary. All questionnaires were completed anon-ymously to ensure confidentiality. The data was collected simultaneously for the majority of countries. The questionnaire was developed in English and administrated in its original language in two countries (India and the United States). Following the recommendations in the literature (Harzing, Reiche, & Pudelko, 2013), the English questionnaire was translated into six languages (Chinese, German, Italian, Russian, Spanish, and Turkish) and back-translated into English to ensure linguistic as well as conceptual equivalence (Brislin, 1980). Two countries (Colombia and Spain) used the Spanish versions but were adjusted for Latin American (Colombia) and

Spanish language differences. In countries where the questionnaire was administered in English (India), students did not report any difficulty in understanding the statements as English was the official language and the language of instruction at the university.

Measures

Cultural Dimensions

Hofstede's (2001) five cultural dimensions are operationalized at the individual level using the 23 items from Yoo, Donthu, and Lenartowicz (2011). Collectivism was assessed with six items (e.g., "group loyalty should be encouraged even if individual goals suffer" and "group success is more important than individual success"). The coefficient alpha reliability was .61, the average variance extracted (AVE) was .50, and the composite reliability (CR) was .66. Masculinity was measured using four items (e.g., "men usually solve problems with logical analysis; women usually solve problems with intuition" and "it is more important for men to have a professional career than it is for women."). The coefficient alpha reliability was .63 (AVE = .50; CR = .66). Power distance was assessed using five items. Sample items are "people in higher positions should not ask the opinions of people in lower positions too frequently" and "people in lower positions should not disagree with decisions by people in higher positions." The coefficient alpha reliability was .61 (AVE = .46; CR = .70). Uncertainty avoidance was measured using five items (e.g., "standardized work procedures are helpful." and "it is important to have instructions spelled out in detail so that I always know what I'm expected to do."). The coefficient alpha reliability was .68 (AVE = .45; CR = .66). The response scales ranged from 1, "strongly disagree," to 5, "strongly agree" for all items that measured the first four cultural dimensions. Finally, the fifth cultural dimension, long-term orientation, was measured using six items. Sample items include "going on resolutely in spite of opposition (persistence)" and "working hard for success in the future." The coefficient alpha reliability was .69 (AVE = .50; CR = .66). Long-term orientation was measured with a scale that ranged from 1, "very unimportant," to 5, "very important."

Emotional Intelligence

The four trait-based dimensions suggested by Wong and Law (2002) are used to measure emotional intelligence. SEA was assessed using four items. Sample items are "I have a good sense of why I have certain feelings most of the time." and "I really understand what I feel." For the pooled sample, the coefficient alpha reliability was .74 (AVE = .50; CR = .75). Others' emotional appraisal (OEA) was measured with four items (e.g., "I always know my friends' emotions from their behavior." and "I have a good understanding of the emotions of people around me."). The coefficient alpha reliability was .76 (AVE = .52; CR = .77). ROE was measured with four items. Sample items are "I am able to control my temper and handle difficulties rationally." and "I have good control of my own emotions." The coefficient alpha reliability was .81 (AVE = .59; CR = .81). Use of emotion (UOE) was assessed with four items. Sample items are "I always set goals for myself and then try my best to achieve them." and "I would always encourage myself to try my best." The coefficient alpha reliability was .69 (AVE = .47; CR = .70). The items contributing to the four dimensions on a scale anchored at 1, "strongly disagree" and 5, "strongly agree."

Controls

We controlled for two demographic variables that may be related to emotional intelligence. Previous studies found that age has an effect on emotional intelligence (see, e.g., Mayer, Caruso, & Salovey, 1999; Tsaousis & Kazi, 2013). Therefore, age was included as a control variable and was measured in years. Prior research on the effect of gender on emotional intelligence is mixed. While some studies suggest that gender has an effect on emotional intelligence (e.g., Day & Carroll, 2004; Mandell & Pherwani, 2003; Van Rooy, Alonso, & Viswesvaran, 2005), other studies have found no significant effect of gender on emotional intelligence (e.g., Nikolaou & Tsaousis, 2002; Whitman, van Rooy, Viswesvaran, & Kraus, 2009). Therefore, we included gender as a control variable. Gender was measured as a dichotomous variable coded as 1 for female and 0 for male. In addition, the questionnaire included questions about citizenship, citizenship at birth, study program, and level of degree program (bachelor/master) to control for sample homogeneity.

RESULTS

Measurement Validation, Common Method Variance, and Descriptive Statistics

We conducted confirmatory factor analysis (CFA) for each country, using AMOS 22 and the maximum likelihood estimation procedure (Arbuckle,

2013) to identify any country-specific components in the measurement model. The chi-square (χ^2) statistic is not an adequate test of model fit given large sample sizes ($n > 250$) (e.g., Cheung & Rensvold, 2002). Consequently, the results of the χ^2 test were not considered critical for evaluating the model fit such that we complement the χ^2 statistic with other measures of fit. We followed the recommendations in the literature (e.g., Browne & Cudeck, 1993) and used the comparative fit index (CFI) and the root mean square error of approximation (RMSEA). Models resulting in CFI values of .90 or higher are considered acceptable (Bagozzi & Yi, 1988). For the RMSEA index, values below .08 are considered indicative of good fit (Browne & Cudeck, 1993). Following the procedure suggested by Byrne (2010), we used the results of individual country CFA to identify those items that build a baseline model for the multigroup confirmatory factor analysis (MGCFA). We deleted several items in the various countries for the cultural dimensions as well as for the emotional intelligence dimensions. All independent and dependent variables were modeled as reflective measures so that items could be removed without affecting their theoretical domain. For further analysis, we used a factor structure that was identical for all nine countries and only used those items that showed high factor loadings and high squared multiple correlations for all nine countries as well as for the pooled sample (Byrne, 2010). The values of the CFI were above the .90 threshold and the RMSEAs were below the .08 threshold for the majority of the nine countries and the pooled sample (Browne & Cudeck, 1993). Overall, the CFA results of the revised measurement model indicate an acceptable fit. In summary, while the measurement model for the emotional intelligence dimensions shows satisfying reliability, the measurement model for the cultural dimensions is not satisfying, in particular for the power distance construct as well as for the uncertainty avoidance constructs. Both constructs have a low AVE (AVE < .50), indicating that the different respective items do not converge properly to the intended factor. There is neither a single item nor a set of items for the two constructs that, if removed, would improve the reliability and the measurement model. Consequently, we decided to keep those items that have been identified in the CFA and MGCFA. The Cronbach alpha values are below the recommended threshold of .70 (Nunnally, 1978) for six of the nine latent variables. According to the literature (Nunnally & Bernstein, 1994), Cronbach alpha values below .70 and over .60 are acceptable for new instruments. In the current study, this in particular applies to the cultural dimension constructs that, to our knowledge, for some of the countries have been translated to the respective national language and tested in the respective country for the first time.

Following the recommendation in the international business as well as in the international human resource management literature (Chang, Van Witteloostuijn, & Eden, 2010; Reio, 2010), we empirically tested whether common method bias affects our results. We used three ex-post approaches to assess common method bias (Podsakoff, MacKenzie, Lee, & Podsakoff, 2003). First, to identify multicollinearity, we examined the correlation coefficients for each country as well as for the pooled sample. We found no highly correlated variables, suggesting that the likelihood of common method bias was low. Second, we used Harman's one factor test and found a very poor fit for the single-factor models for each country sample and the pooled sample, suggesting that the influence of common method bias was minimal. Finally, we used a common method factor and performed CFA for each country and the pooled sample. All item loadings on the common method factor were insignificant for the nine country samples as well as for the pooled sample. While these procedures have their limitations, in summary, the results suggest that common method variance is not a significant issue in this study.

Following the recommendations in the literature, we tested the assumptions of cross-cultural measurement invariance using MGCFA. Measurement invariance is a necessary prerequisite for meaningful cross-cultural comparisons of relationships in international business and international human resource management research (Harzing et al., 2013; Hult, Ketchen, Cavusgil, & Calantone, 2006; Hult et al., 2008; Nimon & Reio, 2011; Schmitt & Kuljanin, 2008; Tsui, Nifadkar, & Ou, 2007). In examining measurement invariance, we constrain factor loadings and variances of the variables to be equal across the nine countries and tested configural invariance, metric invariance, and scalar invariance (Steenkamp & Baumgartner, 1998). To compare relationships across groups, the measurement of constructs needs to show at least partial metric invariance (e.g., Steenkamp & Baumgartner, 1998). The results of the MGCFA for the cultural dimensions as well as for emotional intelligence dimensions are presented in Table 1.

For the cultural dimensions, the results of the MGCFA for the configural model show a satisfactory fit, while the results of the metric model show no acceptable fit. The difference between the configural model and the metric model was above the recommended threshold (ΔCFI = .023), indicating that the factor structure cannot be considered invariant across the nine countries. The results of the partial metric invariance model indicate that the constructs were measured adequately across countries. The difference between the configural model and the partial metric invariance

Table 1.   MGCFA Results for Cultural Dimensions and Emotional
Intelligence Dimensions.

	n	χ^2	df	p	CFI	RMSEA	ΔCFI
Cultural dimensions MGCFA results							
Configural invariance	2,067	1061.00	720	.000	.913	.015	–
Full metric invariance	2,067	1260.10	800	.000	.890	.017	.023
Partial metric invariance	2,067	1154.20	752	.000	.904	.016	.009
Full scalar invariance	2,067	3170.41	920	.000	.462	.034	.442
Emotional intelligence MGCFA results							
Configural invariance	2,067	989.24	462	.000	.935	.023	–
Full metric invariance	2,067	1120.87	518	.000	.926	.023	.009
Full scalar invariance	2,067	1909.73	614	.000	.841	.031	.085

Note: CFA = confirmatory factor analysis; MGCFA = multigroup confirmatory factor analysis, df = degrees of freedom; CFI = comparative fit index; RMSEA = root mean square error of approximation.

model (ΔCFI = .009) was below the recommend threshold (ΔCFI = .01) and, therefore, the factor structure can be considered invariant across the nine countries (Cheung & Rensvold, 2002). The results show an inadequate fit of the scalar model. The comparison between the metric model and the scalar model (ΔCFI = .442) shows that the data did not fit the requirement for scalar invariance and, consequently, the data did not meet the requirement for meaningful comparison of the means across countries.

For the emotional intelligence dimensions, the results of the MGCFA for the configural model as well as for the metric model show a satisfactory fit. The difference between the configural model and the metric model (ΔCFI = .009) was below the recommend threshold (ΔCFI = .01). The results show an inadequate fit of the scalar model. The comparison between the metric model and the scalar model (ΔCFI = .085) shows that the data did not fit the requirement for scalar invariance and, consequently, the data did not meet the requirement for meaningful comparison of the means across countries (Steenkamp & Baumgartner, 1998).

Overall, the MGCFA results support the conclusion that the measurement of the cultural dimensions and the emotional intelligence dimensions can be interpreted in the same way across the nine countries at the metric level, allowing to combine the country samples in a pooled sample. Based on the results of the CFA and the MGCFA, Table 2 presents means and standard deviations for all variables for the pooled sample.

Table 2. Descriptive Statistics.

Variables	Mean	s.d.	1	2	3	4	5	6	7	8	9	10
1. Collectivism	3.25	.81	(.61)									
2. Masculinity	2.73	.97	.01	(.63)								
3. Power distance	2.23	.83	.02	.32	(.61)							
4. Uncertainty avoidance	3.82	.73	.27	.03	−.06	(.68)						
5. Long-term orientation	4.04	.74	.05	.02	−.02	.21	(.69)					
6. Self-emotional appraisal	3.69	.77	.07	.02	−.01	.20	.18	(.74)				
7. Others' emotional appraisal	3.82	.72	.15	−.06	−.06	.18	.18	.46	(.76)			
8. Regulation of emotion	3.54	.86	.11	.02	.01	.12	.13	.45	.24	(.81)		
9. Use of emotion	3.86	.72	.12	−.07	−.07	.19	.29	.35	.34	.31	(.69)	
10. Age	21.54	3.32	.02	.11	.05	.01	−.05	−.03	−.03	−.01	−.01	
11. Gender (female)	.51		−.09	−.36	−.17	.05	.01	−.02	.11	−.13	.06	−.09

Note: $N = 2,067$. All correlations above |0.5| are significant at the .05 level.

Examination of the Research Questions

We utilized the covariance-based approach to structural equation modeling (SEM) to explore our research questions. We examined the proposed relationships using AMOS 22 (Arbuckle, 2013) with the maximum likelihood estimation method. While a partial least squares approach to SEM might better fit the exploratory and predictive nature of this study, we followed Hair, Ringle, and Sarstedt's (2011) rule of thumb and decided to use covariance-based SEM as it allows for MGCFA. Moreover, following the recommendations in the literature (e.g., Iacobucci, Saldanha, & Deng, 2007; Zhao, Lynch, & Chen, 2010), we use SEM and the procedure suggested by James, Mulaik, and Brett (2006) to test the mediating role of SEA, OEA, and ROE in the relationship between cultural dimensions and the UOE. Following James et al. (2006), we compared the proposed full mediation model with a partial mediation model as well as with a nonmediation model. Given the two sequential mediators, namely SEA and ROE, in the relationship between the cultural dimensions and the UOE, we tested the partial mediation model as well as the nonmediation model separately for each of the two sequential mediators. Table 3 presents the different models we explored.

Research Question 1 asked whether SEA mediates the relationship between the cultural dimensions and the emotional intelligence dimensions that represent direct and indirect outcomes of SEA, namely, ROE and UOE. The proposed full mediation model (Model 1 in Table 3) achieved an acceptable fit ($\chi^2 = 1052.99$; df $= 300$; $p = .000$; $\chi^2/df = 3.51$; CFI $= .94$; RMSEA $= .04$). Of the five cultural dimensions, only uncertainty avoidance ($\beta = .19$) as well as long-term orientation ($\beta = .22$) have a statistically significant positive effect on SEA. SEA has a statistically significant positive effect on ROE ($\beta = .62$) and ROE has a statistically significant positive effect on UOE ($\beta = .27$). In answer to Research Question 1, these findings provide initial evidence that SEA mediates the relationship between cultural dimensions and the ROE as well as the UOE.

Research Question 2 evaluated whether OEA influences the UOE. While collectivism ($\beta = .13$), uncertainty avoidance ($\beta = .13$), and long-term orientation ($\beta = .22$) had a statistically significant positive effect on OEA, masculinity ($\beta = -.12$) had a statistically significant negative effect on OEA. Power distance had no significant influence on OEA. OEA had a statistically significant positive effect ($\beta = .30$) on the UOE. These findings, in answer to Research Question 2, provide initial evidence for the mediating role of others' emotional intelligence in the relationship between cultural dimensions and UOE.

Research Question 3 asked whether ROE mediates the relationship between SEA and UOE. As described above, SEA has a significant positive effect on ROE. In addition, collectivism has a statistically significant positive direct effect on ROE ($\beta = .08$). ROE in turn has a statistically significant positive effect on UOE ($\beta = .27$). In answer to Research Question 3, these findings provide initial evidence that ROE mediates the relationship between SEA and UOE and therewith also between the cultural dimensions and the UOE.

In Models 2–5, we further examined the different mediation paths. In Model 2, we examined a partial mediation model in which the five cultural dimensions had paths to SEA as well OEA and, in addition to our proposed model, the five cultural dimensions also had direct paths to ROE. The fit of Model 2 was acceptable and significantly better than the proposed full mediation model evaluated in Model 1. In Model 3, we explored whether a nonmediated model has a better fit with the data compared to Model 2. While the fit of Model 3 was still within an acceptable range,

Table 3. Results of Structural Equation Model Analysis.

Model	Model description	χ^2	df	p	χ^2/df	CFI	RMSEA	$\Delta\chi^2$ test
Model 1 (M1) Proposed full mediation model	Proposed conceptual full mediation model which is depicted in Fig. 2	1052.99	300	.000	3.51	.94	.04	
Model 2 (M2) Partial mediation model: SEA	All five cultural dimensions have paths to SEA and OEA as well as to ROE	1041.87	295	.000	3.53	.94	.04	M2 vs. M1 11.12 (5) p=.049
Model 3 (M3) Nonmediation model: SEA	All five cultural dimensions have paths to ROE and SEA has no path to ROE	1417.67	296	.000	4.79	.91	.04	M3 vs. M2 894.20 (4) p=.000
Model 4 (M4) Partial mediation model: ROE	All five cultural dimensions have paths to SEA and OEA as well as to UOE	938.96	295	.000	3.18	.95	.03	M4 vs. M1 114.03 (5) p=.000
Model 5 (M5) Nonmediation model: ROE	All five cultural dimensions have paths to UOE and ROE has no path to UOE	1027.07	296	.000	3.47	.94	.04	M5 vs. M4 88.11 (1) p=.000
Model 6 (M6) Revised partial mediation Model 1	Only significant paths of all five cultural dimensions to SEA and OEA as well as significant paths from collectivism to ROE and from uncertainty avoidance, masculinity, and long-term orientation to UOE	947.21	301	.000	3.15	.95	.03	M6 vs. M4 8.25 (6) p=.220
Model 7 (M7) Revised partial mediation Model 2	Revised Model 1 excluding the power distance cultural dimension variable; the final model is depicted in Fig. 3	791.47	233	.000	3.40	.95	.03	

Note: SEA = self-emotional appraisal; OEA = others' emotional appraisal; ROE = regulation of emotion.

Model 2 had a significantly better fit compared to Model 3. In summary, these results suggest a direct-only nonmediation (Zhao et al., 2010; no significant indirect effect and a significant direct effect) for the collectivism−SEA−ROE relationship. In Models 4 and 5, we examined the mediating role of ROE in the SEA−UOE relationship as well as the mediating role of SEA and OEA in the relationships between the cultural dimensions and the UOEs. The partial mediation model (Model 4) fits the data significantly better than the full mediation model (Model 1). The results for Model 4 suggest that in addition to the results reported for the previous models, uncertainty avoidance ($\beta = .08$) and long-term orientation ($\beta = .31$) have a statistically significant positive direct effect on the UOE. Masculinity has statistically significant negative direct effect on the UOEs ($\beta = -.10$). Model 4 has a significantly better fit compared to the nonmediated model (Model 5). For reasons of model parsimony, we left nonsignificant paths out in the analysis of Model 6. In Model 7, we also left nonsignificant variables (power distance) out of the analysis. The results of our final revised partial mediation model (Model 7) are presented in Fig. 3.

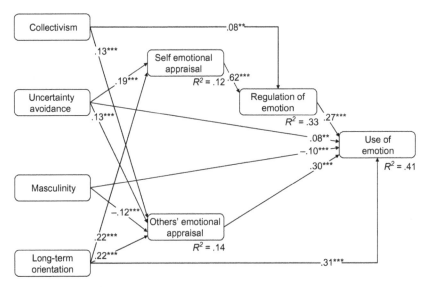

Fig. 3. Results of Structural Equation Modeling Analysis. *Note:* The results of the revised partial mediation model (Model 7) and standardized path coefficients are presented. $N = 2,067$; $\chi^2 = 791.47$; df = 233; $p < 0.000$; $\chi^2/\text{df} = 3.40$; CFI = 0.95; RMSEA = .03. $**p < .01$; $***p < .001$.

In summary, the results of the mediation analysis suggest complementary mediation (Zhao et al., 2010; same sign for significant indirect effects and a significant direct effect) for the six significant indirect relationships between the cultural dimensions and UOE. The variance accounted for (VAF) for the indirect effect of collectivism on the UOE is rather small (33%). The VAF for the indirect effects of uncertainty avoidance on the UOE is moderate (47%). The direct effect ($\beta = .08$) is larger in magnitude than the indirect effects ($\beta = .03$ and $\beta = .039$). The VAF for the indirect effect of masculinity on the UOE is rather small (25%). The direct effect ($\beta = -.10$) is larger in magnitude than the indirect effects ($\beta = -.036$). The VAF for the indirect effects of long-term orientation on the UOE is rather small (25%). The direct effect ($\beta = .31$) is larger in magnitude than the indirect effects ($\beta = .066$ and $\beta = .037$). Results of bootstrapping procedure (Preacher & Hayes, 2008; Zhao et al., 2010) as well as Sobel z-tests (Iacobucci et al., 2007) confirm the SEM mediation analysis by showing that the indirect effects are statistically significant.

DISCUSSION

Meta-analytic evidence suggests that emotional intelligence is an antecedent of a wide range of work-related outcomes, including general performance, job performance, and team performance (Bell, 2007; Joseph & Newman, 2010; O'Boyle et al., 2011; Sharma et al., 2013; Van Rooy & Viswesvaran, 2004) as well as leadership behavior (Harms & Credé, 2010; Walter et al., 2011) and individual health (Schutte, Malouff, Thorsteinsson, Bhullar, & Rooke, 2007). While prior empirical research investigated the outcomes of emotional intelligence, only a limited number of studies investigated the determinants of emotional intelligence. Building on and extending our previous research (Gunkel et al., 2014), we explore the influence of cultural dimensions on a cascading model of the different facets of emotional intelligence as described by Joseph and Newman (2010).

Implications for Theory

Our study makes two main contributions to the existing literature. Our first contribution is to explore the influence of cultural dimensions on a cascading model of emotional intelligence, to provide a more comprehensive understanding of the pathways through which culture influences the different facets of emotional intelligence. Thus, our exploratory study contributes to a better understanding of how different cultural dimensions affect the two emotional intelligence dimensions that have been identified to have the strongest impact on different outcomes, namely, the ROE (Joseph & Newman, 2010) and the UOE (Trivellas, Gerogiannis, & Svarna, 2011). In our previous study (Gunkel et al., 2014), we investigated the influence of cultural dimensions on the four facets of emotional intelligence in a more parallel model. We extend our previous analysis by applying a structural (cascading) model that accounts for the sequential relationships between the distal independent variables (the five cultural dimensions), the mediating variables (self and others' appraisal of emotion as well as the ROE), and the proximal-dependent variable (UOE). This study provides an initial response to Ybarra et al.'s (2013) call to assess the contextual and dynamic nature of emotional intelligence. Using a sample of nine countries that cover eight cultural clusters, the results show that collectivism, uncertainty avoidance, masculinity, and long-term orientation influence in particular three facets of emotional intelligence: SEA, OEA, and the UOE. Our findings indicate that cultures characterized by relatively high degrees of uncertainty avoidance and long-term orientation show a higher degree of SEA. Furthermore, our findings also suggest that cultures characterized by relatively high degrees of collectivism, uncertainty avoidance, femininity, and long-term orientation show a higher degree of OEA.

Our second contribution is to extend the work of Joseph and Newman (2010), who utilized the Mayer and Salovey (1997) conceptualization of emotional intelligence, by examining a cascading model of emotional intelligence based on the Wong and Law's (2002) conceptualization of emotional intelligence. The majority of prior primary studies as well as meta-analytic studies focused on the overall emotional intelligence construct and neglected the specific facets and the interrelationships that ultimately form the emotional intelligence construct. By examining a cascading structure through which different facets of emotional intelligence affect each other, we provide a deeper and better understanding of the mechanism by which the appraisal of one's own as well as others' emotions influence the regulation and use of one's own emotions. Our findings support the proposed cascading model of emotional intelligence. The relationship between SEA and the UOE is fully mediated by ROE. While our findings partially support the proposed mediation mechanism of the relationship between the cultural dimensions and the more proximal facets of emotional intelligence, we also find direct effects of collectivism on

ROE as well as of uncertainty avoidance, masculinity, and long-term orientation on the UOE.

Implications for Practice

The implications for practice are basically the same as those that we identified in our previous study (Gunkel et al., 2014). Managers can benefit from our results by being able to identify employees who might process a higher level of emotional intelligence due to their cultural socialization. This might also help them to identify employees for specific tasks in an organization or to identify those who require training on emotional intelligence. Research has shown that training may have a positive effect on emotional intelligence (Bagshaw, 2000; Cherniss & Caplan, 2001; Clarke, 2010; Dulewicz & Higgs, 1999, 2004; Groves, McEnrue, & Shen, 2008; McEnrue, Groves, & Shen, 2009; Turner & Lloyd-Walker, 2008). Our results indicate that training should be specific to the cultural setting as well as to the two genders. Individuals from countries with high individualism, low uncertainty avoidance, and short-term orientation require a more specific training on the four dimensions of emotional intelligence. Special focus should be placed on educating the trainees on the importance of the investment in time and effort in understanding one's own and others' emotions as well as regulation and UOEs given the importance of emotional intelligence on various management outcomes. Also, gender determines what should be trained. Females might require stronger focus on SEA and ROE, while men may need training on OEA and UOE. Current research in marketing identified emotional intelligence as also a main determinant of economic outcomes in services (e.g., Kidwell, Hardesty, Murtha, & Sheng, 2011). Knowing which employees to train and what to focus on can help practitioners in creating an effective training and development systems.

Limitations and Directions for Future Research

As interpreting the results of our study, the following limitations should be considered that also provide avenues for future research. First, our study is based on a student sample, which, on the one hand, allows comparing homogeneous samples across countries and on the other hand limits the generalizability of the results. Especially, the results for power distance and masculinity could be influenced by the sample. Steel and Taras (2010) note that personal factors, such as age, education, and position, in the corporate ladder might influence the individual culture and therefore the values and norms which students possess might not necessarily reflect the ones of managers who are older, have higher education, and are on high positions in an organization. Future research might consider using a nonstudent sample. Second, we were able to cover only 8 from the 11 cultural clusters described by Ronen and Shenkar (2013). Countries that cover the African, the Arab, and the Nordic cluster are not included in this study. Therefore, our results are not generalizable for countries in these clusters as well as for countries in various subclusters. Future research should aim at covering more countries and regions within the countries in order to provide a more comprehensive analysis. Third, using the recommended translation procedures as well as MGCFA procedure, we have tried to accomplish a comparability of the constructs and the results. Although the reliability for emotional intelligence was good, the reliabilities for the cultural dimensions could be improved. Future research should use already available translations of the constructs of which validity and reliability have already been tested by previous studies in order to contribute to the development and improvement of the existing scales. Fourth, we used the measure proposed by Wong and Law (2002) for emotional intelligence. There are several other measures which could have been used (for an overview and critique see, e.g., Conte, 2005). Therefore, our results are not generalizable for emotional intelligence and future research should consider using other measures. In particular, measures that distinguish between negative and positive emotions might be able to provide a more detailed understanding of culture's influence on emotional intelligence. Finally, the current study is cross-sectional in nature and lacks longitudinal data that would uncover the causal relationships between cultural dimensions and emotional intelligence as well as between the different facets of emotional intelligence. Despite these limitations, our study extends the understanding of the complex relationships between culture and emotional intelligence and begins to disentangle the interrelationships of the different facets of emotional intelligence.

REFERENCES

Abraham, R. (2005). Emotional intelligence in the workplace: A review and synthesis. In R. Schulze & R. Roberts (Eds.), *Emotional intelligence: An international handbook* (pp. 255–270). Cambridge, MA: Hogrefe.

Ang, S., Van Dyne, L., Koh, C., Ng, K. Y., Templer, K. J., Tay, C., & Chandrasekar, N. A. (2007). Cultural intelligence: Its measurement and effects on cultural judgment and decision making, cultural adaptation and task performance. *Management and Organization Review, 3*(3), 335–371.

Arbuckle, J. L. (2013). *Amos version 22.0*. Chicago, IL: IBM SPSS.

Bagozzi, R. P., & Yi, Y. (1988). On the evaluation of structural equation models. *Journal of the Academy of Marketing Science, 16*(1), 74–94.

Bagshaw, M. (2000). Emotional intelligence – Training people to be affective so they can be effective. *Industrial and Commercial Training, 32*(2), 61–65.

Barbuto, J. E., & Bugenhagen, M. J. (2009). The emotional intelligence of leaders as antecedent to leader-member exchanges: A field study. *Journal of Leadership Education, 8*(2), 135–146.

Barsade, S. G. (2002). The ripple effect: Emotional contagion and its influence on group behavior. *Administrative Science Quarterly, 47*(4), 644–675.

Basabe, N., Páez, D., Valencia, J., Rimé, B., Pennebaker, J., Diener, E., & González, J. L. (2000). Sociocultural factors predicting subjective experience of emotion: A collective level analysis. *Psicothema Suplemento, 12*, 55–69.

Bell, S. T. (2007). Deep-level composition variables as predictors of team performance: A meta-analysis. *Journal of Applied Psychology, 92*(3), 595–615.

Bello, D., Leung, K., Radebaugh, L., Tung, R. L., & Van Witteloostuijn, A. (2009). From the editors: Student samples in international business research. *Journal of International Business Studies, 40*(3), 361–364.

Brislin, R. W. (1980). Translation and content analysis of oral and written material. In H. C. Triandis & J. W. Berry (Eds.), *Handbook of cross-cultural psychology* (pp. 389–444). Boston, MA: Allyn & Bacon.

Browne, M. W., & Cudeck, R. (1993). Alternative ways of assessing model fit. In K. A. Bollen & J. S. Long (Eds.), *Testing structural equation models* (pp. 445–455). Newbury Park, CA: Sage.

Byrne, M. B. (2010). *Structural equation modeling with AMOS: Basic concepts, applications, and programming*. New York, NY: Routledge.

Chang, S.-J., Van Witteloostuijn, A., & Eden, L. (2010). Common method variance in international business research. *Journal of International Business Studies, 41*(2), 178–184.

Cherniss, C. (2001). Emotional intelligence and organizational effectiveness. In C. Cherniss & D. Goleman (Eds.), *The emotionally intelligent workplace* (pp. 3–12). San Francisco, CA: Jossey-Bass.

Cherniss, C., & Caplan, R. D. (2001). Implementing emotional intelligence programs in organizations. In C. Cherniss & D. Goleman (Eds.), *The emotionally intelligent workplace* (pp. 286–304). San Francisco, CA: Jossey-Bass.

Cherniss, C., & Goleman, D. (2001). Training for emotional intelligence: A model. In C. Cherniss & D. Goleman (Eds.), *The emotionally intelligent workplace* (pp. 209–233). San Francisco, CA: Jossey-Bass.

Cheung, G. W., & Rensvold, R. B. (2002). Evaluating goodness-of-fit indexes for testing measurement invariance. *Structural Equation Modeling, 9*(2), 233–255.

Clarke, N. (2010). The impact of a training programme designed to target the emotional intelligence abilities of project managers. *International Journal of Project Management, 28*(5), 461–468.

Conte, J. M. (2005). A review and critique of emotional intelligence measures. *Journal of Organizational Behavior, 26*(4), 433–440.

Crowne, K. A., Phatak, A. V., & Salunkhe, U. (2009). Does culture influence intelligence? A study of the influence of cultural context. In C. E. J. Härtel, N. M. Ashkanasy, & W. J. Zerbe (Eds.), *Emotions in groups, organization and culture* (Vol. 5, pp. 275–297). Research on Emotion in Organization. Bingley, UK: Emerald Group Publishing Limited.

Crowne, K. A., Phatak, A. V., Salunkhe, U., & Shivarajan, S. (2011). Exploring intelligences, organizational skills and leadership in Mumbai, India. *International Journal of Business, Humanities and Technology, 1*(2), 44–51.

Day, A., & Carroll, S. (2004). Using ability-based measure of emotional intelligence to predict individual performance and group citizenship behaviors. *Personality and Individual Differences, 36*(6), 1443–1458.

Doherty, R. W. (1997). The emotional contagion scale: A measure of individual differences. *Journal of Nonverbal Behavior, 21*(2), 131–154.

Dulewicz, V., & Higgs, M. (1999). Can emotional intelligence be measured and developed? *Leadership & Organization Development Journal, 20*(5), 242–253.

Dulewicz, V., & Higgs, M. (2004). Can emotional intelligence be developed? *International Journal of Human Resource Management, 15*(1), 95–111.

Ekman, P. (1972). Universal and cultural differences in facial expression of emotions. In J. R. Cole (Ed.), *Nebraska Symposium on Motivation, 1971* (pp. 207–283). Lincoln, NE: University of Nebraska Press.

Fernández-Berrocal, P., Salovey, P., Vera, A., Extremera, N., & Ramos, N. (2005). Cultural influences on the relation between perceived emotional intelligence and depression. *International Review of Social Psychology, 18*(1), 91–107.

Franke, G. R., & Richey, R. G. (2010). Improving generalizations from multi-country comparisons in international business research. *Journal of International Business Studies, 41*(8), 1275–1293.

Goleman, D. (1998). *Working with emotional intelligence.* New York, NY: Bantam Books.

Gross, J. J. (1998a). The emerging field of emotion regulation: An integrated review. *Review of General Psychology, 2*(3), 271–299.

Gross, J. J. (1998b). Antecedent- and response-focused emotion regulation: Divergent consequences for experience, expression, and physiology. *Journal of Personality and Social Psychology, 74*(1), 224–237.

Groves, K. S., McEnrue, M. P., & Shen, W. (2008). Developing and measuring the emotional intelligence of leaders. *Journal of Management Development, 27*(2), 225–250.

Gunkel, M., Schlägel, C., & Engle, R. L. (2014). Culture's influence on emotional intelligence: An empirical study of nine countries. *Journal of International Management, 20*(2), 256–274.

Hair, J. F., Ringle, C. M., & Sarstedt, M. (2011). PLS-SEM: Indeed a silver bullet. *Journal of Marketing Theory & Practice, 19*(2), 139–151.

Harms, P. D., & Credé, M. (2010). Emotional intelligence and transformational and transactional leadership: A meta-analysis. *Journal of Leadership & Organizational Studies, 17*(1), 5–17.

Harzing, A. W., Reiche, B. S., & Pudelko, M. (2013). Challenges in international survey research: A review with illustrations and suggested solutions for best practice. *European Journal of International Management, 7*(1), 112–134.

Hatfield, E., Cacioppo, J. T., & Rapson, R. L. (1994). *Emotional contagion.* Cambridge, MA: Cambridge University Press.

Hofstede, G. (1980). *Culture's consequences.* Beverly Hills, CA: Sage.

Hofstede, G. (2001). *Culture's consequences: Comparing values, behaviors, institutions, and organizations across nations* (2nd ed.). Thousand Oaks, CA: Sage.

Hult, G. T. M., Ketchen, D. J., Cavusgil, S. T., & Calantone, R. J. (2006). Knowledge as a strategic resource in supply chains. *Journal of Operations Management, 24*(5), 458–475.

Hult, G. T. M., Tomas, M., Ketchen, D. J., Griffith, D. A., Finnegan, C. A., Padron-Gonzalez, T. L. ... Cavusgil, S. T. (2008). Data equivalence in cross-cultural international business research: Assessment and guidelines. *Journal of International Business Studies, 39*(6), 1027–1044.

Iacobucci, D., Saldanha, N., & Deng, X. (2007). A meditation on mediation: Evidence that structural equations models perform better than regressions. *Journal of Consumer Psychology, 17*(2), 139–153.

James, L. R., Mulaik, S. A., & Brett, J. A. (2006). A tale of two methods. *Organizational Research Methods, 9*(2), 233–244.

Joseph, D. L., & Newman, D. A. (2010). Emotional intelligence: An integrative meta-analysis and cascading model. *Journal of Applied Psychology, 95*(1), 54–78.

Kidwell, B., Hardesty, D. M., Murtha, B. R., & Sheng, S. (2011). Emotional intelligence in marketing exchanges. *Journal of Marketing, 75*(1), 78–95.

Kitayama, S., & Markus, H. R. (1994). *Emotion and culture: Empirical studies of mutual influence.* Washington, DC: American Psychological Association.

Leung, K. (2008). Methods and measurements in cross-cultural management. In P. B. Smith, M. F. Peterson, & D. C. Thomas (Eds.), *The handbook of cross-cultural management research* (pp. 59–73). Los Angeles, CA: Sage.

Mandell, B., & Pherwani, S. (2003). Relationship between emotional intelligence and transformational leadership style: A gender comparison. *Journal of Business and Psychology, 17*(3), 387–404.

Matsumoto, D. (1989). Cultural influences on the perception of emotion. *Journal of Cross-Cultural Psychology, 20*(1), 92–105.

Matsumoto, D. (1990). Cultural similarities and differences in display rules. *Motivation and Emotion, 14*(3), 195–214.

Matsumoto, D., Nezlek, J. B., & Koopmann, B. (2007). Evidence for universality in phenomenological emotion response system coherence. *Emotion, 7*(1), 57–67.

Mayer, J. D., Caruso, D. R., & Salovey, P. (1999). Emotional intelligence meets traditional standards for an intelligence. *Intelligence, 27*(4), 267–298.

Mayer, J. D., & Geher, G. (1996). Emotional intelligence and the identification of emotion. *Intelligence, 22*(2), 89–113.

Mayer, J. D., & Salovey, P. (1997). What is emotional intelligence? In P. Salovey & D. Sluyter (Eds.), *Emotional development and emotional intelligence: Educational implications* (pp. 3–34). New York City, NY: Basic Books.

Mayer, J. D., Salovey, P., & Caruso, D. R. (2000). Models of emotional intelligence. In R. J. Sternberg (Ed.), *Handbook of intelligence* (pp. 396–420). Cambridge, MA: Cambridge University Press.

McEnrue, M. P., Groves, K. S., & Shen, W. (2009). Emotional intelligence development: Leveraging individual characteristics. *Journal of Management Development, 28*(2), 150–174.

Nikolaou, I., & Tsaousis, I. (2002). Emotional intelligence in the workplace: Exploring its effects on occupational stress and organizational commitment. *International Journal of Organizational Analysis, 10*(4), 327–342.

Nimon, K., & Reio, T. G. (2011). Measurement invariance: A foundational principle for quantitative theory building. *Human Resource Development Review, 10*(2), 198–214.

Nunnally, J. C. (1978). *Psychometric theory*. New York, NY: McGraw-Hill.

Nunnally, J. C., & Bernstein, I. H. (1994). *Psychometric theory* (3rd ed.). New York, NY: McGraw-Hill.

Offermann, L. R., & Phan, L. U. (2002). Culturally intelligent leadership for a diverse world. In R. E. Reggio, S. E. Murphy, & F. J. Pirozzolo (Eds.), *Multiple intelligences and leadership* (pp. 187–214). Mahwah, NJ: Erlbaum.

O'Boyle, E. H., Humphrey, R. H., Pollack, J. M., Hawver, T. H., & Story, P. A. (2011). The relation between emotional intelligence and job performance: A meta-analysis. *Journal of Organizational Behavior, 32*(5), 788–818.

Paez, D., & Vergara, A. (1995). Culture differences in emotional knowledge. In J. A. Russell, J. M. Fernández-Dols, A. S. R. Manstead, & J. C. Wellenkamp (Eds.), *Everyday conceptions of emotion* (pp. 415–434). Dordrecht: Kluwer.

Palmer, B. R., Gignac, G., Ekermans, G., & Stough, C. (2008). A comprehensive framework for emotional intelligence. In R. J. Emmerling, V. K. Shanwal, & M. K. Mandal (Eds.), *Emotional intelligence: Theoretical and cultural perspectives* (pp. 17–38). New York, NY: Nova Science Publishers.

Podsakoff, P. M., MacKenzie, S. B., Lee, J. Y., & Podsakoff, N. P. (2003). Common method biases in behavioral research: A critical review of the literature and recommended remedies. *Journal of Applied Psychology, 88*(5), 879–903.

Preacher, K. J., & Hayes, A. F. (2008). Asymptotic and resampling strategies for assessing and comparing indirect effects in multiple mediator models. *Behavior Research Methods, 40*(3), 879–891.

Reio, T. G. (2010). The threat of common method variance bias to theory building. *Human Resource Development Review, 9*(4), 405–411.

Ronen, S., & Shenkar, O. (2013). Mapping world cultures: Cluster formation, sources and implications. *Journal of International Business Studies, 44*(9), 867–897.

Salovey, P., & Mayer, J. D. (1990). Emotional intelligence. *Imagination, Cognition and Personality, 9*(3), 185–211.

Schlaerth, A., Ensari, N., & Christian, J. (2013). A meta-analytical review of the relationship between emotional intelligence and leaders' constructive conflict management. *Group Processes & Intergroup Relations, 16*(1), 126–136.

Schmitt, N., & Kuljanin, G. (2008). Measurement invariance: Review of practice and implications. *Human Resource Management Review, 18*(4), 210–222.

Schutte, N. S., Malouff, J. M., Thorsteinsson, E. B., Bhullar, N., & Rooke, S. E. (2007). A meta-analytic investigation of the relationship between emotional intelligence and health. *Personality and Individual Differences, 42*(6), 921–933.

Sharma, S., Bottom, W. P., & Elfenbein, H. A. (2013). On the role of personality, cognitive ability, and emotional intelligence in predicting negotiation outcomes: A meta-analysis. *Organizational Psychology Review, 3*(4), 293–336.

Steel, P., & Taras, V. (2010). Culture as a consequence: A multi-level multivariate meta-analysis of the effects of individual and country characteristics on work-related cultural values. *Journal of International Management, 16*(3), 211–233.

Steenkamp, J. B., & Baumgartner, H. (1998). Assessing measurement invariance in cross-national consumer research. *Journal of Consumer Research, 25*(1), 78–107.

Taras, V., Kirkman, B. L., & Steel, P. (2010). Examining the impact of culture's consequences: A three-decade, multilevel, meta-analytic review of Hofstede's cultural value dimensions. *Journal of Applied Psychology*, *95*(3), 405–439.

Trivellas, P., Gerogiannis, V., & Svarna, S. (2011). Exploring workplace implications of emotional intelligence (WLEIS) in hospitals: Job satisfaction and turnover intentions. *Procedia – Social and Behavioral Sciences*, *73*, 701–709.

Tsaousis, I., & Kazi, S. (2013). Factorial invariance and latent mean differences of scores on trait emotional intelligence across gender and age. *Personality and Individual Differences*, *54*(2), 169–173.

Tsui, A. S., Nifadkar, S., & Ou, Y. (2007). Cross-national cross-cultural organizational behavior research: Advances, gaps, and recommendations. *Journal of Management*, *33*(3), 426–478.

Turner, R., & Lloyd-Walker, B. (2008). Emotional intelligence (EI) capabilities training: Can it develop EI in project teams? *International Journal of Managing Projects in Business*, *1*(4), 512–534.

Van Rooy, D. L., Alonso, A., & Viswesvaran, C. (2005). Group differences in emotional intelligence scores: Theoretical and practical implications. *Personality and Individual Differences*, *38*(3), 689–700.

Van Rooy, D. L., & Viswesvaran, C. (2004). Emotional intelligence: A meta-analytic investigation of predictive validity and nomological net. *Journal of Vocational Behavior*, *65*(1), 71–95.

Vernon, P. A., Petrides, K. V., Bratko, D., & Schermer, J. A. (2008). A behavioral genetic study of trait emotional intelligence. *Emotion*, *8*(5), 635–642.

Van de Vijver, F. J. R., & Leung, K. (1997). *Methods and data analysis for cross-cultural research*. Newbury Park, CA: Sage.

Walter, F., Cole, M. S., & Humphrey, R. H. (2011). Emotional intelligence: Sine qua non of leadership or folderol? *Academy of Management Perspectives*, *25*(1), 45–59.

Whitman, D. S., Van Rooy, D. L., Viswesvaran, C., & Kraus, E. (2009). Testing the second-order factor structure and measurement equivalence of the Wong and Law emotional intelligence scale across gender and ethnicity. *Educational and Psychological Measurement*, *69*(6), 1059–1074.

Wong, C.-S., & Law, K. S. (2002). The effects of leader and follower emotional intelligence on performance and attitude: An exploratory study. *Leadership Quarterly*, *13*(3), 243–274.

Ybarra, O., Kross, E., Lee, D. S., Zhao, Y., Dougherty, A., & Sanchez-Burks, J. (2013). Toward a more contextual, psychological, and dynamic model of emotional intelligence. In A. B. Bakker (Ed.), *Advances in positive organizational psychology* (Vol. 1, pp. 167–187). Advances in Positive Organizational Psychology. Bingley, UK: Emerald Group Publishing Limited.

Yoo, B., Donthu, N., & Lenartowicz, T. (2011). Measuring Hofstede's five dimensions of cultural values at the individual level: Development and validation of CVSCALE. *Journal of International Consumer Marketing*, *23*(3/4), 193–210.

Zhao, X., Lynch, J. G., & Chen, Q. (2010). Reconsidering Baron and Kenny: Myths and truths about mediation analysis. *Journal of Consumer Research*, *37*(2), 197–206.

CHAPTER 10

MICROPOLITICAL BEHAVIOR IN THE MULTINATIONAL ENTERPRISE: A LANGUAGE PERSPECTIVE

Rebecca Piekkari and Susanne Tietze

ABSTRACT

Purpose — *In this chapter, we align two approaches on the multinational enterprise (MNE), that is, research on languages and international business, and micropolitics, in order to establish the language-based underpinnings of micropolitical behavior in the MNE.*

Design/methodology/approach — *This theoretical chapter departs from a social, relational perspective on power relationships in the MNE. Power relationships are constituted in multilingual encounters between different language users.*

Findings — *Our analysis builds on the assumption that the mandated corporate language in the MNE, which often is English, results in a language hierarchy. This hierarchy creates inequality and tension between the languages in use in the MNE. However, language agents, that is, headquarters, foreign subsidiaries, teams, managers, and employees*

Multinational Enterprises, Markets and Institutional Diversity
Progress in International Business Research, Volume 9, 259–277
Copyright © 2014 by Emerald Group Publishing Limited
All rights of reproduction in any form reserved
ISSN: 1745-8862/doi:10.1108/S1745-886220140000009010

can – individually or collectively – change, challenge, and disrupt this hierarchical order. Their micropolitical behavior is essential for action as it redraws organizational structure, alters the degree of foreign subsidiary autonomy and control, redefines the privileged and the disadvantaged groups in the MNE, and reinforces subgroup formation and dynamics in multilingual teams.

Research implications *– We highlight the important role played by language agents who sit at the interstices of organizational networks in the MNE. The interplay between their actions and motivations and their historical and situational contexts represents an underexplored and undertheorized area of study.*

Practical implications *– Senior managers in MNEs are frequently very competent or native users of the English language. Appreciating the continued existence of various languages has implications for how different MNE units can effectively connect and operate as an overall entity.*

Originality/value *– This chapter highlights the languages-based mechanisms that underpin power relationships in the MNE.*

Keywords: Micropolitics; language; MNE; power relationship; language agents

INTRODUCTION

Many managers and employees of multinational enterprises (MNEs) use several languages in their communications, whether natural or specialized, on a daily basis (Marschan, Welch, & Welch, 1997; Tietze, 2008). They may negotiate with customers and suppliers in one language, correspond with colleagues in another MNE unit in a second language, and prepare a report for their superior in the matrix structure in a third language. MNE headquarters can decide to mandate a common corporate language in an attempt to facilitate internal communication, formal reporting, and control of foreign subsidiaries (Marschan-Piekkari, Welch, & Welch, 1999a; Neeley, 2013). Nevertheless, this decision "will not render the firm monolingual" (Fredriksson, Barner-Rasmussen, & Piekkari, 2006, p. 409). The parallel use of local languages alongside the common corporate language in the MNE provides space for individuals and organizational units to exercise power (Logemann & Piekkari, 2015; Vaara, Tienari, Piekkari, & Säntti, 2005). They may include and exclude others through language decisions and choice, resist organizational policies and practices, and engage in gatekeeping and boundary spanning behaviors in order to strengthen or weaken their power position in the internal network of the MNE.

However, the MNE has only recently been framed from a micropolitical perspective in order to provide a better understanding of intraorganizational power (Becker-Ritterspach & Dörrenbächer, 2011; Dörrenbächer & Geppert, 2006, 2011; Geppert & Dörrenbächer, 2014). This perspective builds on the understanding that power is embedded in social relationships between the various actors and units of the MNE. In this regard, power is dispersed and distributed across units, and headquarters is only one player among others (Forsgren, 2008). Micropolitics is more concerned with how power relations are constructed and played out in the social fabric of the MNE than with identifying the specific sources of power that actors may draw on. As Dörrenbächer and Geppert (2006, p. 255) explain, the micropolitical perspective examines "conflicts that emerge when powerful actors with different goals, interests, and identities interact with each other locally and across national and functional borders." Hence, it emphasizes the political agency of the various actors and adopts a social rather than a structural approach to power (Dörrenbächer & Geppert, 2006).

In addition to the social, relational take on power, the micropolitical perspective examines power relations in context. MNEs are not placeless, timeless, or agency free but are instead communities rooted in specific cultural and political settings with their own history and tradition. MNE actors, who have their particular identities, are embedded in various institutional contexts that may constrain them but also provide them with the resources necessary to strengthen or defend their position (Morgan & Kristensen, 2006). The proponents of the micropolitical perspective argue that micropolitical behavior needs to be understood as situated activity in its natural organizational and institutional context (Dörrenbächer & Geppert, 2006; Geppert & Dörrenbächer, 2014).

The contribution of this chapter is to marry the micropolitical perspective, which has received limited attention in previous research, with a language perspective on the MNE. Dörrenbächer and Geppert (2011, p. 27) argue that actors constitute power relations "interactively and discursively" when they engage in political activities involving both resistance and negotiations. Their view of power as a social and communicative process invites a language perspective that allows a closer look into the foundations of micropolitical behavior (Geppert & Dörrenbächer, 2014). Instead of concentrating on more subtle cultural differences within the MNE, we focus on language as a day-to-day behavior because it is accessible and salient. Our interest lies in language agents, whether individual or collective, who engage in micropolitical behavior informed by the relevant organizational, cultural, and institutional context.

In order to help set the course of the discussion, we first define the MNE as a multilingual organization. We review a body of recent literature that pays particular attention to the role of languages in the constitution of relationships and structures in MNEs. After describing the internal hierarchy of languages and the concept of language distance, we identify various language agents, both individual and collective, who negotiate order in the MNE. Their micropolitical behavior leads to the redrawing of organizational structures, alterations in the degree of foreign subsidiary autonomy and control, redefinitions of privileged and disadvantaged groups, and the formation of new subgroups in multilingual teams. In doing so, we explicitly establish a mutually reinforcing relationship between the decisions that individuals and organizational units make about language use and micropolitical behavior. We also underline the importance of understanding language agency in context. In the "Discussion" section, we underscore the theoretical advancements and synthesize the key issues facing the field in terms of understanding the MNE as a multilingual meeting ground where aspects of power are rooted in language use. It is worth noting, however, that our aim is not to offer an exhaustive coverage of the literature but rather a more selective review of the contributions made by language-sensitive researchers in the field of international business (IB) that have in our opinion either directly or indirectly examined the relationship between languages and power in MNEs.

MNES AS MULTILINGUAL ORGANIZATIONS

There has been interest in languages in IB research since the 1970s. Studies in international marketing and exporting in particular have highlighted the importance of language when entering foreign markets and selling to overseas customers (Johanson & Wiedersheim-Paul, 1975; Leonidou, 1995; MacDonald & Cook, 1998; Reeves, 1986; Swift, 1991). These early studies conceptualized language primarily as a factor of the external environment rather than a part of the internal environment of the MNE (Brannen, Piekkari, & Tietze, 2014). Questions on how to create integration and effective management processes were addressed mainly from a comparative cultural perspective with the nation-state used as the yardstick.

Since the late 1990s and 2000s, the MNE has increasingly been theorized and empirically investigated from a language perspective that focuses on the role of language in the internal day-to-day functioning of the global firm (Brannen et al., 2014). The advances in information and communication technology coupled with the network structures of organizations have democratized interunit communication in MNEs and increased the need for language skills well below top management (Charles & Marschan-Piekkari, 2002). These contributions have established the MNE as a multilingual organization, which operates not only across national country borders but also across multiple language environments (Brannen, 2004; Fredriksson et al., 2006; Luo & Shenkar, 2006; Marschan-Piekkari et al., 1999a; Marschan-Piekkari, Welch, & Welch, 1999b). The networked MNE is seen to be united by ongoing and recurrent flows of communication carried out in and through a variety of languages (Luo & Shenkar, 2006). This stream of research has effectively replaced the term "multi*national*" with "multi*lingual*."

The research momentum has led to the development of language-sensitive approaches in understanding the MNE and other multilingual organizations (Piekkari & Tietze, 2011; Piekkari & Zander, 2005). Janssens, Lambert, and Steyaert (2004) approached the MNE from a translation perspective and argued that it should be regarded as a translating organization. Barner-Rasmussen and Björkman (2005) established a relationship between a shared language and various organizational mechanisms to achieve cohesion and integration within MNEs. Lauring and Selmer (2011) and Lauring and Tange (2010) in turn examined the consequences of a common corporate language for knowledge sharing and patterns of communication in organizations that are characterized by language diversity. Contexts in flux, which have been triggered, for example, by mergers and acquisitions, have proven to be particularly fruitful arenas for exploring language and communication issues because organizational change typically renders language decisions more visible than stability and *status quo* (De Vecchi, 2012; Piekkari, Vaara, Tienari, & Säntti, 2005; Vaara et al., 2005). Some of these studies have also shed light on the politics of language, which we will now turn to.

Internal Language Hierarchy and Language Distance in the MNE

In the multilingual MNE, some languages are "more equal" than others; this leads to an internal hierarchy of languages rather than a more traditional hierarchy of structure (Marschan-Piekkari et al., 1999b). Typically, the home country language of the parent company is at the apex of the hierarchy, closely followed by English as a common corporate language. The languages used in various foreign subsidiaries located in central and peripheral markets can be found lower down in the hierarchy. The varieties of English also reflect an internal hierarchy with US and British English having a higher value than Indian English, for example (Boussebaa, Schuchi, & Yiannis, 2014). In the following sections, we will unpack the emergence of the language-based hierarchy that forms the basis for an information hierarchy in the MNE. It defines access to information and frequency of interaction, turning some parts of the MNE into "isolated islands."

MNE top management often mandates the use of one or more common corporate language in internal exchanges of the firm (Marschan-Piekkari et al., 1999b; Steyaert, Ostendorp, & Gaibrois, 2011; Vaara et al., 2005). Marschan et al. (1997, p. 591) refer to this administrative tool as "language standardization," which stipulates how and when organizational members should use the company language. A language may also reach the status of a common corporate language through a bottom-up process if it becomes the *de facto* language-in-use in everyday managerial practice (Piekkari, Welch, & Welch, 2014). Language standardization often triggers the creation of an internal language hierarchy, although the term itself implies equality and similarity.

Many MNEs based in both English-speaking and non-English-speaking countries choose English as the common corporate language because of its role as a dominant lingua franca (Tietze, 2008). This has resulted in terms such as "anglicization," "Englishization" (Dor, 2004), "Englishnization" (Neeley, 2012), and "corporate Englishization" (Boussebaa et al., 2014). It is the simplified version of standard English that allows people from different linguistic backgrounds to communicate with each other (Steyaert et al., 2011). It is characterized by company jargon, specific words, and acronyms that differentiate the organization from others and makes sense to insiders of the MNE but not to outsiders (Brannen & Doz, 2012). Louhiala-Salminen, Charles, and Kankaanranta (2005) label it "Business English Lingua Franca" (BELF), which is a shared resource for non-native speakers of English.

The internal hierarchy of languages also privileges the home country language of the MNE and separates it from other less prestigious languages such as those employed in the foreign subsidiaries. This is particularly evident in MNEs headquartered in non-English-speaking countries such as Germany (Fredriksson et al., 2006) or Switzerland, which is known for its official quadrilingualism consisting of German, French, Italian, and Romansh (Steyaert et al., 2011).

The internal hierarchy of languages does not only stratify different languages such as the home country language, the common corporate language, or the subsidiary country language but also distinguishes between varieties of English in terms of the speaker's degree of fluency and the use of appropriate accent. Let us start with language fluency. For some MNE managers and employees, English represents a second, third, or fourth foreign language that needs to be mastered. In the case of limited proficiency, the specialized company terminology and abbreviations may provide them with a short-hand for communicating with each other and for overcoming the language barrier posed by English (Logemann & Piekkari, 2015). For others from Anglophone countries, English is a mother tongue "with all the cultural connotations and subtleties of a 'real' language" (Steyaert et al., 2011, p. 276); it grants them a linguistic advantage. In this regard, native speakers are better positioned than non-natives in the internal language hierarchy of the MNE.

However, even native English speakers are set apart by appropriate accent and register. Boussebaa et al. (2014) investigated two offshore call centers in India that provided business services to Anglo-American MNEs and their foreign customers. Their study shows how Indian employees were trained to speak with the "right" English accent when tasked to serve overseas customers on the phone. However, their customers did not consider the English used by the Indian service providers to be "pure enough" and this gave rise to a hierarchy between different kinds of English (i.e., in terms of pronunciation between Indian English versus American and British English) and reproduced colonial-style power relationships within today's MNEs.

Concomitant with internal language hierarchy, there is also what has been called "language distance" in the MNE (Marschan-Piekkari et al., 1999b, p. 435); it has parallels with the concept of psychic distance (Johanson & Wiedersheim-Paul, 1975). Depending on the fluency of employees in foreign subsidiaries in the relevant languages, perceptions of closeness to headquarters or remoteness from it vary. Those speaking the home country language of the MNE and the common corporate language are closest to headquarters due to their ready access to information and their frequency of interaction and can become powerful players among their counterparts. German and US interviewees of a German engineering company were of the opinion that those based "at the German headquarters were in the location where the bulk of the resources existed, where most decisions were made, and where most people and therefore most development activities resided ... this located them with the 'heart' and 'brain' of the company, where most of the ideas were generated" (Hinds, Neeley, & Cramton, 2014, p. 18). Individuals or units that have a strong link with headquarters can turn into language intermediaries for others that are disconnected or isolated due to limited language resources. In the following discussion, the internal hierarchy of languages is played out as various language agents negotiate and practice language use.

LANGUAGE AGENTS AND MICROPOLITICAL BEHAVIOR

The term "language agent" refers to MNE units such as headquarters and foreign subsidiaries, teams, managers, and employees who individually or collectively negotiate and make decisions about language use. These actors are located at the interstices of MNE networks and "make sense, manipulate, negotiate, and partially construct their institutional environments" (Kostova, Roth, & Dacin, 2008, p. 1001). The decisions made by language agents may take place on a daily, routine basis, or rarely, as one-off corporate decisions concerning the introduction of a new corporate language. The subsequent behaviors reflect intraorganizational power relationships in the MNE. We shall now define language agents and illustrate the kind of changes that they may achieve through micropolitical behavior.

Redrawing Organizational Structure

The language competence of employees in the global network of the MNE influences the ability of various parts of the organization to effectively connect and operate as an overall entity. In a case study of KONE, a Finnish MNE, language skills represented an important component of the subsidiaries' power base (Marschan-Piekkari et al., 1999b). At the time of the study, KONE had a strong regional structure that did not accurately reflect how subsidiaries interacted with each other. The language resources of foreign subsidiaries were like glue, uniting certain units with each other and forming new clusters of, for example, English-speaking, Spanish-speaking, and German-speaking subsidiaries, which differed from the formal structure. In an operative sense, these language clusters facilitated communication and knowledge flows between the respective units and influenced performance outcomes through the sharing of resources. For example, the German and Austrian units benefited from combined management training programs.

The language connections and clusters between subsidiaries reinforced regionalization in the MNE and formed "silos" that tended to impede communication between clusters. This generated a shadow structure, a structural arrangement different from the formal regional lines used in KONE. The concept of shadow structure is useful in explaining how subsidiaries create alliances in order to obtain resources and influence their positions within the global network of the MNE. Taken together, the microprocesses driven by language agents and their maneuvering shaped this emerging structure, rearranged linkages within the organization, and acted as a counter-structuring force in the MNE (Piekkari et al., 2014).

Altering the Degree of Foreign Subsidiary Autonomy and Control

Decisions about language use also affect headquarters−subsidiary relationships in the MNE in important ways. The lack of corporate language competence at the subsidiary level becomes a barrier to communication with headquarters. While this provides some autonomy to the subsidiary in question, it constrains the ability of headquarters to control subsidiary operations. Andersen and Rasmussen (2004) studied Danish firms in France; one of the case companies was a Danish construction machinery firm with two French subsidiaries. The company used English as its corporate language but had only one person at headquarters who could speak French. The French employees were uncomfortable with using English and could not speak Danish. Andersen and Rasmussen (2004, p. 240) comment as follows: "The lack of communication with the French market from the headquarters in Denmark makes the firm extremely vulnerable to sudden changes in the market." The French subsidiaries gained more power and autonomy with regard to the local market where they were embedded. At the same time, the opportunities of the French subsidiary to influence headquarters' attitudes towards its operations, participate in global strategy work, and contribute to general operative procedures were reduced.

The potential consequences of a subsidiary "hiding behind a language" and gaining an overly autonomous position were vividly revealed in the experience of KONE and its newly acquired subsidiary in Italy (Marschan, 1996; Piekkari et al., 2014). KONE's top management had adopted a hands-off approach, placing faith in the efficiency of their formal financial reporting, budgeting, and control system. There were limited Italian skills at headquarters and poor English skills at the Italian end, which enlarged the perceived distance between the units and isolated the subsidiary. In 1995, top management discovered in its Italian units deliberate accounting errors that significantly overstated their profitability (Marschan, 1996). The language distance between headquarters and the foreign subsidiary was too great to facilitate constructive exchange of knowledge.

Redefining the Privileged and the Disadvantaged Groups

As mentioned earlier, cross-border mergers and acquisitions draw attention to the politics of language (De Vecchi, 2012; Piekkari et al., 2005; Vaara et al., 2005). Language choice (i.e., whose language is chosen as the common corporate language to integrate the merging organization) is seen to reflect the relative value and symbolic distribution of resources and power across the parties. These studies engage with the perspectives of the workforce and reveal how the new corporate language redefined the "winners" and "losers" among the various language groups, which were different than before the merger.

Several studies have been conducted on the language policy of Nordea, a Nordic financial institution and its effects on the Finnish branch of the bank (Louhiala-Salminen et al., 2005; Piekkari et al., 2005; Vaara et al., 2005). Swedish was first adopted as the corporate language but later changed to English because of foreign acquisitions. In the early phase of the newly merged bank, Finnish native speakers who were also fluent in Swedish were regarded as privileged and co-opted "little brothers" from the Swedish unit of the bank. Their ability to operate in Swedish, the common corporate language, and Finnish, the subsidiary language, provided them with important positions and opportunities to engage in gatekeeping. While the bilinguals found themselves at the nexus of communications, they were at the same time overloaded with communication and translation activity. Hence, the Finnish speakers sometimes blamed their bilingual colleagues for problems and complications in communication despite the favors provided by them.

On the other hand, the disadvantaged were those who had Finnish as their mother tongue but did not master either Swedish or English.

Consequently, the Finnish voices were silenced (or self-silenced) at meetings and they experienced a loss of professional competence due to their lack of proficiency in Swedish. Lacking opportunities to participate in developmental activities and information networks, they became marginalized and disillusioned (see also Neeley, 2013). This group resisted the new language policy of the bank and distanced itself from organizational goals (Vaara et al., 2005). The corporate language decisions also influenced the relative effectiveness of many organizational systems such as performance appraisal, training programs, career pathing, including "exit choices" and opportunities for promotion which hit the disadvantaged group hard. For example, they were unable to exercise their power to influence performance and appraisal processes (Piekkari et al., 2005).

In the above-mentioned studies, bilingual managers and employees acted as language agents who made local decisions about language use. They frequently maneuvered around headquarters, creating advantageous positions for themselves or their allies. While a common corporate language facilitates postmerger integration, it also influences the relative standing of employees in organizational hierarchies and requires ongoing decision-making and sometimes negotiations over which language to use in which context. It is in the dynamics of these local choices and behaviors that space for both conflict and resolution appears.

Reinforcing Subgroup Formation and Dynamics in Multilingual Teams

Multilingual teams consisting of members from different national and cultural backgrounds provide another fruitful setting for generating a more nuanced understanding language issues and power (Hinds et al., 2014; Kassis Henderson, 2005; Tenzer, Pudelko, & Harzing, 2014). Members of global teams, whether co-located or geographically dispersed, need to interact regularly with each other across national and organizational boundaries. Multilingual teams exercise collective agency through which knowledge is generated and shared in the MNE.

An early study by Kassis Henderson (2005, p. 68) was located in a French MNE where French native speakers and speakers of English and German used "English as the most widely shared language in multilingual teams in MNCs [multinational corporations]." The findings clearly point to the hidden aspects of language use, which continue to influence how communication by team members is received and interpreted. Kassis Henderson (2005) argues that the use of English as a shared language creates false impressions among team members of shared understandings and common interpretive frames. This may lead to miscommunication, negative perceptions of other team members, and serious disruptions in team effectiveness. The study implicitly addresses how language choices may affect team relations, including the attribution of particular intents or characteristics to individuals or groups of speakers of other languages. In this regard, Kassis Henderson (2005) anticipates later work by Hinds et al. (2014) and Tenzer et al. (2014), which provides additional evidence that such attributions are interpreted as political behavior whereby certain language groups attempt to gain an advantage over others.

Hinds et al. (2014) conducted an ethnographic study of six globally distributed software development teams of a German-based MNE. They were interested in finding out whether differing levels of English language competence, which was the mandated language of the German-based MNE and thus on top of the corporate language hierarchy, contribute to subgrouping and subgroup dynamics in daily interaction. The individual teams were distributed across different locations – either Germany and the United States or Germany and India. The authors divided the 96 team members into native English speakers, bilingual speakers, and professional English speakers, that is, all the informants were at least professionally competent in English.

Despite the relatively minor language asymmetries, Hinds et al. (2014, p. 19) found that language was used to "channel and embody power struggles" and negative emotions. The team members distributed across the two locations saw themselves as rivals for critical resources, top management attention, division of labor, and ownership of work. Since many German team members found it difficult to communicate technical and social knowledge in English, they would switch from English to their mother tongue, German, during team meetings in order to consult with their fellow countrymen. US team members objected to these practices of code-switching, mainly interpreting them as an exclusion tactic. One US informant even reported such behavior to top management as a breach of the corporate policy. Those teams that had the most severe power contests also had the most divisive subgroupings based on geography, nationality, and language. The nuanced analysis conducted by Hinds et al. (2014) reveals that power struggles activated subgrouping, thereby reinforcing each other.

Tenzer et al. (2014) investigated how members of multinational teams react to language barriers and how their reactions influence trust formation in teams. Like Hinds et al. (2014), they also conducted a case study in the German context, namely of three MNEs operating in the global automotive sector. The teams used English, German, or a mixture of the two languages in their interaction. The findings by Tenzer et al. suggest that language barriers hampered trust formation and lowered levels of trust. Language barriers generated negative emotions in terms of conflict and tension between team members, which in turn had a detrimental effect on perceived trustworthiness and intention to trust. Similar to the findings by Hinds et al. (2014), team members switched from one language to another during conversations, which created negative emotional reactions in their counterparts. As one respondent put it, "language can be used as an instrument of power, a means to ostracize people. If you want to exclude listeners, you just use a language they don't mastered. In my view, people do this on purpose (Tenzer et al., 2014, p. 524)." Thus, code-switching emerged as an important language-based mechanism leading to conspiracy thinking among team members (see also, Harzing & Feely, 2008; Harzing, Köster, & Magner, 2011). Similarly, team members felt threatened when other members spoke better English. Overall, language use was imbued with emotional insecurities, interpreted as political in character, and considered to be expressive of power in relationships with different language speakers.

Understanding Language Agency in Context

Our previous discussion shows that language agents, both individual and collective, make choices about which language to use. Their agency not only influences and is influenced by the corporate language hierarchy but also by the broader context in which the MNE is embedded. Previous research, which we have already introduced earlier, sheds some light on the contextual factors that shape language hierarchies as well as language use.

The study by Vaara et al. (2005) integrates the historical and political relationship between Sweden and Finland into their analysis of power in the merging Nordic financial institution; this is an unusual approach in this particular body of literature. The introduction of Swedish as the common corporate language recreated the historical structures of domination and reinvented identities of superiority and inferiority between the two nation states. The contribution of the study lies in its treatment of the historical-political relationships between Finland and Sweden that have an enduring influence on contemporary relationships in MNEs. Likewise, the authors continue their exploration of the second corporate language decision to replace Swedish with English as the corporate language from a historical and political perspective. English is by no means an unproblematic or neutral tool in terms of its power implications but expresses Anglo-American cultural dominance. Vaara et al. (2005, p. 621) emphasize that all language decisions "involve specific historical legacies" that manifest themselves in the daily activities of the MNE.

Steyaert et al. (2011) undertook an empirical study of two Swiss MNEs embedded in a domestic linguistic landscape of the four languages mentioned above. The authors wanted to find out how multilingualism plays out in everyday communication at the workplace. One of the MNEs was located in the French-speaking part of Switzerland and this informed the behavior and choices of language agents. The second MNE was also headquartered in the same part of Switzerland, but its operations were global, spanning multiple countries and locations. In this MNE, English was more often used as a language of compromise, in particular at headquarters. Steyaert et al. (2011, p. 270) introduce the concept of a linguistic landscape or "linguascaping" to capture how multilingual organizations try to resolve the complexities and conflicts encountered by their workforce. Their findings clearly show that language agents make decisions in local and situational contexts and that their decisions are not only determined by top-down corporate policies.

Boussebaa et al. (2014) investigated the process of corporate Englishization at two offshore call centers in India that provided services to Anglo-American MNEs and their customers. Focusing on English language "purity" instead of language fluency, they demonstrate how corporate "Englishization" reproduced colonial-style power relationships between offshore call centers and their customers and clients in the West. They draw on the legacy of colonialism in British-Indian relationships to shed light on how power is played out and echo the findings of earlier work by Vaara et al. (2005). Taken together, these studies show that a close examination of language agency warrants attention to the circumstances under which such agency is exercised. External, historical, and political factors, including the broader language environment, often have enduring effects on individual micropolitical behavior.

DISCUSSION

In many regards, the work conducted by situated language agents resonates well with Strauss' (1978) notion of "negotiated order." It views organizations as constructions created by individuals who negotiate and interact with each other on a daily basis in changing organizational contexts (Strauss, 1978; Strauss, Schatzman, Bucher, Ehrlich, & Sabshin, 1964). The negotiation of informal rules (i.e., language use) within formal rules (i.e., corporate language policy and common corporate language) results at best in the establishment of shared meanings. Previous findings in MNEs confirm that such negotiations are prevalent in times of change such as cross-border mergers and acquisitions (Vaara et al., 2005) but also ongoing in project-based multilingual teams (Hinds et al., 2014; Tenzer et al., 2014). The use of power is contextual and contingent on individual choice as well as on situational, organizational, and environmental factors.

The studies reviewed in this chapter deal — directly or indirectly — with how managers and employees in MNEs negotiate the position of English and its relationship with other languages as part of their daily work. Questions of language fluency, language purity, and contextuality create ambiguous spaces where negotiations, language "bartering," and conflict occur. When language agents impose English as the common corporate language in the MNE, they draw on their positional power, but when they make decisions about whether to use English or another language in everyday communications, they are more likely to exercise their agency-based power and take situational expediencies into account. Thus, language users should not be seen as "pawns directed by blunt linguistic dominance but […] as developing a multiple competence which allows them to live in a multioptional context, combing English with other language options" (Steyaert, et al., 2011, p. 277).

Our discussion shows that the role of English is central in addressing questions of language policy and language use because of its status as the global lingua franca in business and management (Nickerson, 2005; Tietze, 2008) as well as in management education (Tietze, 2004; Tietze & Dick, 2013). The English language provides a genuine communicative bridging tool in multilingual situations that facilitates knowledge transfer and integration of disparate units in the MNE (Louhiala-Salminen et al., 2005; Schomaker & Zaheer, 2013). Such a position in itself, however, is an outcome of the particular historical and political processes (Ostler, 2005, 2010) that have catapulted English into this prominent and normalized status. This status is not unproblematic, however. It has been associated with linguistic imperialism, in particular, by Philippson (1992), suggesting that English is far from a neutral medium of communication.

The study of MNEs as multilingual organizations is currently burgeoning (Brannen et al., 2014). An important, though underdeveloped, aspect of language-sensitive research in IB takes the external language environment more strongly into account, including the historical and political legacies that shape how decisions about language choice and use are practiced and received. Future research could constructively focus on the interplay between deep-seated national communicative patterns, which inform the immediate language environment of the MNE as well as the organizational and the individual acts of negotiating a language order within the organization. Such approaches align well with current research on micropolitics in the MNE; they question rationalistic and economically driven approaches to understand intraorganizational power relationships (Geppert & Dörrenbächer, 2014).

CONCLUSION

Drawing together aspects from a micropolitical perspective on the MNC with insights from the stream of languages in IB research (Brannen et al., 2014), we argue that language agents construct power relationships in interactive, discursive ways (Dörrenbächer & Geppert, 2011). The behaviors of language agents are political in character, sometimes "hidden," yet having far-reaching consequences. Language agents stabilize and destabilize established organizational structures, shape streams of knowledge, include or exclude particular language groups from sources of knowledge, and subtly influence the strategic orientation of subunits, which pursue their own, local or individual projects. In doing so, they exercise substantive agency, that is, they do not only mold the process of decision-making through "mere" language work, frequently entailing linguistic translation, but they also shape and influence the very content of decisions as words, ideas, instructions, and initiatives are received, interpreted, and changed at the receiving unit of the MNE. This language work entails transformation and change initiated and continued by language agents. Yet, as has been shown, their degree of agency is relative to their political location and historical legacy.

Future research needs to treat language agents as "embedded agents"; this will enable researchers to interrogate their daily language use in terms of code-switching and translation behavior, while remaining sensitive to political-historical contexts. We believe that in this way, deeper insights into the patterns of political negotiation and bargaining that accompany language choices and decisions in the MNE can be gained.

REFERENCES

Andersen, H., & Rasmussen, E. S. (2004). The role of language skills in corporate communication. *Corporate Communication: An International Journal, 9*(2), 231–242.

Barner-Rasmussen, W., & Björkman, I. (2005). Surmounting interunit barriers. *International Studies of Management and Organization, 35*(1), 28–46.

Becker-Ritterspach, F., & Dörrenbächer, C. (2011). An organizational politics perspective on intra-firm competition in multinational corporations. *Management International Review, 51*(4), 533–559.

Boussebaa, M., Schuchi, S., & Yiannis, G. (2014). Englishization in offshore call centres: A postcolonial perspective. *Journal of International Business Studies*. Retrieved from http://dx.doi.org/10.1057/jibs.2014.25. Advance online publication.

Brannen, M. Y. (2004). When Mickey loses face: Recontextualization, semantic fit and semiotics of foreignness. *Academy of Management Review, 29*(4), 593–616.

Brannen, M. Y., & Doz, Y. L. (2012). Corporate languages and strategic agility: Trapped in your jargon or lost in translation? *California Management Review, 54*(3), 77–97.

Brannen, M. Y., Piekkari, R., & Tietze, S. (2014). The multifaceted role of language in international business: Unpacking the forms, functions and features of a critical challenge in MNC theory and performance. *Journal of International Business Studies, 45*(5), 495–507.

Charles, M., & Marschan-Piekkari, R. (2002). Language training for enhanced horizontal communication: A challenge for MNC's. *Business Communication Quarterly, 65*(2), 9–29.

De Vecchi, D. (2012). What do "they" mean by that? The (hidden) role of language in a merger. *LSP Journal, 3*(2), 71–85.

Dor, D. (2004). From englishization to imposed multilingualism: Globalization, the internet and the political economy on the linguistic code. *Public Culture, 16*(1), 97–118.

Dörrenbächer, C., & Geppert, M. (2006). Micro-politics and conflicts in multinational corporations: Current debates, re-framing, and contributions of this special issue. *Journal of International Management, 12*(3), 251–265.

Dörrenbächer, C., & Geppert, M. (2011). *Politics and power in the multinational corporation: The role of institutions, interests and identities.* Cambridge: Cambridge University Press.

Forsgren, M. (2008). *Theories of the multinational firm: A multidimensional creature in the global economy.* Cheltenham: Edward Elgar.

Fredriksson, R., Barner-Rasmussen, W., & Piekkari, R. (2006). The multinational corporation as a multilingual organisation: The notion of a common corporate language. *Corporate Communications: An International Journal, 11*(4), 406–423.

Geppert, M., & Dörrenbächer, C. (2014). Politics and power within multinational corporations: Mainstream studies, emerging critical approaches and suggestions for future research. *International Journal of Management Reviews, 16*(2), 226–244.

Harzing, A.-W., & Feely, A. J. (2008). The language barrier and its implications for HQsubsidiary relationships. *Cross-Cultural Management: An International Journal, 15*(1), 49–60.

Harzing, A.-W., Köster, K., & Magner, U. (2011). Babel in business: The language barrier and its solutions in the HQ–subsidiary relationship. *Journal of World Business, 46*(3), 279–297.

Hinds, P. J., Neeley, T. B., & Cramton, C. D. (2014). Language as a lightning rod: Power contests, emotion regulation, and subgroup dynamics in global teams. *Journal of International Business Studies*, *45*(5), 536–561.

Janssens, M., Lambert, J., & Steyaert, C. (2004). Developing language strategies for international companies: The contribution of translation studies. *Journal of World Business*, *39*(4), 414–430.

Johanson, J., & Wiedersheim-Paul, F. (1975). The internationalisation of the firm: Four Swedish cases. *Journal of Management Studies*, *12*(3), 305–322.

Kassis Henderson, J. (2005). Language diversity in international management teams. *International Studies of Management & Organization*, *35*(1), 66–82.

Kostova, T., Roth, K., & Dacin, M. T. (2008). Institutional theory in the study of multinational corporations: A critique and new directions. *Academy of Management Review*, *33*(4), 994–1006.

Lauring, J., & Selmer, J. (2011). Multicultural organizations: Common language, knowledge sharing and performance. *Personnel Review*, *40*(1), 324–343.

Lauring, J., & Tange, H. (2010). International language management: Contained or dilute communication. *European Journal of International Management*, *4*(4), 317–332.

Leonidou, L. C. (1995). Empirical research on export barriers: Review, assessment, and synthesis. *Journal of International Marketing*, *3*(1), 29–43.

Logemann, M., & Piekkari, R. (2015). Localize or local lies? The power of language and translation in the multinational corporation. *Critical Perspectives on International Business*, *11*(1) (forthcoming).

Louhiala-Salminen, L., Charles, M., & Kankaanranta, A. (2005). English as lingua franca in Nordic corporate mergers: Two case companies. *English for Specific Purposes*, *24*(4), 401–421.

Luo, Y., & Shenkar, O. (2006). The multinational corporation as a multilingual community: Language and organization in a global context. *Journal of International Business Studies*, *37*(3), 321–339.

MacDonald, S., & Cook, M. (1998). An exploration of the use of language training in exporting firms. Case studies from Northamptonshire. *Local Economy*, *13*(3), 216–227.

Marschan, R. (1996). *New structural forms and inter-unit communication in multinationals*: The case of KONE elevators. PhD dissertation, Helsinki School of Economics, Helsinki, Finland.

Marschan, R., Welch, D., & Welch, L. (1997). Language: The forgotten factor in multinational management. *European Management Journal*, *15*(5), 591–598.

Marschan-Piekkari, R., Welch, D., & Welch, L. (1999a). Adopting a common corporate language: IHRM implications. *International Journal of Human Resource Management*, *10*(3), 377–390.

Marschan-Piekkari, R., Welch, D., & Welch, L. (1999b). In the shadow: The impact of language on structure, power and communication in the multinational. *International Business Review*, *8*(4), 421–440.

Morgan, G., & Kristensen, P. H. (2006). The contested space of multinationals: Varieties of institutionalism, varieties of capitalism. *Human Relations*, *59*(11), 1467–1490.

Neeley, T. (2012). Global business speaks English. *Harvard Business Review*, *90*(5), 116–124.

Neeley, T. (2013). Language matters: Status loss and achieved status distinctions in global organizations. *Organization Science*, *24*(2), 476–497.

Nickerson, C. (2005). English as a lingua franca in international business contexts. *English for Specific Purposes*, *24*(4), 367–380.

Ostler, N. (2005). *Empires of the word. A language history of the world*. London: HarperCollins Publishers.

Ostler, N. (2010). *The last lingua franca: English until the return of Babel*. London: Allen Lane, Penguin Books.

Philippson, R. (1992). *Linguistic imperialism*. Oxford: Oxford University Press.

Piekkari, R., & Tietze, S. (2011). A world of languages: Implications for international management research and practice. *Journal of World Business*, *46*(3), 267–269.

Piekkari, R., Vaara, E., Tienari, J., & Säntti, R. (2005). Integration or disintegration? Human resource implications of a common corporate language decision in a cross-border merger. *International Journal of Human Resource Management*, *16*(3), 330–344.

Piekkari, R., Welch, D. E., & Welch, L. S. (2014). *Language in international business: The multilingual reality of global business expansion*. Cheltenham: Edward Elgar.

Piekkari, R., & Zander, L. (2005). Language and communication in international management. *International Studies of Management & Organization*, *35*(1), 3–9.

Reeves, N. (1986). Education for exporting capability: Languages and market penetration. *Journal of the Royal Society of Arts*, *134*(5355), 182–197.

Schomaker, M. S., & Zaheer, S. (2013). The role of language in knowledge transfer to geographically dispersed manufacturing operations. *Journal of International Management*, *20*(1), 55–72.

Steyaert, C., Ostendorp, A., & Gaibrois, C. (2011). Multilingual organizations as 'linguascapes': Negotiating the position of English through discursive practices. *Journal of World Business*, *46*(3), 270–278.

Strauss, A. L. (1978). *Negotiations: Varieties, processes, contexts, and social order*. San Francisco, CA: Jossey-Bass.

Strauss, A. L., Schatzman, L., Bucher, R., Ehrlich, D., & Sabshin, M. (1964). *Psychiatric ideologies and institutions*. London: Collier-Macmillan.

Swift, J. S. (1991). Foreign language ability and international marketing. *European Journal of Marketing*, *25*(12), 36–49.

Tenzer, H., Pudelko, M., & Harzing, A.-W. (2014). The impact of language barriers on trust formation in multinational teams. *Journal of International Business Studies*, *45*(5), 508–535.

Tietze, S. (2004). Spreading the management gospel –In English. *Language and Intercultural Communication*, *4*(3), 175–189.

Tietze, S. (2008). *International management and language*. London: Routledge.

Tietze, S., & Dick, P. (2013). The victorious English language: Hegemonic practices in the management academy. *Journal of Management Inquiry*, *22*(1), 122–134.

Vaara, E., Tienari, J., Piekkari, R., & Säntti, R. (2005). Language and the circuits of power in a merging multinational corporation. *Journal of Management Studies*, *42*(3), 595–623.

PART III
NEW PERSPECTIVES ON
COUNTRY-SPECIFIC ADVANTAGES
IN INTERNATIONAL BUSINESS

CHAPTER 11

IMPACT OF OUTWARD FOREIGN DIRECT INVESTMENT PROMOTION POLICY: EVIDENCE FROM NEWLY INDUSTRIALIZED, EMERGING, AND DEVELOPING ASIAN ECONOMIES

Filip De Beule, Danny Van Den Bulcke[†] and Haiyan Zhang

ABSTRACT

Purpose — *To analyze the industrial development of South, East, and Southeast Asian nations in terms of investment and trade and how the institutional environment — in particular, the government policy with regard to outward foreign direct investment (OFDI) — has played a role in this respect.*

[†]Danny Van Den Bulcke passed away on January 8, 2014. His two coauthors would like to posthumously acknowledge Danny Van Den Bulcke for his research insights and policy suggestions.

Multinational Enterprises, Markets and Institutional Diversity
Progress in International Business Research, Volume 9, 281–302
Copyright © 2014 by Emerald Group Publishing Limited
ISSN: 1745-8862/doi:10.1108/S1745-886220140000009011

Methodology/approach — *The chapter puts OFDI policy and industrial upgrading in newly industrialized, emerging, and developing Asian economies (NIEDAEs) in historical perspective to attempt to draw inference from their past behavior.*

Findings — *The chapter provides information about each NIEDAE's experience with OFDI policy through a comparative analysis of OFDI promotional policy.*

Practical implications — *A useful source of information about each NIEDAE's OFDI policy approach, the chapter attempts to draw recommendations for OFDI policy.*

Originality/value — *This chapter fulfills an information need and offers practical help to government policy makers.*

Keywords: Outward foreign direct investment policy; Southeast Asia

INTRODUCTION

Although much analysis has focused on the determinants of investment attraction and investment location, not only inward FDI patterns but also patterns of outward foreign direct investment (OFDI) reflect the particular institutional and policy context in which the investing firms have evolved and developed their ownership advantages (Dunning, 2009). For instance, corporate decisions are affected by the legal framework governing international capital flows, as well as by proactive policy measures to assist companies in their internationalization process (UNCTAD, 2006). Given the extent to which incentives and support from the government and other institutions influence the internationalization process of firms, the institutional approach has been added to the classic resource-based and industry-based view to form an integrated framework (Lu, Liu, & Wang, 2011; Peng, Wang, & Jiang, 2008) to analyze investment behavior and strategic choices in the internationalization of firms.

Traditional industrial organization literature indicates that conditions within an industry determine a firm's strategy and performance (Porter, 1980). Attributes of the industry structure, in terms of competitive rivalry, homogeneity of products and barriers of entry and exit shape the extent to which a firm is likely to achieve advantage on a global scale. According to industrial organization thinking, internationalization decisions of a firm

depend upon the degree of rivalry and competition of the particular industry in which it operates (Hymer, 1976; Wang, Hong, Kafouros, & Boateng,
2012). The resource-based view of the firm analyzes more in detail the firm-
level heterogeneous characteristics that make up its competitive advantage
and drives its internationalization.

It is suggested that the strategies of multinational enterprises from emerging economies differ from those from developed countries. Multinationals
from emerging economies invest overseas at a relatively earlier stage of
their development than their counterparts from developed economies
(UNCTAD, 2006). To contribute to the understanding of the internationalization strategy of firms from emerging economies, it needs to be investigated whether factors determining internationalization by firms from
emerging economies differ from those initiated by firms from developed
economies. In particular, the institutional aspect of government policy will
be analyzed in this regard.

In summary, the objective of this chapter is to examine the impact of
OFDI promotion policy from an institution-based point of view, while the
evidence of 10 newly industrialized, emerging, and developing Asian economies (NIEDAEs), including Hong Kong, Singapore, South Korea, Taiwan,
Thailand, the Philippines, Malaysia, Indonesia, China and India will be discussed. This will be confronted to some of the more traditional countries in
the developed world to shed light on the differences and similarities.

REGIONAL INDUSTRIAL UPGRADING: THE ROLE OF INVESTMENT AND TRADE

Although the most important outward investors are still the old triad countries, that is, Western European countries, the United States, and Japan,
more and more developing and emerging countries have joined the ranks of
outward investors as they have climbed the development ladder. Without
any doubt, the most significant global shift in the geography of the
world economy during the past 50 years has been the resurgence of Asia —
especially South, East, and Southeast Asia (Dicken, 2011). These regions
have witnessed a tremendous transformation in their economic structure
over the last half century. During this period a number of countries have
sequentially experienced economic takeoff after Japan, such as the newly
industrialized economies (NIEs) of Korea, Hong Kong, Taiwan, and
Singapore; followed by the so-called ASEAN-4 (Indonesia, Thailand,
Malaysia, and the Philippines), China, and India.

The relative importance of these NIEDAEs is especially marked in the sphere of exports. Indeed, in the global reorganization of manufacturing production and trade the increased importance of Asia as an exporter of manufactures is unique in its magnitude. In 1989, Cuyvers and Van Den Bulcke reflected on the outward oriented development strategy of the Newly Industrialized Countries (NICs) or Economies (NIEs). In 1973, the NICs (Hong Kong, Singapore, South Korea, and Taiwan) accounted for 2.9 percent of world exports. In 1985, this share had more than doubled and reached 7.3 percent. The so-called newly exporting countries (NECs) or ASEAN-4 consisting of Indonesia, Malaysia, the Philippines, and Thailand went from 2.8 percent in 1963 to 5.8 percent in 1980 in total manufactures exported from developing countries. As such, the Southeast Asian economies (Korea, Hong Kong, Singapore, Taiwan, Indonesia, Malaysia, Philippines, Thailand) increased their collective share of total world manufactured exports from a mere 1.5 percent in 1963 to almost 20 percent in 1999 despite the East Asian financial crisis of 1997–1998, which had a devastating effect on most of the East Asian economies. By 2008, this share had declined to 12 percent, largely as a result of the growth of another neighboring country China.

The rise to prominence of NIEDAEs is not only apparent in their exporting importance and patterns but also in their investment behavior. The OFDI stock by these Asian economies has become increasingly noteworthy and prevalent in recent years. According to UNCTAD (2013), OFDI stock from these NIEDAEs reached US$2,954 billion by the end of 2012, representing 12.5 percent of the world total OFDI stock, while the relative share was 2.7 percent in 1980, 2.8 percent in 1990, and 7.9 percent in 2000. While the four NIEs are responsible for a large share of such OFDI, that is, 9 percent in 2012, China and India have rapidly become new sources of OFDI during the last decade. From 2000 to 2012, the share of these two NIEDAEs in the world total OFDI stock respectively increased from 0.35 and 0.02 percent to 2.16 and 0.05 percent in 2012. The share of ASEAN-4 in the global OFDI stock has also increased during this period, that is, from 0.34 percent to 0.77 percent.

It is often believed that the success of Asian economies stemmed from their absolute devotion to economic liberalism and their support of private industry. In reality the governments of the NICs were quite active participants in the economy and have intervened continuously (De Beule & Van Den Bulcke, 2010). Unlike Hong Kong the three other Far Eastern NICs only switched to an outward-looking policy in the early 1960s: Taiwan in 1958–1960, South Korea in 1962–1966, and Singapore in 1965.

South Korea especially provided a good example of direct government intervention and a successful industrial policy.

Of the four economies, Korea undoubtedly started out as the most restrictive toward FDI. The Korean policy was to a certain extent inspired by the Japanese example of twenty years earlier, which basically only allowed the entry of foreign firms when their role was considered compatible with the government's development strategies. The first attempt to draw the attention of foreign capital by South Korea was made in 1960 (Foreign Capital Inducement Promotion Act), but it took a while before foreign firms ventured into the country, however. Fearing some adverse effects from foreign penetration a revision of the attitude was carried out in 1973 when measures were taken to give priority to co-ownership projects with Korean nationals. A second reversal occurred in 1984 when a new "open door" policy was launched by a revision of the 1973 foreign capital inducement act (De Beule & Van Den Bulcke, 2010).

From the early 1950s onwards, Hong Kong pursued a more export-oriented policy, whereas Taiwan and South Korea were at that time still inward looking and following import substitution policies. The policy orientation of Hong Kong was very much linked to its role of commercial entrepot in the Far East, hence, the importance of re-exports. However, Hong Kong also benefited from the advantages of the Commonwealth Preference System during this period (Kam-Hon, 1982). As compared to Hong Kong's *laissez-faire* policy, the other three Far Eastern NICs adopted restrictive measures to protect their own industry. Yet, they also introduced export incentives as part of their economic development strategy (Cuyvers & Van Den Bulcke, 1989).

The economies of Taiwan and Hong Kong during the 1960s and 1970s were strongly based on the development of labor-intensive manufactured exports, particularly to the U.S. market. Both economies produced an enormous range of light, labor-intensive manufactures: beginning with plastic flowers in Hong Kong, extending through a vast range of sporting and travel goods, to the huge garment and footwear sectors. This success had an important demonstration effect on China from the beginning of its reform era, because Chinese policy-makers observed their success and sought to emulate and repeat it through economic reform (Naughton, 2007). In a way they formed the basis for the emergence of the early success of the People's Republic of China (PRC) in its outward looking liberalization policy. The export success of Taiwan and Hong Kong began to have a much more direct effect on the Chinese Mainland in the mid-1980s, when it began to drive a restructuring of East Asian production networks.

Exporters from these two newly industrializing economies were convinced by the increasing wages and costs and currency realignments to move production to lower wage locations. This was made possible because, at the same time, capabilities were rapidly upgrading in both Taiwan and Hong Kong: educational levels soared, supply of engineering and scientific manpower increased, and commercial and financial experience accumulated rapidly. Attracted to higher skill and higher remuneration occupations, employees were pulled away from traditional labor-intensive manufacturers, whose managers had no choice but to look around for other locations. They expanded and deepened the bilateral economic cooperation by first building up cross-border intra-firm labor division and then duplicating and extending the local industries of Taiwan and Hong Kong, which later moved into the East coast of Mainland China (Yang & Huang, 2011).

The opening of PRC to foreign direct investment at the end of the 1970s created a dramatic opportunity to transfer labor-intensive export production to the PRC. This development was part of a worldwide trend toward increasing intra-industry trade. The trend toward the geographical dispersion of production chains led to an increasing share of international trade that is made up of intermediate and capital goods and to mounting FDI to build the required networks. This process was particularly powerful in what is known as "Greater China" because transaction costs for Taiwan and Hong Kong firms to operate in the PRC were low. Proximity, aided by common language and customs, made doing business on the mainland easy and cheap, once the mainland's economic system opened up at the beginning via its special economic zones (De Beule & Van Den Bulcke, 2009). Moreover, low transactions costs made it possible to initially move only the most labor-intensive − typically low-skilled − stages of production onto the Mainland, while retaining the coordinating and controlling activities in Hong Kong or Taiwan. Production chains were quickly created that crossed political boundaries and allowed Hong Kong and Taiwan to specialize in high-value services and technology-intensive production while much of the ordinary manufacturing moved to the PRC.

In the 1980s, Taiwan changed the focus to advanced electronics instead of heavy industry which had received priority in the industrial policy in the 1970s. Taiwan began a campaign to entice skilled overseas ethnic Chinese to return to the island since their technological expertise was crucial in the expansion of these industries. Although foreign investment in Taiwan began to slow down, the island had also become a major outward investor. Taiwanese companies moved production abroad, to locations in Southeast

Asia and in particular China where they took advantage of the same lack of organized labor and the low salaries that had been a feature of Taiwan a few decades earlier (Brown, Hempson-Jones, & Pennisi, 2010).

This restructuring moved remarkably quickly for traditional labor-intensive manufacturing, such as garments and footwear, as this process was basically completed by the early 1990s. For example, while Taiwanese firms moved their footwear production to the Mainland, the United States started to import shoes from China which were in fact "displaced" imported shoes from Taiwan. A similar restructuring of the electronics industry began around 1990. It was followed by many successive waves of relocation, of which the most recent – and one of the most dramatic – has been the transplantation of the notebook computer industry during the first decade of the new millennium. In the personal computer and components industry, production of keyboards and power supply units (the most labor-intensive products) were the first to move to mainland China, because the cost advantages were most marked. They were followed by production of monitors and motherboards, and a steadily expanding range of IT hardware products.

From the middle of the 1980s to the end of the first decade of the new millennium the key story of Taiwan throughout this era, however, was the continued interdependence of the Taiwanese and Mainland Chinese economies despite the increasing differences between their political systems. Like the rest of the world, Taiwan looked to the Mainland as a source of development and expansion, particularly because of its newly emerging consumer base. In 1985, Taiwan's largest trading partner, accounting for almost half its exports, was the United States. In 1998, the United States accounted for a quarter of its exports, while China had risen from nowhere to taking up 23 percent. In 2009, the Mainland and Hong Kong took 41 percent of Taiwan's goods combined, with the United States dropping to a mere 11 percent.

Both Hong Kong and Taiwan have experienced substantial success in upgrading to higher skilled activities, while simultaneously experiencing steadily rising incomes and relatively low unemployment. Hong Kong's restructuring has been especially thorough, as it has shed many industrial functions altogether and moved into greater specialization in services, particularly finance, transport, and telecommunications. In Taiwan restructuring within the manufacturing sector itself has been the most impressive feature. Taiwan has moved into technologically more sophisticated products while shedding low-technology activities. Thus, the upgrading of skills occurred in similar and contradictory ways in Hong Kong and

Taiwan. Hong Kong moved out of manufacturing and into a variety of business services, such as finance, marketing, and accounting. Taiwan has been quite successful in improving technological capacities and moving into production and export of commodities at much higher technological levels, yet it now also seeks to become a business-operations and financial center (De Beule & Van Den Bulcke, 2011).

When China gradually became a more open market-oriented economy over time, other Asian economies also followed suit and China quickly developed into the favorite offshoring destination for final assembly for a whole range of goods. Japan, but also Korea and Singapore became quite substantial investors in China, following the same process that Hong Kong and Taiwan had followed previously.

The economic development paths of these countries have been very much interdependent. Singapore was an early recipient of FDI, and has been attracting MNEs since the 1960s, initially in the electric and electronic sector, before slowly attracting more value-added type activities, and moving from a manufactured-based economy to a service-centered one, attracting RHQ, core business functions and establishing itself as a hub for financial services. Although Malaysia, Thailand, and Indonesia opened their doors later than Singapore, they benefited greatly from MNEs established in Singapore wishing to expand their operations to other countries in the region, and continue to benefit from low-cost factors of production, as well as a favorable international institutional framework institutional facilitating exports from ASEAN operations to third markets in the EU and the United States. The benefits of ASEAN membership, especially gaining from the ASEAN milieu and learning from more successful neighbors, remain accessible today for new members, especially for poorer countries such as Cambodia and Vietnam (Giroud & Mirza, 2010).

Also, as China's modernization drive gained momentum in the late 1980s; many Chinese delegations visited Singapore, a Chinese role model nation that achieved notable economic success through a strong government within 30 years of independence. The Chinese visitors were eager to learn modern management methods, while Singapore was also planning integration with other Southeast Asian economies via regionalization, which focused on overseas investment. As a result, for example, in 1992, the idea of developing a modern industrial township with Singaporean experience was proposed. After rounds of discussions and site surveys, both governments decided to join hands in developing a modern industrial park in the east of the city of Suzhou. The Suzhou International Park (SIP) was founded in 1994 as a cooperation between the governments of China and Singapore and after a hesitant start-up period developed into a successful venture (Pereira, 2001).

With respect to trade, China's economic upgrading led to an increasing share of parts and components being shipped from around Asia to China for final assembly that were consequently exported towards Europe and the United States. As a result, China ran a trade deficit toward Asia while it maintained a more than healthy trade surplus with Europe and the United States, in particular. For leading countries like Singapore this global value chain configuration meant that they have a trade surplus with China supplying them with parts and components, while maintaining a trade deficit with developed countries in Europe and the United States by importing final consumption goods.

As Chinese firms started to upgrade their competitive strengths, they started developing and exporting products themselves instead of relying on export processing by foreign subsidiaries. Given the experience of these Chinese firms in their domestic market, they started targeting customers in other developing countries, especially in Asia. They also supported these exports through trade supporting investments. On the whole, this has led to an increasing trade surplus for China, not only with the developed countries, but also in Asia. As a result, the makeup of China's trade partners has become more diversified: the percentage of trade with China's traditional partners including the EU, the United States, and Japan has declined over time whereas marked growth was spotted in trade with emerging markets such as the ASEAN in recent years. The structure of foreign trade entities in China has also changed as private enterprises took up a higher percentage whereas dependence on foreign-invested enterprises was alleviated since the last few years. As a result, the development in foreign trade was more balanced across different regions of China. Foreign trade in coastal provinces and municipalities including Guangdong and Jiangsu now has a smaller part in total national imports and exports than before, whereas imports and exports in the mid-western region has picked up momentum in the last decade (General Administration of Commerce [GAC], 2014).

Also, due to rising production costs in China, some ASEAN countries, such as Cambodia, Indonesia, Myanmar, and Vietnam, have gained ground as low-cost production locations, especially for low-end manufacturing. As China continues to experience rising wages and production costs, the widespread offshoring of low-cost manufacturing to China has been slowing down and divestments are occurring from the coastal areas. Although there might be efficiency-seeking investment going on within

China, investors – including Chinese – have increasingly found their way to other Southeast Asian nations. Meanwhile structural transformation is shifting FDI inflows in China toward higher technology sectors and services (UNCTAD, 2011).

The rise of NIEDAEs' share of global FDI outflows jumped from below 10 percent before 2008 to around 18 percent in 2010 and 20 percent in 2012. There were important outflows in extractive industries (oil, gas, and minerals) especially from China. In manufacturing the major outward investing sectors are electronics, metal and metal products, motor vehicles, and chemicals. As the global center of electronics production the region is also the major source of FDI in the electronics industry and is in line with the international competitiveness of Asian companies in the industry, particularly the contract manufacturers, which have become the dominant force at the production stage of the global electronics value chain. For instance, the Taiwanese company Hon Hai has become the world's largest contract manufacturer with about US$60 billion of sales and one million employees in 2010. Driven by market- and efficiency-seeking motivations, manufacturers of a wide range of industries have been investing mainly in neighboring countries (UNCTAD, 2011).

In summary, we can conclude that the ASEAN remain competitive in attracting inward FDI thanks to their country-specific advantages (CSAs). By contrast, the competitiveness of the local firms in these economies, with the exception of Singapore and Malaysia's relatively prominent role as ASEAN's outward investors was clearly reflected by the amount of their outward FDI stock. In 2007, the outward FDI stock of Singapore and Malaysia accounted for over 85 percent of Southeast Asia's total outward FDI stock (Gugler & Pananond, 2010). A significant characteristic of these leading multinationals from Southeast Asia is that many of these firms are actually owned by the state. Partial state ownership in private firms is mostly evident among the Singaporean firms. Of Singapore's top 11 multinationals, 6 were partly owned by the Singaporean government, through its main holding company Temasek. However, overseas Chinese groups, such as CP and Kuok group, also have substantial investments abroad. The NIEs have become the largest source of OFDI from Asia since the 1990s, taking over from Japan (see Fig. 1).

Apart from market size, ASEAN also benefits from its location as a natural bridge linking two great economies, China and India – a unique advantage for conducting business. Although some see ASEAN's production base are being "squeezed" by these neighboring economic powerhouses, ASEAN, India, and China complement one another. The two giant

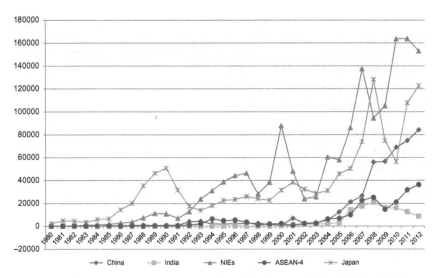

Fig. 1. Outward Foreign Direct Investment Flows, 1980–2012. *Source*: Authors 'calculations based on the UNCTAD FDI database.

economies have become expanding markets for ASEAN exports and also key sources of direct investment into ASEAN. In general, the economies of India and ASEAN have a much greater degree of complementarity than between China and ASEAN. This is because China and ASEAN are highly dependent on FDI flows for their exports and growth dynamics, while India is not so dependent on FDI (Gugler & Chaise, 2010, Fig. 1). Inward FDI in the NICs is thereby not limited to labor-intensive electronics and textiles but extends to capital-intensive chemical industry as well (UNCTAD, 2011).

A new round of industrial restructuring is taking place in China and some low-end, export-oriented manufacturing activities have been shifting from coastal China to low-income countries in Southeast Asia and also Africa. ASEAN's less developed countries also received increasing inflows particularly from China. Also, Laos attracted investment from China in infrastructure such as railway construction (UNCTAD, 2011). Cambodia differs from other countries, as firms located there had moved to the country for the availability of quotas in the United States and Western Europe, exemplifying the role of international trading systems, and customers' recommendations as incentives for FDI (Giroud & Mirza, 2010). For laggard countries, such as Vietnam and Indonesia, this meant that they are now becoming the next investment target, running increasing trade deficits with other Asian nations while increasing their trade surplus with developed markets in the United States and Europe. Other countries, like the Philippines, were less able to upgrade their competitive strengths and are running an increasing trade deficit with the Asian region while also losing developed country export markets.

The results show that ASEAN MNEs possess strong advantages in terms of networking capability and management ability, while others have strong brand reputation and advanced technology. The locational advantages vary among the ASEAN member countries. Singaporean MNEs tend to possess strong CSAs, especially in terms of high-quality human resources and financial system advantages. Thai MNEs enjoy CSAs in terms of resource endowment and market opportunities, in both home and host countries. Malaysian MNEs also have strong CSAs, stemming especially from the government support policy. MNEs from the Philippines, Indonesia, and Vietnam encounter weak CSAs, for example, due to poverty, pervasive corruption, and/or an unstable economy (Nessara & Rugman, 2010).

Asia has witnessed a tremendous rise in the last half century (see Fig. 2). Much of this rise has been realized by what has been termed flying geese industrialization (De Beule & Van Den Bulcke, 2011). This includes Japan as the leading goose, followed by the four Asian NIEs of Hong Kong,

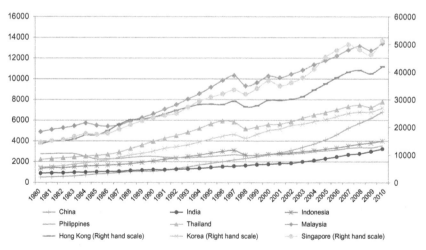

Fig. 2. GDP Per Capita, PPP, 1980−2010. *Source*: World Development Indicators (Worldbank).

Taiwan, South Korea, and Singapore, and two ASEAN countries, Malaysia and Thailand. There is an eerily similar pattern of growth in these Asian nations although at different levels of income. Indonesia and the Philippines missed their takeoff, however, and were surpassed by China. Fig. 2 illustrates how the income per capita of China has surpassed that of both Indonesia and the Philippines over the course of a few decades. China has, to some extent, become another lead goose and has taken countries such as Vietnam, Indonesia, and Cambodia in its wake.

The more direct and intimate trade linkages between Japan and China and driving force of the East Asian trade bloc signify the change of the traditional East Asian flying geese pattern with Japan alone as the leading goose. The rise of China and its leaping over the follower geese of the four NIEs and the ASEAN-4 countries to become the closest trade partner of Japan has shown the difference of its development route from its predecessors. As such, China has broken the rank of flying formation and laid out a next era of development. As a leaping frog China fulfills the conditions required for technological leapfrogging and the shift from lagging to leading. In line with the structural change of the East Asian trade bloc, China has come forward from the outer layer to the innermost core and closely bonded with Japan, meaning that the leapfrogging theorem may provide an explanation (Yang & Huang, 2011).

It very much looks as if the orderly V-formation of the flying geese flock has been disturbed by the rise of China. The intra-regional trade in East Asia consists mainly of parts and components, while the commercial transactions between East Asia and the rest of the world are mostly final goods. With the global financial crisis inflicting heavily on these advanced economies and decreasing their purchasing power, the exports from East Asia weakened. In contrast, the rising domestic demand in the region, especially in the household consumption in China (De Beule & Van Den Bulcke, 2012), came to the rescue of the East Asian countries in the global recession. By fulfilling the conditions of leaping in technology and switching in position from lagging to leading, China may indeed have become from a follower goose to a joint leading goose together with Japan in the new East Asian Flying geese paradigm (Yang & Huang, 2011), aptly called "tandem growth" by Ozawa (2009).

Much of China's economic and technological leapfrogging has been realized by its open door policy's focus on inward foreign direct investment (Luo, Xue, & Han, 2010). In this respect, some Southeast Asian economies have also started using inward FDI to speed up their international competitive position. As these countries are (becoming) some of the most important new locations of production of goods and services; they are also gradually but surely evolving as a source of serious competition for firms in their own domestic markets. A lot of the goods and services from China, for instance, are produced for the export markets, making for some cut-throat competition in the home countries of Western multinationals. This competition is not merely limited to the domestic markets, but is increasingly also spreading to third markets (Zhang & Van Den Bulcke, 1996b). Given the characteristics of the companies from those emerging markets, their products are also better suited for consumers in other emerging third markets. In line with the investment development path (Zhang & Van Den Bulcke, 1996a), these countries are increasingly becoming more important outward foreign direct investors (De Beule & Van Den Bulcke, 2009).

OFDI POLICY OF NIEDAES IN HISTORICAL PERSPECTIVE

Some NIEDAEs' governments have introduced specific promotion policies on OFDI, while others have made specific policy statements encouraging their enterprises to internationalize through OFDI. The so-called "Asian Tigers" from Southeast Asia were among the first developing economies to liberalize and to start promoting OFDI. Improvements in the balance of payments of countries and the build-up of foreign exchange reserves often were necessary but not sufficient conditions for governments to reevaluate their OFDI policy.

During the 1960s and 1970s most governments in developed countries were not very proactive in promoting OFDI either. In fact, outward investment was opposed in many home countries as it was seen as substituting for exports, reducing domestic capital investment, and causing the loss of jobs. Yet, it was also defended to guarantee the growth and prosperity of home-based firms in the contest for worldwide markets. Outward investment therefore became gradually acceptable as necessary to maintain and improve the competitiveness of firms from the countries of origin by exposing them to international markets via direct investment (De Beule & Van Den Bulcke, 2010).

Increasingly, moreover, attention shifted from the macroeconomic impact to micro-economic significance. In a rapidly globalizing world, companies could no longer merely count on their home markets as a relatively secure source of profits (UNCTAD, 2007). Competition from foreign firms became global through imports, inward FDI, and non-equity forms of participation. These various exposures and conditions made it all the more important for firms to pay attention to their competitiveness (Sauvant, 2005). For integrating developing country firms into the global economy OFDI became an important aspect and vehicle of this consideration. That the benefits of internationalization for increasing firm competitiveness became generally recognized is indirectly demonstrated by the fact that also small and medium-sized firms are expanding abroad by OFDI and that more countries are encouraging their firms to do so. In particular, OFDI can help firms increase their revenues, assets, profitability, market reach, and exports (UNCTAD, 2007).

After the Second World War, when developed countries had to cope with the urge of some of their companies to invest abroad, they only hesitantly allowed this because of the looming uncertainty about their future balance of payments developments and the shortages of foreign exchange. To achieve a balance between the need to "control" cross-border capital outflows and the pressure for firms to internationalize was therefore of paramount importance. Once the macroeconomic skies had cleared at the beginning of the 1970s most of the developed countries rather quickly released these restrictions, even though employment concerns almost caused a revival of OFDI controls in a country such as the United States (e.g., the Burke-Hartke proposal in the American Congress).

While some developed countries retained only a few restrictions that were applicable during the 1970s (UNCTAD, 1995), changes in the world economic conditions and the evolving nature and expansion of MNEs transformed the attitudes and policies of the governments of emerging economies toward outward FDI. The globalization of the financial markets and the integration of the value added activities across national borders made international competition more severe. These mounting competitive pressures convinced a number of emerging countries that OFDI had become a necessary strategic option to acquire resources abroad such as raw materials, and to get access to energy, skilled labor, as well as technology and know-how. The policy environment that supports OFDI in general has improved. More countries have removed barriers and simplified regulations for OFDI (UNCTAD, 2007).

For the economies of Southeast Asia, this policy change took place in the second half of the 1980s and early 1990s, that is, Singapore in 1986, Taiwan, Province of China, and the Republic of Korea in 1987, Malaysia and Thailand in 1991. China and India gave a new impetus to their OFDI policy from 1992 onwards (De Beule & Van Den Bulcke, 2010).

During the 1960s and 1970s, developed countries used a number of direct or indirect measures to stimulate their enterprises to venture abroad via OFDI. Essentially, emerging markets, during the 1990s and the first decade of the new millennium relied on the same kind of measures, although there were differences in the intensity with which they were applied. For instance, emerging economies provided incentives to outward FDI long before most controls on inward FDI had been suspended. They also started promoting OFDI well before they had reached the supposedly required stage in the so-called "investment development path" as put forward by Dunning (1981). Also, the existence of direct links between the government and business in several emerging markets — such as for instance China and Singapore — gives a special dimension to the promotional programs and makes it difficult to disentangle the real influence that is exerted on their OFDI policy.

The OFDI promotion policy in NIEDAEs during the last decade consists of a series of measures providing policy statement, regulatory framework, and institutional supports (UNCTAD, 2007). The government of Singapore announced 2004 as the year of internationalization, while the Chinese government established a policy of "go global" in 2000. In 2003, the government of India has specifically encouraged Indian enterprises to go global. In improving OFDI environment, China and India have liberalized their regulatory framework and relaxed exchange controls for OFDI. Supportive measures by the Chinese and Indian governments include also the streamlining OFDI approval procedures, and raising the investment permit ceiling and the conditions governing equity ownership of affiliates abroad. Some NIEDAEs, such as Malaysia and Thailand, have gone beyond liberalization to active promotion — for example, providing institutional support to help their firms internationalize, and organizing OFDI missions to target host countries. Countries such as Singapore, South Korea, and China have supported the creation of foreign enclaves such as industrial parks or special economic zones in host countries. Some even provide incentives and market intelligence information to encourage internationalization of their firms (Singapore). Some countries have private-sector cooperation and networking to promote South-South investment (Malaysia) and investment in other countries (Singapore) (UNCTAD, 2007).

The impact of OFDI on the country of origin illustrates another marked difference in the comparison and assessment of OFDI between developed and emerging economies. While the loss of employment was a very serious concern in developed countries during the 1970s, it is somewhat surprising that this issue is not all that prominent in the discussion about the attitudes of developing countries toward OFDI. This may be due to several reasons. First, this might be explained by the absence of strong trade unions in developing countries. During the 1970s, especially in the United States, but also in the European countries with high rates of trade union membership, the opposition to outward investment was based on fear of permanent job losses and de-industrialization of the economy. Meanwhile, it has been accepted that OFDI does not necessarily lead to unemployment when the core activities are retained at the parent company in the country of origin, or when exporting is not sufficient to maintain foreign market shares because of the competitive strengths of the local firms. Second, to the extent that outward investment from developing countries is resource-seeking and strategic asset-seeking, the employment effects may be negligible. Third, as developing countries still find themselves relatively cost-competitive when compared to developed countries, there is less risk of relocation by efficiency-seeking divestment. This is so because developing countries are increasingly joining the ranks of outward investors at an earlier stage of development (De Beule & Van Den Bulcke, 2010).

In terms of the impact on exports, much of the outward investment is trade creating instead of trade diverting. Most of these emerging countries still find themselves in the "Japanese" phase of their development process (Ozawa, 2008). Most investments are made in trade-supporting market-seeking activities or take place in export-oriented resource-seeking initiatives, although they also focus upon the acquisition of strategic assets, such as knowledge and brands. These emerging multinationals seem to be using these acquisitions as a way to springboard the acquired companies and products to their domestic markets (Fleury & Fleury, 2011).

RECOMMENDATIONS FOR OFDI POLICY

Most developing countries have not yet reached a stage at which a proactive approach to outward FDI is feasible or desirable. Many low-income countries should rather focus on the enhancement of domestic firms' capabilities. Specific policies on outward FDI should be positioned within a national strategy aimed at enhancing international competitiveness. Whether active or proactive promotion of outward FDI is warranted still deserves careful consideration. Also, the criteria applied by governments to discriminate (e.g., size, industry, and host country) among companies that benefit from promotional policies based on incentives or subsidies should seriously be studied before being applied.

The liberalization of OFDI and the introduction of promotional measures in many developing countries were stretched out over a relatively long period of 10 years or more. According to UNCTAD (1995) this was due to the experience of early liberalizers such as Argentina and Chile, which undertook a rapid internal and external liberalization in the late 1970s and were obliged to reintroduce restrictions when their economies suffered from a financial crisis and capital flight associated with external debt problems at the beginning of the 1980s. While it is preferable to loosen the controls rather quickly, it is understandable that developing countries want to continue with the monitoring of their capital flows, to allow for a timely intervention should this become necessary. Perhaps it is even worthwhile considering promoting OFDI without loosening controls entirely. More and more emerging economies are joining the ranks of outward investors at an earlier stage of development, making some form of capital control still necessary. Therefore, most developed countries used to reduce controls before implementing promotion, if at all; while more developing countries already started actively promoting direct investment abroad before abolishing control measures on OFDI. Increasingly, developing countries are taking a different approach toward outward investment than the earlier batch of countries.

When the conditions are ripe to release the restrictions which hindered OFDI, because of the improvements in the macroeconomic situation and the economic environment, countries should not necessarily carry out this process in a too gradual way, as it risks unnecessarily postponing or even canceling worthwhile overseas investments by its firms. This is especially the case for the countries that are latecomers as outbound investors. Their companies no longer have the time to proceed on the basis of the learning approach or the "establishment chain" previously urged by the proponents of the Scandinavian School for internationalizing firms. On the other hand, approval procedures and reporting requirements should be adapted to the internationalization needs and "readiness" of the companies. To put out a schedule of the intended stages and relevant criteria of the promotional measures beforehand might allow for a better planning of the future investment decisions by the companies.

With regard to SMEs it is often true that they are confronted with structural rigidities to venture abroad and that stimulating measures might be defended on the basis of this argument. However, over-stimulation of OFDI, in particular for SMEs should be avoided, as the failure of a subsidiary abroad may cause the whole company to go under. Large established MNEs and business groups should not be the main beneficiaries of a government's promotional efforts, although it may be necessary to ensure that there is a "level playing field."

UNCTAD (2005e, 2005f), more specifically the Trade and Development Board, in 2005 organized a special meeting of experts during which OFDI was praised for its positive effects on enterprise competitiveness. Based on the case studies (UNCTAD, 2005a, 2005b, 2005c, 2005d) commissioned for this meeting, it is suggested that developing and emerging economies should concentrate their promotional policies on SMEs. Yet, except for the study on Singapore which refers to a survey, these reports present little hard evidence on the issue of improved competitiveness because of outward investment or its promotional policies. In a sample of almost 200 Singaporean multinationals two-thirds answered that the impact on their competitive advantage was positive. When specifying the nature of this advantage half of those firms refer to "greater familiarity and experience," while two fifths mention "better reputation." Around one fourth of the responding companies found that the advantages consisted of better managerial experience, better product quality and services, while one-fifth quoted special contacts and connections and specialized resources and materials (UNCTAD, 2005c). It would seem that the link between competitiveness and OFDI is an under-researched area and merits more attention both from academics and policy makers.

Little is also known about the opinion of the general public in developing countries about the promotion of outward investment. Even in developed countries during the 1970s little attention was given to the policy reorientation toward promoting OFDI and the discrete decisions that were taken in this respect, possibly because of the unpopularity of MNEs at that time. Yet, according to Zhang (2003) there was quite some ideological opposition to OFDI in China during the 1990s. To extend OFDI incentives toward foreign-owned subsidiaries in the home country which use it as a platform for investments in neighboring countries or the surrounding region is probably not an immediate concern to those countries. In the United States, to benefit from OPIC's insurance system or other incentives, it is not required that the foreign affiliate is wholly owned or controlled by U.S. investors. However, in the case of joint ventures, only the portion made by the U.S. company is insurable (UNCTAD, 1995). Likewise Singapore does not discriminate between domestic and foreign-owned firms when they request support for their initiatives to put up subsidiaries abroad which are controlled from Singapore. For Singapore this attitude fits into its policy to convince domestic and foreign MNEs to set up a regional headquarter in the country.

While the advantages linked to the activities of MNEs have become more and more appreciated by host and home countries alike, the fact remains that a high proportion of FDI go to a relatively limited number of countries. If successful emerging and developing economies would succeed in targeting lesser developing countries it might be possible to spread out the benefits of FDI more broadly and in a more sustainable way. To the extent that the activities of "Third World MNEs" would be more adapted to the level of development of those countries and the absorptive capacity of their firms, one might wonder if multilateral organizations such as the IFC and MIGA should not play a more active role in stimulating OFDI, or that regional organizations such as ASEAN, SADC, SAARC, and others should perhaps try to activate OFDI in their respective regions.

REFERENCES

Brown, K., Hempson-Jones, J., & Pennisi, J. (2010, November). *Investment across the Taiwan Strait. How Taiwan's relationship with China affects its position in the global economy* (p. 38). London: Chatham House.

Cuyvers, L., & Van Den Bulcke, D. (1989). Some reflections on the "outward-oriented" development strategy of the far eastern newly industrializing countries. In W. M. L. Adriaansen & J. G. Waardenburg (Eds), *A dual economy* (pp. 175–200). Amsterdam: Wolters-Noordhoff.

De Beule, F., & Van Den Bulcke, D. (2009). China's opening up: From Shenzhen to Sudan. In M. van Dijk (Ed.), *The new presence of China in Africa* (pp. 31–52). Amsterdam: Amsterdam University Press.

De Beule, F., & Van Den Bulcke, D. (2010). Changing policy regimes in outward foreign direct investment: From control to promotion. In K. Sauvant, W. Maschek, & G. McAllister (Eds.), *Foreign direct investment from emerging markets: The challenges ahead* (pp. 277–304). New York, NY: Palgrave Macmillan.

De Beule, F., & Van Den Bulcke, D. (2011). International trade and investment patterns: The case of South, East and South-East Asian economies. In M. Dumont & G. Rayp (Eds.), *International business not as usual* (pp. 179–204). Antwerp: Garant Uitgevers.

De Beule, F., & Van Den Bulcke, D. (2012). The impact of the global economic crisis on foreign direct investment: The case of China. In E. Florence & P. Defraigne (Eds.), *Towards a new development paradigm in twenty-first century China: Economy, society and politics* (Vol. 12, pp. 49–65). Comparative Development and Policy in Asia. Abingdon: Routledge.

Dicken, P. (2011). *Global shift: Transforming the world economy*. London: Paul Chapman.

Dunning, J. H. (1981). Explaining the international direct investment position of countries: Towards a dynamic or developmental approach. *Weltwirtschaftliches Archiv, 117*(1), 30–64.

Dunning, J. H. (2009). Location and the multinational enterprise: John Dunning's thoughts, on receiving the journal of international business 2008 decade award. *Journal of International Business Studies, 40*(1), 20–34.

Fleury, A., & Fleury, M. T. M. (2011). *Brazilian multinationals: Competences for internationalization*. Cambridge: Cambridge University Press.

General Administration of Commerce. (2014). *Review of China's foreign trade in 2013*. Beijing: General Administration of Customs of the People's Republic of China.

Giroud, A., & Mirza, H. (2010). MNE linkages in ASEAN. In P. Gugler & J. Chaise (Eds.), *Competitiveness of the ASEAN countries: Corporate and regulatory drivers*. Cheltenham: Edward Elgar.

Gugler, P., & Chaise, J. (Eds.). (2010). *Competitiveness of the ASEAN countries: Corporate and regulatory drivers*. Cheltenham: Edward Elgar.

Gugler, P., & Pananond, P. (2010). The competitiveness of the ASEAN economies: Business competitiveness and international challenges. In P. Gugler & J. Chaise (Eds.), *Competitiveness of the ASEAN countries: Corporate and regulatory drivers*. Cheltenham: Edward Elgar.

Hymer, S. H. (1976). *The international operations of national firms: A study of direct foreign investment*. Cambridge, MA: MIT Press.

Kam-Hon, L. (1982). Development of Hong Kong's place in international trade. *World Economy, 5*, 187–200.

Lu, J., Liu, X., & Wang, H. (2011). Motives for outward FDI of Chinese private firms: Firm resources, industry dynamics, and government policies. *Management and Organization Review, 7*, 223–248.

Luo, Y., Xue, Q., & Han, B. (2010). How emerging market governments promote outward FDI: Experience from China. *Journal of World Business, 45*, 68–79.

Naughton, B. (2007). *The Chinese economy: Transitions and growth*. Cambridge: MIT Press.

Nessara, S. & Rugman, A. (2010). Multinationals and the international competitiveness of ASEAN firms. In P. Gugler & J. Chaise (Eds.), *Competitiveness of the ASEAN countries: Corporate and regulatory drivers*. Cheltenham: Edward Elgar.

Ozawa, T. (2008). *History repeats itself: Evolutionary structural change and TNCs' involvement in infrastructure overseas, flying-geese style*. Working paper Series No. 261. Center on Japanese Economy and Business, Columbia Business School, New York, NY.

Ozawa, T. (2009). *The rise of Asia. The flying geese theory of tandem growth and regional agglomeration*. Chichester: Edward Elgar.

Peng, M., Wang, D., & Jiang, Y. (2008). An institution-based view of international business strategy: A focus on emerging economies. *Journal of International Business Studies, 39*, 920–936.

Pereira, A. A. (2001). *Revitalizing national competitiveness: The transnational aspects of Singapore's regionalization strategy (1990–2000)*. Working Paper No. 161. National University of Singapore, Singapore.

Porter, M. E. (1980). *Competitive strategy*. New York, NY: Free Press.

Sauvant, K. P. (2005). New sources of FDI: The BRICs. Outward FDI from Brazil, Russia, India and China. *Journal of World Investment and Trade, 6*(5), 639–709.

UNCTAD. (1995). *World investment report 1995. Transnational corporations and competitiveness.* New York, NY: United Nations.

UNCTAD. (2005a). *Case study on outward direct investment by Russian firms,* Trade and Development Board, 24 p.

UNCTAD. (2005b). *Case study on outward foreign direct investment by South African enterprises,* Trade and Development Board, 18 p.

UNCTAD. (2005c). *Case study on outward foreign direct investment by Indian small and medium sized enterprises,* Trade and Development Board, 21 p.

UNCTAD. (2005d). *Case study on foreign direct investment by Singaporean firms: Enterprise competitiveness and development,* Trade and Development Board, 24 p.

UNCTAD. (2005e). *Internationalization of developing-country enterprises through outward direct investment.* Issues Note. Geneva: UNCTAD Secretariat.

UNCTAD. (2005f). *Report of the expert meeting on enhancing productive capacity of developing countries through internationalization,* Trade and Development Board, December, 10 p.

UNCTAD. (2006). *World investment report 2006. FDI from developing and transition economies: Implications for development.* New York, NY: United Nations.

UNCTAD. (2007). *Global players from emerging markets: Strengthening enterprise competitiveness through outward investment.* New York, NY: United Nations.

UNCTAD. (2011). *World investment report 2011: Non-equity modes of international production and development.* New York, NY: United Nations.

UNCTAD. (2013). *World investment report 2013: Global value chains: Investment and trade for development.* New York, NY: United Nations.

Wang, C., Hong, J., Kafouros, M., & Boateng, A. (2012). What drives outward FDI of Chinese firms? Testing the explanatory power of three theoretical frameworks. *International Business Review, 21*(3), 425–438.

Yang, T., & Huang, D. (2011). Multinational corporations, FDI and the East Asian economic integration. RIETI Discussion Paper Series 11-E-071. The Research Institute of Economy, Trade and Industry, IAA, Japan.

Zhang, H., & Van Den Bulcke, D. (1996a). China: Rapid changes in the investment development path. In J. H. Dunning & R. Narula (Eds.), *Foreign direct investment and governments.* London: Routledge.

Zhang, H., & Van Den Bulcke, D. (1996b). International management strategies of Chinese multinational firms. In J. Child & Y. Lu (Eds.), *Management issues for China in the 1990s: International enterprises.* London: Routledge.

Zhang, Y. (2003). *China's emerging global businesses, political economy and institutional investigations.* Basingstoke: Palgrave.

CHAPTER 12

AN EXPLORATION OF COMMERCIAL DIPLOMACY AS A SET OF FACILITIES TO SUPPORT INTERNATIONAL BUSINESS TO AND FROM EMERGENT MARKETS

Huub J. M. Ruël and Robin Visser

ABSTRACT

Purpose — *In a globalized world where emerging markets are more important than ever, there is an increasing pressure on international businesses and governments to work together. The set of facilities known as commercial diplomacy combines the interests of both by highlighting new markets and investment opportunities.*

Methodology/approach — *In this chapter, we present a literature review based on 56 relevant publications to assess what we currently know of this important activity.*

Findings — *The results indicate that research on commercial diplomacy consists of many subtopics, resulting in a patchy understanding of the topic as a whole.*

Multinational Enterprises, Markets and Institutional Diversity
Progress in International Business Research, Volume 9, 303–322
Copyright © 2014 by Emerald Group Publishing Limited
All rights of reproduction in any form reserved
ISSN: 1745-8862/doi:10.1108/S1745-886220140000009012

*Research limitations/implications — We discuss why integrative
research focusing on the business—government relationship and the
organization and the value of commercial diplomacy are needed from an
international business perspective.*

Keywords: Commercial diplomacy; trade and export promotion;
literature review; research agenda; international business

INTRODUCTION

Globalization has become the leading mantra for the state of the economy,
with both international trade and foreign direct investment (FDI) increasing
exponentially in the last few decades (Sethi, Guisinger, Ford, & Phelan,
2002). The rise in cross-border business activities has led to increasing
economic interdependencies (Narula & Dunning, 2000) that create opportunities for new political and economic powers to surge. Recently, the developing economies of Brazil, China and India have been exemplary, reflecting
the positive effects of the modern-day global economy (Salmi & Scott-
Kennel, 2012). Such emergent economies and markets are redefining trade
flows and power relations (Levy, 2007) while they are still 'fraught with political, economic, and social instabilities' (Doh & Teegen, 2002, p. 666). The
distinctly different environmental, economical, institutional and relational
aspects of emergent markets, in which the business—government relationship is often strong, render businesses of such economies in better shape to
deal with networking and entry processes in other emerging markets (Lee,
Abosag, & Kwak, 2012).

As their environment becomes increasingly complex and global due to
the rise of emerging economies, businesses are faced with many challenges
in international trade and do not benefit from what potential foreign markets have to offer. As a response, most governments have created a set of
services aimed at assisting businesses with internationalization, which have
seen a steady increase in use (Coolsaet, 2004; Freixanet, 2012; Kotabe &
Czinkota, 1992; Lim, 2008; Richardson, Yamin, & Sinkovics, 2012;
Seringhaus & Rosson, 1994).

A substantial amount of research has gone into such programs and the
context they are used in, yet we still do not understand how these inputs
and outputs are connected. This connection is the intersection of business

and government, and it is important because 'the foreign firm is anxious to avoid the deleterious effects of changes in government policy; to seek the assistance of the government to address any difficulties it experiences in the host country; and to build up a web of contacts and influences that would immunize it from hostility from host country firms and other interested groups' (Sanyai & Guvenli, 2000, pp. 119–120). International business is not just an activity between businesses, it is conducted together with governments and international and societal organizations (Lawton & McGuire, 2001). As 'the work of a network of public and private actors who manage commercial relations using diplomatic channels and processes' (Lee, 2004, p. 51), commercial diplomacy combines the interests of both government and business by highlighting new markets and investment opportunities. In addition, it focuses on business support and promotion rather than economic issues, and as such, it entails more than trade and export promotion (Ruël & Visser, 2012).

The 'need to expand and develop commercial diplomacy is all the more important' (Lee & Ruël, 2012, p. xiv) for two reasons. First, emerging markets drive businesses from Western countries to venture into unknown territories where high-tech exports and innovations need to be marketed to maintain the advantage that Western businesses have. Second, many emerging markets are controlled to a considerable extent by their governments. Successful commercial diplomacy gains access to them, and the idea that successful international business is just a matter of a clear business strategy and good business management is naive and outdated. Benard's (2012) illustration of China's success in employing diplomatic means to secure a prime position in foreign markets for its businesses as opposed to the lack thereof by the United States is a recent and practical example of how diplomacy and business go hand in hand in this new political and economic environment.

The connection between international business, international relations and diplomacy is as old as the existence of international trade. It is time to incorporate the poorly understood international business–diplomacy relationship in the study of international business. Our purpose is to indicate directions for future research on commercial diplomacy from an international business point of view.

In the next section, we will conduct a literature review to clarify what we currently know of commercial diplomacy. In the subsequent section, we will analyze our findings on the state of research on commercial diplomacy. We will then present a research agenda that addresses the key issues and wrap up with a conclusion.

LITERATURE REVIEW

A Methodology to Identify Relevant Publications

We include all possible English commercial diplomacy publications in established journals written in the last 60 years. As there are only 14 publications with commercial diplomacy as a research topic, we widened our search to include relevant related terms such as economic diplomacy, trade promotion, export promotion, trade fairs, trade shows and trade missions. Additionally, we identified key words from publications found in this manner and ran them through several databases. By making use of forward and backward referencing, we identified 56 relevant publications. A categorization showed that 14 deal with commercial diplomacy, 3 with economic diplomacy, 20 with public investment, export and trade programs, 11 with policy and governance and 8 with the business—government interface. Of all the papers, 7% are from before 2000, 29% from the 2000s decade and 64% from the 2010s decade, indicating that the subject is of rapidly increasing interest to researchers.

The Context and Antecedents of Commercial Diplomacy

The policy of commercial diplomacy and the actual activities pertaining to it can be established once (1) the objectives and rationales behind commercial diplomacy are clear, (2) the resources of the home country and the business are defined and (3) the contextual setting is explored and clarified (Reuvers & Ruël, 2012).

The objectives and rationales for the implementation of commercial diplomacy as a policy mainly consist of business—economic reasons such as increased trade and export flows, increased competitiveness of firms in the host country and increased intelligence through networking, as well as macroeconomic reasons such as job creation and improvement of the national economy (Kotabe & Czinkota, 1992; Lee & Hudson, 2004; Saner, Yiu, & Sondergaard, 2000; Wilkinson & Brouthers, 2000a, 2000b; Yannopoulos, 2010). These are thus objectives on the national and organizational levels. The rationale of governments conducting commercial diplomacy as opposed to private agencies is that governments look beyond profit and adopt a view of what is beneficial to the public (Hibbert, 1998) and the economic environment (Naray, 2011; Rose, 2005) and are often more influential than businesses (Ozdem, 2009; Rose, 2005).

Numerous publications deal with home country resources such as the institutional organization (Coolsaet, 2004; Garten, 1997; Hillman & Keim, 1995; Muller, 2002; Naray, 2011; Ozdem, 2009; Potter, 2004; Rana, 2007; Sethi et al., 2002; Sherman & Eliasson, 2006, 2007; Sridharan, 2002; Udovic, 2011; Wu, Li, & Samsell, 2012), the nation's political position (Lee & Hudson, 2004; Li & Samsell, 2009; Morrow, Siverson, & Tabares, 1998; Sridharan, 2002; Van Bergeijk, 1992) and its country's image (Muller, 2002; Yang, Shin, Lee, & Wrigley, 2008) as determinant factors in the development of commercial diplomacy.

Alongside the international setup of diplomatic efforts, the organization of commercial diplomacy in the home country is a major factor in the national policy on commercial diplomacy. National policies need to be and have been shaped to implement and make optimal use of such programs (Coolsaet, 2004; Lawton & McGuire, 2001; Levy, 2007; Muller, 2002; Naidu, Cavusgil, Murthy, & Sarkar, 1997; Sethi et al., 2002).

Usually, most of the diplomatic resources available are allocated for economic and political purposes rather than commercial ones (Muller, 2002; Rana, 2007). As Neumayer (2007, p. 288) succinctly puts it: the 'global pattern of diplomatic representation is significantly determined by geographical distance between countries, the power of both sending and recipient countries and by the degree of their ideological affinity'. Naray (2011) distinguishes five organizational arrangements. In the first one, trade promotion is a part of the trade policy and may thus fall under any ministry that actors are a part of. In the second one, the Ministry of Foreign Affairs (MFA) and Ministry of Trade (MT) jointly coordinate national policy. In the third one, there is a separate office for activities of commercial diplomacy, which is centralized and coordinated by the MFA and the MT. In the fourth one, the MFA is solely responsible for commercial diplomacy, and in the fifth one, commercial diplomacy is essentially delegated to public or semi-private agencies with no hierarchical constraints. Moreover, the organization of individual public actors depends on the national structural arrangement, the effect of which is reflected in the role of the commercial diplomat in terms of the activities performed and his/her personal background (Herbst, 1969; Naray, 2011; Ruël & Visser, 2012).

All this takes place within a context consisting of factors that entail both positive and negative effects on commercial diplomacy. These factors include globalization, technological advances (Henrikson, 2005), changes in the formal domestic and international institutional setting (Henrikson, 2005; Lee, 2004; Lee & Hudson, 2004; Muller, 2002; Neumayer, 2007;

Potter, 2004; Sherman & Eliasson, 2007) and the influence of supranational entities (Lawton & McGuire, 2001; Levy, 2007).

Commercial Diplomacy in Action

The activity of commercial diplomacy pertains to (1) activities and practices and (2) bilateral and multilateral interactions between business and government (Reuvers & Ruël, 2012). Research in this regard includes identifying business-level and agency-level activities as sets of programs (Herbst, 1969; Lee & Hudson, 2004; Naray, 2011; Sridharan, 2002; Wilkinson & Brouthers, 2000b). Furthermore, numerous publications describe specific activities such as export promotion (Czinkota, 2002; Kotabe & Czinkota, 1992), trade shows (Richardson et al., 2012; Seringhaus & Rosson, 1994) and trade missions (Schuler, Schnietz, & Baggett, 2011), as well as the individual actors performing such activities (Bondarouk & Ruël, 2012; Ruël & Visser, 2012). The number of studies in this regard implies that there are myriad ways of looking at the types of activities in commercial diplomacy. Indeed, categorizations exist that distinguish between the gathering and dissemination of information and market research, the development of business and government contacts and the promotion of products and services (Lee, 2004); between trade promotion, protection of intellectual property rights, cooperation in science and technology, promotion of 'made-in' and promotion of FDI (Naray, 2011); and between production planning and support, export information, advice to prospective/inexperienced exporters, marketing support, finance and guarantees and education and training (Naidu et al., 1997). Other authors employ more encompassing aspects such as export promotion and investment promotion (Coolsaet, 2004; Ozdem, 2009).

Reuvers and Ruël (2012) present an integration of the activities put forward by the authors we describe here, and Table 1 presents an overview of their assessment.

On a grander level, several authors describe commercial diplomacy as a set of activities in a national policy setting (Naidu et al., 1997; Narula & Dunning, 1998; Rana, 2001; Stadman & Ruël, 2012). A considerable shift in policy is needed to implement commercial diplomacy (Coolsaet, 2004; Lee, 2004; Muller, 2002; Saner et al., 2000; Udovic, 2011; Wu et al., 2012), and the existence of bilateral or multilateral trade agreements is more a rule than an exception (Rana, 2007; Van Bergeijk, 1992).

Regarding the business−government interaction, several authors describe how businesses can effectively interact with governments and what

Table 1. Typical Activities of Commercial Diplomacy.

Network Activities	Intelligence	Image Campaigns	Business Support
Developing business and government contacts	Gathering/ disseminating commercial information	Promoting goods and services	In negotiations: contract implementation and problem-solving
State visits	Market research	Participating in trade fairs, introducing potential exporters	Gathering export marketing data
Buyer—seller meetings	Reporting to home country	Sensitizing potential foreign investors	Supervision of violations of intellectual property and contracts
Matchmaking	Consultant to both countries	Gathering export marketing data	Advocacy activities
Search for partners/ distributors/ investors/lawyers	Image studies, joint scientific research	Tourism promotion activities	Coordination of legal actions
Personal network		Awareness campaigns	

is needed to this end (Hillman, Keim, & Schuler, 2004; Luo, 2001), how to gain foreign market access, for example, by means of networking (Lee et al., 2012; Sanyai & Guvenli, 2000; Vehof, Ruël, & Telgen, 2012) and how such interaction inadvertently changes policies on commercial diplomacy (Lee, 2004). Corporate political activity is seen as an effective method in the business—government interaction process (Hillman et al., 2004; Saner et al., 2000).

The Value and Effectiveness of Commercial Diplomacy

Research into the value and effectiveness of export promotion programs, trade fairs and trade promotion is extensive and points to the benefits for businesses in various stages of exporting as well as domestic benefits such as an increase in trade figures (Alvarez, 2004; Freixanet, 2012; Kotabe & Czinkota, 1992; Lim, 2008; Wilkinson & Brouthers, 2000a, 2000b, 2006; Yannopoulos, 2010). In a study of the direct effects of export promotion efforts in the foreign market, Rose (2005) shows that bilateral exports rise by 6—10% for each government agency. This should not be surprising; trade fairs have been successful for hundreds of years (Seringhaus & Rosson, 1994), and throughout history there have been many nations that tied trade efforts to diplomatic ones (Edens, 1992; Griffiths, 1970; Lloyd, 1991; Rahusen-de Bruyn Kops, 2002).

The alignment of resources and objectives with certain activities and interaction patterns leads commercial diplomacy to be effective to varying degrees for both governments and businesses, creating value for these actors in the process (Reuvers & Ruël, 2012; Zuidema & Ruël, 2012). Correct alignment leads to economic benefits such as an increase in wealth, knowledge creation, job creation and improved trade, export and investment performance (Alvarez, 2004; Czinkota, 2002; Freixanet, 2012; Kotabe & Czinkota, 1992; Lim, 2008; Rose, 2005; Wilkinson & Brouthers, 2000a, 2006), though this also depends on the international experience and networking capabilities of businesses (Busschers & Ruël, 2012; Spence & Crick, 2004; Yannopoulos, 2010; Zuidema & Ruël, 2012), the organization and alignment between business and government (Freixanet, 2012) and the type of activity performed by governments (Alvarez, 2004; Wilkinson & Brouthers, 2000a). These factors are strongly reliant, however, on the international political context as Van Bergeijk (1992) points out.

From a government point of view, correct alignment may lead to increased economic means to be used for political benefits (Neumayer, 2007) and positive effects on the country image, which, in turn, may lead to an increase in trade (Yang et al., 2008). All in all, positive effects exist on the national and organizational levels (Potter, 2004; Yang et al., 2008).

Several publications address the outcomes of commercial diplomacy. Wilkinson and Brouthers (2006, p. 243) show by means of a statistical analysis that 'both trade shows and programs identifying agents and distributors are positively related with (…) export performance'. Illustrative of this statement is Spence and Crick's (2004, p. 290) finding that 'just under half (…) would not have visited the markets without the trade missions'. Furthermore, the use of investment promotion is revealed by Lim's (2008, pp. 49–50) results that find that 'promotion effectiveness (…) has a positive influence on attracting FDI by the mediation effect between a host country's FDI environment and FDI inflows'. That not all programs are always effective is shown by Alvarez (2004, p. 399), who finds that 'trade shows and trade missions do not affect the probability of exporting permanently, but exporter committees show a positive and significant impact', a statement that is supported by Wilkinson and Brouthers (2000a). Overall, Rose's (2005, p. 13) empirical evidence shows that 'bilateral exports rise by approximately 6–10% for each additional consulate abroad'. These studies confirm that commercial diplomacy is a value-creating activity for both business and government.

FINDINGS

Three Disciplinary Perspectives and Myriad Subtopics

We observe that most publications revolve around an international business, an international relations or a political/economy viewpoint, and that international business is under-represented in terms of topical diversity and scope of research. This is largely in accordance with what Naray (2011) and Lee and Hudson (2004) put forward. They recognized approaches in international relations and diplomacy, the political economy of commercial diplomacy and international trade promotion (Naray, 2011), and international relations and the political economy (Lee & Hudson, 2004). Integrating the findings of these authors with what the publications we investigated show, we confirm that 22 studies adopt an international business approach, 20 studies adopt an international relations approach and 14 studies adopt a political/economy approach.

Studies that take up an international business approach usually discuss the promotion of trade and investment 'from the point of view of international business firms and countries' promotional efforts' (Naray, 2011, p. 128). The activities of commercial diplomacy (see Table 1) are often described in the literature. Studies mainly describe the effectiveness of FDI attraction programs (Lim, 2008; Sethi et al., 2002), the effectiveness of trade and export promotion programs (Alvarez, 2004; Freixanet, 2012; Kotabe & Czinkota, 1992; Wilkinson & Brouthers, 2006; Yannopoulos, 2010), the organization of trade shows, trade fairs and foreign missions (Alvarez, 2004; Richardson et al., 2012; Rose, 2005; Seringhaus & Rosson, 1994; Spence & Crick, 2004; Wilkinson & Brouthers, 2000a), the value of commercial diplomacy (Busschers & Ruël, 2012) and networking activities (Lawton & McGuire, 2001; Lee et al., 2012; Saner et al., 2000; Sanyai & Guvenli, 2000). However, the positive effect of trade and export programs is not ubiquitous as Alvarez (2004), Narula and Dunning (1998), Richardson et al. (2012), Spence and Crick (2004), Wilkinson and Brouthers (2000a) and Yannopoulos (2010) show.

Studies that take up an international relations perspective are still quite limited (Lee & Hudson, 2004). Reuvers and Ruël (2012, p. 9) counter this by saying that many of these studies 'use the international relations perspective to look at all commercial aspects within the broader sense of diplomacy between governments'. This is true for many publications (Coolsaet, 2004; Herbst, 1969; Lee, 2004; Morrow et al., 1998; Muller, 2002; Naray, 2011; Neumayer, 2007; Rana, 2007; Sherman & Eliasson,

2006). The problem that Lee and Hudson (2004, p. 360) recognize in this line of studies is that most of them adopt 'an approach that is based largely on a statist reading of international relations' such as Wu et al.'s (2012) assessment of the governance environment. Hillman et al. (2004), in their conceptual assessment of the business–government relationship, address this issue and call for continuous checks to counter this approach. Some studies do alleviate this problem by accounting for the changing institutional environment that the business–government relationship is subject to (Hillman & Keim, 1995; Zuidema & Ruël, 2012) or by presenting a mathematical model that collects data over several years and thus employs a longitudinal approach (Hibbert, 1998). Furthermore, most studies focus solely on a government point of view, with three publications incorporating elements of a business perspective (Hillman & Keim, 1995; Levy, 2007; Schuler et al., 2011). Three authors adopt only a business point of view (Hillman et al., 2004) or the point of view of individual actors (Bondarouk & Ruël, 2012; Ruël & Visser, 2012).

Studies that take up a political/economy approach have a unique double advantage as they add to 'the theoretical and empirical utility of diplomatic studies as well as international political economy' (Lee & Hudson, 2004, p. 359). Consequently, the publications discuss the home country resources needed for commercial diplomacy in terms of specific programs that are to be implemented (Czinkota, 2002; Wilkinson & Brouthers, 2000b), the institutional implications (Garten, 1997; Sherman & Eliasson, 2007; Sridharan, 2002), agency structure (Ozdem, 2009; Potter, 2004) and whether commercial diplomacy should even be performed by the government (Czinkota, 2002; Garten, 1997; Henrikson, 2005; Ozdem, 2009; Potter, 2004; Rose, 2005; Sridharan, 2002; Wilkinson & Brouthers, 2000b) or at least be left partly to private organizations (Henrikson, 2005; Hocking, 2004; Sherman & Eliasson, 2007). These publications stress the importance and influence of economics on diplomacy and describe how they are intertwined. Any study with a political/economy approach integrates 'market relations with political relations and thus conceptualizes diplomacy as a continuous political–economic dialogue' (Lee & Hudson, 2004, p. 360). Perhaps not surprisingly, all of the studies employ a government point of view. Only Hocking (2004) includes a marginal business point of view.

The current body of work on commercial diplomacy is rather patchy and revolves around subtopics such as the commercial diplomat (Naray, 2011; Ruël & Visser, 2012), government involvement in export promotion (Kotabe & Czinkota, 1992; Wilkinson & Brouthers, 2000a, 2000b), the context of commercial diplomacy (Muller, 2002; Potter, 2004), the national commercial policy (Hibbert, 1998; Naray, 2011), the activities of commercial diplomacy (Coolsaet, 2004; Lee, 2004), the rationale of commercial diplomacy (Hibbert, 1998; Naray, 2011; Ozdem, 2009; Rose, 2005) and the effectiveness of export and trade promotion (Alvarez, 2004; Freixanet, 2012; Rose, 2005).

Diversity in Methodological Approaches

A total of 20 studies makes use of a conceptual or literature study approach while 36 employ some form of empirical research. Of the empirical studies, 14 adopt a (multiple) case study approach, 18 employ statistical analysis of either historical (8) or survey based (10) data, 2 employ surveys and interviews and 2 more add a statistical analysis to the data gathered through means of surveys and interviews.

Of the 56 publications in our literature review, we distinguish four different levels of analysis: (1) a national or supranational level, (2) an organizational (i.e. businesses and government agencies) level, (3) an individual-actor level and (4) a literature review or conceptual model. In our review, 31 adopted a national level, 10 adopted an organizational level, 3 adopted an individual-actor level and 7 conducted a literature review. Only five authors employed multiple levels of analysis in their empirical studies. Narula and Dunning (1998), Levy (2007) and Luo (2001) use both the national and organizational levels; Zuidema and Ruël (2012) use both the national and individual-actor levels but only Naray (2011) uses the national, organizational and individual-actor levels. In only two cases (Naray, 2011; Narula & Dunning, 1998) it becomes clear why the authors chose their specific multi-level analyses.

International Business as an Under-Represented Viewpoint

Research into commercial diplomacy focuses on an international relation, a political/economic or an international business viewpoint. While the first two feature multi-level research from the vantage point of both government and business, research from an international business viewpoint is under-represented. Moreover, in the viewpoints of international relations and political economy, we discern a wide variety of topics ranging from macro-level national policy to micro-level individual-actor research, while the international business research deals mostly with effectiveness studies. The current status of research on commercial diplomacy is one in which core issues have not yet been addressed in a full and proper manner. Therefore, in the next section, we present a research agenda for commercial diplomacy that addresses these core issues in a way that we believe will resolve this problem.

A RESEARCH AGENDA FOR COMMERCIAL DIPLOMACY AND INTERNATIONAL BUSINESS

There is a dire need for more integrative research on the topic of commercial diplomacy as several aspects are severely under-represented. In this section, we will suggest what type of perspective would benefit commercial diplomacy the most. We will give a more detailed description of the specific topics that need attention and present an indication of the manner in which future research should be undertaken.

Future Research and the Necessity of a Disciplinary Approach

While research on commercial diplomacy has been performed from an international relations perspective so far, Reuvers and Ruël (2012) found that commercial elements are largely neglected. Research in the field of international relations would do well to conduct studies in which businesses and governments are examined concurrently as international business is largely neglected in studies on, for example, national policy, although it is directly affected by it. A coming together of the macro-level (national) and the meso-level (businesses and government agencies) is needed. The same goes for political economy even though an inherent characteristic of the political economy point of view is that it is only concerned with government issues.

Naray's (2011, p. 128) observation that most international business studies are undertaken 'from the point of view of international business firms and countries' promotional efforts' echoes in our findings; both national macro-level and organizational meso-level studies exist, yet we found very few cross-overs between the two. This area could be greatly improved by more studies that take a look at both the national and business levels.

RELEVANT TOPICS IN THE COMMERCIAL DIPLOMACY–INTERNATIONAL BUSINESS INTERPLAY

Improving Commercial Diplomacy Using Topics of International Business

Research into the context, antecedents, activities, value and effectiveness of commercial diplomacy is widespread and deals with numerous topics. However, the number of subjects they address results in an understanding that is patchy at best. When it comes to context and antecedents, the focus of attention is on national institutional developments rather than contextual ones. The actual activities of commercial diplomacy are quite well defined, but an overview of national policy is lacking, along with an evaluation of the activities inherent to the practice of commercial diplomacy. This coincides with the limited knowledge on the value of commercial diplomacy as a whole, where the focus is still on the usefulness of specific types of programs for businesses. A broader type of research is needed that incorporates the value of commercial diplomacy as a set of activities and programs and its usefulness on the national and organizational levels.

Considering how the concept of commercial diplomacy is heavily reliant on an international relations perspective, broadening the perspective using specific topics from international business would greatly advance our understanding of the subject. Based on what the literature review has shown us, we believe that three areas of this perspective are of particular interest: (1) the international business–government relationship, (2) the organization of commercial diplomacy and (3) value creation. First of all, commercial diplomacy being subject to the interplay between governments and businesses, the context of the international business–government relationship is a crucial topic (Luo, 2001), which has received hardly any attention from a commercial diplomacy point of view (Reuvers & Ruël, 2012). Secondly, the organizational arrangement of commercial diplomacy affects both governments and businesses on the meso-levels and micro-levels, yet research into this topic from a business perspective is scarce while it may prove highly insightful. Lastly, a lot of research has been made on the benefits of export promotion, yet commercial diplomacy lacks such analyses even though value and value creation are key aspects of the international management perspective (Porter, 1980).

Commercial Diplomacy and the Business—Government Relationship

So far, studies on commercial diplomacy have only scratched the surface of issues in international business—government relations with connotations on their organization (Naray, 2011), the interplay between the national policy on commercial diplomacy and enterprise preferences (Udovic, 2011) and the role of globalization in the formulation of a national policy on commercial diplomacy (Potter, 2004). In order to understand the role of the international business—government relationship in commercial diplomacy, further investigation is needed in terms of expectation management between representatives from both business and government. Such research should be conducted within the context of business—government relationship building by means of certain interaction channels and patterns based on the meso-level and micro-level perspectives. Specific theoretical concepts that could be adopted include business diplomacy, corporate political activity and both formal and informal institutionalism as they are all concepts that revolve around the interaction between actors.

The Organization of Commercial Diplomacy

The macro-level perspective dominates the discussion of organizational issues in commercial diplomacy, focusing on national and supranational policies. Only Naray (2011) approaches commercial diplomacy from a meso-level and micro-level even though the academic literature on organization is abundant. The most urgent topics of relevance to commercial diplomacy are an exploration of the organizational arrangements that actors most benefit from, a comparison of the organization of commercial diplomacy at the macro-level, meso-level and micro-level as well as the inter-level influence. Specific theoretical concepts that could be adopted include network theory, agency theory, contingency theory and knowledge management, as they are all concepts that address organization from a multi-level and individual-actor level.

The Value of Commercial Diplomacy

While research into the subtopics of the value and effectiveness of commercial diplomacy is abundant, we know very little of the value creation process in commercial diplomacy and the factors that determine it.

Once these issues are resolved, further analysis may also clarify the relative impact of macro-level, meso-level and micro-level factors on the value of commercial diplomacy and thus reveal the origin of its added value. Specific theoretical concepts that could be adopted include value creation, exchange value, transaction cost and resource management, as they are all concepts that deal with the origin, translation or capture of value.

METHODOLOGICAL RECOMMENDATIONS FOR FUTURE RESEARCH

To foster the development of theories on commercial diplomacy, future research should use a wider variety of methods. We observe that studies dealing with commercial diplomacy or a related topic such as export or trade promotion mostly employ a conceptual study, a statistical analysis or a case study approach. Only Naray (2011), Sanyai and Guvenli (2000), Kotabe and Czinkota (1992) and Luo (2001) employ multiple methods, involving a combination of surveys, interviews and statistical analysis.

In addition, virtually all publications we found are cross-sectional, and where respondents are needed, the studies rely on single sources, either commercial diplomats or businessmen. In order to add to the empirical findings and to substantiate future research, multi-method studies are needed that (1) deal with commercial diplomacy on the macro-levels, meso-levels and micro-levels at the same time, (2) utilize multiple sources such as commercial diplomats, businessmen and the institutions they are a part of in one study, as well as (3) employ multiple methods for data collection such as surveys, database research, historical research, statistical analysis and case studies.

THREE PATHS TO THE RECONCILIATION OF COMMERCIAL DIPLOMACY AND INTERNATIONAL BUSINESS

At an increasingly faster pace, global economic interdependencies brought about by globalization and the rise of emergent markets are redefining global trade flows and power relations. As a consequence, international business is conducted together with governments and other societal organizations, rendering it no longer just a matter of a clear business strategy and

Table 2. Three Research Areas as Key Directions of Future Research into Commercial Diplomacy.

	International Business–Government Relations and Commercial Diplomacy	Organization and Commercial Diplomacy	Value Creation and Commercial Diplomacy
Key issues	(1) The context of international business–government relationship building, (2) identification of channels and patterns in this process and (3) expectation management between individual actors.	(1) The organizational arrangements that actors most benefit from, (2) macro-level, meso-level and micro-level organizations of commercial diplomacy and (3) the inter-level influence between the macro-levels, meso-levels and micro-levels.	(1) The value creation process in commercial diplomacy, (2) the factors that determine value creation and (3) the relative impact of macro-level, meso-level and micro-level factors
Methodology	Exploratory qualitative and quantitative, multiple-case studies and statistical analysis of interaction pattern correlation employing business diplomacy, corporate political activity and institutionalism.	Comparative qualitative and descriptive, multiple-case study analysis research of different countries and instruments, employing network theory, agency theory, contingency theory and knowledge management.	Meso-level and micro-level explanatory studies employing quantitative methods using value creation, exchange value, transaction cost and resource management.
Output	Insight into how governments and businesses benefit from interaction patterns and channels.	Insight into the effective organization of commercial diplomacy	Insight into the value chain process and the relative impact of macro-level, meso-level and micro-level factors.

good business management. Commercial diplomacy plays a crucial role at this intersection of international relations and international business by providing governments and businesses with a means to interact and facilitate economic development. Our literature review shows that research on commercial diplomacy exists in all forms and on many subtopics, yet the combined understanding of the topic is still rather patchy. Therefore, we conclude that there is a dire need for more integrative research. Based on our findings, we contend that future research should focus on three specific areas of international business (the business—government relationship, organization and value) in order to alleviate the problem of patchiness on the one hand and to strengthen the bond between commercial diplomacy and international business on the other as the two areas are inherently intertwined. Table 2 provides a concise summary of where we believe research into commercial diplomacy should go to reach this goal, as well as how and why.

REFERENCES

Alvarez, R. (2004). Sources of export success in small- and medium-sized enterprises: The impact of public programs. *International Business Review, 13*(3), 383–400.

Benard, A. (2012). How to succeed in business and why Washington should really try. *Foreign Affairs, 91*(4), 91–101.

Bondarouk, E., & Ruël, H. J. M. (2012). Lobbying of commercial diplomats: Institutional setting as a determining factor. In H. J. M. Ruël (Ed.), *Commercial diplomacy and international business: A conceptual and empirical exploration* (pp. 251–291). Bingley: Emerald Insight.

Busschers, S., & Ruël, H. J. M. (2012). The value of commercial diplomacy from an international entrepreneur's perspective. In H. J. M. Ruël (Ed.), *Commercial diplomacy and international business: A conceptual and empirical exploration* (pp. 71–103). Bingley: Emerald Insight.

Coolsaet, R. (2004). Trade and diplomacy: The Belgian case. *International Studies Perspectives, 5*(1), 61–652.

Czinkota, M. (2002). Export promotion: Framework for finding opportunity in change. *Thunderbird International Business Review, 44*(3), 315–324.

Doh, J. P., & Teegen, H. (2002). Nongovernmental organisations as institutional actors in international business: Theory and implications. *International Business Review, 11*(6), 665–684.

Edens, C. (1992). Dynamics of trade in the ancient Mesopotamian "world system." *American Anthropologist, 95*(1), 118–139.

Freixanet, J. (2012). Export promotion programs: Their impact on companies' internationalisation performance and competitiveness. *International Business Review, 21*(6), 1065–1086.

Garten, J. E. (1997). Business and foreign policy. *Foreign Affairs, 76*(3), 67–79.

Griffiths, D. M. (1970). American commercial diplomacy in Russia, 1780 to 1783. *The Willian and Mary Quarterly, 27*(3), 379–410.

Henrikson, A. (2005). Diplomacy's possible futures. *The Hague: Journal of Diplomacy, 1*(1), 3–27.

Herbst, A. (1969). The commercial counsellor's field of activity. *Intereconomics, 4*(10), 323–325.

Hibbert, E. (1998). Evaluating government export promotion: Some conceptual and empirical approaches. *The International Trade Journal, 12*(4).

Hillman, A., & Keim, G. (1995). International variation in the business–government interface: Institutional and organisational considerations. *The Academy of Management Review, 20*(1), 193–214.

Hillman, A. J., Keim, G. D., & Schuler, D. (2004). Corporate political activity: A review and research agenda. *Journal of Management, 30*(6), 837–857.

Hocking, B. (2004). Privatizing diplomacy. *International Studies Perspectives, 5*, 147–152.

Kotabe, M., & Czinkota, M. R. (1992). State government promotion of manufacturing exports: A gap analysis. *Journal of International Business Studies, 23*(4), 637–658.

Lawton, T. C., & McGuire, S. M. (2001). Supranational governance and corporate strategy: The emerging role of the World Trade Organisation. *International Business Review, 10*(2), 217–233.

Lee, D. (2004). The growing influence of business in U.K. diplomacy. *International Studies Perspectives, 5*, 50–54.

Lee, D., & Hudson, L. (2004). The old and the new significance of political economy in diplomacy. *Review of International Studies, 30*, 343–360.

Lee, D., & Ruël, H. J. M. (2012). Commercial diplomacy and international business: Merging international business and international relations. In H. J. M. Ruël (Ed.), *Commercial diplomacy and international business: A conceptual and empirical exploration* (pp. xiii–xix). Bingley: Emerald Insight.

Lee, J. W., Abosag, I., & Kwak, J. (2012). The role of networking and commitment in foreign market entry process: Multinational corporations in the Chinese automobile industry. *International Business Review, 21*(1), 27–39.

Levy, B. (2007). The interface between globalisation, trade and development: Theoretical issues for international business studies. *International Business Review, 16*(5), 594–612.

Li, S., & Samsell, D. P. (2009). Why some countries trade more than others: The effect of the governance environment on trade flows. *Corporate Governance: An International Review, 17*(1), 47–61.

Lim, S. (2008). How investment promotion affects attracting foreign direct investment: Analytical argument and empirical analyses. *International Business Review, 17*(1), 39–53.

Lloyd, T. H. (1991). *England and the German Hanse* (pp. 1157–1611). New York, NY: Cambridge University Press.

Luo, Y. (2001). Toward a cooperative view of MNC-host government relations: Building blocks and performance implications. *Journal of International Business Studies, 31*(3), 401–419.

Morrow, J. D., Siverson, R. M., & Tabares, T. E. (1998). The political determinants of international trade: The major powers, 1907–90. *American Political Review, 92*(3), 649–661.

Muller, M. (2002). South Africa's economic diplomacy: Constructing a better world for all? *Diplomacy and Statecraft, 13*(1), 1–30.

Naidu, G. M., Cavusgil, S. T., Murthy, B. K., & Sarkar, M. (1997). An export promotion model for India: Implications for public policy. *International Business Review, 6*(2), 113–125.

Naray, O. (2011). Commercial diplomats in the context of international business. *The Hague Journal of Diplomacy, 6*, 121–148.

Narula, R., & Dunning, J. H. (1998). Explaining international R&D alliances and the role of governments. *International Business Review, 7*(4), 377–397.

Narula, R., & Dunning, J. H. (2000). Industrial development, globalization and multinational enterprises: New realities for developing countries. *Oxford Development Studies, 28*(2), 141–167.

Neumayer, E. (2007). Distance, power and ideology: Diplomatic representation in a world of nation-states. *Area, 40*(2), 228–236.

Ozdem, M. I. (2009). *Government agencies in commercial diplomacy: Seeking the optimal agency structure for foreign trade policy*. Raleigh, NC: North Carolina State University.

Porter, M. (1980). *Competitive strategy: Techniques for analysing industries and competitors*. New York, NY: Free Press.

Potter, E. H. (2004). Branding Canada: The renaissance of Canada's commercial diplomacy. *International Studies Perspectives, 5*, 55–60.

Rahusen-de Bruyn Kops, H. (2002). Not such an 'unpromising beginning': The first Dutch trade embassy to China, 1655–1657. *Modern Asian Studies, 36*(3), 535–578.

Rana, K. S. (2001). Serving the private sector: India's experience in context. In N. Bayne & S. Woolcock (Eds.), *The new economic diplomacy: Decision-making and negotiation in international economic relations* (1st ed.). Farnham: Ashgate Publishing Limited.

Rana, K. S. (2007). Economic diplomacy: The experience of developing countries. In N. Bayne & S. Woolcock (Eds.), *The new economic diplomacy: Decision-making and negotiation in international economic relations* (pp. 201–220). Aldershot: Ashgate.

Reuvers, S. I. M., & Ruël, H. J. M. (2012). Research on commercial diplomacy: A review and implications. In H. J. M. Ruël (Ed.), *Commercial diplomacy and international business: A conceptual and empirical exploration* (pp. 1–27). Bingley: Emerald Insight.

Richardson, C., Yamin, M., & Sinkovics, R. R. (2012). Policy-driven clusters, interfirm interactions and firm internationalisation: Some insights from Malaysia's Multimedia Super Corridor. *International Business Review, 21*(5), 794–805.

Rose, A. K. (2005). The foreign service and foreign trade: Embassies as export promotion. *World Economy, 30*(1), 22–38.

Ruël, H. J. M., & Visser, R. (2012). Commercial diplomats as corporate entrepreneurs: Explaining role behavior from an institutional perspective. *International Journal of Diplomacy and Economy, 1*(1), 42–79.

Salmi, A., & Scott-Kennel, J. (2012). Just another BRIC in the wall? The rise of the BRICs and educating tomorrow's global managers. *AIB Insights, 12*(3), 3–6.

Saner, R., Yiu, L., & Sondergaard, M. (2000). Business diplomacy management: A core competency for global companies. *Academy of Management Executive, 14*(1), 80–92.

Sanyai, R. N., & Guvenli, T. (2000). Relations between multinational firms and host governments: The experience of American-owned firms in China. *International Business Review, 9*(1), 119–134.

Schuler, D. A., Schnietz, K. E., & Baggett, L. S. (2011). Determinants of foreign trade mission participation. *Business & Society, 41*(1), 6–35.

Seringhaus, F. H. R., & Rosson, P. J. (1994). International trade fairs and foreign market involvement: Review and research directions. *International Business Review*, *3*(3), 311–329.

Sethi, D., Guisinger, S., Ford, D. L., & Phelan, S. E. (2002). Seeking greener pastures: A theoretical and empirical investigation into the changing trend of foreign direct investment flows in response to institutional and strategic factors. *International Business Review*, *11*(6), 685–705.

Sherman, R., & Eliasson, J. (2006). Trade disputes and non-state actors: New institutional arrangements and the privatisation of commercial diplomacy. *World Economy*, *29*, 473–489.

Sherman, R., & Eliasson, J. (2007). Privatizing commercial diplomacy: Institutional innovation at the domestic–international frontier. *Current Politics and Economics of Europe*, *18*(3/ 4), 351–355.

Spence, M., & Crick, D. (2004). Acquiring relevant knowledge for foreign market entry: The role of overseas trade missions. *Strategic Change*, *13*(5), 283–292.

Sridharan, K. (2002). Commercial diplomacy and statecraft in the context of economic reform: The Indian experience. *Diplomacy and Statecraft*, *13*(2), 57–82.

Stadman, A., & Ruël, H. J. M. (2012). Competitors or collaborators: A comparison of commercial diplomacy policies and practices of EU member governments. In H. J. M. Ruël (Ed.), *Commercial diplomacy and international business: A conceptual and empirical exploration* (pp. 183–225). Bingley: Emerald Insight.

Udovic, B. (2011). Slovene commercial diplomacy in the Western Balkan countries. *Communist and Post-Communist Studies*, *44*, 357–368.

Van Bergeijk, P. A. G. (1992). Diplomatic barriers to trade. *The Economist*, *140*(1), 45–64.

Vehof, T., Ruël, H. J. M., & Telgen, J. (2012). Entering the United governments federal procurement market: Success factors and barriers for foreign firms. In H. J. M. Ruël (Ed.), *Commercial diplomacy and international business: A conceptual and empirical exploration* (pp. 227–250). Bingley: Emerald Insight.

Wilkinson, T. J., & Brouthers, L. E. (2000a). An evaluation of government sponsored promotion programs. *Journal of Business Research*, *47*(3), 229–246.

Wilkinson, T. J., & Brouthers, L. E. (2000b). Trade shows, trade missions and state governments: Increasing FDI and high-tech exports. *Journal of International Business Studies*, *31*(4), 725–734.

Wilkinson, T. J., & Brouthers, L. E. (2006). Trade promotion and SME export performance. *International Business Review*, *15*(3), 233–252.

Wu, J., Li, S., & Samsell, D. (2012). Why some countries trade more, some trade less, some trade almost nothing: The effect of the governance environment on trade flows. *International Business Review*, *21*(2), 225–238.

Yang, S., Shin, H., Lee, J., & Wrigley, B. (2008). Country reputation in multidimensions: Predictors, effects, and communication channels. *Journal of Public Relations Research*, *20*(4), 421–440.

Yannopoulos, P. (2010). Export assistance programs: Insights from Canadian SMEs. *International Review of Business Research Papers*, *6*(5), 36–51.

Zuidema, L., & Ruël, H. J. M. (2012). The effectiveness of commercial diplomacy: A survey among embassies and consulates. In H. J. M. Ruël (Ed.), *Commercial diplomacy and international business: A conceptual and empirical exploration* (pp. 105–140). Bingley: Emerald Insight.

CHAPTER 13

THE VAGUENESS OF THE "COUNTRY-SPECIFIC ADVANTAGE" CONSTRUCT: WHICH HOST-CSAS MATTER FOR CHINESE OFDI?

Gilmar Masiero and Francisco Urdinez

ABSTRACT

Purpose — *The purpose of this chapter is to demonstrate that, despite the extensive literature on firm-specific advantages (FSAs) and country-specific advantages (CSAs) produced since Rugman's classic matrix (1981), little progress has been made in empirically operationalizing the second concept.*

Design/methodology/approach — *Through a review of the international business (IB) literature that refers to the CSA concept, we identify the "vagueness" in the usage of this concept. First, we present a concise literature review of the CSA construct, with a link to the "double diamond" theoretical model of Rugman and D'Cruz (1993) and Rugman and Verbeke (1993). Second, we present the results of the bibliographic analysis on the use of the construct by a variety of authors.*

Multinational Enterprises, Markets and Institutional Diversity
Progress in International Business Research, Volume 9, 323–345
Copyright © 2014 by Emerald Group Publishing Limited
All rights of reproduction in any form reserved
ISSN: 1745-8862/doi:10.1108/S1745-886220140000009013

Findings — *We demonstrate the weak conceptual grounding of the CSA concept by reviewing the literature on host-CSAs attracting Chinese overseas foreign direct investment (OFDI). Apart from the fact that various authors use different sources of data, an important reason for contradictory results is the fact that each author tests host-CSA through different indicators. Here, we propose a list of variables and indicators based on the "double diamond" model and test these empirically.*

Originality/value — *IB researchers should start conducting serious studies on home-CSAs and host-CSAs instrumental to attracting investments, defining clear indicators and using replicable data based on publicly available information. This chapter is the first to show that the concepts developed by Rugman (1981) and expanded by Rugman, A. M. and Verbeke, A. (2008) (Internalization theory and its impact on the field of international business.* Research in Global Strategic Management, *14, 155–174) are relevant to advance in the quantitative operationalization of concepts within IB theory.*

Keywords: Country-specific advantages; international business theory; outward foreign direct investments

INTRODUCTION

Despite the extensive literature on firm-specific advantages (FSAs) and country-specific advantages (CSAs) introduced by the classical Rugman matrix (1981) and extended by Rugman and D'Cruz (1993) and Rugman and Verbeke (1993), little progress has been made in the effort to measure the CSA concept empirically. Whereas the concept of FSAs has continued to be measured and developed by researchers of the resource-based view of the firm, such as Wernerfelt (1984), Peteraf (1993) and Barney (1991, 2001), the intuitively rich concept of CSA has been understudied by international business (IB) researchers over the last three decades.

Based on a review of the IB literature referring to the concept of CSA, we conclude that the term has been only vaguely defined. Our chapter seeks to more precisely measure this concept and test its effects in five sections. First, we present a concise literature review of the CSA construct, including its extension in Rugman and D'Cruz's (1993) and Rugman and Verbeke's (1993) "double diamond" model. Second, we present the results of the bibliography analysis on the use of the construct by other authors. Third, we illustrate the vagueness of the construct through the review of the literature on host CSA attracting Chinese OFDI. Apart from the fact that authors use different sources of data, a main reason for opposite results has to do with the fact that each test host CSA through different indicators. Fourth, we test empirically a set of commonly used host CSA on Chinese OFDI. Finally, we conclude highlighting the relevance of our discussion to the theory of International Business. All these sections are developed to answer our research question: What do Chinese multinational enterprises (MNEs) care about when investing in foreign markets?

WHAT IS A COUNTRY-SPECIFIC ADVANTAGE?

The motivations for our study depart from *Fifty years of International Business Theory and Beyond* (Rugman, Verbeke, & Nguyen, 2011). The work will be a classic in years to come due to its excellent synthesis. However, what this chapter reveals is that a whole theoretical structure has been built on what we believe is a concept not thoroughly empirically tested: CSAs.

Even though pioneering works, such as Vernon (1966), Dunning (1980), and Rugman (1980), had included country-specific factors as part of their analysis, these studies had limited their understanding to examining how country-specific factors served as a channel to facilitate learning by MNE and how these learning effects were then employed in international markets (Rugman et al., 2011). That is, the CSAs were seen as FSAs enhancers. The focus in the 1980s was directed at FSA. Internationalization theory economists, such as Buckley and Casson (1976) and Rugman (1981), have developed important explanations about why firms become involved in international production highlighting that foreign direct investment (FDI) should not be analyzed solely at the country level, but also at the firm level, that is, the MNE (Rugman et al., 2011). Multinational firms became the prominent source of FDI inflows and outflows into developed and developing countries as part of the wave of globalization of the 1990s and the first decade of the 2000. Following this viewpoint, internationalization theory scholars emphasized that profit-maximizing firms may seek to internalize their acquisition of intermediate goods and intangible assets of technology, brand, management expertise, etc. across national borders (Buckley & Casson, 2009). They have been doing this due to the market imperfections of the pricing of intermediate goods, information asymmetries, the lack of future markets and many other public goods externalities associated with the government interventions and trade barriers of different national economies. However, Rugman has himself questioned internationalization theory stating that it "lacks serious conceptual grounding and generalizability" (Rugman et al., 2011, p. 14), particularly a clear definition with regards to geographic proximity of experiential learning and which of these concepts impact the decision of FDI and the spread of geographic sales.

In short, the literature lacks clarity on which variables can be used to measure the concept of CSAs. In fact, it seems that there is no such discussion. Rugman's definition of CSA is that they are "the natural resource endowments (minerals, energy, forests, etc.), the quality and quantity of labor force, and associated cultural factors" (Rugman, 2005, p. 34; Rugman, 2007, p. 334; Rugman, Oh, & Lim, 2012, p. 221). The author recognizes both home and host CSA to be important for an accurate analysis and gives a more detailed definition of (host) CSAs when combining it with Dunning's OLI framework (i.e., location advantages) (Rugman, 2010). In other words, what matters is the host-country advantages related to market size, natural resources, infrastructure aspects, education system, governance structures, and other aspects of political and government activity.

Rugman and D'Cruz (1993) and Rugman and Verbeke (2003) considered the CSAs variables in depth based on Porter's diamond. They explain how CSAs are divided into host and home factors, and are formed by four variables, namely supporting industries, factor conditions (resources), demand conditions (customers), and government conditions. Rugman and D'Cruz (1993) devised what they called "double-diamond model" (DDM).

Rugman and D'Cruz (1993) and Rugman and Verbeke (2003) adopted Porter's terminology to clarify how countries explore their CSAs, but since these papers' publication, these dimensions have not yet been tested empirically, perhaps with the sole exception of Moon, Rugman and Verbeke (1998). We argue that it is vital to develop a metric to compare results as well as to validate constructs and concepts.

CSAS IN THE LITERATURE

We undertook a bibliographic analysis to better understand the development of CSA construct in the literature. First, we searched for articles using wide-ranging academic databases such as EBSCO, Science Direct, JSTOR,

Sage, Emerald, Scielo, Spell and Google Scholar. We researched academic peer-reviewed articles and found only three papers containing "Country-Specific Advantages" in its title (De Beule & Duanmu, 2012; Nachum & Rolle, 1999; Shan & Hamilton, 1991), while 176 peer-reviewed papers containing that expression in the title or body of the work.[1]

Second, the selected papers had to fulfill the following points to be included in our bibliographic analysis: (a) use the concept explicitly, (b) define the concept with variables, or (c) try to test it empirically. Among the 176 papers, we only found 13 that satisfied our specified criteria. The details are depicted in Table 1.

Many papers focus on home or host determinants of OFDI, but few refer to Rugman's theory. For instance, Luo and Wang (2012) show, using a survey of 153 MNEs from China, that Chinese overseas investment strategies are influenced by home country environment parameters, traits including economic growth, institutional perceived hardship, competitive pressure, and by their home country operational characteristics, including inward internationalization, innovation orientation, and business development stage. Despite citing an interest in understanding the effect of Rugman's CSA concept, the authors make inferences about *Home Country Effects* without providing a definition of which variables measure this factor and its effect on FDI.

Among the academic sample selected, only four papers define CSAs with testable variables (Buckley, Forsans, & Munjal, 2012; Cho, Moon, & Kim, 2009; De Beule & Duanmu, 2012; Ramamurti, 2008). Ramamurti (2008) defines 10 CSAs variables, but does not test them econometrically. De Beule and Duanmu (2012) analyze how country-, industry- and firm-specific determinants affect Chinese and Indian acquisitions and test 11 CSAs variables: market size, market wealth (GDP per capita), market openness, resources (percentage of ores and metals exports to total merchandise exports by country), patents, trademarks, political stability, rule of law, control of corruption, regulatory quality, and geographical distance. While better rule of law, regulatory quality, and control of corruption are found to be important for India´s although not for China´s acquisitions, political stability proves to be a negative estimator for both countries.

Buckley et al. (2012) examine the complementarity of country-specific linkages with country advantages to explain the foreign acquisitions of Indian MNES. In order to adjust for the shortcomings of the CSAs concept, these authors also use the eclectic paradigm (Dunning, 1977, 1980; Dunning & Rugman, 1985). In order to evaluate home CSAs, the authors

Table 1. Major Studies Employing CSA Concept.

Title	Author(s)/Year	Journal	Use of CSA Concept	Define CSA Variables	Test CSAs
"Country-specific advantage and international cooperation"	Shan and Hamilton (1991)	Strategic Management Journal	✓	—	✓
"Home country and firm-specific ownership advantages: A study of US, UK and French advertising agencies."	Nachum and Rolle (1999)	International Business Review	✓	—	—
"Transforming disadvantages into advantages: Developing-country MNEs in the least developed countries"	Cuervo-Cazurra and Genc (2008)	Journal of International Business Studies	✓	—	✓
"Does one size fit all? A dual double diamond approach to country-specific advantages"	Cho et al. (2009)	Asian Business & Management	✓	✓	✓
"What have we learned about emerging-market MNEs?"	Ramamurti (2008)	For presentation at a conference	✓	✓	—
"Market characteristics and regionalisation patterns"	Seno-Alday (2009)	European Management Journal	✓	—	—
"The evolution of country and firm specific advantages and disadvantages in the process of Chinese firm internationalization."	Marinova, Child, and Marinov (2011)	Advances in International Management	✓	—	—
"EMNEs and knowledge-seeking FDI"	Kedia, Gaffney, and Clampit (2012)	Management International Review	✓	—	—
"Host-home country linkages and host-home country specific advantages as determinants of foreign acquisition by Indian firms"	Buckley et al. (2012)	International Business Review	✓	✓	✓

Table 1. (Continued)

Title	Author(s)/Year	Journal	Use of CSA Concept	Define CSA Variables	Test CSAs
"Why MNCs tend to concentrate their activities in their home region"	Wolf, Dunemann, and Ezzgelhoff (2012)	*Multinational Business Review*	✓	–	–
"Locational determinants of internationalization: A firm-level analysis of Chinese and Indian acquisitions"	De Beule and Duanmu (2012)	*European Management Journal*	✓	✓	✓
"Foreign direct investment strategies by developing country multinationals: A diagnostic model for home country effects"	Luo and Wang (2012)	*Global Strategy Journal*	✓	–	✓
"Home country determinants of outward FDI from developing countries"	Das (2013)	*Margin: The Journal of Applied Economic Research*	✓	–	✓

examine three determinants of MNE capital investment: domestic capital market, foreign exchange rate of the Indian Rupee against the US Dollar, and language proficiency. They find that all these factors are significant and have an expected positive sign helping to explain the level of foreign acquisitions made by Indian MNEs.

In order to examine the effect of locational advantages, the authors consider three sets of determinants: market seeking motives, endowment of natural resources, and endowment of knowledge assets. Their preliminary results confirm the significance of host country's market size. In other words, market-seeking motives measured by the size of the host country's market are significant. As natural resources endowments are not found to be statistically significant, the authors posit that "[...] India might not have reached the point in its development process where it needs to import large amounts of natural resources yet, unlike China" (Buckley et al., 2012, p. 888).

WHAT ARE THE IMPLICATIONS OF THE LACK OF PRECISION?

The lack of empirical definition of CSAs can lead to opposite conclusions since each author uses a different set of indicators. Some IB authors have pointed out the particularities of Chinese OFDI, suggesting that this case might offer refinements to established theories or even their refutation (Liu, Buck, & Shu, 2005; Li-Ying, Stucchi, Visholm, & Jansen, 2013; Ramasamy, Yeung, & Laforet, 2012). In the remainder of this chapter, we delve further into the literature on CSA determinants of Chinese OFDI to precisely explore these contradictions and the questions they raise for IB research.

Based on our review, we believe that the literature arrives at different results not only because of the use of different sources of data, but mainly, because of the different indicators chosen to test the host-country determinants of investments. There is a rich literature regarding Chinese OFDI, especially since 2005, but these studies employ different indicators to empirically test the same hypotheses. As we discuss below, these differences are important and merit further exploration.

China is no longer a mere recipient of FDI, but has become in recent years an active investor in the world. In 2013, three of the ten largest companies in the world were Chinese (Sinopec Group, China National

Petroleum, and State Grid), and the Forbes Global 500 includes 73 Chinese companies. That is nearly 15% of the largest 500.

Liu et al. (2005) reject the idea that Chinese OFDI is a *sui generis* case. They test their model with a GMM regression and their results suggest that the level of economic development, measured by GDP per capita plus human capital, is still the main factor explaining China's rate of OFDI, as it is for other countries. They also found OFDI to be positively influenced by the value of local investments in human capital, which is a determinant of OFDI for other countries.

Morck, Yeung, and Zhao (2008) assert that China's outward investment is mostly driven by acquisitions in neighboring Asian countries and resource-rich parts of Africa. In those acquisitions, natural resources appear to be critical, as Asian and African countries are gaining relevance. Thus, China is depicted as a resource seeker that invests in countries with weak macroeconomic environments.

Buckley et al. (2007) have written an insightful paper in this area. Building on Liu et al. (2005), their motivation was to test the extent to which the mainstream theory that explains industrialized country FDI is applicable to emerging country contexts and whether special explanations nested within the general theory are needed. Through OLS regressions, these authors conclude that Chinese OFDI is associated with host natural resources endowments. However, these authors chose to measure these assets through data on host country's exports of ores and minerals, excluding energy and food investments. They find Chinese OFDI to be associated with high levels of political risk in, and cultural proximity to, host countries throughout, along with host market size and geographic proximity. In this sense, the authors are closer to Morck et al. (2008).

Cui and Jiang (2010) develop a case study based on ten Chinese outward investing firms. Their paper examines ownership with a focus on the choice between a wholly owned subsidiary (WOS) and a joint venture (JV) entry mode. They found that Chinese firms invest overseas to seek various strategic assets, and a full ownership structure (WOS) is considered a proper way to organize. Chinese firms invest overseas to seek technology and brand-related assets to enhance their competitiveness. These companies favor WOS as it is more effective than JV in terms of acquiring, utilizing, and transferring desired assets. Chinese firms value a good relationship with the host country government, and try to establish a harmonious social status within the host country, thereby trying to avoid an exploitative reputation. The CSAs that attract investments differ depending on whether a venture is a WOS or a JV. The authors show that investment decisions are also explained by whether the Chinese enterprise is a state-owned enterprise (SOE) or a privately owned enterprise (POE).

Ramasamy et al. (2012) argue that Chinese firms seem to be investing into countries that do not fit the standard profile of host locations. They test, through a Poisson count data regression model, that Chinese OFDI is attracted to countries that possess large supply of natural resources. They categorize the firms into state-controlled and privately owned according to majority ownership. Afterwards, they report that the determinants of internationalization differ based on ownership: State-controlled firms are attracted to countries with large sources of natural resources and risky political environments. Private firms are more market seekers. This thought-provoking work also measured "natural resources endowments" using data on host countries exports of ores and minerals as Liu et al. (2005) did.

Li (2012) finds that Chinese OFDI generally follows what is predicted by mainstream direct investment theory in terms of host country GDP and geographic distance to parent country, indicating that Chinese OFDI is sensitive to market size and costs. This study also reports strong evidence that Chinese OFDI is attracted to countries with abundant natural resources.

Finally, Li-Ying et al. (2013) chose two Chinese firms that just had started investing and a third one that was in the process of preparing to invest in Denmark. The authors inquire on whether new theories are needed or whether updating the profound and long-tested existing theories of international business to serve a new era of OFDI from emerging markets firms will be sufficient. In contrast to other studies, they cite Rugman, arguing that strategic asset-seeking OFDIs were supposed to have high levels of FSAs and CSAs.

Using Dunning's theory, their study presented a more detailed analysis regarding the O, L, and I advantages that Chinese investing firms in Denmark are perceived to possess and found that these Chinese investing firms had high levels of Oa (asset-based ownership advantage) and Oi (institution-based ownership advantage) but Ot (transaction-based ownership advantage) was largely absent. Furthermore, although Lr (resource-based L advantages) was obviously appreciated in Denmark, Li (institution-based L advantages) presented a mixed picture.

As we have tried to exemplify, since 2005 several investigations on CSA determining Chinese OFDI have been done and there is not much consensus across these results, except for the relevance of natural resources endowments, which has been measured through dubious indicators and which only seem to attract SOE, and not POE which are more market seekers (Morck et al., 2008). By using a clear definition of CSA, empirical research in the area of IB would be more aligned.

In an attempt to standardize the use of CSA indicators and provide a contribution to the literature, we propose some variables and indicators based on the "double diamond" model (Rugman & D'Cruz, 1993; Rugman & Verbeke, 2003). We employ these measures on Chinese OFDI cases, which are described in the following section. Using these variables, we seek to investigate "Chinese CSAs" (Rugman & Li, 2007) and try to answer the research question: What do Chinese MNEs care about when investing in foreign markets?

DATA ANALYSIS AND METHOD

As compared with past empirical work, we believe our specification is more robust as it attempts to fully capture the usefulness of the CSA construct, a task thus far incompletely explored in past research. We tested our hypotheses by operationalizing the four variables in Rugman and D'Cruz's (1993) and Rugman and Verbeke's (2003) DDM. The method used to test our model was ordinary least squares (OLS) regression with robust standard errors to control for heteroskedasticity, which was tested using the Breusch-Pagan/Cook-Weisberg test. The baseline model of this work can be summarized as:

$$\text{Total Chinese OFDI}_i = \beta_0 + \beta_1 \text{ endowed resources} (X_{i1})$$
$$+ \beta_2 \text{ supporting industries} (X_{i2}) + \beta_3 \text{ domestic demand} (X_{i3})$$
$$+ \beta_4 \text{ government conditions} (X_{i4}) + \varepsilon_i$$

The dependent variable, total Chinese OFDI, measures the "*Sum of Chinese OFDI received per country between 2005 and 2012*" was created using the Heritage Foundation's China Global Investment Tracker. This is the only publicly available Chinese OFDI base, which has the advantage that its information can be replicated by all interested readers. Its data is gathered by monitoring companies and foreign sources are also used for data collection. The sample period we considered (2005−2012) was determined by the availability of data from this source. An advantage of this database is that it includes information on transactions of failed and successful Chinese investments, which may overstate the amount of capital inflows. Many projects are announced and never concretized. On the other hand, a caveat of this data sources is that it only registers transactions valued at more than $100 million thereby excluding small projects. Another warning is that only investments announced and published in English sources are included in the database. We base our findings on a sample of 96 countries.[2]

The independent variables use "objective" data (World Bank Data, Correlates of War, and World Distance Calculator) and more "subjective" data (World Economic Forum). We believe that the latter has three advantages over the former and has therefore been included. First, its indicators are created based on a mixture of, on the one hand, statistical data from recognized agencies, notably the United Nations Educational, Scientific and Cultural Organization (UNESCO), the International Monetary Fund (IMF), and the World Health Organization (WHO). The alternative source is based on the World Economic Forum's annual Executive Opinion Survey, which collects an average of a hundred respondents per country making it the largest poll of its kind, collecting the insight of more than 14,000 business executives. Second, the country coverage is extensive and all the 96 countries in our study are included, something that does not happen with other data sources. Third, the subjectivity of the executives is a valuable insight since foreign investment decisions are also based on subjective factors. Therefore, our model contains four independent variables related to endowment resources, supporting industries, domestic demand, and government conditions that are described in detail in Table 2.

Finally, we include a control variable that measures the geographical distance in kilometers between Beijing to the host country's capital.

RESULTS

Our baseline regression is presented in column 1 of Table 3. It reveals that natural resources are an important driver of Chinese OFDI and that specifically energy production is a key. The remaining results presented in Table 3 have three variants, in which with each column, an additional set of measures of the model is added to endowed resources. Column 4, the reader will notice, corresponds to the DDM proposed by Rugman and D'Cruz (1993) and Rugman and Verbeke (2003). The number of observations among the four columns varies due to missing data in some independent variables.

Table 2.   Proposed Indicators to Test Which CSA Attract Chinese OFDI.

Variables	Indicators	Expected Sign (Based on Literature)	Data Sources
Total sum of Chinese OFDI received per country (Y_{f1})	Expressed as the amount of FDI received from Chinese MNEs in million US$.	—	Heritage foundation China global investment tracker
Natural endowed resources (X_{f1})	a. Cereal yield (kg per hectare) b. Land under cereal production (thousand hectares) c. Forest area (thousand sq. km) d. Energy production (thousand kt of oil equivalent) e. Iron and steel production (thousands of tons)	Positive	World Bank Data, and correlates of war
Related and supporting industries (X_{f2})	f. Transport infrastructure (score between 0 and 7) g. Electricity and telephony infrastructure (score between 0 and 7) h. Trustworthiness and confidence (score between 0 and 7) i. Technological adoption (score between 0 and 7) j. Macroeconomic environment (score between 0 and 7) k. Roads, paved (% of total roads, latest available value) l. Private institutions quality (score between 0 and 7) m. Trade in services (% of GDP) n. Ease of doing business rank (1 = most business-friendly regulations, 180 = least business-friendly regulations)	Negative	World economic forum global competitiveness index and World Bank Data

Table 2. (*Continued*)

Variables	Indicators	Expected Sign (Based on Literature)	Data Sources
Domestic demand (X_{i3})	o. Competition (score between 0 and 7) p. Quality of demand conditions (score between 0 and 7) q. Domestic market size (score between 0 and 7) r. Business sophistication (score between 0 and 7) s. GDP per capita (current US$, average 2005–2012) t. Inflation, consumer prices (annual %) u. Unemployment, total (% of total labor force)	Positive	World economic forum global competitiveness index and World Bank Data
Government conditions (X_{i4})	v. Health (score between 0 and 7) w. Primary education (score between 0 and 7) x. Quantity of education (score between 0 and 7) y. Public institutions quality (score between 0 and 7) z. Total tax rate (% of commercial profits) aa. Time to prepare and pay taxes (hours) bb. Time required to enforce a contract (days)	Negative	World economic forum global competitiveness index and World Bank Data
Distance (control variable)	Kms between Beijing and the country's capital	Positive	World distance calculator (GlobeFeed.com)

Table 3. Econometric Results.

Method: OLS Regression with Robust Standard Errors Dependent Variable: Sum of FDI between 2005 and 2012 (US$)	Coefficient t-statistic (1)	Coefficient t-statistic (2)	Coefficient t-statistic (3)	Coefficient t-statistic (4)
Endowed resources (X_{f1})				
Cereal yield	0.172 (0.64)	−0.819 (−1.22)	−0.842 (−1.27)	−1.029 (−1.37)
Land under cereal production	0.0824 0.66	0.0678 0.46	0.0115 0.09	0.0577 0.47
Forest area	1.208 0.48	0.769 0.35	0.457 0.22	−0.835 (−0.44)
Energy production	23.52*** 3.62	25.80*** 3.43	26.05** 3.43	29.74*** 4.96
Iron and steel production	−0.0602 (−1.41)	−0.126* (−2.08)	−0.168** (−2.77)	−0.194** (−2.88)
Related and supporting industries (X_{f2})				
Transport infrastructure		1700.2 1.19	890.2 0.44	1633.5 0.68
Electricity and telephony infrastructure		2374.6 1.67	2668.5 1.57	1875.3 0.72
Trustworthiness and confidence		2084.2 1.46	2722.8 1.26	1698.8 0.57
Technological adoption		−660.2 (−0.29)	−537.7 (−0.27)	−1470.6 (−0.52)
Macroeconomic environment		−1803.8* (−2.35)	−2687.2* (−2.02)	−2700.5* (−2.16)
Paved roads		−70.7 (−1.83)	−73 (−1.53)	−94.08 (−1.77)
Private institutions quality		1117.4 (−0.56)	−163.8 (−0.06)	4263.6 (−0.93)

Table 3. (Continued)

Method: OLS Regression with Robust Standard Errors Dependent Variable: Sum of FDI between 2005 and 2012 (US$)	Coefficient t-statistic	Coefficient t-statistic	Coefficient t-statistic	Coefficient t-statistic
	(1)	(2)	(3)	(4)
Trade in services		−61.59 (−1.69)	−27.82 (−0.80)	−0.506 (−0.01)
Ease of doing business		27.63 1.26	41.51 1.28	17.03 0.38
Domestic demand (X_{f3})				
Competition			1186.1 0.54	328.2 0.12
Quality of demand conditions			6880.5* 2.24	6531.2 1.97
Domestic market size			2673.6 1.77	2058.2 1.03
Business sophistication			−6587.8 (−1.34)	−5800.8 (−1.02)
GDP per capita			0.0835 0.85	0.125 1.07
Inflation, consumer prices			63.12 0.38	−16.55 (−0.11)
Unemployment			−113.2 (−0.71)	56.81 0.34
Government conditions (X_{f4})				
Health				881.5 0.6
Primary education				2686.9 1.15
Quantity of education				−508 (−0.40)

Table 3. (*Continued*)

Method: OLS Regression with Robust Standard Errors Dependent Variable: Sum of FDI between 2005 and 2012 (US$)	Coefficient t-statistic	Coefficient t-statistic	Coefficient t-statistic	Coefficient t-statistic
	(1)	(2)	(3)	(4)
Public institutions quality				-4471.2
				(-1.48)
Total tax rate				-65.61
				(-0.98)
Time to prepare and pay taxes				7.648*
				2.05
Time required to enforce a contract				-0.504
				(-0.20)
Geographical distance	0.195	0.0047	0.191	0.0841
	1.07	0.03	0.91	0.36
Constant	403.1	-10230.5	-22316.9	-22619.6
	0.2	(-1.30)	(-1.21)	(-1.08)
N	96	90	79	79
Mean RSE	7061.7	6756.1	7130.9	7212.7
R^2	0.47	0.59	0.64	0.68

t-statistics in parentheses.
*$p < 0.05$, **$p < 0.01$, ***$p < 0.001$.

From an empirical standpoint, our results call into question the necessity of employing more comprehensive measures to capture CSAs. Only one of the nine indicators of related and supporting industries (X_{i2}), none of the seven indicators of Domestic Demand (X_{i3}), and only one of the seven indicators of government conditions (X_{i4}) were statistical significant in our regression model.

The effect of energy production, measured as *average thousand kt of oil equivalent*[3] is positive and statistical significance in all four columns, which is at first glance promising. However, as McCloskey (1998) notes, statistical significance does not necessarily mean scientific significance. When the coefficient is evaluated in terms of its magnitude, we see that, other things being equal, a country endowed with a 100,000 kt of oil per year, or equivalent, is predicted to receive US$ 2974 million on average in Chinese OFDI. However, using the 95% confidence interval, the preciseness of this effect can be as high as US$4174 or as low as US$ 1774.

The explanatory power of this variable is astonishing as it can predict around 73% of total Chinese OFDI received among the "Top 15 receivers." When we compared the predicted value to the observed investment only in the energy sector, the former overpredicts the latter by just 7.7%. The main destinations of OFDI in energy projects were Canada (33.1 billion), Australia (23 billion), Brazil (19 billion), the United States (14.4 billion), and Iran (13.7 billion). The most prominent investors were CNOOC and Sinopec.

Our results are in agreement with those of Ramasamy et al. (2012), Li (2012), and Buckley et al. (2007) in highlighting the relevance of natural endowments. However, our findings more precisely call attention to the relevance of the energetic variable over other natural resources as the key determinant of CSAs.

Iron and steel production, measured as thousands of tons produced, in 2007[4] has statistical significance, but its explanatory power is much lower. Moreover, the sign of the coefficient for these variables is negative. This suggests, counter intuitively, that the production of iron and steel was not a motivating CSA after controlling for other factors. This was an unexpected result as many authors have called attention to the high demand of steel and iron by China for sustaining urbanization as a key determinant of internationalization (Guo & Fu, 2010; Shen, Cheng, Gunson, & Wan, 2005). Furthermore, as was observed in Table 3, 16% of total OFDI was directed for mining projects. The reason of this counterintuitive result can be explained by the fact that only four observations in the sample

(Australia, Indonesia, DRC, and Peru) concentrate 52% of total investments in mining projects.

The host country´s macroeconomic environment[5] was also statistically significant. Its sign is negative, suggesting that many Chinese flows went to unstable economies with poor macroeconomic environments. This finding is comprehensible and confirms the arguments of other authors about the growing importance of Africa and Latin America in Chinese investments (Morck et al., 2008). The same should be said about the time to pay taxes,[6] which has a positive signal, reinforcing the idea that Chinese investments have grown in underdeveloped countries with weak institutions (Li, 2012).

Contrary to the findings of Buckley et al. (2007), geographical distance was not significant in the model. Unlike trade flows, investments are insensitive to geographical distances, especially when it comes to tracing natural resources around the globe. Contrary to Liu et al. (2005) we did not find GDP per capita, nor human capital indicators (such as primary education and quantity of education) to be statistically significant. As in Mudambi (1995), risk and infrastructural factors (such as roads paved, transport infrastructure, and quality of education) were found to be relatively ineffective in explaining the location of Chinese investment. Policy variables, such as total tax rate and public institutions, were also not significant.

CONCLUSIONS

By advancing the use of quantitative testing concepts of IB theories, we show that theories need to be more robustly tested for the progress of the field. To date, the CSA construct has remained a vague concept and arbitrary variables have been used for its measurement. Of the 176 papers that use the construct, only 13 attempted to test it empirically or to define it in specific terms.

In order to understand the effects of home and host CSA, we propose a set of indicators that measure the term and its multiple dimensions with more conceptual rigor. We then showed results of a single case study on how CSAs help to explain Chinese OFDI. At least for this case, the CSA construct has very limited explanatory power. Not all aspects of the CSA construct are relevant to explaining Chinese OFDI, and even more worrisome, the investment pattern is largely driven by a single variable, energy endowments. Our results clearly point to the need for more robust testing of the measure within and across cases.

NOTES

1. In Google Scholar, the same search found six papers containing "Country-Specific Advantages" in its title, and 574 papers containing that expression in the body of the work, but most of these are secondary references. The three paper difference between both results has to do to with the fact that Google Scholar included Rugman's works, which contained the expression in the title.

2. The distribution of the sample of 96 countries by geographical region is as follows: South America (11%), Caribbean (4%), North America (3%), Europe (18%), Middle East (13%), Northern Eurasia (15%), Oceania (3%), North Africa (5%), Sub-Saharan Africa (15%), Southern Africa (7%), and Other (6%).

3. Refers to forms of primary energy − petroleum (crude oil, natural gas liquids, and oil from nonconventional sources), natural gas, solid fuels (coal, lignite, and other derived fuels), and combustible renewables and waste − and primary electricity, all converted into oil equivalents.

4. The inter-annual variance is minimal and there are no significant differences with data between 2005 and 2012.

5. Indicator created by the global competitiveness index measured by: (a) general government budget balance as a percentage of GDP; (b) gross national savings as a percentage of GDP; (c) annual percent change in consumer price index (year average); (d) gross general government debt as a percentage of GDP; and (e) expert assessment of the probability of sovereign debt default on a 0−100 (lowest probability) scale.

6. Based on World Bank Data data, time to prepare and pay taxes is the time, in hours per year, it takes to prepare, file, and pay (or withhold) three major types of taxes: the corporate income tax, the value added or sales tax, and labor taxes, including payroll taxes and social security contributions.

REFERENCES

Barney, J. (1991). Firm resources and sustained competitive advantage. *Journal of Management*, *17*(1), 99−120.

Barney, J. (2001). Is the resource-based "view" a useful perspective for strategic management research? Yes. *Academy of Management Review*, *26*(1), 41−56.

Buckley, P. J., & Casson, M. (1976). *The future of the multinational enterprise* (Vol. 1). London: Macmillan.

Buckley, P. J., & Casson, M. (2009). The internalisation theory of the multinational enterprise: A review of the progress of a research agenda after 30 years. *Journal of International Business Studies, 40*(9), 1563–1580.

Buckley, P. J., Clegg, L. J., Cross, A. R., Liu, X., Voss, H., & Zheng, P. (2007). The determinants of Chinese outward foreign direct investment. *Journal of International Business Studies, 38*(4), 499–518.

Buckley, P. J., Forsans, N., & Munjal, S. (2012). Host–home country linkages and host–home country specific advantages as determinants of foreign acquisitions by Indian firms. *International Business Review, 21*(5), 878–890.

Cho, D. S., Moon, H. C., & Kim, M. Y. (2009). Does one size fit all? A dual double diamond approach to country-specific advantages. *Asian Business & Management, 8*(1), 83–102.

Cuervo-Cazurra, A., & Genc, M. (2008). Transforming disadvantages into advantages: Developing-country MNEs in the least developed countries. *Journal of International Business Studies, 39*(6), 957–979.

Cui, L., & Jiang, F. (2010). Behind ownership decision of Chinese outward FDI: Resources and institutions. *Asia Pacific Journal of Management, 27*(4), 751–774.

Das, K. C. (2013). Home country determinants of outward FDI from developing countries. *Margin: The Journal of Applied Economic Research, 7*(1), 93–116.

De Beule, F., & Duanmu, J. L. (2012). Locational determinants of internationalization: A firm-level analysis of Chinese and Indian acquisitions. *European Management Journal, 30*(3), 264–277.

Dunning, J. H. (1977). Trade, location of economic activity and the MNE: A search for an eclectic approach. In B. Ohlin, P. O. Hesselborn, & P. M. Wijkman (Eds.), *The international allocation of economic activity* (pp. 395–418). London: Macmillan.

Dunning, J. H. (1980). Towards an eclectic theory of international production: Some empirical tests. *Journal of International Business Studies, 11*(1), 9–31.

Dunning, J. H. (1988). The eclectic paradigm of international production: A restatement and some possible extensions. *Journal of International Business Studies, 19*(1), 1–31.

Dunning, J. H., & Rugman, A. M. (1985). The influence of Hymer's dissertation on the theory of foreign direct investment. *The American Economic Review, 75*(2), 228–232.

Guo, Z. C., & Fu, Z. X. (2010). Current situation of energy consumption and measures taken for energy saving in the iron and steel industry in China. *Energy, 35*(11), 4356–4360.

Kedia, B., Gaffney, N., & Clampit, J. (2012). EMNEs and knowledge-seeking FDI. *Management International Review, 52*(2), 155–173.

Li, T. (2012). Institutional factors matter: Perspectives on China's outward direct investment. Available at SSRN 2196272.

Liu, X., Buck, T., & Shu, C. (2005). Chinese economic development, the next stage: Outward FDI? *International Business Review, 14*(1), 97–115.

Li-Ying, J., Stucchi, T., Visholm, A., & Jansen, J. S. (2013). Chinese multinationals in Denmark: Testing the eclectic framework and internalization theory. *Multinational Business Review, 21*(1), 65–86.

Luo, Y., & Wang, S. L. (2012). Foreign direct investment strategies by developing country multinationals: A diagnostic model for home country effects. *Global Strategy Journal, 2*(3), 244–261.

Marinova, S., Child, J., & Marinov, M. (2011). Evolution of firm-and country-specific advantages and disadvantages in the process of Chinese firm internationalization. *Advances in International Management, 24*, 235–269.

McCloskey, D. N. (1998). *The rhetoric of economics*. Madison, WI: University of Wisconsin Press.

Moon, C. H., Rugman, A. M., & Verbeke, A. (1998). A generalized double diamond approach to the global competitiveness of Korea and Singapore. *International Business Review*, 7(2), 135–150.

Morck, R., Yeung, B., & Zhao, M. (2008). Perspectives on China's outward foreign direct investment. *Journal of International Business Studies*, 39(3), 337–350.

Mudambi, R. (1995). The MNE investment location decision: Some empirical evidence. *Managerial and Decision Economics*, 16(3), 249–257.

Nachum, L., & Rolle, J. D. (1999). Home country and firm-specific ownership advantages: A study of US, UK and French advertising agencies. *International Business Review*, 8(5), 633–660.

Peteraf, M. A. (1993). The cornerstones of competitive advantage: A resource-based view. *Strategic Management Journal*, 14(3), 179–191.

Ramamurti, R. (2008, October). What have we learned about emerging-market MNEs? Insights from a multi-country research project. *Copenhagen Business School conference emerging multinationals: Outward FDI from emerging and developing economies*, Copenhagen, Denmark. Retrieved from http://www.gdex.dk/ofdi/68%20Ramamurti%20Ravi.pdf

Ramasamy, B., Yeung, M., & Laforet, S. (2012). China's outward foreign direct investment: Location choice and firm ownership. *Journal of World Business*, 47(1), 17–25.

Rugman, A. (2007). *Theoretical aspects of multinational enterprises from emerging economies, with particular reference to China*. Unpublished manuscript. Retrieved from http://www3.qeh.ox.ac.uk/slptmd/Rugman.pdf

Rugman, A. M. (1980). Internalization as a general theory of foreign direct investment: A re-appraisal of the literature. *Review of World Economics*, 116(2), 365–379.

Rugman, A. M. (1981). *Inside the multinationals: The economics of internal markets*. New York, NY: Columbia University Press.

Rugman, A. M. (2005). *The regional multinationals: MNEs and 'global' strategic management*. Cambridge: Cambridge University Press.

Rugman, A. M. (2010). Reconciling internalization theory and the eclectic paradigm. *Multinational Business Review*, 18(2), 1–12.

Rugman, A. M., & D'Cruz, J. R. (1993). The "double diamond" model of international competitiveness: The Canadian experience. *Management International Review*, 33, 17–39.

Rugman, A. M., & Verbeke, A. (1993). Foreign subsidiaries and multinational strategic management: An extension and correction of Porter's single diamond framework. *Management International Review*, 33, 71–84.

Rugman, A. M., & Verbeke, A. (2003). Extending the theory of the multinational enterprise: Internalization and strategic management perspectives. *Journal of International Business Studies*, 34(2), 125–137.

Rugman, A. M., & Verbeke, A. (2008). Internalization theory and its impact on the field of international business. *Research in Global Strategic Management*, 14, 155–174.

Rugman, A. M., Verbeke, A., & Nguyen, P. C. Q. T. (2011). Fifty years of international business theory and beyond. *Management International Review*, 51(6), 755–786.

Seno-Alday, S. (2009). Market characteristics and regionalisation patterns. *European Management Journal*, 27(5), 366–376.

Shan, W., & Hamilton, W. (1991). Country-specific advantage and international cooperation. *Strategic Management Journal, 12*(6), 419−432.

Shen, L., Cheng, S., Gunson, A. J., & Wan, H. (2005). Urbanization, sustainability and the utilization of energy and mineral resources in China. *Cities, 22*(4), 287−302.

Vernon, R. (1966). International investment and international trade in the product cycle. *The Quarterly Journal of Economics, 8*(2), 190−207.

Wernerfelt, B. (1984). A resource-based view of the firm. *Strategic Management Journal, 5*(2), 171−180.

Wolf, J., Dunemann, T., & Egelhoff, W. G. (2012). Why MNCs tend to concentrate their activities in their home region. *Multinational Business Review, 20*(1), 67−91.

CHAPTER 14

MULTI-NATIONAL FIRMS, CORRUPTION AND INNOVATION IN RUSSIA

Natalya Smith, Ekaterina Thomas and Christos Antoniou

ABSTRACT

Purpose – *The purpose of this chapter is to examine the relationship between multi-national firms (MNEs), institutions and innovation.*

Methodology/approach – *We empirically examine the link between corruption and innovation within the environment of Russia. The use of data on foreign direct investment (FDI) from both emerging and developed markets provides us an opportunity to test whether the impact on innovation of different types of MNEs varies.*

Findings – *We find that, in the environments with high political risk, corruption may act as a hedge against such risks, boosting the scope and scale of innovation. We, however, find no support for the assumption that the experience at home of emerging country MNEs would offer them the advantage over the developed country MNEs in environments with weak institutions.*

Multinational Enterprises, Markets and Institutional Diversity
Progress in International Business Research, Volume 9, 347–371
Copyright © 2014 by Emerald Group Publishing Limited
All rights of reproduction in any form reserved
ISSN: 1745-8862/doi:10.1108/S1745-886220140000009014

Research implications – *One of the major implications of this study is that, in as geographically large country as Russia, it is critical to consider the factors affecting innovation output at sub-national level.*

Originality/value – *The study is novel as it is the first to examine how innovation is affected by institutions in general and corruption in particular. But in our approach, we use the measure of the actual rather than perceived corruption. Previous studies have largely focused on developed country MNEs; in this study, we examine the impact on innovation of investors from developed as well as emerging economies.*

Keywords: Innovation; MNEs; institutions; corruption; Russia

INTRODUCTION

Innovation, continued improvement and change are the three cornerstones of competitiveness enabling the long-term survival of firms locally and globally (Porter, 1990).[1] International diffusion of technology from foreign-owned firms (MNEs) is one of the key drivers of growth in transition economies where the spillovers could occur, for example, when local firms benefit from the superior knowledge of product or process technology brought about by MNEs (Blomström & Sjöholm, 1999).

A large body of the literature has examined the spillovers from MNEs (Girma & Görg, 2005; Holland & Pain, 1998; Smarzynska, 2004) and the role of institutions in fostering such spillovers (Barrel & Pain, 1999; Jalilian, Kirkpatricket, & Parker, 2007; Rodrik, 2000; Zsuzsa, 2003). Because institutions are the key determinants of corrupt practices (Rose-Ackerman, 1999), their quality matters for attracting MNEs and fostering innovation.

Corruption[2] has most frequently been used as a measure of institutional quality due to its principally damaging economic effect (Aidt, 2003; Jain, 2001). Corruption can 'sand the economic wheel' as investments in innovation may incur higher costs leading to greater inefficiencies and lower profitability (Acemoglu & Verdier, 2000; Mauro, 1995; Rose-Ackerman, 1999; Shleifer & Vishny, 1993). At the same time, corruption may help removing rigid obstacles to investment and foster innovation and growth, that is, 'grease the economic wheel' (Bailey, 1966; Leff, 1964).

Across the globe, there is a high reliance on inward foreign direct investment (FDI) as an explicit means to improved competitiveness. This applies to transition economies alike where FDI may provide a vital source of capital and technology fuelling economic growth. By exploiting their proprietary advantage (e.g. knowledge) generated at home, MNEs also innovate abroad using the resources of the host country (Dunning, 1998; Dunning & Lundan, 1998). That is said, there does not appear to be much of cumulative benefits of technology spillovers emanating from MNEs (Aitken & Harrison, 1999; Damijan, Knell, Majcen, & Rojec, 2003; Sjöholm, 1998; Yudaeva, Kozlov, Melentieva, & Ponomareva, 2003) and the literature is inconclusive at best.

Although the role of (especially) developed countries' MNEs (DMNEs) in fostering innovation has received some great attention from international business scholars (see e.g. Caves, 1996; Driffield, 2001), the recent surge in FDI from emerging countries demands new research focus for the following reasons. MNEs from emerging markets (EMNEs) differ fundamentally from DMNEs as the home—host market characteristics differ fundamentally (Buckley et al., 2007). Such fundamental difference may be, for example, in their institutional development.

As evidenced by *Transparency International Corruption Perception* index, one of the most cited international organisations, the level of corruption in emerging markets is higher than that of the developed countries. Corruption is generally considered an obstacle to foreign investment. However, the literature is unclear on whether the exposure to corruption at home affects the locational decisions of MNEs abroad.

Dealing with corruption at home, for example, may provide a learning experience preparing firms to handle corruption abroad (Habib & Zurawicki, 2002). Although institutions matter for foreign investors (Aidt, 2003; Rose-Ackerman, 1999), there is little empirical evidence as to what the exact effect of corruption on location decisions of MNEs is in this context.

The purpose of this chapter is, therefore, to examine this for the first time in the case of Russia. This presents a preliminary investigation on the impact of MNEs and institutions on the innovation outcome in Russia. The case of Russia is of a significant interest given its evolving institutions and an increasing importance of FDI. The aim of this study is to contribute further evidence to the debate on the role of institutions in shaping innovation in transition economies.

The focus of this chapter is on DMNEs and EMNEs, as the literature argues that EMNEs can take advantage of their experience of dealing with corruption at home to obtain advantage in markets with similar characteristics (Habib & Zurawicki, 2002). This chapter is structured as follows. The section 'MNEs, Corruption and Innovation' reviews the literature on MNEs, corruption and innovation. The section 'Data and Variables' describes the data used in the study. The section 'Regression Analysis' discusses the empirical model used in the analysis. The section 'Results and Discussion' presents the main findings, while the section 'Conclusion' concludes.

MNEs, CORRUPTION AND INNOVATION

Although several empirical studies have examined spillovers from FDI, few statements are universally valid. In many cases, there is somewhat conflicting evidence suggesting that the occurrence of spillovers depends on a complex interplay of both subsidiary-specific and region-specific factors (Aitken & Harrison, 1999; Bertschek, 1995; Blomström & Sjöholm, 1999; Caves, 1974; Damijan et al., 2003; Iammarino, Padilla-Pérez, & von Tunzelmann, 2008; Konings, 2001). It appears that conditions in the host country and the quality of institutions in particular can be crucial for whether positive spillovers from FDI are generated (Barrel & Pain, 1999; Rose-Ackerman, 1999).

While good governance raises productivity prospects for foreign investors, the low quality of institutions increases costs for MNEs (Wei, 2000). For example, poor government efficiency, policy reversals, graft or weak enforcement of property rights increase uncertainty and, therefore, sunk costs for MNEs, determining their investment decisions (Acemoglu, Johnson, & Robinson, 2002; Wei, 2000).

To date, the empirical research examining the relationship between institutions and FDI has focused on the cross-country variation in FDI and on the extent to which the latter is affected by the level of corruption of the host. More often, the studies find a negative relationship in this context (Habib & Zurawicki, 2002; Lambsdorff, 2003; Voyer & Beamish, 2004; Wei, 2000). This is in line with a 'grabbing hand' argument: as bureaucrats in host countries tend to extract high rents from foreign investors (Tanzi & Davoodi, 2000); this increases the cost of doing business in a country (Jun & Singh, 1996; Mauro, 1995) discouraging MNEs from investing.

Corruption has also been considered a 'helping hand' for MNEs (Tanzi & Davoodi, 2000). It can speed up the business processes in overcoming bureaucratic issues and enhance efficiency (Ehrlich & Lui, 1999; Leff, 1964) and help companies gain favourable treatment regarding publicly funded projects (Tanzi & Davoodi, 2000). In general, however, MNEs tend to avoid corruption because 'it is considered wrong and it can create operational ineffi-ciencies' (Habib & Zurawicki, 2002, p. 291). 'Handling corruption makes FDI a challenge for companies from less corrupt countries and can result in a negative FDI decision. Alternatively, exposure to corruption at home pro-vides a learning experience preparing the companies to handle them abroad. Hence, acquiring skills in managing corruption helps develop a certain com-petitive advantage' (Habib & Zurawicki, 2002, p. 295).

Regarding the effect of corruption on innovation, the literature offers two views. Common wisdom views corruption as an obstacle to growth, which 'sand the economic wheel' (Acemoglu & Verdier, 2000; Mauro, 1995; Murphy, Shleifer, & Vishny, 1993; Rose-Ackerman, 1999; Shleifer & Vishny, 1993). Under corruption, investments in innovation may incur higher transactional costs, lower profitability and lead to greater inefficien-cies (Acemoglu & Verdier, 2000). Indeed, the rent seekers are likely to target the innovation sector, which requires more public goods than established industries (Ehrlich & Lui, 1999).

Paying highest bribes allows firms to enter markets even though these firms may compromise on the quality of their products (Mankiw & Whinston, 1986; Rose-Ackerman, 1999). As a result, the entry of rent-seeking firms may hinder innovation in both the established firms and start-up firms. Furthermore, corruption can create obstacles to doing business by undermining property rights protection, impeding innovation and the trans-fer of technology (Fosu, Bates, & Hoeffler, 2006). Regional bureaucrats (by using their offices) create a private market for public goods (e.g. protection of property rights) to which only a limited number of firms can have access through 'facilitation payments' (Hellman, Jones, & Kaufmann, 2003; Levin & Satarov, 2000).

Corrupt firms often report having advanced technologies even when this is not the case (Shleifer & Vishny, 1993). Thus, the amount of innovative activity in corrupt environments might seem larger. Bureaucrats may also reject promising projects and delay innovation until a threshold level of bribe is reached which could be extracted often waiting until the maximum offer is made (Qian & Xu, 1998). Regulations can also create rigidities, slowing down the innovation process, because once bureaucrats realise they can take advantage of regulation they produce more regulation. At the same time, small increases in the penalties to corruption or the effectiveness of detection may result in large increases in the amount of product innova-tion (Veracierto, 2008).

The other view of corruption is that it helps removing rigid obstacles to investment and economic activity and 'grease the economic wheel' hedging against political risks (Bailey, 1966; Leff, 1964). In this capacity, it can allocate investment by the most efficient firms given that they are also able to pay the highest bribes. Corruption can improve time efficiency allowing firms to move in front of bureaucratic lines (Bailey, 1966; Leff, 1964).

Some empirical evidence confirms a positive impact of corruption on growth (Anokhin & Schulze, 2009; Bardhan, 1997; Heckelman & Powell, 2010) and, in some cases, (e.g. incremental innovation) corruption may enable firms to overcome bureaucratic barriers (Bardhan, 1997) and reduce the inefficiency in public administration (Heckelman & Powell, 2010).

By encouraging rent-seeking behaviour, officials can allow firms to win the innovation race. Thus, corruption may act as an incentive for bureaucrats to help fasten the innovation process. Therefore, in governance systems that do not allow much scope for innovation, corruption might facilitate entrepreneurial activities (Heckelman & Powell, 2010). Anokhin and Schulze (2009), for example, using patents and realised innovation (as proxies for the level of innovative activity), observe a curvilinear relationship between innovation, FDI and corruption. The study provides some evidence for the positive and concave relationship between corruption and patents, convex – between corruption, FDI and realised innovation. Innovation was greater when FDI was lower due to the possibility of corrupt nations attracting FDI only from other corrupt nations, which resulted in lower rates of domestic innovation.

MEASURING CORRUPTION

Transparency International highlights the fact that corruption is difficult to capture because it is happening 'behind closed doors'. Subsequently, both measuring corruption directly and quantifying it has proven to be a daunting task. The most widely accepted measure of corruption is the corruption perception index (CPI), an index claiming to 'capture the informed views of analysts, businesspeople and experts around the world' on corruption in different countries (www.transparency.org).

Countries have been ranked with individual scores between 0 and 10, with those scoring low being perceived low corrupt than those scoring high. Although this measure lacks objectivity, it is so far the best the international community has come up with. Based on CPI, one can also see the relative rankings of the home countries of the DMNEs and the EMNEs in our sample score (see Table 1); we have listed those countries scoring the highest

Table 1. Transparency International Corruption Perception Indices of Countries in the Sample.

Home Country	1995	1996	1997	1998	1999	2000	2001	2002	2003	2004	2005	2006	2007	2008	2009	2010
DMNE[a]																
Finland	9.1	9	9.5	9.6	9.8	10	9.9	9.7	9.7	9.7	9.6	9.6	9.4	9	8.9	9.4
Germany	8.1	8.3	8.2	7.9	8	7.6	7.4	7.3	7.7	8.2	8.2	8	7.8	7.9	8	8
The United Kingdom	8.6	8.4	8.2	8.7	8.6	8.7	8.3	8.7	8.7	8.6	8.6	8.6	8.4	7.7	7.7	7.8
The United States	7.8	7.8	7.6	7.5	7.5	7.8	7.6	7.7	7.5	7.5	7.6	7.3	7.2	7.3	7.5	7.1
EMNE[b]																
Belorussia				3.9	3.4	4.1	4.5	4.8	4.2	3.3	2.6	2.1	2.1	2	2.4	2.4
China	2.3	2.4	2.9	3.5	3.4	3.1	3.5	3.5	3.4	3.4	3.2	3.3	3.5	3.6	3.6	3.6
Kazakhstan					2.3	3	2.7	2.3	2.4	2.2	2.6	2.6	2.1	2.2	2.7	2.7
Ukraine				2.8	2.6	1.5	2.1	2.4	2.3	2.2	2.6	2.8	2.7	2.5	2.2	2.3

Source: Transparency International 2011.
[a]DMNE stands for the MNEs from developed countries.
[b]EMNE stands for the MNEs from emerging countries.

and those scoring the lowest according to the CPI. This largely overlaps with our breakdown of the sample in MNEs originating from develop and emerging economies, respectively. This implies that the higher the level of development in an economy the lower the importance and impact of corruption, that is, the better the institutions – as they are believed to be more advanced economies – the less corrupt the socio-economic environments.

The above-mentioned supports the argument that DMNEs are used to operate in more institutionalised environments, while EMNEs will have developed expertise in operating in more unstructured and corrupt contexts hence will be more comfortable than the former ones in entering and thriving in markets resembling the institutional structure of their home economies. This would suggest than in the Russian context, DMNES will face more difficulties than EMNEs to innovate since they will not be able to use the local 'rules of the game' (North, 2005).

We would, therefore, expect the difference in the background of the MNEs in our sample to also play out in our analysis. Unlike previous studies we have not, however, based our understanding on corruption on CPI but have used a quantifiable proxy, the number of economic crimes. The reason for doing this is because we consider the CPI inappropriate for our purposes: firstly, it is not a 'hard' measure, but rather a perceptual one, allowing for high level of subjectivity that can impact the outcome of the analysis significantly and secondly, it only measures perceived corruption at the national level, while we are interested in inter-regional variations, as expressed by the patents registered in the different Russian regions.

DATA AND VARIABLES

Data

All estimations in this chapter are based on the data collected from the Rosstat (Federal State Statics Bureau of the Russian Federation). We use data on DMNEs and EMNEs. Due to data availability, we focus on two sub-samples of MNEs: DMNEs from Germany, the United Kingdom, the United States and Finland and EMNEs from Belorussia, Kazakhstan, Ukraine and China. These foreign investors have equal to or more than 10% share in the capital of a particular firm registered in Russia. The data set specifies the type of investors as companies.

Between 1997 and 2011, across Russia there were on average 8,573 MNEs: 2,958 from emerging economies and 5,615 from developed markets (see Table 2). Our sample accounts for around 53% of the total number of MNEs operating in Russia in 1997–2011 as reported by Rosstat. A brief look at a breakdown of MNEs across 81 regions (for which data are available) shows that on average the inward FDI flow has mainly been concentrated in the Moscow city and Moscow region (with 1,094 EMNEs and 1,631 DMNEs) and Leningrad region and St Petersburg city (with 182 EMNES and 849 DMNEs). Belgorod region had 127 EMNEs and Bryansk — 122, while Kaliningrad has attracted 111 DMNEs. In contrast, the smallest number of EMNEs is located in Tuva, Kabardino-Cherkssia, Khakassia and Yamalo-Nenetsk with one firm, respectively. Kalmykia, Khakassia and Altay are the regions with the lowest number of DMNEs.

Variables

The choice of our control variables was motivated by related literature on the determinants of innovation and the availability of data. A number of

Table 2. The Accumulated Annual Number of MNEs in Russia by the Year of Registration.

Year	$EMNE^a$				$DMNE^b$			
	Belorussia	Kazakhstan	China	Ukraine	Germany	The United Kingdom	The United States	Finland
1998	242	131	733	448	662	713	1,350	492
1999	534	262	1,647	843	1,360	1,350	2,787	1,086
2000	884	411	2,698	1,259	2,116	2,316	4,181	1,698
2001	1,255	536	3,875	1,636	2,883	3,579	5,584	2,306
2002	1,655	649	5,293	2,079	3,682	5,079	6,940	2,875
2003	2,120	785	6,870	2,691	4,542	5,989	8,148	3,422
2004	2,769	975	8,805	3,425	5,516	7,489	9,556	4,061
2005	3,489	1,202	10,208	4,264	6,848	8,982	10,967	4,687
2006	4,333	1,520	11,665	5,220	8,282	9,982	12,153	5,297
2007	5,545	1,922	13,242	6,390	9,736	10,892	13,220	5,862
2008	7,041	2,363	14,594	7,422	11,241	11,800	14,189	6,425
2009	7,889	2,810	15,639	8,526	12,838	12,684	15,061	6,967
2010	8,686	3,257	16,849	9,661	14,316	13,492	15,883	7,435

[a]EMNE stands for the MNEs from emerging countries.
[b]DMNE stands for the MNEs from developed countries.

indicators have been used to proxy innovation with the level of research and development (R&D) expenditure and patent statistics as the most common measures.

Data on both R&D and patents, however, can suffer from a number of problems. For example, R&D can be an input to innovation output rather than a measure of innovation occurring in a country. Because data on R&D rely merely on the linear, technology-driven view of innovation, it may establish no necessary link to any tangible innovation output (Mansfield, 1984).

Patents are considered as a clear output indicator but may not result in commercialisation (Love & Rooper, 1999). Firms sometimes protect their innovations with alternative methods, notably industrial secrecy. Not all inventions are technically patentable. This is, for example, the case of software which is generally legally protected by copyright. Moreover, different companies have different 'propensity to patent' at home and abroad, and this may depend on whether or not they can exploit their inventions commercially (Archibugi & Pianta, 1996).

Although neither of these two measures is perfect; they, however, tend to produce reliable results when researchers control for some obvious biases and confounding correlations. In this chapter, the total count for patents is used as the dependent variable, which is a direct output-based measure of the extent of innovation. To rule out plausible alternative explanations that might influence the likelihood of innovation in regions, we control for several local-level characteristics.

Innovation is largely determined by the quality of supporting market institutions that are the key component of any innovation system (North, 2005). Different proxies have been used to measure the quality of institutions in the context of transition economies. For example, Popov (2001) and, later, Kim and Kang (2009) used the number of reported crimes. Crimes can in fact be interlinked with corruption (Buscaglia & Van Dijk, 2003; Van Dijk, 2007), because corruption[3] tends to be an integral part of organised crime's *modus operandi*.

In this chapter, we use the data on economic crimes reported (*ECCR*), which is the number of economic crimes per capita, the types of crimes that 'rank amongst the most costly of all criminal activities, with dire consequences for societies' (Lame, 2002, p. 11). Examples of economic crimes include embezzlement, insider trading, padding of one's expenses, paying a bribe to get a contract, altering a financial document and individuals receiving money or being promoted for altering a financial document.[4]

The fact that this indicator varies across Russia's regions, gives us some obvious advantage. In addition, we use two alternative proxies for institutions. Both variables are rankings, representing elements in evaluation of the investment environment in Russian regions published by Expert. These are an index of institutional potential (*INST*) and an index of political risk (*POLIT*). Regions are ranked on a scale from 1 (low) to 81 (high) − potential/risk. These correspond to the nature and quality of the institutional environment within Russia.

To account for the fact that MNEs can generate intra-regional spillovers through diffusion of new technologies (Girma & Görg, 2005), we use the accumulated number of (the stock) MNEs. Although it has been acknowledged that FDI stocks can be 'a noisy' measure (Beugelsdijik, McCann, & Mudambi, 2010), it has been frequently used in the country-level studies as a measure of the total amount of value-adding activity performed by MNEs.

The level of technology used by MNEs may depend on the local technological capabilities (Wang & Blomstrom, 1992). If they are low, the level of technology transferred will also remain low. Local firms can increase their level of technological capabilities by continuously investing in R&D (Griscuolo & Narula, 2008). We use R&D expenditures (*RD*) as an innovation input. We acknowledge that while data on R&D may ignore the complex processes of technological accumulation (Feldman, Feller, Bercovitz, & Burton, 2002), it is the greatest source of knowledge generated (Cohen & Klepper, 1992).

We also control for the educational level of population (*LABQ*). LABQ is the number of graduates with technical qualifications and university degree per capita. The growing literature on innovation focuses on the ability of firms to acquire, master and adapt imported technology to benefit from FDI (Girma & Görg, 2005; Griscuolo & Narula, 2008; Mancusi, 2008). Innovation, as a knowledge-intensive activity, is expected to be related to

Table 3. Description of the Variables Used in the Study.

PAT − Number of patent applications
RD − Expenditures on R&D
MNE − Accumulated stock of the number of foreign MNEs
DMNE − Accumulated stock of developed countries' MNEs
EMNE − Accumulated stock of emerging economies' MNEs
LABQ − Number of people with technical qualifications and university degrees per capita
ECCR − Number of economic crimes per capita
INST − Index of institutional potential
POLIT − Index of political risk

Table 4. Descriptive Statistics.

Variable	Obs	Mean	Std. Dev.	Min	Max
PAT	1,245	381	1,020.2	0	13,180
RD	1,397	44,653.7	222,436.7	0.7	3,812,621
MNE	1,135	602	2,731.4	0	35,952
DMNE	1,135	49	197.9	0	1922
EMNE	1,135	36	129.2	0	1577
LABQ	1,351	0.01	0.001	0.001	0.1
ECCR	1,245	2,995	3,053.4	23	25,506
INST	1,410	42.6	24.0	1	81
POLIT	916	45.6	25.4	1	81

Note: See Table 3 for the abbreviations of variables.

Table 5. Correlations Between Variables.

	PAT	RD	MNE	DMNE	EMNE	LABQ	ECCR	INST	POLIT
PAT	1								
RD	0.6974	1							
MNE	0.5091	0.6849	1						
DMNE	0.5314	0.5385	0.8469	1					
EMNE	0.5237	0.7133	0.9546	0.7563	1				
LABQ	0.1501	0.178	−0.1336	−0.2301	−0.0618	1			
ECCR	0.7832	0.6152	0.4399	0.4906	0.4567	0.0814	1		
INST	−0.6395	−0.4313	−0.2481	−0.2735	−0.2252	−0.0921	−0.6871	1	
POLIT	−0.018	0.0534	0.0104	0.0121	0.0016	−0.0322	0.0103	0.0508	1

Note: See Table 3 for the abbreviations of variables.

human capital in multiple ways. Investment in human capital through on-the-job training and education is the driving force behind increases in productivity and competitiveness (Black & Lynch, 1996; Cannon, 2000).

Description of variables is shown in Table 3. Summary statistics of variables is presented in Table 4. In Table 5, we present the correlations between variables.

REGRESSION ANALYSIS

Methodology

As our dependent variable is a non-negative count measure, the ordinary-least squares method was not appropriate. Instead, we used a panel data methodology. This increases the efficiency of results and the reliability of the estimates of the regression coefficients (Baltagi, 2005, p. 5) and because this methodology is designed to account for unobserved heterogeneity (frequently a source of autocorrelation and heteroscedasticity). To decide between fixed (FEs) or random effects (REs), we run a Hausman test (Green, 2008), which supports the use of FEs. The corresponding *p*-values of the test are reported at the bottom of Table 6.

With a count measure as the dependent variable, our analytical choices were either Poisson regression or the negative binominal regression (Cameron & Trivedi, 1986; Hausman, Hall, & Griliches, 1984). Because the dependent variable is over-dispersed, the Poisson assumption that the conditional mean of the outcome was equal to the conditional variance was violated. Consequently, negative binominal was an improvement over Poisson (Green, 2008).[5] Therefore, we run and report the results from the negative binominal regressions in Table 6. Because of the panel data format, we also accounted for the unobserved heterogeneity in our cross-sectional units (region-year). To do so, we included time and regional dummies. We estimate the following model:

$$PAT_{r,t} = \gamma X_{r,t-3'} + \varepsilon_{r,t-3}$$

where $PAT_{r,t}$ is the number of patent applications in a region r at time t ($r = 1, ..., 81$ and $t = 1997, ..., 2011$). $X_{r,\ t-3'}$ is a vector of variables affecting innovation. Our two explanatory variables of interest are MNEs and corruption; these are included in $X_{r,\ t-3'}$.

When relating inputs to innovative output, a time lag has to be assumed (for the reason that R&D is a lengthy process requiring time for attaining a patentable result). Since patenting of innovation can be decided long time before a patent is filed, it is more rational to use the variables lagged at least three times to account for the possible endogeneity (Fritsch & Slavtchev, 2007, 2008). In our context, this means that the innovation output in a given year is reflected in the patents filed three years in the future. Since all the years are used in the regression, we also use the clustering by region.

Table 6 presents our main results. Model 1 is our basic model with *MNE* that includes corruption and the main innovation determinants. Model 4 is our basic model with *DMNE* that includes corruption and the main innovation determinants. Model 7 is our basic model with *EMNE* that includes corruption and the main innovation determinants.

Two alternative measures of institutions are then added to the specification with *INST* controlling for the institutional potential and *POLIT* − for

Table 6. Fixed Effect Regressions.

	(1)	(2)	(3)	(4)	(5)	(6)	(7)	(8)	(9)
RD	0.089**	0.091**	0.081*	0.086**	0.088**	0.066***	0.135**	0.136**	0.143**
	(0.032)	(0.031)	(0.035)	(0.033)	(0.032)	(0.036)	(0.030)	(0.030)	(0.034)
MNE	0.275**	0.283**	0.320*						
	(0.033)	(0.034)	(0.037)						
DMNE				0.298**	0.305**	0.359***			
				(0.037)	(0.037)	(0.042)			
EMNE							0.054***	0.057***	0.069*
							(0.029)	(0.029)	(0.032)
LABQ	0.160*	0.158*	0.213**	0.180**	0.179**	0.238**	0.106	0.106	0.154*
	(0.068)	(0.067)	(0.070)	(0.066)	(0.066)	(0.068)	(0.072)	(0.072)	(0.075)
ECCR	0.090*	0.105**	0.106*	0.091*	0.106**	0.107*	0.124**	0.127**	0.137**
	(0.037)	(0.038)	(0.043)	(0.037)	(0.037)	(0.043)	(0.039)	(0.039)	(0.046)
INST		0.080*	0.084*		0.077*	0.081*		0.017	0.023
		(0.036)	(0.038)		(0.036)	(0.038)		(0.037)	(0.040)
POLIT			-0.044*			-0.042*			-0.045*
			(0.018)			(0.018)			(0.018)
Const	1.373**	0.939***	0.309	1.558**	1.143*	0.570	0.992***	0.887	1.444*
	(0.505)	(0.539)	(0.617)	(0.503)	(0.536)	(0.618)	(0.520)	(0.567)	(0.634)
N	821	821	736	800	800	716	792	792	706
Wald	73.23***	77.06***	168.54***	151.36***	155.38***	178.91***	52.22***	52.27***	59.12***
Hausman	452.39***	195.95***	177.89***	536.98***	255.07***	186.45***	569.56***	629.33***	143.21***

Note: Robust Jackrife standard errors in parentheses; ***$p < .10$, **$p < .05$, *$p < .01$. All models are estimated with a constant and the full control variables. Dependent variable is number of patents filed. See Table 3 for the abbreviations of variables.

political risks – in a region. Model 2 reports the results after adding *INST* into Model 1 with *MNE*. Model 5 reports the results after adding an index of *INST* into Model 4 with DMNEs. Model 8 reports the results after adding an index of *INST* into Model 7 with DMNEs. Model 3 reports the results after adding *POLIT* into Model 2 with MNEs. Model 6 reports the results after adding *POLIT* into Model 5 with DMNEs. Model 9 reports the results after adding *POLIT* into Model 8 with DMNEs.

Table 6 shows all the control variables to be significant (at 1% or above). All our models are statistically significant (at 5% or above). The evaluation of the models is undertaken by applying the Ramsey RESET test. The corresponding *p*-values of the test are reported at the bottom of Table 6. The results show that we cannot reject the null hypothesis suggesting no evidence of misspecification of the functional forms. The signs of the coefficients do not change and the magnitudes are very similar. Therefore, the results presented in this chapter are robust to different specifications.

Interestingly, our results show that corruption in Russia has a positive effect on innovation, 'greasing' the process of innovation. But this result is not surprising because Russia is known for its rigid bureaucracy. That is why it is possible that to overcome excessive bureaucratic barriers to innovation firms in Russia's regions may have used the weaknesses of the institutional environment to their advantage.

That said, the willingness to engage in corrupt activities depends on the penalty imposed and on the probability of being caught. If a region has strong institutions, the probability of getting caught is very high and government officials may find it difficult to engage in corrupt activities. Thus, our sensitivity analysis is concerned with the interaction terms that occur between institutions and corruption.

We use two terms (see Table 7): *ECCR*INST* is the interaction between institutional potential and corruption and *ECCR*POLIT* is the interaction between legislative risks and corruption. In effect, we want to test whether the effect of corruption is significantly different in regions with higher level of institutional quality. We would expect these interaction terms to have a negative effect on innovation if corruption deters innovators ('sand') and otherwise ('grease'). If the coefficient of *ECCR*INST* is positive and significant, then it is interpreted that corruption 'greases' innovation through institutions. If the coefficient of *ECCR*POLIT* is negative and significant, then it is interpreted that corruption 'sands' innovation output through political risks. The results of these regressions are reported in Table 7.

Columns 10, 12 and 14 show that there is indeed the evidence that the effect of corruption on innovation depends on the quality of institutions.

Table 7.   Sensitivity Analysis.

	(10)	(11)	(12)	(13)	(14)	(15)
INST	0.067**		0.079**		0.013**	
	(0.060)		(0.060)		(0.063)	
POLIT		−0.026***		−0.028***		−0.021***
		(0.015)		(0.015)		(0.016)
ECCR	0.098***	0.008**	0.011***	0.005**	0.096***	0.038**
	(0.058)	(0.041)	(0.057)	(0.041)	(0.061)	(0.042)
*ECCR*INST*	−0.001**		−0.001**		−0.001**	
	(0.000)		(0.000)		(0.000)	
*ECCR*POLIT*		0.001**		0.001**		0.001**
		(0.000)		(0.000)		(0.000)
N obs	822	732	801	712	793	702
N groups	77	77	77	77	77	77

Note: Robust Jackrife standard errors in parentheses; ***p < .10, **p < .05. All models are esti-mated with a constant and the full control variables. Dependent variable is number of patents filed. See Table 3 for the abbreviations of variables.

While better institutions *per se* lead to more innovation in regions, regions with higher number of reported crimes (used as a measure of corruption) also have higher innovation output. This can be so because the number of reported economic crimes (the actual corruption) can also indicate the effi-ciency of law and enforcement agencies, which should be taken into account when considering the 'greasing' effect of corruption in Tables 6 and 7.

In similar fashion, Columns 11, 13 and 15 give evidence of corruption (i.e. economic crimes) 'greasing' the innovation through political risks. But when political risks are accounted for, the effect of political risks *per se* on innovation is 'sanding'. That is, in regions with higher political risks (e.g. where risk of expropriation of local governments is higher), the innovation output is lower. What observed when political risks are inter-acted with corruption (measured by economic crimes), however, is that the association with innovation becomes unexpected (i.e. positive).

Scholars have identified close relationships between the state and busi-ness as a central problem of many transition countries (Frydman & Rapaczynski, 1994). That is, innovators can bypass and accept political risks by engaging in illegal dealings with decision-makers able to mediate the impact of political risks. In our case, this is exemplified by the positive interaction effect between political risks and corruption (see Table 7), which is in line with some early research suggesting that in transition coun-tries indigenous firms that belong to foreign or regional private owners are likely to be captors (Yakovlev & Zhuravskaya, 2009).

RESULTS AND DISCUSSION

Our most important findings can be summarised as follows. Firstly, our results support some earlier research that innovation can be facilitated by FDI along with expenditures on R&D and human capital quality (Black & Lynch, 1996; Cannon, 2000; Cohen & Klepper, 1992; Girma & Görg, 2005). Secondly, our research supports the idea that institutional quality matters for innovation. That said, in the case of Russia corruption (proxied by the number of economic crimes) has been 'the grease' for innovation (Bailey, 1966; Leff, 1964). This result is in support of the argument of Bardhan (1997) and the findings of Heckelman and Powell (2010) and Anokhin and Schulze (2009).

Regarding the effect of MNEs on innovation, our results provide evidence of technological transfer stemming from in Russia. Innovation in this market has been indeed facilitated by MNE affiliate's superior knowledge of product, process technology and/or markets (Blomström & Sjöholm, 1999). We also wanted to explore further the argument that the exposure to corruption at home can help firms to deal better with corruption abroad. However, we found that innovation across Russian regions was facilitated by both types of foreign-owned firms, despite the fact that the level of corruption in the locations with higher number of MNEs was also high.

Along with MNEs-related spillovers, the importance of R&D capital and quality of human capital in determining innovation outcome across Russia is also obvious. This result is in line with the previous studies (Black & Lynch, 1996; Cannon, 2000; Cohen & Klepper, 1992; Feldman et al., 2002). The coefficients of these variables are positive but the magnitude of coefficients of R&D and human capital is higher than of that of MNEs. In that, we find a convincing evidence of a positive effect of both tangible and intangible capital on innovation.

Corruption and Innovation

In line with the existing arguments (e.g. see Getz & Volkema, 2001; Shleifer & Vishny, 1993), our results show strong support for the existence of the positive relationship between innovation and institutional potential and of the negative association between political risks and patenting. Institutions matter for fostering innovation.

On the one hand, corruption can discourage investors because doing business in corrupt environments amplifies risk and uncertainties

(Shleifer & Vishny, 1993). On the other hand, acting as a hedge against political risks, corruption can boost the scope and scale of investment (Leff, 1964). But although our empirical evidence shows that corruption in the Russian case may have helped removing rigid obstacles to investment and foster innovation by reducing the inefficiency in public administration (Bardhan, 1997; Heckelman & Powell, 2010), this challenges the view that the transitional period in Russia has been accompanied by increasing formalisation of rules and filling the gaps in the legislative and regulatory basis (Radaev, 2000).

The finding that more economic crimes are associated with more innovation may at first sight seem as an oxymoron. However, it may actually imply that the more economic crimes are reported, the higher the awareness of the problem may be, and the greater the chance these will be effectively addressed, which in turn may enhance the belief of prospective innovators that corruption is being effectively tackled.

In other words, the larger the number of economic crimes being recorded, the higher the possibility that the authorities will do something about it and the bigger the boost to the confidence of companies to innovate and invest in the regional economies. This is in line with the negative relation between political risk (i.e. the legislative risk) and innovation: if economic crimes are not recorded but are prevailing, or if they are recorded but not effectively tackled, companies will be alienated from the poor institutional response reducing their efforts.

Any corrupt deal runs a risk to be detected and punished. The expected bribe revenue for a corrupt official (so-called 'facilitation payment') should be, as a result, higher if a larger payment is expected to be offered by firms. As large-scale innovation projects (e.g. by MNEs) possibly have higher probability of a larger payment being offered by firms-innovators, one could argue that corrupt regional government would prefer large-scale innovation projects. Therefore, firms that are capable of offering higher payments are likely to be those with better access to finance or funding, that is, the MNEs.

Given that MNEs require access to permits and licenses to bring their technologies to markets quickly, they will require passing through the tangled bureaucratic system by paying 'facilitation fees', fuelling more corruption. This said, corruption can mitigate barriers to the growth of firms, misallocates resources and distorts investment priorities or 'sands the economic wheel' as a result (Baumol, 1990).

It was expected that the experience of EMNEs in operating in similar environments (i.e. in environments with weak institutions and higher corruption) would offer them the advantage over DMNEs (that were not supposed to be able to operating in such locations without a struggle to deal with corrupt officials – as discussed above), we found no evidence for this assumption. This fact clearly constitutes a limitation for the study and needs to be adequately addressed.

There are a number of likely explanations with a plausible one being the composition of the data used. The data set available would not allow us a chance to be broken down into patents (our proxy for innovation) filed by DMNEs and EMNEs, respectively. Therefore, our findings about the impact of corruption on innovation are, at best, preliminary. This may also be the reason why no difference between the home countries' background of our MNE sample could be spotted.

Contrary to expectations, the level of perceived corruption in the home economies of the DMNEs and the EMNEs would not have an effect on the level of innovation of these companies when investing in different Russian regions. This is an interesting finding since it could also be interpreted as a deficiency of the dominant measure of corruption, the CPI, in revealing the true exposure of developed economies to corruption.

It may well be that the perceptual index fails in capturing the level of corruption because the perceptions of the respondents are biased, ill-informed or outright misleading, thereby greatly skewing the data. This view is in line with the recent revelations of major corruption cases of MNEs from the developed world (Siemens, ThysseKrup, Ferostahl and MAN from Germany, BAe from the United Kingdom etc.).

These cases have demonstrated that DMNEs engage in corruption and have developed skills to deal successfully with corrupt environments, but the perceptions of the CPI respondents rather seem to refer to the environments in their home markets that are much better regulated and monitored. If this is indeed the case, this would call for a major revision of the composition of the CPI as a measure reflecting the ethical conduct of businesses originating in countries with a perceived low level of corruption.

In order to be able to fully establish the impact of innovation on corruption as expressed by patents filed and the number of economic crimes reported, respectively, we need to have disaggregated data allowing us to refine our sample further. Once these data become available, we will be able to offer further insight into the dynamics at play between MNEs with a different level of exposure to corruption in their home markets and their drive for innovation when confronted with different levels of corruption in the markets they decide to enter.

Given the limitations discussed, our key result is robust because once we control for the institutions in a host region, the positive effect does not disappear. This suggests that when the institutional environment is improved (in this case, more severe penalties for the 'corrupted' are imposed and the likelihood of being caught is enhanced), the innovation outcome will also be fostered.

CONCLUSION

This chapter analysed empirically the impact of MNEs and corruption on innovation in Russia. We argue that in a geographically large country such as Russia, it is indeed important to consider the factors affecting innovation output at a sub-national level. In particular, we focused on the distribution of patent statistics across Russian regions. The main purpose of this chapter was to test the link between corruption and innovation within the environment that have attracted FDI from both emerging and developed markets. We also examined the significance of the traditional determinants of innovation (e.g. R&D expenditures and human capital).

We tried to challenge the idea of corruption to 'grease the economic wheal' (Bailey, 1966; Leff, 1964) but provided some evidence in support to the argument. We disaggregated a sample of multi-national companies into firms that came from less corrupt environments (developed markets MNEs) and more corrupt environments (emerging markets MNEs). This provided an opportunity to test whether the impact on innovation of different types of foreign-owned firms was different. Our results are consistent with the argument that in high-risk political environments, corruption can act as a hedge against political risks, boosting the scope and scale of innovation (Bailey, 1966; Leff, 1964).

This chapter has made an important contribution. More specifically, the study is novel because to the best of our knowledge it is the first to examine the relationships between corruption as expressed by the number of economic crimes (which can be seen as actual corruption rather than a perception) and innovation (as expressed by the number of patents) across Russian regions. Understanding the impact of institutions on business environment is vital as firms can exploit valuable knowledge created or learnt in one country to another (so-called 'world-wide learning') to create a competitive advantage. This is especially important for Russia that is in need of modernisation.

This study, however, is not without limitations. Our first limitation is regarding the proxies that have been used to measure our dependent variable (innovation output) and our key explanatory variable (corruption). In terms of patents, the available data were not disaggregated so the knowledge regarding the ownership of patents filed was not possible to be gathered. That is, the data did not allow us to split patents into those filed by foreign or domestic enterprises.

In terms of economic crimes (as discussed above), the measure of economic crimes used as a proxy for corruption could be also used as a proxy of the efficiency of law enforcement and cannot account for corruption that goes unrecorded, so any limitation or criticism of using crimes would apply.

NOTES

1. Here, we take a broad view on innovation and consider innovation as a process involving generation, adoption, implementation and incorporation of new ideas and practices (Van de Ven, Angle, and Poole, 1989).
2. Or the misuse of public office for private gains as in some cases public office can provide private benefits to politicians (Aidt, 2003; Jain, 2001; Rose-Ackerman, 1999).
3. That includes terms, for example, corporate wrongdoing, management fraud and illegal corporate behaviour (Zahra, 2005).
4. Examples of economic crimes include embezzlement, insider trading, padding of one's expenses, paying a bribe to get a contract, altering a financial document and individuals receiving money or being promoted for altering a financial document.
5. Following Green (2008), we applied a test that directly compares the negative binominal with Poisson regression, which indicated a significant improvement over Poisson.

REFERENCES

Acemoglu, D., Johnson, S., & Robinson, J. A. (2002). Reversal of fortune: Geography and institutions in the making of the modern world income distribution. *Quarterly Journal of Economics, 117,* 1231–1294.

Acemoglu, D., & Verdier, T. (2000). The choice between market failures and corruption. *The American Economic Review, 90,* 194–211.

Aidt, T. S. (2003). Analysis of corruption: A survey. *Economic Journal, 113,* F632–F652.

Aitken, B. J., & Harrison, A. E. (1999). Do domestic firms benefit from direct foreign investment? Evidence from Venezuela. *The American Economic Review, 6,* 605–618.

Anokhin, S., & Schulze, W. S. (2009). Entrepreneurship, innovation, and corruption. *Journal of Business Venturing, 24*(5), 465–476.

Archibugi, D., & Pianta, M. (1996). Measuring technological change through patents and innovation survey. *Technovation, 16*(9), 451–468.

Bailey, D. H. (1966). The effects of corruption in a developing nation. *Western Political Quarterly, 19*, 719–732.

Baltagi, B. H. (2005). *Econometric analysis of panel data*. Chichester: Wiley.

Bardhan, P. (1997). Corruption and development: A review of issues. *Journal of Economic Literature, 35*(3), 1320–1346.

Barrel, R., & Pain, N. (1999). The growth of foreign direct investment in Europe. In R. Barrel & N. Pain (Eds.), Innovation, investment and the diffusion of technology in Europe: German direct investment and economic growth in post war Europe. Cambridge: Cambridge University Press.

Baumol, W. J. (1990). Entrepreneurship: Productive, unproductive and destructive. *Journal of Political Economy, 98*(5), 893–921.

Bertschek, I. (1995). Product and process innovation as a response to increasing imports and foreign direct investment. *The Journal of Industrial Economics, 43*, 341–357.

Beugelsdijik, S., McCann, P., & Mudambi, R. (2010). Place, space and organisation: Economic geography and multinational enterprise. *Journal of Economic Geography, 10*(4), 485–493.

Black, S., & Lynch, L. (1996). Human-capital investments and productivity. *American Economic Review, 86*, 263–268.

Blomström, M., & Sjöholm, F. (1999). Technology transfer and spillovers: Does local participation with multinationals matter? *European Economic Review, 43*, 915–923.

Buckley, P. J., Clegg, L. J., Cross, A. R., Liu, X., Voss, H., & Zheng, P. (2007). The determinants of Chinese outward foreign direct investment. *Journal of International Business Studies, 38*, 499–518.

Buscaglia, E., & Van Dijk, J. (2003). Controlling organised crime and corruption in the public sector. In *Forum on crime and society* (Vol. 3, pp. 1–2). New York, NY: United Nations Publication.

Cameron, C., & Trivedi, P. K. (1986). Econometric models based on count data: Comparisons and applications of some estimators and tests. *Journal of Applied Econometrics, 1*(1), 29–54.

Cannon, E. (2000). Human capital: Level versus growth effects. *Oxford Economic Papers, 52*, 670–677.

Caves, R. E. (1974). Multinational firms, competition and productivity in host-country markets. *Economica, 41*, 176–193.

Caves, R. E. (1996). *Multinational enterprise and economic analysis*. Cambridge:Cambridge University Press.

Cohen, W. M., & Klepper, S. (1992). The anatomy of industry R&D intensity distributions. *American Economic Review, 82*, 773–799.

Damijan, J. P., Knell, M., Majcen, B., & Rojec, M. (2003). The role of FDI, R&D accumulation and trade in transferring technology to transition countries: Evidence from firm panel data for eight transition countries. *Economic Systems, 27*, 189–204.

Driffield, N. L. (2001). The impact on domestic productivity of inward investment in the UK. *The Manchester School, 69*, 103–119.

Dunning, J. H. (1998). Location and the multinational enterprise: A neglected factor? *Journal of International Business Studies, 29*, 45–66.

Dunning, J. H., & Lundan, S. M. (1998). *Multinational enterprises and the global economy*. Cheltenham: Edward Elgar Publishing.

Ehrlich, I., & Lui, F. T. (1999). Bureaucratic corruption and endogenous economic growth. *Journal of Political Economy*, *107*(6), 270–293.

Feldman, M. P., Feller, I., Bercovitz, J. E. L., & Burton, R. M. (2002). University-technology transfer and the system of innovation. In M. P. Feldman & N. Massard (Eds.), *Institutions and systems in the geography of innovation* (pp. 55–78). Boston, MA: Kluwer.

Fosu, A., Bates, R., & Hoeffler, A. (2006). Institutions, governance and economic development in Africa: An overview. *Journal of African Economies*, *15*(1), 1–9.

Fritsch, M., & Slavtchev, V. (2007). Universities and innovation in space. *Industry and Innovation*, *14*, 201–218.

Fritsch, M., & Slavtchev, V. (2008). *Local knowledge sources, spillovers and innovation*. Department of Economics and Business Administration, Friedrich-Schiller-University Jena, Germany, Mimeo.

Frydman, R., & Rapaczynski, A. (1994). *Privatisation in eastern Europe: Is the state withering away*. Budapest: Central European University Press.

Getz, K. A., & Volkema, R. J. (2001). Culture, perceived corruption, and economics: A model of predictors and outcomes. *Business and Society*, *40*(1), 7–30.

Girma, S., & Görg, H. (2005). *Foreign direct investment, spillovers and absorptive capacity: Evidence from quantile regressions*. Discussion paper Series 1, Economic Studies, N. 13.

Green, W. (2008). *Econometric analysis*. Upper Saddle River, NJ: Prentice Hall.

Griscuolo, P., & Narula, N. (2008). A novel approach to national technological accumulation and absorptive capacity: Aggregating cohen and levinthal. *European Journal of Development Research*, *20*(1), 56–73.

Habib, M., & Zurawicki, L. (2002). Corruption and foreign direct investment. *Journal of International Business Studies*, *33*(2), 291–307.

Hausman, J., Hall, B. H., & Griliches, Z. (1984). Econometric models for count data with application to the patents-R&D relationship. *Econometrica*, *52*, 909–938.

Heckelman, J., & Powell, B. (2010). Corruption and the institutional environment for growth. *Comparative Economic Studies*, *52*, 351–378.

Hellman, J. S., Jones, G., & Kaufmann, D. (2003). Seize the state, seize the day: State capture and influence in transition economies. *Journal of Comparative Economics*, *31*(4), 751–777.

Holland, D., & Pain, N. (1998). *The diffusion of innovations in Central and Eastern Europe: A study of the determinants and impact of foreign direct investment*. NIESR discussion papers 137, National Institute of Economic and Social Research, London.

Iammarino, S., Padilla-Pérez, R., & von Tunzelmann, N. (2008). Technological capabilities and global-local interactions: The electronics industry in two Mexican regions. *World Development*, *36*(10), 1980–2003.

Jain, A. K. (2001). Corruption: A review. *Journal of Economic Surveys*, *15*(1), 71–121.

Jalilian, H., Kirkpatricket, C., & Parker, D. (2007). The impact of regulation on economic growth in developing countries: A cross-country analysis. *World Development*, *35*(1), 87–103.

Jun, K., & Singh, H. (1996). The determinants of foreign direct investment in developing countries. *Transnational Corporation Journal*, *5*(2), 67–105.

Kim, B.-Y., & Kang, Y. (2009). The informal economy and the growth of small enterprises in Russia. *Economics of Transition*, *17*(2), 351–376.

Konings, J. (2001). The effect of direct foreign investment on domestic firms. *Economics of Transition*, *9*, 619–633.

Lambsdorff, G. F. (2003). How corruption affects productivity. *Kyklos, 56*(4), 457–474.

Lame, I. Y. (2002). An overview of organised crime. *Proceedings of the first national seminar on economic crime*, The Executive Committee, National Seminar on Economic Crime, Aduja 14.

Leff, N. H. (1964). Economic development through bureaucratic corruption. *The American Behavioral Scientist, 8*(3), 8–14.

Levin, M., & Satarov, G. (2000). Corruption and institutions in Russia. *European Journal of Political Economy, 16*(1), 113–132.

Love, J., & Rooper, S. (1999). The determinants of innovation: R&D, technology transfer and networking effects. *Review of Industrial Organisation, 15*, 43–64.

Mancusi, M. L. (2008). International spillovers and absorptive capacity: A cross-country cross-sector analysis based on patents and citations. *Journal of International Economics, 76*, 155–165.

Mankiw, N. G., & Whinston, M. D. (1986). Free entry and social inefficiency. *Rand Journal of Economics, 17*, 48–58.

Mansfield, E. (1984). R&D and innovation: Some empirical findings. In Z. Griliches (Ed.), *R&D, patents and productivity* (pp. 127–148). Chicago, IL: University of Chicago Press.

Mauro, P. (1995). Corruption and growth. *Quarterly Journal of Economics, CX, 3*, 681–712.

Murphy, K. M., Shleifer, A., & Vishny, R. W. (1993). Why is rent-seeking so costly to growth? *American Economic Review, 83*(2), 409–414.

North, D. (2005). *Understanding the process of economic change*. Princeton, NJ: Princeton University Press.

Popov, V. (2001). Reform strategies and economic performance of Russia's regions. *World Development, 29*, 865–886.

Porter, M. E. (1990). *The competitive advantage of nations*. New York, NY: Free Press, MacMillan.

Qian, Y., & Xu, C. (1998). Innovation and bureaucracy under soft and hard budget constraints. *Review of Economics Studies, 65*, 151–164.

Radaev, V. (2000). Revisited version of the paper presented at the Annual Conference of International Society for the New Institutional Economics, Tubingen, Germany, September 22–24.

Rodrik, D. (2000). Institutions for high-quality growth: What they are and how to acquire them. *Studies in Comparative International Development, 35*(3), 3–31.

Rose-Ackerman, S. (1999). *Corruption and government: Causes, consequences, and reform*. Cambridge: Cambridge University Press.

Shleifer, A., & Vishny, R. (1993). Corruption. *Quarterly Journal of Economics, 108*(3), 599–617.

Sjöholm, F. (1998). *Productivity growth in Indonesia: The role of regional characteristics and direct foreign investment*. Working paper in Economics and Finance, No. 216.

Smarzynska, B. J. (2004). The composition of foreign direct investment and protection of intellectual property rights: Evidence from transition economies. *European Economic Review, 48*(1), 39–62.

Tanzi, V., & Davoodi, H. R. (2000). Corruption, growth and public finances. *IMF Working Paper, 11*, 1–27.

Van de Ven, A., Angle, H. L., & Poole, M. (Eds.). (1989). *Research on the management of innovation: The Minnesota studies*. New York, NY: Harper & Row.

Van Dijk, J. J. M. (2007). *The world of crime: Breaking the silence on problems of security, justice and development across the world.* Thousand Oaks, CA: Sage.

Veracierto, M. (2008). *Corruption and innovation.* Chicago: Federal Reserve Bank of Chicago.

Voyer, P. A., & Beamish, P. W. (2004). The effect of corruption on Japanese foreign direct investment. *Journal of Business Ethics, 50*(3), 211–224.

Wang, J.-Y., & Blomstrom, M. (1992). Foreign investment and technology transfer: A simple model. *European Economic Review, 36*(1), 137–155.

Wei, S.-J. (2000). *Natural openness and good government.* NBER working paper, No. 7765, NBER Program, June 2000.

Yakovlev, E., & Zhuravskaya, E. (2009). State capture: from Eltsin to Putin. In J. Kornai, L. Matyas, & G. Roland (Eds.), *Corruption, development and institutional design.* New York, NY: Palgrave MacMillan.

Yudaeva, K., Kozlov, K., Melentieva, N., & Ponomareva, N. (2003). Does foreign ownership matter? The Russian experience. *Economics of Transition, 11*(3), 383–409.

Zahra, S. A. (2005). Entrepreneurial risk taking in family firms. *Family Business Review, 18*(1), 23–40.

Zsuzsa, L. (2003). Attraction versus repulsion – Foreign direct investment in Russia. *Development and Finance, 1,* 51–62.

PART IV
INSTITUTIONAL DIVERSITY IN THE EMERGING ECONOMY CONTEXT

CHAPTER 15

STRATEGIC ASSET SEEKING BY EMNEs: A MATTER OF LIABILITIES OF FOREIGNNESS – OR OUTSIDERSHIP?

Bent Petersen and Rene E. Seifert, Jr.

ABSTRACT

Purpose – *The chapter provides an economic explanation and perspectivation of strategic asset seeking of multinational enterprises from emerging economies (EMNEs) as a prominent feature of today's global economy.*

Approach – *The authors apply and extend the "springboard perspective." This perspective submits that EMNEs acquire strategic assets in developed markets primarily for use in their home markets.*

Findings – *The authors succumb that the springboard perspective is alluring theoretically as well as empirically as it suggests that when EMNEs acquire strategic assets, they experience liabilities of foreignness (LOF) that are low relative to those of MNEs from developed markets. The authors concede to this LOF asymmetry but also point out that liabilities of outsidership (LOO) can offset or weaken the home-market advantage of some EMNEs when competing with MNEs.*

Multinational Enterprises, Markets and Institutional Diversity
Progress in International Business Research, Volume 9, 375–398
ISSN: 1745-8862/doi:10.1108/S1745-886220140000009015

Research implications − *LOO appears as the more relevant concept to use when explaining strategic asset seeking of EMNEs. A set of propositions are formulated to guide empirical testing.*

Originality/value − *The insights gained from using the springboard perspective and the LOO concept are non-trivial: They basically predict future dominance of 'insider' EMNEs at the expense of MNEs from developed markets.*

Keywords: Conceptual paper; EMNEs; strategic assets; liabilities of outsidership

INTRODUCTION

A remarkable characteristic of emerging-market multinational enterprises (EMNEs) has been their tendency to acquire strategic assets in developed markets. Such assets often include cutting-edge technologies and widely recognized brands (Athreye & Kapur, 2009; Gammeltoft, 2008; Sauvant, Maschek, & McAlliste, 2009; Rabbiosi, Elia, & Bertoni, 2012; Rugman, 2009; UNCTAD, 2006). Lenovo's acquisition of IBM's PC business, Shanghai Motor's purchase of UK-based Rover, TLC's purchase of Thomson TV, and China Zhejiang Geely Holding Group's takeover of Volvo Car Corporation from the Ford Motor Corporation are notable examples. Such strategic asset seeking has been described as a way for latecomers to catch up with multinational enterprises from developed markets (MNEs) and as a fast track to acquiring ownership advantages[1] (Buckley, Elia, & Kafouros, 2010; Cuervo-Cazurra & Genc, 2008; Deng, 2009; Mathews, 2002, 2006; Rui & Yip, 2008; Tang, Gao, & Li, 2008; Wu, Ding, & Shi, 2012).

The springboard perspective (Luo & Tung, 2007; Ramamurti, 2012) submits that EMNEs acquire strategic assets in developed markets not only to attain competitiveness in developed markets, but also − and, perhaps, mainly − for use in their home markets. In a seminal article from 2007, Luo and Tung featured this springboard perspective:

> We suggest that EMNEs systematically and recursively use international expansion as a springboard to acquire critical resources needed to compete more effectively against their global rivals at home and abroad. [...] They are also recursive because such "springboard" activities are recurrent ... and revolving (i.e., outward activities are strongly integrated with activities back home). [...] Springboard links a firm's international expansion with its home base. [...] Viewed in this manner, the global success of such EMNEs is still highly dependent on their performance at home. [...] Furthermore,

it is foolish for these EMNEs to ignore their home markets while multinationals from advanced and newly industrialized countries are strongly attracted to the opportunities, and hence huge profit potential, posed by emerging economies. Because these global rivals face liabilities of foreignness whereas EMNEs enjoy home court advantage, it is counterproductive for EMNEs not to capitalize on their home markets and home bases. (2007, pp. 484–485)

In a more recent article, Ramamurti referred to the springboard perspective in the following way:

EMNEs go abroad to obtain technologies and brands *primarily for exploitation in their home markets, not abroad.* For firms from large, high-growth markets, such as China, Brazil, or India, this makes strategic sense. When EMNEs from these countries acquire companies abroad, they may appear to engage in market-seeking internationalization when, in fact, they are engaged in strategic asset seeking. (2012, p. 43)

This perspective is empirically appealing, especially in the wake of the economic crisis that has affected the western world since 2008. The economic crisis in the developed countries, which has stood in sharp contrast to the uninterrupted growth in the emerging markets, has accentuated the benefits available to EMNEs wishing to follow sourcing-oriented internationalization paths. In other words, EMNEs can derive significant positive effects from engaging in strategic asset seeking in developed markets with the primary objective of exploiting those assets in their home markets. The economic crisis in the developed countries appears to have lowered the costs of acquiring assets, in general, while the continuous growth in emerging markets has increased the value of employing acquired assets in those markets (Sauvant, McAllister, & Maschek, 2010).

However, a pertinent question arises from the springboard perspective: *Under what conditions are EMNEs better positioned than MNEs to exploit assets acquired in developed markets?* In other words, why are EMNEs more able than MNEs to take advantage of advanced technologies and strong brands in developed *and* emerging markets?

The literature on EMNEs' internationalization offers two possible answers to this question. The first is essentially a government-support explanation. Some EMNEs — especially Chinese state-owned enterprises (SOEs) — have access to low-cost, risk-willing capital provided by the government or, indirectly by other SOEs via a cross-subsidizing system (Child & Rodrigues, 2005; Morck, Yeung, & Zhoa, 2008; Nolan, 2001; Sutherland, 2009; Williamson & Zeng, 2009; Yiu, 2010). The required return for the acquired strategic assets is accordingly low. The second answer is a global-consolidator explanation proposed by Ramamurti and Singh (2009) and Ramamurti (2012). In certain mature industries, such as steel and the meat-processing, the champion firms from emerging markets sometimes consolidate the industry on a global scale through aggressive acquisitions. Such firms include Arcelor Mittal Steel founded in India in 1978 as Ispat International (and operated by Lakshmi Mittal since 1995) and Brazil's J&F Participações SA, a holding company that controls world-leading meatpacker JBS SA. Scale and scope economies, as well as potential collusion economies, drive the strategic asset seeking of such "global consolidators" (Ramamurti & Singh, 2009).[2]

Whereas both explanations appear plausible and well documented, they limit the empirical scope and applicability of the springboard perspective. If we accept these two explanations, then the springboard perspective essentially applies only to: (1) Chinese SOEs engaged in acquisitions that the government believes to be of strategic importance and therefore eligible for low-cost, risk-willing capital; and (2) global consolidators from emerging markets. As an additional restriction, Ramamurti (2012) asserts that the springboard perspective only is relevant to EMNEs with large home-country markets, such as China and Brazil. In this light, the springboard perspective has little relevance for the majority of MNEs, which are neither Chinese SOEs nor global consolidators. As such, therefore, the springboard perspective does not seem to qualify as a general model for strategic asset-seeking EMNEs but rather as an explanation for a relatively few "special cases."

However, we extend the literature on EMNEs by arguing that the springboard perspective may apply to a wider population of EMNEs across countries and industries. Our argument revolves around liability of foreignness − LOF (Zaheer, 1995) − and the liability of outsidership − LOO (Johanson & Vahlne, 2009).[3] In short, we argue that asymmetries exist between the LOFs as experienced by MNEs and EMNEs such that, all else equal, it is easier for EMNEs to succeed in developed markets than it is for MNEs to succeed in emerging markets. This LOF asymmetry puts EMNEs in a better position than MNEs to exploit technologies and brands acquired in developed markets in their home markets. Furthermore, we argue that a large home country (such as Brazil, Russia, India, or China) is not an indispensable precondition for the relevance of the springboard perspective, as the perspective may also apply for EMNEs from smaller emerging markets, such as Vietnam or Chile (Del Sol & Kogan, 2007). We suggest that these two extensions of the applicability of the springboard perspective qualify it as a general explanation for EMNEs' acquisitions of strategic assets in western markets.

In addition, our use of the LOF concept rests on the assumption that *all* EMNEs possess an advantage over MNEs with regards to the exploitation of acquired foreign assets in their home market or region. In this regard, we include a discussion of whether this assumption holds true, or whether it is an oversimplification to ascribe insidership to all domestic firms and outsidership to all foreign firms. We acknowledge that far from all EMNEs experience an advantage of insidership in their home market. We assert that every local firm in emerging markets has an advantage over foreign firms in terms of language, culture, business practices, and non-exposure to foreign-exchange risks, but not necessarily with regards to non-discriminatory treatment by national authorities. Hence, some indigenous firms may, in fact, experience a LOO (Johanson & Vahlne, 2009) when it comes to the exploitation of strategic assets in their home countries.

On this background the chapter proceeds as follows: in the next section, we define strategic asset seeking in the emerging-market context. We then discuss how asymmetries in LOF between MNEs and EMNEs with large home-country markets may constitute a necessary and sufficient precondition for the applicability of the springboard perspective (the section on "Liability of Foreignness Asymmetries between MNEs and EMNEs"). In the section "Home Country or Home Region?," we expand the springboard perspective's applicability to EMNEs from small home countries but larger home regions. In the section on "Replacing Liability of Foreignness with Liability of Outsidership," we discuss the implications of using the LOO concept rather than the LOF concept for the springboard perspective. The discussion includes an analysis of probable insider EMNEs, especially SOEs and firms affiliated business groups. In the concluding section, we suggest several avenues for future research, and highlight some limitations of our study.

DEFINING STRATEGIC ASSETS

The springboard perspective aims to explain EMNEs' acquisitions of strategic assets in developed markets. However, what does the term "strategic assets" include? Our answer to this question originates from Dunning's suggestion that motives for foreign direct investment (FDI) fall into several categories: market, resource, efficiency, and strategic asset seeking (Dunning, 1993; Dunning & Lundan, 2008). In this categorization, the strategic-asset motive pertains to FDI that intends to add assets to the acquiring firms' existing portfolios that "they perceive will either sustain or strengthen their overall competitive position, or weaken that of their competitors" (Dunning, 1993, p. 60). In a similar vein, Makino, Lau, and Yeh

(2002), and Wesson (1993) distinguish between asset-exploiting and asset-augmenting FDI, where the latter emphasizes the needs of firms, particularly firms from emerging markets, to gain access to new technologies and organizational capabilities. In terms of overseas R&D investments, Dunning and Narula (1996) develop dichotomies of asset-exploiting and asset-seeking investments. In addition, Kuemmerle (1999) contrasts home-base-exploiting with home-base-augmenting R&D activities, and points out the growing significance of augmenting existing assets by absorbing and acquiring technological spillovers arising from agglomerative effects in specific sectors, specific companies, or others in the host countries.

In line with Dunning's (1993) definition of strategic asset seeking as including assets acquired with the purpose of weakening the competitive position of other incumbent firms, we submit that assets acquired for future use (such as R&D subsidiaries) *and* assets acquired or leased[4] for use in other foreign markets or in the home market should be labeled "strategic." One example would be the undertaking of FDI in a competitor's home market in order retaliate against or prevent that competitor's entry into the MNC's own, lucrative home market (Graham, 1974, 1978; Knickerbocker, 1973). Other examples of strategic asset seeking of particular relevance to the springboard perspective are the acquisition (or leasing/licensing) of technologies or brands in foreign markets for use in the home market and the strengthening of a consumer brand through the opening of outlets in prestigious locations, such as Milan, New York, or Paris.[5]

In contrast to the exploratory and augmenting nature of strategic asset seeking, the three other FDI motives − market seeking, resource seeking, and efficiency seeking − pertain to foreign assets acquired with the aim of immediate, on-location exploitation. A sales subsidiary FDI is motivated by market seeking and it executes immediate, on-site exploitation of an ownership advantage. Resource seeking occurs when, for example, an MNC acquires an iron mine concession. Such assets may or may not yield an ownership advantage (depending on the circumstances under which the concession is acquired), but they are subject to immediate exploitation.[6] Assets acquired in conjunction with efficiency-seeking FDI may pertain to firm- and country-specific advantages (e.g., operational flexibility and low labor costs, respectively). Nevertheless, regardless of which of the two advantages are exploited, the asset's payoff is on site and immediate rather than off site (in another country) and in the future.

In light of this discussion, we define "foreign strategic assets" as know-how, technologies, brands, equipment, buildings, and sites acquired or leased abroad with the aim of creating or extending advantages in the future, or in businesses and territories other than where the assets are currently employed and exploited.

Based on this definition of strategic assets we can proceed to a discussion of the EMNE categories to which the springboard perspective applies.

EXPANDING THE APPLICABILITY OF THE SPRINGBOARD PERSPECTIVE (1): LIABILITY OF FOREIGNNESS ASYMMETRIES BETWEEN MNEs AND EMNEs

The LOF concept is usually attributed to Zaheer (1995), but goes back to Hymer's (1960/1976) thesis on the disadvantages encountered by firms operating in foreign markets. Hymer identified four types of disadvantages faced by foreign firms: (1) foreign-exchange risks; (2) home government restrictions on internationalization; (3) information disadvantages regarding how to do business in a foreign country; and (4) discriminatory treatment by local governments. In our emerging-market context, we focus primarily on the two latter types of disadvantages. In this regard, we align our investigation with Zaheer (1995, 2002), who focused on the structural, relational, and institutional costs of doing business abroad. Zaheer defined structural/relational costs as:

> ... the costs associated with a foreign firm's *network position in the host country* and its *linkages to important local actors*, which are both likely to be less developed relative to those of the local firm, resulting in *poorer access* to local information and resources. (2002, p. 351–352)

Hence, Zaheer (2002) focused on institutional distance, rather than cultural distance. As emerging markets are characterized by an institutional void, one might speculate that the institutional distance perceived by EMNEs and MNEs is asymmetric rather than symmetric, meaning that the perceived distance depends on the direction. More specifically, MNEs are in general perceiving a greater institutional distance to emerging markets than EMNEs to developed markets. Shenkar (2001) highlighted the existence of such asymmetries, albeit in the context of cultural distance:

> Cultural distance symmetry is ... difficult to defend in the context of FDI. It suggests an identical role for the home and host cultures, for instance, that a Dutch firm

investing in China is faced with the same cultural distance as a Chinese firm investing in the Netherlands. There is no support for such an assumption. (2001, p. 523)

O'Grady and Lane (1996) noted that the "psychic distance paradox" applied for Canadian firms entering the US market but not for US firms entering the Canadian market. Similarly, in their large-scale empirical study of psychic distance, Håkanson and Ambos (2010) found asymmetries not only between US managers and their peers in smaller countries, but also for nearly all small-large neighboring country pairs in their sample. Their results speak convincingly against the treatment of cultural and psychic distance as symmetric – the assumption that such distances are perceived as the same regardless of direction is faulty.

There seems to be a growing chorus about the existence of LOF asymmetries, particularly with regard to cultural and psychic distances. However, empirical confirmation of the existence of LOF asymmetries does not necessarily allow us to infer a systematic, one-directional LOF asymmetry between MNEs and EMNEs. Nonetheless, several studies suggest that this is, in fact, the case. As pointed out by Vahlne and Widersheim-Paul (1977) and Ghemawat (2001), well-developed economies have better-developed infrastructures for the collection, analysis, and dissemination of economic data and market information. Furthermore, managers' distance perceptions are influenced by their views and understandings of the political and institutional environments in foreign markets (Henisz & Zelner, 2005; Kostova & Zaheer, 1999). As expressed by Håkanson and Ambos:

> Differences in these [political and institutional] conditions are likely to be especially important when managers from a country with an efficient regulatory environment and transparent governance structure are confronted with poorly developed political and institutional institutions where mores may be governed by informal rules and conventions that may appear strange, inefficient or even corrupt or otherwise immoral. Conversely, however, managers from countries with weak institutional structures may not experience the same difficulties in countries with more developed ones, where individuals' behavior and that of organizations tend to be more transparent and therefore easier to understand and relate to. (2010, p. 199)

Håkanson and Ambos (2010) hypothesized that absolute differences in governance systems and the direction of those differences influence psychic distance perceptions of MNC managers. Hence, managers from countries with stronger institutional structures tend to perceive countries with poorly developed regulatory institutions as less transparent and more difficult to understand. Khanna, Palepu, and Sinha (2005) ascribed the failure of US firms to succeed in emerging markets to their inability to handle institutional void in these markets. The managers of MNEs

don't know the "rules of the game" (North, 1990). Håkanson and
Ambos' (2010) findings supplement earlier arguments in the literature
that focus on the role of absolute institutional distances regardless of
their qualitative direction (Kostova, 1997; Meyer, Estrin, Bhaumik, &
Peng, 2009; Xu & Shenkar, 2002).

Royal Dutch Shell's FDI in Russia serves to exemplify the political and
institutional hazards an MNE may experience in an emerging market:

> Royal Dutch Shell in Russia was forced to give up majority ownership of its Sakhalin
> LNG project to a Russian state-owned enterprise, Gazprom, at less than cost, in part
> because Shell on entry divided Sakhalin ownership between itself (with a majority posi-
> tion) and two Japanese firms, as permitted by the prevailing laws in 1995. This foreign
> majority and complete ownership was in contrast to the presence of Russian partners in
> every other large oil and gas project in Russia that were later implemented. This owner-
> ship problem was compounded by the increasing power of the Putin administration and
> growing doubts about Shell's legitimacy in Russia's oil and gas sector. However, Shell
> did not change its ownership over the next 10 years, until forced to cede majority own-
> ership to Gazprom in 2006. As an MNE in Russia, without the benefit of local partner
> advice and insight, Shell may have been unaware of the growing opposition to foreign
> majority ownership in the oil and gas sector in Russia. Shell's LOF in Russia was
> definitely higher than other EMNEs. (Gaur, Kumar, & Sarathy, 2011, p. 215)

Earlier, we asked why EMNEs might be better positioned than firms
from developed markets to exploit assets acquired in developed markets.
We asserted that the two conventional explanations of cheap capital
(Child & Rodrigues, 2005; Williamson & Zeng, 2009) and global consolidators (Ramamurti, 2012; Ramamurti & Singh, 2009) limited the applicability
of the springboard perspective. However, the perspective's applicability
increases considerably with the supposition that, *ceteris paribus,* LOF in
general is higher for MNEs entering emerging markets than for EMNEs
entering developed markets. Ample evidence in the literature seems to support this suggestion, as developed markets with their economic institutions
of capitalism are more transparent, predictive, and less reliant on existing
social and ethnic networks than emerging markets (Ghemawat, 2001;
Håkanson & Ambos, 2010; Henisz & Zelner, 2005; Kostova, 1997;
Kostova & Zaheer, 1999; Meyer et al., 2009; Peng, Wang, & Jiang, 2008;
Xu & Shenkar, 2002). Accordingly, developed markets are, in general,
more accessible than emerging markets to entrant firms.[7]

Our supposition that LOF is asymmetrical between MNEs and EMNEs
leads to an important deduction. In line with Luo and Tung (2007),
Madhok and Keyhani (2012), and Mathews (2002), but somewhat
counter to Ramamurti's (2012) argumentation and the general premises
of Dunning's OLI model (1980), possession of ownership advantages

(together with L and I advantages) as a precondition for FDI does not apply for EMNEs' engagement in springboard internationalization (i.e., FDI motivated by strategic asset seeking for use in home markets). *It suffices that EMNEs experience lower LOFs than MNEs.* Hence, the assumption of asymmetrical LOFs between EMNEs and MNEs is an adequate explanation of the springboard perspective. In fact, it extends the springboard perspective to apply to all strategic asset seeking EMNEs with large home markets. Hence, the key to understanding the springboard perspective is not (only) the global-consolidator phenomenon, or EMNEs' access to cheap capital and politically motivated FDI, but high LOF faced by MNEs entering emerging markets relative to EMNEs entering developed markets.

The assumption of LOF asymmetry provides us with a relatively simple answer to our research question. The answer to this question can be summarized in two inequalities for two-market models (1) and (2). The first inequality is formulated for a model consisting of a developed market plus an emerging market:

$$SA_{DM}: LOF_{EMNE} (DM) < LOF_{MNE} (EM) \qquad (1)$$

where SA_{DM} = strategic asset acquired or leased by an EMNE in a developed market (DM); LOF = liability of foreignness, which is defined as the difference between the value π of a strategic asset to a local versus a foreign/entrant firm; EM = emerging market. We assume that $\pi(SA_{DM}) - LOF_{EMNE}$ (DM)$\geq$0, and that LOF_{MNE} (DM)=LOF_{EMNE} (EM)=0.

The first of these two assumptions implies that the value of the acquired asset as used in the developed market should not be negative, as a negative value may − in the worst case − completely offset the profit earned in the emerging market. The second assumption simply states that MNEs and EMNEs do not experience any liabilities in developed and emerging markets, respectively. We moderate this assumption in the section "The Applicability of The Springboard Perspective: Replacing Liability of Foreignness with Liability of Outsidership."

The second inequality is formulated for a two-market model, which includes a developed market plus an EMNE's large home market (e.g., Brazil):

$$SA_{DM}: LOF_{EMNE} (DM) < LOF_{MNE} (EM_{HOME}) \qquad (2)$$

where EM_{HOME} = the home market of an EMNE. Similar assumptions apply: $\pi(SA_{DM}) - LOF_{EMNE} \ (DM) \geq 0$, and $LOF_{MNE} \ (DM) = LOF_{EMNE} \ (EM_{HOME}) = 0$.

Based on the arguments made in this section, we can formulate the following proposition:

Proposition 1. Due to prevailing LOF asymmetries between developed and emerging markets, strategic assets currently deployed in developed markets are more valuable to EMNEs than to MNEs to the extent that the assets are exploitable in large home countries, for example, the BRIC countries (Brazil, Russia, India, and China).

EXPANDING THE APPLICABILITY OF THE SPRINGBOARD PERSPECTIVE (2): HOME COUNTRY OR HOME REGION?

In the introduction, we quoted Ramamurti's formulation of the springboard perspective saying that EMNEs go abroad to obtain technologies and brands primarily for exploitation in their home markets, not abroad.

> For firms from *large, high-growth markets, such as China, Brazil, or India*, this makes strategic sense. (Ramamurti, 2012, p. 43; emphasis added)

Ramamurti (2012) limited the applicability of the springboard perspective to EMNES from large, high-growth markets. In order to avoid complicating our discussion, we ignore the question of what is meant by "high-growth" markets and focus instead on the issue of whether Ramamurti's geographical restriction of the springboard perspective is reasonable. We show that a large home-*country* market is not necessarily conditional for − or an antecedent of − the applicability of the springboard perspective.

Cuervo-Cazurra and Genc (2008) found that emerging market multinationals were successful in other emerging markets where they could employ their home-grown ability to manage institutional void. Lall (1983) found that EMNEs outperformed MNEs when they entered emerging markets other than their own home markets. According to Lall (1983), the competitive advantage held by EMNEs originates from lower cost inputs, affiliations with business groups, ethnic connections in the host country, and the possession of technology and management that are adapted to host-country conditions. Lall's (1983) findings have since been echoed by Erdener and Shapiro (2005), Khanna and Palepu (2006), and Thomas,

Eden, and Hitt (2002). These studies suggest that the springboard perspective makes sense *not only* for EMNEs with large home-country markets, such as Brazil, China, and India, but also for firms from smaller emerging markets, such as Vietnam and Uruguay to the extent that these firms view an emerging-market *region* (e.g., ASEAN and Mercosur, respectively) rather than an emerging market *country* as their home market.

Given this background, we reformulate the research question slightly to the following: *Under which conditions does it pay for EMNEs with a small home-country market to acquire or lease a strategic asset in a developed market?* The answer to this question can be summarized by the following inequality, which is based on a two-market model that includes a developed market and an EMNE's home region. The home region, for example, ASEAN, includes the emerging firm's (small) home-country market, for example, Vietnam:

$$SA_{DM}: LOF_{EMNE}\,(DM) < LOF_{MNE}\,(EM_{HOME\text{-}REG})   \qquad (3)$$

where $EM_{HOME\text{-}REG}$ = home region of an EMNE. Similar assumptions apply: $\pi(SA_{DM}) - LOF_{EMNE}\,(DM) \geq 0$, and that $LOF_{MNE}\,(DM) = LOF_{EMNE}\,(EM_{HOME\text{-}REG}) = 0$.

Based on the arguments made in this section, we formulate the following proposition, which is an extension of Proposition 1:

Proposition 2. Due to prevailing LOF asymmetries between developed and emerging markets, strategic assets currently deployed in developed markets are more valuable to EMNEs than to MNEs to the extent that the assets are exploitable in large home countries *or regions.*

THE APPLICABILITY OF THE SPRINGBOARD PERSPECTIVE: REPLACING LIABILITY OF FOREIGNNESS WITH LIABILITY OF OUTSIDERSHIP

Our use of the LOF concept rests on the assumption that all EMNEs possess an advantage over MNEs with regards to the exploitation of acquired foreign assets in their home market or home region. In other words, we have thus far assumed that all EMNEs enjoy an advantage of *insidership* in their home market (i.e., $LOF_{EMNE}\,(EM) = 0$) and that all MNEs experience a disadvantage of *outsidership* in emerging markets.

This section is devoted to a discourse on whether this assumption holds true in reality. In other words, we attempt to investigate whether ascribing insidership to all domestic firms and outsidership to all foreign firms reflects an oversimplification. In this discourse, we maintain the latter assumption, namely that all MNEs experience a LOO (Johanson & Vahlne, 2009)[8] in emerging markets, although we make a few comments on the realism of this assumption in the conclusion. However, we suggest not all EMNEs experience an advantage of insidership in their home markets. We assert that local firms in emerging markets hold an advantage over foreign firms in terms of language, culture, business practice, and non-exposure to foreign-exchange risks, but not necessarily in terms of non-discriminatory treatment by national authorities. Hence, local firms may experience direct or indirect discrimination from the authorities when it comes to the exploitation of strategic assets acquired in developed markets.

As one of the main characteristics of emerging markets is the state's prominent role in the local business environment (e.g., Henisz & Zelner, 2005; Kostova, 1997; Kostova & Zaheer, 1999), direct or indirect discrimination by the state is critical (van Tulder, 2010). Governments in emerging markets often provide overt and covert support to domestic firms in their internationalization operations (Gaur et al., 2011; Luo, Xue, & Han, 2010; Ren, Liang, & Zheng, 2012), but the role of government is more salient in the home market. In particular, we highlight the notion of homegrown (Bhattacharya & Michael, 2008) or national (Sauvant et al., 2009) champions as companies in emerging markets that are especially favored by the federal or local government. Governments can select such local firms with the intention of nurturing them as leaders in certain industries believed to be of strategic importance to the country. As such, national champions are intended to bolster the country against otherwise dominant multinational enterprises from developed markets.[9]

We further assert that the "national champion" qualification is not reserved for SOEs, as any company with strong links to the "political elite" may be eligible for this status. Hence, an EMNE affiliated a business group (BG) may qualify as a national champion. BGs are defined as "firms which, though legally independent, are bound together by a constellation of formal and informal ties and are accustomed to taking coordinated action" (Khanna & Rivkin, 2001, pp. 47–48). As one characteristic of a business group is its "insidership," which is established through close connections to the political system (Granovetter, 1994; Guillén, 2000) (e.g., donations to political parties and partial state ownership), companies organized in these business groups may qualify as national champions.

In some emerging markets, business groups constitute a dominant feature of the private sector (Carney, Gedajlovic, Heugens, van Essen, & van Oosterhout, 2011; Kumar, Gaur, & Pattnaik, 2012; Xavier, Bandeira-de-Mello, & Marcon, 2014). In China, business groups have grown from being non-existent three decades ago to a point where the revenues of the largest 500 business groups contribute about two-thirds of the country's industrial output (Yiu, 2010). The Chinese government has selected the largest 100 business groups as "trial business groups" for internationalization. These business groups are collectively referred to as "national teams" (Nolan, 2001; Sutherland, 2009) and they are directly overseen and nurtured by the State Council. They receive special treatment in the internationalization process, such as smooth processing of their outward FDI project applications, access to foreign currencies (low-interest funding from state-owned banks), direct and indirect subsidies, and domestic tax breaks. As a result of this preferential treatment, business groups dominate China's outward FDI, making up 75% of the total. In 2008, 36 of the 40 largest Chinese MNCs (in terms of FDI assets) were affiliated business groups (Yiu, 2010).

The observation that distinguishable groups of local firms in emerging markets enjoy preferential treatment by the state questions the relevance of differentiating only between local and foreign firms as suggested by the LOF concept. We therefore suggest that foreign firms should fall into the same category as those local firms that do not benefit from privileged treatment by the government and thus experience a LOO. Hence, we reformulate our research question as the following: *Under which conditions can an "insider" EMNE benefit from acquiring or leasing a strategic asset in a developed market?*

The answer to this question is that an insider EMNE will benefit from acquiring or leasing strategic assets in western markets when the following inequality is fulfilled:

$$SA_{DM}: LOO_{EMNE\text{-}INSIDER}\,(DM) < LOO_{MNE}\,(EM) \qquad (4)$$

where SA_{DM} = the strategic asset acquired or leased by an "insider" EMNE ($EMNE_{INSIDER}$) in a developed market (DM), LOO = liability of outsidership, which is defined as the difference between the value π of the strategic asset to an "insider" versus an "outsider" EMNE ($EMNE_{OUTSIDER}$). We make the following assumptions:

$$\pi(SA_{DM}) - LOO_{EMNE\text{-}INSIDER}\,(DM) \geq 0$$

$$LOO_{MNE} (DM) = LOO_{EMNE\text{-}INSIDER} (EM) = 0,$$

$$LOO_{EMNE\text{-}OUTSIDER} (EM) > 0,$$

and

$$SA_{DM}: LOO_{EMNE\text{-}OUTSIDER} (DM + EM) \geq LOO_{MNE} (DM + EM)$$

The last assumption states that EMNEs which are outsiders in their home markets will incur the same (or higher) LOO as MNEs in developed and emerging markets alike.

Based on the above-mentioned arguments, we can formulate three new propositions. However, these three propositions differ from the boundary conditions of the two previous propositions because of the inclusion of LOO assumptions. Proposition 3 concerns the distinction between "insider" and "outsider" EMNEs, and proposes that strategic asset seeking in developed markets is economical for the former but not the latter:

Proposition 3. Strategic assets currently deployed in developed markets are more valuable to EMNEs that are "insiders" − not to EMNEs that experience a liability of outsidership in their home markets and therefore are unable to fully exploit the acquired or leased assets at home.

Proposition 4 revolves around the definition of "insider" EMNEs and proposes that "insiders" consist of SOEs and BG-affiliated firms. As indicated above, many BG-affiliated firms are also SOEs and sometimes BGs are exclusively composed of SOEs:

Proposition 4. EMNEs that are state-owned or included in a business group are "insiders," i.e., they do not experience a liability of outsidership in their home market.

The fifth and final proposition highlights an important exception to the general contention that only insider EMNEs can acquire strategic assets in an economical way. This exception refers to "global consolidators" from emerging markets. Although these MNEs originate from emerging markets, they stand out as economically independent of those markets. They exploit acquired strategic assets on a global scale and not (only) in the home market.

Proposition 5. Strategic assets currently deployed in developed markets may be more valuable for EMNEs that are "global consolidators" − even if they are "outsiders" in their home market in that they are neither state owned nor included in a business group.

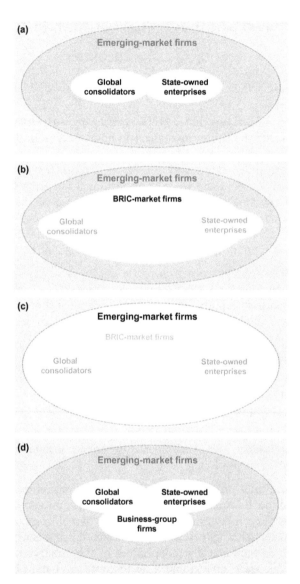

Fig. 1. Applicability of the Springboard perspective. (a) Applicability for global consolidators and EMNEs with Access to low-cost capital. (b) Applicability for all EMNEs from large countries (BRICs). (c) Applicability for all EMNEs (including those from small countries). (d) Applicability for insider EMNEs (i.e., state-owned and BG-affiliated) and global consolidators.

As shown in Fig. 1, four applications, or boundary assumptions (Andersen, 1993), of the springboard perspective emerge. As the boundary assumptions set the limits for the application of the springboard perspective, they point out under which circumstances (for instance, home-market size and LOF asymmetries) the perspective should be used as an explanation of the phenomenon of EMNEs' acquisitions or leasing of strategic assets in western markets.

Fig. 1a depicts the baseline application of the springboard perspective, which is limited to EMNEs that are either state owned or global consolidators (indicated by the white area in the figure). Fig. 1b and c represents two significant expansions of the perspective (grounded on the LOF asymmetry logic). These two presentations encompass all EMNEs from the BRIC countries (Fig. 1b) and all EMNEs − not only those from the BRIC countries (Fig. 1c). In Fig. 1d, the boundary assumptions of the springboard perspective retrench to only comprise "insider" EMNEs (defined as enterprises that are state owned and/or affiliated with business groups) and global-consolidator EMNEs.

CONCLUSIONS AND AVENUES FOR FURTHER RESEARCH

In this chapter, we have analyzed the applicability of the springboard perspective (Luo & Tung, 2007; Ramamurti, 2012) as an explanation for EMNEs' search for strategic assets in developed markets. Our analysis revolved around two concepts: LOF and LOO. We used the LOF concept to infer a considerable expansion of the springboard perspective from applying only to SOEs and global consolidators from large emerging markets to applying to all EMNEs. We argued that the LOF an EMNE experiences in a developed market is low relative to the LOF an MNE experiences in an emerging market. This LOF asymmetry supposition suffices as a potent lever of the scope and relevance of the springboard perspective.

However, the use of the LOO concept, instead of the LOF concept, led us to considerably *narrow* the scope of the springboard perspective in our discourse discussion. We argued that EMNEs that are subject to "outsidership" in their home market are unable to fully exploit the strategic assets they may acquire in western markets. The inverse formulation is that the springboard perspective is relevant only to EMNEs that enjoy "insidership" in their home countries or regions, that is, SOEs or EMNEs affiliated with business groups that have strong ties to the government and other important actors (e.g., local authorities and trade unions) in the emerging market. A germane research avenue − and a huge empirical challenge − is establishing which business groups accommodate insidership.

Irrespective of whether the LOF or the LOO is the better concept to use in ascertaining the boundary assumptions of the springboard perspective, one temporal element of the springboard perspective's basic premise remains important − EMNEs' weak or absent ownership advantages in developed markets. With the rapid development of knowledge-creating institutions in emerging economies, it seems only a matter of time before the insignificance or absence of EMNE ownership advantages in developed markets is a phenomenon of the past. In other words, the applicability of the springboard perspective may be limited in time.

We acknowledge several limitations of our study. Our analysis is limited in terms of nuanced information as to how MNEs may overcome LOFs and LOOs. Luo (2007), for example, highlights successful veteran MNEs in China that have shifted from an early status of "foreign investor" to a new status of "strategic insider" by redefining their strategies and structures to meet internal demands and, thereby, achieve localized value-chain integration.[10] In a recent empirical study, Gammelgaard et al. (2012) analyzed the ways in which MNE subsidiaries reduce their LOO. They found a correlation between performance and strong, local network positions of subsidiaries. Relatedly, we have not discussed MNEs' possibilities to ally with emerging-market firms in order to achieve insidership in emerging markets. Instead, we have assumed that MNEs exploit their assets singlehandedly or sell (or license out) those assets to emerging-market firms for commercialization in emerging markets. Hence, we have not considered the fact that MNEs can form equity joint ventures with EMNEs even though most emerging-market governments now allow for the formation of wholly-owned foreign subsidiaries in their countries. It is also important to note that SOEs in emerging markets are often MNEs' preferred joint-venture partners (Meyer et al, 2009; Yiu, 2010) − allegedly because an alliance with an SOE is a shortcut to insidership and legitimacy in such markets.

Finally, we have not discussed whether the springboard perspective applies only to EMNEs. In other words, we have not addressed whether the springboard perspective can explain the internationalization of (some) MNEs. As argued in this chapter, developed markets are generally more open to entrant firms (including EMNEs) and thus cannot be portrayed as the protected backyards of MNEs. However, the inward internationalization of MNEs, including the surge in MNEs' offshoring of labor-intensive processes to emerging economies, has some resemblances to the springboard perspective. The extent to which this offshoring includes the seeking of strategic assets primarily for use in developed markets is a question worthy of study.

NOTES

1. In the following, the term "ownership advantage" is used interchangeably with "firm-specific advantage."

2. The idea that EMNEs can be industry leaders through sufficiently large acquisitions is developed further by Cantwell and Mudambi (2011).

3. In a revision of their classic Uppsala internationalization process model, Johanson and Vahlne (2009) featured the "liability of outsidership" concept. The authors contend that insidership in relevant network(s) is necessary for successful internationalization. Hence, if a firm attempts to enter a foreign market in which it has no relevant network position, it will suffer from a LOO.

4. Dunning's (1993) FDI motives concern only assets *owned* by the MNE. However, by obtaining user rights, for example, a license to a certain technology, entrant firms may control assets without owning them. We therefore include the leasing of strategic assets as an alternative to the acquisition of such assets.

5. *Natura*, the largest producer of cosmetics and market leader in Brazil, serves as an illustration of the latter. In 2005, *Natura* opened a flagship shop in Paris. Although this move might sound ordinary in the context of increasing globalization and internationalization among emerging-market firms, two factors seem of particular relevance. First, flagship shops are not *Natura*'s major sales channel or expertise. Since the company began internationalizing in the 1970s, it has mainly operated through direct-sales channels. Second, although the company has consistently invested in foreign operations in the last decade (which accounted for 12.3% of its revenues in 2012), such investments were mainly targeted at countries in Latin America. To date, France is the only country outside Latin America in which the company owns sales facilities (Barbosa, 2013).

6. The much vaunted Chinese FDI in natural resource extraction in Africa may constitute strategic assets from a state or government perspective, but less so from the perspective of the individual Chinese MNCs (unless, of course, they are SOEs).

7. To complete the picture, we should add another argument for this asymmetry, which is made by Ramamurti (2012, p. 43), who states that "the LOF problem is more severe in the case of market-seeking internationalization ... than it is for resource-seeking internationalization." In other words, when EMNEs engage in strategic asset or resource seeking in developed markets, they are generally less exposed to LOF than MNEs are when undertaking market-seeking FDI in emerging markets — apparently even without assuming differences between developed and emerging markets in terms of their institutional and political environments.

8. Johanson and Vahlne (2009) contend that outsidership, rather than psychic distance, is the root of uncertainty in foreign operations. An important distinction

between the concepts of LOF and LOO is that the latter considers networks rather than countries as the major focal point for analysis of internationalization. It suggests that "firms' problems and opportunities in international business are becoming less a matter of country-specificity and more one of relationship specificity and network specificity" (Johanson & Vahlne, 2009, p. 1426). Nevertheless, Johanson and Vahlne (2009) recognize an important relationship between these concepts and suggest that the LOF complicates the process of becoming an insider within a country or region relevant network. This view leads Johanson and Vahlne to recognize the need for research that may explain when the LOF or the LOO is the primary difficulty in foreign-market entries – see, for example, Gammelgaard, McDonald, Stephan, Tüselmann, and Dörrenbächer (2012) for a discussion of the relationship between the concepts of "LOF" and "LOO."

9. Consider China's Lenovo as an example. Despite its impressive globalization, Lenovo is still considered to be a "national champion", as it is heavily reliant on profits from the domestic Chinese market to finance its overseas expansion (Deng, 2012; The Economist, 2013, p. 52).

10. It cannot be assumed that an MNE's attainment of insidership is contingent on the time spent and experience gained in the local market. Hence, the "obsolescing bargain model" (Vernon, 1971) predicts that an MNE's bargaining power vis-à-vis the local government is strong at the time of its entry into the foreign market. As such, the MNE initially enjoys an insider position. However, this position is likely to obsolesce as the government's perception of benefits and costs change over time (and as other MNEs enter the market). In the worst case, this trend may eventually ascribe the first-mover MNE an outsider rather than an insider position (Eden & Molot, 2002).

REFERENCES

Andersen, O. (1993). On the internationalization process of firms: A critical analysis. *Journal of International Business Studies, 24*(2), 209–231.

Athreye, M., & Kapur, S. (2009). Introduction: The internationalization of Chinese and Indian firms – Trends, motivations and strategy. *Industrial and Corporate Change, 18*(2), 209–221.

Barbosa, D. (2013, February). Natura não descarta abrir lojas para crescer no exterior. *Revista Exame.* Retrieved from http://exame.abril.com.br/negocios/noticias/natura-nao-descarta-abrir-lojas-para-crescer-no-exterior

Bhattacharya, A., & Michael, D. (2008). How local companies keep multinationals at bay. *Harvard Business Review, 86*(3), 84–95.

Buckley, P. J., Elia, S., & Kafouros, M. (2010). Acquisitions from emerging countries: What factors influence the performance of target firms in advanced countries? *European Journal of International Management, 4*(1–2), 30–47.

Cantwell, J. A., & Mudambi, R. (2011). Physical attraction and the geography of knowledge sourcing in multinational enterprises. *Global Strategy Journal, 1*(3–4), 206–232.

Carney, M., Gedajlovic, E. R., Heugens, P. P. M. A. R., van Essen, M., & van Oosterhout, J. (2011). Business group affiliation, performance, context, and strategy: A meta-analysis. *Academy of Management Journal, 54*(3), 437–460.

Child, J., & Rodrigues, B. (2005). The internationalization of Chinese firms. *Management and Organization Review*, *1*(3), 381–410.

Cuervo-Cazurra, A., & Genc, M. (2008). Transforming disadvantages into advantages: Developing countries MNEs in the least developed countries. *Journal of International Business Studies*, *39*(6), 957–979.

Del Sol, P., & Kogan, J. (2007). Regional competitive advantage based on pioneering economic reforms: The case of Chilean FDI. *Journal of International Business Studies*, *38*(6), 901–927.

Deng, P. (2009). Why do Chinese firms tend to acquire strategic assets in international expansion? *Journal of World Business*, *44*(1), 74–84.

Deng, P. (2012). Effects of absorptive capacity on international acquisitions of Chinese firms. In I. Alon, M. Fetscherin, & P. Gugler (Eds.), *Chinese international investments* (pp. 137–153). Basingstoke: Palgrave Macmillan.

Dunning, J. H. (1980). Towards an eclectic theory of international production: Some empirical tests. *Journal of International Business Studies*, *11*(1), 9–31.

Dunning, J. H. (1993). *Multinational enterprises and the global economy*. Wokingham: Addison-Wesley Publishing.

Dunning, J. H., & Lundan, S. M. (2008). *Multinational enterprises and the global economy* (2nd ed.). Cheltenham: Edward Elgar.

Dunning, J. H., & Narula, R. (1996). The investment development path revisited: Some emerging issues. In J. H. Dunning & R. Narula (Eds.), *Foreign direct investment and governments: Catalysts for economic restructuring* (pp. 1–41). London: Routledge.

Eden, L., & Molot, M. A. (2002). Insiders, outsiders and host country bargains. *Journal of International Management*, *8*(4), 359–388.

Erdener, C., & Shapiro, D. M. (2005). The internationalization of Chinese family enterprises and Dunning's eclectic MNE paradigm. *Management and Organization Review*, *1*(3), 411–436.

Gammelgaard, J., McDonald, F., Stephan, A., Tüselmann, H., & Dörrenbächer, C. (2012). The impact of changes in subsidiary autonomy and network relationships on performance. *International Business Review*, *21*(6), 1158–1172.

Gammeltoft, P. (2008). Emerging multinationals: Outward FDI from the BRICS countries. *International Journal of Technology and Globalisation*, *4*(1), 5–22.

Gaur, A. S., Kumar, V., & Sarathy, R. (2011). Liability of foreignness and internationalisation of emerging market firms. In C. G. Asmussen, T. Pedersen, T. M. Devinney, & L. Tihanyi (Eds.), *Advances in international management: Dynamics of localization: Location-specific advantages or liabilities of foreignness?* (pp. 211–233). London: Emerald.

Ghemawat, P. (2001). Distance still matters: The hard reality of global expansion. *Harvard Business Review*, *79*(8), 137–147.

Graham, E. M. (1974). *Oligopolistic reaction and European direct investment in the United States*. Boston, MA: Harvard Business School.

Graham, E. M. (1978). Transatlantic investment by multinational firms: A rivalistic phenomenon? *Journal of Post Keynesian Economics*, *1*(1), 82–99.

Granovetter, M. (1994). Business groups. In N. J. Smelser & R. Swedborg (Eds.), *Handbook of economic sociology* (pp. 453–475). Princeton, NJ: Princeton University Press.

Guillén, M. F. (2000). Business groups in emerging economies: A resource based view. *Academy of Management Journal*, *43*(3), 362–380.

Håkanson, L., & Ambos, B. (2010). The antecedents of psychic distance. *Journal of International Management*, *16*(3), 195–210.

Henisz, W., & Zelner, B. (2005). Legitimacy, interest group pressures and change in emergent institutions. *Academy of Management Review*, *30*(2), 361–382.

Hymer, S. H. (1960/1976). *The international operations of national firms: A study of direct foreign investment*. Cambridge, MA: MIT Press.

Johanson, J., & Vahlne, J.-E. (2009). The Uppsala internationalization process model revisited: From liability of foreignness to liability of outsidership. *Journal of International Business Studies*, *40*(9), 1411–1431.

Khanna, T., & Palepu, K. (2006). Emerging giants: Building world-class companies in developing countries. *Harvard Business Review*, *84*(10), 60–69.

Khanna, T., Palepu, K., & Sinha, J. (2005). Strategies that fit emerging markets. *Harvard Business Review*, *83*(6), 63–76.

Khanna, T., & Rivkin, J. W. (2001). Estimating the performance effects of business groups in emerging markets. *Strategic Management Journal*, *22*(1), 45–74.

Knickerbocker, F. T. (1973). *Oligopolistic reaction and multinational enterprise*. Boston, MA: Harvard University.

Kostova, T. (1997). Country institutional profile: Concepts and measurement. *Proceedings of the Academy of Management*, 180–184.

Kostova, T., & Zaheer, S. (1999). Organizational legitimacy under conditions of complexity: The case of the multinational enterprise. *Academy of Management Review*, *24*(1), 64–81.

Kuemmerle, W. (1999). The drivers of foreign direct investment into research and development: An empirical investigation. *Journal of International Business Studies*, *30*(1), 1–24.

Kumar, V., Gaur, A. S., & Pattnaik, C. (2012). Product diversification and international expansion of business groups: Evidence from India. *Management International Review*, *52*(2), 175–192.

Lall, S. (1983). *The new multinationals: The spread of third world enterprises*. New York, NY: Wiley.

Luo, Y. (2007). From foreign investors to strategic insiders: Shifting parameters, prescriptions and paradigms for MNCs in China. *Journal of World Business*, *42*(1), 14–34.

Luo, Y., & Tung, R. L. (2007). International expansion of emerging market enterprises: A springboard perspective. *Journal of International Business Studies*, *38*(4), 481–498.

Luo, Y., Xue, Q., & Han, B. (2010). How emerging market governments promote outward FDI: Experience from China. *Journal of World Business*, *45*(1), 68–79.

Madhok, A., & Keyhani, M. (2012). Acquisitions as entrepreneurship: Asymmetries, opportunities, and the internationalization of multinationals from emerging economies. *Global Strategy Journal*, *2*(1), 26–40.

Makino, S., Lau, C. M., & Yeh, R. S. (2002). Asset-exploitation versus asset-seeking: Implications for location choice of foreign direct investment from newly industrialized economies. *Journal of International Business Studies*, *33*(3), 403–421.

Mathews, J. A. (2002). Competitive advantages of the latecomer firm: A resource-based account of industrial catch-up strategies. *Asia Pacific Journal of Management*, *19*(4), 467–488.

Mathews, J. A. (2006). Dragon multinationals: New players in 21st century globalization. *Asia-Pacific Journal of Management*, *23*(1), 5–27.

Meyer, K. E., Estrin, S., Bhaumik, S. K., & Peng, M. W. (2009). Institutions, resources, and entry strategies in emerging economies. *Strategic Management Journal*, *30*, 61–80.

Morck, R., Yeung, B., & Zhoa, M. (2008). Perspectives on China's outward foreign direct investment. *Journal of International Business Studies, 39*(3), 337–350.

Nolan, P. (2001). *China and the global economy*. Basingstoke: Palgrave.

North, D. (1990). *Institutions, institutional change, and economic performance*. Cambridge: Cambridge University Press.

O'Grady, S., & Lane, H. W. (1996). The psychic distance paradox. *Journal of International Business Studies, 27*(2), 309–333.

Peng, M. W., Wang, D., & Jiang, Y. (2008). An institution-based view of international business strategy: A focus on emerging economies. *Journal of International Business Studies, 39*(5), 920–936.

Rabbiosi, L., Elia, S., & Bertoni, F. (2012). Acquisitions by EMNCs in developed markets: An organizational learning perspective. *Management International Review, 52*(2), 193–212.

Ramamurti, R. (2012). What is really different about emerging market multinationals? *Global Strategy Journal, 2*(1), 41–47.

Ramamurti, R., & Singh, J. V. (2009). *Emerging multinationals from emerging markets*. Cambridge: Cambridge University Press.

Ren, B., Liang, H., & Zheng, Y. (2012). An institutional perspective and the role of the state for Chinese OFDI. In I. Alon, M. Fetscherin, & P. Gugler (Eds.), *Chinese international investments* (pp. 11–37). Basingstoke: Palgrave Macmillan.

Rugman, A. M. (2009). Theoretical aspects of MNEs from emerging markets. In R. Ramamurti, & J. V. Singh (Eds.), *Emerging multinationals in emerging markets* (pp. 42–63). Cambridge: Cambridge University Press.

Rui, H., & Yip, G. S. (2008). Foreign acquisitions by Chinese firms: A strategic intent perspective. *Journal of World Business, 43*(2), 213–226.

Sauvant, K. P., Maschek, W. A., & McAllister, G. (2009). Foreign direct investment by emerging market multinational enterprises: The impact of the financial crisis and recession and challenges ahead. OECD Global Forum on International Investment (viii).

Sauvant, K. P., McAllister, G., & Maschek, W. A. (2010). Foreign direct investment by emerging market multinational enterprises, the impact of the financial crisis and recession and challenges ahead. In K. P. Sauvant, G. McAllister, & W. A. Maschek (Eds.), *Foreign direct investments from emerging markets: The challenges ahead* (pp. 3–30). New York, NY: Palgrave MacMillan.

Shenkar, O. (2001). Cultural distance revisited: Towards a more rigorous conceptualization and measurement of cultural differences. *Journal of International Business Studies, 32*(3), 519–535.

Sutherland, D. (2009). Do China's 'national team' business groups undertake strategic-asset-seeking OFDI? *Chinese Management Studies, 3*(1), 11–24.

Tang, F. C., Gao, X. D., & Li, Q. (2008). Knowledge acquisition and learning strategies in globalization of China's enterprises. In I. Alon & J. R. McIntyre (Eds.), *Globalization of Chinese enterprises* (pp. 31–43). Basingstoke: Palgrave Macmillan.

The Economist. (2013). From guard shack to global giant: How did Lenovo become the world's biggest computer company? January 12, 52–53.

Thomas, D. E., Eden, L., & Hitt, M. A. (2002). Who goes abroad? International diversification by emerging market firms into developed markets. Paper presented at the Academy of Management Annual Meeting, Denver, Colorado.

UNCTAD. (2006). *World investment report*. Geneva: United Nations.

Vahlne, J. -E., & Widersheim-Paul, F. (1977). *Psychic distance: An inhibiting factor in international trade.* Working Paper No. 2. Department of Business Administration, Uppsala University.

van Tulder, R. J. M. (2010). Toward a renewed stages theory for BRIC multinational enterprises? A home country bargaining approach. In K. Sauvant, G. McAllister, & W. Maschek (Eds.), *Foreign direct investments from emerging markets* (pp. 61–75). New York, NY: Palgrave Macmillan.

Vernon, R. (1971). *Sovereignty at bay: The multinational spread of US enterprises.* New York, NY: Basic Books.

Wesson, T. J. (1993). *An alternative motivation for FDI.* PhD thesis, Harvard University.

Williamson, P., & Zeng, M. (2009). Chinese multinationals: Emerging through new global gateways. In R. Ramamurti & J. V. Singh (Eds.), *Emerging multinationals in emerging markets* (pp. 42–63). Cambridge: Cambridge University Press.

Wu, X., Ding, W.-L., & Shi, Y.-J. (2012). Motives and patterns of reverse FDI by Chinese manufacturing firms. In I. Alon, M. Fetscherin, & P. Gugler (Eds.), *Chinese international investments* (pp. 107–121). Basingstoke: Palgrave Macmillan.

Xavier, W. G., Bandeira-de-Mello, R., & Marcon, R. (2014). Institutional environment and business groups resilience in Brazil. *Journal of Business Research, 67*(5), 900–907.

Xu, D., & Shenkar, O. (2002). Institutional distance and the multinational enterprise. *Academy of Management Review, 27*(4), 608–618.

Yiu, D. W. (2010). Multinational advantages of Chinese business groups: A theoretical exploration. *Management and Organization Review, 7*(2), 249–277.

Zaheer, S. (1995). Overcoming liability of foreignness. *Academy of Management Journal, 38*(2), 341–363.

Zaheer, S. (2002). The liability of foreignness, redux. *Journal of International Management, 8*(3), 351–358.

CHAPTER 16

REVERSE TRANSFER OF HRM PRACTICES FROM EMERGING MARKET SUBSIDIARIES: ORGANIZATIONAL AND COUNTRY-LEVEL INFLUENCES

Michał K. Lemański

ABSTRACT

Purpose — *The purpose of this chapter is to conceptually analyze reverse transfers of human resource management practices from subsidiaries of transnational corporations in emerging markets to their headquarters in developed countries.*

Methodology/approach — *This is a conceptual chapter based on a review of the pertinent literature. Analysis is performed at the organizational and national levels.*

Findings — *We identify the type of transnational corporation best positioned to learn and utilize the potential of its emerging market subsidiaries to advance its human resource management practices. We further identify the types of practices best suited for reverse transfer.*

Multinational Enterprises, Markets and Institutional Diversity
Progress in International Business Research, Volume 9, 399–415
Copyright © 2014 by Emerald Group Publishing Limited
All rights of reproduction in any form reserved
ISSN: 1745-8862/doi:10.1108/S1745-886220140000009016

Research limitations/implications — *Empirical tests of our propositions are needed. We encourage researchers to extend our research by considering the regional (supra-national), industry and individual levels of analyses.*

Practical implications — *Managers are informed when and where potential for learning new practices is the greatest, and are urged to scrutinize those corporate units where such potentials exist, and yet transfers do not occur.*

Originality/value — *Emerging markets offer substantial learning potential for transnational corporations, yet most recent studies focus on transfer of technology and product innovations from subsidiaries, leaving the transfer of human resource management practices largely unexplored. Therefore, this study advances research on organizational knowledge and innovation management, and organization of transnational corporations.*

Keywords: Reverse transfer; human resource management (HRM) practices; emerging markets; transnational corporation (TNC); subsidiaries; conceptual paper

INTRODUCTION

Transnational corporations (TNCs) increasingly look for new and valuable knowledge in the emerging markets (The Economist, 2010), and the TNC subsidiaries are best positioned to transfer that knowledge to their developed market headquarters and other TNC units (Doz, Santos, & Williamson, 2001; Nohria & Ghoshal, 1997). Examples include subsidiaries of GE in India and Poland transferring new technologies to the GE units in Japan and the United States, and P&G adopting globally new products from South Africa (Bartlett & Beamish, 2011), or transfer of quality management practices from GM subsidiaries in Poland to GM in the United Kingdom (Dobosz-Bourne, 2006).

The potential for reverse transfer of human resource management (HRM) practices from emerging markets, that is, the adoption of HRM practices originating at the emerging market subsidiaries by the headquarters of the developed market TNCs is hindered by a perception of inferior origin at both organizational and national level. The latter can be explained by the theory of dominance effects (Smith & Meiksins, 1995), which predicts that subsidiaries from the emerging market countries will be adopting practices from those countries that are perceived as more developed, and not the other way round. Indeed, empirical tests show that HRM practices in TNCs converge to the global "best practice" model of dominant countries (Pudelko & Harzing, 2007). For example, within the emerging market region of Central and Eastern Europe, firms adopt practices from the more economically developed Western Europe (Michailova, Heraty, & Morley, 2009; Weinstein & Obłój, 2002).

At the organizational level, factors hindering reverse transfer are, in an aggregated form, manifested by the corporate immune system, that is, subsidiary attempts to carry out reverse transfer will be confronted with the headquarters' resistance based on ethnocentrism, suspicion of the unknown, and resistance to change (Birkinshaw & Ridderstråle, 1999). These restrictions are particularly burdening for the reverse transfer of HRM practices from emerging market subsidiaries, which are often viewed by the developed market TNC managers as "the most foreign of all foreign places" (Selmer, 2005, p. 78), and their HRM practices reflect significantly different environments (Budhwar & Debrah, 2005).

Those barriers pose a significant challenge to TNCs, whose competitive advantage relies on the ability to explore the knowledge of all units (Doz et al., 2001). In times when emerging markets are becoming increasingly important for the global economy, to capitalize on their trans-nationality and to fully explore the potential of their network of subsidiaries, TNCs need to find ways to enable reverse transfer of HRM practices from emerging markets.

Our intended contribution is to help TNCs solve this problem and to extend the theoretical understanding of a phenomenon that is potentially very significant, yet relatively new to management research. Specifically, we link streams of literature on reverse transfer (Edwards, 1998; Ferner, 1997; Tempel, 2001) and subsidiary entrepreneurship (Birkinshaw, 2000; Birkinshaw, Hood, & Young, 2005) to suggest the type of a TNC best positioned to utilize the potential of its emerging market subsidiaries for advancing HRM practices and identify the types of practices best suited for reverse transfer to the TNC's developed market headquarters.

In the next section, we shed light on the importance of reverse transfer of HRM practices from emerging market subsidiaries and present challenges to such transfers. Afterward we establish a set of propositions on the type of a TNC and the type of a practice optimally set for reverse transfer from emerging market subsidiaries, and elaborate on them in the following discussion. Finally, we identify practical implications of our work and suggest an agenda for further research.

LITERATURE REVIEW

Relevance of Learning from Emerging Markets

Previous studies focused on reverse transfer from the developed market subsidiaries (Edwards, 1998; Edwards & Ferner, 2004; Edwards & Tempel, 2010; Tempel, 2001; Thory, 2008; Tregaskis, Edwards, Edwards, Ferner, & Marginson, 2010). The last two decades, however, have seen a global rise of the emerging markets, and TNCs have been the first in line to capitalize on this phenomenon. One of the impacts of this has been a change in the balance of the employee voice, which requires TNCs to learn new HRM practices. The number of employees in emerging market subsidiaries now outweighs the number of employees in the home country operations of many TNCs. More importantly, that is not only true for the labor-intensive industries, but also for knowledge-intensive corporations like Accenture or IBM, which now employ more people in emerging markets than in their home country (Guillén & Ontiveros, 2012). Emerging market transnational firms represent one fourth of the 500 largest corporations in the world and nearly one third of the total number of transnational firms (Guillén & Ontiveros, 2012). Since the power of TNCs depends on their knowledge, and power of a particular TNC unit within the TNC depends on its knowledge (Forsgren, Holm, & Johanson, 2005), the developed market TNC headquarters need reverse transfer from their subsidiaries to learn about the growing emerging markets as they increase in importance, not least as a defensive strategy against the "emerging giants" competitors. Further, during the recent crisis, emerging markets economically outperformed the developed market countries (Guillén & Ontiveros, 2012), attracting greater attention of TNCs, who also started to examine the practices used in the emerging market context.

HRM Practices in Emerging Markets

HRM practices reflect the environments in which corporations operate (Björkman, Fey, & Park, 2007) and as emerging and developed market environments differ significantly, so do HRM practices used in both contexts. Due to historical reasons, some areas of organizational practices in emerging market corporations, especially those related to work organization, remain underdeveloped (Budhwar & Debrah, 2005; Horwitz, 2011). For example, in Central and Eastern Europe and in the Soviet Union an inefficient use of human resources was a major weakness during the communist era, and HRM practices in that region, at least to some extent, still reflect the heritage of closed economies (Weinstein & Obłój, 2002). Gurkov and Zelenova (2009) report that some companies in Russia still experience difficulties finding even basic support with state-of-the-art recruitment techniques from the HR department.

The business environment in emerging markets is very dynamic. Adjusting to the fast pace of change in the environment, corporations in emerging markets either develop new HRM practices, or adopt practices from the developed countries. The former are normally set to compensate underdeveloped institutions, for instance, deficiencies in state-sponsored healthcare and social insurance (Gurkov & Zelenova, 2009), while the latter build legitimacy in relations with foreign investors (Nolan, 2010). Since HRM in emerging markets is subject to rapid changes, TNCs should expect the development of new HRM practices in their emerging market subsidiaries (Budhwar & Debrah, 2005; Michailova et al., 2009), which creates potential for reverse transfer.

Reverse Transfer from Emerging Markets

Some practices developed in an emerging market context may not be applicable to the developed market environment. Still, there are others that do not carry the burden of the emerging market origin and can be applied in different contexts, and are suitable for reverse transfer to the developed market headquarters. The criterion is legitimacy, which is required for acceptance and utilization of the diffused practices (Kostova & Roth, 2002).

Perceived legitimacy of HRM practices may, however, be difficult to achieve for emerging market subsidiaries. The perception of subsidiaries by the headquarters depends to a great extent on the local environment, in which subsidiaries are embedded and from which they can learn (Ferner & Varul, 2000; Forsgren et al., 2005). Since their business environment is relatively less developed, the potential for learning practices that could be subsequently diffused to developed market headquarters is limited. In addition, many individuals emigrate from the emerging market countries to the developed ones, frequently within the same TNC. Those migrants, however, often suffer from the "underdog syndrome" (Koźmiński & Yip, 2000, p. 302) and to overcome it and succeed in their new environment quickly adopt headquarters' practices rather than try to promote practices from their home country subsidiaries. This further reinforces perceptions of the dominance of the developed market headquarters' practices.

The challenges posed by an inferior environment are coupled by organizational characteristics. Emerging market subsidiaries have less developed organizational systems and practices, since they are often younger, smaller, and serve less sophisticated customers than the TNC units in developed markets; therefore, TNCs may not find good opportunities to learn new practices from them (Danik & Lewandowska, 2013; Gorynia & Samelak, 2013; Whitley, 2007).

Under some circumstances, however, the emerging market practices can be perceived as legitimate to adopt in the developed market headquarters. Within developed countries of the West, corporations facing pressures similar to those typical to the emerging market environment start seeking for new practices in the emerging East (Ming-Jer & Miller, 2010). For example, massive job losses and perceived job insecurity of employees in the developed countries severely suffering from the economic crisis (e.g., currently Southern Europe) resemble conditions typical to the emerging markets. Corporations in such environments could potentially find practices developed by their emerging market subsidiaries useful in their current situation. There is already some evidence that corporations in Western Europe have changed their HRM practices in response to the economic downturn, for example, cutting expenditures on management development (Schuh, 2012; Sheehan, 2012), and such cost rationalizations open room for the adoption of low-cost practices of emerging market subsidiaries.

Corporate-Level Immune System

The "corporate immune system" defined by Birkinshaw and Ridderstråle (1999, p. 153) as a "set of organizational forces that suppress the advancement of creation-oriented activities" can be found in many, if not all corporations. It can, however, become particularly strong in the context of reverse transfer of HRM practices from emerging market subsidiaries. Particularly one element of resistance to reverse transfer specified by Birkinshaw (2000) sharpens the impact of the corporate immune system on reverse transfer from emerging markets: misunderstanding and lack of trust. As the environment and practices used in the emerging and developed market units differ significantly, there is a greater room for possible confusion about the purpose and outcomes of adopting certain practices. The headquarters' perception of what the best HRM practices are reflects the previous experience of the TNC, rather than current developments in the business environment (Williams & Lee, 2009). For developed market headquarters, adopting ideas through reverse transfer changes the pool of used practices, and requires adaptation to the new situation, which in turn may lead to resistance of those units (Jansen & Szulanski, 2004).

National-Level Influences on Reverse Transfer

National characteristics influence the abilities of corporations to produce and to absorb new organizational practices (Whitley, 2007), and past research has revealed country of origin effects on the type of practices that are diffused, and on the propensity of headquarters and subsidiaries to engage in reverse transfer (Ferner, 1997; Ferner, Almond, & Colling, 2005; Thory, 2008).

Practices used by the developed market headquarters are subjectively perceived as a source of their economic success. Building on the dominance effects theory (Edwards & Ferner, 2004; Pudelko & Harzing, 2007; Smith & Meiksins, 1995), we expect that managers of headquarters located in developed market countries will perceive practices used at their emerging market subsidiaries as less advanced, or even not fulfilling the standards of management in a developed market context, and will not be willing to incorporate practices from a different context, and from emerging market organizations in particular.

Besides the satisfaction of headquarters with own country practices, the headquarters in developed countries may oppose reverse transfers from emerging market subsidiaries fearing of adverse reactions of stakeholders within the TNC home country who, also subject to the national influences, may negatively perceive the adoption of practices from a less developed environment (Stevens & Shenkar, 2012).

PROPOSITIONS

Type of Practices

Adaptation significantly increases the difficulty of cross-border transfer of practices (Jensen & Szulanski, 2004), which puts an additional burden on transfers from emerging market subsidiaries, where the need for adaptation is greater because of differences in institutional environments (Meyer & Peng, 2005). Some subsidiary practices embedded in the emerging market context are therefore difficult to transfer to the developed market headquarters.

Still, there are different practices and organizational structures that can be equally efficient in different countries (Orru, Biggart, & Hamilton,

1991). Explicit HRM practices, such as using of IT HRM systems (e.g., use of payroll software.), or practices reflecting the globally recognized principles like the United Nations Declaration on Human Rights, universal human values like the so-called "golden rule" found in all major religions, which are shared across many contexts and cultures, regardless of the level of their economic advancement (Lubich, 2007). Being free of the liability of an emerging market origin, such practices can be employed in both developed and emerging market TNC units. Examples include cost-saving practices like switching off the lights after leaving the workplace, or recycling office equipment. Such practices are legitimate in the eyes of the headquarters regardless of their origin.

To facilitate international transfer, some TNCs may even promote denationalization of their HRM practices (Tempel, 2001). These should not be seen as "culture-free" practices, but practices free of the emerging market nature. Subsidiaries located in countries that are perceived by the headquarters as less developed will not be able to pursue reverse transfer unless the practices they attempt to diffuse are perceived as compatible with the dominant models (Edwards & Tempel, 2010). The emerging market subsidiaries that develop practices based on universal or "dominant" values enjoy the perception of legitimacy. Hence, we propose that:

Proposition 1a. Headquarters in developed markets will accept reverse transfer of such HRM practices that are representing universally accepted values, or a dominant model of HRM.

At the opposite end of the range, there are such HRM practices that may become valuable in the eyes of the headquarters thanks to their emerging market origin. For instance, during a crisis of the national economy in the developed countries, headquarters may start seeking solutions to environmental challenges. Practices of the emerging market subsidiaries that were developed for precisely such a context enjoy credibility in such a situation since credibility is gained through a demonstrated successful usage (Birkinshaw, 2000). Hence:

Proposition 1b. Headquarters in developed markets will accept reverse transfer of such HRM practices that are set to solve an issue typical to the emerging market environment, and new to the headquarters' environment.

TNC Characteristics

TNC characteristics significantly influence reverse transfer of HRM practices (Edwards & Ferner, 2004; Edwards & Tempel, 2010). Within the

HRM function, when the HRM departments are relatively small, they are responsible for a broader range of tasks and can develop practices for different sub-functions of the HRM system, like recruitment or remuneration. In larger HRM functions, there exists a room for high specialization and focused sub-teams responsible for particular areas of HRM are also small. A relatively small headcount coupled with a similarity of work tasks in both instances create an incentive for the TNC to create international task forces and gives the HRM personnel better chances of transferring practices (Edwards & Ferner, 2004). It also diminishes the effects of the corporate immune system related to the uncertainty, lack of trust, and the lack of knowledge about subsidiary practices. Hence, we propose that:

Proposition 2a. Reverse transfer of HRM practices from emerging markets is likely to occur in TNCs where the organization of the HRM function within the subsidiary network reflects the HRM organization in the headquarters.

Previous research found that organizational slack diminishes the need of innovation and change of practices, and makes transfer of practices abundant (Nohria & Ghoshal, 1997). The existence of organizational slack resources reinforces the satisfaction of the headquarters with their own practices. Such headquarters are less willing to take the risks of adoption of new practices. Some slack is however necessary for reverse transfer, since it allows experimentation and development of new HRM solutions. When the emerging market subsidiaries do not possess organizational slack resources, they perceive themselves as dependent on their parent. Such units tend to only implement headquarters' practices (Kostova & Roth, 2002). Therefore, a TNC where reverse transfer from emerging market subsidiaries is more likely to occur would be one with the headquarters suffering from no slack resources (e.g., home country operations in a crisis), and relatively resource-rich subsidiaries, that is, such which need to innovate because of the dynamism of the emerging market environment, but which still have resources which allow experimentation. Hence, we put our next proposition:

Proposition 2b. Reverse transfer of HRM practices from emerging markets is likely to occur in TNCs where the headquarters do not possess organizational slack, but the subsidiaries do.

Country-level Factors

While the corporate context is very important for reverse transfer to occur, national-level factors also influence the process, and some countries may be more favorable for the transfer of practices than others (Kostova & Roth, 2002). Further, specific characteristics of each country make corporations more or less adept at receiving new practices in comparison with other countries. For instance, the headquarters of TNCs embedded in a business system based on the job experience and the organic development of knowledge, like the Japanese TNCs are, may be less likely to adopt practices than headquarters of other developed market TNCs (Lam, 1997).

More generally, reverse transfer from emerging markets is less likely to be accepted by headquarters of TNCs from coordinated market economies that tend to be dependent on home country labor in key positions and innovative activities (Tregaskis et al., 2010). Similarly, the headquarters of TNCs from countries that have been exposed to globalization only late or in a limited scope may be more reluctant to reverse transfer from emerging markets, simply because the headquarters managers are less familiar with the environment of emerging markets. Further, the TNC units located in liberal markets tend to be more open to radical innovation and new ideas from abroad (Tregaskis et al., 2010; Whitley, 2007). Hence, we propose:

Proposition 3. Reverse transfer of HRM practices from emerging markets is likely to occur in headquarters located in a country characterized by a liberal, rather than a coordinated market economy.

DISCUSSION

While cross-border transfer of practices is never an easy process (Edwards, Almond, Clark, Colling, & Ferner, 2005; Jensen & Szulanski, 2004) and reverse transfer from emerging market subsidiaries is subject to additional obstacles, it is still possible when diffusing practices meet certain criteria, and in certain types of TNC, and located in certain national environments. In line with the past research we acknowledge that, in general, practices diffused from the emerging to the developed market units normally require significant adaptations. But we also indicate that there are practices that are more universal and do not cause additional burden to the adopting unit. Thus, we help to fine tune the literature on reverse transfer of HRM practices (e.g., Edwards & Ferner, 2004) which established that power relations will influence reverse transfer irrespective of the characteristics of the transferred practice, and we argue that the strength of influence of power relations on reverse transfer will vary according to those characteristics.

Further, although dominance effects and corporate immune systems block transfer of some HRM practices from the emerging market subsidiaries, they work selectively and allow transfer of others. Past studies seem to support these arguments. For instance, Birkinshaw et al. (2005) suggest that external actors and forces co-create available options, but ultimately the decision whether to initiate (or not) reverse transfer lies at the discretion of the subsidiary that despite any facilitating or hindering conditions may (or may not) respond to the existing opportunities. We extend those arguments by pointing out few such opportunities, and indicated conditions under which headquarters are more likely to accept reverse transfer of subsidiary practices, even from an origin perceived as inferior. We support the view that even when headquarters do not acknowledge subsidiary efforts, or when the organizational and national-level environment of the headquarters are hostile to subsidiary initiatives, it is still up to the subsidiary to decide on whether to act in an entrepreneurial way. Adding to the recommendations of Birkinshaw (2000) who implicitly advices subsidiary managers to always take more initiatives, even initiatives that go against the official sanctioning of the headquarters, we suggest specific types of initiatives (i.e., practices) and contextual variables (i.e., situations in which the headquarters may be) that make the success of subsidiary initiatives more likely.

While we support the views from the past research that the emerging market origin of practices can be a factor hindering reverse transfer, we support prediction of Stevens and Shenkar (2012) who argue that the specific nationality of origin and its different aspects may play even more important role than the liability of origin. For example, while the Chinese economy still falls under the category of emerging market, because of its size and importance, it could also be perceived as dominant in some business relations. Following the success of the Chinese economy, there is a growing interest in Chinese business practices. We argue that headquarters in countries struggling with rapid economic changes, like for example some developed countries in Southern Europe, can become more open to adopting practices from their subsidiaries that successfully deal with such a turbulent environment.

Considering reverse transfer as a way of increasing competitive advantage leads us to link it with country characteristics representing the internationalization and international competitiveness of the national economy (Ganter & Hecker, 2013). We argue that the level of liberalization and exposure to globalization and international competition increases the propensity of headquarters to accept reverse transfer from emerging markets.

For instance through competition with other international players, including the "emerging market giants," the developed market TNCs learn more about their practices and possibly gain respect for emerging market corporations. The negative perception of the country of origin derived from the general weakness of the national economy can be then outweighed by the relative strength of a particular company. The subsidiary in the respective emerging market, a home for the TNCs competitor, may then naturally become a source of knowledge about the rival's background. If the emerging market competitor demonstrates advantages related to specific HRM practices, the developed market headquarters may want to use their subsidiary to absorb that knowledge from the original context. In more liberal economies a kind of a spillover effect can become visible, that is, when one TNC headquarters start adopting practices from its emerging market subsidiaries, the headquarters of other TNCs may become more open for such transfers.

Finally, as the emerging market countries are aspiring or "emerging" to the standards of the developed countries, they adapt their legal systems and even accept some culture norms of the developed countries. At the same time, the economic success of emerging market countries and mixed performance of the developed market countries blur some aspects of the traditional dominance effects. Hence, we predict that reverse transfer of HRM practices from the emerging market subsidiaries is to become a more frequent phenomenon.

Implications for Future Research

Our analysis also suggests several promising future research avenues. Firstly, as we elaborated on the national-level influences on reverse transfer, the question that emerges is whether there exists a regional-level dominance effect, or immune system? Since differences between regions are greater than within one region (Rugman & Verbeke, 2005), one could expect that practices from countries within the TNC home region may be accepted more readily than those from subsidiaries in other parts of the world. In the Ferner et al. (2005) study of cross-national transfer of workforce diversity policy in US transnationals, it was found that UK HR managers claimed that US policies are not applicable to the European context, and brought up regional-level arguments to fence off the policies that the US headquarters wished to implement.

A promising avenue for future research seems to lie in the regional aspects of ethnocentrism. In particular, future research could cross-compare the impact of economic and culture influences on reverse transfer when studying transfer from, and between, emerging market subsidiaries located in different emerging market regions, for example, Eastern Europe and Latin America.

Future research should also consider different, other than intra-corporate transfer of practices, ways that TNCs can use for learning from emerging markets. One question to explore in future studies would then be whether developed market headquarters learn from subsidiaries of emerging market TNCs operating in the developed countries. Related question promising an interesting area of research is if reverse transfer of practices from emerging market subsidiaries is subject to the same influences in the developed as the emerging market TNCs. Specifically, such research could explore if HRM practices are more likely to be diffused from emerging market subsidiaries to the emerging market headquarters, or do emerging market TNCs rather use their developed market subsidiaries to source new practices.

Finally, those practices that are emerging market specific could possibly be amended and "stripped out" of the emerging market liabilities. By doing so, the headquarters could make those practices applicable to a broader variety of contexts. Indeed, headquarters can play an important role in reverse transfer. Headquarters' involvement in the process of transfer increases chances of adoption, and headquarters do modify subsidiary practices to diffuse them further (Ciabuschi & Martín, 2009), and there exists some evidence of headquarters managers diffusing practices developed by the emerging market subsidiaries without acknowledgment of their origin (Lemanski, 2012). Since such acts can significantly enlarge the pool of available practices and increase organizational potential for learning from subsidiaries, future research should explore the ways that the headquarters uses to refine practices from their emerging market subsidiaries for adoption in other contexts. Specifically, scholars could further explore the question of whether acknowledgment of the emerging market origin of a practice hinders its transfer.

Implications for Practitioners

Managers of TNCs located in developed countries but experiencing crisis or rapid changes in the business environment are encouraged to monitor their emerging market subsidiaries for practices suitable to cope with consequences of the economic challenges in the environment. Similarly, emerging market subsidiary managers who developed solutions to challenges that are typical to the emerging markets but can also appear in the developed countries should actively promote their practices to the headquarters. They should also actively engage in development and sharing of practices rooted in universally accepted or dominant values. To be able to exploit potential for learning practices developed at the emerging market subsidiaries, the TNC should possess certain characteristics. When the TNC managers discover those are missing, they may want to build them, and so tap the benefit of the transnational nature of their corporation.

Finally, our research brings implications for policy makers. As the success of corporations contributes to the success of national economies, and reverse transfer can increase the competitive advantage of both receivers and senders of practices, policy makers in both subsidiary and headquarters countries should support reverse transfer. Particularly, policy makers in the developed countries should promote openness to new knowledge from abroad, which increases innovativeness of the headquarters the country is hosting, not least during the times of rapid economic changes or during an economic crisis.

REFERENCES

Bartlett, C. A., & Beamish, P. W. (2011). *Transnational management: Text, cases and readings in cross-border management* (6th ed.). New York, NY: McGraw-Hill.

Birkinshaw, J. (2000). *Entrepreneurship in the global firm*. Thousand Oaks, CA: Sage.

Birkinshaw, J., Hood, N., & Young, S. (2005). Subsidiary entrepreneurship, internal and external competitive forces, and subsidiary performance. *International Business Review, 14*(2), 227–248.

Birkinshaw, J., & Ridderstråle, J. (1999). Fighting the corporate immune system: A process study of subsidiary initiatives in multinational corporations. *International Business Review, 8*(2), 149–180.

Björkman, I., Fey, C. F., & Park, H. J. (2007). Institutional theory and MNC subsidiary HRM practices: Evidence from a three-country study. *Journal of International Business Studies, 38*(3), 430–446.

Budhwar, P. S., & Debrah, Y. A. (2005). International HRM in developing countries. In H. Scullion & M. Linehan (Eds.), *International human resource management: A critical text*. Houndmills: Palgrave Macmillan.

Ciabuschi, F., & Martín, O. M. (2009). Innovation processes at unit level: A study of headquarters involvement, innovation impact, transfer performance, and adoption success. In J. Larimo & T. Vissak (Eds.), *Research on knowledge, innovation and internationalization* (Vol. 4, pp. 157–183). Progress in International Business Research. Bingley, UK: Emerald Group Publishing Limited.

Danik, L., & Lewandowska, M. S. (2013). Motives and barriers in the field of cooperation between corporations. Research outcomes based on the Polish engineering industry. *Journal of Economics & Management, 14*, 21−34.

Dobosz-Bourne, D. (2006). Reverse diffusion of quality: Evidence from general motors UK and Poland. *Journal for East European Management Studies, 11*(3), 244−266.

Doz, Y., Santos, J., & Williamson, P. (2001). *From global to metanational: How companies win in the knowledge economy*. Boston, MA: Harvard Business School Press.

Edwards, T. (1998). Multinationals, labour management and the process of reverse diffusion: A case study. *International Journal of Human Resource Management, 9*(4), 696−709.

Edwards, T., Almond, P., Clark, I., Colling, T., & Ferner, A. (2005). Reverse diffusion in US multinationals: Barriers from the American business system. *Journal of Management Studies, 42*(6), 1261−1286.

Edwards, T., & Ferner, A. (2004). Multinationals, reverse diffusion and national business systems. *Management International Review, 44*(1), 49−79.

Edwards, T., & Tempel, A. (2010). Explaining variation in reverse diffusion of HR practices. *Journal of World Business, 45*(1), 19−28.

Ferner, A. (1997). Country of origin effects and HRM in multinational companies. *Human Resource Management Journal, 7*(1), 19−37.

Ferner, A., Almond, P., & Colling, T. (2005). Institutional theory and the cross-national transfer of employment policy: The case of 'workforce diversity' in US multinationals. *Journal of International Business Studies, 36*(3), 304−321.

Ferner, A., & M. Varul (2000). 'Vanguard' subsidiaries and the diffusion of new practices: A case study of German multinationals. *British Journal of Industrial Relations 38*(1), 115–140.

Forsgren, M., Holm, U., & Johanson, J. (2005). *Managing the embedded multinational: A business network view*. Cheltenham: Edward Elgar.

Ganter, A., & Hecker, A. (2013). Deciphering antecedents of organizational innovation. *Journal of Business Research, 66*(5), 575−584.

Gorynia, M., & Samelak, O. (2013). An overview of research into the functioning of Polish subsidiaries of transnational corporations (in Polish). *Gospodarka Narodowa, 10*(266), 69−91.

Guillén, M. F., & Ontiveros, E. (2012). *Global turning points: Understanding the challenges for business in the 21st century*. Cambridge: Cambridge University Press.

Gurkov, I., & Zelenova, O. (2009). Managing human resources in Russia. In M. J. Morley, N. Heraty, & S. Michailova (Eds.), *Managing human resources in Central and Eastern Europe*. London: Routledge.

Horwitz, F. M. (2011). Future HRM challenges for multinational firms in Eastern and Central Europe. *Human Resource Management Journal, 21*(4), 432−443.

Jensen, R., & Szulanski, G. (2004). Stickiness and the adaptation of organizational practices in cross-border knowledge transfers. *Journal of International Business Studies, 35*(6), 508−523.

Kostova, T., & Roth, K. (2002). Adoption of an organizational practice by the subsidiaries of the MNC: Institutional and relational effects. *Academy of Management Journal, 45*(1), 215−233.

Koźmiński, A. K., & Yip, G. S. (2000). *Strategies for Central and Eastern Europe*. Houndmills: Macmillan.

Lam, A. (1997). Embedded firms, embedded knowledge: Problems of collaboration and knowledge transfer in global cooperative ventures. *Organization Studies, 18*(6), 973–996.

Lemanski, M. K. (2012). That shiny moon has a dark side too: Reverse transfer of practices and intra-corporate plagiarism. *Proceedings of the 38th annual EIBA conference,* Brighton, UK, 7–9 December.

Lubich, C. (2007). *Essential writings: Spirituality, dialogue, culture.* Hyde Park, NY: New City Press.

Meyer, K. E., & Peng, M. W. (2005). Probing theoretically into Central and Eastern Europe: Transactions, resources, and institutions. *Journal of International Business Studies, 36*(6), 600–621.

Michailova, S., Heraty, N., & Morley, M. J. (2009). Studying HRM in the international context: The case of CEE. In M. J. Morley, N. Heraty, & S. Michailova (Eds.), *Managing human resources in Central and Eastern Europe.* London: Routledge.

Ming-Jer, C., & Miller, D. (2010). West meets East: Toward an ambicultural approach to management. *Academy of Management Perspectives, 24*(4), 17–24.

Nohria, N., & Ghoshal, S. (1997). *The differentiated network: Organizing multinational corporations for value creation.* San Francisco, CA: Jossey-Bass Publishers.

Nolan, J. (2010). The influence of western banks on corporate governance in China. *Asia Pacific Business Review, 16*(3), 417–436.

Orru, M., Biggart, N. W., & Hamilton, G. G. (1991). Organizational isomorphism in East Asia. In W. W. Powell & P. J. DiMaggio (Eds.), *The new institutionalism in organizational analysis.* Chicago, IL: The University of Chicago Press.

Pudelko, M., & Harzing, A. (2007). 'Country-of-Origin', localization, or dominance effect? An empirical investigation of HRM practises in foreign subsidiaries. *Human Resource Management, 46*(4), 535–559.

Rugman, A. M., & Verbeke, A. (2005). Towards a theory of regional multinationals: A transaction cost economics approach. *Management International Review, 45*(1), 5–17.

Schuh, A. (2012). Strategic responses to the global financial and economic crisis in Central and Eastern Europe – The foreign multinational company perspective. In R. Van Tulder, A. Verbeke, & L. Voinea (Eds.), *New policy challenges for European multinationals* (Vol. 7, pp. 393–419). Progress in International Business Research. Bingley, UK: Emerald Group Publishing Limited.

Selmer, J. (2005). Cross-cultural training and expatriate adjustment in China: Western joint-venture managers. *Personnel Review, 34*(1), 68–84.

Sheehan, M. (2012). Investing in management development in turbulent times and perceived organisational performance: A study of UK MNCs and their subsidiaries. *The International Journal of Human Resource Management, 23*(12), 2491–2513.

Smith, C., & Meiksins, P. F. (1995). System, society and dominance effects in cross-national organizational analysis. *Work, Employment and Society, 9*(2), 241–267.

Stevens, C. E., & Shenkar, O. (2012). The liability of home: Institutional friction and firm disadvantage abroad. In T. Devinney, T. Pedersen, & L. Tihanyi (Eds.), *Institutional theory in international business and management* (Vol. 25, pp. 127–148). Advances in International Management. Bingley, UK: Emerald Group Publishing Limited.

Tempel, A. (2001). *The cross-national transfer of human resource management practices in German and British multinational companies.* Munich: Rainer Hampp Verlag.

The Economist. (2010). The world turned upside down. Special report: Innovation in emerging markets. *The Economist*, April 17.

Thory, K. (2008). The internationalization of HRM through reverse transfer: Two case studies of French multinationals in Scotland. *Human Resource Management Journal, 18*(1), 54–71.

Tregaskis, O., Edwards, T., Edwards, P., Ferner, A., & Marginson, P. (2010). Transnational learning structures in multinational firms: Organizational context and national embeddedness. *Human Relations, 63*(4), 471–499.

Weinstein, M., & Obłój, K. (2002). Strategic and environmental determinants of HRM innovations in post-socialist Poland. *International Journal of Human Resource Management, 13*(4), 642–659.

Whitley, R. (2007). *Business systems and organizational capabilities: The institutional structuring of competitive competences.* Oxford: Oxford University Press.

Williams, Ch., & Lee, S. H. (2009). International management, political arena and dispersed entrepreneurship in the MNC. *Journal of World Business, 44*(3), 287–299.

CHAPTER 17

FACING DISCRIMINATION BY HOST COUNTRY NATIONALS – EMERGING MARKET MULTINATIONAL ENTERPRISES IN DEVELOPED MARKETS

Katrin Held and Nicola Berg

ABSTRACT

Purpose — *In developed markets, emerging market multinational enterprises (EMNEs) seem to be more discriminated by host country nationals than foreign developed market multinational enterprises (DMNEs). They are challenged with host country nationals' prejudices and face a stigma of being from emerging markets. While literature agrees that EMNEs suffer from additional disadvantages due to their country-of-origin, research fails to identify those factors that may lead to a higher discrimination against EMNEs than against foreign DMNEs.*

Design/methodology/approach — *Based on institutional theory, we look at institutional-related and resource-related antecedents that have an*

Multinational Enterprises, Markets and Institutional Diversity
Progress in International Business Research, Volume 9, 417–441
Copyright © 2014 by Emerald Group Publishing Limited
All rights of reproduction in any form reserved
ISSN: 1745-8862/doi:10.1108/S1745-886220140000009020

impact on various forms of direct and indirect discrimination by host country nationals.

Originality/value *— Our framework analyzes the crucial differences between host country nationals' perception of EMNEs and foreign DMNEs and the resulting challenges for EMNEs in the developed world. It enhances our understanding of the importance of institutional environments in explaining differences in host country nationals' discrimination against foreign MNEs.*

Keywords: Emerging market multinational enterprises; discrimination; host country nationals; liability of emergingness; developed markets

INTRODUCTION

In foreign markets, multinational enterprises (MNEs) do not only have to face geographic distance and unfamiliarity between home country and a host country, they also have to manage discrimination by host country nationals (Hymer, 1976; Zaheer, 1995). While some MNEs successfully get accepted, others have more difficulties to gain legitimacy in foreign markets. Such unfavorable treatments weaken MNEs' competitive advantage and consequently need to be mitigated (Luo & Mezias, 2002; Luo, Shenkar, & Nyaw, 2002; Suchmann, 1995).

Especially in developed markets, emerging market multinational enterprises (EMNEs) are challenged by unfavorable treatments of host country nationals and face difficulties to win their acceptance. Discrimination by host country nationals can occur in terms of strikes, negative word-of-mouth, defensive requirements and regulations, or boycotts against EMNEs. Discrimination usually derives from host country nationals' fear that EMNEs gain to much control over the targeted economic and financial markets in general and over companies in specific. For example, the Chinese construction company Sany was challenged with such discrimination during their market entry in Germany and the United States. The company was confronted with protests during their acquisition of the German concrete-pump manufacturer Putzmeister since employees feared Chinese acquisition intentions and crucial changes in their working conditions (Galbraith, 2012). Furthermore, Sany needed to file a lawsuit against defensive measures of the US government, because a planned wind farm purchase deal in Oregon was blocked by the US government on the grounds of national security risk (McMahon, 2012). EMNEs like Sany seem to be more affected by country-of-origin disadvantages than their foreign counterparts (Barnard, 2010; Chang, Mellahi, & Wilkinson, 2009). In particular, host country nationals negatively associate EMNEs with home country characteristics, such as a poorer economic development, infrastructure bottlenecks, and inadequate legal rights (Chang et al., 2009). Moreover, EMNEs are mainly characterized as late players in the global competition, usually are more interlinked with their home country government and primarily enter developed markets due to knowledge-seeking motives (Child & Rodrigues, 2005; Goldstein, 2009; Miller, Thomas, Eden, & Hitt, 2009). On the other hand, foreign DMNEs seem to have an advantage in developed markets due to a relatively similar institutional background, longer international experience, and sophisticated firm resources. This raises the question if EMNEs and foreign DMNEs can be perceived by host country nationals in the same way or if EMNEs are challenged with additional disadvantages simply because they are from emerging markets (Madhok & Keyhani, 2012). Madhok and Keyhani (2012) define these disadvantages as liability of emergingness, elaborating that EMNEs face a stigma of being from emerging markets. Therefore, it is crucial to understand to what extent host country nationals, such as prospective applicants, consumers, suppliers, and the host country governments, distinguish in their discrimination against EMNEs and against foreign DMNEs based on certain country-of-origin associations.

Despite the agreement that EMNEs suffer from a liability of emergingess in developed markets, present research fails to identify those factors that may influence EMNEs' additional discrimination problems (Barnard, 2010; Chang et al., 2009; Madhok & Keyhani, 2012). However, in order to overcome these higher risks of being stereotyped and discriminated against, EMNEs need to incorporate the interests of host country nationals since these interest groups have a direct influence on EMNEs' business activities and performance in foreign markets (Clarkson, 1995; Freeman, 1984; Podnar & Jancic, 2006). Therefore, the chapter seeks to compare host country nationals' perception of EMNEs and foreign DMNEs in order to identify differences in their discrimination against EMNEs and DMNEs in a developed market context. Applying institutional theory, we develop a conceptual framework with eight propositions that consider the impact of different institutional and resource-related antecedents on forms of direct and indirect discrimination.

The chapter contributes to literature on liability of foreignness (LOF) by focusing on the previously neglected South-to-North investments. The concept of LOF is well-established in international business literature (Hennart, Roehl, & Zeng, 2002; Mezias, 2002; Newburry, Gardberg, & Belkin, 2006). However, it primarily focuses on the internationalization of DMNEs (Brannen, 2004; Goodall & Roberts, 2003). Regarding EMNEs' internationalization to the developed world, the concept is barely examined (Denk, Kaufmann, & Roesch, 2012). Moreover, while the concept of LOF was mainly used to compare local with foreign companies, we employ the LOF concept as an out-group/out-group construct, analyzing the crucial differences between EMNEs' and foreign DMNEs' liabilities in developed markets (Calhoun, 2002; Chen, Griffith, & Hu, 2006). We present a framework that helps to understand the potential discrimination against EMNEs in developed markets, seeking to answer the following questions: (1) which factors predominantly influence the discrimination against EMNEs by host country nationals, (2) do these factors influence the discrimination against EMNEs and foreign DMNEs in a different way?, and (3) how can EMNEs' liability of emergingness in developed markets consequently be determined?

We proceed as follows: first, literature on institutional theory and discrimination against MNEs is reviewed. Second, we derive propositions regarding factors that influence EMNEs' extra burden of discrimination by host country nationals. After presenting a theoretical grounded framework, we conclude with implications and avenues for future research.

INSTITUTIONAL THEORY AND THE DISCRIMINATION AGAINST EMNEs

According to institutional theory, the institutional environment of a country influences MNEs' practices and behavior in foreign markets (DiMaggio & Powell, 1983; Kostova & Roth, 2002; North, 1990). MNEs internationalizing to a relatively similar institutional environment can more easily adapt to these countries since their business practices, institutional norms, and values are more alike (DiMaggio & Powell, 1983; Meyer, Estrin, Bhaumik, & Peng, 2009). On the contrary, in institutionally distant markets foreign MNEs are unfamiliar with the institutional environment (North, 1990). They have to make an effort to understand the given regulations in the host country and simultaneously have to determine host country nationals' diverse demands and different social values (Elango, 2009; Kostova & Zaheer, 1999; Scott, 1995). As long as companies do not gain social acceptance, credibility, and support from host country nationals, they are in a disadvantageous position compared to domestic companies, which consequently is reflected in a higher LOF (Brouthers, Donnell, & Hadjimarcou, 2005; Suchmann, 1995; Zaheer, 1995).

Eden and Miller (2004) distinguish LOF-related disadvantages into unfamiliarity, relational, and discrimination hazards. Unfamiliarity hazards describe an inadequate knowledge about the host market (Eden & Miller, 2004). Foreign companies lack relevant information about the local demand, distribution channels, or the competitive environment in the market and are not as locally embedded in the host market as their local counterparts (Sethi & Judge, 2009).

Relational hazards derive from controlling and coordinating subsidiaries and organizational practices in foreign markets (Denk et al., 2012; Eden & Miller, 2004). Foreign companies usually face difficulties when they want to transfer their knowledge from the headquarters to their subsidiaries and have to mitigate potential conflicts during their integration of the headquarters' specific business practices (Eden & Miller, 2004).

Research points out that unfamiliarity and relational hazards are shown to decrease over time, because foreign companies learn about the market structures and acquire relevant local market knowledge (Miller & Parkhe, 2002; Yildiz & Fey, 2012). However, costs due to discriminatory behavior by host country nationals are argued to sustain over time (Miller & Parkhe, 2002; Ramachandran, 2010; Yildiz & Fey, 2012). Changing host country nationals' deeply anchored attitudes towards companies from certain countries is very difficult and time-consuming. Thus, especially EMNEs from institutionally distant countries have to intensively invest in building up relationships with host country nationals in order to overcome potential discrepancies between the home and the host countries' institutional environments. As long as host country nationals are not familiar with EMNEs' way of doing business and are not somehow convinced that EMNEs have their best interests in mind, they will discriminate against these new entrants. In conclusion, while EMNEs may manage unfamiliarity and relational hazards over time, they are still highly challenged by discrimination hazards.

According to Eden and Miller (2004) discrimination hazards exist when host country nationals directly or indirectly treat foreign firms in a different way than local companies. Host country nationals who use defensive measures like strikes, regulations, or boycotts directly discriminate against a foreign company. For instance, direct discrimination can result in terms of specific restrictions of the host government to protect domestic firms or specific industries (Ramachandran, 2010). Similar to Sany's experience in the United States, intended acquisitions of US companies by the Chinese telecommunication company Huawei were prohibited by the government due to national security risks. Thus, among others a buyout of an US network equipment maker was scuttled by the government since Huawei would have gained access to highly sensitive telecommunication technologies, also used by the US Defense Department (Globerman & Shapiro, 2008).

Indirect discrimination occurs in preferential treatments of local companies over foreign companies. In this case, host country nationals have a choice between foreign and local companies and indirectly discriminate against the former by favoring the latter as employer of choice, business partner, or client (Eden & Miller, 2004). In our context, indirect discrimination is reflected in applicants' higher attraction towards foreign DMNEs than EMNEs as future employers. According to Alkire and Avey (2013) Western job seekers prefer MNEs from Europe and the United States over Chinese and Indian MNEs since they expect a stable and wealthy environment and consequently a better career enhancement in organizations from developed economies. In line with differences in applicants' attraction towards EMNEs and foreign DMNEs, research on consumers' behavior also investigated that consumers favor products and services from developed markets before they consider to purchase products from emerging markets (Balabanis, Diamantopoulos, Mueller, & Melewar, 2001; Demirbag, Sahadev, & Mellahi, 2010; Johansson, Ronkainen, & Czinkota, 1994). This can be due to the fact that consumers rely on country images to evaluate the quality and reliability of a specific product. As these products derive from stable and wealthy developed markets, consumers associate DMNEs and their products as superior to address the sophisticated consumer demands (Han, 1989; Martin & Eroglu, 1993).

Overall, host country nationals are expected to discriminate more against EMNEs since they especially differ from foreign DMNEs in their home countries' institutional environment (Buckley et al., 2007; Moeller, Harvey, Griffith, & Richey, 2013; Peng, Wang, & Jiang, 2008). These companies derive from emerging markets that are in a stage of economic and political transition, evolving to countries with growth rates above average.

Although the majority of these markets change from centrally planned political systems to more market-oriented systems, their governments are still involved in local companies' business practices (Peng, 2003; Puffer & McCarthy, 2007). Moreover, emerging markets lack sophisticated legal systems and are, due to a late liberalization of their markets, not as globally experienced as their Western counterparts (Hoskisson, Eden, Chung Ming, & Wright, 2000; Wang, Hong, Kafouros, & Wright, 2012). The fact that EMNEs have to catch-up to foreign DMNEs (Hitt, Levitas, Arregle, & Borza, 2000), their different resource endowments (Dunning, Kim, & Park, 2008), and the still existent institutional differences between emerging and developed markets (Hoskisson et al., 2000) may lead to host country nationals' different perception of EMNEs and DMNEs in developed markets. Host country nationals may have doubts about EMNEs' market entry and may question their presence in the specific host country. Thus, in order to gain acceptance and to overcome the outsider status in the host country, foreign companies in general, but EMNEs specifically need to invest in relationships with host country nationals (Calhoun, 2002; Kostova & Zaheer, 1999; Schmidt & Sofka, 2009; Yildiz & Fey, 2012).

Fig. 1 shows potential direct and indirect discrimination against EMNEs among specific groups of host country nationals. The degree of discrimination varies between these groups since they differ in their interests, power, and influence on EMNEs' performance.

ANTECEDENTS INFLUENCING THE DISCRIMINATION AGAINST EMNES IN DEVELOPED MARKETS

In the following, we look at institutional-related and resource-related antecedents that may have an impact on the discrimination against EMNEs and DMNEs, respectively. Institutional-related antecedents are the company's degree of state-ownership on the one hand and the similarity of business practices, requirements, and laws between the foreign company's home country and the host country on the other hand. We expect that EMNEs' home country governments have a different involvement in EMNEs' internationalization and business decisions than the home country governments of DMNEs. Moreover, we expect crucial differences between EMNEs' and foreign DMNEs' business practices since they derive from

Fig. 1. Discrimination against EMNEs among Host Country Nationals.

institutionally different markets. Besides institutional-related antecedents, we also focus on resource-related antecedents, namely the company's marketing, managerial, and technological resources, and the company's international and developed market experience.

Since institutional changes, such as the liberalization of their markets, influence companies' resource endowments, the chapter analyzes resource-related antecedents in the context of institutional theory (Guillén & García-Canal, 2009; Hitt et al., 2000). In contrast to foreign DMNEs, EMNEs do not derive from long liberalized economies and therefore just recently start to access resources and international experience foreign DMNEs already have. Fig. 2 illustrates the conceptual framework.

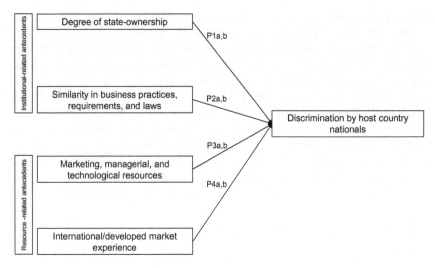

Fig. 2. Conceptual Model.

The Degree of State-Ownership and its Influence on the Discrimination against EMNES in Developed Markets

Regardless of companies' home countries, MNEs with a high degree of state-ownership can face conflicts in simultaneously fulfilling the interests of the company and that of the home country government. MNEs with high state-ownership structures are more likely influenced by the government in their business decisions. This can be reflected in a higher percentage of politically engaged executives in top management teams, who follow the interests of the home country government during their management decisions (Wang et al., 2012). Moreover, the home country government can play an important role in foreign MNEs' internationalization decisions, if they financially support foreign direct investments in specific regions or industries (Luo, Xue, & Han, 2010). Although state-owned companies may also benefit from governmental incentives and financial support (Berning & Holtbrügge, 2012), state-owned MNEs are associated with a higher dependence on their home country government. Host country nationals are expected to treat foreign MNEs with state-ownership structures differently since they question the potential power of the home country government. In this context Turban, Lau, Ngo, Chow, and Si (2001) found that university graduates are less attracted to state-owned MNEs than privately owned MNEs since they expect more autonomy in the latter.

While both state-owned EMNEs and DMNEs might be associated with high governmental influence, host country nationals may lay more interest on the ownership structures of EMNEs since they derive from home countries with a relatively different role of the home country government (Ben-Zeev, Fein, & Inzlicht, 2005; Greenwald & Banaji, 1995). Prior research emphasizes that the home government has a crucial impact on EMNEs in two specific ways. Firstly, in order to boost the home country's liberalization process, EMNEs' internationalization paths and location choices are financially supported by the government, for example, with tax reliefs, credit supports, or preferential foreign exchange policies (Luo et al., 2010). For instance, in their eleventh five-year plan the Chinese government especially supported companies in the oil and gas, electronic, and automotive industry during their internationalization to the developed world (Buckley et al., 2007; Luo & Tung, 2007). However, the higher the financial support by EMNEs' home country governments, the more likely EMNEs feel committed to fulfill the governments' interests, leading to a crucial institutional pressure from home (Cui & Jiang, 2012). As a consequence, EMNEs are challenged to achieve their own goals and simultaneously to satisfy the objectives of the government.

Secondly, looking at the Fortune Global 500 companies from emerging markets, the majority of EMNEs are state-owned companies (Fortune, 2013). These companies are additionally characterized by executive positions majorly assigned to government officials (Holtbrügge & Kreppel, 2012; Wang et al., 2012). For instance, Alexey Miller (Gazprom) was former deputy minister of energy, Igor Sechin (Rosneft) was administration deputy head in the Russian government, and Kirill Androsov (Aeroflot) was former deputy chief of staff, before they accepted management positions in the top five companies in Russia (Puffer & McCarthy, 2007). Companies with executive boards closely linked to the home country government are more likely perceived as biased and politically loyal, addressing the national interests before considering organizational objectives (Globerman & Shapiro, 2008).

In cases like this, host country nationals are expected to develop an unfavorable political image of EMNEs, leading to a higher discrimination against EMNEs compared to foreign DMNEs (Cui & Jiang, 2012). Especially, when the political systems between home and host country differ from each other, host country nationals are expected to have doubts about the way in which politicians rule the specific emerging markets

(Moeller et al., 2013). In this context, Russian state-owned companies could face the risk of being interlinked with recent political developments in the Ukraine. Although they are not involved in these political actions, host country nationals may perceive these companies to follow political interests similar to that of the home country government. Moreover, Chinese companies suffer from their political image and are less attractive to non-Chinese applicants since these applicants disagree with the way the government handles freedom of press and human rights, indirectly discriminating Chinese companies by preferring foreign DMNEs as future employers (Tung, 2007).

Although state-owned DMNEs might also follow political interests when internationalizing to other developed markets, these companies can more readily gain institutional legitimacy for several reasons. Firstly, the majority of DMNEs in the Fortune Global 500 are characterized by private ownership structures, reflecting the minor influence of DMNEs' home country governments. Moreover, the minority of companies that are state-owned are not automatically associated with high intervention of the government since host country nationals may not focus as much on the ownership structure as they may do in the context of EMNEs. Secondly, DMNEs internationalizing to other developed economies, usually originate from countries with a rather similar institutional background, such as relatively similar democratic structures. Host country nationals are expected to imply that also state-owned DMNEs follow the same political interests and are less pressured and controlled by their home country government. Additionally, state-owned DMNEs are usually not financially supported in the way home country governments support EMNEs' internationalization, and consequently are more independent of their government (Guillén & García-Canal, 2009; Mathews, 2002). Consequently, compared to foreign DMNEs, EMNEs may be challenged to overcome their negative political image and the stigma that they are highly dependent on their home country government (Bangara, Freeman, & Schroder, 2012; Brouthers et al., 2005). We propose:

Proposition 1a. The higher the company's degree of state-ownership, the more likely host country nationals discriminate against the respective company.

Proposition 1b. The relationship between the company's degree of state-ownership and host country nationals' discrimination is stronger in the context of EMNEs in developed markets than in the context of foreign DMNEs in developed markets.

Similarity in Business Practices, Requirements, and Laws and its Influence on the Discrimination against EMNEs in Developed Markets

The higher the institutional distance between the home and the host markets, the more challenging it is for foreign MNEs to enter and to become accepted in the respective market (Peng, 2003; Shenkar, 2001). Especially, if requirements and laws differ from those at home, foreign MNEs face barriers in implementing their business practices in foreign markets since they have to adapt to a new institutional environment first (Estrin, Baghdasaryan, & Meyer, 2009; Ferner, Almond, & Colling, 2005). Foreign MNEs that follow relatively similar regulations and requirements in their home country can more easily transfer their business practices in the foreign market and are supposed to face less discrimination by host country nationals than MNEs from institutionally distant markets (Gaur, Delios, & Singh, 2007).

Comparing legal systems of emerging and developed markets, emerging markets are usually described to have unprotected property rights, high levels of corruption practices, and crucial problems with bribery (Hoskisson et al., 2000; Wang et al., 2012). In particular, while in emerging markets sanctions against corruption are still missing, developed markets usually have sophisticated regulatory institutions to control and sanction MNEs' corrupt business practices (Calhoun, 2002; Eden & Miller, 2004). In fact, foreign DMNEs are more likely perceived to follow the rules since they have to face high sanctions if they act in a corrupt way (Cuervo-Cazurra & Genc, 2008). This avoidance of corruption practices is also reflected in DMNEs' highly sophisticated and transparent reporting policies (Transparency International, 2013).

On the contrary, EMNEs are perceived to be confronted with corrupt practices every day and are expected to have experience following illegal business practices to gain competitive advantages in foreign markets. According to Transparency International (2013), Russian and Chinese companies, among other EMNEs, are still not transparent in their business practices and do not fulfill the standards of transparency reporting in developed markets (Transparency International, 2013). While stakeholders in emerging markets may attach less importance to these transparency standards, host country nationals from developed markets demand transparent reporting policies and an adequate ethical behavior. Thus, host country nationals more likely label EMNEs as untrustworthy partners compared to their Western counterparts (Bangara et al., 2012; Brouthers et al., 2005). They are supposed to favor foreign DMNEs over EMNEs since the former follows similar ethical understandings.

EMNEs may also face different labor market regulations, standards in workplace safety, or environmental protection than those at home (Banalieva & Sarathy, 2010; Barnard, 2010). While EMNEs deal with relatively informal agreements at home, they are challenged by approving authorizations and officials in the developed world in order to gain certifications and seals of quality or to manage requested environmental and business directives (Yamakawa, Peng, & Deeds, 2008). When Indian pharmaceutical companies like Dr. Reddy's Laboratories or Ranbaxy Laboratories entered Europe, the United States, and Japan, they faced a very unfamiliar and stringent regulatory environment (Chittoor & Ray, 2007; Pradhan, 2010; Yeoh, 2011). In order to promote a generic product in developed markets, they were challenged with multiple approving authorities, stricter healthcare regulations, and established patent laws (Kedron & Bagchi-Sen, 2012; Yeoh, 2011). On the contrary, foreign DMNEs share relatively similar norms and standards and know-how to manage the relevant regulatory environment. In conclusion, EMNEs face legitimacy problems since they are perceived to be unable to cope with dissimilar regulatory environments. EMNEs face higher institutional pressures from host country nationals and need to intensively invest to develop trustworthy relationships and to convince host country nationals that they will follow institutional rules of the specific market (Elango, 2009; Moeller et al., 2013). Foreign DMNEs, on the other hand, originate from rather similar institutional environments. Host country nationals expect DMNEs to face less institutional problems like corruption, bribery rates, and nontransparent requirements. Thus, they more likely prefer foreign DMNEs over EMNEs since the former follows relatively similar business practices as local companies from that specific developed market. Hence, we propose:

Proposition 2a. The lower the similarity of business practices, requirements, and laws, the more likely host country nationals discriminate against the respective company.

Proposition 2b. The relationship between the similarity of business practices, requirements, and laws and host country nationals' discrimination is stronger in the context of EMNEs in developed markets than in the context of foreign DMNEs in developed markets.

The Influence of Marketing, Managerial, and Technological Resources on the Discrimination against EMNEs in Developed Markets

Individuals are usually more attracted to foreign MNEs with rich resource endowments, such as marketing capabilities or qualitative technological resources. In fact, they can better identify with companies that own well-established brands and consequently they are more willing to support popular foreign MNEs during their market entry (Backhaus & Tikoo, 2004; Berthon, Ewing, & Hah, 2005). Additionally, local companies are usually more attracted to a foreign MNE as their future business partner if the respective company owns strategically relevant managerial and technological capabilities (Hitt et al., 2000). Thus, foreign MNEs with high resource endowments are favored as future business partners over those companies that lack well-established brands, managerial capabilities, or distinctive technologies.

Compared to foreign DMNEs, EMNEs derive from countries that experienced a late liberalization and consequently are in a different stage of internationalization (Dunning et al., 2008). While their foreign counterparts accumulated marketing and technological capabilities due to an earlier liberalization of their home countries, EMNEs lack those capabilities since they just recently started to expand to the developed world (Elango & Pattnaik, 2007; Hennart, 2012; Kedia, Gaffney, & Clampit, 2012; Ramamurti, 2009). Additionally, since EMNEs usually followed the strategy of being a cost leader in emerging markets, they cannot yet address the sophisticated consumer demands in developed markets and lack marketing skills as well as well-known brands (Cayla & Eckhardt, 2007; Luo & Rui, 2009; Luo & Tung, 2007; Salehizadeh, 2007). Thus, they have to catch-up to companies with superior resources and capabilities by acquiring relevant strategic resources (Kedia et al., 2012; Luo & Tung, 2007). Following a springboard approach, these companies indeed augment new strategic resources during their internationalization (Aybar & Thirunavukkarasu, 2005; Mathews, 2006).

Moreover, research found that Western consumers are more attracted to products produced by foreign DMNEs since they are perceived to offer them better quality than products from EMNEs (Demirbag et al., 2010; Kreppel & Holtbrügge, 2012). For instance, during its internationalization in developed markets, the home appliance manufacturer Haier was not as familiar as well-known foreign DMNEs like General Electric, Siemens, Sony, and Whirlpool. Consumers were not aware of Haier's products at all (Liu & Li, 2002) or associated Haier as an exporter of low value-added products that lead to crucial shortfalls in their sales (Klossek, Linke, & Nippa, 2012). Consequently, the risk of being discriminated by Western consumers is more likely and EMNEs and have to adjust their products and services to the different consumer demands.

Lastly, due to the fact that EMNEs enter developed markets to acquire managerial capabilities (Kedia et al., 2012), local companies may assume that they own managerial capabilities that are better than those of EMNEs (Chang et al., 2009). Therefore, local competitors see little benefits in entering business partnerships with these EMNEs and are more likely to refuse cooperation with these latecomers (Hitt et al., 2000). On the contrary, foreign DMNEs are more attractive in the eyes of local companies since they can offer them high resource endowments due to an earlier liberalization of their home countries. Hence, EMNEs face a discriminatory behavior from host country competitors, resulting in higher costs to convince local companies to work together (Denk et al., 2012).

Overall, we assume that there are crucial differences how firms' resource endowments are perceived by host country nationals and consequently how they discriminate against EMNEs and foreign DMNEs. Thus, we propose:

Proposition 3a. The lower a company's marketing, managerial, and technological capabilities, the more likely host country nationals discriminate against the respective company.

Proposition 3b. The relationship between the company's marketing, managerial, and technological capabilities and host country nationals' discrimination is stronger in the context of EMNEs in developed markets than in the context of foreign DMNEs in developed markets.

The Influence of International and Developed Market Experience on the Discrimination against EMNEs in Developed Markets

Petersen and Pedersen (2002) underline that internationally experienced MNEs are more flexible to adapt to a new institutional environment since they can use and combine their accumulated knowledge from prior market entries. Moreover, research found that foreign companies with international experience significantly perform better in foreign markets than those without international experience (Geringer & Beamish, 1989; Luo & Peng, 1999). Thus, experience gained in one country can help to overcome LOF in another country with relatively similar market structures. In fact, MNEs can more easily become familiar with the specific institutional environment, market structures, and local demand if they can rely on prior international experience (Delios & Beamish, 2001; Zaheer, 1995; Zaheer & Mosakowski,

1997). Moreover, compared to inexperienced MNEs, foreign MNEs with a high degree of accumulated international experience can quickly respond to market changes and are more attractive to host country nationals, such as potential job seekers, local business, or the host country government (Gaur & Lu, 2007; Johanson & Vahlne, 1977). For example, prior studies point out that internationally experienced MNEs can offer a better career enhancement and a more diversified work environment to prospective applicants (Lievens, Decaesteker, Coetsier, & Geirnaert, 2001; Newburry et al., 2006).

In our context, EMNEs usually have a competitive advantage in other emerging markets since they are experienced in managing institutional voids such as imperfect regulations or inefficient bureaucracies (Cuervo-Cazurra & Genc, 2008; Hoskisson et al., 2000). Conversely, in developed markets, EMNEs face unfamiliar institutions and have to compete with local as well as foreign well-known DMNEs. DMNEs are more experienced in managing the competitive environment and the local demand in developed markets (Thomas, Eden, Hitt, & Miller, 2007). For instance, they have the knowledge how to attract Western applicants, are experienced with hiring practices, and are better informed about necessary approving authorities than their emerging counterparts. As a consequence, host country nationals may question EMNEs' lack of international and developed market experience and thus their ability to compete with globally experienced foreign DMNEs. Exemplary, future job seekers are supposed to be more attracted to internationally experienced DMNEs since they can better react to the institutional environment, provide more job securities, and international career perspectives (Alkire & Avey, 2013; Cuervo-Cazurra & Genc, 2008; Fombrun & Shanley, 1990). In contrast to DMNEs, EMNEs need more time to acclimatize to the market and to gain legitimacy by relevant players (Thomas et al., 2007). Hence, host country nationals associate EMNEs as inexperienced companies, leading to the following proposition:

Proposition 4a. The lower a company's international (developed market) experience, the more likely host country nationals discriminate against the respective company.

Proposition 4b. The relationship between the company's international (developed market) experience and host country nationals' discrimination is stronger in the context of EMNEs in developed markets than in the context of foreign DMNEs in developed markets.

CONCLUSION, IMPLICATIONS, AND FUTURE RESEARCH

This chapter contributes to international business literature in several ways. Firstly, prior research only vaguely investigates host country nationals' negative attitudes towards EMNEs in developed markets (Barnard, 2010; Chang et al., 2009; Madhok & Keyhani, 2012). We addressed this issue and offer a framework to identify antecedents that may influence why EMNEs face additional discrimination by host country nationals. We argue that due to their different home countries, EMNEs and foreign DMNEs are not equally perceived by host country nationals from developed markets. Thus, host country nationals from developed markets differently evaluate a company's degree of state-ownership, a company's way of doing business, its developed market experience, and its resource endowments if the respective company is from an emerging market. In other words, even if an EMNE has the same ownership structure, firm resources, and experience like a foreign DMNE, host country nationals still might have prejudices towards EMNEs simply because they are from emerging markets. Additionally, host country nationals are more likely to prefer foreign DMNEs simply because these companies have a relatively similar institutional background than those from the respective host country. This bias expressed in host country nationals' higher discrimination against EMNEs can be defined as the liability of emergingness.

Secondly, we contribute to international business literature by determining the difference between LOF and liability of emergingness. Particularly, the chapter contributes to institutional theory by focusing on today's influence of companies' institutional background on host country nationals' acceptance (DiMaggio & Powell, 1983).

Thus, by comparing DMNEs and EMNES that originate from different institutional environments, we want to shed light on EMNEs' potential stigma of being from emerging markets, which goes beyond the classic LOF (Hymer, 1976, p. 35). It seems that EMNEs face home and host country institutional pressure when they internationalize to developed markets. Firstly, during their internationalization to strategically relevant developed markets, they are financially supported by their home country government. At the same time however, they are more likely pressured to follow non-commercial objectives from their home country government since they are more dependent on their financial incentives to enter these competitive developed markets (Cui & Jiang, 2012; Wang et al., 2012). Secondly, since EMNEs have a different institutional background, they are more likely to be treated differently by host country nationals and consequently they face higher legitimacy issues in developed markets (Madhok & Keyhani, 2012; Moeller et al., 2013; Yildiz & Fey, 2012). On the other hand, foreign DMNEs depend less on their home country government to internationalize to strategically relevant developed markets and thus might experience less home country institutional pressure. Moreover, due to their relatively similar institutional backgrounds, for example, similar regulations and legal systems, they are less discriminated by host country nationals.

This chapter also contains promising avenues for future research. Future studies should empirically investigate the indirect discriminatory behavior against EMNEs and DMNEs among different groups of host country nationals. Thus, future studies could investigate differences in Western consumers' purchasing intentions to buy a product from an EMNE versus DMNE or could compare applicants' attraction towards EMNEs with their willingness to work for foreign DMNEs. Additionally, it could be very interesting to compare the discriminatory behavior among the different groups of stakeholders, identifying which group relies on the home country institutional environment the most. Still, there may not only be differences between the groups of host country nationals, but also within one group. Comparing business-to-business sectors with business-to-consumer sectors could give promising insights into EMNEs' liability of emergingness within consumer groups. We can expect that corporate consumers do have better information and knowledge about MNEs' products and services since they directly negotiate with the companies. However, end consumers lack this chance to negotiate and may more likely rely on a company's home country to evaluate the product quality (Keller, 1993). Thus, we anticipate future research to explore if EMNEs from business-to-consumer sectors face higher discrimination hazards than EMNEs conducting business-to-business operations. These studies could also control and analyze the influence of different industries on the discrimination behavior by host country nationals since the magnitude of discrimination against EMNEs could vary between manufacturing, service, or oil and gas industries.

Although this framework is not yet empirically tested, some implications can be derived as well. Managers of EMNEs as well as foreign DMNEs can identify which antecedents influence host country nationals' discriminatory behavior the most and can, if necessary, adjust their business practices to the developed market context. For instance, if the similarity of business practices, requirements, and laws is the one factor crucially influencing the direct and indirect discrimination against EMNEs, EMNEs should integrate controlling systems to sanction corruption or bribery and should implement communication strategies to convince host country nationals of their adequate and ethical business practices. At the same time, in order to secure their superior competitive situation, foreign DMNEs could use these results by outlining their higher transparency standards and trustworthiness to host country nationals. Using specific image campaigns could help foreign DMNEs to communicate their positive company reputations, better product quality, and their higher resource endowments and experience.

Besides our contributions and future research implications, the chapter still has some limitations. Our framework ignores external factors that could moderate the magnitude of discrimination against EMNEs, such as the financial crisis (Sauvant, Maschek, & McAllister, 2009). Although host country nationals might have negative attitudes towards EMNEs and prefer foreign DMNEs, some might be thankful for EMNEs' investments in struggling companies near insolvency. Prominent examples are Chinese acquisitions of struggling Swedish car manufacturers like Saab and Volvo or the German car supplier Saargummi. Thus, especially during the financial crisis, some EMNEs can be seen as saviors rather than as a threat for struggling European companies, leading to a lesser discrimination against EMNEs.

In addition, this framework concentrates on country-of-origin disadvantages. However, EMNEs may also have certain advantages due to their home country environment, for example, they are more flexible to deal with difficult environments or are more able to address consumers at the lower income level with less expensive products and services (Child & Rodrigues, 2005; Cuervo-Cazurra & Genc, 2008; Luo et al., 2010). Hence, the influence of institutional- and resource-related antecedents on the discrimination against EMNEs may be moderated by specific home country advantages.

In conclusion, we hope to steer future research to empirically investigate the differences between the discrimination against EMNEs and foreign DMNEs and to further investigate the existence of the liability of emergingness. Thus, we hope that future empirical studies give insights into today's importance of the home country environment to successfully compete in institutionally distant markets.

REFERENCES

Alkire, T. D., & Avey, J. B. (2013). Psychological capital and the intent to pursue employment with developed and emerging market multinational corporations. *Human Resource Development International, 16*(1), 40–55.

Aybar, B., & Thirunavukkarasu, A. (2005). Emerging market multinationals: An analysis of performance and risk characteristics. *Journal of Asia-Pacific Business, 6*(2), 5−39.

Backhaus, K. B., & Tikoo, S. (2004). Conceptualizing and researching employer branding. *Career Development International, 9*(5), 501−517.

Balabanis, G., Diamantopoulos, A., Mueller, R. D., & Melewar, T. C. (2001). The impact of nationalism, patriotism and internationalism on consumer ethnocentric tendencies. *Journal of International Business Studies, 32*(1), 157−175.

Banalieva, E. R., & Sarathy, R. (2010). The impact of regional trade agreements on the global orientation of emerging market multinationals. *Management International Review, 50*(6), 797−826.

Bangara, A., Freeman, S., & Schroder, W. (2012). Legitimacy and accelerated internationalisation: An Indian perspective. *Journal of World Business, 47*(4), 623−634.

Barnard, H. (2010). Overcoming the liability of foreignness without strong firm capabilities − The value of market-based resources. *Journal of International Management, 16*(2), 165−176.

Ben-Zeev, T., Fein, S., & Inzlicht, M. (2005). Arousal and stereotype threat. *Journal of Experimental Social Psychology, 41*(2), 174−181.

Berning, S. C., & Holtbrügge, D. (2012). Chinese outward foreign direct investment − A challenge for traditional internationalization theories? *Journal für Betriebswirtschaft, 62*(3−4), 169−224.

Berthon, P., Ewing, M., & Hah, L. L. (2005). Captivating company: Dimensions of attractiveness in employer branding. *International Journal of Advertising, 24*(2), 151−172.

Brannen, M. Y. (2004). When Mickey loses face: Recontextualization, semantic fit, and the semiotics of foreignness. *The Academy of Management Review, 29*(4), 593.

Brouthers, L. E., Donnell, E. O., & Hadjimarcou, J. (2005). Generic product strategies for emerging market exports into triad nation markets: A mimetic isomorphism approach. *Journal of Management Studies, 42*(1), 225−245.

Buckley, P. J., Clegg, L. J., Cross, A. R., Liu, X., Voss, H., & Zheng, P. (2007). The determinants of Chinese outward foreign direct investment. *Journal of International Business Studies, 38*(4), 499−518.

Calhoun, M. (2002). Unpacking liability of foreignness: Identifying culturally driven external and internal sources of liability for the foreign subsidiary. *Journal of International Management, 8*(3), 301−321.

Cayla, J., & Eckhardt, G. M. (2007). Asian brands without borders: Regional opportunities and challenges. *International Marketing Review, 24*(4), 444−456.

Chang, Y. Y., Mellahi, K., & Wilkinson, A. (2009). Control of subsidiaries of MNCs from emerging economies in developed countries: The case of Taiwanese MNCs in the UK. *The International Journal of Human Resource Management, 20*(1), 75−95.

Chen, H., Griffith, D. a., & Hu, M. Y. (2006). The influence of liability of foreignness on market entry strategies: An illustration of market entry in China. *International Marketing Review, 23*(6), 636−649.

Child, J., & Rodrigues, S. B. (2005). The internationalization of Chinese firms: A case for theoretical extension? *Management and Organization Review, 1*(3), 381−410.

Chittoor, R., & Ray, S. (2007). Internationalization paths of Indian pharmaceutical firms − A strategic group analysis. *Journal of International Management, 13*(3), 338−355.

Clarkson, M. B. E. (1995). A stakeholder framework for analyzing and evaluating corporate social performance. *The Academy of Management Review, 20*(1), 92−117.

Cuervo-Cazurra, A., & Genc, M. (2008). Transforming disadvantages into advantages: Developing-country MNEs in the least developed countries. *Journal of International Business Studies, 39*(6), 957–979.

Cui, L., & Jiang, F. (2012). State ownership effect on firms' FDI ownership decisions under institutional pressure: A study of Chinese outward-investing firms. *Journal of International Business Studies, 43*(3), 264–284.

Delios, A., & Beamish, P. W. (2001). Survival and profitability: The roles of experience and intangible assets in foreign subsidiary performance. *Academy of Management Journal, 44*(5), 1028–1038.

Demirbag, M., Sahadev, S., & Mellahi, K. (2010). Country image and consumer preference for emerging economy products: The moderating role of consumer materialism. *International Marketing Review, 27*(2), 164–178.

Denk, N., Kaufmann, L., & Roesch, J.-F. (2012). Liabilities of foreignness revisited: A review of contemporary studies and recommendations for future research. *Journal of International Management, 18*(4), 322–334.

DiMaggio, P. J., & Powell, W. W. (1983). The iron cage revisited: Institutional isomorphism and collective rationality in organizational fields. *American Sociological Review, 48*(2), 147–160.

Dunning, J. H., Kim, C., & Park, D. (2008). Old wine in new bottles: A comparison of emerging market TNCs today and developed-country TNCs thirty years ago. In K. P. Sauvant (Ed.), *The rise of transnational corporations from emerging markets. Threat or opportunity?* (pp. 158–182). Cheltenham: Edward Elgar.

Eden, L., & Miller, S. R. (2004). Distance matters: Liability of foreignness, institutional distance and ownership strategy. *Advances in International Management, 16*, 187–221.

Elango, B. (2009). Minimizing effects of "liability of foreignness": Response strategies of foreign firms in the United States. *Journal of World Business, 44*(1), 51–62.

Elango, B., & Pattnaik, C. (2007). Building capabilities for international operations through networks: A study of Indian firms. *Journal of International Business Studies, 38*(4), 541–555.

Estrin, S., Baghdasaryan, D., & Meyer, K. E. (2009). The impact of institutional and human resource distance on international entry strategies. *Journal of Management Studies, 46*(7), 1171–1196.

Ferner, A., Almond, P., & Colling, T. (2005). Institutional theory and the cross-national transfer of employment policy: The case of workforce diversity in US multinationals. *Journal of International Business Studies, 36*(3), 304–321.

Fombrun, C., & Shanley, M. (1990). What's in a name? Reputation building and corporate strategy. *Academy of Management Journal, 33*(2), 233–258.

Fortune. (2013). Fortune Global 500 List. *CNN Money*. Retrieved from http://money.cnn. com/magazines/fortune/global500/2013/full_list/

Freeman, R. E. (1984). *Strategic management: A stakeholder approach*. Marshfield: Pitman.

Galbraith, A. (2012). China's Sany vows no lay offs in Germany. *Wall Street Journal*. Retrieved from http://online.wsj.com/article/BT-CO-20120201-708285.html#

Gaur, A., & Lu, J. W. (2007). Ownership strategies and survival of foreign subsidiaries: Impacts of institutional distance and experience. *Journal of Management, 33*(1), 84–110.

Gaur, A. S., Delios, A., & Singh, K. (2007). Institutional environments, staffing strategies, and subsidiary performance. *Journal of Management, 33*(4), 611–636.

Geringer, J. M., & Beamish, P. W. (1989). Diversification strategy and internationalization: Implications for MNE performance. *Strategic Management Journal*, *10*(2), 109–119.

Globerman, S., & Shapiro, D. (2008). Economic and strategic considerations surrounding Chinese FDI in the United States. *Asia Pacific Journal of Management*, *26*(1), 163–183.

Goldstein, A. (2009). Multinational companies from emerging economies: Composition, conceptualization & direction in the global economy. *The Indian Journal of Industrial Relations*, *45*(1), 137–148.

Goodall, K., & Roberts, J. (2003). Only connect: Teamwork in the multinational. *Journal of World Business*, *38*(2), 150–164.

Greenwald, A. G., & Banaji, M. (1995). Implicit social cognition: Attitudes, self-esteem, and stereotypes. *Psychological Review*, *102*(1), 4–27.

Guillén, M. F., & García-Canal, E. (2009). The American model of the multinational firm and the "new" multinationals from emerging economies. *Academy of Management Perspectives*, *23*(2), 23–36.

Han, C. M. (1989). Country image: Halo or summary construct? *Journal of Marketing Research*, *26*(2), 222–229.

Hennart, J.-F. (2012). Emerging market multinationals and the theory of the multinational enterprise. *Global Strategy Journal*, *2*(3), 168–187.

Hennart, J.-F., Roehl, T., & Zeng, M. (2002). Do exits proxy a liability of foreignness? The case of Japanese exits from the US. *Journal of International Management*, *8*(3), 241–264.

Hitt, M. A., Levitas, E., Arregle, J.-L., & Borza, A. (2000). Partner selection in emerging and developed market contexts: Resource-based and organizational learning perspectives. *Academy of Management Journal*, *43*(3), 449–467.

Holtbrügge, D., & Kreppel, H. (2012). Determinants of outward foreign direct investment from BRIC countries: An explorative study. *International Journal of Emerging Markets*, *7*(1), 4–30.

Hoskisson, R. E., Eden, L., Chung Ming, L., & Wright, M. (2000). Strategy in emerging economies. *Academy of Management Journal*, *43*(3), 249–267.

Hymer, S. (1976). *The international operations of national firms: A study of direct foreign investment*. Cambridge: MIT Press.

Johanson, J., & Vahlne, J. (1977). The internationalization process of the firm – A model of knowledge development and increasing foreign market commitments. *Journal of International Business Studies*, *8*(1), 23–32.

Johansson, J. K., Ronkainen, I. A., & Czinkota, M. R. (1994). Negative country-of-origin effects: The case of new Russia. *Journal of International Business Studies*, *25*(1), 157–176.

Kedia, B., Gaffney, N., & Clampit, J. (2012). EMNEs and knowledge-seeking FDI. *Management International Review*, *52*(2), 155–173.

Kedron, P., & Bagchi-Sen, S. (2012). Foreign direct investment in Europe by multinational pharmaceutical companies from India. *Journal of Economic Geography*, *12*(4), 809–839.

Keller, K. L. (1993). Conceptualizing, measuring, and managing customer-based brand equity. *Journal of Marketing*, *57*(1), 1.

Klossek, A., Linke, B. M., & Nippa, M. (2012). Chinese enterprises in Germany: Establishment modes and strategies to mitigate the liability of foreignness. *Journal of World Business*, *47*(1), 35–44.

Kostova, T., & Roth, K. (2002). Adoption of an organizational practice by subsidiaries of multinational corporations: Institutional and relational effects. *Academy of Management Journal*, 45(1), 215–233.

Kostova, T., & Zaheer, S. (1999). Organizational legitimacy under conditions of complexity: The case of the multinational enterprise. *Academy of Management Review*, 24(1), 64–81.

Kreppel, H., & Holtbrügge, D. (2012). The perceived attractiveness of Chinese products by German consumers – A sociopsychological approach. *Journal of Global Marketing*, 25(2), 79–99.

Lievens, F., Decaesteker, C., Coetsier, P., & Geirnaert, J. (2001). Organizational attractiveness for prospective applicants: A person organisation fit perspective. *Applied Psychology*, 50(1), 30–51.

Liu, H., & Li, K. (2002). Strategic implications of emerging Chinese multinationals: The haier case study. *European Management Journal*, 20(6), 699–706.

Luo, Y., & Mezias, J. M. (2002). Liabilities of foreignness: Concepts, constructs, and consequences. *Journal of International Management*, 8(3), 217–221.

Luo, Y., & Peng, M. W. (1999). Learning to compete in a transition economy: Experience, environment, and performance. *Journal of International Business Studies*, 30(2), 269–295.

Luo, Y., & Rui, H. (2009). An ambidexterity perspective toward multinational enterprises from emerging economies. *Academy of Management Perspectives*, 23(4), 49–71.

Luo, Y., Shenkar, O., & Nyaw, M. (2002). Mitigating liabilities of foreignness: Defensive versus offensive approaches. *Journal of International Management*, 8(3), 283–300.

Luo, Y., & Tung, R. L. (2007). International expansion of emerging market enterprises: A springboard perspective. *Journal of International Business Studies*, 38(4), 481–498.

Luo, Y., Xue, Q., & Han, B. (2010). How emerging market governments promote outward FDI: Experience from China. *Journal of World Business*, 45(1), 68–79.

Madhok, A., & Keyhani, M. (2012). Acquisitions as entrepreneurship: Asymmetries, opportunities, and the internationalization of multinationals from emerging economies. *Global Strategy Journal*, 2(1), 26–40.

Martin, I. M., & Eroglu, S. (1993). Measuring a multi-dimensional construct: Country image. *Journal of Business Research*, 28(3), 191–210.

Mathews, J. A. (2002). Competitive advantages of the latecomer firm: A resource-based account of industrial catch-up strategies. *Asia Pacific Journal of Management*, 19(4), 467–488.

Mathews, J. A. (2006). Dragon multinationals: New players in 21st century globalization. *Asia Pacific Journal of Management*, 23(1), 5–27.

McMahon, D. (2012). China's Sany Group: U.S. discriminates against China firms' investments. *Wall Street Journal*. Retrieved from http://online.wsj.com/news/articles/SB10000872396390444734804578064183506227980

Meyer, K. E., Estrin, S., Bhaumik, S. K., & Peng, M. W. (2009). Institutions, resources, and entry strategies in emerging economies. *Strategic Management Journal*, 30(1), 61–80.

Mezias, J. M. (2002). How to identify liabilities of foreignness and assess their effects on multinational corporations. *Journal of International Management*, 8(3), 265–282.

Miller, S. R., & Parkhe, A. (2002). Is there a liability of foreignness in global banking? An empirical test of banks' x-efficiency. *Strategic Management Journal*, 23(1), 55–75.

Miller, S. R., Thomas, D. E., Eden, L., & Hitt, M. (2009). Knee deep in the big muddy: The survival of emerging market firms in developed markets. *Management International Review*, *48*(6), 645–666.

Moeller, M., Harvey, M., Griffith, D., & Richey, G. (2013). The impact of country-of-origin on the acceptance of foreign subsidiaries in host countries: An examination of the "liability-of-foreignness". *International Business Review*, *22*(1), 89–99.

Newburry, W., Gardberg, N. A., & Belkin, L. Y. (2006). Organizational attractiveness is in the eye of the beholder: The interaction of demographic characteristics with foreignness. *Journal of International Business Studies*, *37*(5), 666–686.

North, D. C. (1990). *Institutions, institutional change, and economic performance*. New York, NY: Cambridge University Press.

Peng, M. W. (2003). Institutional transitions and strategic choices. *The Academy of Management Review*, *28*(2), 275–296.

Peng, M. W., Wang, D. Y. L., & Jiang, Y. (2008). An institution-based view of international business strategy: A focus on emerging economies. *Journal of International Business Studies*, *39*(5), 920–936.

Petersen, B., & Pedersen, T. (2002). Coping with liability of foreignness: Different learning engagements of entrant firms. *Journal of International Management*, *8*(3), 339–350.

Podnar, K., & Jancic, Z. (2006). Towards a categorization of stakeholder groups: An empirical verification of a three-level model. *Journal of Marketing Communications*, *12*(4), 297–308.

Pradhan, J. P. (2010). Strategic asset-seeking activities of emerging multinationals: Perspectives on foreign acquisitions by Indian pharmaceutical MNEs. *Organizations & Markets in Emerging Economies*, *1*(2), 9–32.

Puffer, S. M., & McCarthy, D. J. (2007). Can Russia's state-managed, network capitalism be competitive? *Journal of World Business*, *42*(1), 1–13.

Ramachandran, J. (2010). The liabilities of origin: An emerging economy perspective on the costs of doing business abroad. In T. Devinney, T. Pedersen, & L. Tihanyi (Eds.), *Advances in international management: The past, present and future of international business and management* (Vol. 23, pp. 231–265). Bingley, UK: Emerald Group Publishing Limited.

Ramamurti, R. (2009). What have we learned about emerging-market MNEs? In R. Ramamurti & J. V. Singh (Eds.), *Emerging multinationals in emerging market* (pp. 399–426). Cambridge: Cambridge University Press.

Salehizadeh, M. (2007). Emerging economies' multinationals: Current status and future prospects. *Third World Quarterly*, *28*(6), 1151–1166.

Sauvant, K. P., Maschek, W. A., & McAllister, G. (2009). Foreign direct investment from emerging markets: The challenges ahead. Paper presented at the OECD Global Forum on International Investment, December 7–8.

Schmidt, T., & Sofka, W. (2009). Liability of foreignness as a barrier to knowledge spillovers: Lost in translation? *Journal of International Management*, *15*(4), 460–474.

Scott, R. (1995). *Institutions and organizations*. Thousand Oaks: Sage.

Sethi, D., & Judge, W. (2009). Reappraising liabilities of foreignness within an integrated perspective of the costs and benefits of doing business abroad. *International Business Review*, *18*(4), 404–416.

Shenkar, O. (2001). Cultural distance revisited: Towards a more rigorous conceptualization and measurement of cultural differences. *Journal of International Business Studies*, *32*(3), 519–535.

Suchmann, M. (1995). Managing legitimacy: Strategic and institutional approaches. *Academy of Management Review, 20*(3), 571–610.

Thomas, D. E., Eden, L., Hitt, M. A., & Miller, S. R. (2007). Experience of emerging market firms: The role of cognitive bias in developed market entry and survival. *Management International Review, 47*(6), 845–867.

Transparency International. (2013). *Transparency in corporate reporting: Assessing emerging market multinationals.*

Tung, R. L. (2007). The human resource challenge to outward foreign direct investment aspirations from emerging economies: The case of China. *The International Journal of Human Resource Management, 18*(5), 868–889.

Turban, D. B., Lau, C. M., Ngo, H. Y., Chow, I. H., & Si, S. X. (2001). Organizational attractiveness of firms in the people's republic of China: A person-organization fit perspective. *Journal of Applied Psychology, 86*(2), 194–206.

Wang, C., Hong, J., Kafouros, M., & Wright, M. (2012). Exploring the role of government involvement in outward FDI from emerging economies. *Journal of International Business Studies, 43*(7), 655–676.

Yamakawa, Y., Peng, M. W., & Deeds, D. L. (2008). What drives new ventures to internationalize from emerging to developed economies? *Entrepreneurship Theory and Practice, 32*(1), 59–83.

Yeoh, P.-L. (2011). Location choice and the internationalization sequence: Insights from Indian pharmaceutical companies. *International Marketing Review, 28*(3), 291–312.

Yildiz, H. E., & Fey, C. F. (2012). The liability of foreignness reconsidered: New insights from the alternative research context of transforming economies. *International Business Review, 21*(2), 269–280.

Zaheer, S. (1995). Overcoming the liability of foreignness. *Academy of Management Journal, 38*(2), 341–363.

Zaheer, S., & Mosakowski, E. (1997). The dynamics of the liability of foreignness: A global study of survival in financial services. *Strategic Management Journal, 18*(6), 439–464.

CHAPTER 18

THE PERFORMANCE LOGIC OF INTERNATIONAL DIVERSIFICATION

Jorge Carneiro, Victor Amaral, Henrique Pacheco, Sylvia Moraes and Gilberto Figueira da Silva

ABSTRACT

Purpose — *This study sheds light on the complex relationship between international diversification and firm performance and explores whether future performance expectations seem to drive managerial decisions related to internationalization issues.*

Methodology/approach — *We conducted in-depth investigation of five firms. This qualitative approach is allegedly better equipped to uncover the peculiarities of specific internationalization decisions by individual companies and the performance consequences derived from modifications in the degree of international diversification, which might go unnoticed in large-sample statistical analyses.*

Findings — *In line with Hennart's (2007, 2011) and Verbeke and Brugman's (2009) theoretical arguments, our findings indicate that no universal relationship should be expected between international diversification and firm performance. Rather, the performance consequences of*

Multinational Enterprises, Markets and Institutional Diversity
Progress in International Business Research, Volume 9, 443–475
Copyright © 2014 by Emerald Group Publishing Limited
All rights of reproduction in any form reserved
ISSN: 1745-8862/doi:10.1108/S1745-886220140000009017

internationalization-related decisions depend on the particular combinations of a firm's characteristics and environment contingencies. Given managerial discretion, internationalization decisions would not be randomly made, but rather would be endogenous, and, as such, the relationship between multinationality and performance can only be understood if one takes a contingent approach. Additionally, internationalization decisions seem to be taken within a context of uncertainty regarding the future, which suggests that managers seem to approach internationalization with a long-term perspective and may in fact be "buying real options."

Research limitations/implications − *This study examined only five cases and they all relate to a particular type of firm: all are headquartered in a large emerging market with good domestic growth prospects, and each either is the leader or stands among the largest in its industry in the domestic market. While this relative homogeneity in the selection of the cases minimizes confounding factors, it suggests that findings may be specific to this particular (firm and market) context.*

Practical implications − *Managers should be aware that decisions that modify the international configuration of a firm might have distinct implications across different firms, given the particular (firm, industry, and environment) contingencies. Therefore, no universal normative orientation should be expected between international diversification and performance.*

Originality/value − *Although it is often implicitly assumed that managers make (informed) decisions with the objective of improving their firms' (long-run) performance, there has been little discussion as to whether managers have detailed information about the expected performance implications arising from decisions that change the degree of international diversification of their firm and whether such decisions are driven by expected performance outcomes.*

Keywords: International diversification; firm performance; emerging market multinationals

INTRODUCTION

Research about the impact of international diversification on firm performance has reached mutually contradictory findings (cf. Contractor, 2007; Hennart, 2007, 2011; Verbeke & Brugman, 2009).

While more than one hundred empirical studies (cf. Glaum & Oesterle, 2007; Hennart, 2011) have tried to find a general relationship between international diversification and performance, Hennart (2011) argues that there is no theoretical reason to expect that the degree of internationalization of firms (also referred to as international diversification or multinationality and, hereinafter, DoI) should present a universal relationship with their performance.

Verbeke and Brugman (2009, p. 272) go further and argue that "recommendations [derived from statistical analysis of large samples] on optimizing the level of m[ultinationality] may be of little use to individual companies" because "firms choose a specific geographic scope of their activities to maximize performance, based on internal strengths and weaknesses, and external opportunities and threats," and not on some expectation of a general multinationality—performance relationship.

Regarding "learning," as one of the alleged benefits of internationalization (Kim, Hwang, & Burgers, 1993; Ruigrok & Wagner, 2003), it has been argued that the transfer of knowledge from subsidiaries to headquarters does not happen naturally, but rather depends on explicit and intentional managerial action in order to put up processes and routines that would allow for knowledge transfer (Barlett & Ghoshal, 2002; Hennart, 2007).

Regarding "economies of scale" as another example of alleged benefits of internationalization, Hennart (2007) argues that firms in large domestic markets would not need the international arena to grow as much as firms in smaller domestic markets, where it may be more difficult to reach the minimum efficient scale.

Our main research objective is

- To provide preliminary evidence of the underlying logic that would tie international expansion decisions with performance expectations.

Specifically we want to understand whether firms expand internationally because of (i) some (expected) general "multinationality—performance" relationship or (ii) performance expectations derived from the combination of idiosyncratic firm characteristics and environment contingencies or (iii) some (not easy to articulate) logic of flexibility similar to a real options approach.

LITERATURE REVIEW

Literature presents several potential benefits of internationalization that would motivate firms to expand abroad. Such motivations have been classified by Dunning (1988) in four categories: market-seeking, efficiency-seeking, resource-seeking, and strategic asset-seeking.

Hennart (2007, p. 445) contended that the "M/P [multinationality–performance] literature has posited that international diversification should reduce risk and that it should increase performance because (1) it facilitates the exploitation of scale economies, (2) it gives greater access to resources and greater flexibility in shifting production and sourcing, and (3) it provides more opportunities to learn."

Likewise, Contractor (2007, p. 471) contended that "internationalization is 'good' for company performance over much of the international expansion range [because of]: (1) knowledge [learning] derived from abroad, (2) accessing or arbitraging cheaper inputs, (3) exploitation of firm-specific assets in foreign markets, (4) accumulation of global market power, (5) international scale, (6) lowering of volatility from geographical diversification, and (7) accumulated internationalization experience [learning]."

Overall, the literature suggests three main categories of potential benefits of internationalization: (unit) cost reductions, increase in (operational) flexibility, and revenue boost. Additionally, the benefits of cost reduction can come from scale economies, scope economies (synergies), and learning. Flexibility (and its potential impact on cost reduction or revenue boost) can increase with internationalization by means of better access to, and availability of, production factors (raw materials, labor, and capital), potential exploitation of arbitrage opportunities (changes in exchange rates or interest rates, imbalances in prices or volumes, differences in tax brackets, and related transfer pricing practices), circumvention of possible trade barriers in host countries, and increase in bargaining power with host governments. Internationalization can also naturally lead to revenue increase from the sheer opportunity to sell more or, in some cases, to charge higher prices than would be possible in the domestic market.

Those potential benefits notwithstanding, Hennart (2011, p. 135) questioned whether there is any "theoretical basis for the existence of a relationship between the size of a firm's foreign footprint (its multinationality) and its performance." Glaum and Oesterle (2007, p. 308) argued that "there is the fundamental theoretical question of whether one can expect a systematic positive (or negative) relationship between firms' internationalization processes over time, or their degrees of internationalization at any point in time, and their contemporaneous or subsequent performance." Verbeke and Brugman (2009, p. 265) argued, "firm-level performance depends primarily on the characteristics of the companies' firm specific advantages (FSAs) rather than on their degree of multinationality."

Hennart (2007) urged researchers to better understand the role of managerial action and of organizational processes in the quest to capture the potential benefits of internationalization as well as the impact of the size of the domestic market on the level of internationalization. Although not explicitly mentioned by Hennart (2007), the potential growth opportunities in the domestic market may in fact play a stronger role than market size.

METHODS

Some scholars have called for in-depth case studies in order to clarify and deepen our (currently blurred) understanding of the association between internationalization and performance.

Glaum and Oesterle (2007, p. 315) argued, "[...] the field of International Business and research on the relationship between internationalization and performance would greatly benefit from more in-depth field research, that is, 'clinical' case studies that focus on individual firms and their internationalization processes and experiences over time or research that analyzes such processes on an industry level. Ideally, such research should be longitudinal in nature, relating the firms' specific internationalization processes to their performance over time."

Additionally Glaum and Oesterle (2007, p. 315) contended that "[t]he 3-stage model [cf. Contractor, Kumar, & Kundu, 2007] is based on learning arguments. Hence, it should be tested whether this learning actually takes place and how it works." Much by the same token, Hennart (2007) advocated the study of how organizational mechanisms are put in place so that learning (derived from international operations) is disseminated through and exploited by the firm. Hennart (2007) added that there is a need to investigate the role of managerial discretion and of organizational structures.

In fact, the theoretical performance implications of (changes in) the degree of internationalization are so complex and potentially dependent on several contingencies that they would be better understood through the in-depth investigation of a few cases, rather than through the statistical aggregation of several cases that might differ in several (uncontrolled for) aspects.

Instead of investigating generic impact issues — for example, *what* (shape of the effect of multinationality on performance) or *how much* (magnitude of the effect) in an aggregated sense across multiple firms — this study concentrates on *why* (the motivation) and *how* (the mechanisms by which) firms internationalize, in a quest to uncover the underlying logic that would link particular decisions of international expansion with performance expectations from the decision-maker's perspective.

The research setting of this study is an emerging market – Brazil – which may help shed light on the phenomenon of internationalization, which has been researched mostly in advanced markets contexts ("[v]irtually all such studies [on the internationalization-performance relationship] have focused on advanced nations," cf. Contractor et al., 2007, p. 401).

We conducted in-depth personal interviews in 2013 with five Brazilian firms that stand among the leaders and the most internationalized in their respective industries in Brazil. The interviews were run at the firms' head-quarters with top executives (one executive director or board member in each firm) who were knowledgeable about their firm's internationalization strategies and results. Interviews lasted for about one hour each and were recorded and transcribed.

Before the interview, the research team collected secondary evidence (from the companies' websites, newspaper and business magazine articles, teaching cases, and academic papers) in order to develop a fairly good idea of the internationalization trajectory (dates, countries, entry modes, etc.) of the firms and to customize the interview script accordingly.

The interview script was flexible and, in order to answer our research question, the following main topics guided the conversation:

- motivations to go international
- choice between expanding to more countries (increase in breadth) versus selling more in the current countries (increase in depth) versus selling more in the domestic market
- psychic distance issues
- potential advantages (e.g., lower costs, flexibility, increased revenues) of increasing international breadth
- internationalization depth-related issues (e.g., advantages and disadvantages of foreign sales versus domestic sales, exports versus FDI (foreign direct investment), greenfield FDI versus acquisition FDI, partnerships versus wholly owned subsidiaries, majority versus minority participation in joint ventures; also licensing-related issues, if applicable)
- role of managerial action and of organizational processes/structure (in the appropriation of the potential benefits of internationalization)
- impact of the (large) size of the domestic market and of domestic growth opportunities

- consolidated impacts of internationalization, possible reverse causation (i.e., past performance driving future internationalization decisions instead of the other way around), possible common causation (i.e., identification of factors that might have an impact both on firm's performance and internationalization)

The firms interviewed were (their names have been disguised for confidentiality reasons):

1. F_Poultry – A producer of processed meat (poultry, pork and beef), that also competes in the dairy, margarine, pasta, pizzas, and frozen vegetables segments
2. F_Beef – A producer of processed meat (mainly, beef and poultry), that also competes in leather, products for pets, biodiesel, collagen, and cleaning products
3. F_Pharma – A pharmaceutical lab
4. F_Bus – A manufacturer of bus bodies
5. F_TV – A TV network (production and broadcasting of content), that also competes in several information and media-related businesses (e.g., newspapers, radio, internet)

F_Poultry is the result of a merger, in 2009, of the two largest Brazilian firms in the poultry business. One of these firms was established in 1949 and the other in 1934. The former initiated exports in 1975 and established joint ventures in technology in 1989 (Japan) and in production in 1990 (Portugal); it had processing facilities in Abu Dhabi, Argentina, the Netherlands, and the United Kingdom, with commercial offices in Dubai, Japan, Singapore, and the United Kingdom. The latter started exports in the 1970s, reaching Japan in 1985 and Europe in 1990; it operated one distribution center in Europe and had commercial offices in several countries: Austria, France, Hungary, Italy, Japan, Netherlands, Portugal, Russia, Singapore, Spain, the United Kingdom, and United Arab Emirates.

F_Beef was founded in 1953 and initiated exports to Europe in 1996. Throughout the 2000s it acquired several production facilities in Argentina, the United States, Australia, Italy, Paraguay, Mexico, China, Russia, and Uruguay and distribution facilities in the United States.

F_Pharma was established in 1972 and started exports in 2002. Over the course of the 2000s it acquired or developed production facilities in Argentina, Uruguay, Chile, Bolivia, Venezuela, Colombia, and Peru.

F_Bus was founded in 1949 and started exports (to Uruguay) as early as 1961. In 1971, it entered into a technology transfer agreement with a

Venezuelan firm and opened its first commercial office, in the United States, in 1980. Negotiations with the Japanese for production technology commenced in 1986. The company established wholly owned production facilities in Portugal (closed in 2009), Argentina, Mexico, and South Africa; production partnerships in China, India, Russia (terminated in 2009), Egypt (terminated in 2011), and Canada; commercial offices in China; licensing agreements with China since 1999; and a training center in South Africa.

F_TV was established in 1965 and began to export (to Uruguay) in 1973. It has production facilities in Italy (1985) and Portugal (1993); has licensed content abroad since 1994 and operates an international channel in United States and Japan since 1999; it also has a coproduction agreement with a Mexican firm.

These five companies are particularly relevant to this study because they have a lot of experience in the international arena and can provide evidence of several different approaches to internationalization. Besides, each of them is the leader, or stands among the leaders, in their respective industry in Brazil, thus catering already to a very large share of the domestic market. Such a strong position in the domestic market "imposes" limitations or even constraints on domestic growth.

FINDINGS

In order to facilitate the identification of insights — corroborations with, or contrasts or additions to the literature — we have organized the findings in terms of the following topics:

- motivations to internationalize
- benefits of internationalization
- role of managerial action and of organizational processes and structures
- impact of the size and of potential growth opportunities in the domestic market
- foreign country selection
- foreign entry mode
- control of operations

Motivations to Internationalize

A quest for growth seems to have driven F_Poultry's international expansion in recent years. In the words of the company's Director of Strategic

Planning, Mergers, and Acquisitions: "the orientation of BRF's shareholder is to grow;" "growth is vital for the firm's value and for its perpetuation in the future;" "we focus on growth a lot." Nevertheless, profitability still seems to be one of the most important objectives: "besides profitability, return on assets, there are other metrics that we also seek." In fact, profitability gained even more importance over mere growth since a new board of directors took over in 2013 (Bautzer, 2014), soon after the interview took place.

Initially, F_Beef saw exports as a way to continue to grow after it had become quite large in the domestic market. As reported by a former Director of the Board, "When the firm achieved a certain scale in Brazil, it realized that exporting meat was attractive."

In the early 2000s, F_Pharma's shareholders (the founder and his son) decided that the firm should someday go international, but first they would try to become relevant in the neighboring region (Latin America). The firm has a vision that, by 2015, they will be present in the six countries of Latin America that represent 90% of sales in the region (Brazil with 40%, then, Mexico, Venezuela, Argentina, Colombia, and Chile). Although foreign sales currently represent only 8% of total sales, F_Pharma's International Area and Export Director expects that "by 2020 [foreign sales] will be around 20–25%," that is, "foreign operations will grow much faster than those in Brazil." In 2006, they inaugurated a new factory, which targeted exports from the first day. F_Pharma wants to replicate in other Latin American countries the successful commercial model they developed in Brazil. Unlike several pharmaceutical labs, which take distributors as their primary target (and offer them extended payment terms, discounts, and other commercial advantages), F_Pharma's model is based on close relationships with physicians. As the physicians prescribe a given drug, then drugstores will look for that drug and put pressure on distributors. However, F_Pharma's model does not include personal benefits (e.g., travel, gifts), but rather leverages informational speeches on the therapeutical properties of its products – which represented a change in new markets and demanded substantial effort by F_Pharma's sales force. Overall, a market-seeking motivation has been driving F_Pharma's (recent) expansion abroad.

F_Bus began to export (to neighboring countries in the south of Latin America) because it was cheaper to "drive a bus" into Uruguay and Argentina than into São Paulo or Rio de Janeiro. In addition to the cost argument, F_Bus has targeted foreign countries also because of limitation to growth in the domestic market, especially in the last two decades. As reported by F_Bus' current Director of Investor Relations, "F_Bus already had [at the end of the 1990s] approximately 40–50% of market share in

Brazil. Moreover, F_Bus was thirsty for growth. If we remained only in Brazil, we would forgo growth."

F_TV initially went abroad as a response to unsolicited orders, as pointed out by its Director of International Business: "Some TV channel out there, that wanted content in the Portuguese language, or channels from poor countries (e.g., in Africa);" "it was an entrepreneurial intuition; seize the opportunity; some incidental luck, and transform it." F_TV seems still not to be sure, "whether it is an organization with Brazilian vocation or is, or intends to have, a vocation, a DNA, which could make it, starting from Brazil, a multinational or global company."

Benefits of Internationalization

We will present whether and how the potential benefits of internationalization (cost reduction, flexibility and revenue increase) were achieved, or not, by each of the five firms.

(Unit) Cost Reductions
- Scale economies

F_Poultry's Director said that the firm already works at (plant-wide) minimum efficient scale, so it has no need of international expansion to achieve scale economies: "[The factories] are rather efficient."

F_Beef's interviewee did not explicitly mention any scale benefits from going international. It appears that the firm already operates at an efficient scale in Brazil.

Interestingly, F_Pharma's Director argued that internationalization has helped the firm better utilize the capacity of its factories in Brazil, thus reducing unit costs. The fact is that the laboratory does not sell enough of its own products to be able to exploit the capacity of its factories. It needs to license from other labs and produce their products in its factories. However, in order to be attractive as a potential licensee, F_Pharma would have to lure them with the possibility of selling higher volumes – and the necessary higher volumes could not be obtained solely from the Brazilian market, thus prompting the firm to internationalize to several countries. In the words of F_Pharma's Director: "[...] you start to be more representative, you increase your purchase power, your purchase volume expands, you become more relevant to suppliers [potential licensors], you achieve better terms." F_Pharma maintains that it is easier to increase sales if it uses such (inward) licensing agreements rather than by developing new products. The firm also considers the possibility of (outward) licensing its own products in countries where is does not have a presence. Interestingly, F_Pharma initiated its life as an outsourcer. Today, producing on behalf of others that will stamp their brands represents a small proportion of revenues (about 4–5%); however, it is important because the firm caters to large laboratories, such as Merck, Pfizer Eli Lilly, and Medley.

F_Bus's Director of Investor Relations explains that selling abroad helps the firm dilute its fixed costs: "[...] it is scale economy: the more I sell, the more my fixed cost increases – but not at the same speed," in particular, those costs related to bus-body design and components R&D.

F_TV's costs, related to the production of TV programs, are of a fixed nature. So, the more you sell, the lower the unit cost. However, adaptations are necessary to sell the programs abroad.

- Scope economies (synergies)

F_Beef's former Director explained that the firm decided to diversify over its main beef business by expanding into poultry and pork. This movement aimed at reducing risk: "If you have a serious mad cow disease crisis, [people] stop eating beef, but you still have the chicken." Besides, all these types of meat use "the same distribution channels and the same platform." He also argued that, as the firm becomes larger (also by internationalizing), it can benefit from synergies in administrative and support activities.

The other four firms did not mention anything about synergies.

- Learning

F_Poultry initially reported that learning from abroad "has not been important" for them to apply in Brazil. However, the Director soon added that in the United Arab Emirates they learned about the "cash van," a car operated by an individual salesman that buys little by little of several products in the early morning and then goes about selling those products on the streets. This salesperson starts the day without any order, so, "you have to be one of the first to reach him because he has a limited amount of money and he will buy only cash, because he has no credit rating. You are playing against Gillette, Pantene. You have to wake up early." Another important learning in UAE was that it might pay if you get a local advisor to help obtain certain permits. F_Poultry now plans to apply some of the lessons learned in the UAE in their new foray into China.

F_Beef reported on a lesson learned from direct observation and experience, one that would not be easily learned from consultants, for example. They noticed that in their acquired plants in the United States, they had

Eastern employees who were very good at removing meat from the bone —
they could get 1% more meat than F_Beef's employees in Brazil. And "if
you leave 1% of meat on the bone, you are losing 30% margin." When
asked whether that learning could have been obtained from a consulting
firm or otherwise, he said, "No, no, no. You have to enter; you have to
have a plant. Go there and see what a slaughterhouse is, how they remove
the meat from the bone. [... You have to see it firsthand] in the field." He
also reported that productivity in cattle raising is higher in the United
States: "They kill an ox with an average age of 25 months. Here [in Brazil]
it is 36, 37 months." Of course, there is the fact that in Brazil cattle is raised
on pastures, not fed on industrialized feed, but this fact was not mentioned.
The firm contends, though, that, given the similarity in factories across
acquired firms in Latin America, there has not been much learning. Besides
the FDI-based operations, exports also contribute to learning, at least in
terms of rules and regulations: "This learning is important because you
skip a few steps when you enter the market with your own operation."

F_Bus explained why they started FDI in Portugal: "What was the best
bus technology in the world? It was European. [...] Setra [...], Iveco,
Volvo, Scania, MAN — were the best products. Therefore, F_Bus needed
to be close to the best suppliers of parts and the best vehicle manufacturers.
[...] We went to Portugal; bought a company there. What was the objective? Since it was in Europe, there was proximity with large suppliers of bus
chassis, large suppliers of parts — and to bring that to Brazil. With exports,
I was not able to learn. [...] We started to bring European suppliers to
Brazil. [...] it was part of F_Bus' strategy. Let's bring to Brazil the suppliers
providing the best parts and absorb, that is, learn how to make these products." F_Bus argues that (inward) licensing of technology would not help:
"It was very expensive. And the vehicles that run in Europe cannot do well
in Brazil, especially because of the [differences in the condition of the]
roads."

F_TV's Director contends that, "it makes sense to export whenever you
get a positive operational result," because "the informal practice of being
exposed to other realities brings, organically, learning."

Flexibility
- Costs and availability of production factors

The beef business is characterized by small margins, thus leading
F_Beef to seek out lower priced raw materials, scale gains, and improved
practices. By being international and having revenues in strong currencies, the company is now able to get better financing terms.

As it acquired competitors in Latin American countries, F_Pharma, "gained access to new suppliers [...] and, in some cases, paying lower prices [than the firm had been able to obtain in Brazil]."

F_Bus searches for countries where it can "utilize local labor" or reap tax benefits between exporting a fully assembled vehicle versus a knocked-down vehicle. F_Bus reports that productivity in their Brazilian factories is only 40% of that of the Indian factories and that "India's cost is absurdly low compared to Brazil's." In addition, building a factory in Brazil would cost "three times as much." Therefore, having assembly assets in some countries abroad is paramount to the efficiency of F-Bus. Additionally, having a physical presence in other countries allows the firm to find better purchase bargains and be more competitive, including its position in the domestic market: "Where is steel cheapest today? Canada, Mexico, US, or China? Bring it from there where it is cheaper. We managed to do this global sourcing, reducing product cost. What other Brazilian manufacturer can do that? None. All of them have their factories in Brazil." It was not clear however, whether this global sourcing would also have been possible without investment in foreign assets.

- Circumvention of trade barriers

F_Poultry said that if the firm has production in one Arab country, it is allowed to export to the other Arab neighbors. That is why they chose to have a factory in Abu Dhabi.

F_Beef argues that it is important to have a physical presence in different countries in order to circumvent restrictions to exports to some other countries: "If there were barriers [to export] from Brazil or the US to Asia — from Austria or Australia there are none."

F_Bus said that they chose Egypt, not because of the market per se, but "because Egypt has a free trade agreement with Europe."

- Increased bargaining power with Governments
- F_Pharma explicitly stated that being present in more countries would not affect their bargaining power with Governments. In their words, "we had no great benefit, no great incentive, especially because we do not go for that. We have not noticed any great reaction or any great barrier from Governments or [regulatory] agencies."
- Interestingly, F_Pharma reported on a benefit to its activities in the domestic market. The expansion abroad has helped the firm improve its relationships in Brazil with "regulatory agencies, Government, BNDES [the National Development Bank]," because "the Brazilian Government wants to strengthen the pharmaceutical industry in order to help the

trade balance [since the Brazilian] pharmaceutical industry is a net importer."

Increased Revenues
- Higher volumes

F_Poultry and F_Beef are the largest players in their industries in Brazil and have become this large after a merger and several acquisitions, respectively. Given regulatory restrictions to their growth in Brazil, imposed by CADE (equivalent to the US Federal Trade Commission), F_Poultry, and F_Beef see the external market as a natural way to keep growing.

In fact, F_Poultry has a drive for growth, pointed out earlier. Therefore, expanding abroad can feed firm's appetite for revenue growth.

F_Pharma's reasonably diversified portfolio is essential for success in other countries. This portfolio has been rounded out with licensed products from foreign labs. As F_Pharma acquires another competitor abroad, the portfolio expands. Thus, having already a large portfolio, with multiple offers in each set of drug classes, makes F_Pharma more attractive to physicians who already had relationships with the acquired firms and makes F_Pharma more competitive than local firms.

F_Pharma contends that licensing agreements (whereby the firm gains the right to produce and sell drugs patented by other firms) prohibit the licensed products from being exported to firms outside Brazil, where the licensor may have other licensees. However, F_Pharma can circumvent this restriction by selling the licensed products to its own affiliates in other countries. Of course, in order to do so, F_Pharma needs to have FDI (either in production or in commercial facilities) in foreign countries, so that for accounting purposes, the sale from Brazil is an intra-company transaction.

Markets abroad have long been an opportunity for F_Pharma to sell more: "Our focus was to operate in Latin America, Africa, Middle East, and Asia. We started to export to these countries where there were distributors and local producers that wanted to complete their portfolio with products that we had." The firm expects to increase its sales abroad by 25% in the next 10 years, both "from local production as well as from intra-firm trade" – which will demand that it invests in production or commercial facilities abroad.

F_Bus had a strong position in the Brazilian market: "In the 90s we had 40%-50% of the internal market, and F_Bus was avid to grow. If we stayed only in Brazil, we would forgo growth."

F_TV has a particularity: its operations are of fixed-cost nature and, once broadcast in a given market, its main products (in particular, soap operas and TV series) become obsolete there. So, selling content to other countries – and the company can export to more than one hundred countries today – can be very profitable, although adaptations have to be made, particularly in terms of language translation of the programs: "none [of the firm's business models] has great capital commitment [abroad, but] all of them have the potential for high operating margins." Their revenues come mainly from selling advertising space, so the first FDI "was not close to markets with high advertising investment." On the other hand, F_TV could see a potential opportunity to exploit its excellence in content: "At that time [the 80s] there were few commercial TV channels in Western Europe. In Portugal, Spain, Italy, Germany the great majority was state owned. True; it was not a large market in terms of demand; but neither were there any major producers of content." Therefore, F_TV employed a strategy of preemption (over other possible foreign players) in markets with weak competitors.

- Higher prices

According to F_Poultry, moving forward along the value chain can pay: "Someone that processes [the chicken], that adds value and adds a brand – I want to be this guy in these markets." In fact, F_Poultry has built a strong position in the domestic market by not selling basic products, but rather fully processed, packaged, and branded products.

F_Beef contended that distributors and trading companies account for a large part of the margin: "They [a trading company] will retain half the margin and you the other half. [...] So, if I have a production operation in that country, my platform, and have the logistics, when I export to that country I have everything."

- Arbitrage opportunities

F_Beef reported that different parts of the cattle are valued differently across countries. So, if a firm can export (and only large firms would be efficient enough to export), it will be able to maximize its revenues by charging higher prices for certain parts in countries where they are valued most. Besides, "there are times when margins in the US are bad, but in Brazil they are good" and vice-versa. This means that a high breadth (several countries) would be good to performance in this industry. F_Beef said that the impact of international diversification on performance is so great that some small slaughterhouses in Brazil have become so inefficient that they can survive only by evading taxes.

F_Pharma admits, "producing and selling in Brazil is more profitable [than abroad]." As such, short-term profitability is not the main drive behind internationalization.

F_Bus "seeks internationalization as a way to fight imbalances. [...] One of the objectives of internationalization was to create development buffers and better production dynamics and stability to growth." The fact that the firm has plants outside Brazil allows it to shift production where the exchange rate makes it more favorable to produce abroad. F_Bus maintains that not all export sales would be profitable because freight from Brazil is expensive: "[Vehicles] with low added value are manufactured locally. High value added vehicles can be exported from Brazil." Also, although costs are lower in some countries (e.g., India or China), prices may be also be substantially lower: "The coachwork of a city bus would be sell for US$ 25,000 [in India], whereas in Brazil it would sell for US$ 75,000–100,000." Regarding profitability, the Portuguese operation was not meant to be profitable: "The [short-term] return was not important. We wanted to bring all the best from Europe to Brazil."

- Brand and reputation boosting
- F_Beef contends that (the acquisition of) a well-known brand abroad can help the firm boost its sales in the domestic market.
- F_Pharma believes that, as the firm expands to more countries, it boosts its reputation in the eyes of the doctors who can prescribe their drugs: "Today F_Pharma is a well-known brand in Latin America because we are present in several countries."

Role of Managerial Action and of Organizational Processes and Structures

Although F_Poultry established an international business unit back in 1994, only after 2005 it engaged in "a deeper discussion about going out of Brazil and having assets outside Brazil."

F_Beef made it clear how important it is to have attentive managers: "There is the eye of the owner there;" "the firm's president spent years in the US, managing;" "whatever good there is there, they managed to capture." The story about the role of the firm's president in how they learned to remove one percent more of meat is illustrative. When prompted about whether the company had been able to implement the necessary organizational restructure after having acquired so many firms abroad, F_Beef said that they had been successful (although some business magazine reports and also anecdotal evidence might suggest otherwise). When asked whether a less attentive owner might not have been able to achieve the necessary synergies, F_Beef said, "Maybe not." The company makes a point of transferring the best practices across countries.

Despite having a commercial model that is different from those previously employed by the firms it acquired abroad, F_Pharma understands that it cannot simply replace people. In fact, as a way to learn business practices and rules in the new markets, and as a way to keep relationships with doctors, F_Pharma endeavors to retain 100% of employees, as well as owners and executives, for a at least two to three years. F_Pharma also expatriates some of its staff, in order for them to learn (good) practices abroad and then transfer them to the Brazilian operations as a way to foster mutual learning. Moreover, the firm now has an organizational area dedicated to international operations. The director adds that, "in the future, if we want to be a global company, we will have to develop internal conditions that give support to the global experience."

F_Bus explicitly runs interchange programs whereby Brazilians go to its plants abroad, and foreigners (employees and partners) spend time in Brazil. Furthermore, they rotate employees: "the people that used to be in South Africa are now deployed in India. We run these shifts – they go – return to Brazil – stay for a while – and then go back again." Additionally, videoconferencing is used, and the firm has built a school that helps training foreign employees and inculcating best practices.

F_TV is adamant that, "there has to be some mobilization in order to ensure that learning comes and feeds the organization as a whole." Nevertheless, the Director also adds that, "the informal practice of being exposed to other realities, provides organic learning." Moreover, "the catalyst is a corporate culture that is open to that – a corporate culture that understands that living other experiences gives you access to better practices, which may or may not translate into better activities. I think the best way to do that is through collective commitment; in other words, engaging [the organization] from the top."

Impact of Size and of Potential Growth Opportunities in the Domestic Market

Despite the fact that the Brazilian markets for poultry and beef are quite large and have good growth prospects, F_Poultry and F_Beef are both already so large that the Brazilian authority, CADE, imposes limits to their growth, especially in terms of acquisitions. Thus, exporting and FDI (usually, through acquisitions) become the alternative ways to grow. Nevertheless, F_Poultry's Director argues that there are no impediments to growing organically in the domestic market and that opportunities in terms of innovation still exist. He also contends, however, that this growth (especially by middle class consumers – in terms of both volume as well as value-added products) may meet an end someday; therefore, "the trend to go abroad is natural."

Interestingly, F_Beef also became so large in the United States (after a few acquisitions) that it cannot grow through acquisitions there any longer. Therefore, its alternative is to grow organically or else to search for new countries. F_Beef noticed that being originated from a large domestic market gives the firm some scale advantage: "It starts from a high V_0. [...] Scale is fundamental."

F_Bus brings an interesting perspective to growing domestically versus abroad. With headquarters and factories located in the south of Brazil, it was always cheaper for the company to drive (and sell) its buses into Argentina or Uruguay, and then to Sao Paulo, for example. F_Bus still has a lot of potential to grow in the domestic market, but faces fierce competition; therefore, exporting is an easier way to grow.

F_TV's director argues that, "the greatest inhibitor to going abroad is the size of the domestic market. Brazil is one of the largest advertising markets in the world, one of the fastest growing, and with some of the highest rates of return, where we have absolute leadership, we know with richness of detail about the various stakeholders in the business, the political and regulatory environments, the market and the consumer, and the technology. Any 5% organic growth in the Brazilian market represents, in absolute values, the size of the Portuguese market in one year." As such, the firm has good reasons to concentrate on the domestic market: "Returns here [in Brazil vs. abroad] are higher and risk is lower; that is, it's a risk that I know better how to handle." He continued: "To what extent do the benefits of going abroad overcome the risk exposure?" On the other hand, F_TV acknowledges that, "as the Brazilian market grows, it will attract new entrants," and rivalry will increase. [However], "it makes sense to be present in several countries because the inherent risks in this business are low, and the level of necessary adaptation – regulatory, tax-related or exchange rate-related – is also low relative to the benefits. In other words, it is a high operational margin activity." Therefore, he adds, "it is an ambiguous situation: to have a motivation to go abroad because you have such a large market and [also] to have such a large set of threats here that you have to reposition and become stronger [in the domestic market]." However, back in the 1980s, the company was already a clear leader, although the domestic market was not so well developed or promising. In addition, the Italian market looked quite attractive, so the firm acquired a business there.

Foreign Country Selection

F_Poultry chooses countries for exports based on demand potential, not psychic distance concerns: "We chose the largest [countries]. We look at the consumption of the products that we produce now or we look at consumption trends." However, the largest markets are not always accessible through exports: "I cannot export to Colombia, Peru, or Argentina. [... There are] restrictions because of local policies. They have their trade balance to maintain." The firm has "focused on developing countries," where there is growth potential. In Europe, on the other hand, the current large size of the market is quite attractive and "we want to go on aggregating value to our basic product." Selling to the United States is difficult because they are self-sufficient.

In addition, retail configuration is highly relevant: "India has just 5% of traditional retail. That is bad because it is very difficult to distribute. So then, a higher number is good? Not always: Germany has 83% of traditional retail, but concentration in the top three retailers is huge. It breaks you because of bargaining power." Moreover, the choice of target countries for exports takes into consideration the level of sanitary and commercial (non-sanitary) barriers, and countries for FDI are chosen after checking for the availability of raw materials (e.g., corn for animal feed).

The choice of where to have production facilities is also carefully scrutinized. In Arab countries, if the firm has production in one market, it is allowed to export to the others: "This factory in Abu Dhabi is going to feed distribution and sales in several markets." In order to have FDI in a given country, F_Poultry wants to make sure that it will be either the largest or the second largest player in that country.

F_Beef also argues that the choice of markets is driven by "where there is high demand and high production," not issues related to psychic distance. Additionally, physical presence in some countries is initiated as a way to circumvent barriers: "I cannot export from here. But, if I am out there, operations continue. It is a way to mitigate the risks of sanitary barriers." The choice of locations with low risk of pests is also important when FDI in production (cattle raising) is considered.

F_Bus reported that what counts now is demand. In relation to F_Bus, the target countries are those with low average personal income and large territory (i.e., where buses are needed) and weak local competitors. F_Bus also reported that Egypt was an interesting country, not because of the market there, per se, but "because Egypt has a free trade agreement with Europe." Nonetheless, they began their exports in neighboring countries in South America and first expanded only regionally. Even their first FDI was in a psychically close country: Portugal. "Because of the language [...] 20 years ago nobody could speak English." Therefore, a psychic distance perspective does seem to have played a role. However, it should be noted that the expansion into the first two countries – Uruguay and Argentina – was dictated not only by psychic distance concerns, but also by cost considerations: "At that time [early 60s] difficulties in communications and transport were enormous. Roads were precarious. The route [from the South of Brazil] to Sao Paulo would take a week. There was also a great barrier to reach the Northern states, whereas the South American frontiers were half the distance compared to Sao Paulo." Besides, competition in these neighboring countries was much less fierce than in Sao Paulo or Rio de Janeiro at that time.

Cultural affinities led F_TV's choice of countries: "Our creation and production talent is more representative in Hispanic markets, in Spanish or Portuguese." Additionally, F_TV argues that in some industries, you have to be global; but in the media industry, you can be local or regional.

Foreign Entry Mode

F_Poultry's foreign expansion is still mostly export-based. F_Poultry reported on why it is cheaper to produce chicken in Brazil and export to the Middle East than to produce there: "In order to raise chicken in the Middle East, you need a shed with air conditioning. They do not have grain, water, or the right temperature." The Director adds that the productivity in the field in Brazil is even higher than that of the United States.

F_Poultry tends to believe that entering a new country with greenfield investment in production plants can lead to higher rivalry against competitors (because of the addition of capacity) and possibly lower prices than entering through acquisitions. However, in some countries the firm has not been able to find an appropriate target to buy. Therefore, if it decides to have facilities there, it will have to build them from scratch. This was the case in Abu Dhabi, a plant used as a platform to sell to other Arab countries. F_Poultry operates some distribution assets abroad, but, in most cases, it relies on third-party distributors. If the firm "believes that it can implement better practices and gain competitiveness," it will internalize foreign distribution.

F_Beef has chosen FDI, through acquisition, as the way to grow abroad. Buying out competitors abroad was cheaper for F_Beef than if they had to grow organically. In addition, there was the advantage of buying an ongoing business, which saved time. Besides, acquisitions do not add new capacity, thus averting issues of rivalry. On the other hand, there was, in some cases, some negative legacy, such as poor locations and environmental liabilities.

F_Beef also means to forward-integrate into distribution: "besides improving quality, more added value, the firm stopped selling to distributors – it became its own distributor. This is a systematic process, where you start with margin gain, you remove one intermediary." F_Beef also "buys [meat] from third parties and sells in the market. Once it has all these channels in place, it does not sell only its own meat."

F_Pharma has accumulated extensive experience with acquisitions in Brazil. Therefore, the acquisition of other firms abroad seems to be quite natural for them. Once they have assets (either production or commercial) abroad, they can also start intra-firm sales from Brazil.

F_Bus reports that exporting a fully assembled bus to a distant place is very expensive because a bus "occupies too much space" in a ship. Thus, to distant countries, the firm exports a completely knocked-down or a partially knocked-down bus and then operates assembly facilities there. On the other hand, in relation to close countries, they can export the full bus "running," that is, drive the bus. In terms of FDI, F_Bus prefers acquisitions: "The reason [for the preference of acquisitions over greenfield] is the speed and the chance to make use of the potential that the [target] firm already has in the local market."

F_Bus gets some foreign revenue from licensing to other manufacturers. They say that they are not afraid of being betrayed by a licensee because "F_Bus' brand is stronger than any other one." Besides, when the licensee's employees return to their countries, after having been trained at F_Bus, they become "F_Busnists."

F_TV has opted not to invest heavily abroad. Rather, it uses two types of outward licensing agreements: direct licenses of series, soap operas and documentary films, and licenses of sports broadcasting rights. However, the firm also operates F_TV International, which broadcasts to Latin communities in the Americas and Portuguese-speaking countries and has coproduction of original content abroad.

Control of Operations

F_Poultry prefers to have a majority stake: "Ideally, we would buy 51% on day 1, keep the partner for some time and have some exit strategy for him after we feel comfortable," that is, after they "understand the local rules." Even when it has a minority stake, BRF tries to keep the operational control of the venture. In fact, F_Poultry's Director stated: "In order to build a true multinational, we would like to have fewer partners. Partners sometimes complicate your plan." In Abu Dhabi, F_Poultry partnered with a local firm, but said that it could do it alone if necessary because the institutional environment is safe – unlike that in China.

F_Pharma also prefers a majority stake: "It is fundamental [to have majority control] because it is part of our strategy to control the operations, not the least because we believe that our strategy has great chances of success in those countries." F_Pharma's director goes further: "I do not want to share with anyone; I do not want any partner on my neck." Today, "except for operations in Chile, all others are 100% F_Pharma."

On the other hand, F_Bus prefers partnerships – preferably with the market leader, which has extensive knowledge about the market and relationship with clients – rather than do it alone.

Additional Insights

Cost of Assets Acquisition

F_Beef has grown abroad mostly through acquisitions. The company says that it is important to be selective in choosing the targets. That is, F_Beef seeks firms that are poorly managed or facing financial difficulties – thereby enabling F_Beef to pay a lower price and do the turnaround profitably (as they did in Argentina and the United States). This argument mirrors the resource-based view (Barney, 1986, 1991) as far as the costs of developing or acquiring strategic assets are relevant to performance.

Much by the same token, F_Pharma also searches for firms with unfulfilled potential, usually smaller and cheaper ones, albeit with a strategic asset: relationships with doctors. Such relationships provide the potential to grow – as long as they are given a good portfolio of products to sell. As the Director put it, "the idea was to buy an entrance ticket and not a large operation among the 10 or 15 main ones, but rather buy the number 40 or the number 50 firm in those markets."

Competitive (Ownership) Advantages and Endogeneity Issues
All the Brazilian firms investigated here developed important competitive advantages *prior* to going international. The majority of these advantages were similar to those possessed by "traditional" advanced market MNEs (cf. Ramamurti, 2009) – such as technical expertise and branding.

F_Poultry had achieved production and distribution excellence and had developed strong reputations for its brands (at least in the home country). In order to start FDI in plants to add value to the plain chicken it used to export, F_Poultry chooses places where it already has a large export base – and thus would reap economies of scale in processing activities.

F_Beef developed experience in integrating acquired firms in Brazil, much earlier than it started its forays abroad. The firm had developed high economies of scale and excelled in production. But F_Beef, nonetheless, had somewhat neglected brand development – although they have recently started to compete on branding also.

F_Pharma also achieved economies of scale and excellence in production as it grew its OEM model, but it forwent brand development and product innovation. The acquisitions of other labs in Latin America enlarged its portfolio and enhanced its attractiveness to doctors – the diversified portfolio – and the chances to find other labs to license to F_Pharma ("we could present a market not of 200 million people [Brazil], but of 500 hundred million in all Latin America").

F_Bus excelled in production (learned from diligent study of Japanese production philosophies (e.g., just-in-time and *kanban*)) and in product technology. Their buses are particularly well adapted to the harsh conditions of roads that can be found in other emerging markets. The firm's ties with well-known manufacturers paved the way to brand recognition: "We had the bus body, but there was a Mercedes [with the bus chassis] or a Volvo or a Scania supporting it, that knew us here from the beginning. Then, they [the potential clients] would say, 'The guys in Brazil are good'." F_Bus also developed technical excellence in services as a cornerstone of its competitive strategy; even in foreign countries, F_Bus employs their own staff in technical maintenance facilities.

F_TV was a pioneer in the TV and radio industries in Brazil and developed product excellence (e.g., in soap operas), reaped economies of scale in the domestic market (where it had the largest market share among competitors) and attracted the most talented pool of artists, that is, had workforce excellence.

Given that these firms had built up competitive advantages prior to their internationalization, there may be a complex link between internationalization and performance. Maybe internationalization has helped them enhance their previous competitive advantages (or even develop new ones), but a reverse causation issue may be in place here: possibly the ex ante competitive advantages are driving internationalization process as well an affecting performance.

DISCUSSION

Some interesting insights can be drawn from this study, related to the association between international diversification and performance.

A Real Options Approach to International Diversification

First, it is worth noting that none of the firms interviewed articulated any clear measure of performance associated with increase in their degree of internationalization. Similar to what Pradhan and Aggarwal (2011) reported, it seems that internationalization is not being driven just by short-term returns (if any), but rather by the expectations of upgrading competitive advantages, a quest for growth out of the constrained domestic market and longer term survival. It is as if firms are buying "real options."

Although some firms mentioned profitability and return on assets (e.g., F_Poultry), in most cases they indicated only access to a larger demand pool (i.e., growth) and, in particular, cost reductions and flexibility issues. There was no explicit articulation of profitability prospects (estimates or calculations) associated with any particular international expansion decision (e.g., entry into a new country, development or acquisition of facilities abroad, increasing exports to current countries, etc.). Such "omission" should not be immediately associated with a complete lack of focus on profitability consequences, but rather, may be the result of the difficulty to make sense of the myriad of implications for costs and revenues (and also risk of cash flows) that each internationalization decision entails.

Although all these five firms have already secured a large market share in the domestic market, two of them (F_Poultry and F_Beef) contend that growth opportunities (in particular in terms of revenues rather than volume) in the domestic market have not been exhausted – especially if they increase the offer of value-added products for the wealthy and for the rising middle class. For F_TV, there is still potential to grow profitably in the domestic market; and for F_Pharma, it is still more profitable to sell in Brazil than abroad. Thus, it seems that these firms go abroad not in search of higher short-term profits, but rather as a way to secure new opportunities for the future and to build a safer position.

F_TV's Director, however, explicitly mentioned the importance of getting "a positive operational result" from each export decision. Possibly, this calculation correctly included only the direct marginal costs (fixed and variable) associated with exports and not the sunk costs of developing the TV content (to be primarily sold in the domestic market). Rather surprisingly, the other four firms did not articulate any of such calculations regarding exports.

Cost reductions are more immediately visible (e.g., "driving a bus to Uruguay instead of to Sao Paulo," synergies across international operations) and can be more explicitly articulated. However, the not-so-visible costs of doing business abroad often go unmentioned (maybe even unconsidered in the calculations of expected returns). In fact, the recovery of the financial costs of investments abroad (the cost of capital) was never mentioned by the interviewees. It seems that decisions are based more in the comparison of (increased) revenues and respective (increased) operational costs, thus neglecting the associated capital costs.

The benefits accruing from learning or from acquiring strategic assets abroad (e.g., F_Bus in search of top-level technology) are not easy to anticipate. Therefore, learning expectations and strategic asset seeking (and the consequent benefits) are like buying a real option.

While the idea of real options is appealing, there are "coordination costs that can mitigate benefits of operational flexibility" (Tong & Reuer, 2007, p. 215); such costs, however, have not been explicitly articulated by the firms in the current study. It seems that firms would pay more attention to potential gains derived from flexibility, but would not factor in all of the costs and the risks – in particular, capital costs and switching costs – that can "influence potential operational flexibility in MNCs" (Tong & Reuer, 2007, p. 227). In fact, bounded rationality issues may prevent managers from "bas[ing] international strategy decisions on greatest expected returns given firm attributes" (Powell, 2014, p. 212).

F_Beef made it clear that they sought firms that were under financial difficulties and, therefore, were cheap targets – which could supposedly be turned around through good management. A similar reason was expressed by F_Pharma, which searched for small firms with still unrealized potential. Thus, these firms do seem to consider the costs to develop or to acquire new resources/assets (cf. the resource-based view).

Bounded rationality and risk avoidance concerns, rather than comprehensive economic analyses, may explain why some firms chose psychically close markets for their (initial) expansion. However, for most part, decisions about country selection and foreign entry mode seem to have been dictated by long-term economic prospects (in particular demand expectations). On the other hand, the preference for wholly owned FDI or majority control over 50/50 or minority FDI seems to derive from a cultural trait of Brazilians (the desire to retain decision power) and not from detailed analyses of advantages versus disadvantages.

While the choice of countries seems to be guided by considerations of "L"ocation advantages (e.g., large demand pool, opportunity to acquire low-priced target firms), compatible with the eclectic paradigm (Dunning, 1988), entry modes still seem to follow a pattern of evolving stages in the establishment chain (first exports, then joint ventures, then wholly owned FDI), compatible with the Uppsala model (Johanson & Vahlne, 1977), albeit not totally sequential. This pattern resembles the contention of Contractor et al. (2007, p. 406) that EMNEs would show "greater propensity for non-traditional international expansion strategies, where exporting and FDI are used simultaneously [early on in their lives]." This was indeed the case for F_Pharma and F_Bus, and, albeit to a lesser extent, for F_Poultry (still heavily concentrated in exports, but also moving up to FDI), F_Beef (whose internationalization path is heavily dependent on FDI), and F_TV (still mainly employing exports).

The Complex Association between International Diversification and Performance

The discussion that follows will make it clear that it is not easy to find any single measure of the degree of internationalization construct that would exhibit a universal relationship with performance. In fact, simplistic and aggregated measures — for example, FSTS (foreign sales to total sales) or FATA (foreign assets to total assets) — that have been used in most of the empirical studies on the association between internationalization and performance are too crude to capture the subtleties by which different forms of expanding and operating abroad impinge on performance.

Contrary to often-used argumentation in empirical studies, that internationalization enables firms to gain economies of scale, F_Poultry's case illustrates that this is not always the case – in particular, when the firm already operates at the minimum efficient scale in its domestic market (this point was also raised by Hennart, 2007). So a simple measure of foreign sales (e.g., FSTS) or of foreign assets (e.g., FATA), would not be associated with performance implications in such cases, at least not for that reason.

Besides, FSTS would treat all sales as similar and would not distinguish between profit impacts of selling distinct products – see, for example, the case of low value added vehicles reported by F_Bus. In addition, sales from exports versus from FDI are not distinguishable in FSTS, although the returns from each entry mode may be quite distinct depending on the contingencies.

Moreover, F_Bus makes it clear that it is not the mere volume of foreign sales that counts, but how the firm conducts its operations. Export sales of fully assembled vehicles to close countries would be less costly than export sales of parts to an affiliate followed by an assembly plant and local sale by the affiliate. When exporting to a distant market, the converse would be less costly. Therefore, it is not just FSTS that counts, but also the costs of how you operationalize the sale.

The benefits of arbitrage in the factor markets can sometimes be obtained only if the firm has production facilities in foreign countries, so it can learn about the local suppliers that do not (yet) export to other countries. If the firm only exports, but does not produce in foreign countries, it may not be able to buy from these cheaper suppliers, as illustrated by F_Pharma's case.

The choice of having own distribution assets in the foreign market or relying on arm's length transactions with local distributors is not a universal decision, but will depend on the relative skills of the firm versus potential local distributors, as reported by F_Poultry. Additionally, the choice between production abroad versus exports is not universal: F_Poultry will tend to raise their chicken in Brazil while F_Bus may tend to have some assembly facilities abroad. Once again, increasing FATA may have distinct impacts on performance depending on the particular circumstances of the industry and of the firm. Given that Brazil has some country-specific advantages in chicken breeding, it would be better to raise chicken in Brazil and export them than to raise them elsewhere. Nevertheless, there may be industries in which to have production close to the market represents a better solution. Therefore, there is no simple logic connecting the level of FATA with performance.

Regarding learning, Hennart (2007) argues that oftentimes one can learn from indirect sources — for example, external observation or consultants. F_Beef, however, explicitly said that some learning only occurs by directly being there; thus FDI would be a necessary condition.

In order to gain the benefit of learning from foreign operations, some firms have explicitly implemented organizational processes. This was also the case with F_Pharma, which retained employees of the acquired firms and expatriated some of its Brazilian employees so that mutual learning could take place. Besides, the firm established a dedicated organizational structure to international operations. Such managerial discretion is not captured by FSTS or FATA.

Selectivity in the choice of countries for FDI is also paramount for profitability. F_Bus' Director reported that productivity in Brazil is 40% of that in India and that costs in India are substantially lower than in Brazil. In fact, besides differences in "engineering" (technical) terms, one also has to consider differences in money terms (Itaki, 1991). Thus, it is not just FATA per se, but the "L" advantages of where the firm locates its FDI.

Additionally, FATA will not capture the impact implications of different types of activities abroad — for example, production, distribution (F_Poultry, F_Beef) or maintenance (F_Bus). While F_Poultry has only recently started to invest in more value-added activities abroad (e.g., processing and branding), F_Bus has for quite a long time been advanced in the value chain abroad (by strengthening its brand name, be it through exports or through FDI) and F_TV has always exported high value-added products. On the other hand, F_Beef still concentrates its efforts in the first steps of the value chain (although it is moving slowly into distribution and branding), and F_Pharma has invested in manufacturing, but not R&D, facilities abroad. These different paths to success suggest, again, that FATA is too crude a measure to capture the implications of different internationalization strategies.

Furthermore, FATA does not distinguish between greenfield versus acquisition-based FDI. However, as stated by F_Poultry, the former can have a negative impact on prices (due to capacity addition and consequent increase in rivalry) as compared to the latter.

Simply having more (or fewer) foreign assets cannot be immediately equated with performance implications. F_Beef makes it clear what are the advantages and disadvantages of acquisitions over greenfield investment in its particular case. Additionally, the firms clearly argued about selectivity in choosing "cheap" targets — those firms where the buyer would be better able to increase the difference between (present value of) profit prospects (in the hands of the new owner) and price paid. However, a distinction between acquisition versus greenfield, or information about the price paid for the assets or the prospects of turnaround are not captured by simplistic measures such as FATA.

The choice between greenfield versus acquisition can depend on the firm's past experience with one mode or the other, as illustrated by F_Pharma's case. Although this choice does not make any difference in the FATA measure, it can make quite a difference in performance.

The reports provided by Brazilian executives, as well as anecdotal evidence, suggest that Brazilians strongly prefer to retain control in partnerships. However, being a majority shareholder may not always mean the best for the joint venture, and simplistic measures, such as FATA, would not capture this subtle difference. In addition, owning assets solely versus in partnership can lead to distinct performance implications, as stated by F_Poultry and F_Bus.

F_Phama's case illustrates that different forms of internationalization may lead to different results, and oftentimes such results depend on a combination of internationalization decisions: the impact on sales as a result of licensing drugs from other firms (inward internationalization) will be compounded if F_Pharma also has assets in foreign countries (outward internationalization) and, thus, can sell (intra-company) to them – and vice-versa. Therefore, a single measure of foreign assets (e.g., FATA) would not capture the interaction effect of complementary modes of internationalization.

The size and the growth opportunities in the domestic market might have distinct implications for distinct firms. While growing in the domestic market would tend to be less costly than exporting or investing in assets abroad, some firms that are already very large will be limited by authorities in their growth in the domestic market. For these firms, the impact of internationalization will be greater than for the firms that still have leeway in the domestic market. The case of F_Bus is also illuminating: some foreign markets are closer, and thus cheaper to serve, than the potentially large domestic market.

Furthermore, measures of dispersion (geographic or psychic) may not fully capture the impact of the choice of foreign countries on performance. Admittedly, at a given level of sales, the more similar the foreign market, the lower the probable costs. However, geographically or psychically close countries are not always the most attractive ones in terms of demand potential or in terms of bargaining power with distributors (see F_Poultry's case). It is not so much the *number* of countries that counts, it is *which* countries. F_Poultry, F_Beef and F_Bus make it clear that different countries have distinct growth and profitability prospects.

It is difficult to discern any clear and direct influence of degree and internationalization and performance. Not only is DoI a quite complex construct — whose particular dimensions may exert distinct and complex influences on performance — the mechanism of influence may not be mediated or moderated instead of direct. In addition, a change in one dimension of DoI (e.g., number of countries) is usually associated with changes in other dimensions (e.g., foreign sales), making it difficult to isolate the impact. Besides, a change in one dimension of DoI (e.g., increase in foreign sales) can be the result of several different paths (e.g., more exports, more (outward) licensing, more FDI, and related sales), each of which have quite distinct implications to costs.

Additional Insights

Given that Banalieva and Sarathy (2011) argued that the impact of internationalization on performance would be moderated by the degree of Government support and financing to internationalization, it is worth mentioning that only one of the five firms investigated here (F_Beef) was heavily financed (with equity and debt) by the Brazilian Government through BNDES (the National Development Bank), in a not officially admitted policy of "national champions."

Contractor et al. (2007, p. 408) argued that "older firms are more prone to strategic inertia and less flexible in terms of adapting to changing external conditions[; and t]his may be more valid for the relatively larger emerging market firms, many of which have grown in a protected home market under traditional family controlled environments." All the five firms in this study were family-controlled for many years, but three of them (F_Poultry, F_Beef and F_Bus) are now publicly listed. Maybe expect for F_TV, all the other four firms seem to be quite willing to adapt to new markets and respond to new challenges.

CONCLUSIONS

All in all, the findings suggest that idiosyncratic characteristics of the firms (e.g., size, FSAs), of the industries, and of the host countries (i) affect whether firms tend to internationalize more or less; (ii) affect the advantages of one given entry mode over another; and (iii) play an important role in the impact of internationalization on performance. As such, the effect of international diversification on performance may have an endogenous component. If such variables are not controlled for, empirical results may be misleading.

Matched samples (for example, by employing propensity score matching) would be recommended in order to somehow control for these endogenous effects.

Given the (firm or industry) contingencies, and the multidimensional nature of the "degree of internationalization" construct, it is not possible to formulate a general theory relating level of DoI with level of performance. In fact, the path to international success by firms in a given industry may be distinct from what one would expect to find in other industries. Additionally, firms with different competitive advantages (e.g., low cost vs. differentiation) may choose to structure their international operations distinctively — for example, in terms of country selection or entry mode (exports vs. licensing vs. FDI) or types of activities abroad (e.g., production, distribution, maintenance, etc.). This state of affairs may lead to a situation of equifinality — whereby different paths may lead to similar outcomes.

Thus, one can advocate the use of a more holistic rather than reductionist approach (cf. Venkatraman & Prescott, 1990), whereby one would not search for bivariate relationships between (a given aspect of) degree of internationalization and (a given aspect of) performance, but rather for patterns and combinations of "ingredients" and "causal recipes," as would be provided by a qualitative comparative analysis, QCA (cf. Ragin, 2008) in a cluster-like fashion (Fiss, 2007) or a fuzzy-set logic fashion (Fiss, 2011). Therefore, a configurational approach (e.g., clusters or fuzzy-sets) and the investigation of necessary and/or sufficient conditions (explicitly recognizing that the relationship may not be merely correlational) relating international diversification and performance would be welcome.

Contractor et al. (2007, p. 404) argued, "[s]ince many emerging market firms are small and operate at an uneconomical scale in their domestic markets [which was not the case in the five cases we investigated], even small levels of internationalization may significantly complement their domestic operations." Future studies could examine how smaller and less successful firms differ from large and domestically successful ones in the ways they approach the international arena and in terms of business practices and international performance.

ACKNOWLEDGMENTS

The first author gratefully acknowledges the financial support received from FAPERJ (Fundação de Amparo à Pesquisa do Estado do Rio de Janeiro — Foundation for Research Support of the State of Rio de Janeiro), per grant APQ1 nr. E-26/111.410/2011.

REFERENCES

Banalieva, E., & Sarathy, R. (2011). A contingent theory of internationalization: Performance for emerging market international enterprises. *Management International Review, 51,* 593–634.

Barlett, C., & Ghoshal, S. (2002). *Managing across borders: The transnational solution* (2nd ed.). Boston, MA: Harvard Business School Press.

Barney, J. (1986). Strategic factor markets: Expectations, luck and business strategy. *Management Science, 32*(10), 1231–1241.

Barney, J. (1991). Firm resources and sustained competitive advantage. *Journal of Management, 17*(1), 99–120.

Bautzer, T. (2014). Tempestade na Fábrica [Plant Storm]. *Exame, 48*(7), 38–49.

Contractor, F. (2007). Is international business good for companies? The evolutionary or multi-stage theory of internationalization vs. the transaction cost perspective. *Management International Review, 47*(3), 453–475.

Contractor, F., Kumar, V., & Kundu, S. (2007). Nature of the relationship between international expansion and performance: The case of emerging market firms. *Journal of World Business, 42,* 401–417.

Dunning, J. (1988). The eclectic paradigm of international production: A restatement and some possible extensions. *Journal of International Business Studies, 19*(1), 1–31.

Fiss, P. (2007). Set-theoretic approach to organizational configurations. *Academy of Management Review, 22*(4), 1180–1198.

Fiss, P. (2011). Building better causal theories: A fuzzy set approach to typologies in organization research. *Academy of Management Journal, 54*(2), 393–420.

Glaum, M., & Oesterle, M.-J. (2007). 40 years of research on internationalization and firm performance: More questions than answers? *Management International Review, 47*(3), 307–317.

Hennart, J.-F. (2007). The theoretical rationale for a multinationality-performance relationship. *Management International Review, 47*(3), 423–452.

Hennart, J.-F. (2011). A theoretical assessment of the empirical literature on the impact of multinationality on performance. *Global Strategy Journal, 1,* 135–151.

Itaki, M. (1991). A critical assessment of the eclectic theory of the multinational enterprise. *Journal of International Business Studies, 22*(3), 445–460.

Johanson, J., & Vahlne, J.-E. (1977). The internationalization process of the firm: A model of knowledge and increasing foreign market commitment. *Journal of International Business Studies, 8*(1), 23–32.

Kim, W., Hwang, P., & Burgers, W. (1993). Multinationals' diversification and the risk-return trade-off. *Strategic Management Journal, 14*(4), 275–286.

Powell, K. (2014). From M–P to MA–P: Multinationality alignment and performance. *Journal of International Business Studies, 45*, 211–226.

Pradhan, P., & Aggarwal, R. (2011). On the globalness of emerging multinationals: A study of Indian MNEs. *Economia e Politica Industriale, 1*, 1–18.

Ragin, C. (2008). *Redesigning social inquiry: Fuzzy sets and beyond.* Chicago, IL: The University of Chicago Press.

Ramamurti, R. (2009). What have we learned about emerging-market MNEs? In R. Ramamurti & J. Singh (Eds.), *Emerging multinationals in emerging markets.* New York, NY: Cambridge University Press.

Ruigrok, W., & Wagner, H. (2003). Internalization and performance: An organizational learning perspective. *Management International Review, 43*(1), 63–83.

Tong, T., & Reuer, J. (2007). Real options in multinational corporations: Organizational challenges and risk implications. *Journal of International Business Studies, 38*(2), 215–230.

Venkatraman, N., & Prescott, J. (1990). Environment-strategy coalignment: An empirical test of its performance implications. *Strategic Management Journal, 11*(1), 23.

Verbeke, A., & Brugman, P. (2009). Triple-testing the quality of multinationality – performance research: An internalization theory perspective. *International Business Review, 18*, 265–275.

CHAPTER 19

CHINESE MNCs: AN OVERVIEW OF THE CURRENT STATE OF RESEARCH

Diego Quer-Ramón, Enrique Claver-Cortés and Laura Rienda-García

ABSTRACT

Purpose — *Since the beginning of the 21st century, China's outward foreign direct investment (OFDI) is growing steadily and Chinese multinationals (MNCs) are playing an increasingly important role in the global economy. Thus, the number of papers focusing on China's OFDI and Chinese MNCs has been increasing during the last years. The aim of this chapter is to carry out a review of the empirical papers dealing with Chinese MNCs published between 2002 and 2012 in high-impact international business and management journals.*

Design/methodology/approach — *This chapter reviews 43 empirical papers focusing on Chinese MNCs that were published in nine major scholarly journals between 2002 and 2012.*

Findings — *We report individual and institutional contributions, the theories and methods used, the research topics, and the main findings. We also discuss implications for future research.*

Multinational Enterprises, Markets and Institutional Diversity
Progress in International Business Research, Volume 9, 477–503
ISSN: 1745-8862/doi:10.1108/S1745-886220140000009018

Originality/value – *Some previous literature reviews have dealt with research on China's OFDI and Chinese MNCs. Nevertheless, none of the earlier reviews dealt specifically with empirical papers; neither did they provide an analysis of both individual and institutional contributions.*

Keywords: Chinese MNCs; literature review; empirical papers

INTRODUCTION

Internationalization has traditionally been associated with developed-country MNCs. However, internationalization of firms from emerging economies, in particular from China, is on the rise. OFDI from China multiplied by four between 2007 and 2012, so that, in 2012, Chinese OFDI flows reached $84.2 billion, accounting for 6.1 percent of the world's total (UNCTAD, 2013). As of the end of 2012, Chinese firms have established about 22,000 overseas enterprises in 179 countries and regions (MOFCOM, 2013). Over the recent years, many Chinese companies have made major investments in other countries. The takeover of Canada's Nexen energy group by China National Offshore Oil Corporation (CNOOC), the takeover of the Swiss-Canadian company Addax Petroleum and the partial acquisitions of Repsol YPF Brasil and Syncrude Canada by Sinopec, or the acquisition of a 20 percent stake in Standard Bank of South Africa by Industrial and Commercial Bank of China (ICBC) are some outstanding examples.

Chinese enterprises "going global" are attracting increasing attention among international business scholars and the number of papers focusing on Chinese OFDI appearing in mainstream journals is increasing. After an initial few years when eminently descriptive papers predominated, more recent studies analyzed topics such as the factors that determine Chinese OFDI, the location choice of Chinese MNCs, or the applicability of traditional theoretical frameworks.

Some previous literature reviews have dealt with research on Chinese OFDI. Wei (2010) reviewed some previous studies on OFDI by Chinese MNCs, including 11 empirical papers, although she did not provide a whole description of the journal and paper selection process. Deng (2012) reviewed the scholarship on the internationalization of Chinese firms focusing on 121 articles published in 45 major scholarly journals during the period 1991–2010. Jormanainen and Koveshnikov (2012) examined

50 publications on the internationalization of emerging market multinationals (EMNCs) in 14 top international management journals in the period 2000–2010 (altogether 28 out of 50 articles focused on Chinese MNCs). Berning and Holtbrügge (2012) analyzed 62 articles on Chinese OFDI in 15 peer-reviewed academic journals that were published between 1986 and June 2012. Bai and Johanson (2012) reviewed 42 articles dealing with Chinese firms' internationalization published in five leading international business journals and two dominant Asian journals in management studies from 2005 to June 2012. Finally, Deng (2013) reported a detailed analysis of 138 papers on Chinese OFDI published in 41 journals between 2001 and 2012 from a theoretical advancement perspective.

All the above-mentioned literature reviews covered both empirical and conceptual papers. Nevertheless, none of the earlier reviews dealt specifically with empirical papers focusing on Chinese OFDI; neither did they provide an analysis of both individual and institutional contributions. Therefore, our aim is to fill this gap by carrying out a review of the empirical papers dealing with Chinese OFDI published between 2002 and 2012 in high-impact international business and management journals. More precisely, an effort is made to answer the following questions: Which authors and academic institutions have published the largest number of contributions? What are the main findings and theoretical approaches? What are the issues that have received the most attention? What are the emerging issues on this topic?

The chapter is structured as follows. First, we describe the methodology used, the journals we have chosen, and the papers being reviewed. Individual and institutional contributions are provided in the next section. After that, we report the topics analyzed and the main findings. Finally, we summarize the conclusions, contributions, and limitations of this review, together with suggestions for future research.

METHODOLOGY

Journal Selection

We selected nine outstanding international journals organized in three groups. The first group contains five outlets recognized as leading in the field of international business and management: Journal of International Business Studies (JIBS), Journal of World Business (JWB), Journal of

International Management (JIM), International Business Review (IBR), and Management International Review (MIR). They are all considered to be top international journals indexed in the Social Sciences Citation Index (SSCI) and they have been included in the literature reviews on Chinese OFDI by Bai and Johanson (2012), Deng (2012, 2013), and Jormanainen and Koveshnikov (2012).

The second group consists of two journals focused on business and management in the Asian context, both of them indexed in the SSCI: the Asia Pacific Journal of Management (APJM) and Asian Business & Management (ABM). The APJM is considered the leading journal on business and management in Asia and has been included in the reviews of Bai and Johanson (2012), Berning and Holtbrügge (2012), and Deng (2012, 2013), while ABM was included by Deng (2012, 2013). The third group contains two journals focused on business and management in the Chinese context, both also SSCI-indexed: Management and Organization Review (MOR) and Chinese Management Studies (CMS). MOR, the leading journal on Chinese management, was included by Bai and Johanson (2012), Berning and Holtbrügge (2012), and Deng (2012, 2013), while CMS was included by Berning and Holtbrügge (2012) and Deng (2012, 2013).

Paper Selection

After identifying the journals to be analyzed, the next step was to select the papers to be reviewed. The period analyzed was between January 2002 and December 2012 (inclusive). This time frame was chosen due to the reason that it was not until 2002 when Chinese firms have rapidly increased the scale and scope of their international activities. The year 2001 brought a major boost with China's entry into the World Trade Organization (WTO) and, in particular, with the announcement by the Chinese government of the "go out" policy. This initiative sought to promote the international competitiveness of Chinese companies by reducing obstacles to OFDI.

We only considered papers with an empirical content focusing on OFDI from mainland China. Therefore, conceptual papers and empirical papers including samples of firms from Hong Kong, Taiwan, or Macau were left out. After reviewing their objectives and methodologies, we identified 43 papers which met the criteria for inclusion.

Overall, the 43 papers were distributed as follows: 1 (in 2005), 4 (in 2007), 5 (in 2008), 7 (in 2009), 6 (in 2010), 5 (in 2011), and 15 (in 2012).

Thus, there are no empirical papers on Chinese OFDI published during the period 2002–2004, and there is a sharp increase in the number of published papers in the last year considered. With regard to the research methodology used, there is a clear prevalence of quantitative studies (31 papers, 72.1 percent); 21 of them used secondary data, while 10 were based on surveys. Among the 12 qualitative studies (27.9 percent), 10 papers were based on multiple case studies, while the remaining 2 were single case studies.

CONTRIBUTIONS

Contributions Per Journal

The journal which published the highest number of empirical papers on Chinese OFDI was JWB, with 13 papers (30.2 percent), followed by IBR with 6 papers (14 percent), JIBS, APJM, and JIM, with 5 papers each (11.6 percent). Table 1 reports the distribution of the papers according to the journals in which they were published.

Individual and Institutional Contributions

A total of 95 authors affiliated to 62 institutions appear in the 43 papers published from 2002 to 2012. The majority of institutions are from mainland China (13), followed by the United States (12), the United Kingdom

Table 1. Ranking of Journals Publishing Empirical Papers on Chinese MNCs (2002–2012).

Rank	Journal	Number of Papers
1	Journal of World Business (JWB)	13
2	International Business Review (IBR)	6
3	Journal of International Business Studies (JIBS)	5
	Asia Pacific Journal of Management (APJM)	5
	Journal of International Management (JIM)	5
4	Chinese Management Studies (CMS)	4
5	Management International Review (MIR)	2
	Asian Business & Management (ABM)	2
6	Management and Organization Review (MOR)	1
Total		43

(10), Australia (8), and Hong Kong, China (6). To establish the ranking of authors and institutions, we have used the method employed in other reviews to build total appearances and adjusted appearances (Chan, Fung, & Leung, 2006; Inkpen & Beamish, 1994; Kumar & Kundu, 2004; Lahiri & Kumar, 2012; Lu, 2003; Morrison & Inkpen, 1991; Quer, Claver, & Rienda, 2007; Xu, Yalcinkaya, & Seggie, 2008). To determine which authors and institutions published most papers, we analyzed the total number of contributions and then adjusted the figures by applying the calculation procedure described later. Regarding total contributions, every time an author or institution appeared, this counted as one contribution, regardless of the number of authors credited for a paper or the different institutions that appeared. An author's position in the credits of a paper bore no weight on the calculation. However, in the adjusted calculations, only if a paper was by a single author it was considered a complete contribution for that author and for that institution. If two authors were credited, this counted as half a contribution each, a third if there were three authors, and so on.

Table 2 lists the 31 authors that had made at least 0.50 adjusted contributions in the period analyzed. These authors have been ranked first by the number of adjusted appearances, and then by the number of total appearances. When different authors have the same number of total and adjusted appearances, they are ranked in the same position.

Fuming Jiang (with 2.50 adjusted appearances and five total appearances) heads the ranking. In second place is Lin Cui (2 adjusted appearances), followed by Monica Yang (1.50 adjusted appearances), and Paz Estrella Tolentino, Chuan Zhi Liu, Peter Ping Li, Jan Knoerich, Jing-Lin Duanmu, and Ping Deng (all of them with 1 adjusted appearance).

Table 3 shows the ranking of the 34 institutions that have at least 0.50 adjusted appearances in the period analyzed. This table has been drawn up using the same criteria that was used to establish the ranking of authors.

The ranking is headed by the Australian National University, Australia (with 3.50 adjusted appearances and 4 total appearances). The second-highest ranked institution is the University of London, UK (with 2.78 adjusted appearances). The University of Leeds, UK, is ranked third (with 2.10 adjusted appearances), followed by the Adelphi University, USA (2 adjusted appearances), the Chinese University of Hong Kong, China (1.66 adjusted appearances), the California State University, USA (1.25 adjusted appearances), the Xi'an Jiaotong University, China (1.16 adjusted appearances), and the Sun Yat-sen University, Guangzhou, China (1.12 adjusted appearances).

Table 2. Individual Contributions on Chinese MNCs (2002–2012).

Rank	Author	Institution	Total Appearances	Adjusted Appearances
1	Jiang, Fuming	Australian National University, Australia/University of South Australia, Australia/Curtin University, Australia	5	2.50
2	Cui, Lin	Australian National University, Australia	4	2.00
3	Yang, Monica	Adelphi University, New York, USA	2	1.50
4	Tolentino, Paz Estrella	University of London, UK	1	1
	Liu, Chuan Zhi	Legend Holdings Ltd., China	1	1
	Li, Peter Ping	California State University, USA	1	1
	Knoerich, Jan	University of London, UK	1	1
	Duanmu, Jing-Lin	University of Surrey, UK	1	1
	Deng, Ping	Maryville University of St. Louis, USA	1	1
5	Yiu, Daphne W.	Chinese University of Hong Kong, Hong Kong, China	2	0.66
	Liu, Xiaohui	Loughborough University, UK	2	0.66
	Lau, Chung Ming	Chinese University of Hong Kong, Hong Kong, China	2	0.66
6	Wang, Chengqi	University of Nottingham, UK/Renmin University of China, Beijing, China	2	0.50
	Kafouros, Mario	University of Leeds, UK	2	0.50
	Hong, Junjie	University of International Business and Economics, Beijing, China	2	0.50
7	Young, Michael N.	Hong Kong Baptist University, Hong Kong, China	1	0.50
	Yip, George S.	Capgemini Consulting, UK/LBS, University of London, UK	1	0.50
	Wu, Tzong-Chen	National Taiwan University of Science and Technology, China	1	0.50
	Wiig, Arne	Chr. Michelsen Institute, Bergen, Norway	1	0.50
	Tan, Hao	University of Western Sydney, Australia	1	0.50
	Shieh, Bih-Lian	National Taiwan University of Science and Technology, China	1	0.50
	Schüller, Margot	German Institute of Global and Area Studies, Hamburg, Germany	1	0.50
	Schüler-Zhou, Yun	University of Hamburg, Germany	1	0.50
	Rui, Huaichuan	Brunel University, UK	1	0.50
	Kolstad, Ivar	Chr. Michelsen Institute, Bergen, Norway	1	0.50
	Kang, Yuanfei	Massey University, Auckland, New Zealand	1	0.50

Table 2. (*Continued*)

Rank	Author	Institution	Total Appearances	Adjusted Appearances
	Hyland, MaryAnne	Adelphi University, New York, USA	1	0.50
	Ge, Gloria L.	Griffith University, Gold Coast, Australia	1	0.50
	Ding, Daniel Z.	City University of Hong Kong, Hong Kong, China	1	0.50
	Chen, Yuan Yi	Hong Kong Baptist University, Hong Kong, China	1	0.50
	Chen, Stephen	Macquarie University, Australia	1	0.50

Note: The complete table of individual contributions is available upon request from the authors of this chapter.

Table 3. Institutional Contributions on Chinese MNCs (2002–2012).

Rank	Institution	Country	Total Appearances	Adjusted Appearances
1	Australian National University, Canberra	Australia	4	3.50
2	University of London	UK	5	2.78
3	University of Leeds	UK	4	2.10
4	Adelphi University, New York	USA	2	2
5	Chinese University of Hong Kong	Hong Kong, China	2	1.66
6	California State University	USA	2	1.25
7	Xi'an Jiaotong University	China	2	1.16
8	Sun Yat-sen University, Guangzhou	China	2	1.12
9	Loughborough University	UK	2	1
	Zhejiang University	China	2	1
10	Chr. Michelsen Institute, Bergen	Norway	1	1
	Hong Kong Baptist University	Hong Kong, China	1	1
	Legend Holdings Ltd.	China	1	1
	Maryville University of St. Louis	USA	1	1
	Monash University, Churchill	Australia	1	1
	National Taiwan University of Science and Technology	Taiwan, China	1	1
	University of Alicante	Spain	1	1
	University of Surrey	UK	1	1
11	University of International Business and Economics, Beijing	China	3	0.83
12	Chinese Academy of Social Sciences, Beijing	China	2	0.83
13	Fudan University, Shanghai	China	1	0.66
	Nyenrode Business University, Breukelen	The Netherlands	1	0.66
	Technische Universität Bergakademie Freiberg	Germany	1	0.66
14	Brunel University, Uxbridge	UK	1	0.50
	City University of Hong Kong	Hong Kong, China	1	0.50
	Curtin University, Perth	Australia	1	0.50
	German Institute of Global and Area Studies, Hamburg	Germany	1	0.50

Table 3. (*Continued*)

Rank	Institution	Country	Total Appearances	Adjusted Appearances
	Griffith University, Gold Coast	Australia	1	0.50
	Macquarie University, North Ryde	Australia	1	0.50
	Massey University, Auckland	New Zealand	1	0.50
	Nankai University, Tianjin	China	1	0.50
	University of Hamburg	Germany	1	0.50
	University of South Australia, Adelaide	Australia	1	0.50
	University of Western Sydney	Australia	1	0.50

Note: The complete table of institutional contributions is available upon request from the authors of this chapter.

Theoretical Approaches

As Table 4 reports, a large number of theoretical perspectives have been used to analyze Chinese OFDI. Among the most commonly applied are institutional theory (19 papers) and the resource-based view/organizational capabilities perspective (10 papers). These theories are used as the theoretical foundation for 67.4 percent of the papers we reviewed.

Table 4. Theoretical Approaches on Chinese MNCs (2002−2012).

Theoretical Approach	Number of Papers	Authors
Institutional theory	19	Buckley et al. (2007), Chen and Tan (2012), Cui and Jiang (2009b, 2010, 2012), Deng (2009), Duanmu (2012), Kang and Jiang (2012), Klossek et al. (2012), Kolstad and Wiig (2012), Luo et al. (2011), Quer et al. (2012), Schüler-Zhou and Schüller (2009), Wang, Hong, Kafouros, and Boateng (2012), Wang, Hong, Kafouros, and Wright (2012), Yang (2009), Yang and Hyland (2012), Yiu et al. (2007), and Zhang et al. (2011)
Resource-based view/organizational capabilities perspective	10	Cui and Jiang (2009b, 2010), Lau et al. (2010), Liang et al. (2012), Luo et al. (2011), Schüler-Zhou and Schüller (2009), Söderman et al. (2008), Wang, Hong, Kafouros, and Wright (2012), Xu et al. (2009), and Yiu et al. (2007)
Strategic intent	4	Duanmu (2012), Kolstad and Wiig (2012), Ramasamy et al. (2012), and Rui and Yip (2008)
Economics	4	Chen and Tan (2012), Duanmu (2012), Kang and Jiang (2012), and Tolentino (2010)
Ownership−location−internalization (OLI) model	3	Ge and Ding (2008), Li (2007), and Sun et al. (2012)
Strategy tripod (resource-based view/industry-based view/institutional theory)	2	Lu et al. (2011) and Yang et al. (2009)
Knowledge-based view/organizational learning perspective	2	Kotabe et al. (2011) and Zhao et al. (2010)
Transaction cost theory	2	Cui and Jiang (2009b) and Xu et al. (2009)

Table 4.   (*Continued*)

Theoretical Approach	Number of Papers	Authors
Linkage–leverage–learning (LLL) model	2	Ge and Ding (2008) and Li (2007)
Strategic behavior	2	Cui and Jiang (2009a, 2009b)
Strategic management	2	Knoerich (2010) and Liu et al. (2011)
Entrepreneurship/international new ventures (INV)	2	Liu et al. (2011) and Liu et al. (2008)
Industry-based view	1	Wang, Hong, Kafouros, and Boateng (2012)
Agency theory	1	Chen and Young (2010)
Bargaining power theory	1	Xu et al. (2009)
Organizational control theory	1	Shieh and Wu (2012)
Uppsala model	1	Liu et al. (2008)
Investment development path (IDP)	1	Liu et al. (2005)
Social capital perspective	1	Kotabe et al. (2011)
Comparative advantage theory	1	Sun et al. (2012)
Competitive strategy perspective	1	Fan et al. (2012)
N/A (descriptive studies)	2	Buckley et al. (2008) and Liu (2007)

RESEARCH TOPICS AND MAIN FINDINGS

The 43 papers reviewed have been grouped into seven broad categories. These were created ex post, after having examined each paper being included in this review. Table 5 reports the different categories, the research topics included in each one, and the authors who made the contribution.

Internationalization Drivers

The first category includes topics that deal with factors influencing the internationalization of Chinese MNCs and accounts for 23.3 percent of the total, being the largest group. Seven out of 10 papers included in this category focus on firm capabilities, although 4 of them also analyze them along with industry and institutional factors.

Lau, Ngo, and Yiu (2010) suggest that two capabilities (production and sales, and operation and finance) have significant impacts on Chinese OFDI. In addition, manufacturing competencies also have a negative effect on the acquisition and use of international capital. Liang, Lu, and

Table 5. Categories and Research Topics on Chinese MNCs
(2002–2012).

Category	Topic	Authors
Internationalization drivers 10 papers (23.3 percent)	Firm capabilities	Lau et al. (2010), Liang et al. (2012), and Söderman et al. (2008)
	Firm capabilities and industry factors	Luo et al. (2011) and Yiu et al. (2007)
	Firm capabilities and institutional factors	Wang, Hong, Kafouros, and Wright (2012)
	Firm capabilities, industry, and institutional factors	Lu et al. (2011)
	Industry and institutional factors	Wang, Hong, Kafouros, and Boateng (2012)
	Capital market imperfections, ownership advantages, and institutional factors	Buckley et al. (2007)
	Entrepreneurial and market orientations	Liu et al. (2011)
Cross-border mergers and acquisitions (M&As) 8 papers (18.6 percent)	Motivation for M&As	Deng (2009) and Rui and Yip (2008)
	Influence of isomorphism on M&As decisions	Yang (2009) and Yang and Hyland (2012)
	Completion of Chinese overseas acquisition deals	Zhang et al. (2011)
	Government ownership and cross-border M&As outcomes	Chen and Young (2010)
	Factors affecting the sale of firms from advanced economies	Knoerich (2010)
	Critical perspective on Chinese cross-border M&As	Schüler-Zhou and Schüller (2009)
Entry mode choice 6 papers (13.9 percent)	Determinants of FDI ownership decisions	Cui and Jiang (2009a, 2009b, 2010, 2012) and Shieh and Wu (2012)
	Impact of host country risk and cultural distance on ownership equity and status	Xu et al. (2009)
Location determinants 5 papers (11.6 percent)	Differences between state-owned enterprises (SOEs) and private firms	Duanmu (2012) and Ramasamy et al. (2012)
	Institutional and economic factors	Kang and Jiang (2012) and Kolstad and Wiig (2012)
	Political risk and cultural distance	Quer et al. (2012)
Applicability of FDI and MNC models 4 papers (9.3 percent)	OLI model/LLL model	Ge and Ding (2008) and Li (2007)
	Uppsala model/INV/ entrepreneurship	Liu et al. (2008)
	IDP	Liu et al. (2005)

Table 5. *(Continued)*

Category	Topic	Authors
Comparison with other countries 3 papers (7 percent)	Chinese and Indian MNCs	Sun et al. (2012) and Tolentino (2010)
	Chinese and Japanese MNCs	Yang et al. (2009)
Other topics 7 papers (16.3 percent)	Chinese OFDI and productivity within China	Zhao et al. (2010)
	Managerial ties, knowledge acquisition, and performance	Kotabe et al. (2011)
	Establishment mode and liability of foreignness	Klossek et al. (2012)
	Location and performance	Chen and Tan (2012)
	Global integration	Fan et al. (2012)
	Descriptive studies	Buckley et al. (2008) and Liu (2007)

Wang (2012) analyze the extent to which competitive advantages/disadvantages of Chinese private firms (compared to home market rivals) may drive outward internationalization. Their results suggest that a Chinese private firm's likelihood of venturing abroad is associated with resource endowment advantages vis-à-vis foreign-invested enterprises, organizing capability advantages vis-à-vis state-owned enterprises (SOEs), and organizing capability disadvantages vis-à-vis foreign-invested enterprises. Söderman, Jakobsson, and Soler (2008) suggest that Chinese companies reposition themselves strategically when internationalizing. Chinese companies aiming for a high-price/low-volume position focus more on getting international experience, exploring own advantages and branding, while Chinese companies adopting the prevalent high-volume/low-price position put more focus on drivers like efficiency in production, innovation, service, and volume in order to defend or achieve their strategic position.

Two papers analyze the influence of both firm capabilities and industry factors. First, that of Luo, Zhao, Wang, and Xi (2011), who present a dual strategic intent perspective. Ownership-specific advantages in areas such as corporate governance, inherited advantage from M&As of SOEs, and inward internationalization increase the level of outward internationalization of Chinese private enterprises. Market imperfection residuals, such as industry structure uncertainty, also propel the inclination for internationalization. The second paper is that of Yiu, Lau, and Bruton (2007), who report that the relationship between firm-specific ownership advantages and international venturing is moderated by the degree of home industry competition and export intensity. More precisely, Chinese firms with higher levels of technological capabilities pursue more international venturing when home industry competition is stronger, and those with close home country network ties pursue more international venturing when their export intensity is higher.

Drawing on the resource-based and the institutional views, Wang, Hong, Kafouros, and Wright (2012) suggest that government involvement influences the level of overseas investment, its location (developed vs. developing countries), and its type (resource- vs. market-seeking). However, these effects depend on firms' own resources and capabilities, since not all firms possess equal ability to internalize government-related advantages and respond to institutional pressures. Based on the integrated "strategy tripod" perspective, Lu, Liu, and Wang (2011) examine the impact of firm resources, industry dynamics, and government policies on Chinese OFDI motives. Their results suggest that supportive government policies are important motivators for both strategic asset-seeking and market-seeking OFDI. Firms' technology-based competitive advantages and a high level of R&D industry intensity tend to motivate strategic asset-seeking OFDI, whereas firm's export experience and higher level of domestic industry competition tend to induce market-seeking OFDI.

Wang, Hong, Kafouros, and Boateng (2012) report that government support and the industrial structure of the home country play a crucial role in explaining Chinese OFDI. By contrast, technological and advertising resources of Chinese firms tend to be less important. From a conventional viewpoint, Buckley et al. (2007) find that Chinese OFDI are associated with cultural proximity to host countries. However, Chinese OFDI are attracted, rather than deterred, by political risk. They attribute this unprecedented finding to the low cost of capital that Chinese firms (for the most part SOEs) enjoy as a consequence of home country capital market imperfections. Moreover, the experience of operating in a highly regulated and controlled domestic environment may have equipped Chinese MNCs with the special ownership advantages needed to be competitive in other emerging economies.

Finally, Liu, Li, and Xue (2011), drawing on the entrepreneurship and strategy literature, report that entrepreneurial orientation directly promotes firm's internationalization activities, whereas market orientation has an inverse U-shaped relationship with internationalization activities. Regarding this relationship, as a firm's market orientation increases from a low to a moderate level, its degree of internationalization is likely to increase accordingly. However, when market orientation goes beyond a moderate level, international involvement may decrease, because of high transaction costs and risk aversion.

Cross-Border Mergers and Acquisitions (M&As)

We now turn to the second group of topics, which examines Chinese cross-border mergers and acquisitions (M&As). There are eight papers in this group (18.6 percent of the total). Two papers explore the motivations for M&As. Following the institutional-based logic, Deng (2009) reports that Chinese firms increasingly use cross-border M&As to acquire strategic assets because they are under pressure to conform to the home country institutional environment and the prevailing corporate values and norms. Using a strategic intent perspective, Rui and Yip (2008) suggest that Chinese firms strategically use cross-border acquisitions to achieve goals, such as acquiring strategic capabilities to offset their competitive disadvantages and leveraging their unique ownership advantages, while making use of institutional incentives and minimizing institutional constraints.

Two papers analyze the influence of isomorphism on M&As decisions, drawing on institutional theory. First, Yang (2009) examines whether isomorphism and mimetic, coercive, and normative mechanisms apply to Chinese cross-border M&As. The results show that not all decisions on cross-border M&As react to forces of conformity in the same way. Overtime, the overall degree of conformity in cross-border M&As decreases. Factors that significantly affect the degree of conformity include the experiences of failure of other firms in the industry, regulatory changes in China, and China's entry into the WTO. Second, Yang and Hyland (2012) find that mimetic isomorphism is partially supported by Chinese firms. More precisely, the degree of similarity in two cross-border M&As decisions (the product relatedness and the location of target firms) increases when the number of completed deals initiated by others at a prior time increases and when firms can tell what the most popular decision choice is. However, their results suggest that not all cross-border M&As decisions are influenced by mimetic isomorphism, as evidenced by the lack of support for ownership structure.

The rest of the papers included in this category deal with other topics related to M&As. From an institutional perspective, Zhang, Zhou, and Ebbers (2011) find that the likelihood that Chinese overseas acquisition deals are completed is lower, if (1) the target country has a worse institutional quality; (2) the target industry is sensitive to national security; and (3) the acquiring firm is a SOE. Drawing on the agency theory, Chen and Young (2010) analyze the importance of corporate governance and support the notion that principal–principal conflicts exist in Chinese government-dominated publicly listed firms, that is, that investors or minority shareholders are indeed skeptical of cross-border M&As deals when the government is the majority owner. More precisely, this study reports that government ownership is negatively related to Chinese cross-border M&As outcomes, which are measured by cumulative abnormal returns.

By analyzing Chinese acquisitions of German firms, the exploratory paper by Knoerich (2010) illustrates why managers from advanced economies decide to sell their firms to Chinese bidders. From a strategic management perspective, the findings indicate that this happens mainly because the arrangement allows the German side to expand their business and assure future competitiveness, while at the same time ensuring that the Chinese partner can equally fulfill its own goals, such as efficient allocation of capital, market access, and technological advancement. Finally, drawing on the resource-based view and the institution-based view, Schüler-Zhou and Schüller (2009) offer a critical perspective on China's official OFDI data from 1990 to 2007, suggesting that Chinese firms predominantly seek high-level equity participation in the acquired target companies abroad.

Entry Mode Choice

There are six papers (13.9 percent) in this category. The first topic included five papers which focus on the determinants of FDI ownership choice: wholly owned subsidiary (WOS) or joint venture (JV). Cui and Jiang (2009a) report that a Chinese firm prefers to enter a host country through a WOS when it adopts a global strategy, faces severe host industry competition, and emphasizes asset-seeking purposes in its FDI. A JV is the preferred entry mode when the firm invests in a high-growth host market. In another paper, Cui and Jiang (2009b) find differences between Chinese firms and developed-country MNCs in FDI ownership decisions, with Chinese firms putting stronger emphasis on strategic intent than strategic fit, enjoying government support that eases their assets constraints, and receiving institutional influences not only from the host country, but also from their own government.

Cui and Jiang (2010) also develop a conceptual framework that integrates the resource-based and institution-based views. On the resource side, Chinese OFDI are both asset exploiting and asset augmenting, and accordingly, both transaction costs and strategic intents have an impact on the FDI ownership decisions. On the institution side, Chinese firms adjust their entry strategies to attain regulative and normative institutional legitimacy in host countries. Meanwhile, they also need to comply with the rules set by the Chinese government. Furthermore, Cui and Jiang (2012) find that the effects of home regulatory, host regulatory, and host normative pressures on a Chinese firm to choose a joint ownership structure are stronger when the share of equity held by state entities in the firm is high. Finally, Shieh and Wu (2012) report that host country risk, cultural distance, foreign exchange rate, competitive intensity, subsidiary's capital, investment duration, and location in Ho Chi Minh City are significant factors affecting the choice between a WOS and a JV when firms entering Vietnam originate from the Greater Chinese Economic Areas, including mainland China.

The last paper in this category is that of Xu, Hu, and Fan (2009), who report that both host country risk and cultural distance have significant and negative impacts on the level of ownership equity, but insignificant impacts on ownership status of the investing Chinese company in the target company (largest shareholder, second shareholder, etc.).

Location Determinants

This category comprises five papers (11.6 percent). Two of them analyze differences between SOEs and private firms. First, Duanmu (2012) suggests that Chinese SOEs, compared to their peers without controlling state equity, are less concerned about host country political risk, but more responsive to favorable exchange rate between Chinese Renminbi (RMB) and the host currency. Second, Ramasamy, Yeung, and Laforet (2012) find that while Chinese SOEs are attracted to countries with large sources of natural resources and risky political environments, Chinese private firms are more market seekers.

Two papers focus on institutional and economic factors. First, Kang and Jiang (2012) suggest that institutional factors demonstrate a higher level of significance, complexity, and diversity in determining FDI location choice in comparison with economic factors, while both types of factors influence the FDI location choice of Chinese MNCs. Second, Kolstad and Wiig (2012) find that Chinese OFDI are attracted to large markets (Organization for Economic Co-operation and Development – OECD countries), and to countries with a combination of large natural resources and poor institutions (non-OECD countries).

Lastly, Quer, Claver, and Rienda (2012), building on the institutional perspective, report that location patterns of Chinese MNCs show some characteristics that differ from the conventional wisdom, because a high political risk in the host country does not discourage Chinese MNCs. However, from a more conventional point of view, the presence of overseas Chinese in the host country (considered as a proxy of smaller cultural distance) is positively associated with Chinese OFDI.

Applicability of FDI and MNC Models

The fifth category includes four papers (9.3 percent) assessing the applicability of FDI and MNC models to Chinese OFDI. Li (2007) suggests that the traditional ownership–location–internalization (OLI) model, also known as the eclectic paradigm (Dunning, 1981b), and the newly proposed linkage–leverage–learning (LLL) model of MNC formation (Mathews, 2006) can be readily integrated within a content-process framework of MNC evolution so as to better explain all types of MNC from both developed and developing countries, such as China. Ge and Ding (2008) present a case study of one of the most successful manufacturers in China, the Galanz Group, now the world's largest microwave manufacturer. Their findings suggest that the LLL model provides a robust explanation for the catching-up strategies of latecomer MNCs. The essence of Galanz's model lies in the linkage with foreign MNCs via the original equipment manufacturing route, initially producing microwaves for many different international brands (Child & Rodrigues, 2005). This strategy allowed Galanz to gain access to modern production facilities, advanced technologies, technical assistance, and training.

Liu, Xiao, and Huang (2008) argue that the internationalization behavior of indigenous Chinese private-owned firms can only be partially explained by the Uppsala Model (Johanson & Vahlne, 1977) and the theory of international new ventures (Oviatt & McDougall, 1994). Instead, the so-called "bounded entrepreneurship" may be the key influence on the unique internationalization patterns and competitive positions of these firms. Embedded in a transitional and emerging economy, indigenous Chinese entrepreneurs are bounded by their low education and experience and by unfavorable institutional arrangements. They have limited technological, managerial, and linguistic knowledge. Given the bounded entrepreneurship, some of them

carried out inward-oriented internationalization activities to learn technological and managerial knowledge before they started outward-oriented activities. Despite the insufficiency of knowledge, it is entrepreneurship that has
motivated Chinese firms to expand into the world market.

Finally, Liu, Buck, and Shu (2005) suggest that the patterns of Chinese
OFDI are quite consistent with the refined Investment Development Path
(IDP) hypothesis (Dunning, 1981a; Dunning, Kim, & Lin, 2001;
Dunning & Narula, 1996). More precisely, they report that the level of
China's economic development, proxied by GDP per capita, human capital
development, exports, and inward FDI together affect the magnitude of
Chinese OFDI in the long run.

Comparison with Other Countries

This category contains three papers (7 percent) that compare Chinese
OFDI with that of other countries. Two of them focus on Chinese and
Indian MNCs. First, Sun, Peng, Ren, and Yan (2012), integrating the comparative advantage theory with Dunning's OLI paradigm, develop a comparative ownership advantage framework for cross-border M&As by
Chinese and Indian MNCs. Their findings support the following propositions: comparatively, China have intensive cross-border M&As in manufacturing industries; Chinese MNCs prefer to acquire companies in Asia; both
Chinese and Indian MNCs prefer friendly rather than hostile M&As;
Chinese MNCs prefer to acquire natural resource-intensive firms and backward integration in cross-border M&As; and Chinese SOEs generally play
the lead role in large-scale M&As deals. Second, Tolentino (2010) reports
that although China and India share similar inferences about the casual
relationships concerning OFDI flows, Chinese and Indian MNCs are different from each other because of the varying influence of the unique national
economic characteristics of their countries of origin in explaining the variability in their levels of OFDI flows.

The last paper in this category is that of Yang, Jiang, Kang, and Ke
(2009), who demonstrate that industrial characteristics, firm resources, and
institutional factors can significantly explain the differences and similarities
of international expansion of Chinese and Japanese MNCs. Both China
and Japan actively adopted industrial policies, which provided impetus for
domestic firms to expand abroad. However, in China, inward FDI pre-
ceded OFDI and the leading Chinese MNCs are primarily SOEs.
Moreover, when Chinese firms expand abroad, many of them are more

interested in establishing global brands or accessing technological and managerial know-how which further consolidate their competitive position in the domestic market.

Other Topics

The last category includes seven papers (16.3 percent) dealing with other topics not covered by the above-mentioned categories. Zhao, Liu, and Zhao (2010) look at the effects of China's OFDI on growth in its own productivity. Their findings suggest that Chinese OFDI in developed countries have had beneficial spillover effects in improving total factor productivity growth over the period of study (1991–2007), and that gains in efficiency have been the major reason for this development. Kotabe, Jiang, and Murray (2011) explore the effects of managerial ties with government officials and foreign MNC partners on knowledge acquisition and performance. Their results indicate that both business and political ties have a U-shaped relationship with knowledge acquisition. Moreover, knowledge acquisition could only enhance new product market performance with the presence of realized absorptive capacity.

Klossek, Linke, and Nippa (2012) describe how entry mode choice impacts the strategies adopted by Chinese firms to cope with the specific institutional hurdles of a developed country such as Germany, and how they mitigate their specific "liability of foreignness." Chen and Tan (2012) show how internationalization in the Greater China region (comprising Taiwan, Hong Kong, and Macau), which has cultural similarity and historical links to mainland China, has a particularly significant effect on the performance of Chinese MNCs. Fan, Zhu, and Nyland (2012) find that the majority of factors the international business literature argues affect the global integration of Chinese MNCs in Australia. However, four factors (advertising intensity, premium positioning, country-specific advantages, and formalization) are not deemed significant.

Finally, we review two descriptive studies. First, that of Buckley, Cross, Tan, Xin, and Voss (2008) who identify historic and emergent trends in Chinese OFDI for the period 1991 to 2005 with regard to investment destination, activity type, entry mode choice, and investment motivation. Second, that of Liu (2007) who explains the development path of the Chinese company Lenovo, one of the world's leaders in the PC industry. The emphasis is placed on the story of Lenovo's acquisition of IBM's PC division.

CONCLUSION

This chapter has systematically reviewed the empirical research on Chinese MNCs published in nine outstanding journals between 2002 and 2012. Our results indicate that quantitative papers prevail; the JWB published the most papers during this period; Fuming Jiang and Lin Cui were the most prolific authors; the Australian National University, the University of London, and the University of Leeds contributed the most papers; the most common theoretical approaches were the institutional and resource-based views; and the most frequent research topics were internationalization drivers and cross-border M&As of Chinese MNCs.

There are some limitations to this study. First, the limitation inherent to any literature review: the journal selection. Although all of them are major scholarly journals indexed in the SSCI, empirical contributions appearing in other journals have not been considered. The second limitation refers to the classification of research topics, since some papers might have been included in some alternative category.

In spite of this, this study has made a number of interesting contributions. First, we have provided an overview of the current state of research on China's OFDI and Chinese MNCs. Thus, this literature review enhances the knowledge of a phenomenon that gains increasing importance in the international business field. Second, although there are other reviews on China's OFDI, none of them dealt specifically with empirical papers; neither did they provide an analysis of both individual and institutional contributions.

With regard to future research, we consider that more work is needed in order to analyze if the globalization of Chinese firms as EMNCs represents a challenge for the conventional wisdom, mainly based on developed-country MNCs. Indeed, the interest in EMNCs and Chinese MNCs has generated an epistemological debate among international business researchers. While some scholars argue that the analysis of EMNCs requires new theory (Mathews, 2006), others argue that no new theory is required (Rugman, 2010). A third view suggests that it can be used to extend theory, that is the study of EMNCs helps identify some of the unstated assumptions upon which existing theories have been built and extend their predictions (Cuervo-Cazurra, 2012).

Dunning's OLI model is one of the theoretical perspectives that has been subject of debate. Narula (2012) argues that there is a fundamental principle that applies to all MNCs regardless of nationality: there is a threshold of firm-specific assets (FSA) that the firm must possess for such international expansion to be successful. Moreover, beyond different initial conditions derived from the location-specific assets of the home country, as infant EMNCs evolve, the observable differences between them and advanced economy MNCs will diminish. While acknowledging that some EMNCs have genuine FSAs they can exploit in foreign markets, Hennart (2012) takes a more radical view. He argues that the difficulty the OLI model has in explaining some of the OFDI made by EMNCs, specifically their intangible-asset investments in developed countries, arises from a basic flaw. Many host country resource endowments or location advantages (land, natural resources, labor, and distribution assets) are not freely available to all foreign investors. Intangible-asset seeking OFDI by EMNCs can, thus, be understood as ways by which EMNCs with preferential access to this subset of local resources acquire the complementary FSAs they lack to compete with foreign MNCs – first at home and then internationally.

As occurs with Dunning's OLI model, it is necessary to further investigate the degree to which the international expansion of Chinese MNCs follows the prescriptions of other theoretical approaches in the international business literature. Future work might also focus on some under-researched topics such as how Chinese MNCs choose the type of native or expatriate staff for their foreign subsidiaries, how they deal with corporate governance issues, what factors determine the success or failure of Chinese cross-border M&As, or what are the relationships among strategy, structure, and performance in Chinese MNCs.

REFERENCES

Bai, W., & Johanson, M. (2012). Chinese firms' internationalisation: A review and future research topic. *38th annual conference of the European international business academy (EIBA)*, University of Sussex, UK.

Berning, S. C., & Holtbrügge, D. (2012). Chinese outward foreign direct investment – A challenge for traditional internationalization theories? *Journal für Betriebswirtschaft*, *62*(3–4), 169–224.

Buckley, P. J., Clegg, L. J., Cross, A. R., Liu, X., Voss, H., & Zheng, P. (2007). The determinants of Chinese outward foreign direct investment. *Journal of International Business Studies*, *38*(4), 499–518.

Buckley, P. J., Cross, A. R., Tan, H., Xin, L., & Voss, H. (2008). Historic and emergent trends in Chinese outward direct investment. *Management International Review*, *48*(6), 715–748.

Chan, K. C., Fung, H. G., & Leung, W. K. (2006). International business research: Trends and school rankings. *International Business Review*, *15*(4), 317–338.

Chen, S., & Tan, H. (2012). Region effects in the internationalization-performance relationship in Chinese firms. *Journal of World Business, 47*(1), 73–80.

Chen, Y. Y., & Young, M. N. (2010). Cross-border mergers and acquisitions by Chinese listed companies: A principal–principal perspective. *Asia Pacific Journal of Management, 27*(3), 523–539.

Child, J., & Rodrigues, S. B. (2005). The internationalization of Chinese firms: A case for theoretical extension? *Management and Organization Review, 1*(3), 381–410.

Cuervo-Cazurra, A. (2012). Extending theory by analyzing developing country multinational companies: Solving the Goldilocks debate. *Global Strategy Journal, 2*(3), 153–167.

Cui, L., & Jiang, F. (2009a). FDI entry mode choice of Chinese firms: A strategic behavior perspective. *Journal of World Business, 44*(4), 434–444.

Cui, L., & Jiang, F. (2009b). Ownership decisions in Chinese outward FDI: An integrated conceptual framework and research agenda. *Asian Business & Management, 8*(3), 301–324.

Cui, L., & Jiang, F. (2010). Behind ownership decision of Chinese outward FDI: Resources and institutions. *Asia Pacific Journal of Management, 27*(4), 751–774.

Cui, L., & Jiang, F. (2012). State ownership effect on firms' FDI ownership decisions under institutional pressure: A study of Chinese outward-investing firms. *Journal of International Business Studies, 43*(3), 264–284.

Deng, P. (2009). Why do Chinese firms tend to acquire strategic assets in international expansion? *Journal of World Business, 44*(1), 74–84.

Deng, P. (2012). The internationalization of Chinese firms: A critical review and future research. *International Journal of Management Reviews, 14*(4), 408–427.

Deng, P. (2013). Chinese outward direct investment research: Theoretical integration and recommendations. *Management Organization Review, 9*(3), 513–539.

Duanmu, J. L. (2012). Firm heterogeneity and location choice of Chinese multinational enterprises (MNEs). *Journal of World Business, 47*(1), 64–72.

Dunning, J. (1981a). Explaining the international direct investment position of countries: Toward a dynamic and development approach. *Weltwirtschaftliches Archiv, 117*(5), 30–64.

Dunning, J. (1981b). *International production and the multinational enterprise.* London: George Allen & Unwin.

Dunning, J., Kim, C., & Lin, J. (2001). Incorporating trade into the investment development path: A case study of Korea and Taiwan. *Oxford Development Studies, 29*(2), 145–154.

Dunning, J., & Narula, R. (1996). The investment development path revisited: Some emerging issues. In J. Dunning & R. Narula (Eds.), *Foreign direct investment and governments: Catalysts for economic restructuring* (pp. 1–33). London: Routledge.

Fan, D., Zhu, C. J., & Nyland, C. (2012). Factors affecting global integration of Chinese multinationals in Australia: A qualitative analysis. *International Business Review, 21*(1), 13–26.

Ge, G. L., & Ding, D. Z. (2008). A strategic analysis of surging Chinese manufacturers: The case of Galanz. *Asia Pacific Journal of Management, 25*(4), 667–683.

Hennart, J. F. (2012). Emerging market multinationals and the theory of the multinational enterprise. *Global Strategy Journal, 2*(3), 168–187.

Inkpen, A. C., & Beamish, P. W. (1994). An analysis of twenty-five years of research in the journal of international business studies. *Journal of International Business Studies, 25*(4), 703–713.

Johanson, J., & Vahlne, J. E. (1977). The internationalization process of the firm − A model of knowledge development and increasing foreign market commitments. *Journal of International Business Studies, 8*(1), 23−32.

Jormanainen, I., & Koveshnikov, A. (2012). International activities of emerging market firms: A critical assessment of research in top international management journals. *Management International Review, 52*(5), 691−725.

Kang, Y., & Jiang, F. (2012). FDI location choice of Chinese multinationals in East and Southeast Asia: Traditional economic factors and institutional perspective. *Journal of World Business, 47*(1), 45−53.

Klossek, A., Linke, B. M., & Nippa, M. (2012). Chinese enterprises in Germany: Establishment modes and strategies to mitigate the liability of foreignness. *Journal of World Business, 47*(1), 35−44.

Knoerich, J. (2010). Gaining from the global ambitions of emerging economy enterprises: An analysis of the decision to sell a German firm to a Chinese acquirer. *Journal of International Management, 16*(2), 177−191.

Kolstad, I., & Wiig, A. (2012). What determines Chinese outward FDI? *Journal of World Business, 47*(1), 26−34.

Kotabe, M., Jiang, C. X., & Murray, J. Y. (2011). Managerial ties, knowledge acquisition, realized absorptive capacity and new product market performance of emerging multinational companies: A case of China. *Journal of World Business, 46*(2), 166−176.

Kumar, S., & Kundu, S. K. (2004). Ranking the international business schools: Faculty publication as the measure. *Management International Review, 44*(2), 213−228.

Lahiri, S., & Kumar, V. (2012). Ranking international business institutions and faculty members using research publication as the measure: Update and extension of prior research. *Management International Review, 52*(3), 317−340.

Lau, C. M., Ngo, H. Y., & Yiu, D. W. (2010). Internationalization and organizational resources of Chinese firms. *Chinese Management Studies, 4*(3), 258−272.

Li, P. P. (2007). Toward an integrated theory of multinational evolution: The evidence of Chinese multinational enterprises as latecomers. *Journal of International Management, 13*(3), 296−318.

Liang, X., Lu, X., & Wang, L. (2012). Outward internationalization of private enterprises in China: The effect of competitive advantages and disadvantages compared to home market rivals. *Journal of World Business, 47*(1), 134−144.

Liu, C. Z. (2007). Lenovo: An example of globalization of Chinese enterprises. *Journal of International Business Studies, 38*(4), 573−577.

Liu, X., Buck, T., & Shu, C. (2005). Chinese economic development, the next stage: Outward FDI? *International Business Review, 14*(1), 97−115.

Liu, X., Xiao, W., & Huang, X. (2008). Bounded entrepreneurship and internationalisation of indigenous Chinese private-owned firms. *International Business Review, 17*(4), 488−508.

Liu, Y., Li, Y., & Xue, J. (2011). Ownership, strategic orientation and internationalization in emerging markets. *Journal of World Business, 46*(3), 381−393.

Lu, J., Liu, X., & Wang, H. (2011). Motives for outward FDI of Chinese private firms: Firm resources, industry dynamics, and government policies. *Management and Organization Review, 7*(2), 223−248.

Lu, J. W. (2003). The evolving contributions in international strategic management research. *Journal of International Management, 9*(2), 193−213.

Luo, Y., Zhao, H., Wang, Y., & Xi, Y. (2011). Venturing abroad by emerging market enterprises: A test of dual strategic intents. *Management International Review*, *51*(4), 433–459.

Mathews, J. A. (2006). Dragon multinationals: New players in 21st century globalization. *Asia Pacific Journal of Management*, *23*(1), 5–27.

MOFCOM. (2013). *2012 Statistical bulletin of China's outward foreign direct investment*. Beijing: Ministry of Commerce (MOFCOM) of People's Republic of China.

Morrison, A. J., & Inkpen, A. C. (1991). An analysis of significant contributions to the international business literature. *Journal of International Business Studies*, *22*(1), 143–153.

Narula, R. (2012). Do we need different frameworks to explain infant MNES from developing countries? *Global Strategy Journal*, *2*(3), 188–204.

Oviatt, B., & McDougall, P. (1994). Toward a theory of international new ventures. *Journal of International Business Studies*, *25*(1), 45–64.

Quer, D., Claver, E., & Rienda, L. (2007). Business and management in China: A review of empirical research in leading international journals. *Asia Pacific Journal of Management*, *24*(3), 359–384.

Quer, D., Claver, E., & Rienda, L. (2012). Political risk, cultural distance, and outward foreign direct investment: Empirical evidence from large Chinese firms. *Asia Pacific Journal of Management*, *29*(4), 1089–1104.

Ramasamy, B., Yeung, M., & Laforet, S. (2012). China's outward foreign direct investment: Location choice and firm ownership. *Journal of World Business*, *47*(1), 17–25.

Rugman, A. M. (2010). Book review: Globalization of Chinese enterprises. *The International Trade Journal*, *24*(3), 352–354.

Rui, H., & Yip, G. S. (2008). Foreign acquisitions by Chinese firms: A strategic intent perspective. *Journal of World Business*, *43*(2), 213–226.

Schüler-Zhou, Y., & Schüller, M. (2009). The internationalization of Chinese companies: What do official statistics tell us about Chinese outward foreign direct investment? *Chinese Management Studies*, *3*(1), 25–42.

Shieh, B. L., & Wu, T. C. (2012). Equity-based entry modes of the greater Chinese economic areas's foreign direct investments in Vietnam. *International Business Review*, *21*(3), 508–517.

Söderman, S., Jakobsson, A., & Soler, L. (2008). A quest for repositioning: The emerging internationalization of Chinese companies. *Asian Business & Management*, *7*(1), 115–142.

Sun, S. L., Peng, M. W., Ren, B., & Yan, D. (2012). A comparative ownership advantage framework for cross-border M&As: The rise of Chinese and Indian MNEs. *Journal of World Business*, *47*(1), 4–16.

Tolentino, P. E. (2010). Home country macroeconomic factors and outward FDI of China and India. *Journal of International Management*, *16*(2), 102–120.

UNCTAD. (2013). *World investment report 2013. Global value chains: Investment and trade for development*. New York, NY: United Nations Conference on Trade and Development.

Wang, C., Hong, J., Kafouros, M., & Boateng, A. (2012). What drives outward FDI of Chinese firms? Testing the explanatory power of three theoretical frameworks. *International Business Review*, *21*(3), 425–438.

Wang, C., Hong, J., Kafouros, M., & Wright, M. (2012). Exploring the role of government involvement in outward FDI from emerging economics. *Journal of International Business Studies*, *43*(7), 655–676.

Wei, Z. (2010). The literature on Chinese outward FDI. *Multinational Business Review, 18*(3), 73–112.

Xu, S., Yalcinkaya, G., & Seggie, S. H. (2008). Prolific authors and institutions in leading international business journals. *Asia Pacific Journal of Management, 25*(2), 189–207.

Xu, Y., Hu, S., & Fan, X. (2009). The impacts of country risk and cultural distance on transnational equity investments: Empirical evidence of Chinese enterprises' shareholdings in overseas listed companies. *Chinese Management Studies, 3*(3), 235–248.

Yang, M. (2009). Isomorphic or not? Examining cross-border mergers and acquisitions by Chinese firms, 1985–2006. *Chinese Management Studies, 3*(1), 43–57.

Yang, M., & Hyland, M. (2012). Similarity in cross-border mergers and acquisitions: Imitation, uncertainty and experience among Chinese firms, 1985–2006. *Journal of International Management, 18*(4), 352–365.

Yang, X., Jiang, Y., Kang, R., & Ke, Y. (2009). A comparative analysis of the internationalization of Chinese and Japanese firms. *Asia Pacific Journal of Management, 26*(1), 141–162.

Yiu, D. W., Lau, C. M., & Bruton, G. D. (2007). International venturing by emerging economy firms: The effects of firm capabilities, home country networks, and corporate entrepreneurship. *Journal of International Business Studies, 38*(4), 519–540.

Zhang, J., Zhou, C., & Ebbers, H. (2011). Completion of Chinese overseas acquisitions: Institutional perspectives and evidence. *International Business Review, 20*(2), 226–238.

Zhao, W., Liu, L., & Zhao, T. (2010). The contribution of outward direct investment to productivity changes within China, 1991–2007. *Journal of International Management, 16*(2), 121–130.